Network Propaganda

Network Propaganda

Manipulation, Disinformation, and Radicalization in American Politics

YOCHAI BENKLER

ROBERT FARIS

HAL ROBERTS

OXFORD
UNIVERSITY PRESS

OXFORD
UNIVERSITY PRESS

Oxford University Press is a department of the University of Oxford. It furthers the University's
objective of excellence in research, scholarship, and education by publishing worldwide. Oxford is a
registered trademark of Oxford University Press in the UK and certain other countries.

Published in the United States of America by Oxford University Press
198 Madison Avenue, New York, NY 10016, United States of America.

Library of Congress Cataloging-in-Publication Data

Names: Benkler, Yochai, author. | Faris, Robert, author. | Roberts, Hal (Harold) author.
Title: Network propaganda : manipulation, disinformation, and radicalization in American politics /
Yochai Benkler, Robert Faris, Hal Roberts.
Description: New York, NY : Oxford University Press, 2018. | Includes bibliographical
references and index.
Identifiers: LCCN 2018020121 | ISBN 9780190923624 ((hardback) : alk. paper) |
ISBN 9780190923631 ((pbk.) : alk. paper)
Subjects: LCSH: Presidents—United States—Election—2016. | Communication in
politics—United States. | Political campaigns—United States. | Mass media—Political
aspects—United States. | Social media—Political aspects—United States. | Internet in
political campaigns—United States. | Disinformation—United States—History—
21st century. | Radicalism—United States. | Political culture—United States. | United States—
Politics and government—2009–2017. | United States—Politics and government—2017–
Classification: LCC JK526 2016 .B46 2018 | DDC 324.973/0932—dc23
LC record available at https://lccn.loc.gov/2018020121

1 3 5 7 9 8 6 4 2

Paperback printed by Sheridan Books, Inc., United States of America
Hardback printed by Bridgeport National Bindery, Inc., United States of America

Note to Readers
This publication is designed to provide accurate and authoritative information in regard to
the subject matter covered. It is based upon sources believed to be accurate and reliable and
is intended to be current as of the time it was written. It is sold with the understanding that
the publisher is not engaged in rendering legal, accounting, or other professional services.
If legal advice or other expert assistance is required, the services of a competent professional
person should be sought. Also, to confirm that the information has not been affected or
changed by recent developments, traditional legal research techniques should be used,
including checking primary sources where appropriate.

*(Based on the Declaration of Principles jointly adopted by a Committee of the
American Bar Association and a Committee of Publishers and Associations.)*

You may order this or any other Oxford University Press publication
by visiting the Oxford University Press website at www.oup.com.

Contents

Acknowledgments   vii

PART ONE: *Mapping Disorder*

1. Epistemic Crisis   3

2. The Architecture of Our Discontent   45

3. The Propaganda Feedback Loop   75

PART TWO: *Dynamics of Network Propaganda*

4. Immigration and Islamophobia: Breitbart and the Trump Party   105

5. The Fox Diet   145

6. Mainstream Media Failure Modes and Self-Healing in a
   Propaganda-Rich Environment   189

PART THREE: *The Usual Suspects*

7. The Propaganda Pipeline: Hacking the Core from the Periphery   225

8. Are the Russians Coming?   235

9. Mammon's Algorithm: Marketing, Manipulation, and Clickbait
   on Facebook   269

PART FOUR: *Can Democracy Survive the Internet?*

10. Polarization in American Politics   295

11. The Origins of Asymmetry   311

12. Can the Internet Survive Democracy?   341

13. What Can Men Do Against Such Reckless Hate?   351

14. Conclusion   381

Notes   389

Index   443

Acknowledgments

THIS BOOK REPRESENTS an account and update from what has been a long intellectual journey for each of us. For well over a decade, we have collected and used data to study, understand, and describe the impact of newly emerging digital communication on society, politics, and democracy. We have not undertaken this journey alone, and this book has benefited from the input and support of countless people along the way.

We would first like to thank Ethan Zuckerman for his decade-long partnership with us to support both the intellectual work of this book and the development of the Media Cloud platform that enabled the core analysis in this book. A decade ago, we began developing the technical infrastructure for the data analysis platform which would eventually take the name Media Cloud. Spurred on by debates within the Berkman Klein Center, where Zuckerman, now Director of the Center for Civic Media at MIT, co-founder and co-Principal Investigator of the Media Cloud project, was a fellow and senior researcher, and across the broader academic community, we sought to develop better tools to empirically study the structure and function of digital media. At that time, the open web was the core of digital communication. Much of our attention was directed at studying the impact of blogs on public discourse while Facebook, Twitter, and YouTube were relatively recent additions to the digital landscape. While we debated whether blogging would democratize media production and strengthen, we set about the many years' process of building the Media Cloud platform to collect, parse, and analyze digital media.

This book is the result of many months of effort and has only come to be as a result of the generous input of our friends and colleagues from the Berkman Klein Center and beyond. We are especially indebted to our colleagues Nikki Bourassa, Bruce Etling, and Justin Clark, who have made important substantive contributions to this study, supported the overall research enterprise, conducted analysis, gathered data, provided input and feedback on this book, and shaped our understanding of the issues. Kira Tebbe provided crucial assistance in the final editing and production of the book. Rebekah Heacock Jones helped get this research off the ground with research into political discourse on Twitter. Daniel Dennis Jones worked tirelessly in the production and publication of this work. We benefited from the insights and efforts of Zach Wehrwein and Devin Gaffney, who helps us to track and understand the propagation of frames and narratives from Reddit. Brendan Roach and Michael Jasper provided invaluable research assistance. Jonas Kaiser and Paola Villarreal expanded our thinking around methods and interpretation. Alicia Solow-Niederman worked tirelessly to debug early versions of the analytical methods that were used in this book. Urs Gasser and Jonathan Zittrain have extended valuable support that has enabled us to maintain this research for many years. John Palfrey and Colin Maclay provided critical institutional support for Media Cloud in its early stages.

      We are grateful to our friends and collaborators at the Center for Civic Media at the MIT Media Lab who have worked with us in the development of the Media Cloud platform and contributed to the applied research it has supported. This work has built upon and fostered an unusually close and productive collaboration between our two academic centers. Rahul Bhargava, Linas Valiukas, and Cindy Bishop have helped to extend and translate the ideas and concepts of a large-scale media analysis platform into the current functionality of the Media Cloud platform upon which this research relied. Fernando Bermejo has been a valuable supporter and contributor to our collective work in this field. Natalie Gyenes and Anushka Shah provided research insights and Media Cloud expertise.

      This research has also benefited from contributions of many outside the Berkman Klein community. John Kelly and Vlad Barash provided important insights into the role of social media in the election, leading us to new hypotheses and ideas that shaped the book's development. Matt Higgins helped lay a firm foundation of thought and hypotheses upon which this work was completed. Philipp Nowak provided valuable early research assistance. Participants of Data & Society's Propaganda & Media Manipulation Workshop in May 2017 provided valuable feedback and critical cross-examination that helped steer our earlier work toward this final version. We are also indebted to our editors at the Oxford University Press, Alex Flach and Emma Taylor, without whose initiative and support we would not have translated and extended our research into this book.

The research on the post-election period and additional research necessary to understand the institutional foundations we describe here as well as the production of the book benefited from the support of the Ford Foundation and the Ethics and Governance of Artificial Intelligence Fund. The original study of the election period, upon which significant portions of this book are based, was funded by the Open Society Foundations U.S. Programs. This work would not have been feasible without the investments made by a set of funders who have funded Media Cloud development over the years, including the Bill and Melinda Gates Foundation, the Robert Woods Johnson Foundation, the Ford Foundation, the John D. and Catherine T. MacArthur Foundation, and the Open Society Foundations.

We are also grateful to those who have invested time and resources into developing open tools and data for public interest research. We drew upon TV Archive data collected and made available by the Internet Archive, and used the tools and interfaces developed and made publicly available by the GDELT Project. Gephi, open source network analysis and visualization software, served as the engine for our network analysis.

PART ONE

Mapping Disorder

1

Epistemic Crisis

As a result of psychological research, coupled with the modern means of communication, the practice of democracy has turned a corner. A revolution is taking place, infinitely more significant than any shifting of economic power

WALTER LIPPMANN, Public Opinion, 1922

ON SUNDAY, DECEMBER 4, 2016, a young man carrying an assault rifle walked into Comet Pizza in Northwest Washington, D.C., to investigate reports that Hillary Clinton and her campaign chief were running a pedophilia ring from the basement of the pizza parlor.[1] A week later, a YouGov poll found that, however whacky the story, the young man was not alone in believing it; nearly half of Trump voters polled "gave some credence" to the rumors.[2]

Two weeks earlier, BuzzFeed's Craig Silverman had published an article that launched the term "fake news."[3] Silverman's article examined engagements with news stories on Facebook through shares, reactions, and comments and argued that the best-performing stories produced by political clickbait sites masquerading as actual news sites, often located offshore, generated more Facebook engagements than the top stories of legitimate news sites. On January 6, 2017, the Office of the Director of National Intelligence released a report that blamed Russia of running a disinformation campaign aimed to influence the U.S. election with the aim of helping Donald Trump get elected.[4]

The steady flow of stories reinforced a perception that the 2016 election had involved an unusual degree of misleading information flowing in the American media ecosystem. From claims during the primary that Jeb Bush had "close Nazi ties,"[5] through claims during the general election that Hillary Clinton's campaign was 20 percent funded by the Saudi royal family,[6] the campaign was littered with misleading stories, often from sources that masked their identity or affiliation. Moreover, just as with the alleged pedophilia case,

Network Propaganda. Yochai Benkler, Robert Faris, and Hal Roberts.
© Yochai Benkler, Robert Faris, and Hal Roberts 2018. Published 2018 by Oxford University Press.

many of the stories seemed designed to elicit fear and disgust, as the titles of Breitbart's most widely shared stories on immigration exhibit: "Six Diseases Return to US as Migration Advocates Celebrate World Refugee Day," and "More than 347,000 Convicted Criminal Immigrants At Large in U.S."[7]

The 2016 U.S. presidential election won by Donald Trump followed closely on the heels of the equally shocking success of the Leave campaign in Britain's vote to exit the European Union. Both seemed to mark an epistemic crisis in contemporary democratic societies. As 2016 was drawing to a close, many in the United States and the European Union saw these events as signals that democracy itself was in crisis, buckling under the pressure of technological processes that had overwhelmed our collective capacity to tell truth from falsehood and reason from its absence. Brexit and the rise of far-right parties in countries such as France, Hungary, Austria, and even Sweden signaled a deep crisis in the pluralist, cosmopolitan, democratic project that was at the heart of the project of Europe. The victory of Donald Trump marked a triumph of a radical populist right-wing politics that had long simmered on the margins of the American right and the Republican Party: from the segregationist third-party candidacy of George Wallace in 1968, through Pat Buchanan's primary runs in 1992 and 1996, to the rise of the Tea Party after 2008. These remarkable political victories for what were once marginal ideologies appeared at the same time that democracies around the world, from the Philippines, through India, to Turkey saw shifts from more liberal democratic forms to a new model of illiberal, and in some cases authoritarian, majoritarianism.

Something fundamental was happening to threaten democracy, and our collective eye fell on the novel and rapidly changing—technology. Technological processes beyond the control of any person or country— the convergence of social media, algorithmic news curation, bots, artificial intelligence, and big data analysis—were creating echo chambers that reinforced our biases, were removing indicia of trustworthiness, and were generally overwhelming our capacity to make sense of the world, and with it our capacity to govern ourselves as reasonable democracies.

The first year of the Trump presidency brought no relief. The president himself adopted the term "fake news" to describe all news that was critical or embarrassing. By the end of his first year in office, the president was handing out "Fake News Awards" to his critics, and four in ten Republicans responded that they "considered accurate news stories that cast a politician or political group in a negative light to be fake news."[8] While trust in news media declined in a broad range of countries, the patterns of trust and mistrust differed widely across different countries. Together with Hungary and Israel, two other democracies with powerful right-wing parties, the United States was an outlier: distrust was high on average but markedly higher for one party affiliation.[9]

Echo chambers ringing with false news make democracies ungovernable. We can imagine a pluralist democracy in which populations contested elections and won or lost based on their votes, without ever sharing a viewpoint on what is going on in the world. Partisan press hurling accusations at the other party was, after all, the norm in nineteenth-century America. One party might believe that we are under attack from zombies and vote to counter this existential menace, while another party might believe that we are threatened by a long-term decline in productivity growth and vote to focus on that problem. Whoever won would design policies to counter what they saw as the major policy question of our times. The role of pluralist democracy would be to govern the rules of orderly transition from the zombie slayers to the productivity wonks and back with the ebb and flow of electoral success.

In practice, given the intensity of the "zombie-threat" party's sense of impending doom, such a pluralist democracy would be deeply unstable. Some shared means of defining what facts or beliefs are off the wall and what are plausibly open to reasoned debate is necessary to maintain a democracy. The twentieth century in particular saw the development of a range of institutional and cultural practices designed to create a shared order out of the increasingly complex and interconnected world in which citizens were forced to address a world beyond their local communities, values, and beliefs. The medical profession, for example, rapidly and fundamentally transformed itself after the discovery of germ theory in 1876. Between 1900 and 1910, the American Medical Association grew from 8,400 to 70,000 members. This growth represented the transition from dubiously effective local medical practices to a nationally organized profession acting as an institutional gatekeeper for scientifically-based practices. The same pattern can be found in the establishment of other truth-seeking professions during the early twentieth century, including education, law, and academia. All of these professions organized themselves into their modern national, institutional forms in roughly the first 20 years of the twentieth century. Those years saw the emergence of, among others, the American Bar Association; the National Education Association; and the American Historical, American Economic, American Statistical, and American Political Science Associations.[10]

During this same critical period, journalism experienced its own transformation, into an institutionalized profession that adopted practices we would recognize as modern objective journalism. By 1912 Columbia University's journalism school had been founded, which helped to institutionalize through professional training a set of practices that had developed in the late nineteenth and early twentieth centuries and that we now associate with objective journalism—detachment, nonpartisanship, the inverted pyramid writing style, facticity, and balance. Before this development, none of these attributes were broadly present in journalism.[11] These shifts in the professions in general, and in journalism in particular, were in turn part of the broad shift associated with modernism, employing rational planning, expertise, and objective evidence in both private sector management and public administration.

Since the end of World War II this trend toward institutionalized professions for truth seeking has accelerated. Government statistics agencies; science and academic investigations; law and the legal profession; and journalism developed increasingly rationalized and formalized solutions to the problem of how societies made up of diverse populations with diverse and conflicting political views can nonetheless form a shared sense of what is going on in the world.[12] As the quip usually attributed to Daniel Patrick Moynihan put it, "Everyone is entitled to his own opinion, but not his own facts." Politics was always centrally about identity and belonging and meaning, but in the decades following World War II, democracy operated within constraints with regard to a shared set of institutional statements about reality. Zombie invasions were out.

Zombie invasions are definitely back in. The year following the 2016 U.S. presidential election saw publication of reports[13] and academic papers[14] seeking to categorize the confusion, defining misinformation (the unintentional spread of false beliefs) and disinformation and propaganda (the intentional manipulation of beliefs), identifying their sources,[15] and studying the dynamics by which they spread.[16] This flurry of work exhibited a broad sense that as a public we have lost our capacity to agree on shared modes of validation as to what is going on and what is just plain whacky. The perceived threats to our very capacity to tell truth from convenient political fiction, if true, strike at the very foundations of democratic society. But it is important to recognize that for all the anxiety, not to say panic, about disinformation through social media, we do not yet have anything approaching a scientific consensus on what exactly happened, who were the primary sources of disinformation, what were its primary vectors or channels, and how it affected the outcome of the election. In this book we try to advance that diagnosis by applying a wide range of tools to very large data sets and reviewing the literature that developed over the first year after the election.

The critical thing to understand as you read this book is that the epochal change reflected by the 2016 election and the first year of the Trump presidency was not that Republicans beat Democrats despite having a demonstrably less qualified candidate. The critical change was that in 2016 the party of Ronald Reagan and the two presidents Bush was defeated by the party of Donald Trump, Breitbart, and billionaire Robert Mercer. As our data show, in 2017 Fox News joined the victors in launching sustained attacks on core pillars of the Party of Reagan—free trade and a relatively open immigration policy, and, most directly, the national security establishment and law enforcement when these threatened President Trump himself. Our work helps to explain how a media ecosystem that initially helped the GOP gain and retain power ultimately spun out of control. From the nomination of Roy Moore as Republican candidate for the Alabama special Senate election over the objections of Republican Party leadership to Republican congressman Francis Rooney's call to "purge the FBI," and from the retirement of Paul Ryan from his position as Speaker of the House to evangelical leader Franklin Graham's shrug at Donald Trump's marital infidelities, a range of apparently incongruous political stories can be understood as elements of this basic conflict between Trumpism and Reaganism over control of the Republican Party. In the 2016 election, once the Trump Party took over the Republican Party, many Republicans chose to support the party that had long anchored their political identity, even if they did not love the candidate at the top of the ticket. Indeed, it is likely that the vehemence of the attacks on Hillary Clinton that we document in Chapters 3, 4, 6, and 7 were intended precisely to reduce that dissonance, and to make that bitter medicine go down more easily. Our observations, and the propaganda feedback loop we identify in Chapters 2 and 3 help explain both how such a radicalization could have succeeded within the Republican Party, and how that transformation could achieve an electoral victory in a two-party system that should, according to the standard median voter models favored in political science, have led the party rebels to electoral defeat and swept them into the dustbin of history. We leave until Part Three our historical explanation for how and when that propaganda feedback loop established itself in the right wing of American politics.

The bulk of this book comprises detailed analyses of large data sets, case studies of the emergence of broad frames and particular narratives, and synthesis with the work of others who have tried to make sense of what happened at both abstract and concrete levels. Our goal is to understand which actors were responsible for this transformation of the American public sphere, and how this new public sphere operated through those actors so as to make it so vulnerable to disinformation, propaganda, and just sheer bullshit. Our heavy focus on data is complemented by an effort to make sense of what we see today in historical context, both political and cultural.

We take a political economy view of technology, suggesting that the fundamental mistake of "the internet polarizes" narrative is that it adopts too naïve a view of how technology works and understates the degree to which institutions, culture, and politics shape technological adoption and diffusion patterns. These, we think, were the prime movers of the architecture of American political media, and it is this finding that makes this book, for all its detailed focus on American politics and media, a useful guide for other countries as well. We argue that it would simply be a mistake for countries such as, say, Germany, to look at elections in the United States or the United Kingdom, see the concerns over online information pollution or propaganda, and conclude that the technology, which they too use, is the source of disruption. Different political systems, coming from different historical trajectories and institutional traditions, will likely exhibit different effects of the same basic technological affordances. So it was with mass circulation presses, movies, radio, and television, and so it is with the internet and social media. Each country's institutions, media ecosystems, and political culture will interact to influence the relative significance of the internet's democratizing affordances relative to its authoritarian and nihilistic affordances. What our analysis of the American system offers others is a method, an approach to observing empirically what in fact is happening in a country's political media ecosystem, and a framework for understanding why the particular new technological affordances may develop differently in one country than another.

Dramatis Personae

Media and academic discussions of the post-truth moment have identified a set of actors and technological drivers as the prime suspects in causing the present state of information disorder, such as fake news purveyors, Russians, and so forth. These discussions have also employed a broad range of definitions of the problem. Before turning to our analysis, we offer, first, the list of actors who have been described as potentially responsible for disrupting American political communications, and second, precise definitions of the terms we will use in describing the sources and forms of misperceptions that spread through the American media ecosystem.

"Fake News" Entrepreneurs/Political Clickbait Fabricators.—Before Donald Trump appropriated the term, the "fake news" phrase took off in the wake of Craig Silverman's reporting on BuzzFeed about the success of fake election news stories.[17] This reporting built on Silverman's earlier story describing over 100 pro-Trump websites run from a single town in the former Yugoslav Republic of Macedonia. The Macedonian teenagers responsible had little interest in American politics but had found that by imitating actual news sites, and pushing outlandish hyperpartisan stories, they got lots of Facebook engagements from Trump supporters, which translated into very real advertising dollars.[18] For a while, these websites received a lot of media attention.[19] Their operators had figured out how to leverage a core affordance of Facebook—its ability not only to connect publishers with audiences, but also to generate revenues and distribute them to publishers able to elicit "engagements" on the platform. The social media entrepreneurs who created these sites were the perfect target of anxiety for traditional media: they diverted attention and advertising dollars from "legitimate" media, they manipulated Facebook's algorithm, they were mostly foreign in these stories, and they were purely in it for the money. Here, we call them "clickbait fabricators," and primarily address their role in Chapter 9. By "clickbait" we mean media items designed to trigger an affective response from a user that leads them to click on the item—be it an image, a video, or a headline—because the click itself generates revenue for the clickbait purveyor. While this can easily apply to many news headlines and much of online advertising, "clickbait fabricators" are individuals or firms whose product is in effect purely the clickbait item, rather than any meaningful underlying news or product. We use the "fake news" moniker to introduce them here because it was used early on to identify this particular threat of pollution from political clickbait fabricators. Elsewhere, we avoid the term itself because it is too vague as a category of analysis and its meaning quickly eroded soon after it was first introduced.

Russian Hackers, Bots, and Sockpuppets—Claims of Russian intervention in the U.S. election surfaced immediately after the hacking of the Democratic National Committee (DNC) email server, in June 2016.[20] By the end of the year, it had become an official assessment of the U.S. intelligence community.[21] Over the course of 2017 and 2018 this set of concerns has been the most politically important, not least because of the criminal investigation into alleged connections between the Trump campaign and Russia. Reports and documentation released by congressional committees shone particular attention on Russian propaganda use of Facebook advertising. Facebook itself, and later Twitter, issued reports confirming that they had identified instances of Russian interference. A range of independent academic and nonprofit reports confirmed the effort. The types of interventions described included the email hacks themselves—primarily the DNC and John Podesta emails—which provided grist for the partisan mill in the months before the election; and the use on Facebook and Twitter of automated accounts ("bots"), and "fake" accounts masquerading as something other than Russian agents ("sockpuppets"), which incited people on both the right and the left to protest, and pushed and gave particular prominence to anti-Clinton and pro-Trump messages. We dedicate Chapter 8 to assessing the Russian threat in detail.

The Facebook News Feed algorithm and Online Echo Chambers—A third major suspect was centered on the Facebook News Feed algorithm, although it extended to other social media and the internet more generally as well. To some extent, this was simply a reprise of the nearly 20-year-old concern that personalization of news, "the Daily Me," would drive us into "echo chambers" or "filter bubbles." To some extent it reflected a wave of newer literature concerned in general with algorithmic governance, or the replacement of human, legible, and accountable judgments with "black box" algorithms.[22] In particular it reflected the application of this literature to politics in the wake of a series of experiments published by Facebook research teams on the News Feed algorithm's ability to affect attitudes and bring out the vote.[23] It was this algorithm that rewarded the clickbait sites circulating the hyperpartisan bullshit. It was this algorithm that reinforced patterns of sharing in tightly clustered communities that supported the relative insularity of user communities. As a result, many of the most visible reform efforts in 2017 and 2018 were focused on revisions of the Facebook News Feed algorithm to constrain the dissemination of political clickbait and Russian propaganda. As with the case of the Russians, concern over the Facebook News Feed algorithm in particular, and over algorithmic shaping of reading and viewing habits in general, is legitimate and serious. In our observations, Facebook appears to be a more polluted information environment than Twitter or the open web. In Chapters 2, 3, and 9, we show that sites that are particularly prominent on Facebook but not on Twitter or the open web tend to be more prone to false content and hyperpartisan bullshit, on both sides of the political divide, although there is more than enough pollution on these other media as well. But, we will explain why manipulations of Facebook's platform, like Russian intervention, were nonetheless not the primary driver of disinformation and confusion.

Fake news entrepreneurs, Russians, the Facebook algorithm, and online echo chambers provide normatively unproblematic, nonpartisan explanations to the current epistemic crisis. For all of these actors, the strong emphasis on technology suggests a novel challenge that our normal systems do not know how to handle but that can be addressed in a nonpartisan manner. Moreover, focusing on "fake news" from foreign sources and on Russian efforts to intervene places the blame onto foreigners with no legitimate stake in our democracy. Both liberal political theory and professional journalism consistently seek neutral justifications for democratic institutions, so visibly nonpartisan explanations such as these have enormous attraction. The rest of the actors, described below, lack this nonpartisan characteristic.

Cambridge Analytica—Another commonly blamed actor is the Trump campaign's use of Cambridge Analytica to manipulate behavior using artificial intelligence (AI)-driven social media advertising. The extent to which Cambridge Analytica, a U.K.-based data analytics political consultancy that had used tens of millions of Facebook profiles to develop techniques for manipulating voters, in fact used psychographic data and manipulated targets is debatable. What is clear is that the social media companies, Facebook in particular, helped the Trump campaign, as they would any paying customer, to use their deep data and behavioral insights to target advertising.[24] It is less clear, however, that there is anything wrong, from the perspective of American norms of electoral politics, with this campaign usage of cutting-edge, data-driven behavioral marketing. In 2012, when the Obama campaign used then-state-of-the-art data-driven targeting, post-campaign analyses feted the campaign geeks.[25] If there is a problem here, it is part of a much broader and deeper critique of behavioral marketing more generally, and how it undermines consumer and citizen sovereignty. We outline some of the events and the broader concerns in Chapter 9, explain why the threat is likely more remote than news coverage of Cambridge Analytica implied, and suggest how some of the proposed solutions may, or may not, help with this long-term threat in Chapter 13.

White Supremacist and Alt-Right Trolls—One of the most troubling aspects of the 2016 election and the politics of 2017 was the rise of white supremacists in American politics. As Alice Marwick and Rebecca Lewis carefully documented, white supremacists, neo-Nazis, and other long-standing denizens of the American far-right found fellow travelers in young, net-native subcultures on Reddit, 4chan, and 8chan, graduates of the Gamergate controversy, and other online trolls, to undertake a meme war.[26] The core argument is that these decentralized, politically mobilized, and meme-savvy activists deployed a set of disinformation memes and framings that altered the election. Serious anthropological and computational work, in addition to the work of Marwick and Lewis, supports the argument that these meme campaigns had significant impact on the campaign.[27] Our own work detailed in the following chapters, however, aligns with that of researchers, including Whitney Phillips, Jessica Breyer, and Gabriella Coleman,[28] who were more skeptical of the central role assigned to "alt-right" online activists by some. In Chapter 4 we document how isolated the white supremacist sites were from the overall Islamophobic framing of immigration that typified right-wing media. In Chapter 7 we document how these activists intersected with Russian propagandists to propel stories up the propaganda pipeline, but also suggest that these events were, in the scheme of things, of secondary importance.

The impact of the white supremacists matters a great deal, because fear over their impact has created nettlesome problems for Americans concerned with democracy and the First Amendment; and for Europeans concerned with far-right propaganda on one hand, and the fear of American companies imposing their speech standards on Europeans on the other hand. Far-right activist meme wars undoubtedly represent core political speech, by a politically mobilized minority. It is hard to think of a clearer case for First Amendment protection. But many of the techniques involved in these campaigns involve releasing embarrassing documents, hateful drowning-out of opponents, and other substantial personal offenses. The substantive abhorrence of explicitly racist and misogynistic views and the genuine concern with the effects of the intimidation and silencing campaigns have increased calls for online censorship by privately owned platforms. The most visible results of these calls were the decisions by GoDaddy, Google, and Cloudflare to deny services to the Daily Stormer, a neo-Nazi site, in the wake of the white supremacist demonstrations in Charlottesville, Virginia, in the middle of 2017. In Europe explicitly Nazi content is an easier constitutional case, but questions of what counts as illegal and worthy of removal will remain central. A German law called the 'NetzDG' law, effectively enforced since January 2018, became the most aggressive effort by a liberal democracy to require online platforms to police their systems. Aimed at hate speech in particular, the law imposed very large fines on major online platforms if they failed to remove speech that violates a broad set of German criminal prohibitions, some of which applied to much broader and vaguer categories than obvious hate speech. We offer a more detailed description of this law and its limitations in Chapter 13. That law will undoubtedly inform other countries in Europe and elsewhere as they decide to create their own versions of laws that push private platforms to impose what some would call "editorial control" and others "private censorship." Our data support the more reticent approach, based on the scarcity of evidence of transformational impact of these extremists on the U.S. media ecosystem. Throughout our case studies we observe instances of alt-right memes trickling through the media ecosystem, but to do so they rely overwhelmingly on transmission by the more prominent nodes in the right-wing media network. These major right-wing outlets, in turn, are adept at producing their own conspiracy theories and defamation campaigns, and do not depend on decentralized networks of Redditors to write their materials. Given the secondary and dependent role that these sites have on the shape of the American media ecosystem, the gains from silencing the more insulated far-right forums may be less significant than would justify expansion of the powers of private censorship by already powerful online platforms in relatively concentrated markets.

Right-Wing Media Ecosystem—Our own contribution to debates about the 2016 election was to shine a light on the right-wing media ecosystem itself as the primary culprit in sowing confusion and distrust in the broader American media ecosystem. In the first two parts of this book we continue that work by documenting how the right-wing media ecosystem differs categorically from the rest of the media environment and how much more susceptible it has been to disinformation, lies, and half-truths. In short, we find that the influence in the right-wing media ecosystem, whether judged by hyperlinks, Twitter sharing, or Facebook sharing, is both highly skewed to the far right and highly insulated from other segments of the network, from center-right (which is nearly nonexistent) through the far left. We did not come to this work looking for a partisan-skewed explanation. As we began to analyze the millions of online stories, tweets, and Facebook sharing data points, the pattern that emerged was clear. Our own earlier work, which analyzed specific campaigns around intellectual property law and found that right and left online media collaborated, made us skeptical of our initial observations, but these proved highly resilient to a wide range of specifications and robustness checks. Something very different was happening in right-wing media than in centrist, center-left, and left-wing media.

We will make the argument throughout this book that the behavior of the right-wing media ecosystem represents a radicalization of roughly a third of the American media system. We use the term "radicalization" advisedly in two senses. First, to speak of "polarization" is to assume symmetry. No fact emerges more clearly from our analysis of how four million political stories were linked, tweeted, and shared over a three-year period than that there is no symmetry in the architecture and dynamics of communications within the right-wing media ecosystem and outside of it. Second, throughout this period we have observed repeated public humiliation and vicious disinformation campaigns mounted by the leading sites in this sphere against individuals who were the core pillars of Republican identity a mere decade earlier. At the beginning of this period, Jeb Bush, the son and brother of the two most recent Republican presidents, was besmirched as having "close Nazi ties" on Infowars. By November 2017 life-long Republicans who had been appointed to leading law enforcement positions by President George W. Bush found themselves under sustained, weeks-long disinformation campaigns aimed to impugn their integrity and undermine their professional independence. When a solidly conservative party is taken over by its most extreme wing in a campaign that includes attacks that are no less vicious when aimed at that conservative party's mainstream pillars than they are at the opposition party, we think "radicalization" is an objectively appropriate term.

This radicalization was driven by a group of extreme sites including Breitbart, Infowars, Truthfeed, Zero Hedge, and the Gateway Pundit, none of which claim to follow the norms or processes of professional journalistic objectivity. As we will see time and again, both in our overall analysis of the architecture and in our detailed case studies, even core right-wing sites that do claim to follow journalistic norms, Fox News and the Daily Caller, do not in fact do so, and therefore fail to act as a truth-telling brake on these radical sites. Indeed, repeatedly we found Fox News accrediting and amplifying the excesses of the radical sites. As the case studies in Chapter 5 document, over the course of 2017 Fox News had become the propaganda arm of the White House in all but name. This pattern is not mirrored on the left wing. First, while we do find fringe sites on the left that mirror the radical sites, these simply do not have the kind of visibility and prominence on the left as they do on the right. Second, the most visible sites on the left, like Huffington Post, are at their worst mirrors of Fox News, not of the Gateway Pundit or Zero Hedge. And third, all these sites on the left are tightly integrated with traditional mainstream media sites like the *New York Times* and the *Washington Post*, and most, though not all, of these sites operate either directly under long-standing journalistic norms or are indirectly sensitive to criticism based on reporting that adheres to such norms. As we show in Chapter 3, there is ample supply of and demand for false hyperpartisan narratives on the left. The difference is that the audience and hyperpartisan commercial clickbait fabricators oriented toward the left form part of a single media ecosystem with center, center-left, and left-wing sites that are committed to journalistic truth-seeking norms. Those norm-constrained sites, both mainstream and net-native, serve as a consistent check on dissemination and validation of the most extreme stories when they do emerge on the left, and have no parallels in the levels of visibility or trust that can perform the same function on the right.

We do not expect our findings to persuade anyone who is already committed to the right-wing media ecosystem. The maps we draw in Chapter 2 could be interpreted differently. They could be viewed as a media system overwhelmed by liberal bias and opposed only by a tightly-clustered set of right-wing sites courageously telling the truth in the teeth of what Sean Hannity calls the "corrupt, lying media," rather than our interpretation of a radicalized right set apart from a media system anchored in century-old norms of professional journalism. We take up this issue in Chapter 3 where we compare left and right news sites for their patterns of reporting and correction and where we describe our explicit efforts to find conspiracy theories that made it out of the margins of the left to the center of mainstream media. We dedicate Chapter 6 to exploring the modes of failure of mainstream media in their election coverage, and examine the recipients of the Trump Fake News Awards and how they responded to having made the significant errors that won them that honor. We think that fundamentally, anyone who insists on claiming that we cannot draw conclusions about which side is biased, and which side gravitates more closely to the truth, must explain how the media sources most trusted by consistently conservative survey respondents—Fox News, Hannity, Rush Limbaugh, and Glenn Beck—are the equivalent of the sites that occupy the same positions among consistently liberal respondents: NPR, PBS, the BBC, and the *New York Times*.[29]

The central role of the radicalized right in creating the current crisis of disinformation and misinformation creates a significant challenge for policy recommendations and is not easy to reconcile with democratic theory. It seems too partisan a perspective to convert into a general, nonpartisan policy recommendation or neutral argument about what democracy requires.

And yet, we believe that there is a core set of concerns that transcend party affiliation and should appeal across party lines. First, having a segment of the population that is systematically disengaged from objective journalism and the ability to tell truth from partisan fiction is dangerous to any country. It creates fertile ground for propaganda. Second, it makes actual governance difficult. Other than their major success with tax reform, Republicans found it difficult to govern during the first year of the Trump presidency, despite holding majorities in both houses of Congress and the presidency. In large part, this is due to the inability to bridge the gap between the state of the world as many in their base know it and the state of the world as it is. Third, the divorce of a party base from the institutions and norms that provide a reality check on our leaders is a political disaster waiting to happen—see for instance the primary victory of Roy Moore over Lucas Strange and Moore's subsequent defeat in the general election. However strident and loyal the party base may be, not even a clear majority of Republican voters is exclusively focused on the right-wing media ecosystem. Over time, the incongruence between the reality inside and outside that ecosystem will make it harder for non-base "lean-Republican" voters to swallow candidates that are palatable inside it. Our hope, then, is that perhaps Republicans see in our findings reason enough to look for a change in the dynamic of the media ecosystem that their most loyal supporters inhabit.

Finding nonpartisan or bipartisan solutions in a society as highly polarized as the United States has become difficult, to say the least. But ignoring the stark partisan asymmetry at the root of our present epistemic crisis will make it impossible to develop solutions that address the actual causes of that crisis. Any argument that depends for its own sense of neutrality and objectivity on drawing empirically false equivalents between Fox News and CNN, much less between top left-wing sites like Mother Jones and Salon and equivalently prominent sites on the right like the Gateway Pundit or Infowars, undermines clear thinking on the problem at hand.

Mainstream Media—Most Americans do not get their news from Facebook, and even most Trump voters did not get their news solely from Fox News or right-wing online media.[30] As Thomas Patterson's study of mainstream media coverage of the 2016 election documented,[31] and Watts and Rothschild's study of the *New York Times* in the run-up to the election showed,[32] mainstream media coverage of the election was mostly focused on the horserace, was overwhelmingly negative about both candidates, and treated both candidates as equally unfit for office. One of the starkest findings of our work was the extent to which non-horserace coverage in mainstream media followed the agenda of the right-wing media and the Trump campaign.

As Figure 1.1 shows, Trump got more coverage, and, however negative, the stories still covered his core substantive issues—immigration, jobs, and trade. By contrast, Clinton's coverage was dominated by scandals—emails, the Clinton Foundation, and, to a lesser extent, Benghazi. The effect of this was most clearly shown in a September 2016 Gallup poll that showed that the word Americans most consistently associated with Clinton was "emails," followed by "lie," "scandal," and "foundation." By contrast, for Trump, "Mexico," "immigration," and so forth were more prominent.[33] Given that only a portion of Trump supporters were primarily focused on the right wing, it would have been impossible for this stark divergence of association to arise without the adoption by major media of the framing and agenda-setting efforts of the right wing and the Trump campaign. Patterson's explanation for the negativity in coverage is that journalists have developed professional norms that use cynicism and negative coverage as a sign of even-handed, hard-hitting journalism. Certainly the need to attract viewers and earn advertising revenues is rendered easier by focusing on easy-to-digest exciting news like horserace or scandals than by running in-depth analyses of wonkish policy details. None of these are technological or political drivers. They are the basic

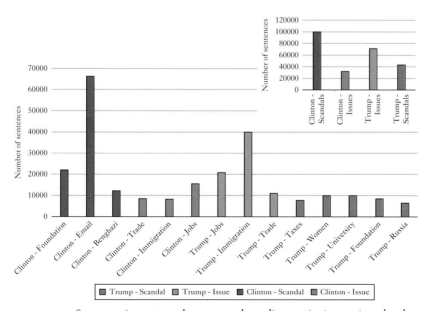

FIGURE 1.1 Sentences in mass-market open web media mentioning topics related to Donald Trump and Hillary Clinton during the 2016 election period.

drivers of advertising-supported media. We document and analyze these dynamics in Chapter 6, in particular the fragility of basic journalistic norms of neutrality in the teeth of an asymmetric, propaganda-rich media ecosystem. It is, we believe, impossible to gauge the effects of any of the other actors or dynamics without considering how they flowed through, and affected coverage by, professional mainstream media that were the primary source of news for most Americans outside the right-wing bubble.

Donald Trump: Candidate and President—All the explanations we have presented to this point ignore a central player in the dynamics of the moment—Donald Trump himself. But as we see repeatedly throughout this book, the president played a central catalyzing role in all these dynamics. In Chapter 4, when we look at the topic of immigration and the peaks and valleys in coverage, there is little doubt that Trump launched his campaign with an anti-immigrant message and continued to shape the patterns of coverage with his own statements throughout. Even Breitbart, clearly the most effective media actor promoting immigration as the core agenda of the election and framing it in terms of anti-Muslim fears, seems to have taken its cues from the candidate no less than Trump took cues from the site. Trump's comments as candidate repeatedly drew heated coverage and commentary from the mainstream press. He used this tactic to hold the spotlight from the beginning to the end of the campaign. Audacity, outrage, and divisiveness fueled his campaign. Trump launched his political career largely on his support of the "birther" movement, and has since embraced a wide range of conspiracy theories, from implying that Ted Cruz's father was associated with the Kennedy assassination, through reviving the Vince Foster conspiracy, to asserting that Hillary Clinton aided ISIS. Since becoming president Trump has repeatedly embraced and propagated conspiracy theories against political opponents, many of which fall within the broad frame of the "deep state," as when he embraced the Uranium One conspiracy theory designed to discredit the FBI and special counsel Robert Mueller's investigation. He has also adopted the term "fake news" to describe all critical mainstream media. It is highly likely his steady drumbeat of condemnation will have only heightened the distrust of media among his supporters.

Trump's use of Twitter has been one the defining facets of his presidency. One way to understand Trump's use of Twitter is as a mechanism to communicate directly with the public, particularly his tens of millions of followers (although it is unknown how many of these are in fact U.S. voters, and how many in fact read his tweets). The picture is more complex than that.

Trump not only uses Twitter to communicate with his followers, but also uses Twitter as a means of exerting power—over the media, the executive branch, the legislature, or opponents. Both as candidate and as president Trump has used Twitter in a feedback loop with the media. There have been several stories that document Trump "live tweeting" cable news, picking up talking points from what the president sees every morning on Fox and Friends, and tweeting them back out to the world.[34] There are many signs that guests that appear on the president's favorite Fox News, for example House Speaker Paul Ryan promoting a spending bill, are in effect performing for an audience of one;[35] others have documented how coverage is crafted to influence Trump.[36] The influence flows in both directions in an unusual multimedia relationship. Not a day goes by without the president's tweets becoming a news story. However outlandish a claim, as soon as the president makes or repeats it on Twitter, it is legitimate news not only on right-wing media but across the media ecosystem. In this manner, Trump has been able to insert himself as the center of media attention at any time and with little effort, and in doing so influence the media agenda. During the campaign, this attention "earned" him vastly greater media coverage than Hillary Clinton got. Over the course of his first year in office, the president has used Twitter to short-circuit normal processes in the executive branch as well, such as firing Secretary of State Rex Tillerson, announcing a ban on transgender troops, and creating "facts on the ground" that his subordinates have had to either explain away or, more often than not, accept and adjust their marching orders. While in principle the president could have used regular appearances at the daily press briefing in a similarly mercurial fashion, there is little doubt that the easy availability of a mass media outlet in the palm of his hand, at all hours of the day, has given the president a new and highly unorthodox lever of power.

Overall, the debate since the election seems to have focused on the presidency of Donald Trump more as the consequence to be explained than as an active player in a positive feedback contributing to information disorder. It might also be argued that the exact opposite is the case. That the media dynamics we observe in 2016 and since the election are the anomalous result of the presence of Trump, a charismatic reality TV personality with unusually strong media skills, first as candidate and then as president. There is little doubt that Trump is an outlier in this sense. Nonetheless, the highly asymmetric architecture of the media ecosystem precedes him, as do the asymmetric patterns of political polarization, and we think it more likely that his success was enabled by a political and media landscape ripe for takeover rather than that he himself upended the ecosystem. Trump, as both candidate and president, was both contributing cause and outcome, operating on the playing field of an already radicalized, asymmetric media ecosystem. As we explain in Chapters 10 and 11, Donald Trump represents the present state of a dynamic system that has been moving Republican politicians, voters, audiences, and media to the right at least since Rush Limbaugh launched this model of mass media propaganda on talk radio in 1988 and became, as the *National Review* wrote in 1993, "the Leader of the Opposition." In that ecosystem, Trump now operates as catalyst in chief.

Mapping the Actors: Politics, Commerce, Technology, and Centralization

In addition to identifying the specific actors responsible for the current crisis, we try to examine over the course of this book the larger drivers behind those specific actors. Our argument is that the crisis is more institutional than technological, more focused on U.S. media ecosystem dynamics than on Russia, and more driven by asymmetric political polarization than by commercial advertising systems. To highlight these larger questions, we have included two figures below. In both figures, we map each of the actors we have identified above along a horizontal axis of political versus commercial orientation. In Figure 1.2, we map the actors with a vertical axis that distinguishes between threats that come from centralized sources, like states or big companies, as opposed to decentralized sources, like grassroots mobilization or small businesses out to make a buck. In Figure 1.3, we map actors along a vertical axis that distinguishes between threats that are seen as caused by technological change versus those seen as coming from institutional dynamics—laws or social norms that shape how we develop our beliefs about what's going on and why.

Three things become quite clear from looking at these maps. First, most efforts to understand the apparent epistemic crisis have focused on technology—social media, the Facebook algorithm, behavioral microtargeting, bots, and online organic fragmentation and polarization. Second, Russia and Facebook play a very large role in the explanations. And third, most of the explanations focus on threats and failures that are politically neutral, or nonpartisan.

Our research suggests that our present epistemic crisis has an inescapably partisan shape. The patterns of mistrust in media and lack of ability to tell truth from fiction are not symmetric across the partisan divide. And the

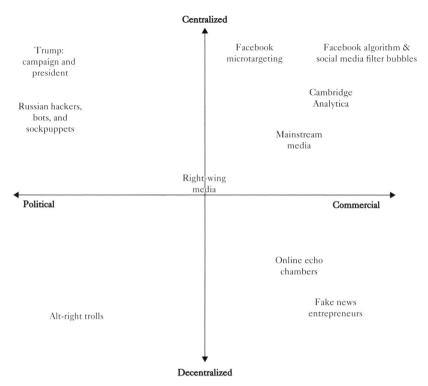

FIGURE 1.2 Threat models distinguished by political vs. commercial orientation and centralized vs. decentralized origins.

fundamental explanation for these differences cannot be laid at the feet of Facebook, Russia, or new technology. They are rooted in long-term changes in American politics. We are not arguing that technology does not matter, that the Russians did not actively interfere with U.S. politics, or that Facebook's algorithm is unimportant. Instead, we suggest that each of these "usual suspects" acts through and depends on the asymmetric partisan ecosystem that has developed over the past four decades. What that means in practice, for Americans, is that solutions that focus purely on short-term causes, like the Facebook algorithm, are unlikely to significantly improve our public discourse.

For others around the world it means understanding the costs and benefits of proposed interventions based on local institutional conditions, rather than context-free explanations based on "the nature" of the technology. Germany's new law, which puts Facebook and Google under severe pressure to censor their users to avoid large fines, may be useful for hate speech specifically, but

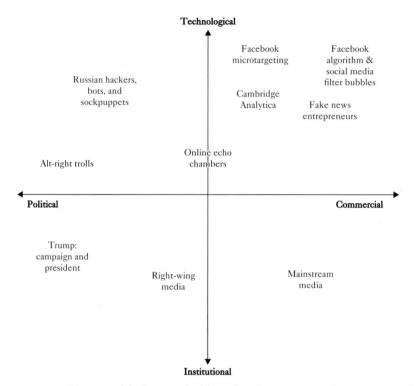

FIGURE 1.3 Threat models distinguished by political vs. commercial orientation and technological vs. institutional origins.

is not likely needed to counter propaganda generally because of the high trust in public media in Germany. This social background fact likely helped keep Russian propaganda on the margins in the 2017 German election, and the highly stable political institutional structures further limited the destabilizing effect of network propaganda and kept the far right at the margins of political significance despite electoral success. On the other hand, perhaps it is precisely Germany's willingness to wade into regulating its public sphere, born of its own bitter historical experience with democratic failure, that has given it its relatively stable media ecosystem. We do not suggest an answer to that question in this book, but we do offer a set of tools and an approach to understanding technology that may help those evaluating that question reach a clearer answer.

Technology does not determine outcomes or the patterns of its own adoption. Specific technologies, under specific institutional and cultural conditions, can certainly contribute to epistemic crisis. Radio during the

Rwandan genocide, and possibly troll-farms in Russia and WhatsApp in India, suggest that technology, in interaction with particular political-institutional conditions, can become the critical ingredient that tips some societies into instability, maybe at local levels or for brief periods. But we have not seen sufficient evidence to support the proposition that social media, or the internet, or technology in itself can be a sufficient cause for democratic destabilization at the national scale. Indeed, our own detailed study of the American case suggests that it is only where the underlying institutional and political-cultural fabric is frayed that technology can exacerbate existing problems and dynamics to the point of crisis. In the 2016 election, it was the already-present asymmetric architecture of news media, and asymmetric attitudes toward professional journalism governed by norms of objectivity, that fed the divergent patterns of media adoption online. It was this asymmetric architecture, and the insularity of right-wing media and audiences from the corrective function of professional journalism, that made that segment of the overall media ecosystem more susceptible to political clickbait fabricators, Russian propaganda, and extremist hyperpartisan bullshit of the Pizzagate variety.

Definitions: Propaganda and Its Elements, Purposes, and Outcomes

The widespread sense that we have entered a "post-truth" era and the general confusion over how we have gotten to this point has led to several careful efforts to define the terms of reference in the debate. The initial surge in "fake news" usage by observers from the center and left was quickly superseded by the term's adoption by President Trump to denote coverage critical of him, and has since essentially lost any real meaning. Influential work by Clair Wardle and Hossein Derakhshan for the Council of Europe and by Caroline Jack at the Data & Society Institute began to bring order to well-known but ill-defined terms like "*propaganda*," "*misinformation*," or "*disinformation*," as well as introducing neologisms like "*malinformation*" to denote leaks and harassment strategies.[37]

In the rest of this section, we present a brief history of the study of propaganda and lay out the definitions of these terms as we will use them through the rest of the book. We focus on the information and communications measures, rather than the harassment and intimidation activities. We anchor our definitions both in the salient forms we observed in our study of communications from April of 2015 to March of 2018 and in the long tradition of propaganda studies.

This segment may be a touch academic for some readers who want to get to the meat of our observations about how propaganda in fact played out in America in the presidential elections and the first year of the Trump presidency. For those readers we offer a brief cheat sheet here and invite you to skip the history and definitions and either go straight to our description of the plan of the book in this chapter or just dive in to Chapter 2.

- *"Propaganda"* and *"disinformation"*: manipulating and misleading people intentionally to achieve political ends.
- *"Network propaganda"*: the ways in which the architecture of a media ecosystem makes it more or less susceptible to disseminating these kinds of manipulations and lies.
- *"Bullshit"*: communications of outlets that don't care whether their statements are true or false, and usually not what their political effect is, as long as they make a buck.
- *"Misinformation"*: publishing wrong information without meaning to be wrong or having a political purpose in communicating false information.
- *"Disorientation"*: a condition that some propaganda seeks to induce, in which the target population simply loses the ability to tell truth from falsehood or where to go for help in distinguishing between the two.

There are more details in the definitions and history, and like all cheat sheets, this one is neither complete nor precise. But these will serve to make sure that if you skip the next segment you will not miss any important aspects of the chapters that follow.

A brief intellectual history of propaganda

Histories of propaganda, including Harold Laswell's field-defining work in the 1920s and 1930s,[38] emphasize sometimes the ancient origins of the use of communications to exercise control over populations and sometimes the Catholic Congregation for the Propagation of the Faith in the seventeenth century. It seems, nonetheless, that the intense interest in propaganda is a distinctly modern phenomenon. Several factors lent new urgency to the question of how governing elites were to manage mass populations: The discovery of "the masses," uprooted by industrialization and mass migration as a new object of concern; the emergence of new mass communications technologies, from the penny presses and mass circulation papers through movies in the nickelodeons to radio in the 1920s; the invention of psychology as a field of scientific inquiry and its application to mass populations; and the urgent need to mobilize these populations in the teeth of total war on a scale never seen before. Propaganda as a field was an application of the modernist commitment to expertise and scientific management, applied to the problem of managing a mass population in time of crisis. Walter Lippmann's words in *Public Opinion* might as well have been written in 2017 about behavioral psychology, A/B testing, and microtargeting as it was in 1922:

> That the manufacture of consent is capable of great refinements no one, I think, denies. The process by which public opinions arise is certainly no less intricate than it has appeared in these pages, and the opportunities for manipulation open to anyone who understands the process are plain enough. The creation of consent is not a new art. It is a very old one which was supposed to have died out with the appearance of democracy. But it has not died out. It has, in fact, improved enormously in technic, because it is now based on analysis rather than on rule of thumb. And so, as a result of psychological research, coupled with the modern means of communication, the practice of democracy has turned a corner. A revolution is taking place, infinitely more significant than any shifting of economic power.
>
> Within the life of the generation now in control of affairs, persuasion has become a self-conscious art and a regular organ of popular government. None of us begins to understand the consequences, but it is no daring prophecy to say that the knowledge of how to create consent will alter every political calculation and modify every political premise. Under the impact of propaganda, not necessarily in the sinister meaning of the word alone, the old constants of our thinking have become variables. It is no longer possible, for example, to believe in the original dogma of democracy; that the knowledge needed for the management of human affairs comes up spontaneously from the human heart. Where we act on that theory we expose ourselves to self-deception, and to forms of persuasion that we cannot verify.[39]

The Committee on Public Information that operated to shape public opinion in support of the American war effort in World War I, the Creel Committee, implemented the idea of applying the best cutting-edge techniques of technology and psychology to engage in the "Engineering of Consent," as one of its most influential alumni, Edward Bernays, would later call it.[40] Bernays, in this regard, embodies the translation of cutting-edge social psychology and the idea of expert engineering into the domain of manufacturing public opinion, and became one of the founders of the public relations industry in the early 1920s. Over the course of the 1920s to 1940s, writing about propaganda that remains influential today was caught between the will to systematize the definition and understanding of propaganda so as to make it an appropriately professional, scientific field of practice, and the negative inflection that the term had received during World War I, when all antiwar efforts were branded "German propaganda." While the negative connotation lingered, the professional orientation toward a managerial definition anchored in psychological manipulation is captured both in Laswell's classic 1927 definition "Propaganda is the management of collective attitudes by the manipulation of significant symbols"[41] and in the state-of-the-art definition adopted by the Institute for Propaganda Analysis in 1937: "Propaganda is the expression of opinions or actions carried out deliberately by individuals or groups with a view to influencing the opinions or actions of other individuals or groups for predetermined ends and through psychological manipulations."

The critical elements of this era of professionalized attention to propaganda were, therefore: (a) an actor with intent to manage a (b) target population's attitudes or behaviors (c) through symbolic manipulation informed by a psychological model of belief or attitude formation and revision, as opposed to rational or deliberative approach. This purposive, managerial approach remains central to self-conscious professional propagandists to this day. The *Army Field Manual of Psychological Operations*, for example, describes the role of PSYOP soldiers to "[i]nfluence foreign populations by expressing information subjectively to influence attitudes and behavior, and to obtain compliance, noninterference, or other desired behavioral changes."[42] These definitions emphasize *the propagandist actor*: an agent who acts intentionally; the purpose: to *influence* or manage a *target population*, which distinguishes propaganda from one-on-one persuasion, manipulation, or fraud; and the means: "*manipulation*," or "expressing information subjectively" in the terms of the PSYOP field manual—that is to say, *communicating* in a manner *behaviorally designed* to trigger a response in the target population to affect *beliefs, attitudes*, or *preferences* of the target population in order to *obtain behavior compliant* with the subjective goals of the propagandist.

The tension between this understanding of propaganda and a more deliberative or participatory view of democracy was already explicitly present in Lippmann's 1922 *Public Opinion*. If, as an empirical fact of the matter, the opinions of citizens as a population are poorly formed and weakly held, and if they are subject to manipulation through ever-more-refined interventions informed by ever-improving scientifically tested social and cognitive psychology, then the idea of deliberative democracy by an informed citizenry exercising self-governance is a utopia. In 1922 Lippmann was still willing to make the argument explicitly, and use it as a basis for an expertise-informed, elite-governed, democracy, recognizing that the inevitability of public opinion being manipulated may as well be used to mobilize support for good policies rather than for exploitation. The same is true for propaganda in markets. Bernays, who had cut his teeth in the Committee on Political Information, would go on to developing marketing campaigns, such as branding cigarettes "torches of freedom" in a 1929 effort to market cigarettes to women.[43] If consumer preferences were manufactured by sellers, and citizens' beliefs were manufactured by elites, then both anchors of liberal market democracies were fundamentally unstable. The use of the term "propaganda" made both of these tensions too palpable, and the term receded from use by expert practitioners, to be replaced by less morally freighted terms: "marketing," "communications," "public relations," or "publicity." "Propaganda," when used by mainstream authors, was left to describe what the Soviet Union did. Mostly, its use shifted to become a critical framework from which to criticize modern liberal market society, most famously in Jacques Ellul's *Propaganda: The Formation of Men's Attitudes* and later Edward Herman and Noam Chomsky's *Manufacturing Consent: The Political Economy of the Mass Media*.

Ellul's now-classic work reoriented the study of propaganda from understanding the practice of intentional management of beliefs and attitudes at the population level to understanding the structure of consciousness in technologically mediated market society. Propaganda was no longer something an actor perpetrates on a population (although it is that too), but the overall social practice and effect that normalizes and regularizes life and meaning in modern, technologically mediated society. "In the midst of increasing mechanization and technological organization, propaganda is simply the means used to prevent these things from being felt as too oppressive and to persuade man to submit with good grace."[44] This focus on how propaganda in this pacification sense is a pervasive characteristic in modern, mass-mediated society, and bridging from political communication to marketing and even education, became the typical approach of a mostly dwindling field of study.[45] Most prominently in this period, Herman and Chomsky's "Propaganda Model" of mass media offered the most explicit application of the term "propaganda" to the claim that "the media serve, and propagandize on behalf of, the powerful societal interests that control and finance them."[46] They delivered a detailed critique of media coverage of a range of politically sensitive topics and described the dynamics of newsroom politics, of ownership and control, media concentration and advertising dependence. Herman and Chomsky assimilate the term "propaganda" into the more general critique of commercial mass media that became prominent from the 1980s to the early 2000s. Other important contributions in this vein, which did not use the terminology of "propaganda" to make their point, include Ben Bagdikian's *Media Monopoly*, Neil Postman's *Amusing Ourselves to Death*, Robert McChesney's *Rich Media, Poor Democracy*, and Ed Baker's *Media, Markets, and Democracy*. This literature examined important failings of the commercial mass media model that typified the state of the media pre-internet, and continues to shed light on some of the failures of media conglomerates and the threats of concentrated commercial media to a well-functioning democratic public sphere. But in appropriating the term "propaganda" to describe the broad structure of ideology in modern, technologically mediated market society, as Ellul did, or the failings of commercial mass media during the rise of neoliberalism, as Herman and Chomsky did, the critical turn removed the term "propaganda" from the toolkit of those who wish to study intentional manipulation of public opinion, particularly as applied to politics.

We do not ignore or reject the validity and value of sustained study and critique of the democratic distortions introduced by commercial mass media, particularly concentrated media. Indeed, one of us relied on it in exploring the role of the internet in reversing some of these destructive characteristics of the commercial mass-mediated public sphere.[47] But the dynamics of the 2016 U.S. presidential election, Brexit, and other political arenas lead us to believe that it would be more useful to adopt the approach of work in the 1990s and 2000s that itself sought to revive the technocratic or scientific study of propaganda as a coherent topic of analysis. This work focused primarily on retaining the negative connotation of propaganda, while overcoming the urge to treat communications from "our" side as "communications," and those of opponents as "propaganda." The primary effort was to coherently distinguish "propaganda" from a variety of other terms that refer to communication to a population that has a similar desired outcome: persuasion, marketing, public relations, and education. The most influential treatment in this technical, observational line of work was Gareth Jowett and Victoria O'Donnell's *Propaganda and Persuasion*.[48] The book offered the most comprehensive intellectual history of propaganda studies, psychological research on the influence of media on attitudes and behaviors, and psychological warfare, and sought to systematize a definition and analysis approach out of that broad survey of the field. We follow that line of work in characterizing propaganda. Our claim for these definitions is not their abstract truth but their utility. We think they can help focus analysis on the set of threats that appear to be most salient in the present state and help define a coherent set of research questions without spilling over into too many associated fields of inquiry.

Definitions: Propaganda and Its Elements

Propaganda

Communication designed to manipulate a target population by affecting its beliefs, attitudes, or preferences in order to obtain behavior compliant with political goals of the propagandist.

This definition focuses the study of propaganda on *intentional* communications that are designed by the propagator to obtain outcomes. Unintentionally false communications that in fact affect behavior, but not by design, would not count. It limits the study to communications *targeted at a population*, excluding interpersonal manipulation or very small-scale efforts to manipulate a small group. This limitation in part is to keep the term in its broad original sense of dealing with mass populations, and in part to avoid confounding it simply with all forms of interpersonal manipulation. It limits the term to purposive behavior intended to affect a *political* outcome desired by the propagandist. In this, we purposefully exclude marketing, which fits all other elements of the definition and which shares many of the practices. We do so because we believe normative judgments about how it is appropriate for parties to treat each other in markets may differ from those we consider appropriate for interactions among citizens and between them and their governments or other political actors. Historically, even in more critical usage, "propaganda" has tended to highlight politics and power rather than commercial advantage, although critical usage has tended to expand the meaning and reach of the political. We recognize that what commentators will consider "political" will vary and that a campaign to market soap may be properly described as political if it is understood to reinforce a certain viewpoint about the appropriate standards by which women should be judged, for example. We certainly do not intend to exclude politics in this sense from our definition of political. Nonetheless, we think that confounding political manipulation with manipulative and misleading marketing for commercial gain will muddy the waters in both. The rise in consumer surveillance and behavioral marketing will certainly require extensive work on measuring and combating such practices. We think it will likely benefit from being part of a renewed literature on misleading advertising and consumer protection and that the study of manipulative marketing and propaganda will share a good bit of empirical overlap in terms of how to identify the practices, measure their effects, and so forth. But we believe there is an advantage to keeping separate the domain of politics, with its normative commitment to democracy, from the domain of commerce, and its normative commitment to welfare, consumer sovereignty, and consumer protection. And using "propaganda" to refer to the political domain is both consistent with longtime usage of the term and allows a more distinct focus for this kind of manipulation from this set of actors who operate within a distinct institutional framework for a set of distinct motivations.

Manipulation

Directly influencing someone's beliefs, attitudes, or preferences in ways that fall short of what an empathetic observer would deem normatively appropriate in context.

We emphasize the *manipulative* character of communications we deem propaganda. But "manipulation" is itself a term requiring definition. By Cass Sunstein's account, "manipulation" entails influencing people in a manner that "does not sufficiently engage or appeal to their capacity for reflection and deliberation."[49] We think this is too restrictive, because there can be emotional appeals that circumvent the rational capacities but are entirely appropriate for the relevant situation—such as a coach rallying her players' spirits at halftime after a disastrous first half. The critical issue is appropriateness for the situation. We adopt a variant of Anne Barnhill's definition that "[m]anipulation is directly influencing someone's beliefs, desires, or emotions such that she falls short of ideals for belief, desire, or emotion in ways typically not in her self-interest or likely not in her self-interest in the present context."[50] We adopt a variant, rather than Barnhill's definition, because in the political context appeals that are not in the self-interest of the individual are common and appropriate for the context, and so we focus instead on the property of appropriateness for the context. Indeed, we consider "autonomy" rather than "self-interest" as the touchstone, and adopt an "empathetic observer" standard, which one of us initially proposed in the context of characterizing modes of communication as appropriate and inappropriate from the perspective of an autonomous subject.[51] The "empathetic observer" differs from the "reasonable person" in that she takes the first-person perspective of the target of the communication, and asks whether that person, knowing the entire situation, including the intentions and psychological techniques of the alleged manipulator, would welcome the allegedly manipulative communication. While manipulation is often aided by cutting-edge behavioral psychology, we do not take the fact of scientifically informed design to be definitional, in the sense that manipulation informed by intuition and pop psychology is no less and no more objectionable for that reason.

What "manipulate" adds to a definition of propaganda, which already focuses on intentional action to shape beliefs, attitudes, or preferences, is the need to explain why the communication falls short of a normative ideal for how beliefs, attitudes, or preferences ought to be shaped. Outright false or materially misleading communications are relatively easy to categorize as normatively inappropriate, but emotionally evocative language presents harder questions. What is the difference between Martin Luther King Jr.'s soaring oratory in the "I Have a Dream" speech, and the Gateway Pundit's anti-immigration article entitled "Obama Changes Law: Allows Immigrants with Blistering STDs and Leprosy into U.S."? Perhaps appeals to strongly negative emotions such as fear, hatred, or disgust should be considered more inappropriate than strongly positive emotions, such as love, patriotism, or pride? One might imagine that from the perspective of democratic engagement, at least, the former would be more destructive to the possibility of public reason-giving and persuasion than the latter, and so from the perspective of a democracy committed to collective self-governance by people who treat each other as worthy of equal concern as citizens, the latter would more readily fall into the category of normatively inappropriate. But some of the worst abuses in human history were framed in terms that in the abstract sound positive and uplifting, be it love of country and patriotism or the universal solidarity of workers. The empathetic observer allows us to ground the difference in arguments about respecting the autonomy of members of the population subject to the intervention. Its risk, of course, is that those who think it is trivially true to think that King's oratory is appropriate and the Gateway Pundit's is not have to contend with the possibility that the readers of the Gateway Pundit are fully aware of the intent and effect of the communication, and desire it no less than the nearly defeated athletes at halftime desire the rousing pep talk from the coach. If that turns out to be sociologically true, then one needs some framework based not on respect for the autonomy of citizens as individuals but based on a more collective normative framework, such as what democracy requires of citizens.

We do not try to resolve that question here but emphasize that some form of manipulation is a necessary part of justifying the normatively negative connotation of "propaganda" and that connotation must have a well-defined normative foundation other than "I don't agree with what they said."

Disinformation

Dissemination of explicitly false or misleading information.

We use the term "disinformation" to denote a subset of propaganda that includes dissemination of explicitly false or misleading information. The falsehood may be the origin of the information, as when Russian-controlled Facebook or Twitter accounts masquerade as American, or it may be in relation to specific facts, as when Alex Jones of Infowars ran a Pizzagate story that he was later forced to retract. We mean to include both "black" and "gray" propaganda in the term disinformation, that is to say, propaganda whose source or content is purely false, as well as propaganda whose source and content is more subtly masked and manipulated to appear other than what it is.

Bullshit—Here we adopt philosopher Harry Frankfurt's by now widely popular definition, which covers communicating with no regard to the truth or falsehood of the statements made. A liar knows the truth and speaks what he knows to be untruthful. The bullshit artist "does not care whether the things he says describe reality correctly. He just picks them out, or makes them up, to suit his purpose."[52] "Fake news" producers in the original meaning, that is, purely commercial actors with no apparent political agenda who propagated made-up stories to garner engagements and advertising revenue, were the quintessence of bullshit artists in this sense. Not all bullshit is propaganda, because its propagators are indifferent to its impact on beliefs, attitudes, or preferences and have no agenda to shape behavior, political or otherwise, other than to induce a click. Here, in our case studies, we repeatedly encounter behavior that may be pure bullshit artistry and may be propaganda, depending on our best understanding of the motive and beliefs of the propagator. Broadcasting propaganda can be enormously profitable. It is hard to tell whether Sean Hannity or Alex Jones, for example, were acting as propagandists or bullshit artists in some of the stories we tell in Chapters 4 through 9. In all these cases, and those of many other actors in our studies, there is certainly a symbiotic relationship between the propagandists and the bullshit artists, with each providing the other with bits of narrative and framing that could be used, copied, circulated, and amplified throughout the network, such that as a practical matter what we interchangeably call commercial bullshit and political clickbait fabricators formed an important component of network propaganda.

Network Propaganda—What we observe in our broad, macroscale studies as well as in our detailed case studies is that the overall effect on beliefs and attitudes emerges from the interaction among a diverse and often broad set of discrete sources and narrative bits. The effects we define below—induced misperceptions, disorientation, and distraction—which contribute to population-scale changes in attitudes and beliefs, come not from a single story or source but from the fact that a wide range of outlets, some controlled by the propagandist, most not, repeat various versions of the propagandist's communications, adding credibility and improving recall of the false, misleading, or otherwise manipulative narrative in the target population, and disseminating that narrative more widely in that population. We call this dynamic "network propaganda" to allow us to treat it as a whole, while, as network analysis usually does, emphasizing the possibility and necessity of zooming in and out from individual nodes and connections to meso- and macroscale dynamics in order to understand the propagation characteristics and effect of propaganda campaigns, and in particular the role of network architecture and information flow dynamics in supporting and accelerating propagation, as opposed to resisting or correcting the propagandist efforts as they begin to propagate.

Propaganda Feedback Loop—This is a network dynamic in which media outlets, political elites, activists, and publics form and break connections based on the contents of statements, and that progressively lowers the costs of telling lies that are consistent with a shared political narrative and increases the costs of resisting that shared narrative in the name of truth. A network caught within such a feedback loop makes it difficult for a media outlet or politician to adopt a consistently truth-focused strategy without being expelled from the network and losing influence in the relevant segment of the public. We dedicate Chapter 3 to describing and documenting the effect.

Propaganda Pipeline and the Attention Backbone—In earlier work, one of us identified a dynamic, "the attention backbone," whereby peripheral nodes in the network garner attention for their agenda and frame, attract attention to it within a subnetwork of like-minded users who are intensely interested in the perspective, and through relatively more visible members of that subnetwork amplify that agenda or frame progressively upward to ever-more publicly influential sites to reach the public at large.[53] He argued that this dynamic was democratizing in that it circumvented the power of major media outlets to set, or sell the power to set, the agenda, and that it allowed for more diverse viewpoints than would normally be admissible in the mass-mediated public sphere to rise to the public agenda. In our work here, we have encountered that same structural dynamic being used to propagate disinformation and propaganda from peripheral nodes into the core. While the mechanisms are identical, we distinguish its use for propaganda purposes (which is determined by the character of the content, not its transmission mechanism) as "the propaganda pipeline" and offer an analysis and case study in Chapter 7.

Effects of Propaganda

Induced Misperceptions

Politically active factual beliefs that are false, contradict the best avail-able evidence in the public domain, or represent patently implausible interpretations of observed evidence.

By "misperception," we follow D.J. Flynn, Brendan Nyhan, and Jason Reifler, who define "misperceptions" as "factual beliefs that are false or contradict the best available evidence in the public domain."[54] By "politically active," we follow Jennifer Hochschild and Katherine Levine Einstein's typology, and focus on what people think they know that is associated with distinctive involvement in the public arena.[55] This limitation flows from our concern in propaganda with politics. Our observations regarding the practices of disinformation in the American public sphere lead us to emphasize that the falsehood of a belief cannot be limited to factual misstatement but must include patently implausible interpretations of observed evidence. We include as "patently implausible" both interpretations containing obvious logical errors and, more controversially, bad faith interpretations or framing that contradicts well-documented professional consensus. While interpretation adds fuzziness to judgments about beliefs, it is impossible to ignore the broad range of disinformation tactics we have observed that construct paranoid conspiracy interpretations around a core of true facts. Limiting our focus to discrete, false statements of fact will cause us to lose sight of more important and more invidious manipulations than simply communication of wrong

Jerry Brown Signs Bill Allowing Illegal Immigrants to Vote - Breitbart
www.breitbart.com/california/.../gov-jerry-brown-signs-bill-allowing-illegal-aliens-vot... ▼
Oct 12, 2015 - On Saturday, California Governor **Jerry Brown** signed Assembly Bill 1461, the New Motor
Voter **Act**, which **will** automatically register people to **vote** through the DMV, and could result in **illegal
aliens voting**. Any person who renewed or secured a driver's license through the DMV may now register
to **vote**, ...

FIGURE I.4 Google search result for Breitbart story on California motor voter law.

facts. For example, in one of its most widely shared immigration-related
stories, Breitbart wrote a factually correct set of statements, that Governor
Jerry Brown of California signed a motor voter law that, if the secretary of
state fails to check the citizenship of applicants, could allow undocumented
immigrants to vote. The story was posted with the URL designation: "Jerry
Brown Signs Bill Allowing Illegal Immigrants to Vote." This then shaped
how the headline appeared in Google searches (Figure 1.4) or the Facebook
newsfeed, so that this was the title as the story appeared in users' normal flow,
creating what we consider an example of a false interpretation of a set of true
facts. While the text of the article included factually correct statements—that
Jerry Brown signed a law that automatically registered eligible voters when
they obtained a driver's license, and that, if the secretary of state of California
should fail to check the eligibility of registrants such a law could result in
undocumented immigrants being registered—the gap between the chain of
unlikely but possible events that would lead to such an outcome and the highly
salient interpretation embedded in the distribution of the story suggests an
effort of intentional manipulation that would lead to "misperception" as we
define it here.

Distraction—Propaganda can often take the form of distracting a population
into paying no attention to a given subject and thus losing the capacity to
form politically active beliefs about or attitudes toward it. As Gary King,
Jennifer Pan, and Margaret Roberts showed in a large empirical study
of Chinese domestic propaganda that the "50 Cent Army"—the tens or
hundreds of thousands of people paid by the Chinese government to post
online to affect online discussion—primarily engages in distraction, rather
than persuasion or manipulation to achieve particular results. Studying over
400 million posts by these paid propagandists, King, Pan, and Roberts argue
that they do not generally engage anyone in debate, or attempt to persuade
anyone of anything; instead, their primary purpose appears to be to "distract
and redirect public attention from discussion or events with collective action
potential."[56]

Disorientation—The emphasis on disorientation appears in the literature on modern Russian propaganda, both in inward-focused applications and in its international propaganda outlets, Sputnik and RT (formerly, Russia Today). Here, the purpose is not to convince the audience of any particular truth but instead to make it impossible for people in the society subject to the propagandist's intervention to tell truth from non-truth. As Peter Pomerantsev put it in *Nothing Is True and Everything is Possible*:

> In today's Russia, by contrast, the idea of truth is irrelevant. On Russian "news" broadcasts, the borders between fact and fiction have become utterly blurred. Russian current-affairs programs feature apparent actors posing as refugees from eastern Ukraine, crying for the cameras about invented threats from imagined fascist gangs. [...] "The public likes how our main TV channels present material, the tone of our programs," [the deputy minister of communications] said. "The share of viewers for news programs on Russian TV has doubled over the last two months." The Kremlin tells its stories well, having mastered the mixture of authoritarianism and entertainment culture. The notion of "journalism," in the sense of reporting "facts" or "truth," has been wiped out. [...] When the Kremlin and its affiliated media outlets spat out outlandish stories about the downing of Malaysia Airlines Flight 17 over eastern Ukraine in July—reports that characterized the crash as everything from an assault by Ukrainian fighter jets following U.S. instructions, to an attempted NATO attack on Putin's private jet—they were trying not so much to convince viewers of any one version of events, but rather to leave them confused, paranoid, and passive—living in a Kremlin-controlled virtual reality that can no longer be mediated or debated by any appeal to "truth."[57]

As we will see, disorientation has been a central strategy of right-wing media since the early days of Rush Limbaugh's emergence as a popular conservative radio talk show host and political commentator with millions of listeners. Limbaugh's decades-long diatribes against one or all of what he calls "the four corners of Deceit"—government, academia, science, and the media— seem designed to disorient his audience and unmoor them from the core institutionalized mechanisms for defining truth in modernity. Repeatedly throughout our research for this book we have encountered truly fantastical stories circulated widely in the right-wing media ecosystem, from Hillary Clinton trafficking in Haitian children to satisfy her husband's unnatural lusts, to Hillary Clinton herself participating in pedophilia on "Orgy Island," to John Podesta's participation in satanic rituals, to the Uranium One story in which the special counsel investigating Russian interference in support of Donald Trump's campaign, Robert Mueller, and the deputy attorney general who appointed him, Rod Rosenstein, were portrayed as corruptly facilitating the Obama administration's sale of 20 percent of America's nuclear capabilities to Russia. These are all stories reported widely in the core sites of the right wing, and polls report that substantial numbers of Republicans claim to believe these stories—whether because they actually believe them factually or because claiming to believe them is part of what identifies them as Republicans.[58] But all of these seem so ludicrously implausible that it is difficult to imagine that they are in fact intended to make people believe them, rather than simply to create a profound disorientation and disconnect from any sense that there is anyone who actually "knows the truth." Left with nothing but this anomic disorientation, audiences can no longer tell truth from fiction, even if they want to. They are left with nothing but to choose statements that are ideologically congenial or mark them as members of the tribe. And in a world in which there is no truth, the most entertaining conspiracy theory will often win.

Propaganda and its effects, in our usage, always involve intention to communicate. A potentially important fact about the internet is that it may also create a good bit of error and confusion that are not the result of anyone's effort to shape political belief. We follow other work in defining misinformation.

Misinformation

Communication of false information without intent to deceive, manipulate, or otherwise obtain an outcome.

This may occur because in the 24-hour news cycle, journalists and others who seek to keep abreast of breaking news make honest mistakes; it may occur because the internet allows a much wider range of people to communicate broadly, and it covers many people without the resources or training to avoid error or correct it quickly. A major line of concern with the internet and social media is precisely that what characterizes our "post-truth" moment is misinformation in this sense. A common articulation of this concern is that as a society we are experiencing the disorientation that results from inhabiting a fast-moving, chaotic process and that the information chaos is an emergent property of a ubiquitously connected, always-on society over which we have no control.

Our data lead us to believe that, at least insofar as political communications are concerned, this diagnosis is false. The much simpler explanation in the political domain is that we are operating in a propaganda-rich environment and that network propaganda is a much deeper threat to democracy than any out-of-human-control emergent socio-technical process. We recognize that misinformation may play a larger role in fields that are not pervasively populated by intentional, well-organized, and well-resourced actors. False beliefs about health, such as anti-vaccine and anti-fluoridation sentiment, may well be more of function of misinformation than propaganda dynamics, as Brittney Seymour and her collaborators have shown.[59] But political communication operates in its own distinct ecosystem and that network is pervaded by propaganda. Describing the evidence that leads us to this conclusion and documenting the highly asymmetric pattern of susceptibility to and diffusion of propaganda and bullshit in the American media ecosystem will take up most of the book. As we will see, our conclusions make it difficult to identify solutions that are consistent with free speech and respect for freewheeling political contestation. We identify some responses, incremental and partial though they may be. We do believe that there are discrete interventions that can help. But the fundamental challenge is not purely or even primarily technological. It is institutional and cultural; which is to say, ultimately, political.

Plan of the Book

In the next chapter we describe our macrolevel findings about the architecture of the American news media ecosystem from 2015 to 2018. We collected and analyzed two million stories published during the 2016 presidential election campaign, and another 1.9 million stories about the Trump presidency during its first year. We analyze patterns of interlinking between the sites to understand the relations of authority and credibility among publishers high and low, and the tweeting and Facebook sharing practices of users to understand attention patterns to these media. What we find is a highly asymmetric media ecosystem, with a tightly integrated, insular right wing, while the rest of the media ecosystem comprises not a symmetrically separated left and a center but rather a single media ecosystem, spanning the range from relatively conservative publications like the *Wall Street Journal* to liberal or left publications like *The Nation* or *Mother Jones*, anchored in the traditional professional media. This basic pattern has remain unchanged in the year since Donald Trump took office, and, as we show in Chapter 11, was likely already in place at least as early as the 2012 election cycle. Chapter 3 presents a model of how such an insular media ecosystem might emerge and how two fundamentally different media ecosystems can coexist—one in which false narratives that reinforce partisan identity not only flourish but crowd out true narratives even when these are presented by leading insiders, and the other in which false narratives are tested, confronted, and contained by diverse outlets and actors operating in a truth-oriented norms dynamic. We then show how parallel but politically divergent false rumors, about Trump raping a 13-year-old and Hillary and Bill Clinton being involved in pedophilia, followed fundamentally different paths through the media ecosystems into which each was introduced. We argue that the difference in how the two highly divergent media ecosystems amplified or resisted the false narratives, not in the initial availability of falsehoods or the enthusiasm with which audiences wanted to hear them, made the Trump rape allegations wither on the vine while the Clinton pedophilia rumors thrived.

In Part Two we analyze the main actors in the asymmetric media ecosystem and how they used it to affect the formation of beliefs and the propagation of disinformation in the American public sphere. Chapter 4 looks at how the more radical parts of the right-wing media ecosystem, centered on Breitbart, interacted with Donald Trump as a candidate to force immigration to the forefront of the substantive agenda in both the Republican primary and the general election, and framed immigration primarily in terms of Islamophobia and threats to personal security. Chapter 5 turns to Fox News in particular. Through a series of case studies surrounding the central controversy of the first year of the Trump presidency—the Trump Russia investigation— we show how Fox News repeatedly mounted propaganda attacks at major transition moments in the controversy—the Michael Flynn firing in March 2017, when Fox adopted the "deep state" framing of the entire controversy; the James Comey firing and the Robert Mueller appointment in May 2017, when Fox propagated the Seth Rich murder conspiracy; and in October and November 2017, when the arrests of Paul Manafort and guilty plea of Michael Flynn seemed to mark a new level of threat to the president, when Fox reframed the Uranium One story as an attack on the integrity of the FBI and Justice Department officials in charge of the investigation. In each case, the attacks persisted over one or more months. In the case of the "deep state," the attack created the basic frame through which the right-wing media ecosystem interpreted the entire investigation. In each case the narrative and framing elements were repeated across diverse programs, by diverse personalities, across Fox News and Fox Business on television and on Fox's online site.

Chapter 6 turns its attention to the failure and recovery modes of mainstream media. Most Americans do not get their news from the right-wing media ecosystem. The 2016 election was heavily influenced by the ways in which those parts of the public sphere anchored around mainstream media operated. In particular, we show how standard journalistic norms of balance and chasing the scoop and the flashy headline create predictable failure modes in the presence of a highly asymmetric and propaganda-rich ecosystem. In the search for balance, professional media outlets emphasized negative coverage and focused heavily on scandals in their coverage of Clinton, particularly on emails and the Clinton Foundation. In search of the scoop, traditional media could not resist email-based coverage, and repeatedly covered it with a mismatch between the actual revelations, which were usually fairly banal, and the framing and headlines, which often overstated the significance of the findings. We use the case of the Clinton Foundation coverage in particular as a detailed case study of how Steve Bannon, Breitbart-CEO turned Trump campaign CEO and later White House chief strategist for the first seven months of the Trump administration, manipulated first the *New York Times*, and then most of the rest of the mainstream media ecosystem, into lending their credibility to his opposition research efforts in ways that were likely enormously damaging to Clinton's standing with the broad electorate. We end Chapter 6 with a study of the several news failures that populated the president's Fake News Awards list for 2017 and show that in all these cases the media ecosystem dynamic of "the rest," outside the right wing, functioned to introduce corrections early and to reinforce the incentives of all media outlets and reporters in that larger part of the ecosystem to commit resources and follow procedures that will allow them to get their facts straight.

Part Three looks at the remaining prime suspects in manipulating the election or political coverage during the election and the first year of the Trump presidency. In Chapter 7 we document a widely reported, but we think relatively less important part of the story—the propaganda pipeline. We show how statements by marginal actors on Reddit and 4chan were collated and prepared for propagation by more visible sites; and we show how this technique was used by both alt-right and Russia-related actors to successfully get a story from the periphery to Sean Hannity. But we also explain why we think that this process depends on actors to which we dedicated Chapters 3, 4, and 5, and why the propaganda pipeline, while open, was of secondary importance.

Chapter 8 addresses Russian propaganda more generally. We describe the existing sources of evidence that overwhelmingly support the proposition that Russia mounted sustained and significant information operations in the United States. We do not raise doubts as to the fact that the efforts occurred and continue. We do, however outline a series of questions about how important the Russian interference really was. Repeatedly, when we assess the concrete allegations made, we suggest reasons to think that these were likely of marginal significance, and mostly jumped on a bandwagon already hurtling down whatever path it was taking rather than giving that bandwagon the shove that got it going. Understanding not only that Russian propaganda efforts happened, but also how effective they were is, we think, critical to putting those efforts in context. Critically, if the biggest win for Russian information operations is to disorient American political communications, in the way we define the term here, then overstating the impact of those efforts actually helps consolidate their success. We do not suggest that we should understate the effects when we do see them. But it is important not to confuse the high degree to which Russian operations are observable with the extent to which they actually made a difference to politically active beliefs, attitudes, and behaviors on America.

Chapter 9 looks at the three major Facebook-based culprits—fake news entrepreneurs, behavioral manipulation by Cambridge Analytica, and plain old Facebook microtargeted advertising. We review the work of others, and complement it to some extent with our own data, to explain why we are skeptical of the importance of clickbait fabricators or Cambridge Analytica. The core long-term concern, we suggest, is Facebook's capacity to run highly targeted campaigns, using behavioral science and large-scale experimentation. In Chapter 13 we address possible solutions regarding political advertising regulation and the adoption, by regulation or voluntary compliance, of a public health approach to providing independent research accountability to the effects of Facebook and other major platforms on the health of the American media ecosystem.

Part Four takes on the claim that "the internet polarizes" or that social media creates "filter bubbles" as the primary causal mechanism for polarization online, as compared to the claim that the highly asymmetric media ecosystem we observe is a function of long-term institutional and political dynamics. Chapter 10 engages with the political science literature on polarization and shows that polarization long precedes the internet and results primarily from asymmetric political-elite-driven dynamics. We believe that that elite process, however, is influenced by the propaganda feedback loop we describe in Chapter 3. We lay out that argument in Chapter 11, when we turn to media history and describe the rise of second-wave right-wing media. We take a political economy approach that explains how institutions, politics, culture, and technology combine to explain why Rush Limbaugh, televangelism, and Fox News were able to emerge as mass media when they did, rather than remaining, as first-generation right-wing media after World War II had, small niche players. We then describe how the emergence of the online right-wing media ecosystem simply followed the offline media ecosystem architecture and, indeed, was left little choice by the propaganda feedback loop but to follow the path that it took. We see that asymmetric polarization precedes the emergence of the internet, and that even today the internet is highly unlikely to be the main cause of polarization, by comparison to Fox News and talk radio. In Chapter 12 we turn to consider what these insights imply for how we think about the internet; whether it can, or cannot, contribute to democratization, and under what conditions. Chapter 13 offers solutions. Unfortunately, the complex, long-term causes we outline do not lend themselves to small technocratic solutions. But we do emphasize adaptations that traditional media can undertake, in particular shifting the performance of objectivity from demonstrating neutrality to institutionalized accountability in truth seeking, as well as reforms in rules surrounding political advertising and data collection and use in behavioral advertising. We consider these all to be meaningful incremental steps to at least contain the extension of the unhealthy propaganda dynamics we observe to deeper and more invidious forms, but we acknowledge that given the decades-long effects of the propaganda feedback loop on the architecture of right-wing media in America, the solution is only likely to come with sustained political change.

In the final chapter, we underscore two core conclusions. First, if we are to understand how technology impacts society in general, and politics and democratic communications in particular, we must not be caught up in the particular, novel, technical disruption. Instead, we have to expand our viewpoint across time and systems, and understand the long term structural interactions between technology, institutions, and culture. Through this broader and longer-term lens, the present epistemic crisis is not made of technology; it cannot be placed at the feet of the internet, social media, or artificial intelligence. It is a phenomenon rooted in the radicalization of the right wing of American politics and a thirty-year process of media markets rewarding right-wing propagandists. We suspect that a similarly broad and long-term lens will be required to properly understand the rise of far-right parties and their information ecosystems elsewhere. At least in the United States, we find here that a failure to do so results in severe misdiagnosis of the challenges we face.

Second, much of contemporary discussion of the causes of crisis confound what is novel and observable with what actually has impact. It is hard to find bots; and when researchers find them, they are new and interesting. But repeatedly in our work they operate as background noise, and do not change the structure of the conversation. It is hard to spot Russians; and when Russia-hunters find them, they are sinister and newly menacing. But our work suggests that, while they were there, and much of what they did is likely illegal, they were mostly jumping on bandwagons already hurtling full-tilt downhill and cheering on a process entirely made in America. It is challenging to measure, and titillating to imagine, young nihilists generating fake news for American consumption and overwhelming traditional media. But when we measure the actual impact, it does not seem to be significant. So too with psychographically-informed behavioral marketing Cambridge Analytica-style.

It is not complacency that we seek to communicate, but the necessity of evidence-based diagnosis. If the evidence is too narrowly focused, or lacks the context to interpret the observations correctly, it will lead us to misdiagnose the problem and to develop solutions for emotionally salient but functionally marginal contributing causes of information disorder. These will, in turn, divert our attention and efforts to the wrong solutions, for the wrong reasons, at the wrong time. In the present crisis of the project of democracy, that is a misdiagnosis that we cannot afford.

2

The Architecture of Our Discontent

TENS OF THOUSANDS of entities form the complex ecosystem of American political media. Americans receive their political information from this diverse set of sources, which aim at a mix of broad and niche audiences. Although a growing proportion of the U.S. population uses Facebook and other social media as primary sources of news, a large portion, particularly those over 50 but even many who are younger, still rely on broadcast television and cable news.[1] Talk radio remains an important source of information and ideology for many Americans. Although the number of people who read newspapers and news magazines is shrinking, it remains significant, and political news is also brought to our attention by many other means, including face-to-face conversations in offline social networks, email, campaign advertising, social media, and family dinners.

To understand media and politics, we must understand the entire ecosystem: the outlets and influencers who form networks, the structure of networks, and the flow of information in networks. The increasing role of online platforms in shaping the media agenda is a challenge for political communications scholars and media observers. Researchers no longer have the convenience of simply looking at major news channels and newspapers to monitor the media agenda. And, conversely, a social-media-oriented strategy that only looks at Twitter or Facebook will miss much of what matters. We have to try to understand the interplay of broadcast news and newspapers with digital news outlets and blogs; of pundits, politicians, and personalities with large followings on social media, as well as the more distributed processes that occur in digital media. Some patterns of information flow emerge from organic, decentralized processes, and some are caused by intentional manipulation and marketing by centralized actors—most prominently political campaigns and state propaganda.

Network Propaganda. Yochai Benkler, Robert Faris, and Hal Roberts.
© Yochai Benkler, Robert Faris, and Hal Roberts 2018. Published 2018 by Oxford University Press.

In this chapter, we provide an overview of the architecture of political communication in America from the spring of 2015, when the 2016 presidential campaign kicked off, until the one-year anniversary of Donald Trump's presidency. We look separately at the structure of communication during the 2016 presidential election and the post-election period and document how that structure remained largely but not entirely stable during Trump's first year in office. In later chapters we complement this broad structural view with case studies that incorporate television and offer broader media coverage and more granular analysis. Here, we provide two types of maps for each period: an open web map, which describes the hyperlinking practices of online media producers on the web, and social media maps, which describe the content sharing practices of Twitter and Facebook users over the same period. These maps and the resulting analysis were developed using the Media Cloud platform and are based on the linking, tweeting, and sharing of just under four million political stories from over 40,000 online news sources. Media Cloud is an open platform for the analysis of online media that provides free access, through code, web tools, and data, to over 800 million stories from about 60,000 regularly crawled sources.[2]

Asymmetric Polarization in the 2016 Presidential Election

We present our data first as a series of network maps that describe news media sources and their relations to each other by different measures. We provide the more technical explanation of the methods, the data used to make these maps, and high-resolution images of each map in the online appendix.

The nodes, or circles, in each map, represent news sources. The size of each node represents its relative prominence by one of three measures. In the open web map, the node size represents the number of media sources that link to a site in the period the map describes. We think of these open-web links as expressions of judgment by online media producers about which sources are more influential as sources to cite. In the Twitter map, the size of the nodes represents the total number of tweets that shared stories from that site. In the Facebook map, the size of the nodes represents the total number of Facebook shares of stories on the site. As a rule of thumb, the sizes on the open web map are mostly determined by thousands of web publishers, those on the Twitter map are determined by millions of tweeters, and those on the Facebook map are determined by tens of millions of Facebook users.

The edges, or **links** between the nodes, are what give the network its architecture. They represent the relationships among the nodes. In the open web map, the architecture is defined by the hyperlinks between media sources. For any pair of media sources, the higher the number of stories on either site that link to the other site, the closer they are drawn together by the model. The structure of the Twitter maps is determined by the media source sharing patterns of Twitter users. In these, we create a link between two sites each time a single Twitter handle shares a story from each of those two sites on the same day. The intuitive interpretation is that if someone shares something from Breitbart and from the Daily Caller, that is an indication that Breitbart and the Daily Caller draw a common set of readers. The greater the number of accounts that tweet out links to the two sites, the closer the sites are on the map. Again, it is hardly surprising that more people who tweet out a Breitbart story will also tweet out a story on the Daily Caller or Fox News on the same day or that more people who tweet out a *New York Times* story will tweet a *Washington Post* story on the same day. Critically, the Twitter-derived networks give us the architecture of attention by politically engaged social media users, while the open web maps are based on the decisions of media producers. This provides us with two very different and important perspectives.

We also produce a second version of the Twitter-based network maps to highlight popularity on Facebook. The architecture of these maps is based on the same patterns of Twitter users in sharing links, but the nodes are sized by the number of shares on Facebook. We use the Twitter sharing architecture for the Facebook maps because the data Facebook made available at the time of this research to public researchers only provided total share numbers and not the network structure of those shares.

The similarity of the architecture of the open web maps compared to the Twitter maps strongly supports the robustness of our observations about that architecture. Particularly in evaluating the changes in 2017, the open web map offers us a measure of change that is insulated from the decisions of the social media companies. In this regard it offers us a baseline against which to evaluate changes in Facebook or Twitter prominence and the extent to which any changes reflect a change in algorithm or a change more generally in attention to that site.

The colors of the nodes reflect the partisanship of attention given to the media sources on Twitter. The partisanship is expressed in quintiles: red for the right, pink for the center-right, green for the center, light blue for the center-left, and dark blue for the left. The scores used to color the nodes reflect the share of that site's stories tweeted by users who also retweeted either Hillary Clinton or Trump during the election. These colors therefore reflect the attention patterns of audiences, not analysis of content of the sites, and are entirely based on user behavior rather than researcher judgment. Dark blue sites draw attention in ratios of at least 4:1 from Clinton supporters; red sites 4:1 from Trump supporters. Green sites were retweeted more or less equally by supporters of each candidate. Light-blue sites draw 3:2 Clinton supporters, and pink draw 3:2 Trump supporters.

The Open Web: 2016 Election

This aggregate view of the open web link economy during the 2016 election period (Figure 2.1) shows a marked difference between the right and everything that is not the right. There is a clear overlap and interaction between the left, center-left, and center media outlets. These are all centered on the cluster of professional, mainstream journalism sites: the *Washington Post*, the *New York*

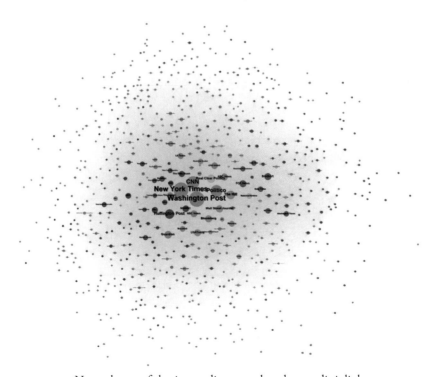

FIGURE 2.1 Network map of election media sources based on media inlinks.

Times, CNN, and *Politico* form a basin of attraction for outlets ranging from the editorially conservative *Wall Street Journal*, ABC News, *Business Week*, or *USA Today*, through the liberally oriented MSNBC. Zooming in (Figure 2.2), we see that the right side of the spectrum, by contrast, has Breitbart and Fox News as its basin of attraction, has almost no overlap with the center, and is sharply separated from the rest of the map. The other leading sites on the right include the *New York Post*, the *Washington Times*, the Daily Caller, the *Daily Mail*, and the *Washington Examiner*. There is almost no center-right, and what there is, anchored around the *National Review*, is distinct from the set of sites anchored by Fox and Breitbart on the right. The Huffington Post, the *Guardian*, and MSNBC receive the largest number of media inlinks on the left, joined by Mother Jones, Slate, Vox, and Salon.

The centrality of the *Washington Post*, the *New York Times*, CNN, *Politico*, and *The Hill* is determined not only by the large number of media inlinks they receive but also by the fact that they receive inlinks from across the network. The *Washington Post*, for example, is referenced by 5,100 unique media sources. The prominence of these large media sources can be explained in part by the reputation and authoritative voice of these long-standing institutions. But

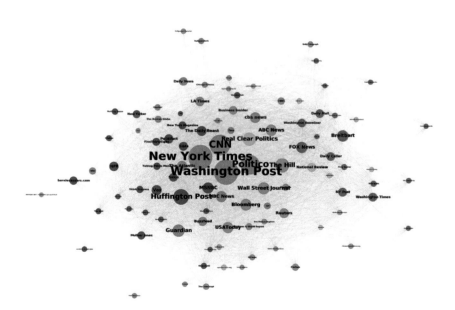

FIGURE 2.2 A closer look at the center of the open web media network map (Figure 2.1).

the sheer volume of stories produced by each outlet is another factor in these patterns. The *Washington Post* produced more than 50,000 stories over the 18-month election period, while the *New York Times*, CNN, and Huffington Post each published more than 30,000 stories.

The open web map—a reflection of which sources media producers deem worthy of citation—offers insights into the views of this elite cohort. As Table 2.1 suggests, this media-centric view attributes most of its attention and authority to professional media outlets, several with quite long institutional histories—legacy media, if you will. The roster of sites

Table 2.1 Top 50 media sources by media inlinks.

Media Source	Media Inlinks	Media Source	Media Inlinks
Washington Post	5100	HillaryClinton.com	1561
New York Times	5026	NPR	1539
CNN	4131	Los Angeles Times	1536
Politico	3866	PolitiFact	1489
YouTube	3846	BuzzFeed	1476
Huffington Post	2963	Yahoo! News	1462
The Hill	2605	National Review	1445
Wikipedia	2437	Slate	1410
Real Clear Politics	2381	New York Post	1407
Guardian	2206	Washington Times	1396
Wall Street Journal	2128	Daily Caller	1390
Facebook	2085	New York Daily News	1354
Business Week	2018	Daily Mail	1352
Breitbart	1990	Business Insider	1348
ABC News	1981	Salon	1340
Fox News	1967	BernieSanders.com	1296
MSNBC	1925	Washington Examiner	1295
USA Today	1921	Mother Jones	1259
NBC News	1897	New Yorker	1210
DonaldJTrump.com	1858	FiveThirtyEight	1177
CBS News	1829	New York Magazine	1173
Vox	1702	Amazon	1096
The Atlantic	1680	Talking Points Memo	1052
Daily Beast	1666	BBC	1043
Reuters	1605	Forbes	1037

that receive many inlinks on the open web includes some newcomers, certainly, but does not mark an epistemic crisis. Both versions of the social media maps, from Twitter and Facebook, replicate some of this attention pattern but exhibit more asymmetry between the right and the rest of the media landscape. And the largest nodes in the Twitter and Facebook maps include substantially more sites that are both relatively newer and do not claim to follow professional journalistic norms. As we will see later, this difference sharpens further when we break the attention down by partisan quintile, rather than taking a broad view of the top sites across the entire spectrum.

Twitter in the 2016 Election Period

The Twitter-based media network map displays many parallels with the open web network map (Figure 2.3). The separation of the right-wing media sphere and the central role played by Breitbart during the election period are even

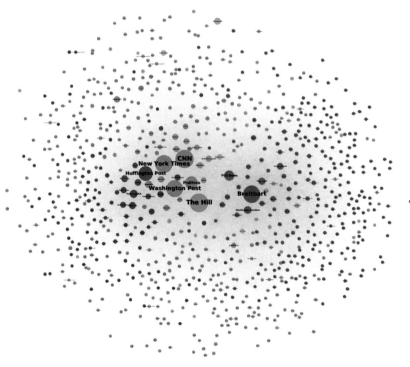

FIGURE 2.3 Network map based on Twitter media sharing, May 1, 2015–November 7, 2016. Nodes sized by number of Twitter shares.

more clearly visible. On Twitter, the left appears to be less integrated with the center-left, suggesting greater polarization on social media than on the open web both on the left and the right. The *New York Times*, CNN, *Washington Post*, and *Politico* remain as important nodes in the center-left along with *The Hill* in the center. The Huffington Post is still the most important media source on the left. On the right, Breitbart overshadows Fox News as the central node of conservative discourse on Twitter, but both rise in the overall hierarchy of sites across the ideological divide, Breitbart to fourth place and Fox to eighth (Table 2.2). Moreover, younger, more net-native, more frankly partisan sites gain significantly in prominence. On the left, Daily Kos, Politicus USA, Raw Story, and Salon gain visibility relative to their place in the link economy. On the right, the *New York Post* and *Washington Times* lose ground, surpassed by the Daily Caller and a newfound prominence for the Gateway Pundit and the Right Scoop.

Because of the influence of bots and coordinated propaganda efforts on Twitter, we tested to see whether the results would change meaningfully if we were to remove all the Twitter handles that would fall under the definition of "bot" according to a slightly revised version of one of the most widely used bot-detection approaches.[3] We also generated the maps by using the simple

Table 2.2 **Media sources most frequently shared on Twitter.**

1	CNN	16	Raw Story
2	The Hill	17	Salon
3	New York Times	18	Gateway Pundit
4	Breitbart	19	MSNBC
5	Washington Post	20	NBC News
6	Huffington Post	21	Wall Street Journal
7	Politico	22	USA Today
8	Fox News	23	Mother Jones
9	Politicus USA	24	Business Week
10	Washington Examiner	25	BuzzFeed
11	Guardian	26	Think Progress
12	Mashable	27	Daily Beast
13	Daily Kos	28	Reuters
14	Daily Caller	29	Vox
15	Yahoo! News	30	ABC News

rule of removing any bot that tweeted more than 200 times per day. Neither of these bot-filtering methods changed any of our results meaningfully. For reasons we will explain in Chapter 7, we are not confident that this approach fully accounts for all bots or in fact finds only bots we should care about, so we leave all the accounts in the next few figures. We are not claiming that intentional, automated, or human manipulation was unimportant in the campaign. We are observing that removing suspected bot handles does not meaningfully change the overall architecture of the media ecosystem.

Facebook in the 2016 Election Period

Using Facebook shares instead of Twitter shares to size the nodes (but still using tweets for the architecture of the network), there is an evident sharpening of the partisan divide (Figure 2.4). The principal nodes that anchor the center and center-left remain unchanged. The most remarkable feature of this map is the overwhelming prominence of Breitbart. Our data certainly support

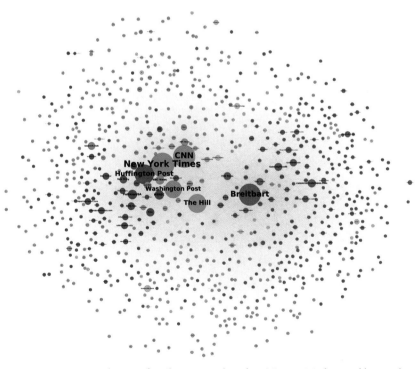

FIGURE 2.4 Network map of media sources shared on Twitter. Nodes sized by number of Facebook shares.

Table 2.3 Media sources most frequently shared on Facebook.

1	New York Times	16	Daily Kos
2	CNN	17	Daily Caller
3	Breitbart	18	Truthfeed
4	Huffington Post	19	Guardian
5	The Hill	20	ABC News
6	Washington Post	21	New Yorker
7	Politicus USA	22	Occupy Democrats
8	MSNBC	23	Addicting Info
9	NBC News	24	Bipartisan Report
10	Vox	25	Slate
11	Conservative Tribune	26	Western Journalism Center
12	Gateway Pundit	27	Daily Newsbin
13	Raw Story	28	Political Insider
14	Fox News	29	Salon
15	US Uncut	30	Mother Jones

Steve Bannon's claim that "Facebook is what propelled Breitbart to a massive audience."[4] More generally, the roster of top sites on Facebook retains some overlap with Twitter, while diverging even further from the popular sites on the open web (Table 2.3). On the left, many of the mainstays of liberal media are popular on Facebook, including the Huffington Post, Vox, Slate, Salon, Daily Kos, and *Mother Jones*. Politicus USA is still important and is joined by a set of newer highly partisan sites further left on the spectrum: Occupy Democrats, Addicting Info, Daily Newsbin, and Bipartisan Report. The most popular sites on Facebook from the right also include a number of more recent highly partisan entrants: Conservative Tribune, Truthfeed, Western Journalism, and the Political Insider.

Asymmetric Patterns of Authority and Attention

The maps offer one way of looking at the asymmetric architecture of the media ecosystem. The asymmetry becomes clearer with simple bar graphs that depict different measures of attention at different points of political spectrum. Figures 2.5, 2.6, and 2.7 show the top 250 sites during the 2016 presidential election by three measures: media inlinks, Twitter shares, and Facebook

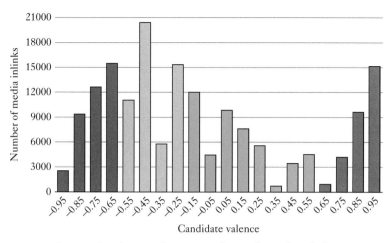

FIGURE 2.5 Partisan distribution of top 250 media sites by media inlinks, 2015–2016.

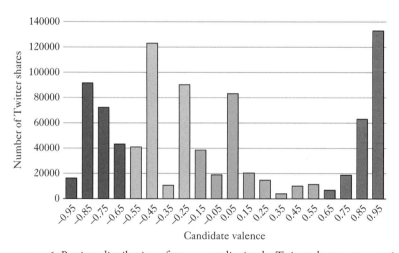

FIGURE 2.6 Partisan distribution of top 250 media sites by Twitter shares, 2015–2016.

shares. In broad outline, these graphs make clearer that attention, whether by Twitter, Facebook, or the more authoritative cross-media links, follows an asymmetric bimodal distribution, meaning that there are two peaks, and the left peak is closer to the center than the right peak. Starting at the center right and moving left we see a more or less normal distribution. Attention and authority both peak at the major professional journalism outlets that make up the center-left category and drop off as one moves left or right from that peak. By contrast, starting at the center-right and moving right, the distribution exhibits a negative skew: the further right an outlet is, the more attention it

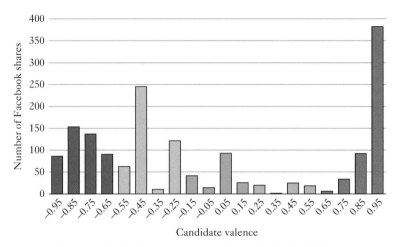

FIGURE 2.7 Partisan distribution of top 250 media sites by Facebook shares, 2015–2016.

gets. This is a fundamentally different structure of attention. People on the left do not emphasize media that draw only left attention, but frequently instead read, share, and quote the mainstream media, the *New York Times, Washington Post,* or CNN. These sites also account for substantial attention from people who otherwise read or write publications from the center, and even center-right.

By contrast, media producers and social media users on the right read, share, and quote almost only right-oriented media, and even among sites in the right quintile, the further right a site is the more attention it gets. The particular prominence of the right-most column in Figure 2.7 reflects the overwhelming prominence of Breitbart, as also reflected in the network maps. The general pattern is consistent across all three measures, although media sources frequently shared on Twitter and Facebook are weighted more toward the extremes, on right and left. This pattern is more pronounced on Facebook than on Twitter. On Twitter, the center-right is the least represented. On Facebook, both the center and center-right garnered relatively little attention. This pattern suggests that social media sharing in general is more partisan than hyperlinking, and sharing on Facebook is more partisan than on Twitter. This finding agrees with prior studies that indicate that more politically engaged citizens are also more partisan, as those sharing political content on Twitter and Facebook are likely those who are politically engaged.[5] Nonetheless, the overall structure, and in particular the clear difference in distribution of attention between the right and the left, remains clear across the open web, Twitter, and Facebook.

Breitbart, Fox News, and Influence in Conservative Media

The 2016 elections showed an unusual pattern of support for Trump as a candidate. Some right-leaning outlets, most notably Breitbart, launched attacks targeted not only at Democrats and Trump's Republican rivals but also at media outlets that did not fully support Trump's candidacy. A review of the stories most widely shared during the primary season shows that Jeb Bush, Marco Rubio, and Fox News were major targets of attack from Breitbart and related sites. The anti-elitist and anti-establishment narrative adopted by Trump and Breitbart led toward attacks on traditional institutions on both sides of the political spectrum.

Competition among the Republican contenders during the primaries had a strong impact on the shape of conservative media. Breitbart rose to serve as a focal point for Trump supporters and media organizations on the far right. This was arguably the largest change in the conservative media sphere, and the increasing role that Breitbart played during the election is clearly visible in our data. One important aspect that is less apparent in the network maps is how Breitbart served as a translator and bridge that helped to legitimate and popularize extreme views on topics such as immigration and anti-Muslim sentiments.

Breitbart and Fox News were the two principal poles of conservative media depicted in the link economy maps. This structure remained stable over the duration of the election. Changes over time are more evident in the Twitter-based maps. Recall that the position of media sources on these maps is shaped by the proclivity for Twitter users to share media sources. The most engaged partisans on Twitter effectively voted on which media sources were complementary, as reflected in the maps by their proximity.

In October 2015, with a broad set of candidates running for the GOP nomination, Fox News and Breitbart occupied similar areas of the map, with Fox News closer to the center and Breitbart further to the right (Figure 2.8).

By February 2016, Breitbart had grown more prominent while Fox had declined. In Figure 2.9, Fox News appears as a smaller node quite distant from the Breitbart-centered right. This shift reflects the fact that Fox News then received less Twitter attention than it did earlier or later in the campaign, and less attention in particular from users who also paid attention to the core Breitbart-centered sites. The March map is similar, and only over April and May did the overall attention paid to Fox and attention from Trump followers recover.

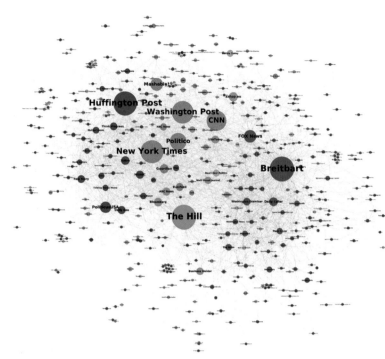

FIGURE 2.8 Network map based on Twitter media sharing, October 2015.

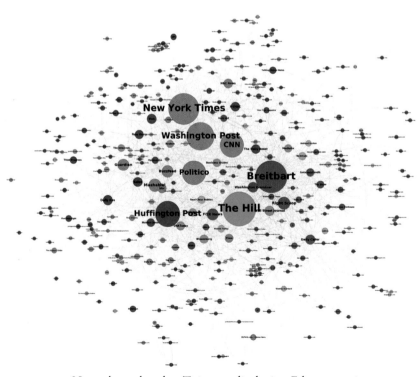

FIGURE 2.9 Network map based on Twitter media sharing, February 2016.

This sidelining of Fox News in early 2016 coincided with sustained attacks against the network by Breitbart. The top 20 stories in the right-wing media ecology during January included, for example, "Trump Campaign Manager Reveals Fox News Debate Chief Has Daughter Working for Rubio." Many of the strongest attacks on Fox were linked to immigration, which, as we document in Chapter 4, was the central agenda of Trump's 2016 candidacy. The five most widely shared stories in which Breitbart referred to Fox were stories intended to brand Fox News as weak on immigration and unseat it as the central arbiter of conservative news. The narrative tied together Breitbart's stance on immigration with its successful framing of immigration as centrally concerned with Muslims, terrorism, and elite corruption:

The Anti-Trump Network: Fox News Money Flows into Open Borders Group

NY Times Bombshell Scoop: Fox News Colluded with Rubio to Give Amnesty to Illegal Aliens

Google and Fox TV Invite Anti-Trump, Hitler-Citing, Muslim Advocate to Join Next GOP TV-Debate

Fox, Google Pick 1994 Illegal Immigrant To Ask Question In Iowa GOP Debate

Fox News At Facebook Meeting Is Misdirection: Murdoch and Zuckerberg Are Deeply Connected Over Immigration

The repeated theme of conspiracy, corruption, and media betrayal is palpable in these highly shared Breitbart headlines linking Fox News, Rubio, and illegal immigration.

These sustained attacks likely contributed to the apparent decline in the standing of Fox News among the most conservative voters. As Breitbart trumpeted at the time,[6] a survey reported that in February 2016 the perception of Fox News among conservative audiences was at its lowest point in more than three years.[7]

Our maps show that, as the primaries ended, attention to Fox recovered and Fox became more closely integrated with Breitbart and the remainder of the right-wing media sphere (Figure 2.10). As right-wing media closed ranks behind their chosen candidate, tensions within the right wing were reduced, and attacks from right-wing media uniformly targeted traditional

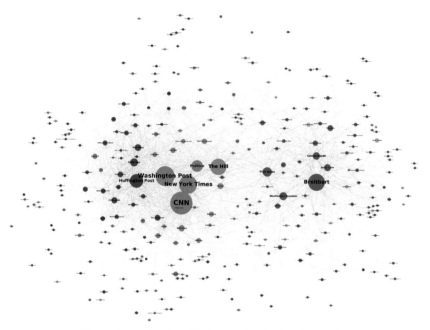

FIGURE 2.10 Network map based on Twitter media sharing, September 2016.

mainstream media. While the prominence of individual media sources in the right-wing sphere varies when assessed by shares on Facebook and Twitter, the content and core structure, with Breitbart at the center, is stable across platforms. Even in the highly charged pre-election months, everyone outside the Breitbart-centered universe formed a tightly interconnected attention network, with major traditional mass-media and professional sources at the core. The right, by contrast, formed its own insular sphere centered on Breitbart.

Post-Election Asymmetry: Fox News Rises on the Right, the Left Tunes in to the Mainstream

The overall architecture of the American political media ecosystem remained as asymmetric in 2017 as it was in the preceding two years. In fact, each segment of the media ecosystem became a clearer version of itself. Outside the right-wing ecosystem, we did not see a leftward polarization but its opposite—an increase in the authority of, and attention paid to, the traditional professional media that occupy the center and center-left, at the expense of the left. On the right, the most important shift was that Fox News reasserted its authority as

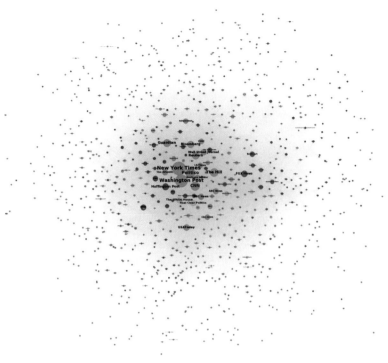

FIGURE 2.11 Network map based on media inlinks, coverage of Donald Trump, November 8, 2016–September 14, 2017.

the central node of the online right-wing media ecosystem. This revival came at the expense of Breitbart, which declined to second place online (leaving aside Fox dominance of conservative television throughout the election and post-election periods). However, Fox News's resurgence did not increase connections between the right and the rest of the network. During the election, Fox online received 40 percent of its inlinks from the right quintile. In the year after the election, Fox received 51 percent of its links from the right quintile. This shift reflected a decline in linking to Fox across-the-board, not only from the left. Indeed, links from the center-right and the center to Fox declined proportionately more than did links from the center-left and left.[8]

The network map shown in Figure 2.11 is based on 1.6 million open web stories related to Trump from the day after the election until mid-September 2017. When compared to the pre-election data (Figure 2.1), the post-election network shows a less prominent right-wing media presence.

Figure 2.12 zooms in to underscore the heightened role of Fox within the right-wing and the general decline in the total number of links to the right, while the center and center-left grew.

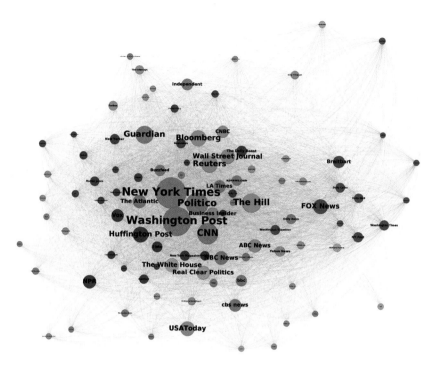

FIGURE 2.12 Core of the network map based on media inlinks, coverage of Donald Trump, November 8, 2016–September 14, 2017.

Figure 2.13 compares inlinks in the 18 months prior to the election, colored by their quintile, to inlinks from Election Day to September of 2017, represented next to them and colored grey for contrast. Links provide a particularly valuable baseline because they are not affected by any of the platform companies' algorithm changes. Facebook, Twitter, or Google may have a modest impact on the media diet of media producers, but cross-media links are deliberate choices of journalists and other online media producers, and are therefore less influenced by the vagaries of platform policies and algorithms. On the left, we see the three most-leftward columns decline in their share of inlinks. The most centrist media sources on the left and those in the center-left gained in inlink shares. These segments, as you recall, are populated primarily by professional journalism outlets. Even within the left, publishers linked more to NPR than to MSNBC or Talking Points Memo. We also see a distinct increase in links to the center in three of its four columns, with the major movers there reflecting an increase in the relative prominence

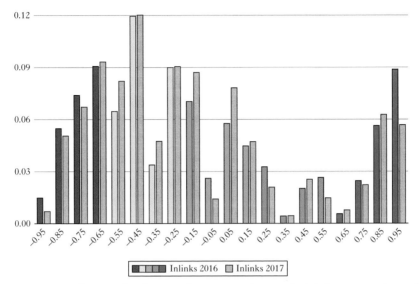

FIGURE 2.13 Partisan distribution of top 250 media sites by inlinks—comparison of pre-election and post-election.

Table 2.4 Cross-media inlinks to each quintile.

	Total inlinks to quintile, in thousands		Share of total	
	2016	2017	2016	2017
Left	204.9	145.2	0.20	0.18
Center-left	440.8	369.7	0.43	0.46
Center	186.1	170.2	0.18	0.21
Center-right	44.2	26.2	0.04	0.03
Right	138.6	100.6	0.14	0.12

of *The Hill* and Reuters, and a decrease for ABC News and the *Wall Street Journal*. On the right, the biggest change is the dramatic decline in Breitbart's relative weight—and remember, this graph reflects not social-media attention but linking, and therefore is not a function of any social media algorithmic changes. This shift represents the structure of authority on the right, primarily a reassertion of authority by Fox News online.

Table 2.4 shows the share each quintile received of the total inlinks during this period. Prior to the election, for all the vehemence and polarization,

Table 2.5a Proportion of all inlinks to top 50 sites on the right, by site.

	Total inlinks, in thousands		Proportion of total inlinks to right quintile	
	2016	2017	2016	2017
Breitbart	16.6	11.8	0.12	0.12
Fox News	14.4	16.5	0.10	0.16
Daily Caller	10.2	8.3	0.07	0.08
Washington Examiner	9.1	7.6	0.06	0.08
NY Post	7.6	6.5	0.05	0.06
DonaldJTrump.com	7.5	2.9	0.05	0.03
Washington Times	7.0	5.2	0.05	0.05
Daily Mail	6.1	4.6	0.04	0.05
WikiLeaks	4.7	0.2	0.03	0.00
Free Beacon	4.3	2.7	0.03	0.03

Table 2.5b Proportion of all inlinks to top 50 sites on the left, by site.

	Total inlinks, in thousands		Proportion of total inlinks to left quintile	
	2016	2017	2016	2017
Huffington Post	25.0	16.3	0.12	0.11
MSNBC	16.9	4.3	0.08	0.03
PolitiFact	11.4	5.5	0.06	0.04
NPR	10.4	14.8	0.05	0.10
Vox	10.2	11.2	0.05	0.08
Daily Beast	9.6	7.4	0.05	0.05
Slate	8.2	6.9	0.04	0.05
Talking Points Memo	7.1	4.2	0.04	0.03
HillaryClinton.com	7.1	0.1	0.04	0.00
Salon	6.8	4.5	0.03	0.03

65 percent of all links went to the center, center-left, and center-right, while the left got 20 percent of the links and the right 14 percent. In 2017, the shares of the left and right both declined as a proportion of overall authority, and the share of the three center quintiles rose to 70 percent. The asymmetry is a

function of the fact that the center right is largely absent in both years, and this does not change meaningfully in 2017.

Tables 2.5a and 2.5b dig deeper into the most influential media on the left and the right. As a proportion of all links that went to the top 50 media outlets on the left and right, the big positive mover on the right was Fox News, and to a lesser extent the *Washington Examiner*, while on the left we saw a significant decline for MSNBC and a substantial increase for NPR and Vox.

Social Media During the First Year of the Trump Presidency

As we saw in the comparison of cross-media links and social media activity prior to the election, the sharing patterns of politically engaged users on Twitter and Facebook offer a view of media activity that is more partisan and more centered around nontraditional news media.

Figure 2.14, based on Twitter sharing patterns, shows the now-familiar highly segregated network structure. The right stands clearly apart from the center, center-left, and left. Unlike the pre-election period, Fox garners the most attention on the right. Figure 2.15, which compares the distribution of

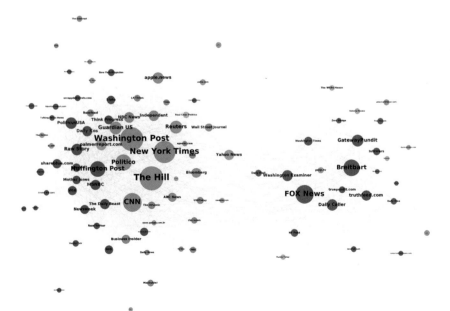

FIGURE 2.14 Network map based on Twitter media sharing, January 22, 2017–January 21, 2018. Nodes sized by number of Twitter shares.

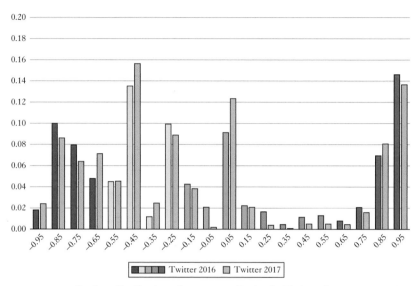

FIGURE 2.15 Partisan distribution of top 250 media sites by Twitter shares—comparison of pre-election and post-election.

attention across the partisan spectrum in the pre-election and post-election periods, shows a remarkable level of consistency across the two time periods. There are some notable changes. Here we see a small increase in the farthest left column, decreased in the next two columns on the left, and then an increase in the most centrist of the left columns. Three of the center-left segments gained in shares along with the segment in the center occupied by *The Hill*. On the center-right and right we see a broad decline except for the two right-most columns, where Fox News's rise reflects in an increase in the second-from-right segment, and the decline of Breitbart and the increase in the Twitter shares of Truthfeed, Zero Hedge, and the Gateway Pundit balance out.

Fox News surpassed Breitbart in both inlinks and Twitter shares. Breitbart continues to have more Facebook shares, but its lead shrinks from 400 percent to only 30 percent, due to both a collapse in Breitbart's numbers and a substantial increase in Fox's numbers (Table 2.6).

Figure 2.16 shows that the big gains in Facebook share are in the center left and center professional media segments, not on the further left. There is steep decline in the far right. As we will show, this is partially a drop in shares to Breitbart but also a decline for other media sources on the far right. The second to the right column, led by Fox, gains slightly.

Directing attention to particular media sources yields clear insights about who gained and who lost ground across the media landscape after the election.

Table 2.6 Breitbart and Fox comparison of pre-election
and post-election periods.

		Media inlinks	Total inlinks	Twitter shares	Facebook shares
Pre-election	Breitbart	1,990	16,649	38,467	83,529
	Fox	1,967	14,420	19,532	19,862
Post-election	Breitbart	1,475	11,821	13,579	31,208
	Fox	1,915	16,493	20,376	24,780

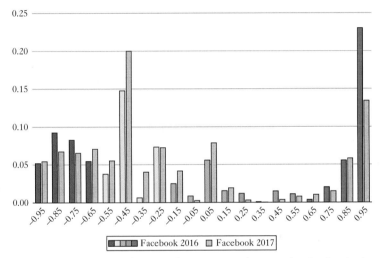

FIGURE 2.16 Partisan distribution of top 250 media sites by Facebook shares—comparison of pre-election and post-election.

Figures 2.17 and 2.18 represent the top sites and their relative changes on Facebook and Twitter comparing the pre-election and post-election periods. The *New York Times, Washington Post*, Fox News, and *The Hill* all increased their share of social attention in 2017 on both Twitter and Facebook. CNN, the Huffington Post, and Breitbart, although still very prominent, declined on both platforms. The shift in media coverage after the election is part of the story as post-election media coverage focused more on reporting and investigative journalism and less on campaign horserace coverage. The trend we see among the most popular media outlets is consistent with a shift in attention to larger established media outlets. Two liberal U.K.-based media outlets, the *Guardian* and the *Independent*, broke into the top 10 in 2017 by

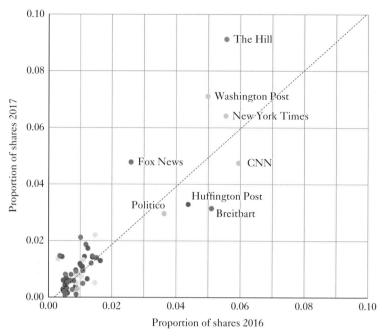

FIGURE 2.17 Proportion of total shares for media sources most shared on Twitter—comparison of 2016 and 2017.

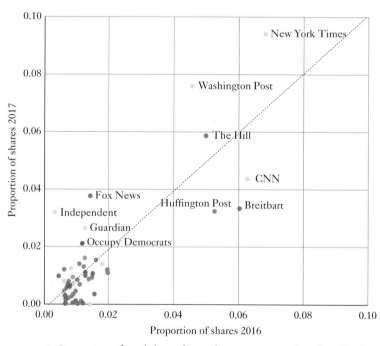

FIGURE 2.18 Proportion of total shares for media sources most shared on Facebook—comparison of 2016 and 2017.

Facebook shares. The rising prominence of Fox News is clear, accompanied by the declining influence of Breitbart on the right.

Occupy Democrats is the only far-left site that gained prominence on Facebook in 2017. These gains occurred before June. Thereafter the site rapidly declined and effectively shifted to new domains: washingtonjournal. com, first, and then washintonpress.com; neither had as much influence as the site had earlier.[9] Palmer Report and Raw Story, other left-wing sites, saw more attention on Twitter in 2017, as seen in Figure 2.19, which shows the movement among second-tier media sources on Twitter. Figure 2.20 shows the corresponding changes for second-tier sites on Facebook. The other sites from the left that increased in 2017 on Facebook include the *Atlantic*, the *New Yorker*, and Slate. On Twitter, the winners on the left include MSNBC, Vox, and *Mother Jones*.

Hyperpartisan and conspiracy-minded sites on both ends of the political spectrum fared poorly on Facebook, presumably falling victim to changes in

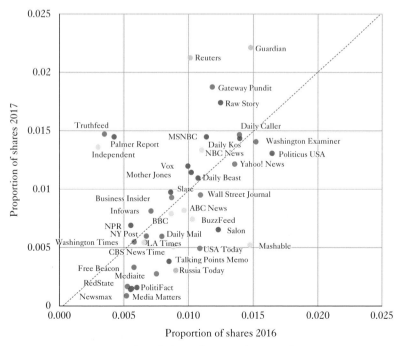

FIGURE 2.19 Proportion of total shares for second-tier media sources on Twitter—comparison of 2016 and 2017.

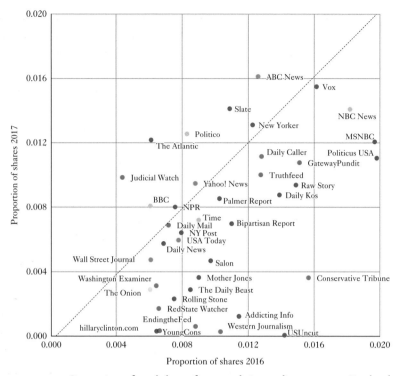

FIGURE 2.20 Proportion of total shares for second-tier media sources on Facebook—comparison of 2016 and 2017.

the Facebook newsfeed algorithm. On the left, the losers include Bipartisan Report, Addicting Info, and Palmer Report (when compared to the prior incarnation of Bill Palmer's site, Daily News Bin). On the right, the slate of hyperpartisan sites declined dramatically, including Conservative Tribune, Western Journalism, Young Cons, Ending the Fed, and Red State Watcher, along with the more popular Daily Caller, Truthfeed, and Gateway Pundit.

On Twitter, there were also far more losers than winners. Overall, the focus of attention shifted toward the top sites and away from second-tier sites. Reuters and the *Guardian* performed better on Twitter in 2017. Looking at Twitter shares on the right, Truthfeed and the Gateway Pundit are outliers, gaining substantially in their share of attention. Infowars also made moderate gains on Twitter, as did the Daily Caller.

Changes on both the left and the right were mixed. As we saw when looking in the aggregate, sites on the left as a whole lost prominence on social media, while sites on the center-left and professional news sites like NPR increased. This did not prevent a hyperpartisan site like the Palmer Report or Raw Story from joining the Huffington Post as the three most tweeted sources in the left media set. Similarly, results on the right were mixed. On the one hand, Breitbart was replaced by Fox News as the leading site, which suggests some moderation of the style and extremity of views sought by viewers and readers. On the other hand, other winners on the right in 2017 on Twitter included Gateway Pundit, Infowars, and Truthfeed, sites that make Breitbart seem moderate. This shift might be more consistent with a different interpretation of the rise of Fox: that the network became a more extreme version of itself in 2017. We examine that question in Chapter 5, when we turn our focus to what happened to Fox News in 2017.

The changes in 2017 on the left and center-left are not consistent with the sense of a pervasive epistemic crisis. If anything, they mark a moderate strengthening of the role of professional journalistic organizations. Certainly, there were outlets on the left that adopted the hyperpartisan strategy of many of the most successful sites on the right. Occupy Democrats and the Palmer Report are the two clearest examples. As we will show throughout Part Two of the book, however, conspiracy theories and disinformation campaigns require more than a single site or two to spin them up to move from isolated chatter to gain broader currency. The architecture of the network in which these left-oriented hyperpartisan clickbait sites operate is fundamentally different from the network architecture which their right-oriented counterparts occupy. And, as we argue in the next several chapters, that architecture and the institutional character of the media outlets that constitute it, more than the Russians, more than the fake news entrepreneurs, more than Facebook advertising, and more than Cambridge Analytica, are most directly responsible for the prevalence and success of disinformation, propaganda, and commercial bullshit in the American media ecosystem.

We began this chapter with an acknowledgment that observing online communications, much less a single medium like Twitter or Facebook, offers only a partial and almost certainly imperfect view of the American media ecosystem. In the run-up to the election, a Pew survey suggested that 57 percent of Americans got their news from television: cable, local, and network news; while 38 percent got their news online.[10] A Pew study from earlier in 2016 found that only 14 percent identified social media as their "most helpful" source for getting information on the election, while cable, local news, network news, and radio were described so by about 60 percent of the audience.[11] A 2017 survey by Hunt Alcott and Matthew Gentzkow similarly found that 14 percent of respondents stated that social media were their "most important" source of election news.[12] Narrowing down more specifically to election news, a Pew survey conducted a few weeks after the election found that Fox News was the primary source of news for 40 percent of Trump voters, alongside CNN (8 percent), the three major networks (12 percent in total), local TV (5 percent), and radio (3 percent), leaving Facebook as the primary source of news for only 7 percent of Trump voters. No print media broke the 3 percent minimum share to be reported in that study. Clinton voters, by contrast, had a more varied diet, with CNN topping at 18 percent, MSNBC (9 percent), local TV (8 percent), NPR (7 percent), the networks (15 percent), the *New York Times* (5 percent), local newspapers (4 percent), and Fox News (3 percent). But Facebook use was quite similar to that of Trump followers, and was the primary source of news for only 8 percent of Clinton supporters.[13]

These observations seem to be at odds with a 2017 Pew survey often cited for the claim that 67 percent of Americans get their news on social media.[14] While that higher number is often cited, it is important to remember that the 67 percent includes 20 percent who say they "hardly ever" get news on social media. The headline finding from that survey might have been entitled: "53 percent of Americans never or hardly ever get their news from social media." Only 20 percent of respondents in that survey said that they often get their news on social media, and another 27 percent said they sometimes do. When asked looser survey questions about their news consumption habits, such as where they got news "often," 57 percent responded that they got news on television, ranging across all cable, network, and local, and another 25 percent get their news from radio, some of which is talk radio and some of which is NPR and networks.[15] Clearly, online news continues to grow as a source of news people often turn to, and will continue to grow in importance. This trend is driven by readers over 50, and in particular over 65, increasing their previously low use of online sources, rather than younger people meaningfully changing their already substantial use of online media.[16] Still, television remains the primary source of news and will likely continue to occupy that spot for several more election cycles.

There are several ways in which we try to expand our data collection and interpret our data to allow us to say more about the overall media ecosystem, and not only about online news sources and social media. First, even if only about half of Americans get their news online often or sometimes, these news readers interact socially, and offline social relations are an important source of news for the majority of the population.[17] Many Americans who do not get their news online are a conversation away from those who are. Second, our data include the online versions of the major television news channels, and while this may not replicate exactly the content of television programming, it represents a reasonable proxy. It also offers us a structural view of how these sources interact with other sources, the patterns of attention they draw, and their relation to other news sites whose content we can analyze in great detail. Third, the prominence of particular sites and stories enables us to identify salient television news coverage that we can then use a database of television broadcasts by major news networks and select local stations maintained by the Internet Archive to study as case studies. This targeting for case studies is further complemented by our ability to analyze YouTube videos, another useful avenue to identify particularly influential television moments. Throughout Chapters 3 to 8 we will combine our online data analysis with television analysis based on these bridges to give a more complete picture of what the media ecosystem looked like even when we do not have a full picture of every communication. Finally, but not least, political and media elites—politicians, pundits, journalists, and activists—all use online media extensively, and their actions are influenced not only by what they read but also by what is written about them and how they perceive this coverage. The combined effect of these approaches gives us a good degree of confidence that our findings reflect something very real about the American public sphere. And our fundamental observations regarding the asymmetric structure of online media receive clear confirmation from a 2014 Pew survey about media consumption and patterns of trust. That survey found that respondents who score as "consistently conservative" on a survey of their political views reported that their most trusted news sources were Fox News, Sean Hannity, and Rush Limbaugh. "Consistently liberal" respondents placed NPR, PBS, and the BBC in those top three most trusted positions.[18] This pattern of trust in television and radio sources—one side trusting a highly partisan commercial outlet and two of the most incendiary personalities in American political media, and the other in three public institutions of the most traditional journalistic form, suggests that the overall pattern of the media ecosystem is highly congruent with the patterns we observe online.

THE CONSISTENT PATTERN that emerges from our data is that, both during the highly divisive election campaign and even more so during the first year of the Trump presidency, there is no left-right division, but rather a division between the right and the rest of the media ecosystem. The right wing of the media ecosystem behaves precisely as the echo-chamber models predict—exhibiting high insularity, susceptibility to information cascades, rumor and conspiracy theory, and drift toward more extreme versions of itself. The rest of the media ecosystem, however, operates as an interconnected network anchored by organizations, both for profit and nonprofit, that adhere to professional journalistic norms. The members of that integrated ecosystem range from traditionally conservative publications like the *Wall Street Journal* or *Forbes* to historically left publications like *Mother Jones* or liberal and progressive activist sites like Daily Kos. This architecture changes the dynamics of information propagation and correction. It imposes higher reputational costs on sites and authors who propagate rumor and provides avenues for relatively rapid fact checking, criticism of false claims, and rapid dissemination of and coalescence around corrected narratives. The insular right wing of the media ecosystem creates positive feedbacks for bias-confirming statements as a central feature of its normal operation. The rest of the media ecosystem comprises sites diverse enough in their political orientation, organizational culture, business model, and reputational needs to create impedance in the network. This system resists and corrects falsehood as its normal operation, even though, like all systems, it also occasionally fails, sometimes spectacularly.

In Chapter 3 we offer a more detailed account of how these different network dynamics might emerge, and use two case studies to show how the architectural differences result, in the case of the right, in high diffusion and amplification of rumors and lies, while on the left, anchored as it is in "the rest" network rather than having its own symmetric echo chamber, rumors and lies get dampened and contained. We return in Chapter 11 to the deeper question of when and why these dynamics developed on the right but not on the left.

3

The Propaganda Feedback Loop

IN CHAPTER 2 we showed that the American media ecosystem consists of two distinct, structurally different media ecosystems. One part is the right-wing, dominated by partisan media outlets that are densely interconnected and insular and anchored by Fox News and Breitbart. The other part spans the rest of the spectrum. It includes outlets from the left to historically center-right publications like the *Wall Street Journal* and is anchored by media organizations on the center and center-left that adhere to professional standards of journalism. There is no distinct left-wing media ecosystem that parallels the right in its internal coherence or insularity from the center.

Throughout the book we document how these segments of the media system operate differently. Here we sketch out a framework for understanding the differences in the incentives, mechanics, and practices between the two parts of the media landscape. The model is a stylized description of the relationships, interactions, and feedback loops between elites, media, and the public. Dynamics on the right tend to reinforce partisan statements, irrespective of their truth, and to punish actors—be they media outlets or politicians and pundits—who insist on speaking truths that are inconsistent with partisan frames and narratives dominant within the ecosystem. Dynamics in the rest of the media landscape, including the left, tend to dampen and contain partisan statements that are demonstrably false. This does not suggest that the center and left are always error-free or pure of heart. In this chapter we describe the reporting on a smear lawsuit alleging that Donald Trump raped a 13-year-old, which suggests that there is ample supply of and demand for nasty falsehoods on the left. In Chapter 6 we will encounter plenty of errors in the mainstream media. What we try to explain here is why on average and at a population level (by which we mean the population of the public, the media outlets, and political elites), we see partisan falsehoods thrive on the right not

Network Propaganda. Yochai Benkler, Robert Faris, and Hal Roberts.
© Yochai Benkler, Robert Faris, and Hal Roberts 2018. Published 2018 by Oxford University Press.

as errors but as design features of the network, and why these design features have made the right-wing ecosystem a richer breeding ground and receptive ecosystem for propagandist efforts, foreign and domestic.

Our basic model initially divides the political landscape into political elites, media outlets, and the public. We assume, for purposes of this basic model, that members of the public consume news because they want to know what is going on in the world and how their political leaders are doing, but also want to get information that confirms them in their worldview and identity. They operate under motivated reasoning, which is to say, the basic psychological model that states that we tend to believe what we want to believe, seek out confirming information, reject or discount disconfirming evidence, and to do otherwise requires hard cognitive and emotional work. Members of the public get some gain from knowing what is really going on and some gain from being reinforced in their beliefs. And they incur some discomfort or cost from being misinformed, and from being challenged in their beliefs. They look for media outlets and politicians that will inform them as best as possible without suffering too much cognitive discomfort. Media outlets seek to attract large audiences, whether to make money, in the case of for-profits, or to better fulfill their mission, in the case of nonprofits. This involves interactions between reporters, editors, and owners, all of whom themselves operate under motivated reasoning and are perfectly able to lie to themselves to reduce the tensions between their often conflicting goals. Politicians want to be elected and achieve their policy goals. Although politicians find ways to reach out directly to their constituents, they must work through media outlets to reach a larger public. Politicians must also be informed both about the state of the world and about their voters' perceptions of the state of the world, and must balance between these goals when they are in tension. For this purpose, politicians consume the media their voters do. Pundits occupy a position between politicians and media outlets, unconstrained by the need to be re-elected but more constrained by their need to attract audiences to media outlets. In that regard, they are less constrained by facts than politicians, and more like media outlets in their responsiveness to audience preferences. Political activists occupy a spot somewhere between politicians and the public, more focused on substantive victories than on re-election and less sensitive to criticism from media than politicians, but more capable of strategic directed action than members of the public. For simplicity, we focus on the politicians to stand in for political elites more generally.

Media and politicians have the option to serve their audiences and followers by exclusively delivering messages that confirm the prior inclinations of their constituents, or by also including true but disconfirming news when the actual state of the world does not conform to partisan beliefs. For media, this is the key distinction between partisan media and objective media. Partisan media are oriented more toward offering identity-confirming information to partisan audiences while objective media strive for accuracy and aspire to neutrality. Audiences in turn can accept or reject the information from politicians and media, and can decide to continue to follow or abandon the politicians and outlets who deliver the news, whether good or bad. The media outlets, politicians, and public all choose each other iteratively, engaging in the sorting and matching game over time that brings together political affinity groups.

Imagine a media ecosystem in what we call a "reality-check dynamic" (Figure 3.1). Here, media outlets more or less follow institutionalized truth-seeking norms, and aim for more-or-less centrist or neutral perspectives to reduce—to the extent possible—the discomfort that their audience experiences when truth-seeking news is disconfirming. Outlets compete on the truth and freshness of their news, and the search for scoops and sensationalism is in tension with the internal norms and the fact that other

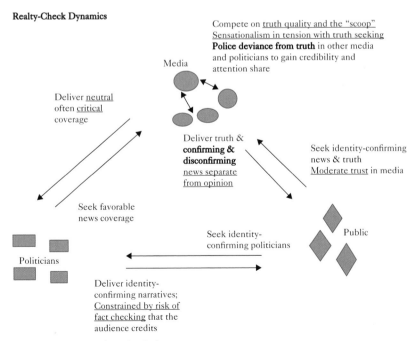

Realty-Check Dynamics

Compete on truth quality and the "scoop"
Sensationalism in tension with truth seeking
Police deviance from truth in other media
and politicians to gain credibility and
attention share

Media

Deliver neutral
often critical
coverage

Deliver truth &
**confirming &
disconfirming**
news separate
from opinion

Seek identity-confirming
news & truth
Moderate trust in media

Seek favorable
news coverage

Seek identity-
confirming politicians

Public

Politicians

Deliver identity-
confirming narratives;
Constrained by risk of
fact checking that the
audience credits

FIGURE 3.1 The reality-check dynamic.

outlets will try to build their own credibility and audience in part by policing them if they get it wrong. They deliver both confirming and disconfirming news to their readers/viewers, and separate news from opinion. Politicians need media outlets to communicate to voters and must navigate this media ecosystem and are constrained in what they can get away with. They try to deliver identity-confirming statements to their voters, but have to keep reasonably close to the truth, at least as reported in media their voters consume, to avoid the reputational harm of being portrayed as dishonest. The media, in turn, report on these politicians in neutral terms and police them for the truth-value of their statements as they police each other. In this dynamic members of the public will receive a mix of truth along with both bias confirmation and disconfirmation. Centrist members of the public are the happiest while media criticism flourishes on the wings—neither of which is getting exactly the trade-off that it wants between partisan confirmation and truth. Levels of trust in any given medium are moderate, because each has occasionally been found in error by its competitors, and each has delivered their audience some disconfirming news.

Now, a new media outlet is launched that adopts a different strategy by emphasizing partisan-confirming news over truth and helping segments of the public to reduce their discomfort by telling them that the outlets providing disconfirming news are not trustworthy. Members of the public who tend to seek confirmation more than truth reward this outlet with attention. Some politicians seek out those outlets and those members. Members of the public now have media outlets and elites confirming their prior beliefs, contrary to what they hear on other media, and are also told by these outlets and elites that other media that contradict what they say are themselves biased and hence untrustworthy. The public that buys into this adjust their levels of trust in other media downward. This reduces the psychological cost of tuning in only to the bias-confirming outlets, as they are now more confident that the partisan good news they hear is true and conflicting news from other outlets is false. Politicians who thrive in this media ecosystem will have done so by aligning their positions and narratives with like-minded publics and supportive media sources or by shifting the narrative in a direction that the public and media are willing to follow. Ideological positions, interpretations of real-world events, and partisan talking points are jointly negotiated by elites, partisan media, pundits, and political activists. News media reject the separation of news and opinion, and compete by policing each other for deviance from identity confirmation, not truth. They similarly align their coverage of politicians to offer favorable coverage to identity-confirming politicians and attacks on opponents, and when they police deviance from politicians, it is identity confirmation, not truth, that they police. All these are intended to help sustain a steady flow of identity-confirming news to audiences who tune in to get precisely that from their media. Subsequent politicians who now enter the arena will find it harder to rely on the mainstream media to challenge assertions made by politicians focused on bias-confirming statements. The public that occupies the partisan media ecosystem no longer believes the external lying media. Challengers within the party are forced to use the same partisan media, subject to the same trade-offs between truth and bias confirmation as the incumbent. Incumbents and challengers consume the partisan media more, because they need to understand what their public believes, what they must confirm, and what parameters shape the way in which they can challenge incumbents. We call this dynamic the "propaganda feedback loop," because once it is set in motion the media, elites, and public are all participants in a self-reinforcing feedback loop that disciplines those who try to step off it with lower attention or votes, and gradually over time increases the costs to everyone of introducing news that is not identity confirming, or challenges the partisan narratives and frames (Figure 3.2). Audiences in this loop will exhibit high trust in identity-confirming media, and low trust in external media. Politicians are not constrained by media policing truth when they

Propaganda Feedback Loop

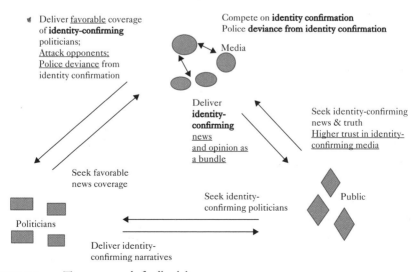

FIGURE 3.2 The propaganda feedback loop.

deliver identity-confirming news to outlets, but rather by media policing the consistency of their statements with party identity.

Propaganda as we define it in Chapter 1—the manipulation of public beliefs, attitudes, and behaviors for political ends, framed in terms that reinforce partisan narratives—is much easier to insert into a system whose audiences, outlets, and elites have nothing to gain by disputing or disbelieving it and everything to lose by doing so, and will survive longer and propagate further in it. The network takes these inputs and converts them into a partisan package delivered to its various constituents: a steady flow of bias-confirming stories that create a shared narrative of the state of the world; a steady flow of audiences, viewers, or clicks for the outlets; and a steady flow of voters highly resilient to arguments made by outsiders on outlets that are outside the network. Outlets within the network are not designed to check or refute propaganda as long as it is consistent with the partisan narrative. There is nothing to gain and everything to lose. Our discussion in Chapter 2 of what happened to Fox News during the primaries and since the election follows these contours precisely. This does not mean that partisan audiences are not exposed to arguments from the other side. Research shows that engaged partisans are indeed aware of the arguments and reporting from the other side,[1] but partisan news audiences simply discount opposing views. When the propagandist's efforts are exposed to external criticism and fact checking, the mechanisms that developed for reducing the cost of disconfirmation— lower attention and lower trust to external media—kick in to insulate the propagandists' efforts from this external criticism.

By contrast, a media ecosystem that operates under the reality-check dynamic, will tend to be more robust to disinformation operations because each outlet in this system gains from exposing the untruth and loses from being caught in the lie or error. Its audiences are less likely to trust any media source in particular, and more likely to check across different media to see whether a story is, in fact, true. Politicians operating within this type of media system will tend to experience resistance when they lie, even if the lies initially confirm the biases of their voters, because the voters will soon learn that the politician lied and reality is not as rosy as the politician promised. The politicians and outlets face starkly different incentives than politicians who operate in the partisan media ecosystem, and the outlets have developed norms and institutions that reflect those incentives and stabilize the truth-seeking behavior.

Nothing prevents the opposite wing of the political system from developing a parallel partisan media ecosystem, and there are many well-functioning democracies with a frankly partisan press, particularly in multipolar political systems. But once one wing has established the strategy of partisan bias confirmation, the centrist media with their truth-seeking institutions and reputations suddenly deliver a new benefit to partisans of the opposite pole— as objective external arbiters they can offer institutionalized credibility to reinforce their view that what their opposition is saying is false. Once one partisan media pole is established, the coverage of existing objective media outlets takes on a partisan flavor without any shift in their own focus on objectivity.

The mainstream media will be able to reconcile their goals of truth-seeking and confirmation from the center with providing a steady flow of partisan-confirming news for the wing in opposition to the wing that is already in the grip of the propaganda feedback loop. The outlets that formed the partisan ecosystem have a first-mover advantage over outlets that try to copy them on the opposite side, because as they decrease the value of the mainstream media to their own audiences, they increase it for the putative audiences of their opponents. The further the first-moving partisan media ecosystem goes down the path of its own propaganda feedback loop, the greater its tendency to produce untrue statements, and the greater the opportunities for reality-check centrist media organizations to deliver news that is both truthful and pleasing to partisans from the other side. Creating a second partisan media ecosystem then becomes more difficult as their potential audience now receives partisan confirmation from centrist objectivity-seeking outlets, and the incremental identity-confirmation benefit they offer their audience is reduced.

In the real world, as opposed to the model, there are of course elements of these two media models found in different media on both sides of the political spectrum. The left includes hyperpartisan media sources, and there are many professional journalists on the right who adhere to standards of objective journalism. The differences lie in the relative power and prominence of the different parts of the system. On the left, politicians and partisans have to navigate the scrutiny and fact checking of objective media sources to reach broader audiences. On the partisan right, the gatekeepers are Fox News, talk radio, Breitbart, and the Drudge Report.

We return in Chapter 11 to examine the historical development of the right-wing media ecosystem, and argue that Rush Limbaugh, and after him Fox News, triggered a propaganda feedback loop that shaped the right-wing media ecosystem as we observe it today. The leading right-wing online media of 2018 were introduced into what was already a decade or two of that feedback loop. Even Breitbart was founded in 2007, almost twenty years after

Limbaugh became nationally syndicated. The other major right-wing net-native sites like the Daily Caller are of even more recent vintage. By contrast, when the Huffington Post emerged in 2005, the left was still attentive to media functioning roughly within a reality-check dynamic, however strained by failures in coverage of the Iraq War and weapons of mass destruction (WMDs).

Here, we turn to two case studies to put some narrative meat on this rather bare-bones model. The first takes an imperfect but nonetheless best-there-is accounting of how much lying there is on the various television networks, and who does the lying where. The second takes the most directly comparable rumors during the election period—an allegation that Trump raped a 13-year-old and allegations tying Clinton to pedophilia—and traces how each fared in the two parts of the media ecosystem. Both cases offer concrete examples of how, a propaganda feedback loop operated on the right, while on the left, an ample supply and appetite for bias-confirming news was contained by the reality-check dynamic.

Who Lies on TV?

It is hard to conduct a large-scale study of the prevalence of false statements on different media, because it is difficult to find unambiguously objective arbiters, and harder still to find arbiters who make their data available in a way that is readily available to aggregate at the news outlet level. Several studies since the 2016 election have sought to use consensus across several fact-checking sites to identify false stories. The limitation of those approaches is that most sites do not organize their findings in ways that are conducive to studying specific outlets or sources. We used PolitiFact, which is the only major fact-checking site to aggregate its findings by media outlet and which reports stories that they determined to be true as well as false. This therefore allows for at least a baseline sense of what proportion of the statements for a given media outlet that were suspicious enough to check ended up being true or false. PolitiFact was accused of political bias a few years ago after a George Mason study found that PolitiFact rated statements by Republicans as false more often than they rated statements by Democrats as false. This finding, which was not accompanied by any effort to independently assess the fairness of the underlying decisions, was interpreted by conservative media as evidence that PolitiFact was biased, rather than that the prevalence of lying on the right might actually be higher.[2] Without valid independent evaluation of the actual truth or falsehood of the claims assessed, it is of course impossible to tell whether

PolitiFact found more lies on the right than on the left because the site was biased in its selection of stories to check or in its determination of the facts, or whether, in fact, right-wing politicians lie more often than do those on the left.[3] That possibility, that the difference is in base rates of lying, rather than the bias of the fact checker, is further supported by some early studies of the *Washington Post*'s Fact Checker, which also found more lying on the right than on the left.[4] Nonetheless, because this basic question of selection bias is not resolvable by outside observers, we offer the following analysis merely as an initial qualitative illustration of this systematic difference. We do not present it as quantitative evidence of its existence, and caution against overinterpreting it in quantitative terms.

PolitiFact is run by professional staff of the *Tampa Bay Times*, which is owned by the Poynter Institute. The site's staff select statements to be checked based on whether they are rooted in a verifiable fact, whether the editors believe the statements might be misleading, and whether they are publicly significant. In other words, we should expect to see a relatively high base rate of false statements in the full set, because stories only get checked if they at least raise suspicion in the minds of a professional reporter and fact checker. As a rough measure of the partisan bias of the site, we can compare PolitiFact's findings on prominent politicians and pundits from the two sides of the aisle. For example, as of December 2017 the Republican and Democratic leadership had remarkably similar proportions of statements rated by PolitiFact as "mostly false" or worse: Mitch McConnell (43 percent), Paul Ryan (43 percent), Nancy Pelosi (41 percent), and Chuck Schumer (42 percent) were practically indistinguishable in terms of the likelihood that the statements they make that seem suspicious enough to warrant fact-checking turn out in fact to be mostly false or worse. Similarly, Rachel Maddow (48 percent) is not systematically different in PolitiFact's measurements than Bill O'Reilly (53 percent) or Sean Hannity (50 percent), all of whom are quite different from, say, Rush Limbaugh (81 percent) and possibly Glenn Beck (59 percent). These numbers show the high ratio of false statements in the stories selected for checking. The overall rates per channel that we describe below do not represent the proportion of false statements out of all statements on the channel, but only the proportion of those statements treated as fishy enough to check. And while the site indeed checks more statements by these right-wing personalities than by the left-wing personalities, the similarities in findings of falsehood suggest that Politifact is not politically biased in its determinations of truth or falsehood. .

Comparing Fox News to CNN, MSNBC, and ABC is revealing.[5] As Figure 3.3 shows, the proportion of Fox News statements that are mostly false

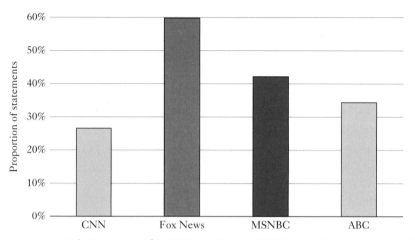

FIGURE 3.3 PolitiFact scoring for CNN, Fox News, MSNBC, and ABC. Proportion of statements scored mostly false or worse.

or worse is almost 50 percent higher than for MSNBC, and more than twice that of CNN.

More revealing yet is the proportion of false statements on each channel that are made by conservative speakers, both paid hosts and pundits and unpaid interviewees. As Figure 3.4 shows, part of the Fox News business model seems to be to pay conservative hosts and pundits to make statements that confirm the biases of its viewers, whether these statements are false or not. MSNBC seems to use a similar approach, but may be less disciplined about it. Most interesting perhaps is that 60 percent of false statements that PolitiFact found on CNN were made by conservative interviewees, some paid pundits, most not, while only 20 percent of such statements were made by liberals. Similarly, nearly 50 percent of the false statements on ABC were made by conservative speakers, and only 21 percent by liberals.

These findings suggest that Fox News and MSNBC are mostly mirror images of each other and follow a fundamentally different model than CNN or ABC. Both Fox News and MSNBC follow a bias-confirming strategy, while CNN and ABC are following roughly a neutral, balanced-perspective strategy. The differential lying by conservatives on CNN and ABC, in turn, is consistent with what we outline in the propaganda feedback loop: politicians who serve a population that is itself trapped in a bias-confirming media ecosystem will tend to lie more often on average than those who serve a constituency that follows neutral channels. For a politician who depends on votes of a public that is mostly inside the propaganda feedback loop, being

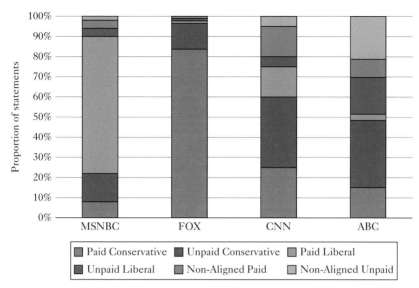

FIGURE 3.4 PolitiFact scoring for CNN, Fox News, MSNBC, and ABC. Proportion of false statements by political alignment by speaker and whether they are paid by the channel.

"caught" in making identity-inconsistent statements even on mainstream media is more costly than being "caught" lying on those media. The difference in rates of making false statements on media persists on CNN and ABC, which suggests that MSNBC's market share is too small, and liberals and Democrats use too many other media that do not follow the bias-confirming strategy to drive liberal politicians and pundits to lie quite as often as their conservative counterparts.

A Case Study in the Effects of the Propaganda Feedback Loop vs. the Reality-Check Dynamic: Clinton Pedophilia vs. Trump Rape in the 2016 Election

There is quite possibly no crime so widely reviled in America as sexual abuse of children. During the campaign, accusations relating to pedophilia were reported against both candidates. Accusations against Clinton ranged from the core story of Bill Clinton (and later Hillary) flying to "orgy island" on the "Lolita Express," to claims that Clinton's State Department was involved in child trafficking of 33 children after the Haitian earthquake, to satanic rituals and "Pizzagate." For Trump, they were focused on allegations in a civil suit that the candidate had raped a 13-year-old in 1994. One can get a sense of the vehemence on the left, manifest in an Occupy Democrats headline from October 24, 2016: "Trump allegedly tied-up 13 year-old girl he raped, struck her in the face." This headline appeared over a story that included sentences such as: "The imagery of a nude, seething, sweating Trump having his way with a defenseless teenager is enough to induce vomiting" leaving little doubt as to the intended effect on readers.[6] The Huffington Post analysis of the story, while more measured in tone, argued that the story deserved significant attention, and was itself the most widely shared story of rape or pedophilia thrown at either candidate throughout the entire campaign. In fact, it had over five times as many Facebook shares (over 1.25 million) as the most widely shared story about Clinton pedophilia.[7] There was no lack of appetite on the left to hear disgusting stories about Donald Trump.

We can look at the spread of these narratives in online media by counting the number of sentences that mention either the Clinton pedophilia frame or the Trump rape frame. We start by looking at the frequency of these frames on the right and the left that are popular on Facebook but have little or no presence in the open web link economy and Twitter. As we explained in Chapter 2, sites with this attention profile include some of the worst offenders in terms of hyperpartisan bullshit on both sides of the aisle—Bipartisan Report, Addicting Info, and Occupy Democrats on the left, and Truthfeed, Ending the Fed, and Western Journalism, on the right. Looking at these sites (Figure 3.5), we see a symmetric pattern: the sites on the left scream "Trump Rape!"; the sites on the right scream "Clinton Pedophilia!"

The difference between the left and the right is not at the extreme margins, but in the transmission to the mainstream and in the amplification effects of the propaganda feedback loop as opposed to the resistance of the reality-check dynamic. We can run the same textual comparison on the sites that receive the most media inlinks from other sites, which is a useful measure of the sites considered most authoritative (Figure 3.6). The accusations against Trump, although they offered an easy opportunity to report allegations made in publicly available court filings, received a fraction of the attention that the accusations against Clinton received among these top media. In fact, the top media on the left wrote more than twice as many stories, and almost three times as many sentences, about the pedophilia accusations against Clinton as they did about the allegations against Trump. The right, by contrast, wrote consistently more damning stories and sentences about their opponent.

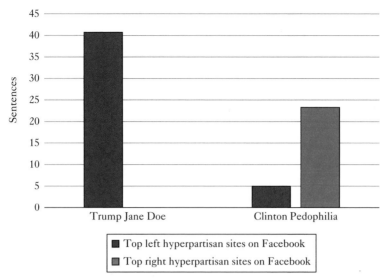

FIGURE 3.5 Coverage of the "Trump rape" and "Clinton pedophilia" frames on Addicting Info, Bipartisan Report, and Occupy Democrats on the left and Truthfeed, Ending the Fed, and Western Journalism on the right.

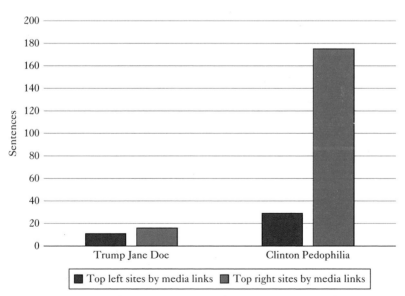

FIGURE 3.6 Coverage of the "Trump rape" and "Clinton pedophilia" frames by the 10 most linked sites on the left and right during the election.

Overall, the number of stories that the Facebook hyperpartisan sites publish is smaller than the larger, better-staffed sites. The overall magnitude of sentences is therefore lower, but the pattern of symmetric polarization among the hyperpartisan sites is clearly visible in the supply of disgusting, stories intended to provoke partisan rage. The critical difference made clear in the two sets of charts is that on the left, those media higher up the food chain that lend credibility to stories and amplify them to larger audiences refused to pick up the storyline and bring it to the wider public.

We can observe the extent to which the right-wing media was different in its treatment of these incendiary stories by comparing top-performing media by quintile across Facebook, Twitter, and links (Figures 3.7a–c).[8] The same picture emerges; the pattern remains stable as we compare the top media by linking, tweeting, and Facebook sharing across the five partisan-attention quintiles. A key difference is that the pattern is less symmetric on Facebook, with substantially more coverage on the right than the left. With the larger number of media outlets included in this view, the craziest sites on the left are diluted, while the bench is deeper on the right. Facebook remains the only medium on which sites on the left give more attention to the Trump rape allegations than the Clinton pedophilia allegations. Systematically the top

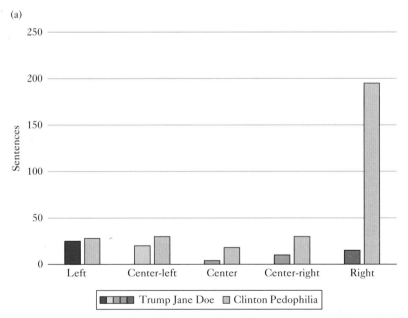

FIGURES 3.7A Coverage of the "Trump rape" and "Clinton pedophilia" frames by the 10 most tweeted sites during the election by quintile.

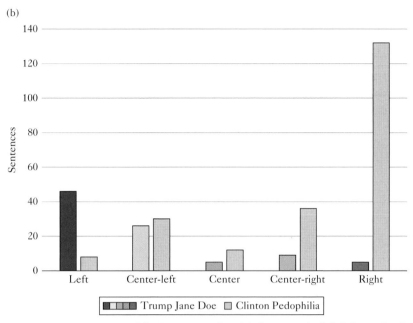

FIGURES 3.7B Coverage of the "Trump rape" and "Clinton pedophilia" frames by the 10 most Facebook-shared sites during the election by quintile.

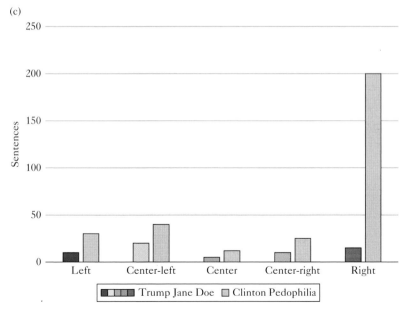

FIGURES 3.7C Coverage of the "Trump rape" and "Clinton pedophilia" frames by the 10 most linked sites during the election by quintile.

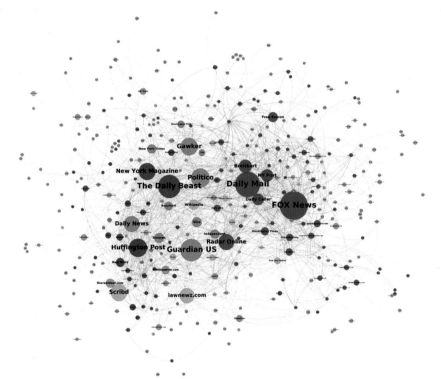

FIGURE 3.8 Network map of media sources reporting on "Trump rape" and "Clinton pedophilia" stories, May 2015–November 8, 2016.

right-wing sites repeat the Clinton pedophilia stories several times as often as any other quintile does, and other than on Facebook, there is no symmetrically excessive attention being paid on the left to the mirror-image story intended to elicit visceral disgust toward Donald Trump. Even on Facebook, where we do see the left quintile pushing the Trump rape narrative, it does so to a substantially smaller degree than the right pushes the pedophilia stories on Facebook. The asymmetry we observe in the architecture of attention appears to be replicated here in the emphasis that the sites themselves pay to producing feelings of outrage and disgust in their audience. The top media by all metrics on the right are in the thrall of the propaganda feedback loop. They must participate to retain credibility. The top media in the rest of the media ecosystem are constrained by the inverse dynamic. They cannot participate if they are to retain credibility and audiences. And the reason they cannot participate is revealed when we move from looking at overall emphasis to the network architecture of the two frames.

Figure 3.8 describes the network of sites that reported both frames, with edges and node sizes determined by hyperlinks into the story. One feature pops out at anyone who has already been exposed to our maps in Chapter 2. The top sites on the center-left and center that normally occupy the central position in our map—the *New York Times*, the *Washington Post*, CNN, *The Hill*—played a peripheral role in this map. The map is driven by partisan sites, not by mainstream media. The second feature is that the Daily Beast, the *Guardian*, Gawker, and *New York Magazine* play a central role on the left and center-left, while Fox News and the *Daily Mail* are the basin of attraction on the right. This offers us very clear targets to examine the diffusion dynamics in the two networks.

Jane Doe and the Trump Rape Accusations

On June 20, 2016, an anonymous "Jane Doe" filed a lawsuit against Donald Trump, accusing him of having raped her 22 years earlier, when she was 13, at an event organized by Jeffery Epstein. On June 29, Lisa Bloom, legal analyst for NBC News, published a piece on the Huffington Post that went through the complaint and argued that the media should cover the case, rather than turning a blind eye as it did in the Bill Cosby case. Bloom argued that Trump's overt misogyny, past accusations of sexual assault against him, Trump's known and publicly admitted long-term relationship with Epstein, and the highly unusual presence of sworn affidavits—one from the victim herself and another from a witness—make the case particularly worthy of attention. Bloom concluded her piece with a clear challenge: "What do you call a nation that refuses to even look at sexual assault claims against a man seeking to lead the free world? Rape culture. We ignore the voices of women at our peril." Bloom's piece was shared over a million times on Facebook. It was followed on July 7 by a piece on MSN, which made roughly the same argument as in Bloom's closing line, and which became the second-most Facebook-shared story addressing either of the two rumors.

On that same day the *Guardian* published a story that led with, "Lawsuits accusing Donald Trump of sexually assaulting a child in the 1990s appear to have been orchestrated by an eccentric anti-Trump campaigner with a record of making outlandish claims about celebrities."[9] The story highlighted an earlier debunking story on Jezebel, which had framed its own discussion with the statement: "The allegations are beyond the pale, even for Trump, and there's little sourcing for them beyond the lawsuit itself."[10] Anna Merlan's story in Jezebel recounted, among other details, how both Gawker and

Jezebel had been approached by an "Al Taylor," who put them in touch with a conservative NeverTrump activist, Steve Baer, and tried to sell them on the rape story, and how both outlets decided to reject the proffered "evidence" and not report on the story. The *Guardian* story then dug deeper and found that "Al Taylor" was likely Norm Lubow, a former producer for the Jerry Springer Show, and proceeded to recount the many times in which Lubow had been involved in generating fake conspiracies. Two weeks later, on the eve of the Republican convention, the Daily Beast dug deeper into the NeverTrump angle, and how the activists created the story but then fell into a cycle of mutual recriminations.[11] There were very few stories after the *Guardian* or Daily Beast stories that reached any prominence at all on the left or center-left, except much later, and those that did outside of the hyperpartisan set like Occupy Democrats all noted and linked back to the *Guardian*, Daily Beast, and several other debunking or critical stories, such as coverage on LawNewz. And what about Gawker's prominence in the map? Gawker, which had chosen not to buy into the Trump rape case, found itself a part of the "Clinton pedophilia" frame through the good graces of Fox News.

What prevented the "Trump raped a 13-year-old" frame from taking off on the left was not a lack of audience desire to receive strong, visceral confirmation of their hatred of Trump. Nothing could be more bias-confirming for Trump opponents. The tremendous success of the Huffington Post and MSN stories during the week of June 29–July 7 exhibits that the desire to believe such a story about Trump existed in spades. It was not the absence of political clickbait fabricators who were trying to push the story to their financial benefit. The passage we quoted from Occupy Democrats and the supply of Trump rape stories from that kind of political clickbait site we showed in Figure 3.5 establish that there were efforts to capitalize on supplying more of this type of story. What prevented this disinformation effort from taking root was the network dynamic whereby diverse sites, many operating on norms dedicated to evaluating the veracity of a story rather than its fit to political purpose or clickbait value, check each other. Even in the absence of the more traditional mainstream press (except the *Guardian*), the presence and attention of both journalists and readers to diverse sites was enough to enforce a hard constraint on the ability to disseminate politically affirming falsehoods.

Jeffrey Epstein, the Lolita Express, and Orgy Island

The prominence of Fox News in the pedophilia narrative underscores that network propaganda is not primarily a story about marginal sites being amplified by big sites, although it sometimes exhibits that dynamic, too. What we see when looking at the Clinton pedophilia frame on the right is a dynamic that rewards the most popular and widely viewed channels at the very top of the media ecosystem for delivering stories, whether true or false, that protect the team, reinforce its beliefs, attack opponents, and refute any claims that might threaten "our" team from outsiders. The Clinton pedophilia story was not primarily a bottom-up, Reddit-imposed, post-truth moment that was then reinforced by higher level media. It was first and foremost the product of a propagandist dynamic between Fox News, as party propaganda organ, and Donald Trump, who, after winning the Indiana primary on May 4, 2016, became the presumptive party nominee. The Clinton pedophilia story was a direct response to the first round of media attacks on Trump for his treatment of women. Fox News's critical contribution to the Clinton pedophilia narrative was the most widely tweeted, most widely Facebook-shared, and third-most widely linked Fox News story published in May 2016 of any election-related story. Indeed, the story remained the most widely shared Fox News story on Facebook throughout the entire campaign out of nearly 6,500 Fox News stories in our set. And it was in May that Fox News return to the fold, after having been browbeaten by Breitbart and shunned by Trump supporters while the primary was still contested, as we saw in Chapter 2.

On May 13, 2017, Fox News online published a story entitled "Flight logs show Bill Clinton flew on sex offender's jet much more than previously,"[12] a story that Fox sent out for syndication via RSS and apparently on Facebook with the more "clickbaity" title: "JET PURV-EYED FOR BILL Clinton a frequent flyer on sex-offender's plane."[13] The story resurfaced a story that had been reported by Gawker a year earlier, but embellished it with a new set of "flight logs showing the former president taking at least 26 trips aboard the 'Lolita Express'—even apparently ditching his Secret Service detail for at least five of the flights, according to records obtained by FoxNews.com." The story then wove various elements from Epstein's own prosecution to embellish the details of Orgy Island. That same day, Breitbart reported on the Fox News story to its readers,[14] as did the British tabloid the *Daily Mail*,[15] one of the most linked and shared sites among Trump supporters. The Daily Caller[16] and *Washington Times*[17] reported on it the next day.

On May 14, the *New York Times* published online a scathing story entitled "Crossing the Lines: How Donald Trump Behaved with Women in Private," which started with a description of how Trump had asked a young woman, Rowan Brewer Lane, to change out of her clothes and into a bikini at a pool

party at Mar-a-Lago, a pattern of behavior the Times called "a debasing
face-to-face encounter between Mr. Trump and a young woman he hardly
knew," based on interviews with over 50 women.[18] One must assume that
the Times had contacted the Trump campaign for its response before the
May 14 online publication. The story was printed in the May 15 *Sunday
Times*. In a dynamic typical of the network diversity of the non-right media
ecosystem, the next morning, on May 16, MSNBC ran a 17-minute segment
of "Morning Joe" eviscerating the *New York Times* for poor reporting, and
leading with a segment from a Fox News interview with Rowan Brewer Lane,
where Lane rejected the interpretation of the *Times* article, saying that Trump
"treated her like a gentleman."[19] After about 10 minutes of criticism of the
Times's journalistic decisions in developing and publishing the stories, the
conversation shifted to assessing what impact it would have on the campaign,
and the panelists all agreed that it would be "gloves off" as far as looking at
Bill Clinton sex stories. At that point Donny Deutsch raised the Epstein story
and emphasized that it would be a likely target for a significant push. Three
hours later, in another MSNBC show, conservative talk show host Hugh
Hewitt repeated the Deutsch point.[20]

Like "Morning Joe" on MSNBC, Sean Hannity ran a segment on his May
16 show, which also began with an interview with Lane, who claimed her
words were taken out of context and blamed the Times piece as being a hit
piece. Newt Gingrich followed Lane and said:[21]

> GINGRICH: Well, look, The New York Times is totally in the tank
> for Hillary Clinton. They're faced with this terrible story about Bill
> Clinton flying around the world with a convicted pedophile, actually
> leaving his Secret Service agents behind on at least five trips to go off
> with his guy by himself for whatever reason. And so they basically
> wanted to smother a real scandal involving Bill Clinton once again
> with this made-up story.

The Daily Caller added another round, reporting that "Former President
Bill Clinton is set to campaign in the U.S. Virgin Islands Monday where his
friend and convicted pedophile Jeffrey Epstein operated 'Orgy Island,'"[22]
while Breitbart used the Deutsch's comment on Morning Joe to publish
the headline: "'Morning Joe' Panel: Clinton Connection with Billionaire
Pedophile Jeffrey Epstein Will 'Blow Up' Campaign."[23]

The next day, May 17, "Special Report with Bret Baier" ran a segment that
began with the words "there's smoke, and where there's smoke, it's worthy

of an investigation."[24] The story essentially repeated for Baier's TV audience the detailed account that Fox News had published online four days earlier, showing the image of the flight logs "and Orgy Island," and emphasizing and analyzing the significance of the absence of Secret Service agents on some of these flights.[25] And again, on May 18, Gingrich returned to the Epstein "Orgy Island" story on Fox News's "On the Record" with Greta Van Susteren, an interview that the Daily Caller dutifully reported.[26] On May 19, Hannity interviewed Donald Trump for his response to the *Times*'s story, an interview during which Trump and Hannity emphasized the refutations by several women mentioned in the story and during which Trump underscored that Bill Clinton had been accused of rape, referring to the Juanita Broderick accusations.[27] The Epstein "Lolita Express" story returned periodically in the major right-wing outlets over the remainder of the campaign, as a general trope standing in for Bill Clinton's sexual misbehavior more generally. A June 2016 report on Breitbart excerpted a portion of a transcript from Rush Limbaugh, where Limbaugh says: "if there ever is a man who has had numerous affairs in the Oval Office, outside the Oval Office, in the governor's office in Arkansas, around the world, palling around with noted pedophile Jeffrey Epstein—why does Bill Clinton get the benefit of the doubt? After all of these years, there ought to be a reaction. Common sense would say, 'You know what? This many allegations, there has to be something there.'"[28] In July, as the Clinton Foundation story that we discuss in Chapter 6 was taking off, Malia Zimmerman, who had authored the original May 13 story based on the flight logs, published another piece, entitled "Billionaire Sex Offender Epstein once claimed he co-founded Clinton Foundation," a claim that the *Daily Mail* faithfully repeated, crediting Fox News.[29]

The announcement by James Comey that the FBI was reopening the Clinton email investigation because of emails found on Anthony Weiner's laptop provided a new opportunity for reviving the pedophilia conspiracy theory. On November 2, True Pundit, a particularly consistent purveyor of disinformation and conspiracy theories, published a story in which it said that "NYPD and FBI sources" confirmed "they now believe Hillary Clinton traveled as Epstein's guest on at least six occasions, probably more,"[30] as well as noting the earlier stories that had "confirmed" that Bill Clinton had traveled more than 20 times to the island and that Huma Abedin and Weiner were cooperating with the FBI. That same day, the story was repeated and linked to by YourNewsWire.[31] As we will see in Chapter 8, both True Pundit and YourNewsWire are among the sites that could plausibly be Russian gray propaganda sites, although YourNewsWire seems to be more of a "useful idiot" site than a gray site. The following day, November 3, Michael Flynn, then of the Trump campaign and later briefly national security adviser, tweeted out a link to the True Pundit story, attached to a message that read: "U decide—NYPD Blows Whistle on New Hillary Emails: Money Laundering, Sex Crimes w Children, etc… MUST READ!"[32] On November 4, Erik Prince, founder of Blackwater USA, later Trump transition team member, and brother to Education Secretary Betsy DeVos, spoke in an interview on the Breitbart XM radio show and broadcast the True Pundit story in all its significant details. As Breitbart described the interview, "Prince claimed he had insider knowledge of the investigation that could help explain why FBI Director James Comey had to announce he was reopening the investigation into Clinton's email server last week." Prince claimed that his informants told him: "They found State Department emails. They found a lot of other really damning criminal information, including money laundering, including the fact that Hillary went to this sex island with convicted pedophile Jeffrey Epstein. Bill Clinton went there more than 20 times. Hillary Clinton went there at least six times," he said.[33] The story leaves little doubt that Prince's "inside" sources were likely the True Pundit story—whether he read it directly, picked it up by following Flynn on Twitter, or read the YourNewsWire repeat.

Unlike many of the other stories, which tried to insinuate that Bill Clinton traveled to Orgy Island (a fact that, though oft-repeated, was inconsistent with the flight logs, which showed Clinton on other trips on the plane, none to the Caribbean), Prince's broadcast of True Pundit's story took elements of the story developed by Fox News in May and created a new layer of fabrication from them. The numbers used evoke the earlier story lines—more than 20 times clearly connects to the "at least 26 flights" from the Fox News online and Bret Baier stories, and Hillary's alleged six visits relate to the number of times the Secret Service was not on board. In combination, True Pundit, Flynn, and Prince sent Hillary to Orgy Island repeatedly. The validation of this storyline by Prince and Breitbart helped to make this new twist the primary narrative in the Clinton pedophilia libel. WND, a popular site on the right, cited the Breitbart story on Erik Prince's radio interview under the headline "Source: FBI Has Evidence Hillary Visited Orgy Island; Huma Abedin said to be cooperating with investigators."[34] Other visible right-wing sites, IJR, Western Journalism, and Conservative Tribune, all linked to and repeated various variations on the story over the following 24 hours, along with several other, more peripheral sites.

If the quintessential moment that captured the sense of epistemic crisis in America was the day on which an armed 20-something walked into a pizza parlor in search of the Clinton pedophilia ring, a close study of the ways in which the association between Clinton and pedophilia emerged points the finger at the very top sites in the right-wing media sphere as the primary culprits in feeding and sustaining this crisis. Russians may well have joined in the fun at various points, as we will see in Chapters 7 and 8. Alt-right agitators happily contributed memes and associations, as we show in Chapter 7. But these exotic explanations seem entirely unnecessary when the political leadership and leading media outlets of the American Republican Party were all repeating the lies as truths in outlets watched, heard, and read by millions of people. Newt Gingrich, former Speaker of the House of Representatives, made the accusation on-air, interviewed by Sean Hannity and by Greta Van Susteren on Fox News. Bret Baier, anchoring Fox News's prime-time news show ran a detailed segment on the accusations of Bill Clinton flying to Orgy Island on the Lolita Express. Fox News online published the underlying materials. Rush Limbaugh discussed the allegation as something everyone knows. Trump's campaign adviser and national security adviser in waiting, Michael Flynn, tweeted it out. Breitbart, the most widely shared right-wing online site whose on-leave CEO Steve Bannon was then running Trump's campaign, aired an interview constructed of pure disinformation. It seems highly unlikely that any of the people involved—Prince, Flynn, or the publishers of Breitbart— thought that the accusation that Hillary Clinton had flown six times to Orgy Island was anything other than utterly false, and yet they published it four days before the election on Breitbart's radio station and online. Not one right-wing outlet came out to criticize and expose this blatant lie for what it was. In the grip of the propaganda feedback loop, the right-wing media ecosystem had no mechanism for self-correction, and instead exhibited dynamics of self-reinforcement, confirmation, and repetition so that readers, viewers, and listeners encountered multiple versions of the same story, over months, to the point that both recall and credibility were enhanced. It is hardly surprising, then, that a YouGov poll from December 2016 found that over 40 percent of Republican respondents thought that it was at least somewhat likely that someone was running a pedophilia ring out of the Clinton campaign.

OUR OBSERVATIONS ABOUT the asymmetric shape of the American networked public sphere show that we do not have a fully polarized media ecosystem, in which both Democrats and Republicans occupy symmetrically closed media bubbles with symmetric, but opposing, self-reinforcing views. Instead, both pre- and post-election, a substantial portion of Republicans and self-identified conservatives occupied a self-reinforcing bubble, while

Democrats and Independents occupied a media sphere anchored by more traditional media outlets that continue to practice the norms of objective journalism, surrounded by more partisan net-native outlets, many of which also adhere to truth-seeking norms rather than purely partisan advantage. The incentives for elites, and the feedback mechanisms between media, elites, and the public, therefore diverged between the two spheres. The center and left dynamics combine networked media and major media outlets, with the latter playing a moderating effect on partisan bullshit and on politicians who still have to worry about fact-checking sites giving them too many Pinocchios, and the former checking the more traditional media from becoming too complacent or comfortable with conventional wisdom, and were able to adhere to truth-seeking norms because their audience, in turn, was ready and able to distinguish truth from falsehood and reward the former. That still leaves plenty of room for partisanship—in agenda setting and topic selection, in perspective and framing—but it appears to significantly constrain disinformation. The interaction between these diverse media sources, their audiences, and political elites creates resistance to the spread of falsehoods, even when politically convenient. The right followed a distinctly different media model, with outlets and elites providing reinforcement and legitimation to partisan propaganda. In this insular ecosystem, subject to the dynamics of propaganda feedback loops, politicians are more or less immune to fact checking because their core audiences treat the professional fact-checking process as itself partisan, and media outlets, audiences, and elites all discipline each other to remain true to faith and confirm party beliefs and ideology on pain of exclusion and demotion—at the ballot box or in the market for attention.

In Chapter 11 we describe how this asymmetric media architectures resulted in highly divergent levels and patterns of trust in media, patterns that offer substantial support for our observations and represent one component of the propaganda feedback loop, on one hand, or the reality-check dynamic, on the other hand. Conservative audiences tend to focus their attention more intensely on fewer sources, which are purely conservative, and to trust these sources much more than liberals do. Consistently conservative respondents trust Fox News, Hannity, Limbaugh, and Glenn Beck much more than they trust ABC, CBS, or NBC, and trust CNN or public radio even less. Consistently liberal audiences, by contrast, spread their attention and trust more broadly, and focus on major mainstream publications and channels.

Parts Two and Three of the book demonstrate that the difference in media ecosystem architecture, the dynamics they set in place, and the divergent patterns of attention, authority, and trust they reflect resulted in different susceptibility to manipulation, propaganda, and belief in false factual claims. Russian propaganda seems to have targeted both sides, and Facebook clickbait sites tried to manipulate denizens of all sides of the American public sphere. But, just as we saw in the case of the competing Trump rape and Clinton pedophilia frames, the responsiveness and success appear to have been very different in the two parts of the media ecosystem. In the right-wing media the propaganda feedback loop enabled conspiracy theories, false rumors, and logically implausible claims to perform better, survive longer, and be shared more widely than were parallel efforts aimed at the left.

Our explanation of the difference between the right and the rest is grounded in historically-specific changes in media institutions and cultural practices, rather than in technological or psychological factors. It is not that Republicans are more gullible, or less rational, than Democrats. It is not that technology has destroyed the possibility of shared discourse for all. It is the structure of the media ecosystem within which Republican voters, whether conservatives or right-wing radicals, on the one hand, and Republican politicians, on the other hand, find themselves that made them particularly susceptible to misperception and manipulation, while the media ecosystem that Democrats and their supporters occupied exhibited structural features that were more robust to propaganda efforts and offered more avenues for self-correction and self-healing. Nonetheless, as we will show in Chapter 6, this media ecosystem still suffers from significant failure modes that are tied to the norms of journalism and the very competitive dynamics that usually protect the system from manipulation. And it was precisely those failure modes that enabled Donald Trump the candidate and his allies in Breitbart in particular to frame the Clinton candidacy almost entirely in terms of corruption. In Part Four, after we describe the actual dynamics of disinformation in the different parts of the media ecosystem, we return to describing the institutional, political, and cultural roots of the asymmetry between the right and the rest, and how the propaganda feedback loop took hold in the right wing of American politics.

PART TWO

Dynamics of Network Propaganda

Political communications usually focus on three primary mechanisms by which media ecosystems affect politics: agenda setting, priming, and framing. Agenda setting is focused on shaping what questions are salient in audiences' minds.[1] Priming focuses on what standards they should use to evaluate candidates or positions on these salient issues.[2] Framing is a more gestalt idea. It relates to the context within which an issue, opinion, or claim is made, and influences our understanding of and attitudes toward it. Consider the politics of drugs in a gubernatorial race as an example of the three different types of effects. Whether to think about drugs and drug use, as opposed to, say, education policy or jobs, as the important political issue of the election is agenda setting. Whether to assess the incumbent governor's performance on the issue of drugs by focusing on changes in the number of overdose deaths of habitual drug users or by focusing on the number of kilos seized and prosecutions brought is a priming question. And whether to think about drug use as a criminal-enforcement issue or a public health issue is a framing question.[3] Whether one thinks of drug use in the frame of "crime" or in the frame of "public health" or whether one is primed to focus on public health measures or criminal enforcement measures has enormous practical implications for where elected and appointed officials put the state's efforts and which classes of policy responses seem reasonable or whacky. As we will see in Chapter 4, for example, the major agenda-setting success of the Donald Trump campaign and Breitbart was to make immigration the core substantive agenda item in the 2016 election. Using text analysis and other measures of salience, we will see that right-wing media framed immigration primarily in terms of fear of Muslims and Islamic terrorism, rather than framing the question in terms of solving the problems of undocumented immigrants in the United States, or of Latin American immigration, as it was in the rest of the media ecosystem. Because of that successful framing, Trump voters were primed to look for progress on that front first and foremost, which helps explain why the newly sworn President Trump rushed to issue his "Muslim ban" within a week of taking office.

How do agenda setting, framing, and priming map on to the questions of propaganda? What might it mean to say that if political party A wants the election to focus on issue A rather than B, that would be "manipulating" public opinion, or in any sense be "false"? At the simplest level, one could pretend to be what one is not and inject agenda-setting or framing narratives into the political debate. So, for example, if we believed that the origin of the large email dumps and the incessant focus on Hillary Clinton emails were in fact the product of Russian hackers and sockpuppets masquerading as American media outlets and activists (spoiler alert for Chapters 6 and 8: we do not), we would call the successful agenda-setting campaign "propaganda" in the sense that the origin of the campaign is masked in order to achieve a manipulative propagandist purpose.

Beyond origin, in principle, though we do not observe it in the American system in the period we asses, one could keep up a steady flow of communications intended to deflect public attention from what you are actually trying to achieve and crowd the agenda with side issues. For example, you might really want to make sure you can pass a massive tax cut that would benefit rich donors, but, knowing that your voters are fed up with tax cuts, distract your target population by persuading them that the most important issue of the day is Muslim immigration and that you will give them what they want on that front. More realistically, given that the actual 2017 tax reform was experienced as defeat by the Trump wing of the Republican Party, if your real belief is that immigration is the major issue, but that focusing on Muslim rather than Latin American immigration would make it easier to sustain the alliance between the white-identity and Christian-identity wings of your coalition, you might emphasize the frame of Muslim immigration even if you knew that, in fact, it was a marginal factor in actual patterns and effects of immigration. Recall that the touchstone of propaganda is the intention of the propagandist.

More pervasively, the salience of an agenda item and its framing are the product of narratives about what the agenda item is, why it is important, how we should fit the flow of daily stories into it, and so forth. If these stories, in their individual detail and their overall effect, are manipulative, false, or materially misleading, we can describe even the broader shift in agenda and frame that they achieve as "propaganda." Much of what we see in Chapters 4 to 6 is the "who" and "how" of network propaganda. We see a network of sites, some peripheral, but more importantly central, keeping up a steady flow of false or misleading stories that together add up to a narrative of Muslim immigration threat (Chapter 4), the deep state attempting to overturn the 2016 election (Chapter 5), or that, whatever you think of Donald Trump, Hillary Clinton is a corrupt, vile criminal who as secretary of state sold out her country to terrorism-supporting Arab sheiks and Russian oligarchs (Chapters 4 and 6).

In Chapter 4, we describe how Breitbart, interacting with Donald Trump the candidate, forced immigration to become the main Republican election agenda, despite the desire of party leadership to stay away from that issue, by keeping up a steady flow of misleading stories that associated immigration with terrorism, the spread of incurable disease, criminality, and abuse of the welfare system. We then dig deeper into text analysis to explain how Islamophobia allowed Breitbart to serve as a bridge between the frank racism and anti-semitism of the white nationalists and the more muted racial anxiety of the more mainstream white- and Christian-identity pillars of the Republican coalition. We conclude by exploring how the network of right-wing sites interacted during the month before the election to weave together the Islamophobia frame and the "Clinton corruption" frame to make for a coherent narrative that left wavering Republicans no choice but to hold their noses and vote for Trump.

In Chapter 5, we shift to focus particularly on Fox News and the central role that it played during the first year of the Trump presidency in creating a narrative that deeply challenges the rule of law in America. Working from the broad frame of the "deep state," through the specific conspiracy theories of Seth Rich and Uranium One, we document how the reassertion by Fox News of its leading role in the right-wing media ecosystem, which we showed in Chapter 2, was achieved by the network effectively turning itself into the president's personal propaganda network. Throughout these stories, Fox led and interacted with the rest of the right-wing media ecosystem to combat civil servants, national security, and law enforcement agents, many of whom were lifelong Republicans, who put their commitment to their civic role ahead of partisan loyalty. Inside the propaganda loop, the choice of these Republican public servants, based on the possibility of objective truth—that there is a truth of the matter about what did or did not happen, and of what is or is not legal—is simply incomprehensible. Inside that loop, such choices necessarily imply corruption or betrayal. We document how, both online and on television, Fox led a persistent campaign at peak moments in the development of the Trump-Russia controversy, to impugn the intelligence community and federal law enforcement agencies in order to protect the president.

In Chapter 6, we turn to examine the operation of mainstream media in a propaganda-rich environment. We begin with the election period and document how internal dynamics of news reporting led mainstream media to emphasize the email investigation over substantive discussion of politics. We dedicate the bulk of the chapter to describing how Breitbart exploited the hunger for scoops and the public performance of objectivity and critical remove of mainstream journalism to harness the credibility of the *New York Times*, and later other major publications, to propagate and accredit the "Clinton corruption" frame. We conclude the chapter with a review of how media outlets in the self-correcting media ecosystem outside the propaganda loop dealt with errors and failures by describing the failures and corrective mechanisms surrounding the recipients of President Trump's Fake News Awards for 2017. Because one of our findings is that mainstream professional media still play a critical role in shaping the American media ecosystem, we think it particularly important to document and identify failure modes in the presence of asymmetric propaganda dynamics and to help professional journalists adjust their practices and self-conception to fit this highly asymmetric system with which they interact. As we underscore in our "solutions" Chapter 13, one of the core recommendations of our work is that professional journalism has to revisit how it performs its commitment to objectivity—shifting from neutrality among competing views to a more scientific sense of provisional assertions of "objective" truth based on fairly disclosed and framed best evidence as the fundamental touchstone of that commitment.

4
_____

Immigration and Islamophobia: Breitbart and the Trump Party

ON JUNE 17, 2015, Donald Trump launched his campaign with this now-famous statement:

> The U.S. has become a dumping ground for everybody else's problems.
> *[Applause]* Thank you. It's true, and these are the best and the finest.
> When Mexico sends its people, they're not sending their best. They're
> not sending you. They're not sending you. They're sending people that
> have lots of problems, and they're bringing those problems with us.
> They're bringing drugs. They're bringing crime. They're rapists. And
> some, I assume, are good people.[1]

Immigration was to become the topic most associated with Donald Trump's candidacy, as we saw in Figure 1.1. It became his primary agenda item, and his supporters were primed throughout this period to judge him by how he implemented his core agenda. In terms of framing, as we will see in this chapter, despite Trump's initial emphasis on Mexico, and even though as a matter of practical policy, immigration in the United States involves Latino immigrants much more than immigrants from Muslim countries, over the course of the campaign immigration came to be framed primarily in anti-Muslim terms.

The centrality of immigration as an agenda item and its framing as centrally concerned with Muslims, and in particular with "radical Islamic terrorism,"[2] explain why within a week of coming to office President Trump signed the first version of his "Muslim ban." This executive order sought to stop all

Network Propaganda. Yochai Benkler, Robert Faris, and Hal Roberts.
© Yochai Benkler, Robert Faris, and Hal Roberts 2018. Published 2018 by Oxford University Press.

immigration from several Muslim-majority countries, purportedly to prevent the entry of terrorists. The order was poorly conceived as a matter of policy and constitutionality, and had to be revised several times before it could pass judicial scrutiny. But it was first and foremost a symbol of faith—Donald Trump keeping faith with the central claim of his run—that America was deeply threatened by Muslim immigrants and that immigration was a leading vector for physical threats to Americans—Islamist terrorists, crime, and disease. Because immigration, particularly with this anti-Muslim inflection, plays a central role in the rise of far-right parties in Europe, understanding the media dynamics around the emergence of immigration as the core agenda shaping feature of the Trump candidacy and its framing in Islamophobic terms offers a clear bridge between the American-centered analysis we offer here and the dynamics that are putting stress on Europe's pluralistic, democratic institutions as well.

Agenda Setting: This Election Is About Immigration

In 1980 Ronald Reagan concluded his nomination acceptance speech with an embrace of immigration from all over the world:

> Can we doubt that only a Divine Providence placed this land, this island of freedom, here as a refuge for all those people in the world who yearn to breathe freely: Jews and Christians enduring persecution behind the Iron Curtain, the boat people of Southeast Asia, of Cuba and Haiti, the victims of drought and famine in Africa, the freedom fighters of Afghanistan and our own countrymen held in savage captivity.

He then called the assembled to pray. This view of immigration was not meaningfully contested in the Republican Party at the time. During the primaries, Reagan and George H.W. Bush were asked in one of their debates whether "the children of illegal aliens should be allowed to access Texas public schools free," or should they be required to pay a fee. Bush emphasized the immigrants' humanity and their hard-working families, and insisted that their children should be given everything that society gives to their neighbors, and that 6- and 8-year-olds should not be kept uneducated or "made to feel they are living outside the law." Reagan responded with a greater focus on national security, emphasizing that high unemployment in Mexico could lead to a revolution and create hostile relations. On this basis he emphasized the need for free flow of labor across the border, rather than building a fence, as the only safety valve against that threat.[3]

Unsurprisingly in that political environment, Reagan signed an immigration reform bill in 1986 that strengthened border security while granting amnesty to all immigrants who had entered illegally before 1982.

It was in 1992 that Pat Buchanan first ran in the Republican presidential primary with a campaign that called for a fence on the southern border and touted an anti-immigrant, anti-trade, "America First" message. Buchanan, who had worked for the Nixon administration, was primarily known as the conservative firebrand on CNN's "Crossfire" and the nationally syndicated television show, "The McLaughlin Group." He repeated the run in 1996. In neither case was he successful. Throughout the 1990s and up until 2006, attitudes toward immigrants in general and on the question of whether they were a benefit or a burden to the country, were largely similar among Republican and lean-Republican voters and Democratic and lean-Democratic voters.[4] Following the collapse of a series of bipartisan efforts to pass comprehensive immigration reform in 2005, 2006, and 2007, led by both Republican Party and Democratic Party leadership and supported by President George W. Bush, partisan views on immigration began to diverge sharply. Part of this may be due to Latino voters, who, disappointed with the Republican Party's opposition to comprehensive immigration reform, shifted from a near even split of Republicans and Democrats toward a more consistently Democratic vote. While George W. Bush had won 44 percent of the Hispanic vote, Mitt Romney won only 27 percent of that vote.[5] Part of the effect was likely accounted for by the broader political polarization dynamics we discuss in Chapters 10 and 11. Be that as it may, the Republican National Committee's postmortem of the 2012 election, written by a taskforce formed by then-RNC Chair Reince Priebus, who later became Donald Trump's first White House chief of staff, explicitly emphasized the long-term threat of losing Hispanic voters as a block and insisted that Republicans had to find a way to appeal to Latino voters and that "among the steps Republicans take in the Hispanic community and beyond we must embrace and champion comprehensive immigration reform. If we do not, our Party's appeal will continue to shrink to its core constituencies only. We also believe that comprehensive immigration reform is consistent with Republican economic policies that promote job growth and opportunity for all."[6] Going into the 2016 election, at a bare minimum the Republican establishment wanted to emphasize growth, tax cuts, and deregulation, not immigration, and it certainly did not want Republicans to run on an agenda hostile to immigrants. Throughout the primaries, Fox News largely downplayed immigration, except in response to comments such as Trump's announcement of his candidacy. But candidate

Trump, in a mutually reinforcing dynamic with Breitbart and the ecosystem of sites around it, would not follow the GOP playbook.

Immigration was Breitbart's issue long before Trump gave it the perfect candidate. Figure 4.1 tracks the number of sentences per day that mentioned variations of the term "immigration" between the re-election of Barack Obama in November 2012 and the end of Trump's first year in office across four of the top right-wing sites—Fox News, the *New York Post*, Breitbart, and the Daily Caller—as well as the *Wall Street Journal* to represent business-conservative opinion, and CNN, as a baseline for mainstream media.

Figure 4.1 makes clear that Breitbart consistently produced substantially more stories that mention immigration than any of these other leading sites both during the 2014 fights over President Obama's efforts to revive comprehensive immigration reform and during the primary. Breitbart's rise within the right wing accelerated after it expanded its staff and opened offices in Texas and London in February of 2014,[7] likely funded by a $10 million investment from Robert Mercer.[8] Its prominence was revived in response to the Trump announcement of his campaign and his placing immigration at the center of his candidacy. Beginning in July 2015 and continuing through Election Day in 2016, Breitbart carried between two and five times as much coverage that mentioned immigration as any of the other sites, including the major right-wing sites. Overall, as Figure 4.2 describes, nearly 1 out of every 25 sentences in Breitbart's election-related corpus over the course of the election period mentioned immigration, between two and three times as many as other major publications across the partisan spectrum. Nonetheless, analyzing the peaks

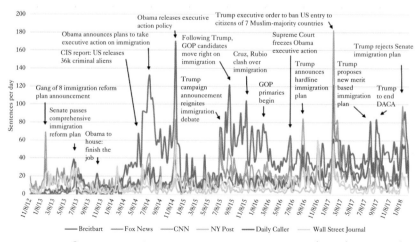

FIGURE 4.1 Sentences mentioning immigration across six top media outlets, November 2012–February 2018.

and troughs of coverage during the 2016 election, all but one of the peaks are responses to statements that Trump made on the campaign trail. Recognizing this allows us to put things in perspective. While as we document in a good bit of detail here, Breitbart was the lead singer in the anti-immigrant right-wing choir, Trump was very much chorus master.

Breitbart played a large role by not only producing its own immigration stories but also acting as a source of stories and authority for other sites on the right and as the center of attention among social media users who shared content from right-wing sites on Twitter or Facebook. As a source of authority, Breitbart and the anti-immigration think tank, Center for Immigration Studies (CIS), were the only right-partisan sites in the 10 most linked-to sites discussing immigration. Table 4.1 lists the top 20 sites by number of inlinks from a topic analysis of all stories during the election period that covered "immigration."

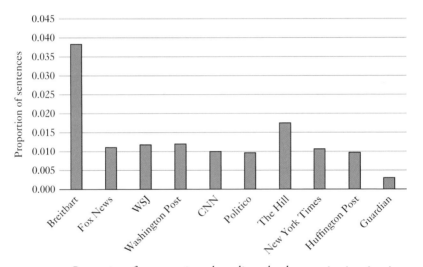

FIGURE 4.2 Proportion of sentences in each media outlet that mention immigration.

Table 4.1 Most linked-to sites discussing immigration during the election.

Media Source	Media Inlinks	Stories
Washington Post	723	2572
New York Times	719	2135
Pew Research Center	708	309
Breitbart	497	2300
Guardian	462	2795
Migration Policy Institute	412	357
Reuters	404	1169
Center for Immigration Studies	365	500

(Continued)

Table 4.1 (Continued)

Media Source	Media Inlinks	Stories
Politico	361	749
Wikipedia	346	776
CNN	338	1016
Huffington Post	328	1905
DonaldJTrump.com	327	9
US Citizenship and Immigration Services	304	128
Fox News	297	1128
Vox	253	1027
USA Today	250	761
The Hill	242	509
Real Clear Politics	238	484
Washington Examiner	221	366

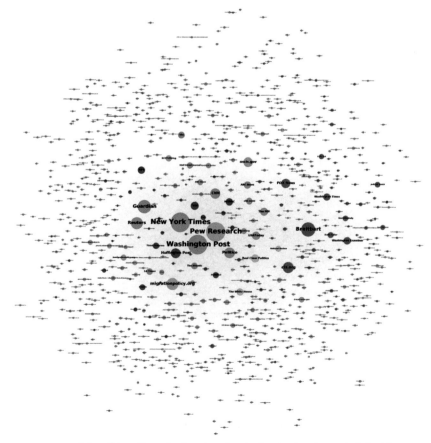

FIGURE 4.3 Map of sites discussing immigration during the election period. Architecture and node sizing by media inlinks.

Figure 4.3 shows a network map of the linking patterns among immigration-related stories and sites. This map shows that Breitbart, CIS, and Fox News were the major sources of authority on the right and were insulated from the rest of the media ecosystem, which was anchored around the *Washington Post*, the *New York Times*, and the Pew Research Center.

One way of assessing the distinct nature of the right wing from the rest of the map is to run a community-detection algorithm on the map. These algorithms are designed to analyze the network and identify sets of sites that are sufficiently interconnected to each other to form a distinct subnetwork, or community, within the whole. We ran the commonly used Louvain community detection algorithm several times, tuning it to produce more or fewer communities. Figures 4.4 and 4.5 show that the subnetwork

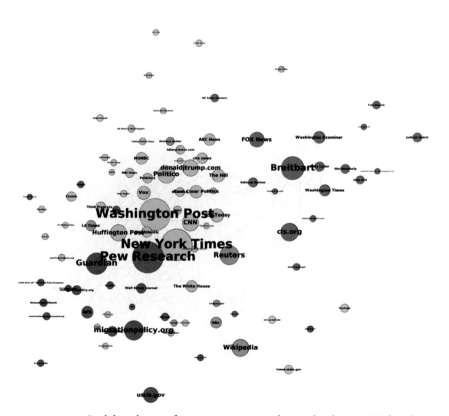

FIGURE 4.4 Link-based map of immigration stories during the election. Node colors reflect modularity class, Louvain community detection, resolution 1.0.

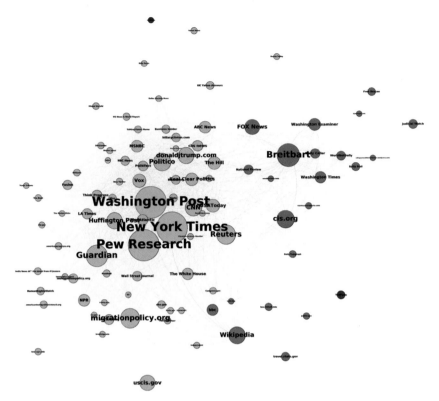

FIGURE 4.5 Link-based map of immigration stories during the election. Node colors reflect modularity class, Louvain community detection, resolution 2.0.

anchored around Breitbart, Fox, and CIS is more homogenous and retains its coherence as a community even as distinctions begin to emerge in other parts of the network.

When measured by social media sharing, Breitbart again dominates the network, and the right is even more clearly separated from the rest of the network. Figure 4.6 shows the network with nodes sized by Facebook shares. The *Wall Street Journal* appears far from the right-wing ecosystem on the issue of immigration, reflecting the fact that its immigration coverage maintained its business-friendly free trade stance even as most other right-wing media had reoriented their immigration coverage into the Breitbart orbit.

In general, the list of top sites by Twitter sharing includes more of the right-wing sites than was true of the list of top sites by links from other top sites (Table 4.2).

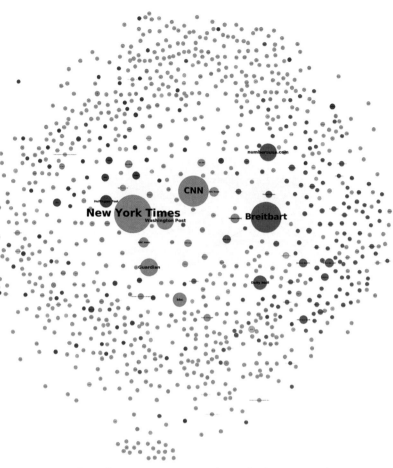

FIGURE 4.6 Map of sites discussing immigration during the election period. Architecture by co-tweets. Nodes sized by number of Facebook shares.

Table 4.2 Most tweeted sites discussing immigration during the election.

Media Source	Twitter Shares	Stories	Facebook Shares (thousands)
Breitbart	50913	1767	15037
Guardian	22718	1222	7732
New York Times	21668	1484	19122
Reuters	19585	928	1058
Fox News	19267	1154	2436
Wall Street Journal	16744	595	1167

(*Continued*)

ganda114   NETWORK PROPAGANDA

Table 4.2 (Continued)

Media Source	Twitter Shares	Stories	Facebook Shares (thousands)
Pew	13397	172	274
Huffington Post	13243	793	4814
Washington Post	12574	904	7477
Yahoo! News	11793	1044	2906
BBC	10628	1155	5582
Los Angeles Times	10439	484	1157
Washington Examiner	10393	1836	1581
Business Insider	8442	263	918
Judicial Watch	7283	74	2495
Infowars	6556	207	1996
Daily Mail	6445	959	5636
NPR	5993	338	2007
The Hill	5828	368	1911
Washington Times	5810	508	875
Daily Caller	5349	263	923
Think Progress	5151	202	97
Free Beacon	4945	73	472
Vice	4784	225	602
Forbes	4701	258	538

Framing: Immigration Is About Personal Security, Particularly Fear of Muslims and Islamic Terrorism

While for most of the American media ecosystem immigration in America was primarily focused on undocumented immigrants who were already in the United States, or on the southern border and immigration from Mexico and elsewhere in Latin America, the Breitbart-centered right-wing media ecosystem framed immigration primarily in terms of fear of Muslims, Islam, and Islamic terrorism. We can get an initial feel for what this frame looks like by reading the headlines of the 20 immigration-related stories published on Breitbart and most widely shared on Facebook (Table 4.3). Sixteen of these 20 stories were framed in terms of a Muslim threat, three of these combined fear of Muslims with other themes. Not a single story of these top 20 was focused purely on immigration from Latin America, and only two included that concern alongside fear of Muslims.

Table 4.3 **Most Facebook-shared immigration stories on Breitbart, election period; by frame.**

Title	Jobs	Political power	Burden on the state	Disease	Crime	Mexico, Latinos, the Wall	Muslims & Islamic terrorism
WATCH: The Anti-Migrant Video Going Viral Across Europe							√
Jerry Brown Signs Bill Allowing Illegal Immigrants to Vote		√					
WATCH: Migrants Dislike Food, Demand TVs, Threaten to Go Back to Syria							√
Social Security Administration Confirms: Illegal Aliens to Begin Collecting Benefits in 2017			√				
EXCLUSIVE REPORT: 8 Syrians Caught at Texas Border in Laredo						√	√
Clinton Cash: Khizr Khan's Deep Legal, Financial Connections to Saudi Arabia, Hillary's Clinton Foundation Tie Terror, Immigration, Email							√
Paul Ryan Tells Sean Hannity He Will Not Support Any Cuts to Muslim Immigration: Not Who We Are							√

(Continued)

Table 4.3 (Continued)

Title	Jobs	Political power	Burden on the state	Disease	Crime	Mexico, Latinos, the Wall	Muslims & Islamic terrorism
Paris Terrorist Was Migrant Who Registered as a Refugee in Greece							√
Donald Trump Calls for Complete Shutdown of Muslims Entering the United States							√
After Paul Ryan Funds Visas for 300,000 Muslim Migrants, House Republicans Give Him Standing Ovation							√
Hillary Clinton: We Cannot End Terrorism Without Gun Control							
Paul Ryan Betrays America: $1.1 Trillion, 2,000-Plus Page Omnibus Bill Funds	√			√	√	√	√
Panic Mode: Khizr Khan Deletes Law Firm Website that Specialized in Muslim Immigration							√
Exclusive: Phyllis Schlafly Makes the Case for President Trump: "Only Hope to Defeat the Kingmakers"	√		√				√

Table 4.3 (Continued)

Title	Jobs	Political power	Burden on the state	Disease	Crime	Mexico, Latinos, the Wall	Muslims & Islamic terrorism
Shock Poll: 51% of U.S. Muslims Want Sharia; 25% Okay with Violence Against Americans							√
Clinton to Resettle One Million Muslim Migrants During First Term Alone							√
South Carolina House Passes Bill Excluding Sharia Law from State Courts							√
Report: Every Deported Illegal Household Saves Taxpayers More than $700,000			√				
White House Celebrates Muslim Holiday on Day Muhammad Murders Four Marines							√
Rand Paul: Restrict Immigration from Muslim Nations							√

Things look more or less the same when looking at the top most tweeted stories (Table 4.4). Here, 14 of the 20 stories are framed in terms of fear of Muslims, three in terms of Latin American immigration, either alone or in combination with Muslim immigration.

And again, looking at the stories with the highest number of links on the web, we see only a slight shift toward other topics, but still 60 percent of the coverage focused on fear of Muslims (Table 4.5).

Table 4.4 Most tweeted immigration stories on Breitbart, election period, by frame.

Title	Jobs	Burden on the state	Disease	Crime	Mexico, the Wall	Muslims & Islamic terrorism
More Than 347,000 Convicted Criminal Immigrants at Large in U.S.				√		
London's Islamist-Linked Mayor Tells U.S. Audience: "Immigrants Shouldn't Assimilate"						√
Mexico Helping Unvetted African Migrants to U.S. Border, Many From Al-Shabaab Terror Hotbed					√	√
Six Diseases Return to US as Migration Advocates Celebrate "World Refugee Day"			√			
Paul Ryan Says U.S. Must Admit Muslim Migrants, Sends Kids to Private School that Screens Them Out						√
Immigration to Swell U.S. Muslim Population to 6.2 Million						√
Under Secretary Clinton, U.S. Permanently Resettled 31,000 Somali Migrants						√

Table 4.4 (Continued)

Title	Jobs	Burden on the state	Disease	Crime	Mexico, the Wall	Muslims & Islamic terrorism
Killer Illegal Immigrant Entered U.S. as "Unaccompanied Child"				√	√	
Federal Data: U.S. Annually Admits Quarter of a Million Muslim Migrants						√
No Assimilation Needed in U.S., Obama Tells Millions of Migrants						√
More than 30 Immigrants Admitted to the U.S. Recently Implicated in Terrorism						√
Jeff Sessions Pushes Back Against Hillary Clinton's "Radical" Suggestion of a Global Right to Immigrate	√					
EXCLUSIVE: Illegal Immigrant with Drug-Resistant TB to Be Released into US, say Arizona Reps			√			
Ten Times in Past Two Years Terrorists Slipped Through Immigration Process into U.S.						√

(Continued)

Table 4.4 (Continued)

Title	Jobs	Burden on the state	Disease	Crime	Mexico, the Wall	Muslims & Islamic terrorism
In Wake of Orlando Shooting, Paul Ryan Pushes Business Deregulation; Says U.S. Can't Pause Muslim Migration						√
Only Ten Percent of Migrant Influx Has Reached Us So Far, Says German Minister						√
U.S. Resettled Nearly Three Quarters of a Million Migrants from Countries that Execute Gays						√
30 Million Illegal Immigrants in US, Says Mexico's Former Ambassador					√	
Since 9/11 U.S. Has Accepted over 2 Million Migrants from Majority Muslim Nations						√
Ryan's Strategy to "Keep the American People Safe" Fails: U.S. to Issue Visas to 300,000 Muslim Migrants						√

**Table 4.5 Most linked-to immigration stories
on Breitbart on the open web, election period, by frame.**

Title	Jobs	Burden on the state	Political power	Disease	Crime	Mexico, Latinos, the Wall	Muslims & Islamic terrorism
Federal Data: U.S. Annually Admits Quarter of a Million Muslim Migrants							√
Immigration to Swell U.S. Muslim Population to 6.2 Million							√
Congress Votes to Fund Nearly 300,000 Visas For Muslim Migrants in One Year							√
Six Diseases Return To US as Migration Advocates Celebrate "World Refugee Day"				√			
Report: Nearly 2.5 Million Immigrants from "Predominantly Muslim Countries" Reside Inside U.S. Right Now							√
London's Islamist-Linked Mayor Tells U.S. Audience: "Immigrants Shouldn't Assimilate"							√
Scott Walker Stands for American Workers on Immigration	√						
Hatch, Rubio, Flake Co-Sponsor Bill to Increase H-1B Guest-Worker Visas	√						

(Continued)

Table 4.5 (Continued)

Title	Jobs	Burden on the state	Political power	Disease	Crime	Mexico, Latinos, the Wall	Muslims & Islamic terrorism
More than 90 Percent of Middle Eastern Refugees on Food Stamps	√						√
Immigration Agents: ISIS May Exploit America's Weakened Immigration System to Attack U.S.							√
Muslim Immigration Puts Half a Million U.S. Girls at Risk of Genital Mutilation							√
Unholy Alliance: Christian Charities Profit from $1 Billion Fed Program to Resettle Refugees, 40 Percent Muslim							√
Obama Invites 18.7 Million Immigrants to Avoid Oath of Allegiance, Pledge to Defend America							
Immigration Expert: U.S. to Resettle Nearly One Million Muslim Migrants Under One Term of Clinton Presidency							√

Table 4.5 (Continued)

Title	Jobs	Burden on the state	Political power	Disease	Crime	Mexico, Latinos, the Wall	Muslims & Islamic terrorism
30 Million Illegal Immigrants in US, Says Mexico's Former Ambassador						√	
U.S. Tuberculosis Cases Rise as Foreign-Born Patients Triple 1986 Caseload Percentage				√			
Illegal Immigrants Accounted for Nearly 37 Percent of Federal Sentences in FY 2014					√		
Paul Ryan Tells Sean Hannity He Will Not Support Any Cuts to Muslim Immigration: "That's Not Who We Are"							√
Measles Outbreak in Memphis Began at Mosque				√			√
New California: Mass Immigration Turning Virginia Blue			√				

By diverse measures of "top," these lists of top immigration stories from Breitbart offer an immediate sense of the more quantitative text analysis to which we now turn to understand how the right differed from the rest of the media ecosystem. They emphasize Muslim immigrants and a fear of Islamist terrorism more than they focus on Hispanic or Latin American immigration, and they work to evoke fear and disgust through claims that immigrants are disease carriers and criminals. The appeal to visceral feelings becomes clearer yet when looking at the top immigration headlines of the Gateway Pundit, the fifth-most tweeted and third-most Facebook-shared site on the right across the entire election coverage, which made sure no one would miss the message. Its most shared stories included titles like:

> Droves of African Migrants Amass at Mexican Border Waiting U.S. Asylum Under Secret Obama Pact
>
> Obama Changes Law: Allows Immigrants with Blistering STDs and Leprosy into U.S.
>
> Muslim Immigrant Arrested After Purchasing Firearm for ISIS Attack on U.S. Soil
>
> Trump Was Right => At Least Nine American Members of ISIS Were Immigrants to U.S.

To expand our view from this top-level analysis, we look at many thousands of sources, of which about 4,000 sources published more than three immigration-related stories over the entire election period. This broad lens allows us not only to understand the frame produced by Breitbart but also to examine the influence of explicitly white-nationalist publications on the debate and begin to consider to what extent these sites influenced the 2016 election, in particular through framing and pushing the immigration debate. Our analysis suggests that white nationalists actually played a peripheral role. To the extent they had an influence it was only through the bridging function that Breitbart played—cleansing their rhetoric from its most explicitly anti-semitic and racist rhetoric, and turning it into the Islamophobic language that the lists above illustrate. VDARE, the most widely linked and influential of the white-nationalist sites, was the only white-nationalist site that reached the top 100 most linked sites in the immigration set. When measured by tweets or Facebook shares, it did not break the top 1,000 sites. The Daily Stormer, one of the more notorious neo-Nazi sites, did not break the top 1,000 sites by linking, or the top 3,000 by Facebook sharing.

Working in collaboration with our colleague Bruce Etling, we analyzed over 180,000 immigration-related stories, training eight different machine learning algorithms to identify stories as "white nationalists," right, center-right, center, center-left, and left. We deviate in this from our standard partisanship metric in order to get purchase on the influence of the white nationalists. Out of the "right" set we drew 36 sites that were categorized as "white nationalist" by the Southern Poverty Law Center, Wikipedia, and an analysis of election-related Twitter clusters by an analytics firm with which we have often collaborated, Graphika.[9] We then created sets of sites that our retweet-partisanship scores identified as we described in Chapter 2, except that we excluded from that set any sites that we already identified as white nationalists. We trained eight algorithms on 3,000 stories from these five quintiles plus the nationalists to recognize whether a given story falls into one or another of the categories. We analyzed the remainder of the 180,000 stories using these algorithms and treated a story as within a given category when at least six of the eight algorithms agreed on which category the story fit in. The algorithms had the hardest time distinguishing between center, center-left, and left stories, and had the highest accuracy in identifying white-nationalist stories. Figure 4.7 portrays six word clouds that present the top 100 words among all the stories that our classifier labeled as white nationalist and each of the five usual quintiles. We use a standard TF-IDF scheme, which looks for which words that appear most frequently in a document such as this (say, a story categorized as "white nationalist" or "left") relative to how often it appears in the overall set of documents. The terms in green in the center are the most typical of stories in that quintile or set.

What becomes eminently clear in looking at these word clouds is that white nationalists are distinctly characterized by their unabashed anti-semitism and blatant racism, whereas what characterizes the right quintile without the white nationalists, consistent with what the lists of most shared stories from Breitbart showed, is an emphasis on Muslims, Islam, and terrorism. The center focuses mainly on Mexico, with some attention to Muslims, the center-left combines a focus on Mexican and other Latin American immigration with a clear emphasis on the Syrian refugee crisis and asylum seekers, and the left focuses on deportation, families, and the undocumented as well as Muslim immigration and the war in Syria. To some extent what is surprising is the fact that the center-right publications seem to have been drawn into emphasizing Muslims and Islam more than any term denoting a focus on Latin American immigration.

Figure 4.8 uses this data to plot typical sites among the six categories on a multidimensional scaling plot. In this plot, each site is plotted between the various segments based on the proportion of stories on that site that at least six of our algorithms agreed were typical of one or another of the quintiles or segments. Several things emerge from this plot. First, media sources across the center-through-left spectrum make up a single cluster, with minor differences separating them. Just as we saw when mapping based on links, tweets, and Facebook shares, here too the center, center-left, and left formed a single media ecosystem that discussed similar items in similar language. Second, the language that white nationalists use puts them on an entirely different

FIGURE 4.7 Words most representative of immigration in stories classified by our algorithms as white nationalist (top left), right (top right), center-right (mid-left), center (mid-right), center-left (bottom left), and left (bottom right).

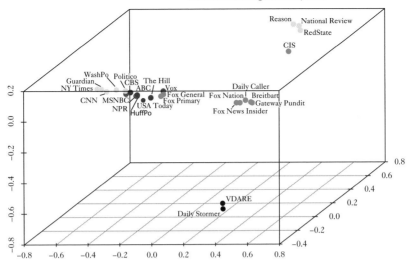

FIGURE 4.8 Multidimensional scaling plot of top sites, Fox subsets, VDARE, and Daily Stormer.

plane from everyone else. No site that was not on our original list of white-nationalist sites had more than 2 percent of its stories categorized by our algorithms as "white nationalist" by its language. Third, Fox News pursues a mixed strategy online. We divided the Fox oeuvre into four buckets. We separated Fox stories from before May 2016 (fox_primary) from Fox stories from May to November (fox_general) to see whether Fox significantly changed its coverage of immigration after Donald Trump won the election. We also analyzed Fox stories from two distinct brands: Fox News Insider and Fox Nation. The text analysis shows that Fox moved only slightly from the center to the right in the transition from the primaries to the general election. Instead, it served its audience right-wing immigration fare through its Fox News Insider and Fox Nation properties, both of which clustered tightly with Breitbart, the Daily Caller, and the Gateway Pundit. Fourth, and finally, the center-right, although its influence was small in the overall election, did in fact have a focus and a way of talking about immigration that was highly distinctive and different from either the right or the larger cluster made of center-through-left outlets.

The major Fox News site's position close to the center is easy to understand when looking at its most widely tweeted stories about immigration, which, like the center, emphasize Mexican immigration over Muslim immigration, along with a focus on waste of public money and arguments that emphasized crime and personal insecurity. Nonetheless, these have a somewhat different tone to the headlines we saw from Breitbart or the Gateway Pundit.

> ICE spends millions flying illegal immigrant children across U.S.
>
> Con game? Immigrants lying about abuse to stay in the U.S.
>
> Mexico warns Texas not to refuse its immigrants' babies U.S. birth certificates
>
> US, Mexican governments helping Haitian migrants enter country, lawmaker says
>
> US immigration policies allow gangs to thrive in violence-plagued NY community, say critics
>
> Mexico issuing transit visas to African migrants flocking to U.S.-Mexico border

Although Breitbart assiduously avoided the frankly anti-semitic language that so clearly marked the white nationalists, journalistic reporting has certainly identified it as a bridge between the white nationalists and the rest of the media ecosystem.[10] In our own data, this can be seen most clearly by following the trajectory of the term "globalist" and how it came to be used by Breitbart to denote opponents who historically would have been referred to as "neoliberals" or "neoconservatives," or as "free-traders" or "internationalists."

Figure 4.9 is a histogram of the average number of sentences per day that use the term "globalist" across VDARE, as a marker for the white nationalists; Alex Jones, who used the term early in his conspiracy theories; and Breitbart from April 2015, when the presidential campaign began, to March of 2018. The histogram makes very clear that the term "globalist" was primarily a VDARE construct in 2015, although Breitbart used it occasionally late in that year, and that Breitbart picked up the term at the height of the primary season and then really leaned into it around the party conventions, through the fall of the election, and since.

It is also clear that coverage outside the right-wing media ecosystem clearly understood that "globalist" was a dog-whistle reference to the cabal of Jewish bankers who have filled the imagination of anti-semites at least since the Rothschilds replaced the Jewish moneylender in the Christian pantheon of villains. Looking at coverage of that term by all the media we code as center-right, center, center-left, and left from April 2015 to December of 2015, just before it was embraced by Breitbart, there was no ambiguity by anyone reporting on usage of the term that that is exactly what it is meant to evoke (Figure 4.10). The term "globalist" is surrounded by "cabal," "banksters,"

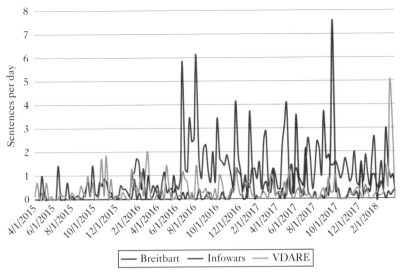

FIGURE 4.9 Sentences per day mentioning "globalist" in open web media, April 2015–April 2018.

FIGURE 4.10 Coverage of the use of the term "globalist" in media from the center-right to the left, April–December 2015.

"neocons," and the acronym "NWO" (for the "New World Order" conspiracy theory that the globalists are seeking to impose is at the center), and "Hillary" is accompanied by "jewish."

That recognition does not disappear as Breitbart begins to adopt the term, even though the site otherwise explicitly and vocally supports the right wing

of Israeli politics, which is to say its governing coalition. Figure 4.11 shows
that coverage from the center-right through the left still sees the anti-semitic
overtones of the term, as "Hillary" continues to be associated with "jewish,"
but the emphasis has shifted to using the term against other opponents,
particularly in reporting on how Fox Business host and longtime anti-
immigration voice Lou Dobbs applied the term in a new context—to Evan
McMullin's challenge to Trump in Utah, deriding McMullin as "nothing but
a Globalist, Romney and Mormon Mafia Tool." (Figure 4.12).

FIGURE 4.11 Coverage of the use of the term "globalist" in media from the center-right
to the left, January–November 2016.

FIGURE 4.12 Lou Dobbs tweet deriding Evan McMullin as a "Globalist, Romney and
Mormon Mafia Tool."

Source: https://twitter.com/LouDobbs/status/790024160160411648.

After President Trump took office, as his lead adviser Steve Bannon continued to use "globalist" to describe allegedly coherent competing ideologies, the recognition was lost that "globalist" is not a description of actual positions anyone takes, but a veiled reference to a global conspiracy of Jewish bankers. As Figure 4.13 shows, coverage of the term from the center-right to the left no longer notes its particular anti-semitic frame.

Few examples capture the transition more clearly than an April 20, 2017, story from the *New York Times*, where the *Times* reports on yet another twist in the Trump administration trade policy. After describing a set of pro-trade moves, the Times, apparently oblivious to the origins of the term, cheerfully lists the Jews and Jewish bankers in Trump's orbit as it explained:

> The flurry of activity amounts to a comeback by nationalists like Mr. Bannon, who views trade as crucial to Mr. Trump's populist appeal but whose star has dimmed after clashes with globalist-minded aides like Jared Kushner, Mr. Trump's son-in-law, and Gary D. Cohn, the former Goldman Sachs banker and lifelong Democrat who is head of the National Economic Council.
>
> The outcome of the debate between nationalists and globalists remains far from settled.

FIGURE 4.13 Coverage of the use of the term "globalist" in media from the center-right to the left, November 2016–April 2018.

And there you have it. From VDARE conspiracy theory to *New York Times* matter-of-fact reporting in less than 18 months, all through the good graces of Breitbart and Bannon.

The fear and loathing of immigrants, so frequently associated with white-identity movements in the United States and so visible in right-wing media immigration coverage during the election, led many to argue that the white nationalists were a major player during the 2016 campaign. Our data suggest that, if they did have a major influence, it was only through Breitbart and the bridging function that it played in transposing the basic frames of the white supremacists to the rest of the right-wing media ecosystem. But whether or not we focus on that bridging function, there is no question that the interaction between Trump the candidate and Breitbart the media outlet set the message that was at the heart of the campaign. That message set the agenda, declaring that immigration was the most important issue. That message framed immigration as primarily about fear of Muslims, and to some extent Africans and Mexicans, who would bring crime, disease, and terrorism. And it was a message that needed little help from the fringe. It was central to Donald Trump's campaign itself, and central to the way that the most influential media outlets in the right-wing media ecosystem framed the immigration debate.

Mobilizing Fear and Loathing: The Clinton Foundation and Islamophobia

As we will see in Chapter 6, defining Hillary Clinton in terms of corruption was the central success of the Trump campaign and the right-wing media ecosystem during the 2016 election. Coverage of the Clinton Foundation in particular played a substantial role in a successful campaign, long engineered by Bannon and Breitbart, to shape the post-convention debate over the course of the month of August 2016, and to orient the debate around allegations of corruption surrounding the foundation. But for purposes of this chapter, with its focus on the interaction between the candidate and political elites and the core of the right-wing media ecosystem to frame the election around Islamophobia, we focus instead on how the Clinton Foundation was made to do double duty—in the mainstream, discussed primarily in August 2016, it was about potential conflicts of interest. But in September and October, as mainstream media moved their attention to the presidential debates and the Hollywood Access video that captured Donald Trump making lewd comments about women, coverage of the Clinton Foundation became a vehicle for reinforcing the core Islamophobic frame that was at the heart of the immigration agenda. In the telling of the right-wing media ecosystem, Clinton was a traitor who collaborated with the enemy. And the enemy was Muslim, and mostly Arab.

Figure 4.14 shows monthly network maps from July to October 2016 of stories related to the Clinton Foundation on right-wing sites. These maps show that, in August, when mainstream media were focused on the Clinton Foundation story, the right-wing media were sparsely connected, directing most of their attention via cross-media links to amplifying the legitimating stories in the mainstream press. In July, September, and October, by contrast, the right-wing network was more densely interconnected, and the Daily Caller and Breitbart played a central role.

The Daily Caller in particular played a central role in setting up the Clinton Foundation topic in July. The site continued to play a significant role during the fall by publishing stories that found little purchase outside the right-wing media ecosystem but that stoked the anti-Clinton fervor

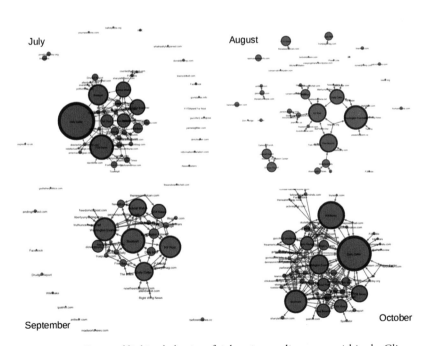

FIGURE 4.14 Directed linking behavior of right-wing media sources within the Clinton Foundation topic during the months of July, August, September, and October 2016.

among core Trump followers. These stories claimed that Clinton's behavior was criminal rather than merely questionable. In a campaign that expressed deep anti-Muslim sentiment, a repeated theme was that Hillary Clinton was seriously in hock to Muslim nations. It is here that the stories become a more explicit disinformation campaign.

On July 13, 2016, just as the focus on the Clinton Foundation was about to intensify, the Daily Caller published one of its most highly tweeted stories, "New Ties Emerge Between Clinton And Mysterious Islamic Cleric." Above the fold, the story is breathless:

> A newly-released email and lobbying documents filed with Congress reveals new ties between Clintonworld and members of a network operated by a mysterious Islamic cleric from Turkey. Connections between Clinton and acolytes of the imam, Fethullah Gulen, could muddle the complex relationship between the U.S. and Turkey, a key NATO ally, if the former secretary of state wins the White House.[11]

The story weaves Clinton Foundation donations into a tapestry of insinuations of corruption and influence by Gulenists in the Clinton Foundation and State Department. Many of the discrete incidents reported are likely factual. Reading carefully and skeptically below the fold reveals a loosely connected set of observations about a network that threatened the Turkish president Recep Tayyip Erdoğan in his own country, but that was likely more Western-oriented and less Islamic in its political orientation than Erdogan's own party. The overall tenor and import, however, was intended to produce a belief that Clinton was working closely with a subversive "Islamic cleric."

The most tweeted stories in October from the Daily Caller make its stance clear and are consistent with our observations about the immigration subtopic and the overall prominence of anti-Muslim stories in the right-wing quintile. The most tweeted story was headlined "Clinton Charity Got Up To $56 Million From Nations That Are Anti-Women, Gays," accompanied by the image reproduced in Figure 4.15 and describing various contributions to the foundation from the Gulf States and Saudi Arabia.

The second-most tweeted story ran under the headline "WIKILEAKS: Here's How The Clinton's Free Private Jet Scam Works."[12] It offered a case study in how disinformation is created by weaving bits and pieces of evidence into a fundamentally misleading presentation that, again,

FIGURE 4.15 Image shared by the Daily Caller alongside the article "Clinton Charity Got Up To $56 Million From Nations That Are Anti-Women, Gays."

implied inappropriate connections between Hillary Clinton and influential Muslims. Above the fold it read:

> Ira Magaziner, the CEO of the Clinton Health Access Initiative, asked former President Bill Clinton to thank Morocco's King Mohammed VI for "offering his plane to the conference in Ethiopia."
>
> "CHAI would like to request that President Clinton call Sheik Mohammed to thank him for offering his plane to the conference in Ethiopia," Magaziner gushed in a November 22, 2011 email released by WikiLeaks.
>
> Clinton frequently has expected free, luxurious private jet travel during his post-presidential life. Clinton, his wife and daughter have artfully secured free air travel and luxurious accommodations since they left the White House. It's an effective way to accept gifts of great value without declaring them for the Clinton Foundation.
>
> "It's highly illegal and it's likely that the owners of these aircraft took tax deductions as a gift to the Clinton Foundation," Charles Ortel, a Wall Street analyst and critic of the Clinton Foundation, told The Daily Caller News Foundation.

Later in the same story the Daily Caller reported: "In the Moroccan case, Clinton was able to fly for free, jetting 3,367 miles from Rabat, Morocco, to Addis Ababa, Ethiopia, on the King's specially equipped 747-400 jumbo jet." Further along it made this seemingly incriminating statement: "But neither the Clinton Foundation nor CHAI have listed any 'non-cash contributions'—such as free jumbo jet travel—on their 2011 tax return for the free use of the aircraft."

Reading the actual email on which the story is based makes clear that the story is pure bunk. The email, part of WikiLeaks' Podesta emails dump,[13] included the quoted words, but stated nearly the opposite of what the story implies:

> CHAI would like to request that President Clinton call Sheik Mohammed to thank him for offering his plane to the conference in Ethiopia *and expressing regrets that President Clinton's schedule does not permit him to attend the conference.* (emphasis added).

In other words, according to the email there was no flight, and Bill Clinton did not go to the conference. Moreover, the email says that the offer came from "Sheikh Mohammed," not "King Mohammed," two very different titles. If anything in the Daily Caller story is true, it is likely that the person the story describes as "Sheikh Mohammed Hussein Al-Amoudi," a businessman who is not the king of Morocco but whom the story describes as organizing the conference in Ethiopia, offered the flight. But leaving King Mohammed of Morocco out of the story would have made it harder to weave in the factoid that "[n]ot including the flight, King Mohammed has donated at least $28 million to the Clinton Foundation." After we published this story in our August 2017 report, the Daily Caller called us and asked for our data; they questioned one of us about his personal political campaign donations, presumably trying to find embarrassing information. In the end, they just removed the story from their site and issued a retraction. But that was long after the campaign had ended and the role the story was meant to play had run its course.

Here, as elsewhere in the campaign, emails played a critical role as concrete, material "evidence" for fantasized conspiracy. As Richard Hofstadter presciently wrote in his classic piece on the paranoid style in American politics,

> A final characteristic of the paranoid style is related to the quality of its pedantry. One of the impressive things about paranoid literature is the contrast between its fantasied conclusions and the almost touching concern with factuality it invariably shows. It produces heroic strivings for evidence to prove that the unbelievable is the only thing that can be believed.
>
> But respectable paranoid literature not only starts from certain moral commitments that can indeed be justified but also carefully and all but obsessively accumulates "evidence." The difference between this

"evidence" and that commonly employed by others is that it seems less a means of entering into normal political controversy than a means of warding off the profane intrusion of the secular political world. The paranoid seems to have little expectation of actually convincing a hostile world, but he can accumulate evidence in order to protect his cherished convictions from it.[14]

The ability to scour emails for "evidence" and to locate, quote, and link to actual secret documents offers a paradise for paranoid logic. In large bodies of documentation almost anything can be found in writing if one is engaged in motivated observation and reasoning. The fact that the emails were private and were pried loose from unwilling hands (whether through Freedom of Information Act litigation or hacking) enhanced their claim to veracity. Precisely because these were private conversations among the conspirators that they wished to deny the public, the emails became totems of truth in the paranoid imagination of the world.

Another major feature of network propaganda is the repetition of claims and statements so that they become familiar and easily recalled. (For example, the Daily Caller "jet scam" story ends, for good measure, with a reprise of the "Lolita Express" story as "perhaps the most notorious freebie flights" Clinton took.) Unsurprisingly, therefore, the next most tweeted story from the Daily Caller, published on the same day by the same reporter as the "jet scam" story, was "Hillary's Two Official Favors To Morocco Resulted In $28 Million For Clinton Foundation."[15] The major part of the story was an utterly unsubstantiated and unsourced claim that in 2011 Clinton had gotten EPA head Lisa Jackson to try to shut down Mosaic Fertilizer, described as America's largest phosphate mining company, in exchange for a $15 million donation to the Clinton Foundation from King Mohammed VI of Morocco, ostensibly to benefit Morocco's state-owned phosphate company. The only evidence of Clinton's supposed control over Jackson, which would allow the secretary of state, without any authority and contrary to law, to direct a regulatory action by an agency, was that two years later, in 2013, Jackson would join the board of the Clinton Foundation. As the foundation's disclosure form shows, Jackson was paid exactly $0 for this "reward."[16]

The Daily Caller story did not offer any details as to what regulatory action Jackson supposedly took at the behest of Hillary Clinton. The article reported vaguely, "The regulatory assault against the U.S. phosphate agency began in earnest when Jackson launched a barrage of intimidating regulatory initiatives against Mosaic." Indeed, the article noted that there had been environmental concerns about phosphate production since 1979, "but the EPA did little to address concerns related to phosphates until Jackson's 2011 moves." Jackson's and Clinton's powers were supposedly so great that "the regulatory assault on the U.S. phosphate industry encompassed several agencies," including the Department of Homeland Security. And, to top it all, the EPA threatened Superfund penalties (the agency's primary mechanism to force and fund cleaning up land contaminated by industrial waste) that could have bankrupted Mosaic. The story offered nothing to explain how an interdepartmental intervention like this could all have originated with the secretary of state based on a personal relationship. It did not note that the Department of Justice Environment and Natural Resources Division had described in its "Accomplishment Report" for fiscal year 2010 a consent decree with Mosaic to spend $30 million to update its site in Uncle Sam, Louisiana, and "cease sulphuric acid production in Bartow, Florida."[17] Nor did it mention that in 2015 Mosaic agreed to a consent decree with the Department of Justice, the EPA, and the EPA's state equivalents in Florida and Louisiana to establish a $1.8 billion fund to clean up hazardous waste at six Florida and two Louisiana sites.[18] The idea that multi-agency cooperation on this level between departments with strong histories of independence and encompassing the federal government and two states, would arise from the request of a secretary with no authority in the matter, endure for years after both she and Lisa Jackson had left government, and result in such a large court-approved settlement, is nothing short of fantastical. It is typical of the paranoid style of reasoning in American politics that such conspiracies loom, and fear and distrust are used to bridge the yawning gaps in logic and evidence.

Despite the absence of detail or evidence, the story quoted two Republican representatives, Dennis Ross, whose district includes a Mosaic facility, and Marsha Blackburn, who had initiated the letter to the IRS on which the Daily Caller began its reporting in late July. According to the story, Ross said, "An environmental concern never existed. This targeting was all done as a payback to Morocco for donating millions of dollars to the Clinton Foundation," and Blackburn said, "These facts seem to reveal the possibility of more pay-to-play activities at the Clinton Foundation." And yet, again, less than a year earlier Mosaic had agreed to create a $1.8 billion cleanup fund in a consent decree not only with the EPA but with the Department of Justice and the Florida and Louisiana environmental agencies as well. Active participation of elected politicians, acting as a source or attesting to the credibility of the story, underscores the extent to which it is a mistake to understand the present epistemic crisis in technological terms, or purely in terms of Russian intervention. And while it is in principle possible that the author and publisher of these stories were themselves too far gone through the looking glass to recognize the yawning gaps in their own logic, the much more natural explanation is that they were simply propagandists, intentionally manipulating their audience on the eve of the election to help mobilize their base to vote out of fear and hatred of their opponent. Partisan propaganda, intended to achieve political advantage, sometimes driven and often supported by political elites indifferent to the truth, is a central part of the story. This interaction between partisan media and party elites is a constituent dynamic of the propaganda feedback loop.

The sheer implausibility of the story did not prevent other outlets from repeating it. Fox News republished Pollock's story essentially unchanged,[19] whereas more extreme outlets led with the subtext, as in this headline: "LEAK—Muslims Paid Hillary $28 MILLION To Do THIS, It's SICK."[20] The anti-Muslim theme was reinforced in the next most tweeted Daily Caller story about the Clinton Foundation in October, "Here's A (Dirty) Laundry List Of The Clinton Foundation's Most Questionable Foreign Donations."[21] Other than the Russian donation said to have been tied to the Uranium One deal, all the foreign donations noted were from Muslim-majority countries— Saudi Arabia, Morocco, Indonesia, Algeria, Kuwait, Qatar, and Oman.

The Podesta email dump provided a new cache of evidence with which to work. The Daily Caller story most linked to (as opposed to most tweeted) in October 2016 was "Hillary In Leaked Email: Saudi Arabia And Qatar Are Funding ISIS," which exposes another characteristic of network propaganda: the reworking of stories into a shared folklore.[22] The Daily Caller story itself was reasonable in its basic frame. It cited an email from Clinton to John Podesta in which Clinton outlined a plan to defeat ISIS. This anti-ISIS plan emphasized arming the Iraqi Kurdish Regional Government with heavier weapons than had been done in the past, supporting special operations, and seeking help for the Free Syrian Army or similar moderate paramilitary groups in Syria. Clinton added: "While this military/paramilitary operation is moving forward, we need to use our diplomatic and more traditional intelligence assets to bring pressure on the governments of Qatar and Saudi Arabia, which are providing clandestine financial and logistic support to ISIL and other radical Sunni groups in the region." Focusing on this language, the Daily Caller story reminded its readers that Qatar and Saudi Arabia had both donated to the Clinton Foundation and reported that "[t]he Clinton campaign has not replied to a Daily Caller inquiry about whether the Clinton Foundation will return donations from these two nations that, according to Hillary Clinton, fund ISIS." In context of the repeated flow of stories connecting the Clinton Foundation to Arab and Muslim funders, the implication that she knew that these donors had funded ISIS was far less benign.

That thesis was at the heart of the story that became the most Facebook-shared October story on Ending the Fed (Figure 4.16), the site that filled five of the top 10 spots on BuzzFeed's list of most widely shared "fake news" stories. Ending the Fed's headline read: "IT'S OVER: Hillary's ISIS Email Just Leaked & It's Worse Than Anyone Could Have Imagined."[23] It opens with the sentence "Today Wikileaks released what is, by far, the most devastating leak of the entire campaign. This makes Trump's dirty talk video look like an episode of Barney and Friends." Offering a screenshot of the email from the WikiLeaks site, the story states:

> Assange promised his latest batch of leaks would lead to the indictment of Hillary, and it looks like he was not kidding. The email proves Hillary knew and was complicit in the funding and arming of ISIS by our "allies" Saudi Arabia and Qatar!

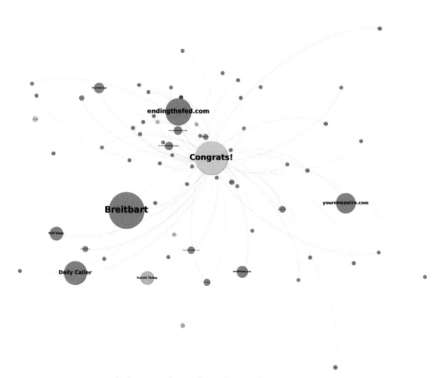

FIGURE 4.16 Sites linking to the WikiLeaks email entitled *Congrats!*, which includes the statement regarding ISIS and Saudi and Qatari funding. Nodes sized by the number of Facebook shares the sites received for all email-linked stories on each site.

The media is yet to report on this, even though Wikileaks has a 10 year history of being 100% accurate in their leaks, never once releasing info that proved to be false.

... *Can you guess why?*

Maybe it has something to do with the fact that The Saudi's brag about funding 20% of Hillary's Presidential campaign, and along with Qatar, are among the largest donors to the CLINTON FOUNDATION.

While the original Daily Caller article presented a plausible framing—Clinton should return donations given by governments that were also supporting ISIS—the Ending the Fed story ramped it up, claiming that the email proved that "Hillary knew and was complicit in the funding and arming of ISIS by our 'allies' Saudi Arabia and Qatar." Not only that, it alleged that the media were not reporting on this because the Saudis bragged that they funded 20 percent of Clinton's presidential campaign and were among the largest donors to the Clinton Foundation. One can read the paragraph as many times as one wishes and still come up short in explaining how a series of non sequiturs adds up to the idea that Hillary Clinton admitted to funding and arming ISIS. However, the repeated insinuations that the Clinton Foundation was a funnel through which various Muslim governments (especially Saudi Arabia) got Clinton to do their bidding, and the intentional conflation of foundation donations and personal speaking fees with pay-to-play corruption, had long been circulating throughout the right-wing media environment.

The 20 percent funding claim originated in a June 14 story on Zero Hedge[24] and was repeated and amplified that same day by Fox News[25] (Fox has since removed the evidence of its republication of this story from its site and blocked its archiving by the Internet Archive) and Infowars.[26] The origin of the story raises many questions. Apparently on Sunday, June 12, the Jordanian Petra News Agency published a story claiming that the then-Deputy Crown Prince Mohammed bin Salman had provided an exclusive interview in which he claimed that Saudi Arabia had provided 20 percent of the Clinton campaign's funds. The report was soon removed, and the Petra News Agency issued a press release asserting that its system had been hacked and that the hack was the source of the bogus report.[27] Before the story was removed, however, it was captured by a Washington-based think tank, the Institute for Gulf Affairs, whose focus is the Saudi government's human rights violations and the cozy relationship between the United States and the Saudi royal family. The story was then published on June 13 in Middle East Eye (MEE),[28] a U.K.-based site that describes itself as independent but is reported by a wide range of outlets to have diverse and conflicting political interests.[29]

Despite MEE's retraction of the story, it had been picked up by Zero Hedge and amplified through the network of paranoid right-wing sites. RT also reported on the hack and the story, emphasizing the angle that MEE had reported that it had been pointed to the Jordanian agency's error by the Podesta Group, the lobbying firm cofounded by John and Tony Podesta, which, it said, counts Saudi Arabia as a lucrative client.[30] Like the emails, a document that was published and then removed offers a peek into occult knowledge that confirms conspiracy. Making the accusation by planting such a document in a remote site would offer it enormous credibility within the network of conspiracy theorists. Certainly, it is not impossible that the young, soon-to-be-elevated crown prince made a strategic error in an interview with the Jordanian news agency, and Saudi diplomatic power was brought to bear to release a bogus retraction and hacking story. For this to be the case one would have to assume that the prince in fact made such an embarrassing mistake and was nonetheless elevated to crown prince within a few months, and that, contrary to law, the Clinton campaign in fact received tens of millions of dollars in donations from a foreign government.

The alternative explanation is that the Jordanian agency was in fact hacked by someone who intended to harm both the Saudi government and the Clinton campaign. Such a hack would be similar to the hack of the Qatari news agency, which has variously been blamed on Russia[31] or the United Arab Emirates.[32] Even if a Muslim or Arab adversary aimed the original hack primarily at the Saudi government, its importation into the U.S. campaign fed into a strong racist, anti-Muslim narrative. The image of a laughing Clinton, on the background of squinting or self-satisfied Arabs and piles of dollars that accompanied the Infowars republication of the Zero Hedge story, leaves little for interpretation (Figure 4.17).

Even if we accept that Ending the Fed (which ceased operations shortly after Trump's election) was a quintessential "fake news" site, a clickbait fabricator designed to make money by reaping Facebook advertising dollars, it did not rely solely on making up stories out of whole cloth, as in the notorious story claiming that the pope had endorsed Donald Trump, to serve as clickbait. It depended more heavily on stories from major nodes in the right-wing media ecosystem—from Zero Hedge to Fox News and Infowars—that created, replicated, and offered credence to various elements of stories that could then be recombined into new, believable conspiracy theories. If Ending the Fed had a meaningful role in influencing the debate; it was the amplification of already circulating tropes whose currency and efficacy depend on their being broadly familiar and intuitively recognizable—like canonical folk tales—to their readers. Such sites should be considered important if there is measurable reason to think that their amplification contributed substantially to the effect produced by the network as a whole. The prominence of Ending the Fed on Facebook, coupled with the fact that a sizable group of voters used Facebook as a major source of news, suggests that such an amplification effect is at least possible. As we explain in more detail in Chapter 9, measuring that influence would be difficult because credibility in the field depends on embeddedness in an epistemic network, and truth or falsity will depend heavily on the familiarity and identity value of the elements of the story.

The "Hillary helped fund and arm ISIS" story depends on a rich shared narrative created by media that have longer and deeper purchase on the minds of those who are exposed to it. If such stories were believed, it is almost certainly because the sustained effort to tie all these themes together was central to the right-wing media ecosystem, as the sixth-most Facebook-shared Breitbart story of the entire 18-month period suggests: "Clinton Cash: Khizr Khan's Deep Legal, Financial Connections to Saudi Arabia, Hillary's Clinton Foundation Tie Terror, Immigration, Email Scandals Together." In the paranoid imagination, all threads tie together.

And then there is Sean Hannity, host of the most-watched show on Fox News. On the same day that the Ending the Fed story came out, Hannity ran a segment, with Sebastian Gorka, who would become a deputy assistant to the

FIGURE 4.17 Infowars story reporting on Zero Hedge's story that links Hillary Clinton's campaign to Saudi funding, June 14, 2016.

president during the first seven months of the Trump administration, built around the ISIS funding email. Hannity opened the segment with the words:

> more headaches for the Clinton campaign because of the Wikileaks email dump. According to the hacked e-mails back in 2014, Hillary Clinton sent an email to John Podesta claiming Saudi Arabia and Qatar were both giving support to ISIS and other extremist groups. Mind you, Saudi Arabia has given up to $25 million dollars to the Clinton Foundation. In addition to that, according to the Washington Post, the royal Saudi family, well, they gave the Clinton Library around 10 million, and the Clinton Foundation took in between $1 and $5 million from the government of Qatar.[33]

What followed was a diatribe of how "America's national interest will be in the auction block if she becomes Commander in Chief. It will be the highest bidder, whether it's the Saudis or the Russians." And the corrupt media were not going to ask Clinton the hard questions. A week later Donald Trump, during the third presidential debate, interjected "she gave us ISIS as sure as you are sitting there."[34]

Ending the Fed's story had a truly mind-boggling 750,000 Facebook shares. Sean Hannity has over three million viewers.

And over 70 million viewers watched the third presidential debate.

AS A CANDIDATE, Donald Trump ran an outsider's campaign and used immigration, which he insisted on framing in terms of "radical Islamic terrorism," as a battering ram against the walls of the Republican Party establishment. The first year of the Trump presidency was marked by escalating rhetoric against incumbent establishment Republicans, a large number of primary challenges from the far-right candidates against incumbents, and a wave of retirements by Republican incumbents ahead of the 2018 elections and the primary challenges they were sure to bring. In May 2018 immigration became the issue on which the House self-styled "Freedom Caucus," the most radical wing of the Republican House members, blocked passage of a farm bill that would have achieved the goals of two major parts of the Republican establishment—providing large payments to farmers in core rural states in the Republican heartland, and encumbering food assistance for poor people consistent with the long-term goal of Reagan Republicans to reduce welfare payments. And while Trump did not invent the anti-immigration, anti-trade populism on the America right, his candidacy certainly was the fulcrum for that wing to achieve its most significant victory, and his presidency has provided the platform around which that battle is being fought.

5

The Fox Diet

For years we've been telling you, journalism is dead.

SEAN HANNITY

ON NOVEMBER 28, 2017, the forty-fifth president of the United States asked his 50 million Twitter followers why "our deep State authorities" were not investigating "Crooked Hillary" and whether the lack of investigation was evidence of a rigged and corrupt system. He concluded this remarkable tweet by calling on the two most widely viewed hosts on Fox News: Tucker Carlson and Sean Hannity (Figure 5.1).

An American president turning on his own national security establishment for failing to attack his political opponent exhibits a troubling authoritarian bent. The fact that he leaned on Hannity and Carlson should, by the end of 2017, have come as no surprise. By that point Fox News had become the lead player in what had become the president's personal propaganda network in his battles against the intelligence community, the media, and, increasingly

Donald J. Trump ✔
@realDonaldTrump

Charles McCullough, the respected fmr Intel Comm Inspector General, said public was misled on Crooked Hillary Emails. "Emails endangered National Security." Why aren't our deep State authorities looking at this? Rigged & corrupt?
@TuckerCarlson @seanhannity
10:45 PM - Nov 28, 2017

FIGURE 5.1 Donald Trump tweet, November 28, 2017.

Network Propaganda. Yochai Benkler, Robert Faris, and Hal Roberts.
© Yochai Benkler, Robert Faris, and Hal Roberts 2018. Published 2018 by Oxford University Press.

over the course of the year, his make-or-break- struggle against the very idea of professionalism in law enforcement and through it the rule of law.

This chapter consists of three detailed case studies of how Fox News actively used its position at the core of the right-wing media ecosystem to support the president in the central political controversy of his presidency: the investigation led by special counsel Robert Mueller into the allegation that Russia had intervened in the U.S. election in support of the candidacy of Donald Trump, and the question of whether it had done so in coordination with the Trump campaign. The first study describes the emergence of the "deep state" as the overarching frame through which the story came to be understood in right-wing media as a partisan effort to unseat Donald Trump directed by holdovers from the Obama administration in the intelligence community and law enforcement. The next two studies involve discrete elements of this overarching frame. One case involves the argument that Democratic activist Seth Rich was murdered to hide the fact that he, not Russia, was responsible for leaking the Democratic National Committee (DNC) emails. The other case involves use of a story surrounding a company called Uranium One to attack the integrity and independence of the key law enforcement officers involved in the special counsel investigation. The timing and pattern we show in these case studies strongly suggest that they were launched for the specific partisan purpose of deflecting the Trump-Russia allegations and undermining the special counsel investigation. And in the two specifically fact-based cases, we show that Fox News actively promoted these stories despite the fact that they were repeatedly fact checked and debunked by a wide variety of professional journalists.

In Chapter 2 we saw that the overall architecture of the American media environment consists of two highly asymmetric networks and that the right was structurally different from the rest. In Chapter 3 we explained the propaganda feedback loop and the reality-check dynamic that could explain the emergence of such an asymmetric system, and the susceptibility of the former to the dissemination and accreditation of disinformation and propaganda. In Chapter 4 we showed how Breitbart and Donald Trump as a candidate interacted to use the propagandist affordances of the right-wing media ecosystem to take over the Republican Party and to mobilize its base in the general election. Here, we document how Fox News reasserted its role at the center of the right-wing media ecosystem by becoming the central node of network propaganda on behalf of an embattled president, on the issue that most threatened his legitimacy and possibly his tenure in office. Journalists and academics observing the American media system recognize their own biases, and many are therefore reticent to point the finger at Fox. Here, we use our large data sets and analytic tools as a source of objective validation that what we are seeing is really there, in the content and propagation dynamics of the frames and stories we cover. These data warrant the conclusion that Fox shares little but a few visual trappings with the world of professional journalism at the core of the rest of the U.S. media system. It is, across its online and television properties, America's leading propaganda outlet.

Deep State: Fox News vs. the National Security Establishment

Prior to 2017 usage of the term "deep state" had been almost entirely reserved for references to political dynamics in Turkey, Egypt after the Arab Spring, and occasionally other Middle Eastern countries. It was generally only used in reference to the United States at the periphery, either by the libertarian right or the civil-libertarian left. As recently as February 2017, Chris Wallace on Fox News skeptically explained the term as he introduced Rush Limbaugh, the dean of right-wing talk radio: "You also use a phrase which I have to say that I only heard for the first time in the last couple of weeks, the 'deep state.' And that's the notion that there's an Obama shadow government embedded in the bureaucracy that is working against this new president."[1] Limbaugh responded, "Well, I would love to claim credit for that, but actually, I think a reporter by the name of Glenn Greenwald at The Intercept who has got a relationship with—what's his name? Assange. I think he actually coined the term. And I think it works. I don't think—who is driving this business that the Russians hacked the election? It's the Democrat Party. It's Hillary. It's Obama."

Limbaugh was referring to Glenn Greenwald, a longtime defender of civil liberties and critic of the national security establishment, best known for his role in reporting on the disclosures by Edward Snowden and Chelsea Manning. On January 11, 2017, Greenwald published a piece, entitled "The Deep State Goes to War with President Elect, Using Unverified Claims, as Democrats Cheer." [2] A week earlier, the Office of the Director of National Intelligence had reported, with little supporting evidence, that the intelligence community had high confidence that Russia had hacked the DNC emails and meddled in the U.S. election. That same week BuzzFeed had published the Steele Dossier, an opposition research dossier that first laid out the allegations of Trump relations with Russia.[3] Greenwald claimed that the CIA had long sought to increase its war-making capacity in Syria and to escalate conflict with Russia. He also claimed that Hillary Clinton had supported these goals and that Trump had opposed them. The next day Tucker Carlson invited Greenwald to explain his criticism of Democrats and mainstream media to roughly three million viewers on Fox News.

By the time Limbaugh appeared on Fox News in mid-February, the frame had shifted. Despite citing Greenwald for credibility, Limbaugh's interview captured the essence of an entirely different and new turn that the "deep state" frame was to take in 2017: "It's the Democrat Party. It's Hillary. It's Obama." Before the 2016 presidential election, the term had been applied from both ends of the political spectrum—libertarians on the right and the civil-libertarian left—to describe a set of entrenched interests that superseded both parties and kept both under control. It was a rarely used term that was the direct descendant of President Dwight D. Eisenhower's parting warning about the power of the "military-industrial complex," not a partisan cudgel. Use of the term, which appeared rarely prior to 2016 election, took a sharp upturn in early 2017 (Figure 5.2).

If we analyze the words used in association with "deep state" before and after Election Day 2016, the shift is clear. Figure 5.3 compares an image of the words most associated with "deep state" from 2012 until Election Day 2016 (panel a) and an image of words associated with the term from Election Day until March 2018 (panel b). The images rely on the widely used Word2Vec

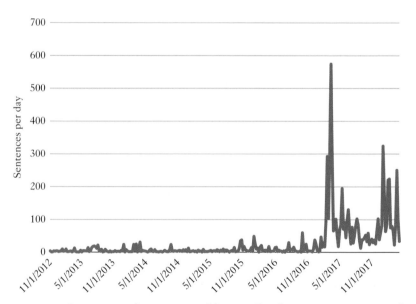

FIGURE 5.2 Sentences per day mentioning "deep state" in the top 50 mainstream media and top 50 digital native media, November 2012–March 2018.

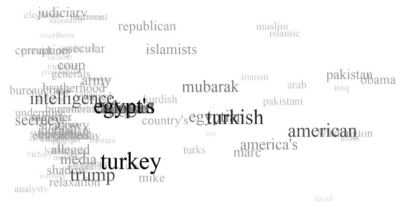

FIGURE 5.3A "Deep state" in top media, November 2012–November 2016.

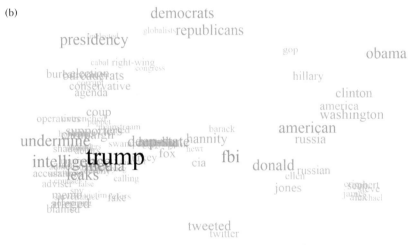

FIGURE 5.3B "Deep state" in top media, November 2016–March 2018.

algorithm to show words that appear more commonly together in the text as clustered together, while separating word clusters that are usually distinct from each other. Before the election of Donald Trump, "deep state" was overwhelmingly used to describe Middle Eastern power structures, primarily the battles of Erdogan against the original bearer of the "deep state" name; the Turkish military and intelligence agencies; and around the reassertion of control by Egypt's military after the failed Arab Spring. After the U.S. presidential election the usage was overwhelmingly domestic, emphasizing "Trump" in connection with "intelligence," "leaks," "undermine," "coup," "Fox," "Hannity," and "Newt." Separate clusters associated "Obama," "Hillary," "Washington," and the "GOP" on one hand, and "Democrats," "Republicans," and "globalists," on the other hand.

Buried right underneath the central word "Egypt" in Figure 5.3a are two names, whose size and location on the map suggest they are similarly central to this period. The first, "Erdogan," is less surprising. The second, "Lofgren," is tied to the "Mike" that appears more visibly right under "Turkey." Both identify the most influential effort to import the term to describe American politics before the 2016 election. In February 2014 Mike Lofgren, who retired in 2011 from a nearly 30-year career as a congressional staffer Republican in the House and Senate, published on the Bill Moyers website an essay entitled "Anatomy of the Deep State."[4] In this essay, Lofgren wove together an image of a power structure anchored by the major security and intelligence agencies, military contractors, and core players in the financial and technology industry, all of whom were:

> [D]eeply dyed in the hue of the official ideology of the governing class, an ideology that is neither specifically Democrat nor Republican. Domestically, whatever they might privately believe about essentially diversionary social issues such as abortion or gay marriage, they almost invariably believe in the "Washington Consensus": financialization, outsourcing, privatization, deregulation and the commodifying of labor. Internationally, they espouse 21st-century "American Exceptionalism": the right and duty of the United States to meddle in every region of the world with coercive diplomacy and boots on the ground and to ignore painfully won international norms of civilized behavior.

It is to this explicitly anti-establishment frame that retired Republican Congressman and twice grassroots libertarian candidate in Republican presidential primaries Ron Paul was clearly referring when he became the first person to use the term in the post-election period in a November 10 interview on Fox Business[5] and then again in a November 11, 2016 interview on RT.[6] And it is in this same sense that libertarian Doug Casey decried under the Zero Hedge persona of Tyler Durden the next day, "I've said for years that the Demopublicans and the Republicrats are just two wings of the same party. One says it's for social freedom (which is a lie), but is actively antagonistic to economic freedom. The other says it's for economic freedom (which is a lie), but is actively antagonistic to social freedom. Both are controlled by members of the Deep State."[7]

The "deep state" framing changed in response to a December 9 story by the *Washington Post* entitled "Secret CIA assessment says Russia was trying to help Trump win White House"[8] and to the Obama administration announcement that it had tasked the intelligence community with producing a report on cyberattacks in the 2016 election. The next day, an unsigned piece under the Tyler Durden pseudonym on Zero Hedge decried "A 'Soft' Coup Attempt." Russia Insider published a similarly framed attack, decrying "Silent Coup in Progress: American Intelligence Agencies Are Trying to Stop Trump From Taking Office."[9] The "coup" construct, together with the "deep state" frame reappeared in a piece published on December 12 on antiwar.com, informationclearinghouse.info, and Veterans News Now,[10] thought to be a Russian gray site.[11] That same day Paul Joseph Watson of Infowars ran a video segment that received half a million views on YouTube that laid out the "deep state" theory of the Trump-Russia allegations.[12]

A story on Breitbart under the pseudonym Virgil reframed the "deep state" to include all the forces arraigned against Donald Trump: Democrats, the mainstream media, and the Washington swamp.

> Do the Democrats want Donald Trump to become the 45th president? Of course not. And how about the Democrats' handmaiden, the Main Stream Media? Do they want Trump in the White House? Of course not. And how 'bout all the other affluent residents of the Washington "swamp," which Trump has pledged to drain—do you think any of *them* want Trump? Of course not. Together, these anti-Trump constituencies help form what has been called the Deep State . . .[13]

The story went on to include a quote from the Daily Beast alleging that agents within the CIA didn't like Michael Flynn and "hate[d] Trump's guts." Virgil theorized that "liberal Democrats have controlled the executive branch for 16 of the last 24 years, and so there had been plenty of time to cultivate liberals— even liberal activists—within the ranks and to bring them to the pinnacles of bureaucratic power." About the military, the piece acknowledged that "[t]o be sure, the vast bulk of our nation's warriors are staunch believers in Douglas MacArthur's trinity of "duty, honor, country. . . .' Yet still, during the Obama years, such patriots have been layered over by liberal apparatchiks. And the same left-pushing syndrome has been equally true of all federal security agencies."

All the elements of the reframed "deep state" were laid out in this piece. The "deep state" was no longer a nonpartisan permanent power that protected an oligarchy and was equally immune to both parties' democratic claims. Now the "deep state" was a partisan effort to portray Donald Trump's victory as a Russian hack instead of the democratic victory of American populism over the Washington establishment. This framing pitted the Trump forces of good against Democrats, Obama holdovers in the national security establishment (and later law enforcement), the mainstream media, and anti-Trump Republicans.

This new partisan "deep state" frame lay dormant for a month after its initial birth (except for claims on Infowars by Trump associates Roger Stone and Alex Jones that they had each been targeted for assassination by the "deep state").[14] Greenwald did not advance this partisan frame in his January piece in The Intercept, which was still focused on the persistent power of the CIA, its history of lying, and his argument that the CIA was resisting Trump because Trump threatened its policy preferences. The partisan frame re-emerged in response to the news that Michael Flynn was forced to resign his position as national security adviser on February 13, 2017, ostensibly for misleading Vice President Mike Pence about having had a phone conversation with the Russian ambassador before President Trump took office. The next few days saw an explosion of stories and YouTube videos discussing the Flynn resignation in terms of the "deep state." The most highly tweeted story on February 14 was a story by Eli Lake on Bloomberg, entitled "The Political Assassination of Michael Flynn," in which Lake argued that "[s]electively disclosing details of private conversations monitored by the FBI or NSA gives the permanent state the power to destroy reputations from the cloak of anonymity. This is what police states do," and that "Flynn was working to reform the intelligence-industrial complex, something that threatened the bureaucratic prerogatives of his rivals."[15]

Infowars had several segments on YouTube with viewership numbers ranging from 50,000 to over 200,000, including the second- and sixth-most tweeted stories in our set from that day. The top 10 tweeted stories were rounded out by Breitbart stories, PJ Media, a Judicial Watch YouTube video, and the appearance of the story entitled "It[']s over Folks: The Neocons and the 'Deep State' Have Neutered the Trump Presidency" by an author writing under the pseudonym The Saker on Paul Craig Roberts's site and on Zero Hedge. The Saker's website tagline is "Stop the War on Russia," and the piece claimed, "Ever since Trump made it to the White House, he has taken blow after blow from the Neocon-run Ziomedia, from Congress, from all the Hollywood doubleplusgoodthinking 'stars' and even from European politicians. [. . .] In order to defeat Trump, the US deep state has had to terribly weaken the US and the AngloZionist Empire."[16] Over the next several days, Breitbart continued to attract attention with its "deep state" coverage, as did Infowars, YouTube videos, and Zero Hedge guest posts.

During February, Fox News began to introduce the "deep state" frame, but still ambivalently. On the morning of Flynn's resignation, Fox News commentator and former left-wing U.S. Representative Dennis Kucinich used the "deep state" frame on the "Mornings With Maria" show on Fox Business,[17] and that evening Sean Hannity invited Bloomberg's Eli Lake to discuss his claim that Flynn's removal was a "political assassination" by the permanent state. Later that same week, Rush Limbaugh jumped on the bandwagon and brought it with him to the interview on Fox News on Sunday with Mike Wallace that we described at the opening. Nonetheless, through February, Fox News was still generally skeptical of the frame. Wallace asked Limbaugh whether this all sounded too conspiratorial; an earlier online Fox News story, entitled "Trump knocks down 'Deep State' claims," concluded that "what Trump made clear in his press conference today is that he sees it for what it is: the political and ideological struggle that always buffets behind-the-scenes Washington, not a part of a vast conspiracy."[18]

Fox's stance on the "deep state" changed after President Trump first tweeted on March 4, "Terrible! Just found out that Obama had my 'wires tapped' in Trump Tower just before the victory. Nothing found. This is McCarthyism!" and then compared it to Watergate in a subsequent tweet that morning. Figure 5.4 documents the explosion of coverage of the deep state frame using media attention measured by open web stories, tweets, and Google searches.

The publication of the Steele dossier by BuzzFeed and the Flynn firing appear as the first spikes in attention. The sharp uptick across all three measures in March coincides with the president's tweets. That was also when Fox News embraced the term both online and, more importantly, on television. Lou Dobbs's March 26 interview of Fox analyst Andrew Napolitano on the topic became the most widely viewed video on YouTube that month,[19] and Dobbs returned to the topic two days later to accuse the "deep state" and the "national left-wing media" of "a full-on assault on the President of the United States."[20] Not to be undone, Hannity cheerfully added the authoritarian terminology of "purge" on March 10: "Deep-state Obama holdovers embedded like barnacles in the federal bureaucracy are hell-bent on destroying President Trump. It's time for the Trump administration to purge these saboteurs."[21]

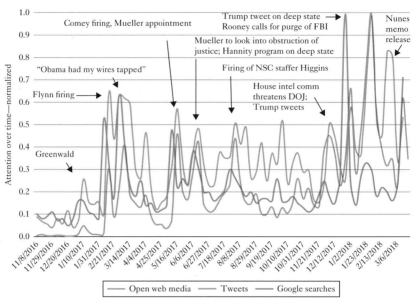

FIGURE 5.4 Level of attention by open web stories, tweets, and Google searches, January 2017–March 2017.

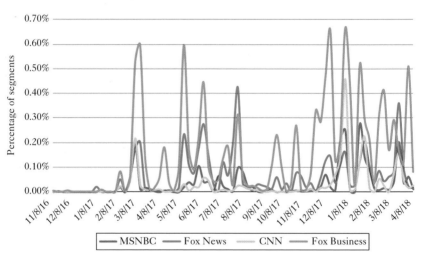

FIGURE 5.5 Percentage of 15-second segments mentioning "deep state" on MSNBC, CNN, Fox News, and Fox Business.

The continuous interplay between Dobbs, Hannity, Carlson, and others on Fox Business and Fox News became the dominant pattern on network news, as Figure 5.5 shows. The peaks in 2017 coincide with the appointment of Robert Mueller, the first disclosures of the Trump Tower meeting, the search of Paul Manafort's home, and the Flynn guilty plea. This pattern strongly implies that repeated invocation of the "deep state" frame is intentionally deployed when the president is most under threat from the investigation. We offer more details for the May and October–November spikes in this chapter, with the Seth Rich and Uranium One case studies. In Chapter 8, we explore in more detail the July–August spike, where we discuss the Guccifer 2.0/Forensicator story as a suspected Russian influence campaign.

The rest of the media ecosystem had an ambivalent relationship with the "deep state" framing. Some, like Greenwald, saw an underlying truth of the matter—that the national security establishment was in fact going after Trump because he opposed their agenda and that having the CIA intervene in politics in this way was a graver threat to democracy than a Trump presidency. Greenwald's interview with Amy Goodman on "Democracy Now!" became the most watched video on the "deep state" in February 2017.[22] Others reported on this spectacle of the Republican Party, which had long branded itself as stronger on national security, attacking the revered national security establishment as partisan and corrupt. But there was little to fact check about the "deep state" that could anchor a counternarrative. As a result, when we map the networks of authority and social media attention, the mainstream professional media are secondary. Breitbart, Fox, and the president's Twitter account anchored the "deep state" frame, as Figure 5.6 shows. (We include Twitter and YouTube in Figure 5.6, the map of web linking, because half of the inlinks to Twitter in this set are to tweets by the president, and so it offers some insight into his role in the frame; and because YouTube served as a major distribution platform.)

The web-linking map also shows the large role that Infowars played on YouTube (accounting for four of the top 10 most watched videos), the distinct network around Zero Hedge, and the independent and large role that the Intercept played as a distinct center of gravity away from either the right-wing or mainstream ecosystems.

When we move from attention and authority among publications and media producers to mapping the attention of politically engaged Twitter users, the picture changes dramatically. Everyone but the right-wing media ecosystem fades away. On Twitter, the frame is purely internal to the right-wing ecosystem. The *New York Times* and the Intercept recede, and the craziest sites—the Gateway Pundit, Infowars, True Pundit, and Truthfeed—congregate around YouTube, while Breitbart, Zero Hedge, and Fox News make up a distinct cluster at the center of the map.

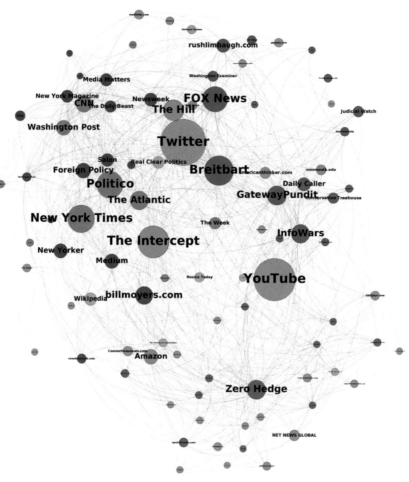

FIGURE 5.6 Network map of "deep state" stories. Architecture and node sizing by media inlinks.

When we zoom in and remove YouTube, the architecture remains unchanged.

It is important not to read Figures 5.6 and 5.7 as marking yet again a marginalization of Fox. Alex Jones's most widely viewed YouTube video about the "deep state" drew about half a million viewers, one-sixth of the daily viewership of either Hannity or Carlson, and most of them got anywhere from 50,000 to 250,000 views. As we showed in Chapter 2, over the course of 2017, Fox News reclaimed its central role in the right-wing

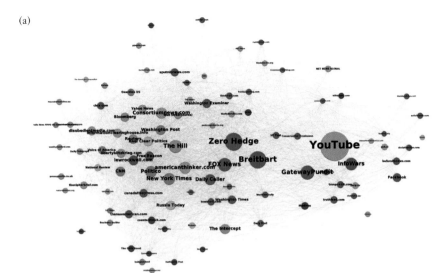

FIGURE 5.7A "Deep state" on Twitter. Nodes sized by number of Twitter shares. Architecture by co-tweeting patterns.

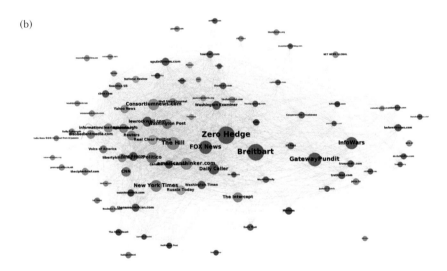

FIGURE 5.7B "Deep state" on Twitter with YouTube removed.

media ecosystem across the broader range of stories that make up the political agenda. Moreover, using overall traffic analysis from web metrics firm SimilarWeb, it is clear that Fox News dominated in terms of actual traffic to the site, both in terms of total number of visits and in terms of unique visitors (see Figure 5.8).

As we look at the reshaping of the new "deep state" frame from its original, nonpartisan concern into a distinct narrative about a partisan attack on Donald Trump, we can certainly find critical moments at which Breitbart played a central reframing role. And we certainly find plenty of the craziest conspiracy theories hovering at the margins. But as we move now to analyze how this broad frame was translated over the course of 2017 into repeated concerted efforts to defend the president from the Russia suspicion, we see Fox News taking center stage in a much clearer and more distinctive way by deflecting attention and blame, interpreting the investigation in deeply partisan terms, and sowing confusion and doubt. And it is here too that the broad and loose gestalt frame takes on distinct falsifiable forms whose pattern fits that of a sustained disinformation campaign by a propaganda outlet, rather than as episodic errors by a journalistic outlet.

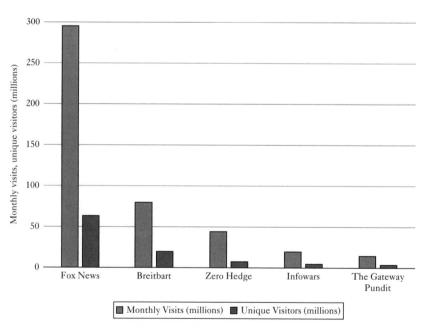

FIGURE 5.8 Average monthly visits and unique visitors, 2017–2018, SimilarWeb.

Seth Rich: Fox News vs. the
Intelligence Community

No single case more clearly exhibits the characteristics of a disinformation campaign aimed to divert attention from the president's political woes than Fox News's coverage in May of 2017 of the conspiracy theory that DNC staffer Seth Rich was murdered because he, rather than state-backed Russian hackers, was the source of the DNC emails disclosed in the middle of the 2016 campaign.

The question of who hacked into the Democratic National Committee's email server and passed the stolen emails on to WikiLeaks was a central locus of the fight over Russian intervention in the 2016 presidential election. Competing narratives emerged to answer the question. The first was that Russian state actors hacked the DNC computer system. A different version painted it as the work of a lone hacker. A third account was that a DNC insider leaked the emails out of disaffection with the internal corruption of the party. If the Russian state was responsible, Trump's victory would look less like a genuine American populist victory. If, by contrast, the emails were leaked by a disgruntled insider, Trump's victory would look even more like a popular rejection of "the swamp," so much so that even honest Democrats could no longer abide. This discrete factual dispute therefore became central for months over the course of 2017.

The DNC blamed the attack on Russian information operations in its original public announcement on June 14, 2016. Throughout the summer and fall of 2016, several technology publications and security firms published reports that supported the Russian theory. At the same time two alternative theories developed in the right-wing media ecosystem, and episodically on the left as well. One theory was that a young DNC staffer, Seth Rich, was the source of the leak. Seth Rich had been murdered in Washington, D.C., on July 10, 2016, and the theory was that the murder was orchestrated by the Clinton campaign, and by some accounts by Clinton herself. The second theory was that a lone hacker who took the name "Guccifer 2.0" was responsible for the attack. We return to that theory and how it played out in Chapter 8, where we discuss it in context of Russian white and gray propaganda.

The first spike in attention to the Seth Rich story occurred in July 2016 (Figure 5.9), right after Rich's murder. A second spike was in early August, after Julian Assange offered a reward for information about his murder and first implied that Rich had been WikiLeaks' source of the DNC emails. Both these early peaks are dwarfed by the coverage in May 2017, when Fox News

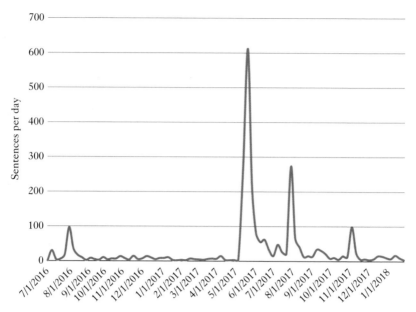

FIGURE 5.9 Sentences per day mentioning Seth Rich in open web media, July 1, 2017–January 31, 2018.

took over, as well as the July–August 2017 peak associated with the revived "Guccifer 2.0" theory.

Conspiracy theories began to bubble up almost immediately after Seth Rich was shot in the early morning hours of July 10, 2016. By July 12 YouNewsWire.com was already weaving tweets from several sources, including @Ricky_Vaughn99, into a story entitled "DNC Election Fraud Whistleblower Found Murdered."[23] Over the next few weeks, YourNewsWire.com published several more stories that ultimately made it one of the two sites whose stories on the Seth Rich conspiracy theory were most widely shared on Facebook, alongside Gateway Pundit. YourNewsWire.com played an early central role in propagating the Pizzagate conspiracy, and in Chapter 8 we discuss whether it better fits the "gray propaganda" or "useful idiot" category in relation to Russian propaganda. @Ricky_Vaughn99, described by the Southern Poverty Law Center as "one of the most prolific and longstanding Alt-Right personalities," was suspended from Twitter a few weeks before the election.[24] Over the next few days, the conspiracy theories remained mostly on marginal sites, although it did appear on a few sites with moderate audiences, like 100percentfedup and Dennis Michael Lynch.[25]

The story picked up again in late July, after two Reddit threads tried to revive the theory.[26] The Reddit threads pointed to an NBC Nightly News interview in which Julian Assange denied evidence that the DNC emails had been hacked by Russians.[27] The story received more attention this time from more influential conspiracy sites. This round of attention included a story by Truthfeed, which relied primarily on a tweet by the alt-right handle @ JaredWyand,[28] a YouTube video by One America News Network that received over 90,000 views,[29] and a few days later, a story in the Gateway Pundit.[30] The presence in this storyline of well-known alt-right handles like @Ricky_Vaughn99 or @JaredWyand offers some evidence of the influence of the alt-right. But they played a relatively marginal role and relied on more visible influencers to move from their own networks to the broader network. This reliance on more central right-wing actors is part of what leads us to put these actors in the second or third tier of concerns over disinformation.

Coverage expanded to broader media outlets only after Assange, on August 9, tweeted a $20,000 reward for "information leading to the conviction for the murder of DNC staffer Seth Rich," and implied in an interview on Dutch TV that Rich may have been the source of the DNC email dump and that his death may have been tied with that fact.[31] The story was only covered by broader major media after that interview. As we saw in Chapter 3 with the pedophilia and rape assertions, conspiracy theories that germinate in the nether regions of the internet stay there unless they find an amplification vector. In this case Julian Assange lent the story visibility and credibility. But interest in the story rapidly tapered off, only to reappear on a much grander scale, as Figure 5.9 makes clear, and on a much more important platform in the middle of May 2017.

The pattern of coverage in May of 2017 strongly suggests that the re-emergence of the Seth Rich conspiracy theory almost a year after it had receded was part of an intentional effort to shield the president from mounting pressure surrounding his ties to Russia. On May 9, 2017, Donald Trump fired the director of the FBI, James Comey. The next day, Trump hosted Russian Foreign Minister Sergey Lavrov and Russian Ambassador to the United States Sergey Kislyak in the White House. On May 16, the *New York Times* reported that a memo written contemporaneously by Comey documented that Trump had asked Comey to drop the investigation of Trump's former National Security Advisor, Michael Flynn.[32] With pressure mounting on May 17, Deputy Attorney General Rod Rosenstein appointed Robert Mueller as special counsel to investigate the allegations of connections between the Trump campaign and Russia. A comparison of May 2017

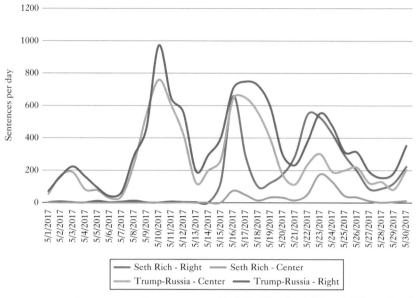

FIGURE 5.10 Sentences per day mentioning "Seth Rich" or both "Donald Trump" and "Russia," May 2017. All media sources coded right and center.

sentences mentioning Trump and Russia and Seth Rich among all media we code as "right" and "center" in May 2017 exhibits a clear interference pattern (Figure 5.10). (Center-left and left publications followed an almost identical pattern to the center, each publishing more stories than the center.) There are two peaks in coverage on the center related to the Comey dismissal and the Comey memo. The right exploded with Seth Rich coverage on May 16, the day the *Times* reported the Comey memo.

At 4:30 a.m. on May 16, 2017, the Washington, D.C., local Fox 5 reported that a private investigator hired by Seth Rich's family, Rod Wheeler, had communicated to Fox 5 that Seth Rich had been in touch with WikiLeaks before his death and that a source inside the D.C. police told him that the police were told to stand down the investigation.[33] At 5:40 a.m., Fox and Friends interviewed the Fox D.C. reporter[34] and developed its own story, which first ran at 6:17 a.m., that repeated the story and vouched for Wheeler's credibility.[35] That story ran again an hour later.[36] Online, Fox News published Malia Zimmerman's version of the story, the version that would ultimately be the basis of lawsuits that Wheeler, and later Rich's family, filed against Fox.[37] That evening Sean Hannity made the connection to the Russia investigation explicit. After telling the basic story, Hannity ran an interview he did with

Julian Assange in January 2017, in which Assange said that the email dumps were not from a state actor (the screen suggests they were talking about the Podesta email dump, not those from the DNC). Hannity then told his audience "let me connect the dots from here," and delivered the core point:

> If this is true, and Seth Rich gave Wikileaks these DNC emails, which, ultimately led to the firing, remember, of Debbie Wasserman Schulz on the eve of the DNC convention, this blows the whole Russia collusion narrative completely out of the water.[38]

Hannity then went on to explain to his listeners that there are:

> Five forces aligning against President Trump. You've got the destroy Trump propaganda media, the destroy Trump Democrats, the Washington Deep State establishment, meaning some members of the intelligence community, you've got weak establishment Republicans, and the NeverTrumpers, they now seem to be working together, in an unprecedented attack on the sitting president.[39]

By that evening, however, Wheeler had already told CNN that he did not have evidence of emails between Rich and WikiLeaks, and that the information he had referenced in the Fox 5 interview was information he had received from a Fox News reporter, whom he did not name in that CNN interview. That CNN story had already made public that his services had been paid for by Ed Butkowsky, a Trump supporter, occasional Fox News commentator, and Breitbart contributor. Twenty-four hours later, Fox 5, the local Fox affiliate, published a clarification that Wheeler had "backtracked" on his statement.[40] The retraction by Wheeler did not tamp down the story even though Wheeler's statement was the entire basis of the initial reports. On May 21, Newt Gingrich, former Republican Speaker of the House and architect of the Republican Party's turn to a more rigidly partisan strategy in the early 1990s,[41] once again repeated the claim on "Fox and Friends," a statement to which PolitiFact awarded its "pants on fire" rating[42] and FactCheck.org covered in an assessment entitled "Gingrich spreads conspiracy theory."[43] On May 23, Fox online retracted the original Zimmerman story.[44] Two days later the ABC affiliate in Washington, D.C., owned by conservative Sinclair Broadcasting, gave the story another lease of life.[45] The station published a report by "the Profiling Project," a group funded by Republican lobbyist Jack Burkman with a near-obsessive attachment to the Seth Rich conspiracy story.[46] Fox

News D.C. then dutifully reported on the Burkman profiling project with a story entitled "Independent Group releases new report on Seth Rich murder investigation."[47] A few days later RT ran a segment of Cross Talk, attempting to rehabilitate the story,[48] but by that point most of the coverage had receded. Later that year Wheeler filed a defamation action against Fox News, in which Wheeler alleged that the Seth Rich article was an intentional effort to "put to bed speculation that President Trump colluded with Russia in an attempt to influence the outcome of the Presidential election."[49] The pattern of reporting, the repetition, and the framing, particularly in Hannity's retelling, is certainly consistent with intentional misdirection.

Mapping the network of stories on Seth Rich offers a clear view of the central role played by Fox News and Fox DC as sources of authority and stories, but also the extent to which conspiracy sites played in propagating the conspiracy theory on Facebook. Both maps below use the linking patterns of websites as the architecture of the network. The first map (Figure 5.11) sizes nodes based on inlinks, identifying the nodes that were influential as sources

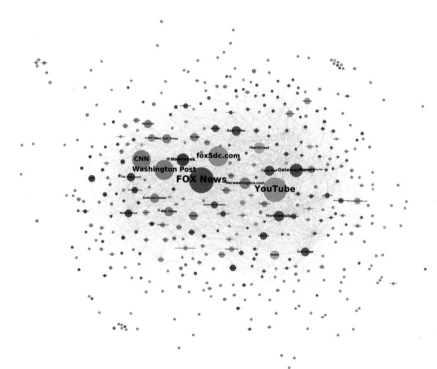

FIGURE 5.11 Network map of media sources mentioning Seth Rich in stories. Architecture and nodes sizing by media inlinks.

for other media producers. It shows the central role that the Fox DC affiliate and Fox News played in developing and propagating the story to other media, and how central YouTube was to disseminating Fox News network programming online, particularly Hannity. It also shows the central role the *Washington Post* and CNN played in criticizing Fox.

The second map (Figure 5.12), with node sizes based on Facebook shares, emphasizes the media outlets that wrote stories that were more widely shared on Facebook. Its most remarkable feature is how central the Gateway Pundit and YourNewsWire.com were on Facebook. YourNewsWire.com's most popular stories on Facebook appeared in July–August 2016. Its core role appears to have been to implant and spin up the Seth Rich conspiracy theory. The Gateway Pundit had stories that were frequently shared on Facebook both in the original effort to point the finger away from Russia and toward the DNC in July–August 2016 and during the May 2017 Fox-led effort to revive the story. YourNewsWire.com was not a marginal flash in the pan. In the first quarter of 2018, according to SimilarWeb metrics, YourNewsWire.com had

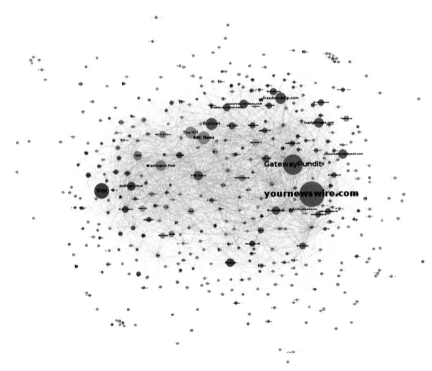

FIGURE 5.12 Seth Rich conspiracy diffusion on the right, and debunking on the left. Nodes sized by Facebook shares.

about one-third the number of monthly visits of the *National Review*, three-quarters the audience of Reason, and more than 30 percent more visits than the *Weekly Standard*. The Gateway Pundit, in turn, had 50 percent more visits than the *National Review*. From the election these ratios remained roughly stable throughout 2017 and early 2018.[50] *The Hill's* relatively prominent place was driven by stories about Wheeler's lawsuit, the Fox News retraction, and Hannity losing advertisers over his Seth Rich conspiracy campaign. Vox's most shared story on Facebook was an essay describing the linkages between the epistemic crisis and social-identity theory.

Uranium One: Fox News vs. the Rule of Law and the Idea of Professional Journalism

On September 19, 2017, FBI agents broke down Paul Manafort's door and executed a search warrant as part of the investigation led by Robert Mueller. Two days later, Mueller requested phone records from Air Force One related to the claim that President Trump had dictated the misleading initial response to revelations of Donald Trump Jr.'s now famous June 9 Trump Tower meeting with a Russian attorney. Trump Jr. appeared to believe the attorney was working with Russian state authorities to get dirt on Hillary Clinton. Mueller also issued a subpoena to Facebook for records of accounts tied to suspected Russian operations. Congress, in the meantime, was considering steps to protect Mueller from the threat of being fired.[51]

By the first week of October, concern over Russian interference in the 2016 election mounted, as Facebook disclosures of Russian advertising purchases gave shape to the previously more amorphous sense of Russian efforts.[52] At the same time, the investigation surfaced the fact that the president's daughter and son-in-law were using private email accounts, possibly for government-related work, again drawing the president's family into the maelstrom.[53] By the end of the second week in October, reporting emerged that the president's legal advisers were cooperating with the investigation and considering how to permit the president to sit for an interview with Mueller.[54]

The following week, the Uranium One story erupted with an intensity and vehemence not seen at any point since Peter Schweizer first published the allegations in April 2015 (we describe the role of the Uranium One story in pre-election debates over the Clinton Foundation in Chapter 6). Over the coming weeks, as Michael Flynn's plea bargain and cooperation with the investigation were announced, reporting on Uranium One as "the real

Russia scandal" reached a fevered pitch. Newt Gingrich called it "the greatest corruption scandal in American history" on Hannity.[55] Sebastian Gorka, former deputy assistant to the president, claimed that "this is equivalent to what the Rosenbergs did, and those people got the chair."[56]

In reality, it turns out that Hillary and Bill Clinton were not quite the twenty-first-century heirs to Julius and Ethel Rosenberg. What instead happened was that Hannity, Gingrich, and the rest of the right-wing media ecosystem were resurrecting a two-and-a-half year old story with a completely new twist—framing it as an attack on the integrity of special counsel Robert Mueller and deputy attorney general Rod Rosenstein. The original story had been told in *Clinton Cash: The Untold Story of How and Why Foreign Governments and Businesses Helped Make Bill and Hillary Rich*, published in May 2015 by Peter Schweizer. Schweizer was at the time a "Breitbart Senior Editor at Large."[57] He cofounded with Steve Bannon the organization that funded his research on the book, the Government Accountability Institute (GAI).[58] The GAI was funded by Robert Mercer, a major investor in Breitbart and a super PAC donor to the Trump campaign.[59] At the time the book was published, Clinton Cash received wide coverage. Most prominently, the *New York Times* published an extensive piece based on the research materials in an advance copy of the book, titled "Cash Flowed to Clinton Foundation Amid Russian Uranium Deal."[60] The heart of the story was that the Russian atomic energy company Rosatom purchased a Canadian firm, Uranium One, which had acquired uranium extraction rights around the world, including to 20 percent of uranium deposits in the United States (the deal did not include a license to export the uranium). The chairman of Uranium One had, over the prior years, made over $2 million in donations to the Clinton Foundation, and as Rosatom announced its intention to purchase Uranium One, Bill Clinton received $500,000 for a speech he made to a Russian bank that was promoting Uranium One stock and had ties to the Kremlin. The Times's angle in the 2015 story was buried in the tenth paragraph:

> Whether the donations played any role in the approval of the uranium deal is unknown. But the episode underscores the special ethical challenges presented by the Clinton Foundation, headed by a former president who relied heavily on foreign cash to accumulate $250 million in assets even as his wife helped steer American foreign policy as secretary of state, presiding over decisions with the potential to benefit the foundation's donors.

As we will see both here (Figures 5.18, 5.19a, and 5.19b) and in Chapter 6, the *Times* story provided legitimation and validation for a broad and aggressive set of political attacks on Hillary Clinton as having given control of over 20 percent of American uranium to the Russians. These attacks were fact-checked extensively. The *Washington Post* Fact Checker awarded four "Pinocchios" to the claim that "Hillary Clinton gave uranium to the Russians." The *Post* explained: "The State Department was one of nine agencies on the committee that approved the deal. The deal was also separately approved by the Nuclear Regulatory Commission. There is no evidence Clinton herself got involved in the deal personally, and it is highly questionable that this deal even rose to the level of the secretary of state."[61] Moreover, the company being bought held uranium extraction rights but not an export license that would have allowed it to take uranium, once extracted, out of the country. Fact Checker found that "[t]he author of 'Clinton Cash' falsely claimed Hillary Clinton as Secretary of State had 'veto power' and 'could have stopped' Russia from buying a company with extensive uranium mining operations in the U.S. In fact, only the president has such power."[62] PolitiFact gave a "mostly false" grade to a version of the story that Trump offered as a candidate in June 2016 and it added a point-by-point response to efforts by the author of *Clinton Cash* to sustain the claim.[63] As the *New York Times* wrote in April 2015, the Clinton Foundation raised "special ethical challenges" when Hillary Clinton was secretary of state, but as it also stated in the tenth paragraph of that story, "[w]hether the donations played any role in the approval of the uranium deal is unknown."[64] To anyone not enmeshed in the right-wing echo chamber, the story recounted by Hannity, Gingrich, Lou Dobbs, and Judge Jeannine—and more than anyone, Donald Trump—that Hillary Clinton as secretary of state gave Russia 20 percent of our uranium, is simply false. Its truth did not increase with repetition or the incendiary vehemence of its delivery.

Searching for Uranium One in our corpus of stories from the pre-election and post-election periods offers a sense of how unusual the spike in coverage of the story was over the month beginning in the third week of October 2017 (Figure 5.13). Even the initial spike in coverage, which followed the release of Schweizer's book and the big *New York Times* story about it, was a fraction of the October–November 2017 spike. The campaign-period coverage of the topic in August 2016, when there was much focus on the Clinton Foundation, was dwarfed by comparison.

We can get some quantitative purchase on the shift in emphasis in the discussion by comparing the results of a standard clustering algorithm

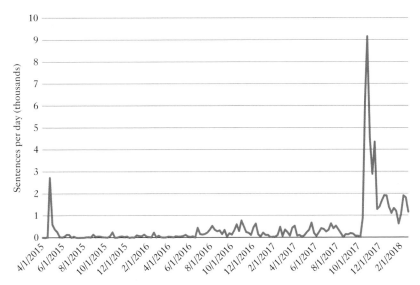

FIGURE 5.13 Sentences per day mentioning Uranium One in open web media, April 1, 2015–February 25, 2018.

FIGURE 5.14 Word2Vec clustering of terms in Uranium One–related stories, April 1, 2015–October 14, 2017.

(Word2Vec) that draws a spatial arrangement of words that often appear together (Figure 5.14). Looking at Uranium One coverage online from April 2015 to October 2017, there are two main clusters: those anchored in "Hillary Clinton" associated with "Russia" and a large cluster around "Clinton

Foundation." Bridging the word "uranium" and the foundation cluster are words related to the mining business: "mining," "investors," and "transactions."

The pattern of usage after October 15, 2017, reflects the shift in the media framing of the topic (Figure 5.15). In addition to the foundation-related cluster, a new cluster emerged around the terms "dossier," "allegations," "scandal," and "probe." These clusters are bridged by the term "prosecutor." In the latter half of October 2017, the Uranium One story had been promoted in conservative media as a counternarrative to the Mueller investigation and coverage of the two had become tangled up.

A different perspective is offered by mapping the web-linking structure of Uranium One media coverage. Figure 5.16, which is based on all the sites that published stories on Uranium One from April 2015 to February 2018, exhibits a highly atypical structure, with a core of right-wing sites clustered tightly around the *New York Times* and *The Hill*. On the left (in deep blue), the primary sources are Fact Check and PolitiFact, and the story that makes the *Washington Post* relatively prominent is the *Post's* fact-checking story, which gave the Uranium One story four Pinocchios. Few images reflect so clearly how the *New York Times* coverage of the Uranium One story was used as a key source of legitimation for the right.

Additional insights can be gleaned by decomposing the image into three distinct periods: the initial release of the *Clinton Cash* book in April–May 2015

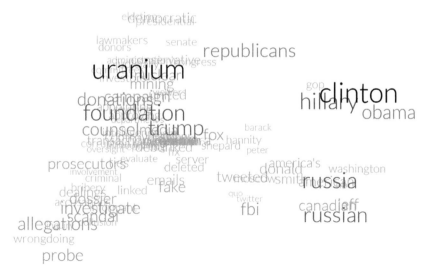

FIGURE 5.15 Word2Vec clustering of terms in Uranium One–related stories, October 15, 2017–February 27, 2018.

(Figure 5.17a); the August 2016 period associated with the Breitbart release of the *Clinton Cash* movie (Figure 5.17b); and the October 2017 coverage (Figure 5.18). In the first two periods we see very clearly that coverage was anchored in the legitimating power of the *New York Times* story, which drew upon a prepublication copy of the Schweizer book. We will return to this in Chapter 6. By October 2017, although the *New York Times* story continued to play an important role as a source of authority, coverage in *The Hill* largely took over.

The quantitative measures and maps point us toward the timing of key events and inflection points, and provide macrolevel validation that something significant was going on, as well as identifying the most influential media sources. However, getting into the guts of what happened requires a more detailed examination of the stories themselves.

FIGURE 5.16 Network map of Uranium One stories, April 2015–February 2018. Architecture and node sizing by media inlinks.

(a)

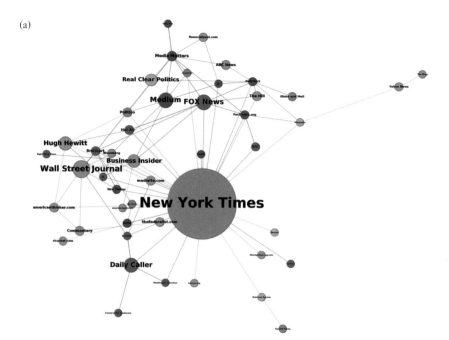

FIGURE 5.17A April–May 2015.

(b)

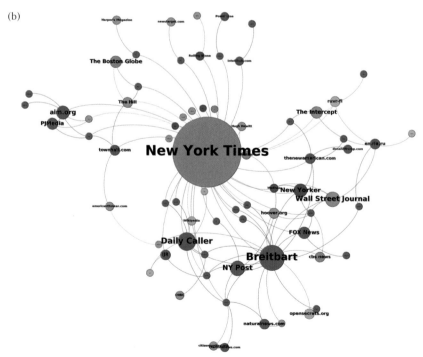

FIGURE 5.17B August 2016.
Network map of Uranium One stories. Architecture and node sizing by media inlinks.

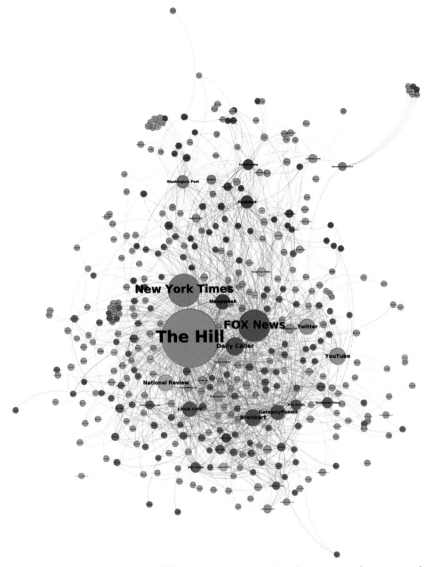

FIGURE 5.18 Network map of Uranium One stories, October 2017. Architecture and node sizing by media inlinks.

On October 17, 2017, John F. Solomon coauthored a detailed piece of investigative reporting on the Uranium One story in *The Hill*. Solomon, executive vice president at *The Hill*, is the former editor-in-chief of the *Washington Times* who was hired away by Sinclair Broadcasting to serve as chief creative officer for its relaunch of Circa News.[65] Circa also published a piece based on the same revelation that same day.[66] The opening three paragraphs of the Solomon article set the stage.

> Before the Obama administration approved a controversial deal in 2010 giving Moscow control of a large swath of American uranium, the FBI had gathered substantial evidence that Russian nuclear industry officials were engaged in bribery, kickbacks, extortion and money laundering designed to grow Vladimir Putin's atomic energy business inside the United States, according to government documents and interviews.
>
> Federal agents used a confidential U.S. witness working inside the Russian nuclear industry to gather extensive financial records, make secret recordings and intercept emails as early as 2009 that showed Moscow had compromised an American uranium trucking firm with bribes and kickbacks in violation of the Foreign Corrupt Practices Act, FBI and court documents show.
>
> They also obtained an eyewitness account—backed by documents— indicating Russian nuclear officials had routed millions of dollars to the U.S. designed to benefit former President Bill Clinton's charitable foundation during the time Secretary of State Hillary Clinton served on a government body that provided a favorable decision to Moscow, sources told The Hill.

Despite the insinuation of payments from Russians to the Clinton Foundation, the remainder of the story explained that the FBI was investigating Russians who were abusing their position while directing the U.S. operations of the Russian company that bought Uranium One. The charges alleged that the Russians offered contractors no-bid inflated price contracts in exchange for kickbacks. The Russian executives were cheating the Russian owners of Uranium One to enrich themselves at the expense of shareholders or other owners of the firm. Indeed, the remainder of the story has very little to say about the Clintons, dedicating a mere 100 additional words to recalling Schweizer's book. The emphasis, instead, was on the nefarious character of Russian corruption and the supposed failures of the Department of Justice in investigating, charging, and reporting on the matter.

"The Department of Justice (DOJ) continued investigating the matter for nearly four more years," Solomon and Spann wrote, "essentially leaving the American public and Congress in the dark about Russian nuclear corruption on U.S. soil during a period when the Obama Administration made two major decisions benefiting Putin's commercial nuclear ambitions." This is where they introduce the new element into the story, finding fault with the Department of Justice. This element remains prominent and distinct, as the word clouds make clear, throughout the coverage over the next several weeks. The story in *The Hill* makes an explicit connection between that alleged failure and the compromised position of the central figures of the Trump-Russia investigation and lays the groundwork for what will follow in the next three weeks of coverage:

> The investigation was ultimately supervised by then-U.S. Attorney Rod Rosenstein, an Obama appointee who now serves as President Trump's deputy attorney general, and then-Assistant FBI Director Andrew McCabe, now the deputy FBI director under Trump, Justice Department documents show. Both men now play a key role in the current investigation into possible, but still unproven, collusion between Russia and Donald Trump's campaign during the 2016 election cycle. McCabe is under congressional and Justice Department inspector general investigation in connection with money his wife's Virginia state Senate campaign accepted in 2015 from now-Virginia Gov. Terry McAuliffe at a time when McAuliffe was reportedly under investigation by the FBI. The probe is not focused on McAuliffe's conduct but rather on whether McCabe's attendance violated the Hatch Act or other FBI conflict rules.
>
> The connections to the current Russia case are many. The Mikerin probe began in 2009 when Robert Mueller, now the special counsel in charge of the Trump case, was still FBI director. And it ended in late 2015 under the direction of then-FBI Director James Comey, whom Trump fired earlier this year.

The Hill story then reported that the investigation ended with a whimper when the defendant pleaded guilty to one charge of conspiracy to commit money laundering. The authors implied that the plea, the understated announcement from the Department of Justice, and the fact that the evidence cited for the plea only covered actions that occurred after approval of the Uranium One deal all suggested that the Department of Justice was at least derelict in its handling of the matter. The piece closes with a quote from a Republican former representative that leaves the impression of a cover-up: "Not providing information on a corruption scheme before the Russian uranium deal was approved by U.S. regulators and engage appropriate congressional committees has served to undermine U.S. national security interests by the very people charged with protecting them."

The story in *The Hill* by Solomon and Spann received some immediate coverage in mainline publications, including Newsweek, Bloomberg, and Yahoo! News, but took off like wildfire in the right-wing media ecosystem. On the day it was published, we collected over 40 stories that picked up the original story: from Fox News and the New York Post, through Breitbart and the Daily Caller, to the Gateway Pundit, Infowars, and Truthfeed. Several YouTube videos were made about it. One, made by an alt-right activist, received over 48,000 views,[67] while Alex Jones's Infowars version received 42,000. The Gateway Pundit, as usual, cut to the chase with a headline: "DEEP STATE SWAMP: Comey, Mueller, Rosenstein, Are Linked to Clinton Uranium One Deal—MOST CORRUPT OFFICIALS EVER!." Alex Jones, not to be undone, titled his segment "BREAKING: Mueller Transferred Uranium To Russia, Hid Clinton Crimes." For all the excitement online, the Uranium One story is not actually a story about social media or online dissemination, but a traditional media story. All the stories published on October 17 combined received slightly over 400,000 Facebook shares, about half of which were of *The Hill* story itself, and almost all the remainder distributed between the *New York Post* and Breitbart. Rush Limbaugh raised *The Hill* story on his talk radio show that day, saying:

> The FBI, folks, we have learned that there was collusion between the FBI and the Obama administration and the Russians in 2009 and 2010 over this uranium deal. Real collusion! Much more collusion than whatever Russia was doing by spending a hundred thousand dollars buying ads on Facebook. This is a blockbuster story, and it comes from our old buddy John Solomon, used to be at Circa, used to be at AP, used to be at the Washington Times, now he is at TheHill.com.
>
> This really is a bombshell, except outside of TheHill.com it's being ignored because it totally upsets every premise behind the get-Trump investigation. While they have no evidence of any collusion by Trump with Russia or versa-vice-a, there is all kinds of evidence that the FBI has had since 2009 and 2010 and suppressed over the Clintons, Bill and Hillary and the Canadian mogul that donated to their foundation and the transfer of United States American uranium

to Russia. Bill Clinton personally was enriched by thousands and thousands of dollars, as was the Clinton Foundation, the Crime Family Foundation.[68]

But the real powerhouse driving the story became Fox News.

As the map in Figure 5.20 shows, Fox News served alongside *The Hill* as a prominent node in the coverage. YouTube also clearly played a significant role. To understand that role, we analyzed the 92 YouTube videos that received links from stores related to Uranium One over the course of 2017. We coded them all, after removing the four which were off-topic. In Figures 5.19a and 5.19b, which depict the top 10 and top 30 videos by number of views, respectively, we see that the "Hannity Show" on Fox News is by far the most popular. Five of the top 10 videos are Hannity shows. The first- and third-most watched videos were two different versions of the same October 19 Hannity monologue, which we discuss in detail below. The second-most watched video in the set is from the Young Turks, a YouTube news and commentary program. They offered a middle-of-the-road validation of *The Hill* story and then a debate between its two hosts as to the validity and legitimacy of

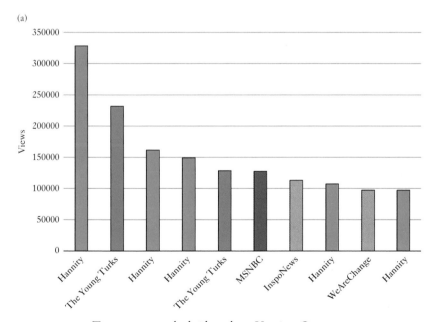

(a)

FIGURE 5.19A Top 10 most watched videos about Uranium One, 2017.

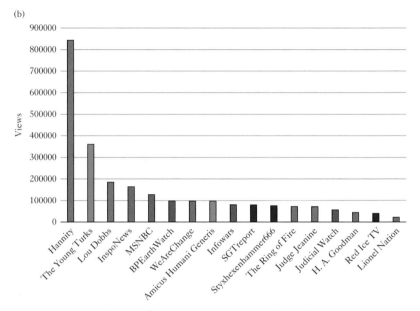

(b)

FIGURE 5.19B Total views of the top 30 most watched YouTube videos on Uranium One by producer, 2017.

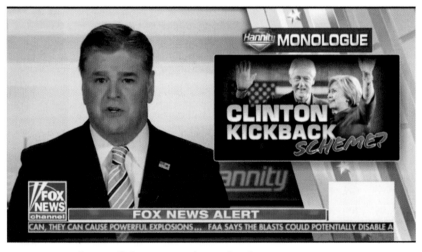

FIGURE 5.20 Screen of Hannity monologue, October 19, 2017.

concerns. An MSNBC segment debunking the Hannity storyline made the top 10, along with two more independent productions that repeated and validated the Hannity claims (InspoNews and WeAreChange).

Expanding the set to the top 30 increases the diversity of outlets but not the lopsided nature of the coverage. Lou Dobbs and Judge Jeannine join from the Fox lineup, as does Alex Jones's Infowars lower down the viewership distribution. We also begin to see independent right-wing sites, including four that are explicitly alt-right or white-identity sites. Only a single video among these 30 top videos by viewership joins the MSNBC rebuttal.

On the day of the original *Hill* report, Fox Business led television coverage with mentions in three shows: "After the Bell" at 4:00 p.m.,[69] "Making Money with Charles Payne" at 6:00 p.m.,[70] and "Lou Dobbs Tonight" at 7:00 p.m. Dobbs spoke with former Deputy Assistant to the President Sebastian Gorka who, after throwing an aside at James Comey for "almost single-handedly" destroying the reputation of the FBI, declared that an FBI source was going on record with evidence of "pay for play, of corruption occurring, and people will have to go to prison, because, it's going to be a humdinger."[71] The next day, Fox News aired segments about Uranium One on their two most highly rated shows, Hannity and Tucker Carlson. The Hannity segment included an interview in which Gingrich introduced a version of a claim he would repeat, that this was "the biggest scandal in history." Following these reports, in the early morning hours of October 19, President Trump tweeted: "Uranium deal to Russia, with Clinton help and Obama Administration knowledge. Is the biggest story that Fake Media doesn't want to follow!"

Later that day, Trump again emphasized the story and its significance to the ongoing investigation of his own campaign with Russia in a television interview:

> If the mainstream media would cover the uranium scandal and that Russia has 20% of the uranium for whatever reason, and a lot of people understand what those reasons may be—I think that's your Russia story. That's your real Russia story, not a story where they talk about collusion, and there was none. It was a hoax. The real Russia story is uranium and how they got all of that uranium, vast percentage of what we have. That is, to me, one of the big stories of the decade.[72]

Harris Faulkner and Neil Cavuto ran segments on these comments on Fox that day, but the most important piece was Hannity's monologue that night.

Hannity's October 19 monologue, which ran nearly 15 minutes, became the most viewed YouTube video on this controversy. But while its half million views make it dominant on YouTube, it's important to remember that the same show got over three million viewers on cable, assuming that Hannity had an average-for-him audience that evening. Hannity's segment opened with a dramatic statement:

> Tonight, massive bombshell breaking news developments in <u>the biggest scandal ever involving Russia</u>. We will continue to do what the <u>corrupt lying mainstream media will not do</u> because we will prove they are complicit in what is a <u>huge coverup</u>. We will explain how the Clintons and Obama administration created a massive national security crisis by handing Vladimir Putin and Russia 20% of America's uranium, which is the foundational material to make nuclear weapons and tonight we will explain in detail who and how many people knew that the Russians had infiltrated America's uranium market and how all of this was before the Uranium One deal.[73]

The opening includes the three elements of misdirection. First, Uranium One, not the Trump-Russia investigation, is the really big scandal involving Russia. Second, any media organization that tells you otherwise is part of "the corrupt lying media." And finally, all this is a huge cover-up involving the very people now investigating Donald Trump. Hannity then claimed that Bill Clinton had been paid $500,000 and cited both *The Hill* and the Circa reports that the FBI had evidence that "includes eyewitness accounts, that the Russian nuclear officials were funneling millions and millions of dollars to the Clinton Foundation while Hillary was actually serving as Secretary of State and *personally* signing off on the Uranium One deal. According to both explosive reports, the Obama Administration hid the evidence of this Russian bribery plot from Congress."

As Hannity was saying these words, the screen behind him showed an image of the Clintons with the words "Clinton Kickback Scheme?" *The Hill* report at no point said that Hillary Clinton had personally approved the deal—there is no evidence she was involved at all, the State Department was one of nine agencies that voted unanimously, and the Nuclear Regulatory Commission separately signed off on the deal. And the "eyewitness accounts" reported by *The Hill* were of kickbacks from American contractors of Russian companies to the Russian executives. The kickbacks had nothing to do with the approval or the Clintons. Hannity's audience, however, was actively led to believe that all the evidence pointed to kickbacks from the Russians to the Clintons for the approval of the uranium deal. That assertion was purely fabricated.

The fundamental purpose of the revival of the story became clear toward the end of the segment. Hannity turned from old adversaries to new, just as *The Hill* piece did:

> Of course these names will all sound familiar. The deputy Attorney General today, Rod Rosenstein, of course is second under the department of justice, under our attorney general Jeff Sessions. Then we have Andrew McCabe. They oversaw the FBI operation into the Russia bribery case. They clearly were well aware about what was taking place. They need to be put under oath. They need to tell us, why were they silent? Then Robert Mueller, too. He should not be leading any probes into Russian collusion. Guess why? He should be answering questions about the real Russian scandal. He should be put under oath. The conduct of Rod Rosenstein, McCabe, Mueller, it's inexcusable. There's a massive conflict of interest. They told nobody and in no way can they be trusted to conduct a fair investigation into anything—it's time for them to literally resign—get out of the way or come public with everything they know. That's my position. I think they've been compromised. Especially when it comes to Russia. It's well past time for many of them to go. These people are corrupt and they've been compromised.[74]

Robert Mueller was a Republican who was appointed by George W. Bush to be the director of the FBI and who oversaw the reorganization of the FBI into a counterterrorism agency after 9/11. James Comey was a registered Republican for most of his adult life and had served as deputy attorney general under George W. Bush. As FBI Director, Comey likely tipped the 2016 presidential election to Donald Trump with his October surprise announcement about the Clinton email server investigation. Rod Rosenstein's conservative credentials were such that he was nominated to become a federal appellate judge by George W. Bush. He was blocked by Maryland's two Democratic senators and held up in a Senate Judiciary Committee controlled by Democrats. Andrew McCabe was a career FBI agent who told ABC News that "I have considered myself to be a Republican my entire life," adding "I've voted for every Republican candidate for president in every election, except the 2016 one, in which I did not vote."[75] Fox News subjected these mainline law-and-order Republicans to the libel that they corruptly aided Russia in strengthening its nuclear weapons capability while weakening ours. Yesterday's "Heroes of the Revolution" were overnight denounced as today's counterrevolutionaries.

Hannity ended the segment as he started it, with an attack on the media. On the backdrop (Figure 5.21), a slide depicted the logos of CNN, the *New York Times*, the *Washington Post*, ABC, CBS, NBC, and MSNBC, while Hannity said: "Finally, you've got the liberal media. For years we've been telling you journalism is dead. They've been lying to you, the American people, for well over a year about Russia, Russia, Russia. The press has been spreading fake news conspiracy theories almost 24/7 nonstop. Why are they so silent in this case?"[76]

In this one brief quote, Hannity explained precisely why American conservatives distrust professional journalism. In the upside down world of the man who peddled in "Orgy Island" smears, cribbed "spirit cooking" conspiracies from Infowars, and trumpeted the Seth Rich conspiracy, these professional journalism outlets have been "spreading fake news conspiracy theories almost 24/7 nonstop." As he put it, "For years we've been telling you journalism is dead."

Hannity had it right. Right-wing media have been attacking mainstream journalism for decades. The theme of mainstream media bias has been a fixture of right-wing media at least since the 1944 launch of right-wing magazine *Human Events* by remnants of the America First Committee that had opposed U.S. entry into the war against Nazi Germany, and was an oft-repeated theme in the other media outlets that made up the first wave of postwar conservative media that we will describe in Chapter 11.[77] But Rush Limbaugh, as he launched the second-generation right-wing media ecosystem, gave the attack on mainstream media its hyperbolic anti-journalism tone. Limbaugh christened

FIGURE 5.21 Screen of Hannity monologue, October 19, 2017.

CNN the "Clinton News Network" in 1999, described the *New York Times* as "a coordinated leftist house organ," and called the *Times*'s editor Howell Raines "Mullah" Raines, featuring his picture on his "website wearing a superimposed turban" in 2002.[78] And in 2011 Limbaugh coined the term "The Four Corners of Deceit," that "in our culture . . . altogether combined, suffice to lie to students and the American people. The Four Corners of Deceit are government, academia, science, and the media."[79] Fox News's own "Fair and Balanced" motto has from the start primed its viewers that other outlets are not. The continuously stated message is that all media not dedicated to a right-wing view are biased and partisan and that only those that are right-wing partisan are truthful and fair. That message was touted from the bully pulpit of the presidency weekly during the first year of the Trump, capped by President Trump's 2017 Fake News Awards to CNN, the *New York Times*, the *Washington Post*, ABC News, and so forth (Figure 5.22).[80]

And the FAKE NEWS winners are...gop.com/the-highly-ant…

9:00 PM - Jan 17, 2018

The Highly Anticipated 2017 Fake News Awards

2017 has been a year of unrelenting bias, unfair news coverage, and even downright fake news.

gop.com

FIGURE 5.22 Donald Trump tweet announcing the 2017 Fake News Awards.

In Chapter 11 we describe the extensive evidence of asymmetric patterns of distrust in media in the United States. In particular the data describe a long-term pattern among conservatives that combines extremely low and decreasing trust in most media outlets and media in general, combined with a level of trust in Fox News that is extraordinarily high for any media source. Liberals and people with mixed liberal and conservative views spread their attention more evenly. And while liberals and moderates on average have much higher trust in media as a whole, they are generally more skeptical of any given outlet and trust no single outlet to the high degree that conservatives trust Fox. The attacks on journalism that we describe throughout this book almost certainly influence these patterns of trust and explain how conservatives have come to trust Hannity and Limbaugh as liberals trust the BBC and PBS.

On October 20, the day after Hannity's extraordinary segment on Uranium One, Fox and Friends ran a segment about the Uranium One deal in which the spoken text was "the BIG Russia story is the fact that Bill and Hillary Clinton, because of her position as Secretary of State, were able to cash in one of the largest scandals that have ever involved the United States."[81] The big block letters at the bottom of the screen read: "Trump: Fake Media Excusing Dem Russia Deal." As the text shifted to emphasizing that this story was about nuclear weapons capability, Mueller's stint at the FBI, and Loretta Lynch at the Department of Justice, the bold caps under the screen scrolled

FIGURE 5.23 Screen appearance on Fox and Friends, October 20, 2017.

the outlandish claim that "Russia Got 20% of U.S. Nuke Industry Under Obama." (Figure 5.23)

That evening, Lou Dobbs interviewed Peter Schweizer, author of *Clinton Cash*, on his Fox Business show, opening with how vindicated Schweizer must feel. On October 24, Hannity returned to the Uranium One story, interviewing former Speaker Newt Gingrich. Gingrich opened his segment by calling the story "the greatest corruption scandal in American history," bigger, he said, than the Teapot Dome in the 1920s, worse than the Grant administration in the 1870s, arguably the most corrupt administration in American history.[82] That same evening, Lou Dobbs on Fox Business opened his show with the words:

> Incriminating evidence, tying former President Clinton to the Uranium One scandal. The former president, Hillary Clinton, the Obama Administration are NOW, now, clearly in focus in what appears to be a *quid pro quo* deal that gave Russia ownership of a fifth of US uranium. NOW, those carping about Russian collusion with the current administration, they are silent as the REAL collusion involving collusion has been staring everyone straight in the face for years.

Three days later, Hannity aired a Sebastian Gorka interview, comparing the Clintons' involvement in Uranium One to the Rosenbergs handing over nuclear bomb design secrets to the Soviet Union, and helpfully reminding viewers that the Rosenbergs had been executed for their deeds.[83] One or more Fox programs returned to this "biggest scandal," every day for the remainder of the month. It then died down for a while until November 14–15, when Jeff Sessions announced that the Department of Justice would take a closer look at the allegations, and then testified on the Hill about Russian influence during the 2016 election.

As Figures 5.24a and 5.24b show, the peaks in coverage on Fox Business and Fox News are closely aligned with coverage on the web. Certainly, there was a lot of coverage online throughout this period, but online audiences were dwarfed in comparison to the reach of Fox television. Given the sustained, repeated attention paid to the Uranium One story, at all hours of the day nearly every day, and the tenor and tone of these Fox News stories as they spun vastly overstated, often simply false versions of the events, combining actual spoken words with strong on-screen imagery, it would be

(a)

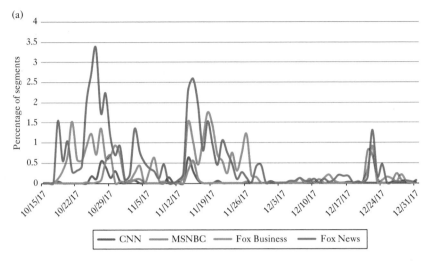

FIGURE 5.24A (Top) Percentage of 15-second segments mentioning Uranium One by television stations, October 15–December 31, 2017.

(b)

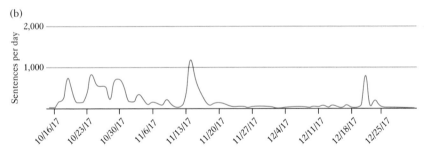

FIGURE 5.24B (Bottom) Sentences per day mentioning Uranium One in open web media, October 15–December 31, 2017.

difficult to see the coverage from October to November 2017 as anything but a coordinated, sustained propagandist effort by the cable television network to shift attention to Uranium One as the "real Russia scandal" and to discredit the president's opponents and discredit the ongoing investigation against him. Whatever efforts anyone else made on Facebook, Twitter, or the open web were largely secondary to the efforts of the most important source of news for nearly half of Trump's voters: the network that 65 percent of Republicans trust; indeed, the only source of news that they consistently trust.

6

Mainstream Media Failure Modes and Self-Healing in a Propaganda-Rich Environment

IN THE PRECEDING three chapters we examined the propaganda feedback loop, how it forms, and how it facilitates disinformation and the manipulation of beliefs of a population. But our observations about the highly asymmetric nature of the American media environment, and the survey-based evidence we described in Chapter 2, which suggests that no more than 30 percent of the American population inhabits the insular, propaganda-rich right-wing media ecosystem, indicate that whatever one thinks of the result of the 2016 election, it could not have been purely the result of right-wing propaganda. Here, we identify two central attributes of mainstream media and professional journalism—balance and the scoop culture—that shaped election coverage, and in some cases made them particularly susceptible to being manipulated into spreading right-wing propaganda.

Balance and Negativity

Despite the dispersion of attention and the large number of media and channels available to them, as Americans were beginning to tune in to election coverage over the summer and early fall of 2016, one word was repeatedly on their minds when they thought of Hillary Clinton: *email*. Over the 10 weeks from July 11 to September 18, 2016, Gallup included in their U.S. Daily Tracking poll the question "What have you read, seen, or heard about Hillary Clinton or Donald Trump in the past several days?" In eight of those 10 weeks,

Network Propaganda. Yochai Benkler, Robert Faris, and Hal Roberts.
© Yochai Benkler, Robert Faris, and Hal Roberts 2018. Published 2018 by Oxford University Press.

(a) What Americans Have Heard or Read About Hillary Clinton

What specifically do you recall reading, hearing or seeing about Hillary Clinton in the last day or two?

GALLUP DAILY TRACKING
JULY 17–SEPT 18, 2016

(b) What Americans Have Heard or Read About Donald Trump

What specifically do you recall reading, hearing or seeing about Donald Trump in the last day or two?

GALLUP DAILY TRACKING
JULY 17–SEPT 18, 2016

FIGURE 6.1 Words most used to answer the question: "What have you read, seen, or heard about Hillary Clinton or Donald Trump in the past several days?" July 11–September 18, 2016. Created by Gallup.

Republished with permission of Gallup, Inc., from GALLUP, "Email" Dominates What Americans Have Heard About Clinton by Frank Newport, Lisa Singh, Stuart Soroka, Michael Traugott and Andrew Dugan. Election 2016, September 19, 2016; permission conveyed through Copyright Clearance Center, Inc.

the top word in response was "email" (Figure 6.1), and even during the convention week, it was the second word after "convention." Comparing the word clouds that Gallup produced from this survey data is one of the most vivid illustrations of how candidates can be framed in entirely different ways.[1] "Lie," "scandal," and "foundation" were not far behind "emails" in framing Clinton's candidacy in the minds of American voters.

We analyzed the text of all the stories that mentioned either candidate's name in the top 50 media sources measured by media inlinks for the 18 months prior to the election. This list (included in the online appendix)

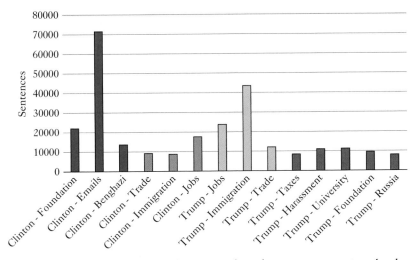

FIGURE 6.2 Sentences in mass-market open web media mentioning topics related to Donald Trump and Hillary Clinton during the 2016 election period.

features primarily mass-market media. Our findings dovetail remarkably well with Gallup's public opinion polls about what people associated with each candidate. As Figure 6.2 shows quite clearly, sentences that included both the terms "Clinton" and "emails" far outstripped other meaningful combinations we searched for either candidate, while sentences that included "Trump" and "immigration" outstripped the various other, more scandal-related terms associated with Trump. That does not mean that Clinton coverage outside the right-wing media ecosystem was necessarily negative and that coverage of Trump was neutral or positive. In fact, most of the media coverage was negative for both candidates, as Thomas Patterson and his collaborators showed.[2] But the Gallup data strongly suggest that however negative the orientation of the stories, the residual in voters' minds was that Trump was associated with immigration, and Clinton, with emails. Our results across top-performing media are confirmed by the more detailed and deep analysis of *New York Times* coverage by Duncan Watts and David Rothschild. Consistent with Patterson's findings, Watts and Rothschild showed that horse-race-style stories dominated coverage, but that for the remainder, scandals outstripped substantive policy stories. Most damningly, coverage of emails associated with Clinton vastly outstripped discussion of her policy positions. As they put it in reference to the days after the Comey announcement about reopening the email investigation, "To reiterate, *in just six days,* The New York Times *ran as many cover stories about Hillary Clinton's emails as they did about all policy issues combined in the 69 days leading up to the election*" (emphasis in the original).[3]

Where did the email coverage come from? We have already seen how central emails were to the efforts to rally the base and harness hatred and revulsion as motivators in the election—in the pedophilia stories and in the stories claiming Clinton was corruptly colluding with Arabs and Muslims. There, the emails offered the quintessential illusory anchor that feeds the pedantry of the paranoid mind otherwise unmoored in reality. But what about the mainstream? A review of the ebb and flow of email-related stories reveals that it was not fake news sites that framed the Clinton candidacy in terms of emails. Nor was it Russian propagandists. Russian propaganda definitely contributed to the email discussion. And Russian hackers obtained and then released the DNC and Podesta emails. But as we look at the pattern of attention to emails over the course of the 18 months leading up to the election, a much more banal story emerges. Figure 6.3 offers a timeline, broken down by quintile, of the number of sentences per day that mentioned "Clinton" and "emails" in the same sentence, from March 2015, when the *New York Times* broke the story that Clinton had used a private email server during her tenure as Secretary of State,[4] until Election Day.

The first overall feature that the timeline reveals is that there is no significant difference in the pattern of coverage between the top right-wing publications and the top center and center-left publications. The ebb and flow of attention across the media quintiles is highly correlated and, if anything, is led by the professional journalism–oriented outlets. The second overall feature is that while Republican candidates certainly took advantage of Clinton's woes, and the stories include many instances of Republican candidates referring to Clinton's emails as a major issue during both the primary and general elections, most of the events are driven by the actions of civil servants that were then covered by professional journalists, each following more or less standard professional norms. Of the 16 coverage peaks, 5 follow email releases or formal reports from the State Department, and 4 more, including the two most significant bumps in coverage, followed the FBI investigation, in particular the July announcement by James Comey that the investigation was closed and the last-minute reopening and reclosing of the investigation around Anthony Weiner's laptop. Only one peak was associated with the Benghazi committee hearings. Two peaks related to court victories by Judicial Watch, an organization that has been using Freedom of Information Act (FOIA) litigation to go after the Clintons since 1994. Judicial Watch was being funded primarily by the Scaife Foundation, which was founded by Richard Mellon

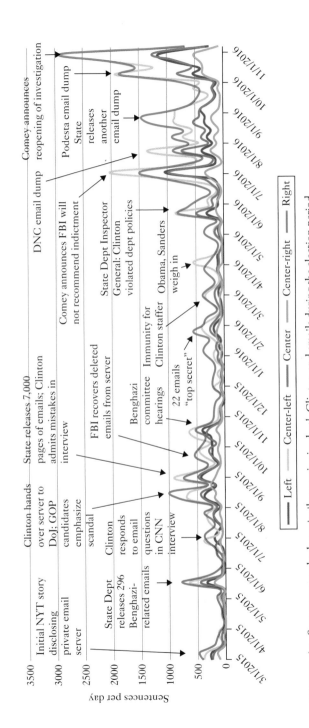

FIGURE 6.3 Sentences per day by quintile mentioning both Clinton and emails during the election period.

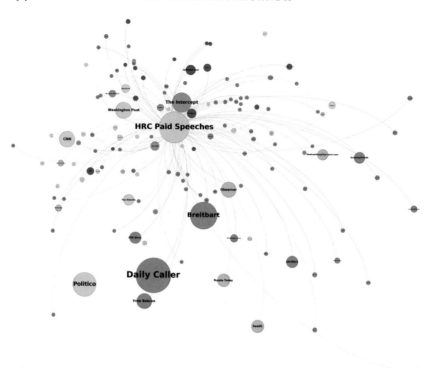

FIGURE 6.4 Media sources that linked to Hillary Clinton's "public and private position" email. Nodes sized by number of media inlinks.

Scaife, whom the *New York Times* described as "one of the leading financiers of the right-wing effort to bring down the Clintons."[5] Those court decisions forced first Clinton staff, then Clinton herself, to answer questions about the emails. Two more peaks were media-created events surrounding media interviews with Republican candidates. Outside of the State Department emails, only the Podesta email dump created a real spike in media coverage, and that was the only spike where email coverage was clearly led by coverage on the right wing of the media ecosystem—as we saw with the Hillary-Saudi Arabia-Qatar-ISIS email.

Figures 6.4 and 6.5 are bimodal maps; one set of nodes in the map are of specific emails and another set of nodes are the sources that linked to them. These maps make quite clear that there were specific emails in the dumps— both the Podesta dump and the DNC dump—that drew attention outside the right-wing media system. In particular, an email from the Podesta dump involving Hillary Clinton's statement that "you need both a public and a private position," and an email from the DNC dump suggesting she had given Clinton questions from town hall events in advance, which cost Donna

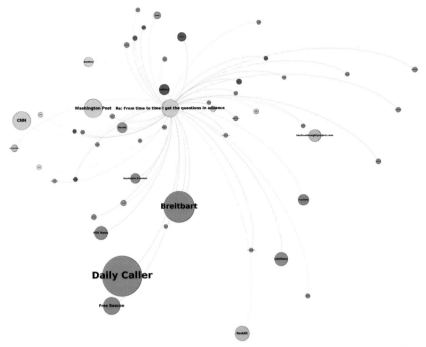

FIGURE 6.5 Media sources that linked to email suggesting Donna Brazile gave Hillary Clinton town hall questions in advance. Nodes sized by number of media inlinks.

Brazile her position as CNN commentator. The major outlets on the right are still highly influential (network nodes are sized by media inlink count), but the *Washington Post*, CNN, and *Politico* in the center-left, and the Huffington Post and Salon on the left also link to one or both emails.

But looking beyond these discrete instances, the overall pattern of coverage in mainstream professional media makes clear that most of the email-related stories were not from the DNC or Podesta email dumps; more coverage was devoted to the slowly unfolding saga of Clinton's use of a private email server while in office as secretary of state. It is a story of civil servants at the State Department and the Justice Department doing their jobs, first to declassify and release the emails, then to determine whether maintaining the private server had violated Department policy, and finally to determine whether there were grounds for prosecution. One could come up with "deep state" conspiracy theories about how these civil servants intentionally sabotaged the Clinton campaign, and some on the "clickbaity" left indeed tried to do so. But the more likely albeit banal explanation is that a politician made a mistake in office, and her actions collided with professional norms applied conscientiously by civil servants, FBI investigators, and journalists. Her political opponents then took advantage of her error and were able to spin, emphasize, and perhaps overblow the importance of that story.

If there is fault in the incessant coverage of emails, it is a fault in patterns of compliance with professional media norms, not in their violation. Patterson's explanation of the negative coverage he found, aligning with the conclusion of Watts and Rothschild, was that a core driver of the email focus was misapplication of the objectivity norm as even-handedness or balance, rather than truth seeking. If professional journalistic objectivity means balance and impartiality, and one is confronted with two candidates who are highly unbalanced—one consistently lies and takes positions that were off the wall for politicians before his candidacy, and the other is about as mainstream and standard as plain vanilla—it is genuinely difficult to maintain balanced coverage. The solution was uniformly negative coverage, as Patterson and colleagues showed, and a heavy focus on detailed objective facts. The emails were catnip for professional journalists. They gave journalists something concrete to work with. They had the aura of salacious reporting of uncovered secrets, while being unimpeachably factual and professional. And they allowed the mainstream publications to appear balanced in that their coverage of the two candidates was equally hard-hitting and tough. The need to publicly perform balance also exposed mainstream media to the standard practice of "working the ref." We already saw in Chapter 5 how right-wing outlets complain that the media is biased and liberal. In addition to disorienting their own viewers and denying them alternative pathways to check propagandist claims to which they are exposed, these attacks tend to push mainstream reporters and editors to seek out stories that will exculpate them from the accusation. As a result, the search for publicly performing neutrality becomes a vulnerability that right-wing propagandists can and do exploit. We return at the end of this chapter to what can stand in for neutrality: the pursuit of objectivity as an open, self-correcting pursuit of truth irrespective of its partisan spin or orientation, however one-sided this may seem in an environment that is, by its very architecture, prone to asymmetric patterns of falsehood.

Scoops and Headlines in a Propaganda-Rich Environment: Bannon Harnesses the Times

As the Democratic National Convention wrapped up at the end of July 2016, Hillary Clinton's poll advantage was at the highest it would ever reach. The normal post-convention bump in polls was enhanced by a powerful speech given by Khizr Khan, an immigrant from Pakistan and father of a fallen U.S. Army captain, Humayun Khan. Donald Trump's response to the speech, in which Khizr Khan offered to lend Trump his copy of the U.S. Constitution, was seen by many as denigrating a Gold Star family. Over the course of August, however, the topic of conversation had shifted to the Clinton Foundation, and in particular to allegations that Hillary Clinton had offered quid pro quo favors, trading State Department access and influence in exchange for donations to the Clinton Foundation. A review of media coverage related to scandals for either candidate shows quite clearly that the Clinton Foundation story had early prominence in April and May 2015, and then lay mostly dormant until it was picked up again in August 2016 (Figure 6.6). The story's re-emergence 15 months after its initial publication damaged Clinton and was likely a major factor in her steady decline in the polls, a slide that continued until the debates and the damaging Hollywood Access video improved her standing.

As we described in Chapter 5, the Clinton Foundation claims were based primarily on Breitbart editor-at-large Peter Schweizer's book *Clinton Cash*. The book had been funded by the Government Accountability Initiative, cofounded by Steve Bannon and Schweizer with funding from Robert Mercer. Schweizer gave the *New York Times* access to research materials and an advance copy of the book, and the *Times* published a story that became the most important source of legitimation and validation for the attacks on the Clinton Foundation, entitled "Cash Flowed to Clinton Foundation Amid Russian Uranium Deal."[6] The *Times* did not disclose Schweizer's affiliation with Breitbart or the Mercer funding behind the book, validating him instead as a former fellow at Stanford University's "right-leaning Hoover Institute." The headline clearly implied corrupt deal making, while the body was more measured and included an admission, buried in the tenth paragraph, that there was no evidence of corruption.

Despite the *Times*'s "scoop," most of the discussion of the Clinton Foundation during the first wave of coverage in the spring of 2015 centered in the right-wing media sphere. Breitbart, Free Beacon, the *Washington Examiner*, Fox News, Hot Air, Newsbusters, and the Daily Caller were among the media sources that produced the most stories mentioning the Clinton Foundation in May 2015. *Politico*, Yahoo! News, and *The Hill* were also in the top 10. By June 2015, the stories that continued to circulate did so almost exclusively in the right-wing media sphere. Despite not making the top 10 in number of stories, the *New York Times* was third among media sources shared on Facebook in May 2015, while all other top-10 sites were right-wing media.

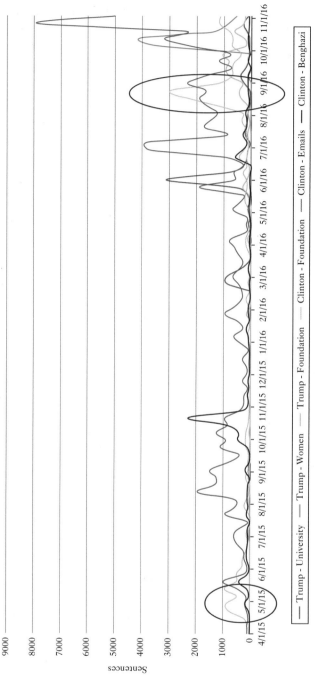

FIGURE 6.6 Sentences per day mentioning various topics over the course of the campaign in open web media. Clinton Foundation spikes are circled. The highest overall peaks correspond to Benghazi, Trump and women, and Clinton's emails.

Legend: Trump - University — Trump- Women — Trump - Foundation — Clinton - Foundation — Clinton - Emails — Clinton - Benghazi

The *Times*'s story about the Russian uranium deal was the reason, and it was the second-most shared story on Facebook related to the Clinton Foundation in May 2015. The most shared link was a petition launched by Judicial Watch to "Demand Answers on Clinton Corruption."

One major role of stories from the *Times* and other traditional professional media was to offer legitimacy to the claims made by Schweizer in *Clinton Cash*. Breitbart's top three most shared stories on Facebook in May 2015 were titled:

11 Explosive Clinton Cash Facts Mainstream Media Confirm are Accurate

REVEALED: Washington Post Uncovers 1,100 Hidden Foreign "Clinton Cash" Donations

Devastating Timeline Reveals the Transfer of Half of U.S. Uranium Output to Russia as Hillary Clinton's Foundation Bags $145 Million

These stories relied on the *Times* story for confirmation. As the Trump campaign sought to resurface the Clinton Foundation allegations, the early 2015 *New York Times* story became the second-most shared story about the Clinton Foundation on Facebook in August 2016.

How did this year-and-a-half-old story become so central to the campaign in August 2016? On July 23, the eve of the Democratic National Convention, Breitbart launched the movie version of Schweizer's *Clinton Cash*, a version edited to appeal to supporters of Bernie Sanders. The site's announcement makes this intention as clear as can be. In its initial report on the release, Breitbart quoted MSNBC and the Guardian as sources, asserting that the movie was "devastating" or "designed to stir up trouble" at the convention. The Breitbart story emphasized that "[t]he *New York Times, Washington Post,* ABC News, and other Establishment Media have verified and confirmed the book's explosive revelations that Hillary Clinton auctioned State Department policies to foreign Clinton Foundation donors and benefactors who then paid Bill Clinton tens of millions of dollars in speaking fees."[7] Breitbart approvingly embraced *Time* magazine's report that it was "aimed at persuading liberals" and "likely to leave on-the-fence Clinton supporters who see it feeling more unsure about casting a vote for her."[8] Throughout August, alongside the *New York Times* uranium story, the freely available YouTube distribution of *Clinton Cash* was the next most shared link about the Clinton Foundation on Facebook.

Our own analysis of YouTube sharing patterns underscores the extent to which the video version of Clinton Cash did double duty—both aimed to split Bernie supporters from Clinton and rally the party base. We analyzed the most tweeted YouTube videos in our election period Twitter set and mapped them based on how they were tweeted with other videos (Figure 6.7). The location on the map is determined by how often a video link is tweeted with another Twitter video. The size of the node is determined by how often a video was tweeted. And the color, unlike most of our other maps, is determined by a Louvain community detection algorithm, one of the standard algorithms used in network analysis to identify what parts of a network form a community in terms of similar patterns of linking. The map shows not only that the *Clinton Cash* YouTube video was the most widely tweeted video throughout the election but also that it straddled the line between core Trump supporters (based on its location in the network) and Bernie supporters (based on the

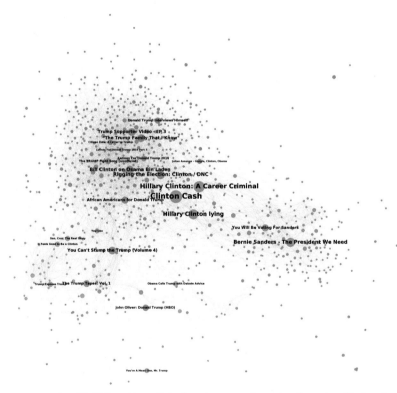

FIGURE 6.7 YouTube videos linked to by campaign-related stories. Nodes sized by number of tweets, edges represent co-sharing by the same Twitter user, and colors by Louvain community detection.

community detection algorithms, which places it clearly within the Bernie community).

On July 15, 2016, a week before the video version of *Clinton Cash* was released by Breitbart, Representative Marsha Blackburn sent a letter cosigned by 64 of her House Republican colleagues to the heads of the FBI, FTC, and IRS demanding that they investigate the allegations of corruption at the Clinton Foundation. A week later the commissioner of the IRS wrote a perfunctory response, informing the representative that he had forwarded the letter to the IRS office responsible for examining exempt organizations.[9] Four days later, on July 26, the second day of the Democratic Convention, the Daily Caller reported on this letter under the headline "EXCLUSIVE: IRS Launches Investigation of Clinton Foundation."[10] The next day, Fox News, crediting the Daily Caller's "exclusive," reported under the headline "IRS looking into Clinton Foundation 'pay-to-play' claims" that "[t]he IRS confirmed in a letter it is looking into claims of 'pay-to-play' practices at the Clinton Foundation, after dozens of Republican lawmakers requested a review of potential 'criminal conduct' at the organization founded by the family at the center of this week's Democratic National Convention."[11]

On July 29 the *New York Post* published an editorial asking why Hillary had not boasted about the Clinton Foundation at the convention. The *Post* speculated that it was because the Foundation was being investigated by the FBI over "intersections" between the Foundation and the State Department, "like her role in handing Russia exclusive mining rights to 20 percent of US uranium reserves via a company that donated millions to the foundation."[12] This editorial was, in turn, referred to by Fox News[13] and Breitbart.[14] The next day Fox News reported that "'Clinton Cash' Author Doubts IRS Will Thoroughly Investigate Clinton Foundation."[15] The pattern here is important and distinct. The stories are repeated and linked to internally within the network of sites. They receive reinforcement through repetition and variation of sources. Readers within this tightly interconnected network of sites will have encountered at least a headline associating Clinton, the foundation, and corruption several times, from diverse sources. It will make it easier to remember the association, reinforcing recall. The repetition in multiple stories also increases the credibility of the story. It is precisely this architecture of reciprocal citation and reinforcement in a tightly-knit network of media outlets that led us to characterize the phenomenon as network propaganda.

The central role of the Daily Caller, and the legitimating role of the *New York Times'* 2015 story, become clear on the map of the Clinton

Foundation stories in the last week of July 2016 (Figure 6.8). The distinct separation usually evident between the right-wing media sphere and the rest is gone, and instead the Daily Caller, Breitbart, and Fox are all clustered around the *New York Times* as a result of linking to its 2015 coverage as a source of validation for their current set of stories. The large Scribd node represents links to the IRS letter in response to the Blackburn letter.

The direction and size of the links in the map also show the extent to which Breitbart and Fox linked to the Daily Caller and also how they all linked to the *New York Times* and the *Washington Post* to legitimate the claims. The selective and strategic use of media usually criticized by the right is highlighted by the links from Breitbart, Fox News, and the Trump campaign site to PolitiFact during this week in late July 2016. These links primarily focused on an April 2015 PolitiFact assertion that a specific claim in Schweizer's book was truthful: Bill Clinton was indeed paid $500,000 or more for each of 13 speeches, only two of which occurred while Hillary was not secretary of state. Needless to say, the links from right-wing sources to PolitiFact did not include a June 30, 2016, report on Trump's claim that

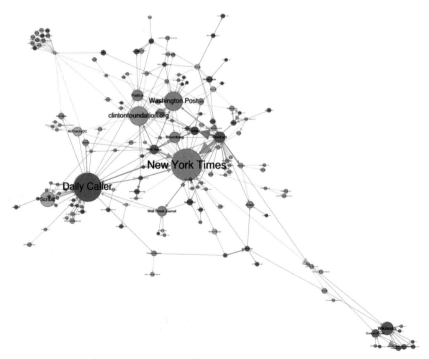

FIGURE 6.8 Online linking practices for stories about the Clinton Foundation during the Democratic Convention, July 25–August 1, 2016.

Clinton was paid to approve the Russian uranium deal, which they found to be mostly false.[16]

If we look at the number of sentences that mentioned the Clinton Foundation or *Clinton Cash* over the period from mid-July to mid-September, when this issue was most salient, the pattern becomes clear: right-wing media coverage of this topic was more extensive during this period and generally preceded coverage by other parts of the media ecosystem by a day or two. And, perhaps counterintuitively, the most pronounced effect was on center-left media—that is, mostly traditional professional media.

We see the first bump in right-wing coverage corresponding to the July 23 release of *Clinton Cash*. It can be seen more clearly if we zoom in on the period just before the August 9 bump.

Because these graphs describe the number of sentences across media quintiles that were *published* on these days, it does not include the influence of stories published much earlier in the campaign period that were linked to—most importantly, the *New York Times* story about the Uranium One deal. This influence comes across very clearly when we observe the word cloud that typifies the right-wing media discussion of the Clinton Foundation: the most distinct word in these media is "uranium" (Figure 6.10a). This word is notably absent in coverage of the Clinton Foundation from the left-center (Figure 6.10b).

As the sentence-count line chart (Figure 6.9 on the next page) makes clear, the next major movement in the story occurred around August 9, 2016. On August 7, the Rebuilding America super PAC published a 30-second television ad reviving the allegations, in which the *Washington Post* fact-checking process gave the ad three Pinocchios.[17] On August 9, Judicial Watch released a batch of emails it had obtained through FOIA litigation. Judicial Watch alleged that these emails exposed specific communications from Doug Band to Huma Abedin and Cheryl Mills at the State Department seeking special access for Gilbert Chagoury, whom Judicial Watch describes in its press release as "a close friend of former President Bill Clinton and a top donor to the Clinton Foundation."[18] As the Figure 6.11 visualization shows, the following day, August 10, was the first time that center-left media covered the Clinton Foundation significantly more than the right media, and Figure 6.12 shows that the words that typified center-left coverage indicate that the story linking Abedin, Chagoury, and Mills were a significant part of that coverage spike.

Fox television coverage played an integral part in propagating the Clinton Foundation frame to broader audiences. Consistent with what we saw

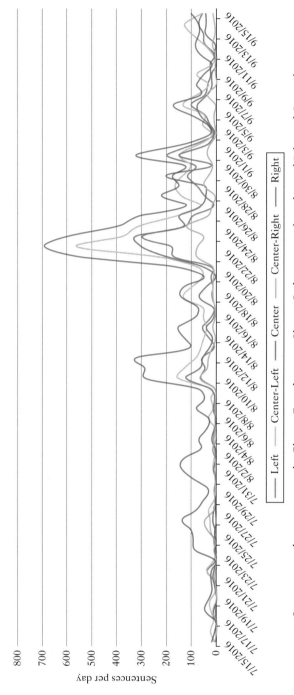

FIGURE 6.9 Sentences per day mentioning the Clinton Foundation or *Clinton Cash* in open web media, mid-July–mid-September 2016.

(a)

● **Right**

uranium investigating charity documentary breitbart skolkovo allegations fbi dnc america's haiti convention pay-to-play facebook khan favors online united exposes flowed ties laureate laundering partners premiere caller sanders disclosed participated canadian education contributors charitable headline tax links thedcnf investors blackburn launches graphic cuban institute supporters tens editor-at-large commission funneled dozens abedin accountability viewers crime john bestselling topics journal trending nations coincided spokesman

FIGURE 6.10A Words used most frequently by right open web media mentioning the Clinton Foundation or *Clinton Cash*, July 23–August 5, 2016.

(b)

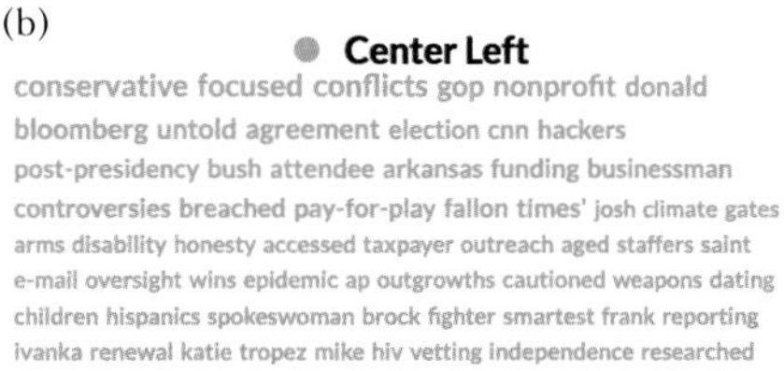

● **Center Left**

conservative focused conflicts gop nonprofit donald bloomberg untold agreement election cnn hackers post-presidency bush attendee arkansas funding businessman controversies breached pay-for-play fallon times' josh climate gates arms disability honesty accessed taxpayer outreach aged staffers saint e-mail oversight wins epidemic ap outgrowths cautioned weapons dating children hispanics spokeswoman brock fighter smartest frank reporting ivanka renewal katie tropez mike hiv vetting independence researched

FIGURE 6.10B Words used most frequently by center-left open web media mentioning the Clinton Foundation or *Clinton Cash*, July 23–August 5, 2016.

online, the Internet Archive's selection of television transcripts indicates that television coverage that mentioned the Clinton Foundation before August 10 was seen almost exclusively on Fox News, Fox Business, and local television Fox affiliates. After August 10, CNN joined the Fox networks, but on local channels the story remained primarily the focus of Fox affiliates (Figures 6.13 and 6.14).[19]

By August 18, although coverage had declined, the reporting raised enough questions to inspire a formal response; Bill Clinton announced that the foundation would stop taking foreign donations if Hillary Clinton was elected president.[20] Bill Clinton's promise did little to quiet the story. On August 22 Donald Trump publicly called for the appointment of a special prosecutor to investigate the claims of a corrupt quid pro quo relationship between the State Department and the Clinton Foundation. That same day, Bill Clinton published a more detailed letter stating that if Hillary Clinton was elected, the foundation would cease accepting foreign donations and transition out of operations that depended on matching funds from countries where its programs operated, and that he would step down from a position on the foundation's board and stop raising funds for the foundation.[21] That same day, Judicial Watch released a second batch of emails. This string of events attracted even more coverage, and most importantly, a broad range of sources outside the right-wing sphere.

The number of sentences referring to the Clinton Foundation was well over twice as large August 22 to 26 as it had been during the prior August 10 to 12 peak. Television coverage, too, was substantially higher (except at the outlier Fox affiliate in Raleigh, North Carolina, which had covered the first round extensively), and this time, among the national networks, CNN

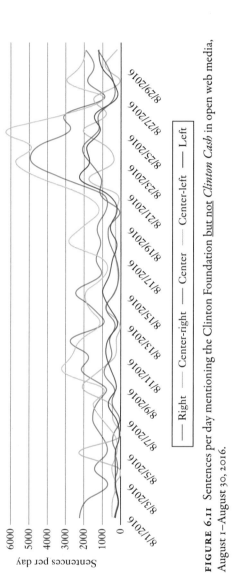

FIGURE 6.11 Sentences per day mentioning the Clinton Foundation but not *Clinton Cash* in open web media, August 1–August 30, 2016.

clinton trump foundation
campaign hillary emails republican
donald presidential donor aides democratic
abedin rally lebanon ryan nominee server election gop
judicial chagoury media violence washington paul cnn john
virginia obama baldwin nbc mills billionaire americans donations rnc
ohio conservative michael abolish bothers e-mails photo hayden cheering
florida applause chris ballots collins calling america illegal united scaife
lebanese messages debates batch fundraiser poll huma children fbi senate johnson
charity ties susan economy staffer oppose university loved suggesting pac gilbert congress
reward kaine informing ambassador ap's cuomo accusing tweets dnc temperament granholm
presidency pennsylvania super exchanges politico's deleting mateen opponent vickers inciting

FIGURE 6.12 Words used most frequently by center-left open web media mentioning the Clinton Foundation, August 10, 2016.

and MSNBC covered the story as much as Fox News did (Figure 6.13). CBS and the other networks' local affiliates also covered the story extensively (Figure 6.15).

A map of media attention August 22 to 26 shows that while the *New York Times* and the *Washington Post* continued to be major nodes, Judicial Watch played a key role in the narrative with its new trove of emails obtained under FOIA (Figure 6.16). CNN and *Politico*, which were generally prominent in the debates but had not been during the earlier spike in interest in the Clinton Foundation on August 9–10, took a more prominent role. So too did the Associated Press (AP) and the *Wall Street Journal*, neither of which previously played a significant role. The most linked-to stories in the *New York Times* on those days included a general background story covering the Bill Clinton announcement about his stepping down if Hillary was elected, the Trump campaign's emphasis on the foundation, and a story on the Judicial Watch email release.

Social media attention, by contrast, centered on Judicial Watch and, to a lesser extent, Breitbart, as Figure 6.17, with nodes sized by Facebook shares, makes clear.

The stories from traditional professional media over this period underscore the difficulty mainstream media faced in reporting on an issue of such sensitivity and complexity in the teeth of a sustained communications effort

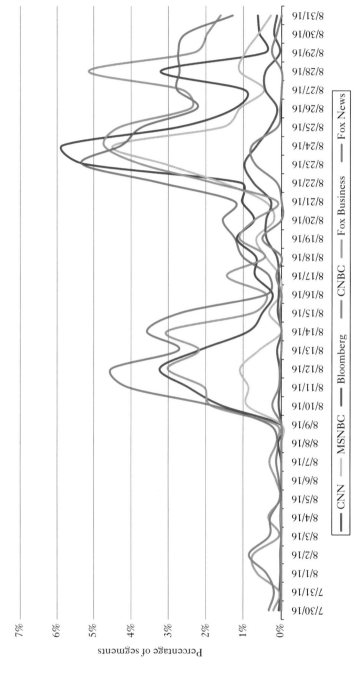

FIGURE 6.13 Percentage of 15-second segments that mention "Clinton Foundation" by national networks, July 30–August 31, 2016.

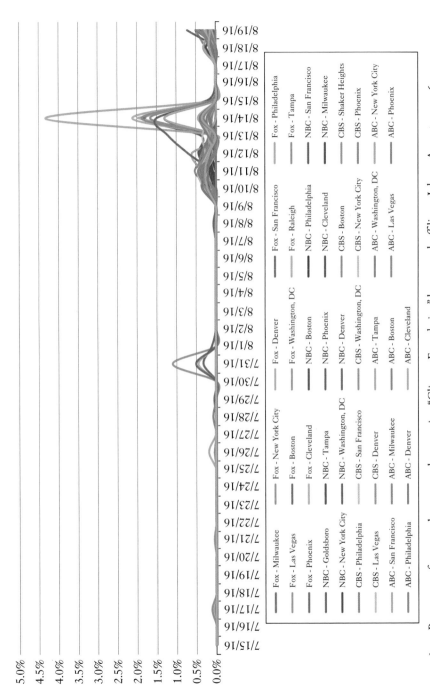

FIGURE 6.14 Percentage of 15-second segments that mention "Clinton Foundation" by network affiliates, July 15–August 19, 2016.

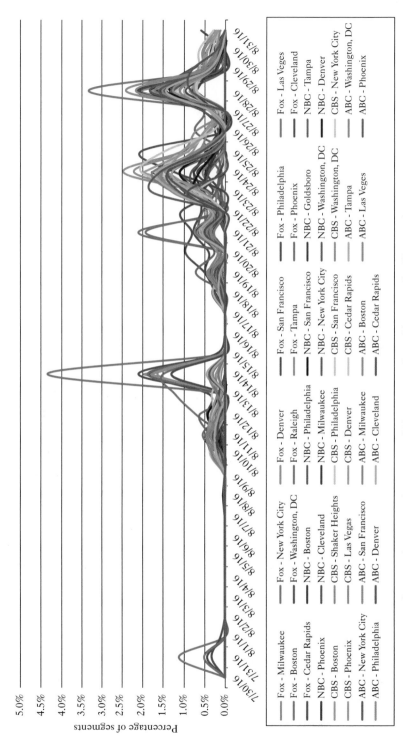

FIGURE 6.15 Percentage of 15-second segments that mention "Clinton Foundation" by network affiliates, July 30–August 31, 2016.

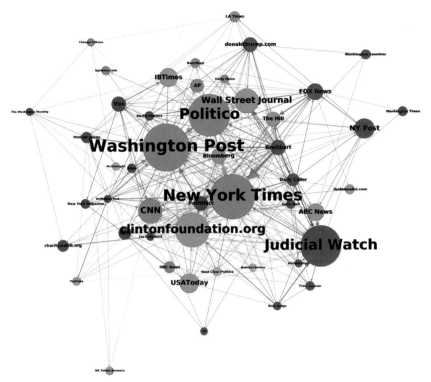

FIGURE 6.16 Directed linking behavior of media sources within the Clinton Foundation topic, August 22–August 29, 2016.

from a motivated party: the right-wing media ecosystem. Balance demanded hard-hitting reporting. And coverage needed eye-catching headlines. The most linked-to and Facebook-shared story from the *Washington Post*, for example, was titled "Emails reveal how foundation donors got access to Clinton and her close aides at State Dept."[22] The opening paragraph read: "A sports executive who was a major donor to the Clinton Foundation and whose firm paid Bill Clinton millions of dollars in consulting fees wanted help getting a visa for a British soccer player with a criminal past." The *16th and 17th paragraphs* read:

> There is no indication from the emails that Abedin intervened on behalf of Casey
>
> Wasserman, an L.A. sports executive who in 2009 asked Band for help getting a visa for a British soccer star trying to visit Las Vegas. Band indicated that the office of Sen. Barbara Boxer (D-Calif.) had

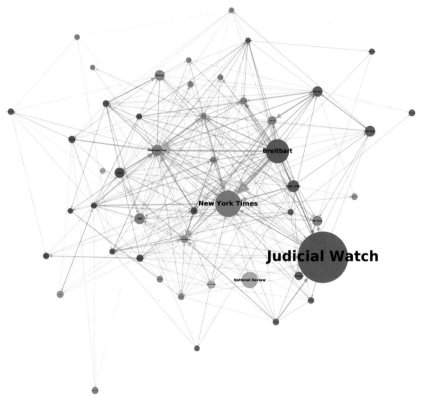

FIGURE 6.17 Directed linking behavior of media sources shared on social media within the Clinton Foundation topic, August 22–August 29, 2016. Nodes sized by number of Facebook shares.

already declined to help, given the player's criminal record. A Boxer spokesman described the request to her office as "routine" but one with that Boxer did not assist, "given the facts of the case."

"Makes me nervous to get involved but I'll ask," Abedin wrote to Band in May 2009 after he forwarded her an email from Wasserman.

Band responded: "then don't."

In other words, for those brave few who read past the intervening 15 paragraphs, the story would more accurately have begun: "Emails reveal that donors sought access, but Clinton aides refused them when they deemed the requests inappropriate." The fifth paragraph, which followed two more claims of potential conflicts, stated: "The emails show that, in these and similar cases, the donors did not always get what they wanted, particularly when they sought anything more than a meeting." This and many other stories used the three events—the Trump call for an investigation, the Judicial Watch email release, and the Bill Clinton email about his role in the foundation—together as evidence that the foundation was an appropriate focus of news coverage. Just as the *New York Times* had done with the Uranium One story, the *Washington Post* here led with the insinuation of potential corruption—a much juicier angle—rather than with the absence of evidence of actual wrongdoing, and then it buried that truthful concession deep in the middle of the story. This is simply the framing corollary to the "If it bleeds, it leads" trope. In this case, Judicial Watch and the Trump campaign were doing what media activists have been doing forever: staging events that would motivate professional media as a way of setting the agenda. What we see here is a successful operation to put red meat too juicy to pass up in front of traditional media. And the availability of new emails, this time obtained legally through FOIA rather than by illegal hacking, gives the reporting the grounding in objective fact that satisfies the professional norms and gives cover to the sensationalist framing necessary to publish front-page news.

The fact that the traditional professional media were the targets of intentional manipulation does not absolve them of responsibility for checking the materials put in front of them, much less of supporting a Trump campaign narrative. In this regard, the Associated Press offers an example of particularly poor reporting. The unusually large presence of the AP as a node in the link economy that week is due to a story that appeared on Twitter as follows: "BREAKING AP Analysis: More than half those who met Clinton as Cabinet secretary gave money to Clinton Foundation." The study was quickly debunked, and within two weeks, the AP had issued a retraction of that assertion and deleted the tweet. The gist of the story was that the AP uncovered 154 people without official positions with whom Clinton had met, and of these 85 had connections with foundation donors. The AP story focused on Nobel Peace Prize winner Muhammad Yunnus, an introduction to the Kennedy Center's chairman at a Kennedy Center awards ceremony, and a conversation with the head of the MAC Cosmetics AIDS charity arm about raising funds for an AIDS education campaign. As Matthew Yglesias put it the morning after the story came out: "The State Department is a big operation. So is the Clinton Foundation. The AP put a lot of work into this project. And it couldn't come up with anything that looks worse than helping a Nobel Prize winner, raising money to finance AIDS education, and doing an introduction for the chair of the Kennedy Center. It's kind of surprising."[23]

But as the preceding figures make clear, by the time the AP issued the retraction of the headline (though not the story itself), the spikes in coverage had already occurred, and the story had made its impact. In particular a big spike in television coverage on non-Fox-affiliated local television channels happened on August 24, immediately after the AP story and after *New York Times* and *Washington Post* stories on August 22 and 23. This coverage, in turn, brought the issue to a broader public.

The critical lesson of this chapter of the Clinton Foundation story is that the manipulation was not a result of Facebook fake news or of the fragmentation of public discourse. Precisely because the majority of Americans do not get their news from Facebook or from the right-wing media ecosystem, it was necessary for the actors on the right—Bannon and Schweizer through the Government Accountability Institute (GAI), Breitbart, Fox, the Daily Caller, and Judicial Watch—to frame a story that was attractive enough for mainstream media to cover and to provide reason for mainstream voters to doubt Hillary Clinton's integrity. There simply are not enough voters who get their news largely from the right-wing media ecosystem to win an election. Right-wing media must harness broader parts of the ecosystem to achieve their strategic goals. In this case, they kept the story alive with several distinct media "hits"—the release of a book while offering careful "exclusive" access to major newspapers; a film; multiple releases of email dumps; and responses by political actors to these media events (from the congressional representatives' letter to the IRS to Donald Trump's public statements). Right-wing media succeeded in pushing the Clinton Foundation to the front of the public agenda precisely at the moment when Clinton would have been anticipated to (and indeed did) receive her biggest bounce in the polls: immediately after the Democratic convention. And as we saw in Chapter 4, even after mainstream interest receded, the validation from mainstream media continued to add credibility to the much more sinister, tribal narratives surrounding the foundation that we saw emerging in both the pedophilia and Islamophobia narratives.

Truth Under Fire: Error Correction and Self-Healing Among Winners of Trump's Fake News Awards

In Chapters 3 and 5 we saw that the same Fox News reporters and shows repeatedly played central roles in the various disinformation campaigns. Malia Zimmerman wrote the initial pieces in both the "Lolita Express" Clinton pedophilia story and the Seth Rich story. Hannity, the network's biggest star, was central to those two as well as Uranium One. Lou Dobbs pushed the "deep state" framing and Uranium One. Fox and Friends was central in propagating the Seth Rich conspiracy theory. Bret Baier was central on the Lolita Express. The reporters who played prominent roles in propagating these false stories paid no professional price, because the network they work for is a propagandist, not journalistic, enterprise.

Central to the practice of objectivity as truth seeking is not infallibility but institutionalized error detection and correction. This is as true for journalism as it is for the scientific method, though the speed of publication, sensitivity to markets, and levels of evidence necessary in each enterprise differ significantly and result in different institutional details. And for all the differences between them, the projects of journalism and science are both committed to norms of truth seeking anchored in a reality that is prior to and external to opinion and perspective. It is fundamentally different from the project of denying the possibility of truth beyond partisan perspective.

As we showed in Chapter 5 and return to in Chapter 11, professional journalism has been under sustained attack from right-wing media since the emergence of Rush Limbaugh to national prominence in the late 1980s early 1990s. The presidency of Donald Trump saw an unprecedented escalation in the war on journalism and a challenge to the very possibility of institutionalized truth seeking, as opposed to partisan perspective. In the teeth of this attack, both mainstream and net-native outlets continued to practice mutual checking and verification, as well as relying on internal controls to impose checks, communicate error, and discipline reporters who circumvented these checks.

Here we review what happened to the major media stories that received President Trump's and the Republican Party's Fake News Awards of 2017.[24] Rather than circling the wagons, in most of these cases news organizations exposed, admitted, and corrected errors over very short timelines, through both internal processes and network processes of mutual monitoring. The dynamic is fundamental to error avoidance, detection, and correction in a well-functioning media ecosystem and is exactly the opposite of the mutually reinforcing roles that entities in a network subject to the propaganda feedback loop exhibit. We lay it out here because, after decades of media criticism from both the left and the right, it is hard for many to accept that there is something very real about the project of objectivity-as-truth seeking and that this has real consequences for the construction of understanding and resilience to bullshit. Even if in theory perfect objectivity is unattainable and truth necessarily provisional, in practice, in the lived experience of media ecosystems, organizations set up to pursue those goals function differently and pose different levels of resistance to propaganda and bullshit than those designed to produce a post-truth world.

On December 1, 2017, ABC News's Brian Ross falsely reported that retired General Michael Flynn would, as part of his plea deal, testify that then-candidate Trump himself had instructed Flynn to contact Russian officials during the campaign. Several hours later, the network issued a correction, in which it explained that its source had contacted the network to explain that the story was inaccurate and that what he had said was that during the campaign the candidate had asked Flynn to find ways to repair relations with Russia, and it was only after the election that then-President-elect Trump asked Flynn to contact Russian officials to discuss working jointly against ISIS.[25] That evening CNN reported on the error, emphasizing that the report had caused a major drop in the Dow Jones, that ABC had learned that its story was in error at 6:00 p.m. that evening, and that Ross would issue a correction on-air at 6:30 p.m.[26] CNN later described how, under pressure, ABC tweeted and posted a correction, rather than a clarification. The next day the *Times*, the *Post, Politico*, and other sites reported on the error and the retraction, and Ross was suspended for four weeks. Raw Story and Newsweek published reports of the original incorrect ABC report, but then appended the ABC correction.[27] The only stories we identified in our set that could be considered amplifications or versions of the story that went uncorrected was a Think Progress report on the mistaken ABC claim, that did not later append a retraction,[28] and a report in the Palmer Report, published before and without reference to the ABC story, claiming that Flynn "is testifying that Donald Trump and Jared Kushner ordered him to be the point man for communicating and conspiring with the Russian government during the election," and did so before the ABC report and without reference to it (and also without foundation).[29] The basic dynamic we observe is self-correction within hours, extensive reporting by other major outlets within the center, center-left, and left of the mistake and the correction, the disciplining of the reporter who made the error, and minimal detectable repetition of the false report even on marginal sites on the left.[30]

On December 8, 2017, CNN published a report that mistakenly stated that Donald Trump Jr. had received a website and decryption key to preview emails before they were made public by WikiLeaks. The original report claimed, based on sources, that the email to Trump Jr. was dated September 4, 2016. A few hours later, the *Washington Post* obtained a copy of the alleged email and reported that it had been sent September 14, 2016, not September 4, and thus came after, not before, the emails had already been reported on publicly. By 6:05 p.m. that day, CNN had issued a correction to its story, credited the *Washington Post* for its find, and linked to the *Post* story as well as to the text of the email showing the September 14 date prominently. Except for one, every story we could find updated the story to include the correction. Raw Story, a left-wing online news organization founded in 2004, is the one exception we found; Raw Story published a story based on the original CNN report but without reporting on the correction.[31] A partisan site like Talking Points Memo issued a blaring, all caps headline that focused on the correction, not the allegation.[32] Across major mainstream and left media the report was on the mistake, the correction, and how it handed the right a weapon in claiming that all the reporting against the president was fake news. Reporting on the right did just that.

The next recipient of the fake news awards was a report in *Time* magazine that President Trump had removed a bust of Martin Luther King Jr. from the Oval Office. *Time* reporter Zeke Miller mistakenly reported on inauguration day that MLK's bust had been removed from the White House. He corrected the error and apologized by email, Twitter, and an online correction to the *Time* story. The story got practically no repetition or amplification, and primarily was reported on the right, as an example of "fake news" by mainstream media, and to some extent elsewhere as an example of how right-wing media or the president use failures to attack the media. A somewhat similar pattern occurred when *Washington Post* reporter Dave Weigel tweeted out a photo showing a Trump rally in Pensacola, Florida, with seats half empty, a photo that turned out to be premature as the stands later filled up. The photo was not part of an actual story published by the *Post*. In a tweet the president demanded an apology and retraction. In a response tweet, Weigel responded "Sure thing: I apologize. I deleted the photo after @dmartosko told me I'd gotten it wrong. Was confused by the image of you walking in the bottom right corner."[33] A few more of the Fake News Awards went to trivial stories, such as a Newsweek story that Poland's first lady had refused to shake Trump's hand, or a CNN story mocking the president for his boorishness in overfeeding decorative fish during a visit to Japan. Stories of greater significance included a CNN story, prior to James Comey's Senate testimony, which anticipated that he would refute President Trump's claim that Comey told him that he was not under investigation. The report was retracted as soon as Comey's testimony was pre-released and included no such affirmation.[34] Another award went to Paul Krugman for writing a blog post at 12:42 a.m. the night of Trump's election, as stock markets were dropping, in which Krugman flippantly wrote: "It really does now look like President Donald

J. Trump, and markets are plunging. When might we expect them to recover? Frankly, I find it hard to care much, even though this is my specialty. The disaster for America and the world has so many aspects that the economic ramifications are way down my list of things to fear. Still, I guess people want an answer: If the question is when markets will recover, a first-pass answer is never."[35]

Calling this kind of flippant opinion statement "fake news" seems more like taking a victory lap over a mistaken prediction made publicly by a vexing opponent than anything else.

The most dramatic story of significance began on the evening of Thursday, June 23, 2017. CNN had published a report, based on a single anonymous source, claiming that the Treasury Department was looking into a meeting between the chief executive of a Russian investment fund, itself subject to sanctions and under Senate Intelligence Committee investigation, and a Trump transition team official, Anthony Scaramucci, a few days before the inauguration.[36] Later that same evening Breitbart and Sputnik each published a detailed criticism of the piece.[37] By the next day CNN had disabled links to the story and, possibly under pressure from BuzzFeed to explain why the story had been removed,[38] appended an editor's note that read: "Story did not meet CNN's editorial standards and has been retracted. Links to the story have been disabled. CNN apologizes to Mr. Scaramucci."[39] The original CNN tweets that pushed out the story were deleted and replaced with links to the editorial note instead. By Monday morning two reporters on the story, and the executive editor of CNN's investigations unit who was responsible for them, had resigned. As with the other cases we have described, all the reporting that followed, both on CNN itself and on other mainstream outlets, was about the mistake, the resignations, and the importance of maintaining the highest standards and responsibility in the teeth of the sustained attack by the president on the trustworthiness of the media.

It is important to focus specifically on what was wrong about the CNN story. There was no disagreement that Scaramucci had in fact met Kirill Dimitriev in Davos, or that the Russian Direct Investment Fund he headed was under U.S. sanctions. Bloomberg had conducted an interview with Scaramucci in Davos at the time, and he acknowledged the meeting and connected it to intentions to bridge relations.[40] The CNN report linked to that Bloomberg interview, which had been published in January under the title "Trump Aid Talks Investment with Sanctioned Kremlin Fund" and correctly quoted Scaramucci's response to Bloomberg, referring to Dmitriev: "What I said to him last night, in my capacity inside the administration, I would certainly reach out to some people to help him." The CNN report described Senators Elizabeth Warren and Ben Cardin's demand sent to incoming Treasury Secretary Steven Mnuchin that he investigate the meeting, and linked to Mnuchin's pro forma response letter, that, if confirmed, he would "ensure that the appropriate Department components assess whether further investigation of this matter is warranted."[41] The error was in relying on a single congressional source, probably a Democratic staffer, to open and frame the entire piece with "Senate investigators are examining the activities of a little-known $10-billion Russian investment fund whose chief executive met with a member of President Donald Trump's transition team four days before Trump's inauguration." The assertion that the Senate was actively investigating the meeting, and the implication, based on a single source, that more facts were emerging than those reported in January, cost the three reporters their jobs.

The sole example we found of substantial diffusion of what remained a fundamentally uncorrected error relates to an August 7 story in the *New York Times*. The *Times* reported that it received a leaked draft of the scientific report on climate change by 13 federal agencies, that the conclusions and findings stood in stark contradiction to the administration's agenda on the environment and climate science, and that the scientists were concerned the administration would suppress it.[42] The most extreme follow-on to the story, published on a site called EcoWatch, interpreted the *Times* story as "while the administration tries to suppress its agencies talking about climate change, a leaked report has concluded that millions of Americans are feeling the effects of climate change right now."[43] *Vanity Fair* quoted the *Times* report under the headline "Damning Federal Climate Report Leaked Before Trump Can Suppress It."[44] Other reports offered somewhat less sensational versions, focused more on the likely true claim that some scientists working for the federal government feared the administration would suppress a report whose conclusions were so directly opposed to the administration's position on climate change. That same day, one climate scientist involved in writing the report pointed out that there was no leak and that the draft report had been out and available in public during the comment period and remained available on the Internet Archive.[45] That evening a political scientist quoted in the *Times* story as having worked on the report tweeted that the report had been out since January, and the next morning noted that a side-by-side comparison showed that the report the *Times* obtained was the same one as the version that had been on the Internet Archive since January and that a draft of the report was still available for purchase from the National Academies of Sciences.[46] On August 9 both the *Washington Post* online and Fox News criticized the *Times* for the misleading implication that the draft report had not been made public. They argued correctly that by claiming to have obtained and published a leaked, previously unpublished report, the *Times* implied that the administration's failure to publish was evidence that fears that the report would be suppressed were well founded.[47] The *Times*'s correction was minimal. It acknowledged the prior availability of the report and emphasized instead the reporting that government scientists and scientists involved in writing the report were concerned that the administration would not formally release the report. While not an impossible reading of the original *Times* story, the implication captured by the Vanity Fair headline we quoted above is certainly what gave the *Times*'s story its claim to be front-page news. The report was ultimately released by the administration in November 2017, and the *Times* never really acknowledged that its framing had been misleading.

COMPARING THE URANIUM One, Seth Rich, and Lolita Express and Orgy Island diffusion patterns we observed in earlier chapters on the one hand, and the various winners of the "fake news awards" on the other hand, underscores the fundamentally different dynamics in the right wing as compared to the rest of the American political media ecosystem. When observing right-wing conspiracy theories, we saw positive feedback loops between the core of that network—composed of Fox News, leading Republican pundits, and Breitbart—and the remainder of the online right-wing network. In those cases we saw repetition, amplification, and circling of the wagons to criticize other media outlets when these exposed the errors and failures of the story. By contrast, the mainstream media ecosystem exhibited intensive competition to hold each other to high journalistic standards, and a repeated pattern of rapid removal of content, correction, and in several cases disciplining of the reporters involved. Moreover, in none of these cases did we find more than a smattering of repetition and amplification of the claims once retracted. In the one case where we are not convinced that the retraction was sufficient, the *Washington Post* published a criticism of the misleading *New York Times* story, and most of the stories that repeated the claims focused on the likely truthful aspect of the report—that there are government climate scientists concerned that the administration would suppress climate science reports—rather than on the sensationalistic and conspiratorial implication that only through the leak to the *New York Times* could these scientists prevent the suppression and that the leak was some heroic act of whistle-blowing.

As our data show, the fundamental architecture of information flow in the two clusters is different. As the case studies show, the organizational practices and consequences for reporters are different. And the narrative sharing practices of the network of sites that diffuse the stories follow fundamentally different pathways. It would be truly remarkable if falsehoods diffused and decayed symmetrically in two networks exhibiting such fundamentally different structure and dynamics. And, as we have consistently seen throughout this book, they do not. Conspiracy theories, falsehoods, and rumors that fit the tribal narrative diffuse more broadly and are sustained for longer on the right than in the rest of the media ecosystem. As such, it would be surprising if people who occupied the right wing of the network were not more susceptible to such falsehoods, be their origin commercial or political, domestic or foreign.

PART THREE

The Usual Suspects

In Part Two we covered the actions of what we perceived to be the primary actors of network propaganda and the American political media ecosystem more generally. Here, we turn to the primary culprits that have received more sustained public attention as the alleged causes of our present moment of information disorder. In Chapter 7 we briefly consider the argument that alt-right activists hacked the media ecosystem by inserting various destructive memes into the mainstream media that helped Donald Trump win the election. There has been excellent work focused on the alt-right, on Reddit and 4chan, aiming to document the efforts of these communities to propagate their views across the media environment. Here, we offer a brief case study where that pathway in fact succeeded, and we offer it as an example of what we call the propaganda pipeline—the path from the periphery to the core through a series of well-known amplification sites, most prominently Infowars and Drudge. That said, we argue that the pipeline, while real, was not as important as the intentional efforts of larger, more central propagandist media, and indeed, depends on those media's willing adoption of the memes generated on the periphery to have a broader impact. In Chapter 8, we spend a good bit of time assessing the evidence of the existence, pathways, and impact of Russian information operations. In Chapter 9, we conclude with considering the three main threats related to Facebook: Facebook microtargeting and dark ads, Cambridge Analytica, and commercial clickbait factories. We explain why we think that the behaviorally informed, microtargeted dark ads are likely the most important novel threat to democratic practice independent of the overall architecture of the media environment, but caution that there is no evidence that they have already played the role that they hypothetically could play. We also suggest that both the Cambridge Analytica and commercial clickbait threats were overstated.

The Propaganda Pipeline: Hacking the Core from the Periphery

"If there's a story that can hurt Hillary, I want it in the news cycle," Cernovich said. "When I first started, that meant figuring out how news cycles work." One way to propel a story into the mainstream is to get it linked by the Drudge Report. "If it's on Drudge, then it's on 'Hannity,'" Cernovich said. "If it's on 'Hannity,' then Brian Stelter's talking about it on CNN." The Drudge Report favors big newspapers and established right-wing blogs; Danger and Play is not on the list. "If I have a really hot story, I might leak it to someone at Breitbart, or to someone else who can get the Drudge link." That journalist usually returns the favor by embedding a Cernovich tweet in the story.[1]

THUS FAR WE have documented our claim that the media ecosystem in both the right and the rest is largely dominated by top-performing media sites, their publication decisions, and their interactions with each other. In this, our work deviates from the standard narrative that followed the election of 2017, which emphasized Facebook advertising, alt-right trolls, and Russian propaganda efforts. We do need to qualify our findings in one important respect. The internet is wide open. It is populated with a diverse set of political actors, all of whom want to influence the public debate. And some of these actors are quite sophisticated in how they take advantage of the media ecosystem architecture to insert their narratives, memes, and frames into the network directly and through the major propagation outlets. We call this process the "propaganda pipeline," exemplified perfectly by the quote from Mike Cernovich, whom Andrew Marantz from *The New Yorker* dubbed "the meme mastermind of the alt-right" in the piece from which we quote the opening of this chapter. In our work on the early stages of the various conspiracy theories we repeatedly interacted with such efforts, some of which in fact succeeded in reaching a broader audience through the pipeline.

Our observations lead us to believe that these efforts, while real and observable, were not determinative in the election or the first year of the Trump presidency. The major frames of this period were immigration and Islamophobia, Hillary Clinton emails and the Clinton Foundation, and the assault on the rule of law and journalism implied by the "deep state" frame. The top media outlets and political elites, not Redditors or meme propagators from the alt-right, were primarily responsible for distributing these frames widely. As we described in Chapter 3, this is even the case with the Clinton pedophilia narratives, where some of the peripheral actors had their greatest success. The Fox News versions of the Clinton pedophilia stories were overwhelmingly more visible than the version that started on Reddit and was accelerated by Cernovich and then-Sputnik reporter Cassandra Fairbanks, which we describe here. These efforts exist. Media outlets and observers should be aware of them. Sometimes they even succeed. In the case we describe here, they made it to *Hannity* and the *Washington Times*, and from there across the right-wing media ecosystem. But it is important not to overstate their importance in the overall dynamic of network propaganda. And because these dynamics seem to suggest a symbiotic relationship between the alt-right and Russian information operations, our story here is also a down payment on Chapter 8, where we dig deeper into Russian intervention.

Spirit Cooking

"*LEAKED EMAIL appears to link Clinton Campaign Chairman to bizarre occult ritual*," tweeted Sean Hannity at 11:50 a.m. on November 4, 2016, linking to a radio and online segment on the topic. Hannity (who later removed the page from his archives) linked to a story from LifeZette—the website founded by Laura Ingraham—headlined: "WikiLeaks: Clinton Campaign Chair Participated in Occult Magic: Emails reveal Podesta attended 'Spirit Cooking' event that has been described as Satanic." That same morning, the *Washington Times* published a story entitled "Wikileaks: Podesta invited to 'Spirit' dinner: host's known 'recipes' demand breast milk, sperm," crediting the Drudge Report as having broken the story. At 8:19 a.m. on November 4, Drudge, under the typically understated headline "WIKI WICCAN: PODESTA PRACTICES OCCULT MAGIC," had posted a link to a segment by Alex Jones's Infowars (more than half of Infowars referrals from other sites come from Drudge). And Infowars was clearly the source of Hannity's insight, as Hannity's headline doesn't even bother to vary the adjectives from the Infowars headline: "'Spirit Cooking': Clinton Campaign Chairman Practices Bizarre Occult Ritual" (Figure 7.1). [2] The Infowars story was built primarily around a post that Cernovich had published on his blog, Danger and Play, several hours earlier, as well as two posts by Cassandra Fairbanks, then a Sputnik news reporter, who published posts that themselves wove together Reddit and 4chan posts with tweets and interview quotes from Cernovich and other alt-right personae.

The story began with an email from the set of John Podesta emails that had been hacked by Russian agents and released on WikiLeaks in October 2016. The "spirit cooking" email was from Tony Podesta to his brother John, forwarding an invitation from performance artist Marina Abramovic "to the Spirit Cooking dinner at my place." The occult sex ritual framing and the striking image of Abramovic holding a bloody, skinned goat's head are both borrowed directly, with credit, from the story Cernovich posted the night before.[3] Cernovich, who also propagated the Pizzagate story, came to broader public attention when Donald Trump Jr. tweeted that he would have been awarded a Pulitzer "in a long gone time of unbiased journalism."[4]

Most of the Infowars story was, however, indebted to two Fairbanks stories. Fairbanks had apparently started her activism and writing career on the left, protesting the failure to prosecute the 2012 rape in Steubenville, Ohio, and covering Black Lives Matters events. As she told the BBC,[5] during the primaries she had supported Bernie Sanders and was thinking of supporting Jill Stein, but decided in June 2016 that Trump was her candidate and set out to persuade her Twitter followers. In her WeAreChange signature line, Fairbanks described herself as "a DC-based writer and political commentator who has been published in a range of outlets including Sputnik News, International Business Times, Teen Vogue, and TeleSUR." In exchanges with Guccifer 2.0, as we will see in Chapter 8, she described Sputnik as her "day job." She continued writing for Sputnik throughout 2017, but moved to the Gateway Pundit in 2018.

Fairbanks's late-night November 3 spirit cooking story mostly described Abramovic's performances without much commentary and embedded a video and images of the performance. Fairbanks's story was not written in an outraged tone, allowing the artist's intentional effort to disturb her audience to speak for itself. At 1:00 a.m., WikiLeaks tweeted that story.[6] WikiLeaks was also the first public-facing Facebook page to share the spirit cooking story.

The Infowars story amped up the volume by explaining that spirit cooking was "'a sacrament in the religion of Thelema which was founded by Aleister

FIGURE 7.1 "Spirit cooking" stories as seen on Infowars, *Washington Times*, and Hannity.

Crowley' and involves an occult performance during which menstrual blood, breast milk, urine and sperm are used to create a 'painting.'" To deepen the conspiracy, the Infowars story picked up the pizza storyline that would become the foundation of Pizzagate soon after the election: "Some are even linking the spirit cooking revelation to claims that the Podesta emails contain 'code for child sex trafficking' that is hidden behind mentions of types of food." The source cited for this proposition was another story by Fairbanks, also posted November 3. Fairbanks's story, "Internet Is On Fire With Speculation that Podesta Emails Contain Code For Child Sex,"[7] reported what others were saying, rather than making her own claim, and ended with a modifier of "Whether this is a case of confirmation bias, or something more sinister—one thing is certain: People really do not trust Hillary Clinton—to the point where thousands of people are actually having serious discussions about whether or not she is involved in a child sex ring." Whatever the modifier, the article combined a Reddit post with a string of tweets to incorporate three more strands in the narrative.

First, Fairbanks described a Reddit post[8] connecting the story to the case of Laura Silsby and her Baptist missionary organization: The New Life Children's Refuge. Silsby and 9 of her colleagues tried to transport 33 children out of Haiti and to the Dominican Republic in the aftermath of the 2010 Haitian earthquake. The 10 missionaries were charged with kidnapping and held for three weeks pending investigation and charging. Their lawyer had requested that Hillary Clinton, then-secretary of state, intervene, but the State Department limited its engagement to standard consular services for the situation.[9] A week later, Bill Clinton, who was coordinating the U.N. relief efforts, made a public plea for the U.S. and Haitian governments to resolve the issue of the 10 American missionaries. Ultimately, 9 of the 10 were released, and Silsby was convicted of a lesser offense and sentenced to six months imprisonment. At the time, the Fox News coverage of the event was highly sympathetic to Silsby, describing her as a "40-year-old businesswoman" who thought the children she was trying to help were "orphans whose homes were destroyed in the earthquake."[10] By 2016, the story received a less anodyne treatment. In Fairbanks's telling, "Silsby was found guilty in Haiti of child trafficking in 2010, after she attempted to cross the Haiti-Dominican Republic border with 33 Haitian children—all but one of the children had at least one living parent and were not orphans. Nine others who were arrested along with her were freed, thanks to the efforts of the Clintons." Fairbanks followed this framing with a pullout of a Mike Cernovich tweet asking, "Were 33 children for Bill Clinton and Jeffrey Epstein's 'use'? Forget corruption, these emails expose connections to child sex trafficking," relating the story back to the

Lolita Express storyline we encountered in Chapter 3. Fairbanks returned to the Lolita Express story in the conclusion of the piece, where she quoted from an interview she conducted with Cernovich: "Cernovich added that because of the facts that Clinton's top aide Huma Abedin's husband is currently under investigation for sexting a minor, and Bill Clinton flew on convicted pedophile Jeffrey Epstein's private jet (which is called 'The Lolita Express'), the whole inner circle deserves scrutiny."

The final strand in the story is pizza—or rather, the belief that the use of words that related to food items represent code for criminal sex trafficking. For this part, Fairbanks moved from Cernovich to another alt-right persona, the @JaredWyand Twitter handle. Wyand is an online persona associated with the alt-right who, after having been banned from Twitter, was warmly embraced by the Daily Stormer for postings such as "The Media is nothing more than the propaganda arm for our Zionist occupational government" and "This is all orchestrated by Jews to topple Western Civilization and reshape it in their vision."[11] The @JaredWyand Twitter handle had been central to several distinct campaigns tied to Russian interests—a Twitter campaign to negate allegations of Russian doping at the World Anti-Doping Agency, Twitter campaigns around the Vault7 leak of CIA cyber surveillance and warfare tools, and one of a cluster of accounts active on the French far right during the 2017 French presidential election, and was actively tweeting on six of the top 10 most widely reported stories linking to any of the Podesta emails.[12] Fairbanks used the JaredWyand tweets as the basis to report that "[t]heories and screenshots began to swirl, claiming that bizarrely-worded emails about food were codes for child sex trafficking." Fairbanks qualified her reporting with "It is important to note that this is originated on anonymous message boards, and the 'keywords' were not listed in any of the emails." This disclaimer, however, was immediately followed by several tweets from JaredWyand and the interview with "lawyer and popular author/journalist" Mike Cernovich repeating versions of the idea that it was code. The start of the article includes, as an example of the "code for child sex" in the title, an image that Fairbanks described as "Asian girls eating pizza" (Figure 7.2).

The first appearance of the term "pizza" in combination with pedophilia or child sex in our data set is in a November 3 Reddit post, "Someone tell me I'm wrong!" That post listed all the various ways in which the word "pizza" appeared in the Podesta emails, and speculated that pizza is a code word for sex trafficking in children.[13] The next appearance is another Reddit post, which collects a set of Reddit threads that bear on the theory.[14] And the third appearance is Cassandra Fairbanks' post from WeAreChange that

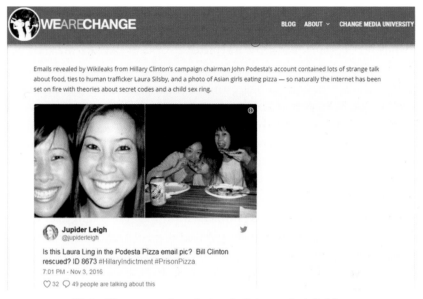

Emails revealed by Wikileaks from Hillary Clinton's campaign chairman John Podesta's account contained lots of strange talk about food, ties to human trafficker Laura Silsby, and a photo of Asian girls eating pizza — so naturally the internet has been set on fire with theories about secret codes and a child sex ring.

Jupider Leigh
@jupiderleigh

Is this Laura Ling in the Podesta Pizza email pic? Bill Clinton rescued? ID 8673 #HillaryIndictment #PrisonPizza
7:01 PM - Nov 3, 2016
♡ 32 ♡ 49 people are talking about this

FIGURE 7.2 WeAreChange story introducing the "pizza pedophilia" frame.

pulls these theories together.[15] The "Comet Pizza" aspect of the story was added on November 7 and took on a life of its own.[16] WikiLeaks picked up Fairbanks' Abramovich story at 1:00 a.m. on November 4. Seven hours later, the Infowars segment curated both of Fairbanks's November 3 stories and Cernovich's into a collection of insinuations that the spirit cooking email was tied to occult satanic sex practices and that these were, in turn, linked to trafficking in children, to the "Lolita Express," and to the use of pizza-related code words to stand for sex trafficking. Amplified within minutes by Drudge, the core insinuation made it to Hannity and the *Washington Times* three or four hours later. Over the course of the day, versions of the story were repeated on Gateway Pundit (which included Michelle Malkin's tweet promoting attention to #SpiritCooking),[17] Truthfeed, WND, Western Journalism, Ending the Fed, and Before It's News.

Assuming that after Infowars and Drudge dissemination was primarily through direct exposure of these highly visible sites, with our colleague Justin Clark we examined 76,127 tweets from 19,696 accounts that mentioned spirit cooking, Abramovic, or otherwise met a broad search for tweets related to the conspiracy before publication of the Infowars story. Of these, nine tweets from eight accounts were from Twitter handles identified by the House Intelligence Committee as Russian-operated accounts. Two of these preceded the WikiLeaks tweet. As a robustness check, we compared these tweets to the broader private list of Twitter handles central to other Russia-related campaigns, which we described in the Jared Wyand context, and found that accounts that had participated in at least three such campaigns accounted for about 4 percent of the accounts, and 8 percent of the tweets prior to the Infowars story. Similarly, they accounted for 7 percent of the tweets that mentioned @Wikileaks, and 6 percent of the tweets aimed at Alex Jones with this story. The time signature of these tweets and accounts is more or less flat as a proportion of tweets, accounting for between 5 percent and 15 percent of the tweets in any given minute between publication of the Fairbanks story and the Infowars story. That temporal signature is more consistent with a background presence and continuous engagement of active Twitter accounts that were also involved in Russian campaigns than with a coordinated campaign to influence WikiLeaks or Alex Jones to publicize this particular story, or to amplify it to a degree not otherwise consistent with background attention among right-wing and conspiracy-minded Twitter users looking for such stories to amplify.

The spirit cooking story perfectly encapsulates the propaganda pipeline from the periphery to the core, drawing in the various suspects in producing information disorder and the relationships among them. One suspect is the Russian information operation. Certainly, the email hack itself was Russian. Cassandra Fairbanks, a Sputnik reporter, wrote the report that curated and transmitted the Reddit, Twitter, and 4chan memes into a package that was then tweeted and shared on Facebook by WikiLeaks overnight and became the basis for an Infowars story by morning. The JaredWyand handle had appeared in other Russia-consistent campaigns quite prominently, most clearly the arguments against the World Anti-Doping Agency's sanctions against Russian athletes. The low-level background presence of known or arguably Russian Twitter handles in the propagation period is also observable. The Reddit and 4chan posts themselves, by contrast, are consistent with models in work that focuses on how alt-right trolls on these platforms experimented with memes that they tried to insert into mainstream media.[18] These were early[19] posts that got out a few hours ahead of the story,[20] and some developed quite imaginative conspiracy theories around pizza party invitations.[21] The involvement of Cernovich also connects the story to the alt-right, as does Jared Wyand, assuming he represents an authentic alt-right persona rather than a Russian plant. Ending the Fed is one of the most successful original "fake news" sites from the November 2016 BuzzFeed story. All the dramatis persona of information disorder are here. And yet, the amplification depended first on WikiLeaks' Twitter and Facebook accounts, then on Alex Jones and Drudge, and then on the rapid and enthusiastic embrace by all the major nodes in the right-wing propaganda network over the course of several hours. It would have been standard practice for a well-balanced media ecosystem to simply refuse to touch such a far-fetched story or actively to debunk it. But the cultural and commercial model of the outlets that picked up the story was not aimed at producing objective journalism. It was designed to produce cathartic outrage in its readers and viewers and to be rewarded by clicks and views. It was aimed to produce a sense of "us against them." Its goal was to disseminate images, descriptions, and video clearly intended to evoke a visceral reaction of disgust, and through that disgust to mobilize viewers, readers, and listeners to political action. And as we saw in Chapter 3, the two parts of the American media ecosystem differ systematically in the incentives and institutional constraints media outlets face. On the right, in particular, the propaganda feedback loop had made the cost of publishing falsehood that is consistent with partisan bias low, and the opportunity to present the publication as being at the forefront of the truth-telling brigade valiantly uncovering corruption, perfidy, and perversion by the opposing party was highly valued. As we saw in both Chapters 3 and 6, in the rest of the media environment the opposite incentives operated, and the institutional structures and attention patterns of audiences made amplifying these kinds of falsehoods more costly.

While the propaganda pipeline can, then, work to transmit narratives from the periphery to the core, our analysis suggests that the major frames and narratives of the campaign and the first year of the Trump presidency did not arise from this pattern. Even the Clinton pedophilia narrative was driven first and foremost by Malia Zimmerman's and Bret Baier's stories on Fox News in May 2016, which were then revived on Breitbart radio and online by Erik Prince, as we described in Chapter 3, not by the spirit cooking and Pizzagate stories that came from the periphery. Indeed, the Pizzagate story started exactly as the spirit cooking story started—on 4chan and Reddit, picked up and curated by Cernovich and Fairbanks, and then rolled up and propagated by Infowars—but never made it up further through the pipeline. The pipeline exists. The trolls, propagandists, and marginal figures know about it and want to leverage it. But it can only work with willing and active complicity of outlets higher up the chain—Drudge, Hannity, and the rest of the more visible members of the media ecosystem. And their complicity, in turn, depends on the architecture of the network within which they themselves sit, the incentives it gives them, and the institutional constraints it imposes or fails to impose on them.

8

Are the Russians Coming?

BY EARLY 2018 only the willfully blind or complicit could continue to reject the proposition that Russia has been running information operations for years aimed at intensifying political divisions and weakening democracy in the United States and Europe. From diverse perspectives and efforts, accounts by journalists and academics, intelligence agencies in the United States and Europe, and the special counsel investigating relations between the Trump campaign and Russia have supported this finding. Even the Trump-supportive House Intelligence Committee investigation confirmed that Russia had mounted cyberattacks on American targets and used social media to sow discord during the 2016 election. A weaker European Union, and a more fractured U.S. polity and inwardly-focused U.S. foreign policy, would leave Russia with greater leeway to pursue its own foreign policy goals, and a steady stream of news about Western democracies in disarray offers legitimacy for Vladimir Putin's own brand of strongman illiberal populism. If we were persuaded that Russian propaganda and interference were the primary reason that the United States elected a president so congenial to Russia's interests; that the third largest economy in Europe, the United Kingdom, had voted to depart the Union; that Spain and Catalonia came to the verge of splitting; or that Italy's Euroskeptics won a majority of the seats in Italy's parliament, we would be observing the most dramatically successful attack on democracy since the end of World War II.

Three primary sources of skepticism, or at least caution, about the Russian interference hypothesis emerged during the year after the election. First, supporters of President Trump resisted the implication that Trump's election was a victory for Russian information warfare not the American people. Second, veteran watchers of the controversy over weapons of mass destruction and intelligence on Iraq, and the media groupthink failures that

Network Propaganda. Yochai Benkler, Robert Faris, and Hal Roberts.
© Yochai Benkler, Robert Faris, and Hal Roberts 2018. Published 2018 by Oxford University Press.

accompanied them, took the interagency consensus on Russia with a grain of salt. Both of these lines of skepticism were on display in Chapter 5: the Fox News interventions for the former, and the Glenn Greenwald articles for the latter. The third form is standard academic working skepticism. This is simply the result of applying rigorous standards of proof to claims and assessing the stronger and weaker aspects of claims by these standards. In this chapter we apply this standard and explain why we are persuaded by the weight of the evidence that there was a sustained Russian effort; but we offer reasons for caution around some of the more expansive narratives—that the social media environment was overrun by Russian bots or that street protests in America were fomented to a significant degree by Russian agitation. We emphasize the difference between proof of the existence of Russian efforts and proof of their impact and suggest that the evidence of impact is less clear. In particular we are guided by the observation that the primary goal of Russian disinformation is to instill a sense that *"Nothing is True and Everything is Possible,"*[1] or to "dismiss, distort, distract, and dismay."[2] If that is the case, then to overstate the prevalence and effect of Russian attacks is to aid their success. Just as terrorism succeeds most when it evokes an overreaction and causes a society to respond from fear and anger rather than calculation, so too will Russian active measures have their largest effect through evoking a harmful autoimmune response from the countries under attack.

Our primary contribution here is to examine the interaction between the asymmetric architecture of the American media ecosystem that we discovered in our own work and the presence of the Russian efforts. In a nutshell what we observe is that Russian efforts take advantage of existing fissures and pathways. The differences between the right-wing media ecosystem and the ecosystem occupied by the rest, from the center to the left, make the former more susceptible to propagandist efforts than the latter. The insular, domestically produced network of sites and social media diffusion networks that traffic in politically motivated falsehoods, coupled with the persistent attacks on mainstream media and other evidence-based institutions and expertise, have made the right wing of the American media ecosystem more susceptible to penetration, less resilient, and less capable of self-correction. When Russian propaganda efforts are consistent with right-wing American framings and beliefs, these falsehoods are able to insert themselves, propagate, and gain credence in the right-wing media ecosystem. By contrast, similar efforts aimed to leverage left-wing biases have to overcome the basic checks provided by a media ecosystem inhabited by professional-norms-oriented media outlets.

Russian Origins

Vladimir Putin's first term in office from 2000 to 2008 was marked by a highly restrictive policy toward mass media but permissive policy toward online communication. Internet penetration in Russia was low, and the reputational costs of a significant crackdown on a symbolically important but politically marginal medium likely outweighed the perceived political risks associated with letting the internet flourish. By the end of Putin's first two terms, LiveJournal had become the dominant blogging platform, and a report authored by Bruce Etling, one of us (Faris), and several other of our colleagues concluded "the political blogosphere appears to remain a free and open space for Russians of all political stripes to discuss politics, criticize or support government, fight corrupt practices and officials, and to mobilize others around political and social causes."[3] It was into this relatively open, highly contested networked public sphere that Dmitry Medvedev entered, earning the nickname "Blogger-in-Chief" from one observer.[4] In support of his activity, Medvedev's government began to redirect youth movements originally developed to counter any Russian "color revolution" efforts on the streets to online activity, and trolls and bots made their first observed appearance in Russian online debates.[5]

The major change, however, coincided with Putin's return to office in 2012 and in response to the most sustained and forceful protests since the implosion of the Soviet Union. A combination of changes in ownership and direct legal pressure forced online platforms Yandex, Vkontakte, and LiveJournal to suppress oppositional voices, and media critical of the government were forced to change leadership, often leading reporters to emigrate and set up shop abroad. Moreover, the wide-open, commercial nature of the Russian internet before 2012 gave birth to companies highly proficient in search engine optimization and commercially oriented trolling. These capabilities became the foundation of the new state-managed online information campaigns against opposition leaders.

In 2013 independent Russian investigative journalists published the first reports on the Internet Research Agency (IRA), which would ultimately be indicted by Robert Mueller in 2018. Registered in 2013, the IRA would become a troll factory, employing paid agents to shape online conversations. Russian investigative reporters critical of the government went undercover and reported repeatedly on the agency from 2013 to 2015.[6] Looking at the research on online communications in Russian politics from the first decade of the twenty-first century, it seems quite clear that the capabilities deployed against the United States in the 2016 election cycle and beyond were still in their infancy by the time they were deployed. There was one investigative journalism piece by Russian expats as early as 2003 observing patterns of information manipulation by "Internet brigades" within the Russian media ecosystem. That report was also the basis of the first academic English-language description of Russian "third generation controls" on internet discourse in 2010 by Deibert and Rohozinski.[7] Deibert and Rohozinski identified coordinated campaigns by " 'Internet brigades' to engage, confuse, or discredit individuals or sources. Such action can include the posting of prepackaged propaganda, *kompromat*, and disinformation through mass blogging and participation in Internet polls, or harassment of individual users, including the posting of personal information."[8] The most publicly prominent voice raising the alarm about this class of attacks on democracy was Evgeny Morozov in *The Net Delusion* in 2011, who offered it as a frontal assault on the then-prevailing wisdom that the internet democratizes political discourse.[9]

The early investigative journalism and academic work on the Russian internet was complemented by national security research following the Ukranian crisis of 2014.[10] Reports from researchers studying Russian national security, including think tanks in Central and Eastern Europe and some in NATO, began to evaluate operations in Russia and its near sphere, from Georgia to Ukraine, Moldova, and beyond. By March 2015 the European Council was concerned enough to form the European Union's East StratCom Task Force to deal with the dangers of Russian information operations in the "Eastern Partnership" countries—Armenia, Azerbaijan, Belarus, Georgia, Moldova, and Ukraine. This body of research precedes the U.S. election and identified strategies remarkably congruent with those observed in other countries by diverse researchers who are not all on the same page. For skeptical Americans concerned that the Russia story is a groupthink overreaction to the election, this body of research should offer some increased confidence that it is real. Perhaps, as some suggest, present Russian doctrine merely updates Soviet "active measures." Perhaps it reflects adaptation and extension of strategies that Russian military and intelligence leaders believe the United States used to undermine Russia in its own sphere of influence. The most obvious trajectory is that what we saw in Russian operations in America is merely an extension of the strategies that the Russian state developed to quell domestic political debate after the 2011–2012 protests. Whatever its origin, the sum of the extensive Russia-centered literature is to document that present Russian doctrine and practice, at home, in its near periphery and increasingly in the European Union, involves extensive information operations of roughly the form observed in the United States during the election period and since. These techniques include breaking into computer systems to obtain compromising information and releasing it in public; creating false accounts on social media to propagate opinions and reports; leveraging the affordances of social media advertising platforms; and combining white propaganda on RT and Sputnik with gray and black propaganda sites and social media accounts to disseminate and add credibility to false information and propagate destabilizing disinformation.

Hacking and Doxxing

Beginning a week after Hillary Clinton formally secured a majority of the Democratic delegates to the convention, and culminating in a big WikiLeaks email dump on the Friday before the Democratic National Convention opened, someone began to release batches of emails on a site called DCLeaks, emails obtained by hackers from the email system of the Democratic National Committee (DNC). The crux of the most damaging emails, particularly those released by WikiLeaks on the eve of the Democratic National Convention on July 22, 2016, showed that DNC leadership had strongly favored Hillary Clinton over Bernie Sanders, despite the organization's commitment to neutrality among the primary candidates. This forced the resignation of then-DNC Chair Debbie Wasserman Schultz.[11]

Hacking into opponents' email and computer systems, obtaining compromising information, and then "leaking" it back out to the public as part of an online propaganda campaign is a technique Russian propaganda efforts have used repeatedly in Russia and abroad.[12] Immediately after the first DNC breach, CrowdStrike, the security firm hired by the DNC to investigate the breach, came out with a report claiming that the hack had been perpetrated by two Russian groups, Fancy Bear and Cozy Bear. One was allegedly associated with the GRU, Russian military intelligence, the other was possibly associated with the FSB (successor to the KGB).[13] Over the next few months, other information security firms and expert groups such as FireEye and ThreatConnect added their own independent assessments, concluding that the digital forensic evidence supported the proposition that the DNC hack was perpetrated by Russian operations.[14] In October and December of 2016, the Department of Homeland Security and the FBI released joint statements asserting that the DNC hack was likely directed by the Russian government and that the attacks and subsequent leaks were "consistent with the methods and motivations of Russian-directed efforts."[15]

On January 6, the Office of the Director of National Intelligence (ODNI) released a joint assessment by the FBI, CIA, and NSA that included a broader and more detailed set of assertions.[16] This assessment attributed the DNC and Podesta email hacks to Russian state actors (although on this question the report was heavy on "trust us" and light on forensic details). It also claimed that these were part of a broader propaganda and social media campaign (again, though, focused on RT rather than any more exotic efforts). And it explicitly rejected the idea that Russia had tried or succeeded in any way in tampering with the 2016 vote-tallying process. Pushing back on the findings of this report was a central feature of the Seth Rich story we noted in Chapter 5. We return to that theme here in the context of describing white and gray propaganda. For now, we accept the consensus of diverse commercial information security firms, technology trade press investigations, mainstream media reports, and the consensus assessment of the U.S. intelligence community.

Social Media Influence: Sockpuppets, Bots, Cyborgs, and Ads

The indictment issued by Robert Mueller against the Internet Research Agency, Yevgeny Prigozhin, and other Russian nationals offered detailed allegations regarding the pattern of Russian intervention, combining false accounts on Facebook and Twitter, bots, strategic targeted advertising bought under false identity, and mobilizing real-space protests by unwitting Americans.[17] The core strategy, according to the indictment, was to increase disaffection, distrust, and polarization in American politics. The practical targeting seemed intended to boost enough of the white-identity vote to drive voters to the polls in states that made the difference, to suppress enough of the black vote, and to suppress enough of the left vote or divert it to Green Party candidate Jill Stein, to tip the election. Given the baseline purpose of undermining trust in democratic institutions, however, simply sowing these divisive themes would have been a perfectly reasonable consolation prize. There were two core claims in the indictment. First, it claimed that the defendants had infiltrated social media networks through the use of false accounts, whether fully automated (bots), humans masquerading as someone other than who they are (sockpuppets), or some combination of the two (cyborgs). Second, it claimed that they bought targeted political advertising online under false accounts and presented themselves as authentic American political activists to spread divisive narratives, organize real-world protests, and push stories that undermined Hillary Clinton and supported Donald Trump. We take this indictment not as proof but as one piece of evidence among many pointing toward the reality of Russian interference in the election. We will use its precision and confidence later in this chapter to raise questions about the likely actual impact on the election and the American public sphere more generally.

The indictment's allegations are congruent with independent reports by investigative journalists, disclosures by Facebook, Twitter, and Google in their testimonies to the House and Senate intelligence committees, and academic studies of Russian operations. Following the first round of committee hearings, Facebook issued a report in April 2017 on "information operations" that was widely read to cover Russia's activities, although it avoided saying so. In anticipation of the second round of congressional hearings, Facebook released an updated report,[18] as did Twitter.[19] Facebook, Twitter, and Google returned to testify in late October, when the most extensive disclosures occurred. Democrats on the House Intelligence Committee released a sample of ads that had been shown on Facebook and that, according to the company, had been purchased by agents of Russia. The ads disclosed various groups masquerading as American activists on both the right, such as Defend the 2d, Secured Borders, and Stop A.I. (where A.I. stood for "All Invaders," not "artificial intelligence") and the left, such as Blacktivists and LGBT United. These releases included methods clearly intended to instigate street clashes, such as publishing ads for opposing protests on the same day across the street from each other, one called "Stop Islamization of Texas" and the other called "United Muslims of America." Facebook's testimony reported that the Internet Research Agency campaign had published 80,000 posts that were shown directly to over 29 million people.

A team led by Young Mie Kim of the University of Wisconsin leveraged the Facebook groups identified by the minority report of the House Intelligence Committee to produce the best study of Facebook advertising by, among others, suspicious Russian groups. They found that 5.6 percent of the Facebook ads served to their large, nationally representative sample of subjects were from one of these sites, and their work obviously identified only a lower bound of Russian intervention using purchased ads.[20] Facebook also testified that Russians had used Instagram to share over 120,000 photos from 170 accounts. And committee Democrats released a list of over 2,700 Twitter handles that have since become the canonical set in efforts to study Russian influence on Twitter. Twitter claimed that the handles had posted over 130,000 tweets during the election period. Beyond these, Twitter testified that the company had identified 36,000 Russia-linked bots that had shared 1.4 million tweets that received about 288 million views. Google, for its part, testified that it believed the Internet Research Agency had bought ads on YouTube, ran 18 channels, and uploaded over 1,100 videos, which they reported as having received very few views: a total of 309,000 views spread across the 1,100 videos. All three companies emphasized that, while the absolute numbers seem large, they represent tiny slivers of the total amount of posts, tweets, videos, and other engagements and uses of their respective sites.[21]

Both before and after these reports, journalists reported a series of stories fleshing out these techniques. A report in the Daily Beast, for example, was the first to document a real-world anti-immigrant protest in Twin Falls, Idaho. The rally was organized using Facebook events by the Russian-controlled site Secured Borders.[22] CNN similarly reported and offered details of the incendiary efforts of Blacktivist, a month before the details about the account emerged in congressional testimony. The *Wall Street Journal* reported that four of these highly divisive accounts, Secured Borders, Blacktivist, Heart of Texas, and Being Patriotic, had between them nearly a million followers.[23] The *New York Times* tried to track down "Melvin Reddick of Harrisburg Pennsylvania," who used Facebook to promote DCLeaks, the site initially used to tease the DNC emails before the broader release on WikiLeaks. They were unable to locate anyone in the United States who matched the profile, but a Brazilian site took interest and with help from their readers located the man, a Brazilian national, whose picture was used in the account.[24]

As a report from the Atlantic Council's Digital Forensics Labs makes clear, however, the most extensive and in-depth reporting came from independent Russian journalists, some working abroad for fear of retaliation, who uncovered much of this activity.[25] Polina Rusyayeva and Andrei Zakharov, journalists at RBC, a media group that has published stories critical of business interests close to Valdimir Putin and come under pressure from the Russian government for it,[26] published the most comprehensive leaked set of Facebook, Twitter, and Instagram accounts run by the Internet Research Agency in the U.S. election. These included accounts aimed at African American audiences, such as Blacktivist or DON'Tshoot; accounts aimed at anti-immigrant sentiment, such as Secured Borders and Stop all Invaders; at Republicans, such as TEN_GOP and Tpartynews; and at police officers, such as Back the Badge or Pray4Police; and so forth.[27]

Some more detail on the commonly-used terminology is useful. "Bots" refer to fully automated accounts or scripts that simply share, tweet, or retweet news headlines, with or without links, retweet other accounts, or exhibit similarly simple actions in high volumes with minimal human supervision. "Sockpuppets" usually refers to fully human accounts that pretend to be people they are not. We prefer "sockpuppets" to "trolls," because the "trolls" term has been used in two quite different meanings in the debate. In long-standing studies of 4chan and other internet countercultures, the term had quite distinct meanings that were more nihilist than programmatic. As three of the leading scholars of these hacking and trolling subcultures argue, by 2017 "trolling" in American usage had come to mean too many things in too many contexts to continue to be a useful analytic category.[28] In Russia-centered studies, by contrast, "trolls" means human participants paid to intervene in an online conversation to shape it in favor of whoever is paying them. That was the *Russian* usage, identified in Russia, by the *Novaya Gazeta* report that first outed the Internet Research Agency.[29] We prefer "sockpuppet" to "human" because we think it important to separate out instances where human beings are presenting their own real persona, even if paid, and those where an individual takes on one or more persona that they manage in a fully human process but present to the outside world as someone other than who they are. We mean this to cover individuals paid to post repeatedly, captured by the "50 Cent Army" metaphor applied to both China and Russia, whether they do so by controlling one account or several. Increasingly these actors use scripts and supervised automation to increase their effectiveness. Accounts that use these practices are increasingly described as "cyborg" by social media researchers.[30]

White Propaganda, Gray Propaganda, and Useful Idiots

There are several other major pieces of the Russian interference puzzle: the role of the state-owned RT and Sputnik in developing and reporting stories targeted at specific countries; the role of apparently local media outlets that are in fact run by Russian agents; and the role of genuinely local media that propagate Russian-developed narratives, wittingly or unwittingly, either to push a political agenda or to attract readers and advertising dollars. The latter are the "useful idiots." In Cold War–era propaganda studies, "white" propaganda referred to communications by an outlet acknowledged to be of one party or another, where the information was more or less accurate but framed to favor that party. "Black" propaganda referred to spreading lies and deception through falsely described sources. "Gray" propaganda was somewhere in between.

The January 6, 2017, ODNI report focused heavily on RT as a major source of propaganda. The report particularly emphasized a number of statements that RT editor-in-chief Margarita Simonyan made to various Russian and foreign outlets. Those statements explicitly described RT's role as a state-funded outlet to serve as an important part of Russia's defense system in the information wars.[31] In our own studies RT was a moderately visible site during and after the U.S. election, shared more by Trump followers than Clinton followers, by a 3:2 ratio. The relatively low direct visibility of RT, however, understates the impact of the site through repetition of its stories on other sites in the network. Some of those propagandist sites are masked Russian outlets (gray propaganda), and some are pawns who repeat the Russian line for their own purposes.

Infowars, the eighth-most tweeted site on the right, repeatedly republishes RT content. A BuzzFeed investigative report found that Infowars had republished over 1,000 stories with an RT byline between 2014 and 2017, without RT's permission.[32] Analyzing the text of stories in our own 2017 set, we found 431 stories in which a sentence of at least 32 words on Infowars was identical to one found on RT. Those stories account for about 3 percent of the Infowars stories in our 2017 dataset. The stories generally either simply republish RT content or quote and link to the site. Sean Adl-Tabatabai, the author of YourNewsWire.com, which has risen to a position of significant visibility in the right-wing media ecosystem and played a prominent role in propagating Pizzagate and the Seth Rich conspiracy, responded to an interview question from the *Evening Standard* with "I love Russia Today!" The *Evening Standard* author described RT as "one of his most cited sources" and followed up with: "You are aware that it's Russian propaganda, right?" to which Adl-Tabatabai responded, "Well, the BBC is British propaganda. It's the same thing."[33] In other words, it would be a mistake to imagine that the primary role of RT is to propagate content directly through social media campaigns. Rather, the evidence suggests that RT intentionally serves as a source and hub of a much more diffuse network of sites that reuse narratives the station produces.

In the other direction, RT and Sputnik offer accreditation for others who carry the Russian line. For example, in the case of the campaign to smear the White Helmets, a humanitarian organization in Syria, RT and Sputnik gave significant prominence and repetition to blogger Vanessa Beeley, associate editor of 21stcenturywire.com, who was at the epicenter of the Russian-led disinformation campaign.[34]

In our study of the "deep state" frame, we found that RT gave Ron Paul a platform to propagate the idea just after the election, that Sputnik published a piece by an editor of 21stcenturywire.com, and that both sites repeated this frame often throughout 2017. Zero Hedge offered guest publishing slots for The Saker (described in Chapter 5), who runs a site with quite a bit of Russian apologia, as well as an early piece from the Strategic Culture Foundation,[35] a Moscow-based think tank that *Politico* described as a part of Russian influence efforts.[36] Despite these traces of Russian efforts, the most important anchors of the deep state frame were American and came from diverse political orientations. The Virgil posts on Breitbart and its full-throated embrace by Fox offered a quite distinct frame from the Greenwald pieces. But it would be a stretch to imagine that either Greenwald or Breitbart needed Russian prompting to frame their criticism as they did. Similarly, in Chapter 7 we saw the central role that Cassandra Fairbanks, then working for Sputnik but publishing on WeAreChange, played in weaving together the spirit cooking and Pizzagate narratives. Reddit users and alt-right characters concocted those narratives from the Russian-hacked Podesta emails and fed them into stories that WikiLeaks, Infowars, and Drudge pushed up the propaganda pipeline.

From our observations of the last three years, there is one example that might count as a significant temporary success of the interplay between white, gray, and black propaganda. It involves the Guccifer 2.0–Adam Carter–Forensicator line of attack on the Russian origins of the DNC hack, which was interwoven with the Seth Rich conspiracy theory we encountered in Chapter 5, but was quite distinct. In particular this line of attack was more directed toward harnessing the national security skepticism that characterized the Greenwald posts than the partisanship of the Breitbart/Fox variety. We say that this story "might" count as a success because the evidence that it was primarily a Russian effort, as opposed to genuine pseudonymous critics of the national security establishment or fans of WikiLeaks, who were then aided at the margins by Russian propagandists, is circumstantial. We say the success was "temporary," because it succeeded in changing the public narrative around the DNC leak for about two months in the middle of 2017 before the orientation of the narrative returned to the original configuration of the right in opposition to the rest of the media ecosystem.

As we described in discussing hacking and doxxing, by the time that the ODNI released its January 6, 2016, report, there was broad consensus that the DNC had been hacked by Russian operations and that the "Guccifer

2.0" persona who claimed responsibility was a Russian cover (an allegation later elaborated and supported in a July 2018 indictment by the special counsel). On February 8, 2017, a person writing under the pseudonym Adam Carter first published what would become a regularly updated blog post describing the reasons to doubt that Guccifer 2.0 was in fact part of a Russian information operation. He argued that Guccifer 2.0 was an effort by the Clinton campaign or the DNC to point the finger at Russia and discredit WikiLeaks.[37] The primary evidence was that metadata from the documents Guccifer 2.0 released suggested that the document was in fact created by a person with ties to the Democratic National Committee. On February 17, as the deep state narrative was spinning up in response to the Michael Flynn resignation, a different person going by the handle tvor_22 and the Cyrillic нет (nyet) published a later-deleted post on Medium that analyzed the documents made public by Guccifer 2.0. That post argued that the extremely obvious ways that Guccifer 2.0 "hid" clues of being Russian were best explained as efforts by the DNC to hide the origin of the leaks, by the CIA to besmirch Russia, or by Russia to sow disinformation and chaos.[38] On March 8, tvor_22 published another deeply ironic post suggesting that the Russian Bear "paw prints" all over the alleged hacks were so laughably clumsy that they were more likely to be CIA false flag operations than actual Russian operations.[39] Whether this account was a bemused hacker ironically taking on an obviously made-up Russian persona to state that the paw prints were too obviously Russian to have been really Russian, or whether it was a Russian information operation pretending to be such a bemused hacker, is anyone's guess.

On March 20, 2017, the House Intelligence Committee ran its Hearing on Russian Active Measures. Representative Adam Schiff's opening statement underscored the sustained Russian attack, connecting the DNC hack, the DCLeaks site, and the Guccifer 2.0 diversion operation as elements in the attack on the American presidential campaign.[40] In response Sputnik News reporter Cassandra Fairbanks tweeted "Pretty sure Guccifer 2 is not a 'creature of Russia,' @RepAdamSchiff" and attached a screenshot of a direct message exchange she had had with Guccifer 2.0 on August 24, 2016. In that exchange she offered to interview Guccifer 2.0, and he answered that he would rather that she interview him for her WeAreChange blog, saying "I don't like sputnik coz it's Russian."[41] Who exactly might be persuaded by a Sputnik reporter sharing a purported screenshot from an alleged Russian agent claiming that he is not in fact a Russian agent, is a curious question. These Fairbanks tweets were then included in the Adam Carter blog as part of the evidence that Guccifer 2.0 was not a Russian job. The Senate Select

Committee on Intelligence then held its open hearings on disinformation and Russian active measures on March 30.

Following the congressional hearings, April saw an uptick in Seth Rich and Guccifer 2.0 conspiracies. On April 8, former Playboy model Robbin Young published a set of purported screenshots from Twitter direct message exchanges with Guccifer 2.0. In one of the messages Guccifer 2.0 asked for help investigating "the real story of his life and death … his name is seth, he was my whistleblower."[42] That same day the WikiLeaks Twitter account tweeted Young's DMs, linking Adam Carter's site, which hosted a copy of the DM exchange.[43] Stories on Heat Street and republished on Zero Hedge with the clickbaity title 'Guccifer 2.0' Chat With Nude Model Sparks New Conspiracy Theories About Seth Rich Murder" followed,[44] joining the Gateway Pundit.[45] Fox and Friends then also reported on the Robbin Young–Guccifer exchange as raising the question of Seth Rich's murder, although added that "it's not clear if the messages are, in fact, authentic."[46] Toward the end of April, Cassandra Fairbanks returned to the conversation with two stories in Big League Politics. In the first, she used alleged screenshots from Twitter DMs with Guccifer. She described her relationship with Guccifer as involving the writing of a story about the leaks. "At this point," Fairbanks wrote, "I was still supporting Sanders in the primary." Among those chats, she reported, Guccifer 2.0 tied the death of Shawn Lucas, who had served papers on the DNC alleging primary fraud against Sanders, to that of Seth Rich.[47] In the second, she reported on Adam Carter's allegations that Guccifer had deliberately planted Russian fingerprints on his account.[48] It was clear that at this point the Guccifer 2.0 story was trying to attract left-wing partisans whose skepticism of the national security establishment would outweigh their partisan proclivity to believe the worst of Donald Trump. Between the Guccifer 2.0 persona, Fairbanks's position at Sputnik, the timing surrounding the congressional hearings into Russian interference, and the party most likely to benefit from this shift in blame, circumstantially this storyline exhibits more hints of a Russian effort than does the Seth Rich episode, which would soon took center stage in May and June.

On July 8, 2017, the *New York Times* published its first story on the famous Trump Tower meeting arranged by Donald Trump Jr. with Natalia Veselnitskaya.[49] The next day, they followed up with reporting that Trump Jr. had been enticed to the meeting with the prospect of damaging information on Hillary Clinton. That same day, an individual working under the pseudonym the Forensicator published an analysis of the Guccifer 2.0 metadata, introducing a new factor into the analysis of the email leak/

hack: the data transfer rate at which the files were copied was too high for any existing broadband connection to sustain, much less from an international connection.[50] The story was then reported on Disobedient Media[51]—a website that is hard to peg as either clearly left or right—generally skeptical of powers that be, but with a heavy focus on WikiLeaks and Julian Assange (when we observed the site, four of twelve stories under "U.S. Politics" concerned Assange; another four covered the Nunes memo). Adam Carter is the site's technology writer. Its cofounder and contributor, William Craddick, is also a contributor to Zero Hedge, where his profile proudly announces that he "[d]iscovered and published the Clinton-Silsby human trafficking scandal"[52] that we encountered in Cassandra Fairbanks's posts in Chapter 7.

From there, the story spread through the by now usual suspects on the right: the Free Republic, the Gateway Pundit, Zero Hedge, and BB4SP, with a Zero Hedge story getting the extra credit of citation by the Daily Stormer prefaced by "Well, if the Jews and their shills thought this was the end of their troubles, they were wrong."[53] Unsurprisingly, RT carried the story as well.[54] The story also appeared on a subreddit for supporters of Bernie Sanders, r/WayOfTheBern. There, the post laid out the Adam Carter and Forensicator analyses and concluded: "In short, *Russiagate is a hoax concocted by the DNC in collaboration with Crowdstrike, and given the stamp of approval by Deep State tools—hand-picked by James Clapper—eager to defame Russia. The Democrats and the MSM subsequently embellished this narrative by claiming that the Trump campaign somehow had 'colluded' in Russia's non-existent interference.*" (emphasis in original). [55] The post was clearly trying to leverage the dual valence of the "deep state" frame—appealing to the older, more general anti-national-security-establishment frame—even as the frame continues to do work on the right in its new, more partisan form. Despite this one appearance on the left, the story remained almost exclusively in right-wing media for the next two weeks.

On July 24, 2017, a group of former U.S. intelligence professionals published an open letter to the president on consortiumnews.com, questioning the consensus view of the active intelligence community that the DNC hack was perpetrated by Russian intelligence.[56] Veteran Intelligence Professionals for Sanity (VIPS) had formed to protest manipulation of intelligence that led to the Iraq War.[57] The group who signed this open letter consisted, among others, of William Binney, Kirk Wiebe, and Ed Loomis, individuals who had been at the center of exposing the elements of the illegal surveillance programs initiated by the Bush administration after 9/11. These revelations later exploded in 2006, and parts were later corroborated in the materials by Edward Snowden. These were no crackpots or Russian stooges but respected professionals with a personal history of calling foul, getting it right, and for some of them, being persecuted for it by the Bush and Obama administrations. Some were heroes to libertarians and civil libertarians alike. The memo relied on the work and logic of the Forensicator and Adam Carter, which identified the "key fact" that

> someone working in the EDT time zone with a computer directly connected to the DNC server or DNC Local Area Network, copied 1,976 MegaBytes of data in 87 seconds onto an external storage device. That speed is much faster than what is physically possible with a hack." (emphasis in the original). It thus appears that the purported "hack" of the DNC by Guccifer 2.0 (the self-proclaimed WikiLeaks source) was not a hack by Russia or anyone else but was rather a copy of DNC data onto an external storage device.

They surmised from the metadata that downloading the volume of materials in the specified time would have required a download speed of 22.7 megabytes per second (slightly over 180 megabits per second). Using average speeds from speedtest.net, the authors of the VIPS memo argued that such speeds were not available in the United States from broadband providers but that that speed was very close to the speed usually obtained in downloading to a USB thumb drive. The memorandum hypothesized from these facts that a likely scenario was that the DNC wove a story of Russian interference to discredit any wrongdoing that the emails exposed, as well as to turn it to the disadvantage of Donald Trump, tarring him with being the preferred candidate of Vladimir Putin. The story was initially republished on a few left-wing sites and on the Antiwar blog, got substantial coverage on the right, and was picked up by RT and Sputnik as well.

On August 9 *The Nation* published a long piece by Patrick Lawrence, detailing the VIPS claims as well as the underlying work that Forensicator and Adam Carter had published.[58] The next day, Bloomberg published a column by Leonid Bershidsky. Bershidsky had been a journalist in Russia and wrote very publicly about his disillusionment with Russia when he emigrated to Germany after the Crimea annexation. His column suggested that the VIPS analysis and *The Nation* story demanded more serious coverage from traditional media. He further argued that the participation of such highly respected professionals warranted more than the back-of-the-hand treatment they had received from mainstream media.[59] *New York Magazine* and the

Washington Monthly published stories criticizing *The Nation* story, but with little analysis.[60] Salon published a piece summarizing the VIPS argument, claiming that mainstream media were ignoring the story because it was an embarrassment that they had all rushed to the wrong judgment and lamenting that the VIPS memo was receiving attention almost exclusively by right-wing media.[61]

Indeed, on the right all the top sites immediately picked up *The Nation* story and used its provenance as a major source of legitimation as a Breitbart headline makes clear: "Left-Wing Magazine The Nation Report Puts 'Russian Hack' DNC Narrative in Freefall."[62] Tucker Carlson interviewed Bill Binney on his show and framed the VIPS claims as "not just that the President Trump didn't collude with Russia, you're calling into question the core allegation; that Russia is responsible for hacking into the DNC server."[63] The VIPS memo did nothing of the sort. It made no claims at all about the broader "collusion" question and focused very specifically on evidence regarding the DNC hack. Nonetheless, the chyron filling the bottom of the screen cycled between "Former NSA Technical Director, Trump-Russia Collusion Story is Bogus, Agenda-Driven," and all caps "FMR NSA TECH DIR: NO PROOF OF COLLUSION."

Figure 8.1 bears attention. Carlson hosted Binney for five and a half minutes. For much of this time Binney focused narrowly and technically on the forensic evidence surrounding the DNC hack itself. His jargon was likely opaque to most TV viewing audiences. Carlson nodded gravely and

FIGURE 8.1 Bill Binney interview on Tucker Carlson, August 14, 2017.

listened intently. Binney said nothing about the Trump Tower meeting or the question of whether or not there was or was not collusion between the Trump campaign and Russian state operatives. But the core message was impossible to miss. An unimpeachable expert offered detailed technical analysis that refuted the core claim of the Trump-Russia investigation.

Figure 8.2 describes the link network of stories surrounding the Guccifer 2.0 analysis that resulted in this remarkable interview. It leaves no doubt as to the centrality of the interventions by Forensicator (both the WordPress blog and the publication on Disobedient Media) and by the Adam Carter blog (g-2space). It leaves no doubt that *The Nation* adoption of this storyline was key. The Intercept, as we will soon see, was actually part of the rejection of the theory, not its adoption, and came much later, in the autumn of 2017.

In the meantime, it seems that some of *The Nation*'s staff were rebelling against the publication of Lawrence's piece. By August 15, the *Washington*

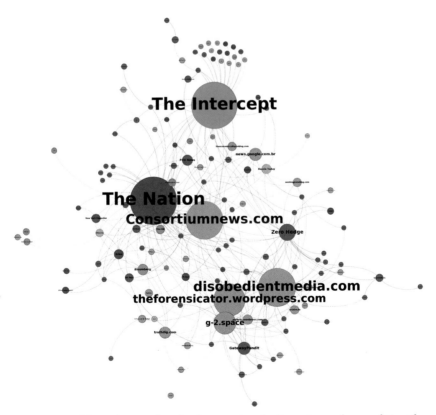

FIGURE 8.2 Network map of stories that mention the Forensicator theory of Guccifer 2.0. Architecture and node sizing by media inlinks.

Post reported that, under internal pressure from journalists at *The Nation*, the magazine was conducting a post-publication review.[64] On September 1, 2017, *The Nation* appended an editor's note to the original August 9 story and published a collection of pieces on the VIPS memo.[65] Those pieces included the results of an independent investigation of the VIPS memo that *The Nation* had asked Nathan Freitas of the Guardian Project to conduct, a countermemo by dissenting members of VIPS, including some like Thomas Drake and Jesselyn Radack, who had long been allied with Binney and other signatories on the original VIPS memo, and a response by the authors of the original VIPS memo. The Freitas memo offered a detailed technical analysis that explained how the Forensicator memorandum went well beyond the data available and how the original VIPS memo had extrapolated further beyond the Forensicator's analysis.[66] The VIPS dissenters also focused on the extent to which the Binney group had jumped to conclusions beyond those warranted by the Forensicator's analysis, rather than raising the less sensational but legitimate questions of why the intelligence community has not released detailed evidence supporting the claim that Russians had hacked the DNC servers.[67] The original VIPS memo authors responded, primarily emphasizing the devastating damage that the intelligence errors leading up to the Iraq War had caused and warning of the danger that we were, once again, suffering from a similar bout of groupthink.[68]

Major media outlets reported on the follow-up coverage in *The Nation*, which was viewed as a near-retraction of the original story in *The Nation*. Right-wing media covered the same collection of stories as an indication that *The Nation* caved in to mainstream anti-Trump media pressure. The story re-emerged in November, when two veteran national security reporters, Duncan Campbell and James Risen, reported in the Intercept that CIA Director Mike Pompeo had met Bill Binney at President Trump's request. The most notable feature of this story was that it was published in the Intercept, founded by Glenn Greenwald, who had been the most important source of skepticism of the Russia hypothesis outside of the right-wing media ecosystem, and who had long worked with national security whistle-blowers among the VIPS memo authors and dissenters. The November 7 story about the Binney-Pompeo meeting, however, emphasized the extent to which the VIPS-Binney-Forensicator theory had by now been abandoned and used the meetings primarily as a signal of concern that Pompeo was bending the CIA to serve Trump's agenda rather than preserving the independence of the agency. Other publications in the mainstream and left emphasized the impropriety of the Trump's intervention and the danger posed by a CIA director willing to bend the agency's mission to help the president politically. Publications on the right, by contrast, framed the meeting as further support for Binney's theories.

The Guccifer 2.0 case and those of Infowars, 21stcenturywire.com, True Pundit, YourNewsWire.com, and Zero Hedge, all present the basic difficulty of sorting out which of these are gray or black propaganda outlets, as opposed to honest critics promoted by propagandist outlets on one hand, and useful idiots just out to make a point or a buck, on the other.

True Pundit, a site founded in March 2016, has grown explosively during the first year of Trump's presidency and was identified by the German Marshall Fund's Hamilton 68 project (an online dashboard offering visualizations of "topics and URLs promoted by Russia-linked influence networks on Twitter") as one of the sites most widely promoted by Russian social media operations.[69] It showed up in our observations as one of the most tweeted sites involved in the propagation of the deep state frame. Practically nothing is known about the origins or authors of this successful site. A bit more is known of YourNewsWire.com. The site was described by Snopes as a "notorious fake news generating site," in the context of refuting its theory that the June 2017 suicide bombing at the Arian Grande concert in the Manchester Arena, in which 22 people were killed and over one hundred injured, was a false flag operation.[70] It has the dubious honor of a perfect "pants on fire" score from PolitiFact.[71] A *Hollywood Reporter* profile of the two owner-authors, a couple living in Los Angeles, noted in passing that an unnamed British paper had reported that "a European Union task force set up to combat Russian propaganda had classified the outlet as a proxy."[72] Digging deeper into the British press coverage, however, about the Brit who moved to Los Angeles with his American husband and makes a living by spinning checkout-counter-tabloid material, some of which is written by his mother, suggest that Sean Adl-Tabatabai is more an Alex Jones wannabe than a chapter from *The Americans*.[73] Because of all the negative coverage, Google removed the site from its advertising network in 2017, and it remains to be seen what impact this will have on the site. While the couple told *Hollywood Reporter* that the move had cost them a 60 percent drop in their revenues, data from the first quarter of 2018 show that the site had retained its level of traffic, with monthly visits roughly halfway between the *Weekly Standard* and *Reason* magazines—a position it had held without much variation throughout the preceding 18 months. One of Zero Hedge's lead authors resigned from the site in mid-2016, telling Bloomberg in the process that he was fed up with cranking out stories that fit the model of "Russia=good. Obama=idiot. Bashar al-Assad=benevolent leader. John Kerry=dunce. Vladimir Putin=greatest leader in the history of statecraft."[74] Nonetheless Lokey, the former Zero Hedge contributor, also told Bloomberg that these guidelines were honed carefully to increase clicks rather than for a political purposes.

Perhaps investigative journalists or law enforcement agencies can find smoking gun evidence that one or another of these actors is in fact a Russian agent. We have not found such evidence in the public record. But the actual observed patterns of behavior suggest that whether there is a formal relationship or whether these sites merely repeat the party line because it fits their ideology or contributes to their bottom line is substantially less important than understanding that these sites behave in this manner and that we are able to tag such sites as repeat offenders when it comes to spreading Russian propaganda. For purposes of legal responsibility, knowledge and intent are critical. For purposes of understanding what sites often serve as pathways for Russian propaganda, witting, unwitting, or witless matters a great deal less than the fact of being such a conduit.

Caution, After All

We began this chapter with the claim that one would have to be willfully blind or complicit to deny the fact that there has been a sustained Russian attack on the American media ecosystem aimed at sowing division and disinformation. The evidence we described in condensed form should be enough to support that assertion. There are simply too many diverse sources to ignore: government and nongovernment, for profit and nonprofit, defense-centered and internet-research-centered, American and European, all of which confirm the general pattern and many of the details that support the claim that Russia mounted a sustained campaign against the United States as well as various countries in Europe.

But evidence of sustained effort is not the same as evidence of impact or prevalence. It would be profoundly counterproductive to embrace the narrative that we can no longer know what is true because of Russian bots, sockpuppets, or shady propaganda. Indeed, having us adopt that attitude would mark a remarkable success for that Russian effort: the success in denying democracy one of its core pillars—the capacity to have a public debate based on some sense of a shared reality and trust in institutions. To be clear, we do not claim that the following pages "prove" that Russian efforts didn't matter. We offer them rather as examples of the kind of perspective and scrutiny we think necessary before one moves from alert to panic in understanding the threat of the attack.

Hacking and Doxxing Minimal Effects

While the Podesta emails may have been released primarily to rally the base, it is very clear from the timing and context that the DNC email hack and its release on DCLeaks and WikiLeaks was intended to deny Clinton the support of disappointed Sanders supporters. In that regard, it represented a relatively obvious target, given the contentiousness of the primary, and, as we saw in Chapter 6, paralleled the strategy Breitbart pursued with the release of the *Clinton Cash* video that same weekend before the convention.

How important were these hacking attacks? We have already seen in Chapter 6 that "emails" was the word most closely associated with Clinton in the run-up to the election, but we also saw that media attention was primarily driven by State Department releases and to a lesser extent Judicial Watch Freedom of Information Act (FOIA) victories. The DNC and Podesta emails certainly produced increased attention, particularly the latter, but the response even to the Podesta emails was dwarfed by the Comey announcement about reopening the State Department server investigation. The emails certainly provided fodder for right-wing media. They were at the heart of Pizzagate. But they were not at all at the root of the much more widely held Clinton-pedophilia conspiracy theory concerning the Lolita Express, which, as we saw in Chapter 3, was rooted in FOIA-enabled reporting by Fox News using flight logs and earlier Gawker reporting. The Seth Rich and Guccifer 2.0 conspiracies certainly played repeated roles over the course of 2017 as means of diverting attention from Russia-related news that was embarrassing to Donald Trump, but, as we saw in Chapter 5, the heavy lifting on Seth Rich was done by Fox rather than by Russian active measures.

If we look at the direct functional target—splitting Sanders supporters from Clinton—the hacking operations seem to have failed. Reviewing the coverage of the DNC email leaks reveals that, as we have repeatedly seen, the media ecosystem occupied by the Sanders left lacked the kind of conspiracy-amplification sites so typical of right-wing media. The stories from the emails did in fact emerge and were covered by both left and center-left media. But

(a)

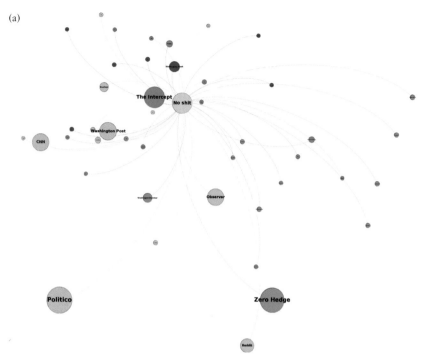

FIGURE 8.3A Media sources that linked to the initial leaked "No shit" email. Nodes sized by number of media inlinks.

then they receded. The most widely shared email from the DNC dump was an email from Amy Dacey to Brad Marshall, both of the DNC, entitled "No shit." In that email Marshall proposed planting a question in a Sanders event in which Sanders would be asked about his religion. Marshall wrote, "I think I read he is an atheist. This could make several points difference with my peeps. My Southern Baptist peeps would draw a big difference between a Jew and an atheist." This original email was covered by the *Intercept, Washington Post*, CNN, and *Politico*, coverage that was quite prominent when measured by media inlinks (Figure 8.3a). Marshall then followed up with "It's the Jesus thing," to which Dacey responded, "AMEN."[75] This latter part of the exchange got more attention on Facebook generally, in particular on the right (Figure 8.3b).

After the mainstream coverage, however, no major Facebook- or Twitter-driven sites kept the story alive on the left, so the impact of the story was small. We see an even starker rightward bias when we look at the other major

(b)

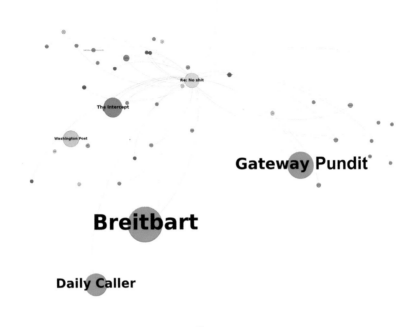

FIGURE 8.3B Media sources that linked to the final "AMEN" response in the exchange. Nodes sized by number of Facebook shares.

Facebook-shared email that could have inflamed the left. Entitled "re: Alaska 'Counter' event," the email mentioned an informant inside the Bernie campaign helping the DNC. Here coverage stayed purely within the right-wing media ecosystem, primarily the Gateway Pundit and to a lesser extent sites like beforeitsnews.com and dcclothesline.com (Figure 8.4).

To the extent that the DNC leaks were intended to splinter the Democratic Party, they appear to have largely failed, and they appear to have failed largely because the media ecosystem on the left did not follow the same practices that were available for the propagandists to harness when they aimed at the right. The stories were reported in major publications and minor; they took their course; but they did not devolve into polarizing hatred-inducing stories of the kind we saw in Chapters 3, 4, and 7.

FIGURE 8.4 Media sources that linked to the leaked "Re: Alaska 'Counter' Event" email. Nodes sized by number of media inlinks.

Infiltrating Social Media
Using Social Media to Introduce Frames

Claims about social media amplification need to address not only the presence of a campaign but also the impact that a campaign has on framing, agenda setting, or behavior on a scale large enough to shape events. We can take, for example, one of the very specific allegations in the Mueller indictment: "Defendants and their co-conspirators began purchasing advertisements that promoted a post on the ORGANIZATION-controlled Facebook account 'Stop A.l.' The post alleged that 'Hillary Clinton has already committed voter fraud during the Democrat Iowa Caucus.'" The

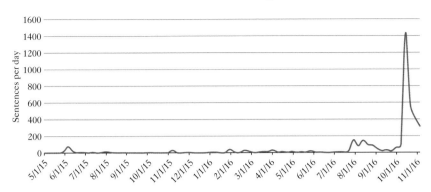

FIGURE 8.5 Sentences per day mentioning "voter fraud" during the election period.

indictment went on to identify communications by the Russian-controlled Twitter handle @Ten_GOP on August 11, and then again on November 2, alleging primary and intended general election voter fraud by the Clinton campaign.

For purposes of understanding whether the acts are illegal, the marginal impact on agenda setting during an election cycle is irrelevant. If an accountant steals $5,000 from a billionaire client, her theft is no less a crime for the fact that the billionaire will not miss the $5,000. But if we are trying to put the acts in context, we need to understand what role that particular intervention might have played in the overall "voter fraud" frame and how it played out in the election. Looking at our election data, Figure 8.5 makes clear that there is in fact a distinct uptick in the use of the "voter fraud" in early August (you need to look carefully not to be confounded by the huge upsurge in mid-October).

If Russians injected that meme into the American election, even if they were not responsible for the later upsurge, that would indeed be a major concern. Zooming in on mid-July to mid-August, however, Figure 8.6 suggests that the uptick in use of the term "voter fraud" precedes August 4, when the indictment alleges a Russian Twitter campaign to push the term. Indeed, the term peaks on that day and declines thereafter.

What precipitated that spike in early August was not Russian bots, sockpuppets, or targeted advertisements but a candidate's strategy. On July 27, during a Reddit AMA (Ask Me Anything) forum, Trump was asked, "We firmly believe Hillary will try and steal this election through vote fraud, especially given recent events. What is your campaign doing to ensure that we have a fair election?" His answer was, "Voter fraud is always a serious concern

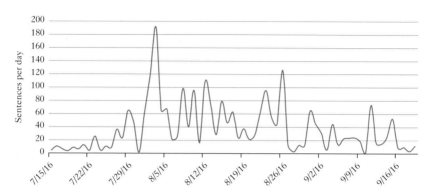

FIGURE 8.6 Sentences per day mentioning "voter fraud," July 15–September 20, 2016.

and authorities must be vigilant from keeping those from voting that are not authorized to do so."[76] The candidate's assertion of voter fraud got coverage in the *Washington Post*, on ABC News, on the "PBS NewsHour," in the *Guardian*, and in the *Miami Herald*, alongside the *New York Post*.

On July 29 a court in North Carolina struck down that state's voter ID law, holding that it had discriminatory intent and targeted African Americans "with almost surgical precision."[77] That same day courts in Wisconsin and Kansas similarly struck down as unconstitutional laws passed by Republican state legislatures involving voter ID and other restrictions. These decisions were widely reported across the media and launched a series of attacks by the Trump campaign. That same day, Breitbart published an interview with Roger Stone under the title "Roger Stone on the Milo Show: How Trump Can Fight Voter Fraud."[78] There Stone alleged that voter fraud was widespread and stated that, "[i]f there's voter fraud, this election will be illegitimate, the election of the winner will be illegitimate, we will have a constitutional crisis, widespread civil disobedience, and the government will no longer be the government."[79]

At a campaign rally on August 1 Trump picked up the theme, alleging that the Democratic primary had been rigged and that "I'm afraid the election is going to be rigged, I have to be honest."[80] Later that day he appeared on Hannity[81] and claimed that the 2012 election and Democratic primary had been rigged and that the general election might be. The next day Trump appeared on the "O'Reilly Factor,"[82] then still the most popular show on Fox News,[83] claiming that people were going "to vote 10 times" because of the court decisions striking down the voter suppression laws in North Carolina, Wisconsin, and Kansas. O'Reilly and Hannity each boasted audiences of roughly three million viewers. Rush Limbaugh ran a segment that day that repeated Trump's campaign speech statement. Although Limbaugh, not a Trump supporter in the primaries, questioned the campaign tactic as defeatist, he nonetheless reinforced the message by saying of Trump's claim, "And, of course, there's gonna be some people who believe this because there have been elections where there has been fraud. I mean, everybody knows this."[84] Limbaugh's audience, though hard to gauge accurately, is estimated to be between 15 and 20 million listeners a week. On that same day, Trump again repeated the claim in an interview published in the *Washington Post*, saying, "there's a lot of dirty pool played at the election, meaning the election is rigged."[85] The following two days, coverage of this voter fraud claim in its various iterations spiked across the entire political spectrum. The proposition that Russian ads on a Facebook account had a meaningful impact on pushing the voter fraud frame *after* it had been pushed repeatedly by the Republican candidate and covered across the major media ecosystem for several days, including the most highly watched right-wing talk shows, strains credulity.

The same goes for the alleged November 2 tweet that the indictment describes. The tweet from @TEN_GOP stated "#VoterFraud by counting tens of thousands of ineligible mail in Hillary votes being reported in Broward County, Florida." But again, the big spike in coverage of voter fraud followed an early morning October 17 tweet, in which Trump wrote: "Of course there is large scale voter fraud happening on and before Election Day. Why do Republican leaders deny what is going on? So naive!" Nancy Pelosi and Harry Reid released a joint statement in response,[86] calling on Republicans to affirm the fairness of the democratic process. Broad public coverage ensued. By November 2, the issue had mostly receded yet again, and again, it is difficult to conclude that the @TEN_GOP had a significant incremental contribution. Moreover, Pelosi and Reid were fighting an old battle that had simply been rekindled by Trump in his various comments, both in August and in October. The North Carolina, Wisconsin, and Kansas laws which were struck down were all based on the oft-repeated but never proven claim that voter fraud is widespread in the United States. An NBC story by Zachary Roth that sought to put Trump's August 1 and 2 comments in context,[87] emphasized that it recapitulated misstatements that John McCain made in 2008.[88] Those misstatements had resulted in a Public Policy Polling finding in 2009 that over 50 percent of Republicans believed Acorn had committed voter fraud and stolen the election for Obama.[89] He traced the claims further back yet, to the 2004 Bush campaign and the 1996 Bob Dole campaign as well. The Russians pushed a false narrative persistently repeated by Republican elites in an effort to justify laws known to disproportionately decrease eligible Democratic votes, particularly among Black and Latino populations. They introduced nothing new. As Limbaugh said, "I mean, everybody knows this."

Using Social Media to Suppress and Split the Democratic Vote

The indictment also alleges that the Russians used Instagram accounts they called "Woke Black" and "Blacktivist" to send messages to dissuade black voters from voting or to divert their vote to Jill Stein. If we consider Jill Stein, in the three states where her vote margin was larger than the Trump/Clinton difference—Michigan, Wisconsin, and Pennsylvania—at least according to exit polls, Stein drew 1 percent or at most 2 percent of the Black vote, less than pre-election polling suggested.[90] More importantly, a pre-election Bloomberg report on the Trump campaign's media campaign quoted an unnamed "senior official" as saying, "we have three major voter suppression operations underway," one of which was to emphasize Clinton's use of the term "superpredator" in 1996 to discourage black voters from showing up at the polls.[91] That report described in detail a campaign, using Facebook to post messages and videos that featured the recording of Clinton's comment, targeted using Facebook's capabilities to make sure that "only the people we want to see it, see it." The interviewee from the campaign boasted that "[w]e know because we've modeled this" that "[i]t will dramatically affect her ability to turn these people out." And that same report quotes Steve Bannon, then running the Trump campaign, as saying, "I wouldn't have come aboard, even for Trump, if I hadn't known they were building this massive Facebook and data engine." Again, as with the "voter suppression" frame, it is difficult to lend credence to the proposition that the Internet Research Agency, through Instagram posts, made a meaningful marginal impact in comparison to the directed efforts of the Trump campaign working with Facebook's political marketing team.[92]

Unlike many other aspects of the allegations, however, the questions of voter suppression through targeted advertising are eminently resolvable, if we have the right disclosure system in place. Unlike Twitter, Facebook actually has the real identity of every account holder. And Facebook also has a record of the entire set of communications to which an account holder was exposed. It would not be too difficult to run a comparison between all the accounts exposed to Russian advertising interventions and accounts of otherwise demographically similar matched accounts—say, Black registered voters in Florida in the same congressional districts or smaller geographic settings— and then match the voter rolls with the real identities of the Facebook account holders. We could then know, to a high degree of confidence, whether being exposed to these Russian ads was significantly associated with lower turnout than among matched Facebook users who were not exposed to the advertising. It is precisely to conduct such investigations that it would be important to produce a record of all targeted advertising, and to make it available, under constraints appropriate to preserve the privacy of the individuals and the integrity of the voting process, for researchers who study the effect of online communications on American democracy.

Real-World Protests

Perhaps the most exotic Russian interventions involve the orchestration of real-world rallies. These are included in the Mueller indictment, in the congressional hearings record, and in several news reports. The idea that Russians impersonating Americans get real Americans to actually get out on the streets and protest has a spy movie quality to it that is irresistible. Two cautions must, however, be kept in mind. First, the reported demonstrations were a drop in the bucket on the background of the steady stream of campaign events, not least among these mass appearances by the candidate or surrogates in which masses of people shout in unison, "Lock her up! Lock her up!" At the time, the Russia-induced protests drew little attention, and it is hard to imagine that this handful of secondary pro-Trump or anti-Clinton events had a meaningful impact on the election or the level of animosity between the two parties in the run-up to the election. The second is that these protests were not only relatively small, but whatever traction they had was in the context of a much broader and deeper political animosity that was not of Russian making.

The very first such report, in the Daily Beast, concerned an effort by the Secured Borders persona to mount an anti-immigration rally in Twin Falls, Idaho.[93] As a Daily Beast story explained, Twin Falls had been the target of a long-standing hate campaign starting with a January 2016 story that reported on Chobani's plan to hire immigrants, entitled "American Yogurt Tycoon Vows to Choke U.S. With Muslims." Infowars ran stories, among them pearls such as "500% increase in tuberculosis in Twin Falls," and "Idaho Yogurt Maker Caught Importing Migrant Rapists." Chobani sued, and as with Pizzagate, Alex Jones was forced to settle.[94] Breitbart, for its part, fanned the flames of anti-immigrant fervor with a different hyped-up version of a case of sexual assault dealt with by Idaho's juvenile justice system.[95] Despite the fertile ground laid by right-wing media, only 48 people registered at the event site, and, according to the Daily Beast, only four claimed to have gone. The city's mayor, however, told the *New York Times* that "after two years of 'robust debate' over the city's refugee resettlement program, which dates to the 1980s, it was 'kind of surreal' to discover that Russia had joined in."[96] Again, though, it's important to recognize that however surreal the discovery, its actual impact on the debate in Idaho or in Twin Falls was, for all practical purposes, nil.

Twitter Bots and Shaping the Debate

Finding bots is hard. Finding Russian bots is even harder. They operate on a very large scale and therefore are only amenable to automated searching. In order to train a machine learning algorithm, one needs a large training set of accounts one knows for sure are "bots" or "Russians" and ultimately both. This is the "ground truth" that is the weakest link—because no matter how sophisticated the algorithm, or how many data points it relies on, all the algorithm does is identify more instances of the entities that were in its training set. If we are uncertain as to whether the entities in the training set are bots or Russians, we will be equally uncertain about the entities the algorithm identifies as similar to them. There are several efforts aimed at identifying such accounts. Some simply look at the posting rate of Twitter accounts and assume that accounts tweeting more than some threshold number of posts are bots.[97] We used a variant of this approach to filter the most obvious bots from our Twitter maps. Some, most prominently the Indiana University group headed by Filippo Menczer that developed the Botometer and Hoaxy, and its graduates, try to diagnose individual accounts based on a broad range of characteristics.[98] Again, we used a variant of this approach as well to test whether bots influenced our overall structure. In the Russian context, efforts by Joshua Tucker's lab at New York University (NYU) have provided some powerful initial results.[99] Others try to take an approach that moves away from diagnosing whether an individual account is a bot or not, and instead asks whether a network of accounts is a coordinated effort, whether fully automated or not.[100] Similarly, distinguishing whether an account is or is not "Russian" as opposed to, say, a party whose interests are aligned with those of Russian propagandists is at least as difficult as deciding whether a clickbait factory is a Russian propaganda site or merely a nihilist out to make a buck. The Hamilton 68 project, which has garnered a lot of media attention because of its attractive visualizations and ease of use, relies on 600 hand-selected accounts whose nature and justification the project will not disclose publicly. They may be completely right, but it is difficult to rely on such an opaque process that purports to rely on such a small set of accounts. By contrast, the

SMaPP Lab project at NYU analyzes accounts that announce their primary language as Russian, and so is very likely to be right about the Russian origin of the accounts, and uses a robust hand-coding approach in determining what is, and is not, a bot; but as its creators clearly explain, this will not cover most of the interventions in the U.S. context, which are masked as Americans. Several researchers take an approach similar to the one taken by Young Mie Kim and her colleagues to quantify Russian Facebook advertising, which we noted earlier in this chapter—that is, using as their basis Facebook or Twitter accounts identified publicly by the companies or congressional committees as "Russian." This approach is reasonably sound to set a lower bound on the activity but will clearly understate its actual level.

The projects we describe are the best of class in what they do at present. They should be encouraged and improved, published and cited. But they should not form the basis of reporting, with the kind of certitude one often reads in media accounts, that some large percentage of Twitter activity or a particular campaign are bots at all, much less Russian bots. The space is in continuous flux; the campaign strategies of the propagandists shift and mutate, and the research is getting better fast. For all we know, by the time our book is out the problem of bot detection and Russian operations detection will be solved. But we doubt it.

Beyond identification, the more important question is effect. The support of an army of bots does not necessary mean that a story is going to take off and be picked up by real accounts. For example, we analyzed all the emails on WikiLeaks, including those released by the State Department associated with the Clinton private server, the DNC hack, and the Podesta hack, and all the stories that linked back to any one of those emails, to create a bimodal map of emails and stories. This map allows us to identify the emails that appeared most frequently in media stories, who had produced the story, and the extent to which those stories had influence by any of the measures we have been using throughout the book—Facebook shares, tweets, and media inlinks. One of the most curious standouts is an email included in only six stories. By comparison, the most covered emails appear in anywhere from 60 to over 240 stories.

Yet one of the stories about this email was among the most highly tweeted stories in our entire set. The email was a 2010 email, related to the Chelsea Manning leaks to WikiLeaks. It was dated five days before the publication of the embassy cables leak, but after publication of the Afghanistan and Iraq war logs leaks, from then-Director of Policy Planning at the State Department, to then-Secretary of State Clinton, attaching a memo outlining "possible legal and nonlegal strategies re wikileaks."[101] The story that was most promoted on

Twitter was from True Pundit, emphasizing that Clinton was willing to use "nonlegal means" as evidence for the core claim in the story—that Clinton was promoting a drone strike on Julian Assange (then in London . . .) to stop publication of the embassy cables.[102] Given that the claim that Clinton wanted to order a drone strike on Assange got no traction more broadly, this particular case suggests some caution before assuming that a substantial Twitter promotion campaign will necessarily promote a story in the media agenda. The sparse attention from other media stories and the minuscule number of stories about it (Figure 8.7), combined with the remarkably high tweet count strongly suggest that the story was the subject of a synthetic Twitter promotion campaign. While it is possible that such a campaign could

AN SP MEMO ON POSSIBLE LEGAL AND NONLEGAL STRATEGIES RE WIKILEAKS

Russia Today

truepundit.com

FIGURE 8.7 Map of emails hosted on WikiLeaks and sources linking to them.
The only two sites that reported on the "legal and nonlegal means" email from the State Department–released set were True Pundit and RT; the True Pundit story was among the most tweeted among stories that linked to an email.

reflect True Pundit's purchase of a viral marketing campaign, none of the other stories True Pundit published about the emails received more than one or two tweets. More likely, given that RT was the only other site to report on this email, is that the Twitter campaign was in fact Russia-directed. This would also be consistent with a later 2017 finding by Hamilton 68 of a brief period when True Pundit was again highly pushed by what they define as Russian bots.[103] And again, given that no other True Pundit story in our email set was accompanied by a similarly large Twitter campaign, it seems more likely that Russian propagandists found a story that they decided to promote, but that it turned out to be of little interest to the right-wing media sphere as a whole, apart from other Russian propagandists.

The basic point is a simple one. We are not denying that there have been repeated Russian Twitter and Facebook campaigns aimed to push one narrative or another. It is worthwhile to try to identify these and to flag them as Russian efforts, so as to enable Americans who want to avoid being drawn in, because of the Russian origin of the attempt, from being duped. But it is critical to understand that without pickup from more influential media somewhere in the American public sphere, these Russian efforts will languish unnoticed. In order for Russians to be influential, their efforts must flow through the media ecosystem Americans inhabit. It is there that stories flourish or falter. The American media ecosystem is as resilient to Russian propaganda as it is resilient to all other falsehoods, whatever their source. And as we saw in our discussion of Russian white and gray propaganda, there is a part of the American media ecosystem for which knowing that the origin of a story is Russia is no reason to ignore it, as long as it aligns with the tribal narrative they are pushing. Willing embrace of divisive Russian propaganda, not innocent error because of Twitter and Facebook manipulation, is the core challenge.

LOOKING AT THE Russian interference in the U.S. 2016 election suggests three conclusions. First, both Americans and Europeans assessing the Russian threat need to be cautious in assessing the actual danger. Many current efforts are, justifiably, focused on the genuinely challenging problem of detection. Doing this critically important work creates a strong bias to assume that the hard-won successful observations of intervention are a sign of large impact and threat. However, trying hard, as the Russians clearly are, does not equal actual success in affecting the outcomes or attitudes of a society at large. And other countries, particularly those that have a pattern of trust in major media more similar to Germany's, like Sweden or Canada, may be a lot more resilient to information operations than countries with more dysfunctional media ecosystems, like the United States. Each country has to make its own internal assessment of its genuine susceptibility and tailor its responses to its real threat model, rather than to the perceived technical possibility of intervention as itself the threat. Second, given that generalized trust is an important ingredient in any democratic society, it is important not to overstate the impact of Russian propaganda and thus feed that generalized distrust. If Russian propaganda is in fact shaping events, we need urgent action. If instead it is simply an ever-present irritant, we need to put it in its right place. Inducing overreaction would be a major success for Russian information operations.

But the most important implication is for American conservatives, particularly economic and national security conservatives rather than white-identity conservatives. They have a genuine conflict on their hands. There is mounting evidence that "the Fox News effect" has given the Republican Party a clear edge in the past several election cycles. There is, it seems, a clear short-term partisan advantage of going along with the style and focus of these right-wing media outlets. But competition among outlets seeking to attract conservative audiences has resulted in a feedback cycle, as sites vie to produce more outrage and anger and get ever more extreme in their framing. If Breitbart's third-most shared headline on immigration is "Six diseases return to U.S. as Migration Advocates Celebrate 'World Refugee Day,'" then Gateway Pundit will respond with its second-most shared headline on the subject, "Obama Changes Law: Allows Immigrants with Blistering STDs and Leprosy into U.S." And so the cycle continues. Infowars may circulate conspiracy theories about "Jeb Bush: Close Nazi Ties Exposed," but it is Fox News hosts who consistently and repeatedly imply that the investigation into Russian interference is a "deep state" conspiracy to reverse the outcome of the 2016 election. This competitive dynamic among right-wing media increases the shrill, conspiracy-tainted tone and content of coverage and makes right-wing audiences ever more susceptible to manipulation.

The result is a United States that is vulnerable to disinformation campaigns, both foreign and domestic. That susceptibility does not come from Russia, though Russia clearly has been trying to exploit it. That susceptibility does not come from Facebook, though Facebook has clearly been a primary vector online. It comes from three decades of divergent media practices and consumption habits that have left a large number of Americans, overwhelmingly on the right of the political spectrum, vulnerable to disinformation and ready to believe the worst, as long as it lines up with their partisan identity. And that susceptibility should be, in the long term, unacceptable to conservatives every bit as much as it is to all other Americans despite its short-term electoral benefits.

9

Mammon's Algorithm

MARKETING, MANIPULATION,
AND CLICKBAIT ON FACEBOOK

FACEBOOK SITS AT the center of the epistemic crisis after 2016. In the immediate aftermath of the election, Craig Silverman's stories on BuzzFeed focused on the "fake news" clickbait fabricators that garnered more Facebook engagement than traditional media outlets. In the middle of 2017, Facebook's willingness to sell advertising to Russian operatives and its hosting of a number of prominent Russian sockpuppet groups put it in the hot seat. By early 2018 the long-simmering story of Cambridge Analytica, the U.K.-based data analytics firm that had obtained tens of millions of Facebook profiles in order to develop techniques for manipulating voters, boiled over and spilled onto Facebook's lap.

The fundamental problem is that Facebook's core business is to collect highly refined data about its users and convert that data into microtargeted manipulations (advertisements, newsfeed adjustments) aimed at getting its users to want, believe, or do things. Actors who want to get people to do things—usually to spend money, sometimes to vote or protest—value that service. Describing this business as "advertising" or "behavioral marketing" rather than "microtargeted manipulation" makes it seem less controversial. But even if you think that microtargeted behavioral marketing is fine for parting people with their money, the normative considerations are acutely different in the context of democratic elections. That same platform-based, microtargeted manipulation used on voters threatens to undermine the very possibility of a democratic polity. That is true whether it is used by the incumbent government to manipulate its population or by committed outsiders bent on subverting democracy. The clickbait factories, the Russians,

Network Propaganda. Yochai Benkler, Robert Faris, and Hal Roberts.
© Yochai Benkler, Robert Faris, and Hal Roberts 2018. Published 2018 by Oxford University Press.

and Cambridge Analytica all took advantage of the intentional design of Facebook's system. We dedicated Chapter 8 to the Russians and discuss the other two here. And while we remain unpersuaded by the evidence that any of these three distinct abusers made a significant impact on the election, the basic business of Facebook, when applied to political communication, presents a long-term threat to democracy. We dedicate a good bit of Chapter 13 to addressing how at least political advertising can be regulated to constrain the abusive potential of the model.

The Basic Threat: Platforms of Persuasion

Less than a month before Election Day, two reporters for Bloomberg, Joshua Green and Sasha Issenberg, were given access to the inner workings of the Trump digital campaign.[1] The context, as they describe it, was that "[a]lmost every public and private metric suggests Trump is headed for a loss, possibly an epic one." They wrote their story before James Comey's October surprise—his announcement that the FBI was reopening an inquiry into Hillary Clinton's use of a private email server—shifted the course of the election. Green and Issenberg followed Brad Parscale, the head of the Trump digital campaign. Parscale was authorized to tweet on Trump's behalf, and Green and Issenberg describe him shooting off a message while Trump was onstage at a campaign event: "Crooked @HillaryClinton's foundation is a CRIMINAL ENTERPRISE. Time to #DrainTheSwamp!"

In October 2016, the Trump campaign had what appeared to be a highly sophisticated digital campaign that was focused on 13.5 million voters in 16 battleground states that they believed were persuadable. As Green and Issenberg told it, the strategy was not to expand the electorate but to shrink it through targeted voter suppression campaigns. The campaign messaging was explicitly negative and focused on three target populations that the Clinton campaign hoped to win by a large margin: African Americans, young women, and "idealistic white liberals." The Trump campaign had long sought to discourage supporters of Bernie Sanders from converting to Clinton voters and tried to exploit and exacerbate divisions on character and policy. For Sanders supporters, Clinton was weak on trade policy, having tried to thread the needle between prior support for the Trans-Pacific Partnership and the political climate that had soured on free trade agreements. The Trump campaign also sought to drive a wedge between Clinton and African American voters by highlighting Clinton's use of the term "superpredators" in a 1996 speech. Trump had tweeted earlier in August "How quickly people forget that Crooked Hillary called African-American youth 'SUPER PREDATORS' - Has she apologized?"

The centerpiece of the digital campaign was named Project Alamo and included voter information data that was used for fundraising and digital political advertising. The voter data base, which included data provided by the Republican National Committee (RNC) and Cambridge Analytica, reportedly had 4,000 to 5,000 data points on 220 million Americans. By the end of the campaign, the digital platform had elicited several million small donations that totaled more than a quarter billion dollars. While prospects for the Trump campaign did not look promising in mid-October, the campaign had come a long way since June 2016, when it appeared to be dead in the water. Then, the campaign had little to no money in the bank, a total of 30 staffers on its payroll, and virtually no ad spending in swing states.[2] Many thought at the time that Trump would outsource the campaign to the RNC, though relations between the Trump team and the RNC were tepid at best. A month prior to the July convention, Trump had replaced campaign manager Corey Lewandowski with Paul Manafort and had hired Parscale to lead his digital campaign. Parscale had no experience in politics but had built websites for the Trump family businesses. Whether by necessity or design, the campaign focused its attention on the digital campaign and allocated its available funding to buying ads on Facebook.

It is remarkable that the Trump campaign was able to spin up a competitive campaign over the next several months with so little experience and using a thoroughly heterodox approach. For the digital campaign, the answer lay in Facebook. The social media giant had built out capabilities specifically tailored to make it a powerful, affordable, and indispensable tool for political campaigns. By partnering with firms such as Acxiom, Facebook allowed campaigns to target voters drawing on multiple sources of data that linked together Facebook accounts with email addresses, postal addresses, phone numbers, and any number of data points on specific American voters.[3] Facebook provided an interface that allowed campaigns to target specific voters, geographic regions, or demographics or to send ads to hyperspecific segments of the population based on this personal data. This capability was coupled with tools—designed first for commercial applications—to quickly evaluate how well different alternatives of the same message elicit engagement in the target audience. This A/B testing supported broad-scale experimentation and removed much of the guesswork from advertising. Green and Issenberg reported that during the campaign, the Trump campaign created "100,000 distinct pieces of creative content." African American

audiences were reminded of Clinton's superpredator remark while likely
Sanders supporters were told about how the DNC rigged the primaries for
Clinton.

Data-rich behavioral microtargeting approaches to political campaigning
are not new. As *Politico* reported on the work of Karl Rove in the 2004
campaign: "Microtargeting became the rage of the 2004 campaign after Rove
green-lighted a project to use a wider array of databases to identify potential
Bush voters. The campaign bought data that allowed it to cross-reference
religious affiliations, shopping habits and club memberships to unearth
pockets of Bush supporters in normally hostile or inscrutable areas."[4] More
prominently, the Obama presidential campaign of 2008 and particularly the
much-lauded "nerds" of Obama's 2012 campaign used data-intensive methods
to model voter behavior and target specific groups for their messaging and
engagement efforts.[5] Clinton hired some of those celebrated nerds for her
campaign.[6] And the success of the Obama campaign efforts drove the RNC
to invest in their own data collection and analytics in preparation for the
2014 and 2016 elections. Those RNC efforts were complemented by the
Koch brothers major investments in data mining to identify voters and test
the effectiveness of various campaign strategies[7] and by Robert Mercer's
investment in Cambridge Analytica.[8]

The ideas of using internet technologies to collect data and using as many
data points as possible to deliver as microtargeted a message as possible are
not new. But the dynamics that have increased the efficacy of big data analysis
in general were at work here as well: Facebook's massive footprint; the
increased storage and processing capacity to allow major platforms to refine
and scale data analysis; and the development of machine learning algorithms
to extract meaning from ever larger data sets. And Facebook has carved out
a uniquely powerful position in the world of political campaigning. Not
only does the company provide access to tools that leverage fine-grained
data on tens of millions of Americans, but, as Daniel Kreiss and Shannon
McGregor showed, Facebook offered to embed company representatives
within campaigns to work elbow to elbow with campaign staff.[9] For Parscale,
the transition from business to politics was an easy one: "I always wonder why
people in politics act like this stuff is so mystical. It's the same shit we use in
commercial, just has fancier names."[10] In a "60 Minutes" interview on CBS
after the campaign, Parscale told viewers, "I understood early that Facebook
was how Donald Trump was going to win. Twitter is how he talked to the
people. Facebook was going to be how he won." As our analysis of mainstream
media coverage in Chapter 6 and of offline media in Chapter 11 make quite

clear Trump supporters primarily used some combination of Fox News, broadcast television, and talk radio as their primary media, and Trump's candidacy benefited from an extraordinary amount of mainstream media coverage that had an estimated value in the billions of dollars.[11] But there is no reason to doubt Parscale's assertion that Facebook was the life blood of the Trump digital campaign, and more importantly, the focus of a majority of the spending of the overall campaign.

Writing in the *New York Times* just after Obama's November 2012 re-election, Zeynep Tufekci sounded an early alarm on the downsides of big data-fueled political campaigns.[12] She emphasized two primary concerns that remain in play today. The first concern is campaigns taking "persuasion into a private, invisible realm" where opponents and watchdogs have no ability to respond. The second concern is that the science of persuasion is getting better and the ability to manipulate voters through the digital realm is heightened, offering an inroad for influencing voters through emotion and irrational biases. Tufekci followed in 2014 with an expanded academic critique of "computational politics" that turns "political communication into an increasingly personalized, private transaction and thus fundamentally reshapes the public sphere, first and foremost by making it less and less public . . ."[13] Many of the concerns she articulated then played out in spades during the 2016 campaign, particularly the application of microtargeting in combination with dog-whistle politics and fear mongering that tore at deep social divides in the United States. The infrastructure for harvesting behavioral data online continues to advance by linking together data gathered on a range of different services and platforms. Dipayan Ghosh and Ben Scott describe in detail the many layers and techniques used to collect, aggregate, and utilize user data to carry out propaganda on the internet.[14] The range of approaches they describe were developed with commercial applications and advertising dollars in mind and repurposed for political ends. They say, "The simple fact that disinformation campaigns and legitimate advertising campaigns are effectively indistinguishable on leading internet platforms lies at the center of our challenge."

The most extensive study published to date on microtargeted Facebook political advertising was done by a team led by Young Mie Kim of the University of Wisconsin. Kim and her collaborators recruited a nationally representative sample of about 9,500 subjects to install a browser extension that collected data about ads they had been served in the six or so weeks leading up to the 2016 election. They analyzed the roughly five million ads that their subjects had been served, of which about 1.6 million were political ads. They found that about 11 percent of the ads were from "suspicious groups," meaning groups banned by Facebook, lacking content after Election Day, or lacking profile information. Another 5.6 percent were delivered by groups identified as Russian-operated by the House Intelligence Committee. This is clearly a lower bound on the prevalence of Russian Facebook advertising. Twenty percent of the ads were from "astroturf" or otherwise unregistered groups, and another 20 percent were from legitimate nonprofits that had not reported to the Federal Election Commission (FEC) as a political action committee (PAC) or any other electioneering activities or independent expenditures (the ads were issue ads—ads that support an issue, not explicitly a candidate—so reporting was not necessarily required). Only about 11 percent were from groups actually registered with the FEC, and another 5 percent were of various questionable news sites. The largest category of ads, slightly over one-quarter, were "other"—sensationalist clickbait and links to meme generators. Examining who was targeted by these ads, Kim and her coauthors found that the ads were targeted at battleground states, and perhaps the most troubling finding was that households earning less than $40,000 were most heavily targeted with advertisements focusing on immigration and racial conflict. The study did not, however, report individual level microtargeting, as opposed to broader geographic or demographic targeting.

Tufekci's work and Ghosh and Scott's work suggest that large-scale data analysis will eventually make microtargeting much more effective than it is now. Because manipulations will happen at the level of the individual user, campaigns will be able to sharpen messages, including those intended to elicit fear and loathing or to intimidate voters from turning out, free of the relative moderation enforced by public scrutiny. Kim's study suggests that we have a little bit of time to address the concern but that solving the problem only for explicit formal electioneering will not solve the much more pervasive problem of "dark ads," advertisements seen only by their narrowly-targeted intended recipients, and therefore unavailable for public scrutiny, and dark money, political funding whose sources are not disclosed. Indeed, the primary finding is that Facebook makes it easy and cheap for even unsophisticated, informal groups to leverage microtargeting techniques. It is precisely because of this longer-term threat that in Chapter 13 we emphasize the importance of disclosure requirements and even more so the creation of a comprehensive public record of all the ads, electioneering and issue ads, in a way that makes them accessible to third parties for continuous monitoring and exposure.

Plumbing the Political Soul: The Dirty Tricks Crew

The concern over the role of psychological profiling in political persuasion hit the headlines in 2018 over the tactics and role of Cambridge Analytica. Cambridge Analytica was founded in late 2013 by Robert Mercer and Steve Bannon. An offshoot of SCL, a British strategic communications company, Cambridge Analytica was created to utilize cutting-edge data analysis techniques to provide insights on audiences to inform public communication and persuasion efforts. The investment provided Mercer and Bannon with a key entity in the political communications and influence game. The company has engaged in political campaigns around the globe and frequently touted its "special sauce"—psychographic profiling techniques meant to uncover political leanings of voters that would not otherwise be apparent, perhaps even to the voters themselves, and to offer guidance on how these voters might be more effectively persuaded by striking specific deep-seated emotional chords. The company derived this technique from research at the University of Cambridge. The researchers who conducted the underlying academic research (but were not associated with Cambridge Analytica), Michal Kosinski, David Stillwell, and Thore Graepel, combined personality surveys with Facebook data to show that "digital records of behavior, Facebook Likes, can be used to automatically and accurately predict a range of highly sensitive personal attributes including: sexual orientation, ethnicity, religious and political views, personality traits, intelligence, happiness, use of addictive substances, parental separation, age, and gender."[15] After Cambridge Analytica failed to convince these researchers to work with them, the company hired Alexander Kogan to replicate their methodology. Kogan created a Facebook app, recruited participants on Mechanical Turk to take a survey and download an app that harvested their Facebook data and data from their network of friends. This presumably enabled them to map personality traits against behavior on Facebook, for example, what people "liked," which would then allow them to make similar personality inferences about any Facebook user, and they now had data on 87 million Facebook users.

After the November 2016 election, Cambridge Analytica eagerly took credit for the "pivotal role" they played in the unexpected success of the Trump campaign. Parscale offered a different narrative that downplayed the role of Cambridge Analytica and reserved more of the credit for the Trump digital team. Many observers voiced great skepticism over the hype of psychometrics that Cambridge Analytica was selling,[16] some referring to the product as snake oil.[17] Ultimately, the company acknowledged that it had not used its psychographic special sauce for the Trump campaign. The company did reportedly contribute to the Trump campaign in other ways, however, by supplying data, coordinating ad spending, and providing strategic advice.

The saga of Cambridge Analytica took a downward turn in March 2018. A former employee and whistle-blower, Chris Wylie, revealed that Cambridge Analytica had collected Facebook data on false pretenses—forcing Facebook to publicly acknowledge this issue—and had not deleted the data when required to do so. A more damaging revelation occurred when executives of the company, including CEO Alexander Nix, were recorded by an investigative team from Channel 4 News in Britain claiming to have entrapped politicians using bribes and sex workers.[18] The recorded conversations also captured the managing director, Mark Turnbull, describing the use of questionable tactics to surreptitiously influence public discourse by tapping into the deep-seated fears of voters: "You just put information into the bloodstream of the internet, and then you watch it grow, give it a little push every now and again, over time to watch it take shape." This was done, he said, in a way that is "unattributable, untrackable." In the taped conversation, the Cambridge Analytics team also took credit for crafting the "defeat crooked Hillary" campaign, and Nix reported that they provided for the Trump campaign "all the research, all the data, all the analytics, all the targeting, we ran all the digital campaign, the television campaign, and our data informed all the strategy." In May of 2018, the company closed down without ever demonstrating the effectiveness of its behavioral profiling approach.

A key outstanding question is how persuasive microtargeting tools based on social media usage actually are. This may seem like a silly question given all the money spent on online advertising and the value the stock market places on data-driven marketing potential. But it is in fact remarkable how little credible evidence there is that targeted political advertising based on social media usage works any better than techniques that already existed 15 years ago or even longer.[19]

The best publicly available scientific evidence that Facebook-based psychographic data is effective, and, indeed, possibly more effective than existing marketing techniques, comes from a pair of papers coauthored by two of the original 2013 paper authors using Facebook data to identify personality traits, Kosinski and Stillwell, along with other collaborators. In 2015 they published an article that showed that machine prediction of personality was more accurate than human prediction.[20] In 2017, they published an article showing that advertising designed to fit the recipient's personality attribute (e.g., giving an extrovert and an introvert different tenor and frame to advance the same product or purpose) performed better for people who possess that attribute than advertising designed for people with its opposite (that is, showing an introvert an advertisement designed for an extrovert; or showing a person low on openness and advertisement designed to fit a person high on that measure).[21] First, although the 2015 paper did show that machines could predict personality traits better than people, they could only do so slightly better, and both humans and machines did either a touch worse or a touch better than a coin toss. Second, the 2017 paper is the strongest published evidence supporting the idea that personality traits predicted from Facebook usage can be used to design advertising that affects behavior and, indeed, that it improves on existing marketing techniques.

The effect sizes in this 2017 study, however, suggest that the concerns about Cambridge Analytica's impact are likely exaggerated. The 2017 paper reported on the results of three experiments. The first experiment matched the ad type to the personality type and did not significantly change click-through rates. On average it increased actual buying among those who did click through 1.54 times. To get a sense of the order of the effect, in that experiment they ran the manipulation on over *three million* people and achieved 390 individual purchases, including purchases by people on whom the manipulation did not work as expected. The second experiment focused on openness. It showed an effect on low openness users, but not on high openness users, and had some effect on click-through and conversion, but again, achieved 500 app installs out of over 84,000 manipulations. The much higher conversion rate is likely due to the fact that installing the app was free. Voting, in this regard, is more likely to be similar to actually paying money than installing a free app. The third campaign compared a company's standard marketing message with a personality-fit message. The personality-informed ad improved the conversion rate from 0.32 percent to 0.37 percent, an increase of 0.05 percent—that is, for every 10,000 people who were exposed to the advertisement, 5 more people installed the app using the psychographically informed advertising than would have been predicted to install after seeing the standard advertising the company was already using. In a state like Pennsylvania, which saw slightly over 6.1 million voters in 2016, if you correctly identified every single voter's personality (and remember, the 2015 paper suggested the level of accuracy between 50 percent and 60 percent), and every personality trait were as effective as the most effectively manipulated personality trait, and you reached every single potential voter, and got this level of improvement, you could shift about 3,000 votes more than standard techniques (assuming that political advertising pre-Facebook psychographics data and commercial marketing pre-Facebook psychographics data are roughly equivalent in effectiveness). Trump beat Clinton in Pennsylvania by about 44,000 votes. If, more plausibly, the effect size were like the effect the researchers saw when they actually asked people to buy something, the effect would be a few hundred votes across the entire state.

Even this low estimate vastly overstates the likely impact. Recall that the accuracy of identifying the users' personality should halve the effect. Worse, misidentified targeted appeals have been shown, in a study of the effect of canvassing in Wisconsin in the 2008 election, to actually turn off voters who are misidentified and who do not want to be contacted, and turn them against a candidate.[22] Another study suggested that narrowly targeted appeals turn off some voters while appealing to others, but it is unclear whether the gains among the latter outweigh the losses among the former.[23] More generally, not everyone uses Facebook often enough to be a useful part of a target audience, and we should expect to see the efficiency gain from a microtargeted advertising campaign decline as one moves from the most predictably sensitive potential voters to those who are less clearly identifiable to those who will actually respond negatively, creating an upper bound on the effectiveness of a campaign well below the maximum theoretically reachable population.[24] All this ignores the fact that the advertising is conducted in the context of a blitz of advertising, backed up by door-to-door canvassing, phone banking, and a range of outreach strategies based on a wide range of prior data from real-world activity, from voting patterns and political donations, through memberships, mailing lists, and other commercially available transactional marketing data.

We are not arguing that psychographically microtargeted advertising can never work or will never work. Nothing in the available public record excludes it from becoming the kind of advertising juggernaut that it was hyped up to be in Nix's public presentations. But unless Cambridge Analytica somehow succeeded within the span of two years in vastly improving on the techniques developed by the academics who invented the techniques on which the company was founded, it seems more likely that the Cambridge Analytica public announcement greatly exaggerated their role in the Trump campaign than that the Trump digital team dramatically underplayed the company's contribution. The impact of the more sophisticated versions of psychographics that raised alarms also appear to be overblown.

What is clear is that Facebook was a far more important tool for the campaign and that its microtargeting functionality is considered by political consultants to be a potent and widely used campaign tool. Facebook's initial public response to the Cambridge Analytica story emphasized the "breach of trust" on the part of Cambridge Analytica—the fact that the company harvested the data of millions of Facebook users without complying with the company's terms of service. From the perspective of basic threat to democracy, however, the privacy violation was significantly less important than the fact that Facebook collects and uses all these data, and that it imposes on its users terms of service that certainly allow the company and its clients, if not outsiders like Cambridge Analytica, to use the data as manipulatively as they choose. For all the reasons we outlined in our skepticism about Cambridge Analytica's impact, we should be similarly cautious to impute to Facebook magical powers of persuasion. Nonetheless, it is plausible that microtargeting will improve as the algorithms for identifying personal characteristics improve; that it will be more effectively targeted only at those subjects most likely to be affected as desired; and that voter suppression campaigns on social media in particular may put a candidate over the top in very close campaigns. There is no evidence to confirm that this is true. Using tailored advertisements to change hearts and minds, and more importantly voter behavior, is still primarily an act of faith, much like most of the rest of online advertising.[25] In Chapter 13 we do, however, suggest that the basic risk of undermining voter autonomy and the almost certain erosion of our collective confidence in the legitimacy of election outcomes are sufficient grounds to recommend that individually tailored, or too narrowly targeted advertising techniques should be constrained in the political context. At a minimum we argue that platforms like Facebook should be required to maintain all of their ads and ad experiments in a publicly accessible database, so that abusive practices can be exposed by opposing candidates or independent researchers.

Clickbait Fabricators Meet Facebook's Algorithms

> *"If there's one fundamental truth about social media's impact*
> *on democracy it's that it amplifies human intent—both good*
> *and bad. At its best, it allows us to express ourselves and take*
> *action. At its worst, it allows people to spread misinformation*
> *and corrode democracy."*

These words were written not by a technology pundit or new-media critic but by a Facebook product manager focused on civic engagement. He goes on to say: "I wish I could guarantee that the positives are destined to outweigh the negatives, but I can't."[26]

The success of Facebook is a story of scale. The company figured out how to maintain a platform that serves over two billion users as well as advertisers who generate tens of billions of dollars in revenue, and the only way to do this was to create automated interfaces that require few humans in the loop. Advertisers need not ask for permission to place an ad, and user interactions are governed by algorithm.

The Facebook News Feed algorithm, from which almost half of adult Americans get news at least sometimes,[27] has altered the media landscape. In particular, it has given rise to a large number of new media organizations, many of which exist only thanks to advertising revenue they receive from publishing on Facebook. Just as Web 2.0 did for the first generation of bloggers, for these entities, Facebook dismantled the obstacles for participation in the news ecosystem, and unlike Web 2.0 and bloggers, solved the revenue question in the same platform. Capital requirements are modest. The ticket to success is figuring out how to work with the algorithm that determines how many people will see your articles, and this depends in large part on the actions of readers. If you can figure out how to get people to click on your article, you are in business.

This has provided opportunities for smaller media organizations to compete for attention with large well-funded and established media sources. By serving up a stream of news stories coming from many media sources, the distinction between sketchy and reputable news sites is diminished. We see audiences that focus attention not only on the *New York Times* but also on the Palmer Report, and we see the overlap in audiences of Fox News and Truthfeed. This does not mean that hyperpartisan clickbait always wins on social media, or that all small media on Facebook are clickbait fabricators. But the economic rewards of producing media that use anger, outrage, ridicule, and tribal bonding are immediate and significant. Producing political clickbait is cheap enough to sustain a modest small business—individuals can sit at home and make a living producing bullshit that gets people to click on it for the entertainment value—or real business, as entrepreneurs have set up shop to produce many of these clickbait fabrication plants on both sides of the political divide.[28] As a challenge to democracy, we can think of the political effects of clickbait factories as emissions of the commercial model of Facebook. They are external costs imposed on democracy as a side effect of the business model of matching advertising dollars to clicks, in the presence of human users whose cognitive apparatus includes the capacity for both system one (autonomous, rapid, unconscious) and system two (slow, reflective) decision-making.[29] Unsurprisingly, clickbait fabricators have figured out that people are quicker to click on materials that trigger system one automatic unreflective responses than materials that appeal to system two controlled reflective decision-making.

Before we shake our heads at the upstarts, it is important to recognize that the tension between making money and writing high-quality news stretches back at least to the early penny presses and the need to sell copy. The corrupting influence of the need to sell to the widest possible audience has been a central and oft-repeated theme of media criticism at least since Harold Innis's *Bias of Communications* in 1951. At some level, Facebook clickbait is simply the grandchild of the tabloid headline and the *Sun's* page 3, which, in turn, is simply the more frankly licentious cousin of the organizational pressures that drove the *New York Times* and *Washington Post* to choose the sensationalist and overblown headlines they did for the Clinton Foundation stories we described in Chapter 5. At another level, many of these sites, which often peddle pseudoscience conspiracy theories as gladly as they peddle political conspiracy theories, are merely the present-day incarnations of supermarket checkout-counter tabloids. And if we use those as a baseline, we should remember that in the 1992 election, the last fully pre-internet election, about 5 percent of the respondents to the Pew media survey reported that they *regularly* read the *National Enquirer*, the *Sun*, or the *Star*. That was roughly as many as those who said they regularly watched the "MacNeil/ Leherer NewsHour" on PBS or C-SPAN (6 percent each).[30]

Our own data support the proposition that the economic incentives and ease of reach that Facebook offered did, in fact, result in Facebook's political content exhibiting more extreme partisanship than either Twitter or the open web. Political clickbait sites were most commonly found on the far edges of the political spectrum and were significantly more pronounced on the right. As we saw in Chapter 3, at the extremes, clickbait sites popular on Facebook were happy to peddle in pedophilia and rape stories on both the right and the left, but the pattern did not extend as far or as deep on the left as on the right. The political extremes are the habitat of the politically active, those that are most likely to engage in directionally motivated reasoning and willing to tolerate hyperpartisan media that often sacrifice accuracy and nuance in favor of sensational and politically biting content. When we view the most prominent media during the 2016 election by cross-media linking, Twitter shares, and Facebook shares (Tables 9.1–9.5), we see that in the center the top sites are generally consistent across these three measures. In the center-left and center-right, there are modest differences. When we move to the left and right, the differences are substantial. On the left, Occupy Democrats, Addicting

Table 9.1 Most popular media on the left
from May 1, 2015 to November 7, 2016.

Rank	Inlinks	Twitter	Facebook
1	Huffington Post	Huffington Post	Huffington Post
2	MSNBC	Politicus USA	Politicus USA
3	Vox	Daily Kos	MSNBC
4	Daily Beast	Raw Story	Vox
5	HillaryClinton.com	Salon	Raw Story
6	NPR	MSNBC	Daily Kos
7	PolitiFact	Mother Jones	New Yorker
8	Slate	Think Progress	Occupy Democrats
9	Salon	Daily Beast	Addicting Info
10	BernieSanders.com	Vox	Bipartisan Report

Table 9.2 Most popular media on the center-left
from May 1, 2015 to November 7, 2016.

Rank	Inlinks	Twitter	Facebook
1	Washington Post	CNN	New York Times
2	New York Times	New York Times	CNN
3	CNN	Washington Post	Washington Post
4	Politico	Politico	NBC News
5	Guardian	Guardian	US Uncut
6	NBC News	Mashable	Guardian
7	CBS News	NBC News	Time
8	The Atlantic	BuzzFeed	Politico
9	LA Times	Time	Daily News
10	BuzzFeed	BBC	The Atlantic

Info, and Bipartisan Report, classic examples of hyperpartisan media, were popular on Facebook but not on Twitter or in the link economy. On the right, the top sites on Facebook include Conservative Tribune, Truthfeed, Western Journalism, Political Insider, and Ending the Fed.

Throughout this volume, we have treated hyperlinks as a core measure of authority and credibility among media producers. A high imbalance between that measure and Facebook shares seems to be highly predictive of

**Table 9.3 Most popular media on the center
from May 1, 2015 to November 7, 2016.**

Rank	Inlinks	Twitter	Facebook
1	The Hill	The Hill	The Hill
2	Wall Street Journal	Yahoo! News	ABC News
3	Business Week	Wall Street Journal	Yahoo! News
4	ABC News	USA Today	USA Today
5	USA Today	Business Week	Wall Street Journal
6	Reuters	Reuters	Business Insider
7	Yahoo! News	ABC News	Mediaite
8	Business Insider	Business Insider	Reuters
9	Forbes	Mediaite	The Intercept
10	CNBC	Forbes	Forbes

**Table 9.4 Most popular media on the center-right
from May 1, 2015 to November 7, 2016.**

Rank	Inlinks	Twitter	Facebook
1	National Review	Russia Today	Real Clear Politics
2	Observer	Real Clear Politics	National Review
3	RedState	RedState	Observer
4	Weekly Standard	National Review	TMZ
5	Russia Today	TMZ	Russia Today
6	Reason	Weekly Standard	RedState
7	The White House	Observer	Federalist
8	McClatchy DC	Federalist	Free Thought Project
9	TMZ	The Resurgent	Patheos
10	Morning Consult	Reason	The Resurgent

a site being political clickbait. Among the 10 most popular sites on Facebook on the left were three media sources that were nearly invisible in the link economy: Addicting Info, Bipartisan Report, and Occupy Democrats. Though extremely popular on Facebook, these sites received 53, 37, and 25 inlinks, respectively, out of the 235,000 inlinks of this sample. More than a third of those links, in turn, were among these same three sources. Similarly, on the right, five sites among the top 10 had vanishingly small footprints in

Table 9.5 Most popular media on the right
from May 1, 2015 to November 7, 2016.

Rank	Inlinks	Twitter	Facebook
1	Breitbart	Breitbart	Breitbart
2	Fox News	Fox News	Conservative Tribune
3	DonaldJTrump.com	Washington Examiner	Gateway Pundit
4	New York Post	Daily Caller	Fox News
5	Washington Times	Gateway Pundit	Daily Caller
6	Daily Caller	Right Scoop	Truthfeed
7	Daily Mail	Daily Mail	Western Journalism
8	Washington Examiner	Infowars	Political Insider
9	WikiLeaks	New York Post	Ending the Fed
10	Free Beacon	Washington Times	New York Post

the link economy. The Conservative Tribune received just 45 inlinks from this sample, half of which came from Ending the Fed. The inlinks to Western Journalism number 130, half of which came from the Conservative Tribune. The Political Insider was the recipient of 66 links. Truthfeed received 46 inlinks, 40 of which came from the Gateway Pundit, and Ending the Fed had four inlinks. Sites that were low on inlinks but popular on Twitter or both Twitter and Facebook were at least highly partisan, and in many cases also among the worst offending conspiracy sites. During the election, low inlink sites on the left included Politicus USA and Raw Story, both of which were popular on both Facebook and Twitter. On the right, The Gateway Pundit ranked third on Facebook and fifth on Twitter during the election period, but was cited infrequently with only several hundred inlinks. Infowars ranked ninth on Twitter and eighteenth on Facebook, but received a small number of citations in the link economy. Another media source popular on social media but with very low traction in the link economy was the Right Scoop. It ranked seventh on Twitter and seventeenth on Facebook, but had only 221 links.

Most sites that were particularly dependent on Facebook for attention, whether left or right, followed similar recipes. They engaged in little or no original reporting and freely borrowed from other sources, producing short posts or articles with provocative titles intended to drive social media traffic. Most of them were not only highly partisan but also featured the most

Table 9.6 13 media sources that received a disproportionate amount of attention from Facebook compared with Twitter and media inlinks during the 2016 presidential election.

Addicting Info
Bipartisan Report
Conservative Tribune
Daily Newsbin
Ending the Fed
Occupy Democrats
Political Insider
RedStateWatcher
The Onion
Truthfeed
US Uncut
Western Journalism
Young Cons

questionable reporting, and have been frequently cited in discussions of fake news and criticized by fact-checking sites.[31] It is important to emphasize that not all sites with this kind of profile are clickbait fabricators. The *New Yorker* has a much higher footprint on Facebook than on Twitter, largely due to the Facebook popularity of the Borowitz Report, a satirical take on current events and news. Its most popular story was titled "Stephen Hawking Angers Trump Supporters with Baffling Array of Long Words." Similarly, the satirical publication *The Onion* has high Facebook sharing numbers and low tweets or links.

By combining relative attention on Twitter, Facebook, and the link economy, we are able to place media sources in groups that are highly suggestive of their position in the larger media sphere. A distinct set of websites received a disproportionate amount of attention from Facebook compared with Twitter and media inlinks. From the set of media sources that were in the top 100 by inlinks or social media shares during the 2016 election, 13 sites fell into this category (Table 9.6). Many of these sites are identified by independent sources and media reporting as examples of inaccurate if not blatantly false reporting. Both in form and substance, the majority of this group of sites are aptly described as political clickbait. Again, this does not imply equivalency across these sites. The satirical site *The Onion* is an outlier in this group, in that it is explicitly satirical and ironic. The others engage in highly partisan and dubious reporting without explicit irony.

How important were these sites in the overall scheme of the election? Without quantifying how much of the overall communications environment was exposed to false stories produced by these clickbait factories, it is impossible to evaluate whether they had an impact, or whether they are even news. The most rigorous effort to quantify the question of exposure to "fake news" on Facebook during the months leading up to the 2016 U.S. presidential election was an article by economists Hunt Allcott and Matthew Gentzkow.[32] Allcott and Gentzkow surveyed 1208 adults about their media use and exposed them to a series of stories, some true, some false, that had been circulated during the three months before the election, and some that were "placebos"—stories they had made up for the experiment that had not in fact circulated at all. Their first finding was that about 70 percent of respondents recalled seeing the big true stories they included in their survey, and just under 60 percent of the respondents believed these stories. By contrast, only 15 percent of respondents reported remembering any of the fake news stories they asked about, and 8 percent reported that they had believed them. For comparison, 14 percent reported that they recall having seen the placebo stories, and 8 percent reported remembering that they believed them. Allcott and Gentzkow calculate that a fake headline was about 1.2 percent more likely to be remembered than a placebo that was never published. Using these numbers, they calculated that an average American adult would have seen about 1.14 fake stories during the election cycle. They complement this survey data with traffic data that suggests that traffic to the top 665 top news sites in their set was roughly 19 times as high as traffic to the 65 fake news sites they identified, and that even on those sites no more than 60 percent of the stories were fake. The fundamental point of Allcott and Gentzkow's work is that even if Facebook clickbait-type fake news had a large audience in absolute terms, on the order of hundreds of millions of visits, this still translates into a tiny fraction of the campaign news-related websites that people visited, and an even tinier fraction of the stories to which they were exposed. A later paper by Andrew Guess, Brendan Nyhan, and Jason Reifler confirmed Alcott and Gentzkow's core finding, that relative exposure across the American media ecosystem was likely low. They used data collected from the browsing habits of a representative sample of U.S. users and found that while quite a few Americans (1 in 4) "visited a fake news site" at least once, only about 2.6 percent of articles Americans read about politics in September and October of 2016 were from such sites.[33] This level of exposure is consistent with the 5 percent who responded in 1992 that they regularly got news from tabloids. Furthermore, Guess, Nyhan, and Reifler found that consumption of stories was much more concentrated by comparison to bare exposure to such sites. About 10 percent of the most highly partisan among the observed population accounted for 60 percent of the stories visited, further limiting the likely persuasive effect, as opposed to the identity-affirming and entertaining effect, of political clickbait.

Despite their likely small effect on the election, political clickbait sites drew extensive public attention as the initial suspects in causing information disorder. The fact that they were so clearly prominent on Facebook put pressure on the company to do something. And because the company is so powerful relative to those who publish on it, it began to experiment over the course of 2017 and 2018 with a range of measures intended to tamp down on these clickbait sites. These included various configurations of affordances that allowed users to identify suspicious stories for factchecking, collaborated with factchecking organizations to check these, and then added a flag when fact checking organizations had disputed the articles, or added related information tags. After these initial efforts proved less than entirely successful, the company changed the News Feed algorithm to promote materials preferred by users' friends rather than those that used commercial promotion. If we look at the 13 sites listed in Table 6.9, we see that most of them in fact declined. Addicting Info, Bipartisan Report, and Truthfeed declined to almost no traffic over the course of 2017 to early 2018, according to data from SimilarWeb. The three sites that had the highest number of visits, Conservative Tribune and Western Journalism on the right and Occupy Democrats on the left, also suffered dramatic drops over the course of 2017. Occupy Democrats declined dramatically in May of 2017, relabeled itself Washington Journal and then Washington Press, and ultimately lost about two-thirds of its audience. Conservative Tribune and Western Journalism both dropped dramatically in September, losing about 60 percent of their audience, and Western Journalism continued to decline to near obscurity thereafter. Conservative Tribune stabilized at about 40 percent of its earlier audience and remains the most visited of this list of sites. The Daily Newsbin also largely disappeared, but its author, Bill Palmer, switched to publish the Palmer Report, which sustained about five million visits a month from about a million unique visitors over the course of 2017. The rest of the sites on this list have largely declined. Only *The Onion* maintained and even increased the number of visits it receives, consistent with the fact that it is a completely different kind of site.

What are we to make of these declines? On the one hand, the fact that they declined equally on the left as on the right argues against the complaints by right-wing sites that Facebook was discriminating against them because of their political viewpoint, and strongly suggests that the company was simply weeding its garden. It just so happens that, because of the propaganda feedback loop, there were a lot more weeds on the right than on the left. Consistent with this broad symmetric effect, Figure 2.20 in Chapter 2 compared the relative prominence on Facebook of sites between the election period and 2017. It exhibited no discernable pattern of anti-right sentiment—with sites on the left and right equally receding over the course of 2017.

Despite these declines, some of the worst and most influential offenders have not only survived, but increased their visibility and shares. Infowars and the Gateway Pundit both increased their Twitter footprint and maintained their overall visibility at around 20 and 15 million visits a month, respectively. True Pundit came out of nowhere to fill the shoes of disappearing sites like Ending the Fed, growing from a few hundred thousand monthly visits in early 2017 to over 3.5 million in early 2018. YourNewsWire maintained its position, hovering between three and five million visits despite the changes in algorithms and being denied access to the Google ad network. The Daily News Bin was superseded by the Palmer Report without a blip.

It remains to be seen how well Facebook can continue to weed its garden. But one suspects that Facebook clickbait sites are here to stay, just like spammers and search engine optimizers. There is an opportunity to make a buck. There are publishers who will find ways to exploit the platforms and their affordances to go after that buck. Some of these publishers will do so in ways that pollute the system on which they feed. Criticism of the platform companies will lead these platforms to keep fighting the polluting publishers. Just like spam, clickbait fabricators will require continuous treatment. Just like spam, these polluters will adapt and avoid detection and suppression. Just like spam, the platforms will play catchup, but will continue to weed. And, just like spam, although politically-inflected commercial clickbait will continue to be an irritant, there is no reason to think that it will play a significantly more important role than it played in the 2016 election. An irritant. Not a crisis.

PART FOUR

Can Democracy Survive the Internet?

"Can Democracy Survive the Internet?" was the provocative title of an April 2017 article by Stanford professor Nathaniel Persily in the journal *Democracy*. It perfectly captured the deep anxiety that the election of Donald Trump, and before it the success of the Leave campaign over whether Britain should leave the European Union, created for many observers of politics across the North Atlantic. The former featured an outsider who violated every rule of what would historically have destroyed a campaign within weeks of its launch; the latter, a campaign to effect a radical departure from decades of British commitment to the European Union. Both seemed to win against all that conventional wisdom could muster. Something had happened that was fundamentally different from everything that had gone before, and the question was how to understand this radical departure. The core thrust of the anxiety was that the Big New Thing was the internet: technology changed how citizens and voters engaged each other; how elites engaged masses; and how people were, or were not, able to distinguish fact from fiction. Persily's characteristically nuanced analysis suggested three primary effects. The internet destabilized established institutions—most importantly, political parties and media—allowing marginalized voices and outsiders to reach out directly to audiences, but equally so allowing demagogues and nihilists to disseminate propaganda and "fake news." Anonymity and lack of accountability allowed Russia to inject its influence. And the internet enabled not only hypertargeted advertising but also the development of filter bubbles and echo chambers that made users embrace their side's partisan messaging without question.[1] In the previous chapters we already outlined our skepticism about the actual incremental impact of several factors: Russia's very real efforts, commercial bullshit sites, and hypertargeted advertising based on psychographics. The Russians tried but were unlikely to have been a critical factor. The commercial bullshit artists made some money, but were peripheral. And while Facebook's data team certainly did make it possible for a complete outsider running with little help from party institutions to identify millions of voters and reach out to them effectively, the Cambridge Analytica manipulative advertising and the dark ads part of the story was still, in 2016, more of a red herring than the game changer some made it out to be.

The echo chambers and polarization concerns are recurring themes in discussions of the internet and democracy, at least since Cass Sunstein first published Republic.com in 2001.[2] The filter-bubble concern has been salient at least since Eli Pariser published *The Filter Bubble* in 2011. Sunstein's basic argument, which remained at the core of the two later editions in 2008 (Republic.com 2.0) and 2017 (#republic), is that the internet and social media's capacity to allow people to curate what they read, see, and hear will interact with our baseline social-psychological tendency to seek out evidence that fits our preconceptions (confirmation bias), congregate with others who are like us (homophily), and avoid information that does not fit what we know and like to hear confirmed. Furthermore, relying primarily on experimental work in the behavioral sciences, Sunstein argued that when people talk only to like-minded people, and do not get exposed to opposing views and arguments except in the context of oppositional argument, each group gets more entrenched in its own views and perceptions. Fragmentation of the media ecosystem leads to polarization both in the sense of segregated spheres and in the sense of increasingly extreme versions of the opposing views coming to the fore. The innovation in Pariser's intervention was to shift agency from the many diverse users choosing to self-segregate, to the companies that design the engagement algorithms. For Sunstein, what drove polarization were choices people made when offered the ability to consume only bias-confirming news and hanging out only with allies. Pariser argued that it was the algorithmic choices of social media and internet firms that pushed people into these media consumption and communication practices. What drives us to see content that reinforces our views were not our own choices, but algorithms that observed us, learned our responses, and fed us more of what increased our engagements. Although in both arguments the solution was to get internet and social media companies to serve us more varied information diets, in Sunstein's case this suggested that companies nudge us to see things that we don't naturally gravitate toward. Sunstein's argument is based on a conception of deliberative democracy, or perhaps republican civic virtue, which requires our engagement with opposing views and an agenda set by general news reports even if, left to our autonomous choices, we would rather not. Pluralist views of democracy, by contrast, could be quite comfortable with highly segregated information spaces, in which groups contesting for political power define competing positions crisply and resolve their differences not by agreeing, but by peacefully counting votes at the polls. By contrast, Pariser's diagnosis required a less normatively-freighted framework to justify roughly similar interventions. If the polarization and segmentation we see were not the outcome of decisions that citizens make for themselves, but rather the product of choices companies make for their users, then regulating these companies to offer a more varied diet that was healthier for democracy did not require us to adopt any particular version of democratic theory. All that was needed was a commitment to the proposition that members of a democratic polity should be able to choose for themselves what they read, see, and hear, rather than have it thrust upon them by companies whose interests are fundamentally commercial, not political. The negative political communications patterns that resulted from these company choices were simply emissions from the commercial companies into the political media ecosystem; byproducts that needed to be regulated to keep from harming democracy.

Our data, particularly the highly asymmetric structure of the networked public sphere, question both diagnoses. If "the internet" is what leads to polarization and increasing extremism we observe, then one would expect to see the media ecosystem develop symmetric patterns of polarization. We should have expected to see (as early studies relying on less data did see) a symmetric pattern of segmentation, assuming that users on the left and the right operate under similar social psychological dynamics and algorithmic decisions. What we observe instead is that everyone outside of the roughly 30 percent of the population that pays attention primarily to right-wing media exists in a mixed-media ecosystem that is not fragmented and is more or less normally distributed in its attention around a core of traditional professional media outlets. People on the left certainly read left-oriented materials, but they also read and engage with publications and media outlets anchored in the professional journalistic norms. These are precisely the kinds of generalized information intermediaries that played the role of shared agenda setting from the end of World War II to the 1980s. . Moreover, polarization is a process that took a sharp upturn among political elites in the mid-1970s, well before TCP-IP had even been defined as the internet protocol or Mark Zuckerberg was born. Rush Limbaugh had already been declared honorary member of the class of Republican House Freshman when Newt Gingrich led the Republican "Contract with America" 1994 capture of the House.

Both the extensive political science literature on polarization and the rich literature on American media history argue against "the internet did it" narratives. Instead, we suggest that technological, institutional, and political dynamics have been interacting for over 40 years to lead the Republican Party and Republican voters to gradually become more extreme versions of themselves, without operating symmetrically on the Democratic Party and its supporters or on most Independents. The 2016 presidential election was the moment at which these long-term dynamics reached an inflection point in the Republican Party, but not among Democrats. These dynamics explain how Jeb Bush, the son and brother of the two most recent Republican presidents, can be castigated for his "close Nazi ties" by the eighth-most tweeted media site on the right; or how Sean Hannity and his guests on the most highly watched cable television program on the most highly watched cable news channel can vilify lifelong Republican law enforcement agents as agents of "the deep state" who are personally corrupt and conflicted out of a major national security investigation. As we have seen repeatedly throughout the preceding chapters, the prominent outlets on the left and center simply do not exhibit a parallel structure, content, or vehement outrage that we observe on the right. These facts are as inconvenient to academics seeking a nonpartisan, neutral diagnosis of what is happening to us as they are to professional journalists who are institutionally committed to describe the game in a nonpartisan way. Both communities have tended to focus on technology, we believe, because if technology is something that happens to all of us, no partisan finger pointing is required. But the facts we observe do not lend themselves to a neutral, "both sides at fault" analysis. Our lived experience is one in which a highly partisan House committee "absolves" the president of allegations that are under active investigation by an independent counsel and that president then tweets: "As the House Intelligence Committee has concluded, there was no collusion between Russia and the Trump Campaign. As many are now finding out, however, there was tremendous leaking, lying and corruption at the highest levels of the FBI, Justice & State. #DrainTheSwamp."[3] Only a conscious and frank assessment of why the two sides of the divide developed such different dynamics will help us avoid the vortex.

In Chapter 10, we review the literature on polarization and see that polarization long precedes the internet and is rooted in asymmetric political-elite-driven dynamics. In Chapter 12, we turn to media history and recount the rise of second-wave right-wing media, beginning with Rush Limbaugh and the shift of televangelism into political coverage. Again, asymmetric polarization precedes the emergence of the internet. We then turn to evaluate various hypotheses about why the differences between the left and the right emerged as they did and cover both psychological explanations and historical-institutional factors. We cannot exclude psychological explanations that claim to identify systematic cognitive and affective differences between conservatives and liberals, but we offer reasons to see the asymmetry more as a function of historical contingency and institutional-political factors interacting with universally applicable models of motivated reasoning than a result of any intergroup psychological differences. As such, we think that while path-dependency will make addressing our present crisis difficult, it will not require going against "human nature" in any deep sense, but "merely" formidable political will on the part of *both* Republicans who still reject their party's takeover by its radical wing, and Democrats who will have to work with those Republicans to re-establish a more symmetric political and media ecosystem.

10

Polarization in American Politics

Polarization of Political Elites

In September 2017, a seven-term moderate Republican representative from Pennsylvania, Charlie Dent, indicated that he would not seek re-election. In his announcement, he decried the rancorous atmosphere in Washington afflicted by "increased polarization and ideological rigidity that leads to dysfunction, disorder and chaos."[1] He was not alone. When LoBiondo Frank of New Jersey followed suit, he declared: "Regrettably, our nation is now consumed by increasing political polarization; there is no longer middle ground to honestly debate issues and put forward solutions." Prior to the 2018 midterm elections, an unusually high number of incumbent Republican senators and representatives announced that they would retire from Congress rather than seek re-election.[2] Polarization was not the only factor at play. Some were facing increasingly competitive elections and the possibility of losing the power and leverage of being part of the majority party. However, increasing polarization and acrimony in Congress was a frequently cited factor, accentuating the fact that this is a conspicuous and unfortunate aspect of political life in the United States today, even among those who have at times helped to further and deepen legislative polarization. And, as we will see here, political polarization in the United States appears to be asymmetric, and more pronounced among Republicans than Democrats.

Polarization in American politics is most reliably measured in the actions of elected officials and is almost certainly led by people who spend their time thinking about politics and acting within it rather than people who turn to politics episodically, usually in the run-up to elections. A particularly vivid way of demonstrating polarization is to generate network maps, based on congressional voting records, in which House representatives are the nodes and shared roll call

Network Propaganda. Yochai Benkler, Robert Faris, and Hal Roberts.

votes between pairs of representatives are the edges. In a 2015 paper, Clio Andris and her collaborators showed that the parties were well separated in the 1940s and 1950s, began a resorting process in the mid-1960s that lasted into the 1980s, and have been well separated again since the mid-1980s.[3] Figure 10.1 shows clearly the pattern over the entire post–World War II era.

FIGURE 10.1 Partisanship in voting patterns in the U.S. House of Representatives, 1949–2011.

The pattern will be immediately legible to anyone with a passing familiarity with American politics since the New Deal. The New Deal and the Fair Deal relied on a compromise between Northern Democrats, who emphasized economic security and poverty alleviation, and Southern Democrats, who supported these goals in principle but only if they were designed so as not to undermine the Southern Jim Crow racial caste system.[4] The clearly observable mixing from the late 1960s to the late 1980s suggests that an important factor in the present pattern of polarization is the gradual working out of the competing forces of incumbency and party realignment caused by the passage of the Civil Rights Act of 1964. Bill Moyers quotes Lyndon Johnson as having told him, on the night he signed the Civil Rights Act of 1964, "I think we just delivered the South to the Republican Party for a very long time."[5] Kevin Phillips's 1969 book, *The Emerging Republican Majority*, was considered at the time the blueprint for Richard Nixon's Southern Strategy.[6] As Phillips put it,

> The presidential election of 1968 marked a historic first occasion—the Negrophobe Deep South and modern Outer South simultaneously abandoned the Democratic Party. And before long, the conservative cycle thus begun ought to witness movement of congressional, state and local Southern Democrats into the ascending Republican Party.[7]

In his 1969 review of the book, the *Times's* political reporter Warren Weaver Jr. characterized Phillips's argument, "the Democratic Party ... will consist largely of treacherous Yankees who forsook the Republican party over the past 30 years, Jews, Negros, some stubborn Scandinavians and the liberal establishment." The "Southern" part of the strategy meant that "[f]ull racial polarization is an essential ingredient of Phillips's political pragmatism."[8] Ignoring the incendiary language, part anachronism part animus, Phillips's maps of the realignment and the basic predictions about the geographic segmentation and sorting of the two parties were remarkably prescient. The element missing from the analysis was that the New Left and the women's movement would evoke in evangelicals a parallel backlash. That backlash complemented the white-identity pillar of the emerging Republican majority with the pillar of the newly politicized evangelical Christian movement that came into its own in 1979 when Jerry Falwell founded the Moral Majority.

The polarization that followed the realignment of Southern Democrats into the Republican Party did not result in symmetric polarization between the parties. DW-NOMINATE, the academic standard for measuring the partisan alignment of members of Congress, was pioneered by political scientists Keith Poole and Howard Rosenthal and later extended in collaborative work with Nolan McCarty.[9] This technique leverages the voting behavior of members of Congress to quantitatively estimate their locations on the political spectrum. On a scale of 1.0 to –1.0 for conservative to liberal, the measure incorporates how often any given member votes with members from the other party as a measure of their ranking from centrist (0.0) to partisan (1.0, –1.0). Looking at all the roll call votes of all members of Congress who have ever served in the U.S. Congress, this approach is also able to record changes in partisanship over time, and in particular how far from the perfectly centrist position various members are. Because individual representatives are relatively stable in the degree to which they are conservative or liberal over a career, DW-NOMINATE uses the fact that various members of Congress overlap in tenure and compares how new members of one or the other party vote relative to already-serving members of that party to compare partisanship over time.

Looking at partisanship and polarization of members of Congress since the Gilded Age, from 1870 to 1900, it is quite clear that Republicans saw a long gradual shift toward more centrist views over the seven decades from the election of Teddy Roosevelt until 1968 (Figure 10.2). Northern Democrats shifted from being more moderate or centrist than Republicans on the eve of World War I, to being more liberal, or further from the perfect centrist position, than their Republican counterparts. This long-term move to the left ended in the mid-1950s. The issue positions associated with liberal and conservative political ideology have changed, but Northern Democrats' voting patterns have remained remarkably consistent in their ideological position over the past six decades. Southern Democrats were the most polarized by this measure before World War I—that is, they were most likely not to vote with members from the other party. From World War I to the New Deal, Southern Democrats became the most centrist in the sense that they were the most likely to vote with Republicans. They occupied this position until 1968. Republicans then began to transition toward a caucus made up of members who took more consistently conservative positions, with a sharper swing beginning in 1977. Meanwhile, Southern Democrats began a long-term convergence with Northern Democrats, with smaller inflection points in 1991 and 1998, as electoral trends accelerated or decelerated the speed with which Southern Democrats were replaced by Southern Republicans. The remaining Southern Democrats were increasingly from majority-minority districts and voted squarely with the Northern Democrats. The Southern Democrats converged to the orientation of the Northern Democrats, who changed the

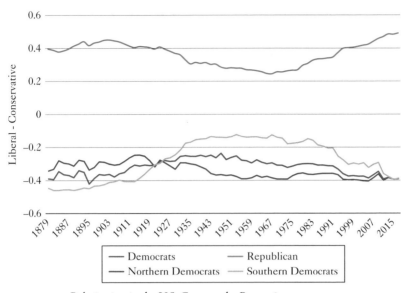

FIGURE 10.2 Polarization in the U.S. Congress by Party, 1879–2015.

Source: https://voteviewblog.com/2015/06/10/more-on-assymmetric-polarization-yes-the-republicans-did-it/.

least over this period of time, arriving back at a DW-NOMINATE score of −0.4, where they had been since the mid-1950s. The Republicans continued to become increasingly conservative. By 2000, Republicans had become more conservative than Democrats were liberal, and on the eve of the 2016 election, Republicans were more conservative than they had been at any point since the Gilded Age. While DW-NOMINATE has become quite standard in political science, there remains a lively academic debate over the comparability of these scores, particularly over very long periods of American political history.[10] Some are not, as we are, persuaded that DW-NOMINATE is the best available measure for tracking these changes.[11] But given that Poole and Rosenthal have done this continuously since 1983, we think that the measures are robust at least for understanding patterns of polarization in the past half century.

These patterns suggest a basic underlying dynamic that is tied to the three pillars of the present Republican coalition. First, the white-identity pillar, the intentional product of the Southern Strategy that was so clearly represented in the tenor of the immigration coverage we described in Chapter 4. Second, the pillar of evangelical Christians, who have been a mainstay of the Republican party since the election of 1980, and whose politicization was driven by a backlash against the politics of the 1960s, the sexual revolution, and the destabilization of the traditional patriarchal family structure by the Women's Movement. And the third, the emergence of organized business in the 1970s, and the deep strategic turnaround that American businesses undertook in response to a series of political losses in the 1960s, particularly under the auspices of the U.S. Chamber of Commerce and the Business Roundtable. As Jacob Hacker and Paul Pierson documented in *Winner-Take-All-Politics*, political contributions by this movement followed very different patterns for Republicans and Democrats. The former received sustained, party-building and movement-building contributions; the latter received primarily rewards for individuals who were reliable allies rather than for the party as a whole.[12] The first two pillars of the Republican coalition—white identity and political evangelicism—are defined in terms of social identity, rather than practical needs, and are therefore particularly amenable to the organization of a party based on a shared ideology, rather than shared interests. The third, business-oriented pillar is more results-focused, but the results it sought were deregulation and tax reduction—that is, reduced state capacity. The veto-rich American legislative system made developing a strategy based on ideological purity—and the gridlock likely to result—congruent with that goal. Grover Norquist's tax pledge, initiated in 1985, is the quintessential example of taking the most practical of political questions—how much money to raise and spend—and turning it into an ideological litmus test with a single right answer: "no new taxes." As Matthew Grossman and David Hopkins argued in *Asymmetric Politics: Ideological Republicans and Group Interest Democrats*, the Republican Party can therefore function as a party committed to ideological purity,[13] punishing moderates who try to compromise to get things done with contested primaries and lost funding. By contrast, the Democratic Party has a long pattern of interest-group coalition politics. It therefore focuses on delivering to its various constituent interest groups the policy outcomes that keep them in the tent. This focus on results means that Democrats value half loaves, whereas Republicans often interpret a half loaf as a full betrayal. Representatives faced with such asymmetric responses among their supporters and funders are likely to adapt their behavior, and the resulting asymmetric patterns of behavior are perfectly consistent with these different incentive structures set up by the two major parties in American politics.

Polarization of the Public

Given the evident and growing partisan divide in Congress, it is natural to surmise that this is accompanied by and fueled by rising polarization of the public. However, despite broad agreement among scholars and political observers that elite polarization is a reality, there is less consensus about whether the electorate is as highly polarized, or has been polarizing at all. The fact that voters are sending representatives to Congress that are acting in increasingly partisan ways is not by itself enough to establish that the mass public is similarly polarizing or that elite polarization is rooted in mass polarization.[14] This pattern of voting more extreme representatives into office could simply be the result of there being fewer moderate candidates to attract the votes of moderates. As the differences in party candidates grow over time, centrist voters are left with more extreme options that do not reflect their moderate views. According to this view, voters are not the instigators of elite polarization but passive victims of the forces of elite polarization, which leave them fewer and fewer centrist options. Independent voters or voters that lean slightly to the right or left would have to choose between staunch liberals or conservatives.

There are many conceptions of polarization and many of the disagreements among scholars stem from different definitions and measures of polarization.[15] There are many ways in which the electorate on the left and right may pull apart. There are policy differences across a range of economic and social topics from taxation and trade policy to guns, abortion, and minority rights. Politics is also deeply personal, and partisans tend to dislike one another.

Among those who study polarization of the broader public, there is wide consensus on two key points. First, voters are better sorted than in the past. Democrats now more reliably identify as liberal while Republicans now more consistently identify as conservative. The southern realignment among voters is a big part of this, but increased ideological-partisan sorting has occurred across the country.[16] The correlation of party and self-reported ideology has increased from 0.28 in 1972 to 0.58 in 2012.[17] Since fewer people who identify as Democrats now hold conservative views and fewer people who identify as Republicans hold liberal views, this sorting process has led to less overlap in the political orientation and attitudes of the parties and greater homogeneity within parties. However, political sorting does not necessarily entail diverging views on issues. Sorting can in principle produce more homogenous parties without voters taking on more extreme positions on particular issues. The process of political sorting could simply be reshuffling voters into more coherent groups where party identities and opinions are more homogenous. A second point of consensus is that voters who are most active politically are more polarized. In the words of Alan Abramowitz and Kyle Saunders: "The most interested, informed, and active citizens are much more polarized in their political views."[18] Activists, however, constitute a small minority of the public. If defined by those who work on campaigns, they make up about 5 percent of the eligible electorate. The number is higher if based on the number who contribute to campaigns: about 10 percent of the electorate.[19]

There is less consensus about what has happened to the majority of Americans who are not highly engaged partisans of either party and are not as polarized as the most engaged citizens. Morris Fiorina and his coauthors have been the leading academic voices expressing skepticism over ideological polarization of the broader public.[20] Their principal argument is that while the political elite and political activists have been growing apart ideologically, the large majority of the public have had and continue to hold moderate positions on the issues. Long-term trends of two likely signals of polarization—strong identification with one of the parties and strong identification with conservative or liberal ideology—do not reveal a clear pattern of polarization. In periodic surveys conducted over many years, the proportions of the electorate that respond as strong liberals, conservatives, Democrats, or Republicans have not increased significantly over the past several decades.[21] Alan Abramowitz and his coauthors offer a different interpretation of the available data and report that the number of ideological moderates has been declining. Drawing on American National Election Studies data, they make the case that the number of political moderates is shrinking, as evidenced by a growing proportion of survey respondents that report strong partisan identities.[22]

Both Fiorina and Abramowitz express concern about the negative implications of growing partisanship among political elites. They differ, however, in the role of the public in this growing divide. For Fiorina, the majority of American voters are not the instigators of political polarization and are not well served by the divisive political system created by elites. In their 2012 book *Disconnect*, Fiorina and Abrams write:[23]

> In America today, there is a disconnect between an unrepresentative political class and the citizenry it purports to represent. The political process today not only is less representative than it was a generation ago and less supported by the citizenry, but the outcomes of that process are at a minimum no better. The present disconnect is cause for concern and not something that can be discounted as either normal or unimportant.

For Abramowitz, the American public plays a more significant role in the disconnect and hence bears more of the responsibility as well:

> There are large differences in outlook between Democrats and Republicans, between red state voters and blue state voters, and between religious voters and secular voters. The high level of ideological polarization evident among political elites in the United States reflects real divisions within the American electorate.[24]

Recent work challenges the notion that voters are more moderate than their elected officials while also drawing into question the definition and measure of what constitutes a political moderate. Based on voter surveys, David Broockman finds not only that many voters hold a mix of conservative and liberal positions but also that many voters also hold extreme positions on issues.[25] On immigration, for example, approximately one-quarter of those surveyed supported a ban on immigration until the border is fully secured and were in favor of deporting all undocumented immigrants. He concludes that the opinions of the public are not in fact more moderate than those taken by elected representatives. By a common measure of ideology, those that favor a mix of liberal and conservative policies would be classified as moderate regardless of the extremity of their views on the individual policies. Once the extremity of views on particular issues is taken into account, Broockman shows that the electorate appears substantially less moderate. He also observes that while highly knowledgeable and engaged American voters tend to have more ideologically consistent views, they do not generally hold more extreme views on specific issues.

Elite Polarization and Political Identity: Do Leaders Matter?

The literature we have surveyed to this point makes two things clear. First, political elites have polarized asymmetrically. Congressional Republicans have become continuously more conservative and ideologically pure over the past 50 years, while congressional Democrats have converged to the degree of partisanship that has characterized Northern Democrats since the mid-1950s. Second, while partisan activists have polarized, it is much less clear whether the majority of the population has similarly polarized. The remaining question is how polarization among elites and activists is likely to affect the majority of the population that does not pay as much attention to politics on a regular basis.

Long-standing research in political science rejects the idea that voters choose candidates who most closely match their opinions on policy issues. In a seminal 1964 paper, Philip Converse provided an early empirical foundation for a premise that is now widely accepted, at least among political scientists: a large majority of Americans do not have consistent and reliable ideological beliefs. Converse found that only about one in six could "assign the terms 'liberal' and 'conservative' correctly to the parties and say something sensible about what the terms meant."[26] These findings have been replicated many times over the past five decades. In recent work, Donald Kinder and Nathan Kalmoe replicated much of Converse's seminal study. They found that the basic description of voter attitudes and behavior articulated many decades ago has changed only modestly.[27] They found that for most people, self-reported ideology had no influence over opinions on a wide range of topics, including immigration, affirmative action, gun control, health policy, foreign aid, tax policy, and social security. There were two exceptions: abortion and lesbian, gay, bisexual, and transgender (LGBTQ) rights. However, once the authors control for religious beliefs, the impact of ideology on these topics disappeared as well. Following in this line, Christopher Achen and Larry Bartels dismantle what they describe as the "folk theory" of democracy: the idea that people have informed policy preferences and then vote for candidates that best match their policy preferences, which in turn promotes elected officials that serve the interests of their electorate. Instead, they conclude that voters are mostly disinterested in politics, ill-informed about political matters, and likely to make their voting choices based on a set of factors that have no relationship to the proposed agenda and competence of their favored candidate.[28]

An alternative to the well-informed rational voter theory is that individuals are driven primarily by partisan identity. This model, frequently known as the Michigan model, was developed by political scientists in the 1950s and articulated in the 1960 classic *The American Voter*. The core premises of this model are that voters inherit a partisan identity early in life from their family and social environment, and that this affiliation, typically with the Democratic Party or Republican Party, shapes political values and perceptions of political affairs. The essence of this model, that for most voters the foundations of political thinking and decisions are social, has held up well over the years.[29] Americans organize opinions on politics and current affairs around their attitudes toward social groups.[30] Kinder and Kalmoe also find that party identification is more stable over time than ideological affiliation and that this is rooted in social ties: "public opinion arises primarily from the attachments and antipathies of group life." Voters apparently establish their party affiliation first and then adapt their views of issues and ideology to align with party. They estimate that those who base political perspectives on group identity—the ideological innocents—outnumber voters with strong ideological and issue-based opinions by a factor of 5 to 1. This distance between ideology and affiliation is not an impediment for political engagement. Partisanship presents more opportunities for citizens to express their affiliation and take action, whether by voting, working for a campaign, attending rallies, or contributing to campaigns. "Parties are material realities in a way that ideologies are not."[31]

The key role of partisan affiliation in determining the views and actions of the electorate through a top-down process is clearly evident in the responsiveness of partisans to political leaders. Voters take cues from political elites on questions of policy. They tend to first choose their favored leaders, and then adopt the political views and stances of the leaders.[32] This phenomenon was demonstrated in an innovative study carried out with the cooperation of state legislators. Working with researchers, legislators sent out issue positions to constituents but with randomly assigned content, some with extensive justification and others with little background. They found in subsequent surveys that voters frequently adopted the positions of legislators even when little justification for the positions was provided. Moreover, legislators were not viewed more negatively when the position statements were in opposition to voter positions. Voters require little convincing to adopt new policy positions, and where the positions of elected officials conflict with voter positions, voters are willing to look beyond that.[33] A study carried out in the wake of the 2016 election took advantage of Donald Trump's "ideological schizophrenia" to assess the influence of political leaders on voter opinion.[34] They found that "low-knowledge respondents, strong Republicans, Trump-approving respondents, and self-described conservatives are the most likely to behave like party loyalists and simply accept the Trump cue—in either direction." When Trump promoted a conservative position, his supporters agreed. When Trump adopted a more liberal position, they agreed.

Partisan responses to the cues of the political leaders applies also to the positions taken by leaders from the opposite side. The response of Democrats to the positions staked out by Trump are a good example of this. Among Democrats there was a marked shift in political values on topics where Trump took strong controversial positions. There was an increase, from 50 percent to 64 percent, in the percentage of Democrats who believe that immigrants strengthen the country because of their hard work and talent.[35] Similarly, there was a large increase from 2015 to 2017 among Democratic survey respondents who view racial discrimination as the main impediment to Blacks "getting ahead."

The implication of the work on the plasticity of voters' policy preferences and their responsiveness to cues from leaders of parties—parties they adopt as a matter of identity—is that patterns of polarization among political leaders can affect patterns of polarization in the public. It means that leaders have considerable latitude to define what it means to be a Republican or Democrat, or what it means to be conservative or liberal. It is whatever they say it is. In ideological terms, partisanship is more flexible and less prescriptive. In the 2016 election, this explains how Trump was able to reset party doctrine on issues such as trade and Russia while still holding a vast majority of the GOP vote. But it also offers a transmission mechanism for the well-measured asymmetric polarization among elected representatives to the broader population of party identifiers.

From Social Identity to Affective Polarization

The fact that social identity begets party affiliation helps explain not only why leaders can induce populations to shift positions over time but also why polarization can take on such deeply affective negative responses to partisans of the other party.[36] Expressive partisanship has a strong emotional component that provides a stronger driver for engagement and activism compared to involvement based on intellectual grounds.[37] People choose sides and become emotionally invested in promoting their side and opposing the other side. These group bonds then determine opinions on issues and the interpretation of political events. As Lilliana Mason writes, political sorting creates a stronger overlap in social identities that exacerbates polarization. Increasing partisan and ideological alignment results in greater partisan bias, activism, and anger. "Partisan identities have become increasingly aligned with religious and racial identities. Republicans tend toward Christian and white identities, and Democrats tend toward non-religious and non-white identities. With these highly aligned identities, people tend to be more sensitive to threats from outsiders, reacting with higher levels of anger than those with cross-cutting identities."[38] Even without any change in the underlying distribution of issue opinions, sorting can fuel greater enmity toward the opposing party and inspire more activism. "The effect is an electorate whose members are more biased and angry than their issue positions alone can explain."[39] And ethnic identity has come to play a particularly large role in this dynamic. Donald Kinder and Cindy Kam show how the definition of in-groups and out-groups based on ethnic background exerts an influence on political attitudes across a range of issues, including immigration, social support programs, and policies to counteract terrorism.[40]

It is hardly news that in-group/out-group dynamics involve as much negative response to the out-group as it does positive response to the in-group. Utilizing survey data, Miller and Conover demonstrate that "stronger partisan identities, more than ideological identities or preferences, are associated with a greater sense of partisan hostility—specifically, party rivalry and anger."[41] They report that those with the strongest partisan identities maintain the most hostile and uncivil attitudes and that they are also the most likely to vote. These dynamics readily explain the extraordinary passion and enthusiasm of Trump political rallies, which was both a point of pride for the campaign and a shock for many, particularly the unmistakable rage of many Trump supporters. Anger and outrage has always played a motivating and instrumental role in political mobilization, but the emotionally charged atmosphere of the 2016 campaign reached levels not seen in the United States in many years. And the anger and frustration palpable in demonstrations of "The Resistance" since inauguration day is hardly the stuff of rational democratic discourse, any more than Hillary Clinton's infamous "basket of deplorables" was an invitation to pragmatic dialog. But the 2016 election was simply the working out of the much longer trend of growing animosity and distrust between liberals and conservatives. This partisan hostility, referred to as affective polarization, has risen sharply over the past two decades. According to Pew Research Center survey data, the number of Republicans that view Democrats unfavorably has risen from 74 percent in 1994 to 91 percent in 2016. Democrats that view Republicans unfavorably has increased from 59 percent to 86 percent over the same time period. In surveys carried in 2014, Pew researchers found that 36 percent of Republicans and 27 percent of Democrats responded that the opposing party's policy agenda "threaten the nation's well-being."[42]

Based on survey data that includes "thermometer" ratings of in-groups and out-groups, Shanto Iyengar, Gaurav Sood, and Yphtach Lelkes described a significant chilling of feelings for the other party among Republicans and Democrats. Over the past several decades, these ratings of the out-party have declined 15 points on a 100-point scale, while in-group feelings have been stable. Surprisingly, perhaps, partisan affective responses are stronger in the data Iyengar, Sood and Lelkes analyze than are affective responses to race or religion, a finding that Iyengar and Sean Westwood confirmed in a series of studies specifically focused on comparing racial to partisan animosity.[43] Consistent with the asymmetric partisanship literature, they also find that while the negative affective response has increased significantly across the partisan divide, it has increased more for Republicans than for Democrats. In 1960, practically no Democrats or Republicans reported that they would be "somewhat or very unhappy" if their child married a member of the other party. By 2010, one-third of Democrats and one-half of Republicans responded that they would have that response to their child marrying a member of the opposite party.[44] In more recent work, Iyengar and Westwood moderated that finding by testing it across a wider range of measures, finding that negative out-group affect was high among Democrats and Republicans broadly speaking to a roughly similar extent, although they did find that when comparing Democrats and Republicans who were "strongly partisan . . . outparty animus is significantly higher among Republicans."[45]

Abramowitz and Steven Webster use the term "negative partisanship" to highlight the fact that the growing hostility voters feel toward the other party is not matched by a stronger affinity for their own party: "A growing proportion of Americans dislike the opposing party more than they like their own party." They hypothesize:

> The rise of negative partisanship in the American electorate appears to be part of a vicious cycle of mutually reinforcing elite and mass behavior. Confrontational politics in Washington and in many state capitols is causing Democratic and Republican voters to develop increasingly negative views of the opposing party and to vote along party lines from the top of the ticket to the bottom. Negative views of the opposing party among voters, in turn, encourage political elites to adopt a confrontational approach to governing. Given these mutually reinforcing patterns of elite and mass behavior, negative partisanship is likely to remain an important feature of American politics for the foreseeable future.[46]

Polarization Before Considering Media Dynamics

Before we turn to considering media and political communications, let us evaluate where we are. There is very good evidence that party elites, and elected representatives in particular, have experienced significant party polarization in the sense that liberals and conservatives have mostly sorted themselves into Democrats and Republicans, respectively, and that the most visible component of this move was the realignment of Southern Democrats to the Republican Party. It is also clear that this movement was asymmetric and that since 1968 Republicans have continuously moved to the right, while Democrats have converged more or less to the location of Northern Democrats in the mid-1950s. It is clear that party activists, ranging in number between 5 percent and 10 percent of the voting population, have similarly polarized in their positions. And it is quite clear that the broader population, if it has polarized at all, has polarized affectively—in the way it feels about the other party—rather than programmatically, or the practical policy preferences it holds. The long-term and regional trajectory of these patterns strongly argues against the internet being a prime driver of polarization. Part of the story relates to the gradual sorting of the parties by ethnic identity—with Democrats relying more heavily on nonwhite voters, and Republicans relying overwhelmingly on non-Hispanic white voters. For both sides the roots of this dynamic are in the 1960s—the success of the civil rights movement and the successful harnessing of the white backlash by the Republican Party, and the response to demographic changes that followed the adoption in 1965 of a much more open immigration policy. Another part of the story reflects the response of religious Americans, particularly Christians, and among them particularly evangelicals, to the sexual revolution and the women's movement, such that today evangelicals are a critical pillar of the Republican coalition. These dynamics initially manifested in the centrality of abortion, and more recently LGBTQ rights, as a party-identity litmus test. Yet another part of the story reflects growing economic inequality and insecurity, and the successful harnessing of identity concerns and ideological purity by the pro-business wing of the Republican Party to divert attention from the practical effects of its sustained political campaign against unions, regulation, taxation, and redistribution.

There is, in other words, plenty at work before we start to consider partisan media generally, and the internet and social media in particular. And as we turn now to consider media, we have to keep in mind how the media ecosystem interacts with these long-standing structural shifts in the shape of polarization and partisanship in America. As the preceding 10 chapters already tell in great detail, there is little surprise in store in the next chapter. Yes, media matters. Our observations of the past three years online and our review of the recent media history of the United States both suggest that right-wing media has been performing different roles for

Republicans than left-wing media has played for Democrats. We observe in the real world the pattern we outlined in Chapter 3 as the propaganda feedback loop. The asymmetry, and the feedback loop it triggered, has its roots in talk radio since 1988 and in Fox News since 1996. And Fox, in particular, continues to play a more important role in the process than the internet.

The Origins of Asymmetry

*No one, today, can be simultaneously honest, informed,
and successful in the Republican Party.*

WILLIAM RUSHER, Publisher, *National Review*, 1960 (lamenting
Barry Goldwater's loss of the party's nomination to Richard Nixon)[1]

FACEBOOK DIDN'T CREATE the asymmetric architecture of the American
public sphere. Nor did the internet or the blogosphere. The asymmetry is
already clear in patterns of attention to cable news networks and talk radio.
As Jeffrey Berry and Sarah Sobieraj document in their book, *The Outrage
Industry*, left-wing partisan commentators like Lawrence O'Donnell on
MSNBC can be every bit as vehement and emotional in the outrage business
as right-wing partisans like Sean Hannity. Among stories suspect enough
to be checked by PolitiFact, Rachel Maddow's mostly-false or worse ratio
(48 percent) is not meaningfully different than Hannity's (50 percent). But
liberal audiences do not pay attention to, or trust, their partisan commentators
at rates even approaching those that typify conservative audiences. In the run-
up to the 2012 election, Fox News viewership outstripped that of MSNBC
and CNN; Maddow was drawing audiences one-third the size of the then-
most popular conservative commentator, Bill O'Reilly.[2] By November 2016,
Adweek reported that "Fox News beat CNN and MSNBC combined across
all dayparts."[3] Since Donald Trump's election, MSNBC has seen a relative
increase in viewership, but still, of the top five rated cable news shows, only
Rachel Maddow was present on the left, behind Sean Hannity and Tucker
Carlson, and ahead of Laura Ingraham and Bret Baier.[4] Consistent with the
ratings of individual shows, a Pew survey found that only 9 percent of Hillary
Clinton voters reported using MSNBC as their primary source of news about
the election. The corresponding number for Trump voters and Fox News was
40 percent.[5] The asymmetry in talk radio is even starker. There is, effectively,
no nationally syndicated liberal talk radio to speak of. From Rush Limbaugh,

Network Propaganda. Yochai Benkler, Robert Faris, and Hal Roberts.
© Yochai Benkler, Robert Faris, and Hal Roberts 2018. Published 2018 by Oxford University Press.

through Sean Hannity, to Mark Levine and a host of others vying for the same market, talk radio captures tens of millions of listeners weekly, and it is almost exclusively right-wing outrage.[6] Berry and Sobieraj also document the differences in language and rhetorical devices employed by different outrage outlets. Liberal media tend to have more mockery and direct confrontation between opponents; conservative media have few head-to-head confrontations but more misrepresentative exaggeration, insulting language, and name-calling, along with ideologically extreme activation language.[7] Compared to liberal outlets, conservative programs live on outrage; the likelihood that a given program was conservative, as opposed to liberal, increased linearly with the number of instances where one of their categories of "outrage expression" appeared in a program.[8] Perhaps unsurprisingly, getting your news from outrage merchants does not help you get a handle on reality. As Joanne Miller and her collaborators and, independently, Adam Berinsky have shown, for Democrats, the more knowledgeable they are about politics, the less likely they are to accept conspiracy theories or unsubstantiated rumors that harm their ideological opponents. But for Republicans more knowledge results in, at best, no change in the rate at which they accept conspiracy theories, and at worst, actually increases their willingness to accept such theories.[9]

There have been numerous experiments aimed at creating left-wing equivalents of the mainstays of right-wing media, most prominently Air America's effort to replicate conservative talk radio in 2004 and MSNBC's strategic shift toward creating a left-oriented mirror to Fox News in 2006. In the early stages of Web 2.0, which coincided with the George W. Bush administration and the Iraq and Afghanistan wars, a flourishing left-wing political blogosphere emerged alongside and in interaction with both mainstream media and the Democratic Party. None of these were able to replicate the industrial organization, market success, or political and cultural significance of the right, and none of these succeeded in creating a symmetrically polarized media ecosystem with balance between the left and right. Instead the left remained firmly anchored, together with the center, in "the reality-based community," while the right largely shifted to a revival of the nineteenth-century partisan press. As Theda Skocpol and Vanessa Williamson put it in their study of the rise of the Tea Party:

> American democracy is, in an important sense, caught betwixt and between in the new media world. The frank, exuberant, all-around partisanship of the nineteenth century is not quite what we now have. True, there are both liberal and conservative bloggers, and on the tube,

the Fox political slant is weakly countered by liberal-slanted shows on MSNBC. But mostly what America has right now is a thousand-pound-gorilla media juggernaut on the right, operating nineteenth-century style, coexisting with other news outlets trying to keep up while making fitful efforts, twentieth-century style, to check facts and cover "both sides of the story."[10]

It would be difficult to offer a more succinct encapsulation of what our data describe. Both the macroscale architecture our data uncover, and the detailed, microlevel data we collect on specific case studies support this basic asymmetry.

Origins

Partisan press was as American as apple pie in the nineteenth century. Vitriol, partisanship, and smear campaigns were the order of the day. But as Michael Schudson's classic work showed, American journalists in the 1920s began to develop norms and institutions that made objectivism and fact-based reporting—removed from partisan opinion—the hallmark of the profession.[11] The process was very much an application to journalism of the much broader emergence of managerialism, or Weberian rationality, to all social systems. From Taylorism and Fordism in industry, through the rise of the administrative state and the expert agencies, architecture and urban planning, to the professionalization of science and what we now think of as "the professions," the era of modernism saw a broad reorganization of social relations across diverse domains into structures oriented around expertise, objectivity, and evidence.[12]

As norms of objectivity developed for the mainstream, political suppression muted the left and right wings of the American sphere. The revolution in Russia and America's entry into World War I drove the first Red Scare. The judicial opinions that laid the foundations for what would become, decades later, the Supreme Court's First Amendment decisions that permitted speech to be suppressed only if it presents a "clear and present danger" were dissenting opinions or later-overturned decisions surrounding suppression of socialist antiwar efforts—*The Masses*,[13] *Schenck*,[14] and Oliver Wendell Holmes's dissent in *Abrams*.[15] Five times Socialist presidential candidate Eugene Debs was imprisoned for 10 years under the Espionage Act, although later pardoned by President Warren G. Harding. As radio burst onto the scene as the new mass medium in the 1920s, efforts to produce left-wing media encountered regulatory resistance. In 1925, the Chicago Federation of Labor launched WCFL. In 1927, the Socialist Party of America launched WEVD (after Eugene V. Debs). Both outlets came under severe pressure from the Federal Radio Commission as propaganda stations and were forced to accept lower-power, constrained licenses that significantly inhibited their growth and adoption.

On the right Father Coughlin became a mass phenomenon and is the direct lineal ancestor of Rush Limbaugh and conservative talk radio. Beginning his career with religious broadcasts in the late 1920s, Coughlin shifted in the 1930s from purely religious broadcasting to politics. Initially he mixed ardent anti-communism with an embrace of the New Deal. After 1934, however, Coughlin became both anti–New Deal, denouncing it as creeping communism, and increasingly pro-Fascist, anti-semitic, and antiwar. Unlike the socialist and labor stations, which the Federal Communications Commission (FCC) had constrained from the start, Father Coughlin may have reached as many as 30 million listeners.[16] And his broadcasts became a classic case study in early research on propaganda.[17] In 1939, after the war began in Europe, guidelines from the National Association of Broadcasters on selling time to "spokesmen on controversial public issues" and the threat that failure to comply with these would result in FCC nonrenewal of licenses forced Coughlin off the air. It would be five decades before his conspiracy-theory-laden, emotional, propagandist style would return to the airwaves, one year after the FCC finally repealed the fairness doctrine.

During the war, Henry Luce, the head of Time Inc. and publisher of dozens of magazines, responded to concerns about a growing regulatory state and encroaching wartime propaganda by putting in motion a process whose conclusion would become the institutional heart of the post–World War II professional ethos: the 1947 Report of the Commission on Freedom of the Press. The principal concern to which the commission responded was the increasing power of media companies and the prospect of greater censorship by the government under the guise of ensuring that media served American interests. The commission brought together 12 intellectuals to study the role of media and took on the name of its head, Robert Hutchins, the president of the University of Chicago. This coterie of upper-class white men met periodically over a four-year period and issued in 1947 a scathing report on media practices at the time. The legal scholar C. Edwin Baker described the work of the Hutchins Commission "the most important, semiofficial, policy-oriented study of the mass media in U.S. history."[18]

The Hutchins Commission defined the key functions of media as follows:

> First, a truthful, comprehensive, and intelligent account of the day's
> events in a context which gives them meaning; second, a forum for
> the exchange of comment and criticism; third, a means of projecting
> the opinions and attitudes of the groups in the society to one another;
> fourth, a method of presenting and clarifying the goals and values of
> the society; and, fifth, a way of reaching every member of the society
> by the currents of information, thought, and feeling which the press
> supplies.

They concluded that the media was failing to meet these goals:

> These needs are not being met. The news is twisted by the emphasis
> on firstness, on the novel and sensational; by the personal interests of
> owners; and by pressure groups. Too much of the regular output of
> the press consists of a miscellaneous succession of stories and images
> which have no relation to the typical lives of real people anywhere.
> Too often the result is meaninglessness, flatness, distortion, and the
> perpetuation of misunderstanding among widely scattered groups
> whose only contract is through these media.

The commission concluded that the failures of media put freedom of
expression at risk: "Press practices at times have been so irresponsible that
if continued society is bound to take control for its own protection." They
ultimately recommended self-regulation and called on media to commit itself
to take its social responsibilities more seriously.

In politics bipartisanship reigned ,and the mainstream dominated in
the post–World War II years. The New Deal and Fair Deal saw progressive
Democrats and Southern Democrats ally around programs that alleviated
poverty and stabilized economic security while largely excluding Black
populations from many of their benefits.[19] Treaty of Detroit labor relations
(agreements beginning in 1950 between the United Auto Workers and the
Big Three automobile manufacturers that set labor and wage standards
across large industrial sectors and were the foundation of post-war industrial
peace and middle-class wage growth) and the sustained economic growth
they enabled led to relatively widespread sharing of the returns, and the
dominance of Keynesianism took much of the sting out of economic policy
politics. The horror of Nazism and the solidarity of wartime experience

largely discredited the America First wing of the American right. And the
Cold War largely united Democrats and Republicans at the expense of the
left under McCarthyism.

Against this political background, and in the media and regulatory
environment of postwar America, right-wing media remained on the
periphery of mass channels. Clarence Manion's "Forum" was the most
successful radio program on the right and was popular from its launch in
1954 to its end in the late 1970s. The weekly program played a significant
role in the rise of the postwar conservative movement, supported the Barry
Goldwater candidacy, and worked in constant cooperation with the *National
Review* and other conservative outlets. It was nonetheless limited to what a
weekly show could do in terms of mass coverage.[20] On the left, the Cold War
and the Second Red Scare, McCarthyism, and the implementation of Treaty
of Detroit labor relations through a more or less centrist accommodation
between New Deal Democrats and Eisenhower-Nixon Republicans, meant
that left-wing media were marginalized. While efforts like Pacifica Radio,
launched in 1946, existed throughout this period, these remained relatively
localized and did not reach national influence.

Magazines, with respectable but limited circulation in the tens of thousands
up to around 200,000, continued to provide a forum for partisan commentary
and news. On the left, *The Nation* had been published since 1865, and *The
Progressive* and *The New Republic* (until it was bought in 1974 and moved
right) operated since the rise of the Progressive movement before World War
I. *Mother Jones* and *The American Prospect* joined them in later decades. On
the right, *Human Events* launched in 1944 as a vestige of the America First
antiwar movement, and developed over the 1950s and 60s as a major voice in
the rise of the conservative movement. *National Review*, of course, became the
sine qua non of conservative media within a few years of its founding in 1955.[21]
And while these conservative publications and the "Manion Forum" formed
an interconnected network of outlets, with some shared publication facilities
and with mutual recognition and praise, they never reached the scale and
scope of either Coughlin's audience or what would emerge in the 1990s. The
only moment when conservative publications reached a truly mass audience
was the publication of three self-published paperbacks in the run-up to the
1964 election, which were published outside of the right-wing media network
but sold a total of 16 million copies, containing various conspiracy theories
to suggest a Lyndon Johnson presidency would be a disaster (including, in
A Texan Looks at Lyndon, insinuating that Johnson had an interest in the
John F. Kennedy assassination that preceded his rise to the presidency).[22]

The Goldwater candidacy and anonymous donor purchases of these books in order to distribute them as campaign paraphernalia combined to make these paperbacks instant successes, but subsequent efforts to replicate their success after Johnson won the election faltered.

Ultimately, the first generation of right-wing media was unable to overcome then-prevailing structural barriers to success. Most Americans got their news from the three broadcast networks. Radio still operated under strict group ownership limits, which meant that national syndication required negotiations with many independent station owners. Broadcast operated under the FCC's fairness doctrine, whose core requirements were that broadcasters cover matters of public importance and that they do so fairly, mostly in the sense that they air competing positions. The doctrine was often associated with a right of reply for politicians who were subject to personal attack and other elements of the broader "public trustee" doctrine that held that private broadcasters holding licenses to public airwaves should act in managing those airwaves as a trustee for the real owners—the American people. While the fairness doctrine did not often result in complete silencing, it made many broadcasters skittish about airing programming that they thought might trigger an obligation to grant free response time to those attacked in these broadcasts. Daily newspapers were local and largely independent. All these conditions made it hard for first-generation postwar right-wing media to reach mass distribution on a national scale. Indeed, the anchor tenants of the first-generation right-wing media system were never, or almost never, economically sustainable as businesses. They relied on donations from listeners, a handful of ideologically committed wealthy individuals, and some corporate sponsorship. On the left these same economic barriers joined the more direct effects of anti-Communist sentiment and political and legal constraints stretching from the first Red Scare into the 1960s.

The one enduring legacy of that post–World War II generation of right-wing media was the basic rhetorical frame of liberal media bias. As Nicole Hemmer traces in great detail, *Human Events* imparted that sense that mainstream media was biased against conservative beliefs from its earliest days. By the 1960s the insistence that mainstream newspapers were biased and that it was necessary to produce media that were objective, but not impartial, was a basic tenet of conservative media. Hemmer describes a moment when, as part of the years-long battle between the UAW and the Kohler Company about whether Kohler would be a union shop, Manion offered Herbert Kohler an open channel to air his views. The union threatened to sue the station, and, fearing liability, the network of Mutual stations that aired the

"Manion Forum" canceled that day's show. Manion responded by setting up his own network, syndicating his show to independent broadcast stations and setting up the first prototype of a conservative network. A basic theme emerged throughout the network of conservative publications in the 1950s and '60s. Mainstream media were biased against conservative views; the FCC's fairness doctrine, and the norms of objectivity held by Northeastern publishing, radio, and television elites all excluded conservative views from the media; and the only answer was to create mass-scale media that would balance out that broad media bias by taking a conservative perspective on what to report and how to report on it. That viewpoint of liberal media bias was embraced and repeated vocally by Spiro Agnew, and later by Richard Nixon as the Nixon administration struggled with increasing pressure from traditional journalistic sources—from the Pentagon Papers to Watergate. But that era also coincided with professional journalists receiving the highest levels of trust and positive public opinion, among both Democrats and Republicans, that has been recorded in the General Social Survey.[23]

Just as there was right-wing criticism of mainstream media, there was a steady flow of left-wing media criticism, most famously Edward Herman and Noam Chomsky's *Manufacturing Consent*,[24] but no less so Ben Bagdikian's *Media Monopoly*[25] and work by Robert McChesney, Ed Baker, and others, about the extent to which mainstream media reflect the perspectives and interests of corporate owners, government insiders, and the national security establishment. It was precisely that sense that underlay some of the early enthusiasm associated with the emergence of the internet as a democratizing medium, freeing individual and informal networks of individuals to play a greater role in setting the agenda, reporting the news, and mobilizing in a new networked public sphere.[26] But because a left-wing mass media ecosystem never emerged in the same way as it did in the 1990s on the right, this left-wing version of the media-bias argument remained largely within the academic and activist domain and never became a basic narrative shared by large parts of the population. But on the right, televangelism, talk radio, and ultimately Fox News were able to reach mass audiences that eluded the first generation of postwar conservative media, and it was these outlets' mass appeal that successfully generalized the "liberal media bias" frame to large parts of the population. That imbalance between the left and right's ability to develop highly partisan mass media outlets, rather than the absence of a left-wing critique of media, accounts for the clear asymmetry in levels of trust in media between right-leaning and left-leaning mass audiences.

After Disco: Talk Radio, Televangelism, and Cable News

Over the course of the 1970s, 1980s, and 1990s, a series of technological, institutional, and political changes removed each of the structural barriers that had contained the first generation of right-wing media and created the conditions for the emergence and dramatic success of the second generation right-wing media system that undergirds today's asymmetric architecture, anchored by Fox News and talk radio.

The 1970s saw substantial moves to deregulate cable and remove many of the byzantine constraints that the FCC had placed on it during the 1960s and early 1970s at the behest of incumbent television broadcasters.[27] At the same time, several technological developments increased cable channel capacity and the reach of national networks. Satellite distribution of content to local cable ground stations allowed Ted Turner to launch TBS as the first national cable network. Developments in compression, set-top box, and later hybrid fiber-coaxial systems dramatically increased channel capacity over the course of the 1980s and 1990s, making room for more niche-programming channels to develop. One of the earliest format innovations was CNN. In 1980, when it launched, CNN was a far-out idea—a 24-hour news channel in an era when the major news networks were losing money on creating a 30-minute show at prime time. Its audience grew dramatically over the course of the 1980s. Beginning with a paltry 1.3 million households at a time when network news was viewed by tens of millions across the three networks, CNN quickly grew and within a decade matched the big three networks in news audience. In 1991 the Iraq War marked the coming of age of CNN, as it became the go-to source, and in the early stages the only source, with coverage from inside Baghdad. By 1992 Pew found that about 30 percent of Americans who said they got their presidential election news on TV got it on CNN.[28] It was only at that point, with the business model proven and the technological trajectory toward increasing channel capacity settled, that two more 24-hour news channels—Fox and MSNBC—joined the fray in 1996.

Another major media development in the 1970s and 1980s was the emergence of televangelism and evangelical Christian broadcasting. Despite their long presence as part of the American religious experience, in the 1940s and 1950s evangelicals were largely marginalized on the airwaves through the combined efforts of the major mainline religious organizations and the broadcast networks.[29] Religious broadcasting during that period was treated as part of the broadcasters' public interest obligations, which the

FCC allowed broadcasters to satisfy by airing mainline religious broadcasts on a "sustaining" basis—that is to say, unpaid.[30] In 1960–1961, the FCC made two regulatory changes that would ultimately enable televangelism to replace mainline churches on the airwaves. Intense lobbying by evangelical broadcasters led the FCC to change its rules in 1960 to permit broadcasters to treat paid religious programming to count against their public interest obligation. And evangelical broadcasters paid. By the end of the 1970s, paid evangelical programming used this opening to almost entirely displace mainline religious programming on mainstream broadcast stations. In 1961 Congress also passed the All Channel Receiver Act, which required all TV sets to be enabled to receive Ultra High Frequency (UHF), not only the established Very High Frequency (VHF) channels. This change made the largely fallow UHF licenses usable, and these became the basis for a new crop of Christian broadcasters. By 1978 there were 30 new religious stations. More importantly, syndication of the top 10 religious programs, through paid programming, accounted for half the religious programs aired. As cable capacity and adoption expanded, cable reception in turn evened out the quality differential between UHF and VHF stations, and the new possibility of combining cable local distribution with the satellite national syndication that had enabled Turner's launch of TBS, also enabled Pat Robertson to launch the Christian Broadcasting Network (CBN) a few months later. Robertson had purchased a defunct broadcast license in 1961 and began broadcasting his "700 Club" in 1963. By the mid-1980s CBN's viewership was third only to CNN and ESPN.[31] This rise in audience share for Christian broadcasting coincided with a reorientation of evangelicals toward politics. In support of this reorientation, Robertson changed the format of the "700 Club" in 1980 to include the first investigative journalism and news reporting segments aired by religious broadcast.[32] The reach of these broadcasts is a matter of some controversy, but 20 million American households is a reasonable estimate of the number who watched at least some religious programming in the 1980s.[33] While televangelism viewership declined in the wake of the scandals that hit televangelists in 1987, most prominently Jim and Tammy Bakker, the new role of evangelicals as a major pillar of the conservative Republican coalition made sure that Christian broadcasting remained an important and distinguishing element of the right-wing media ecosystem—one that came out of a distinctly different moral universe than the framework that underlay the objectivity norms of professional journalism.

Like cable and televangelism, AM talk radio emerged out of an interaction between technological and regulatory changes. The tragic story of how David

Sarnoff—legendary radio pioneer, head of RCA, and founder of NBC—used litigation and FCC channel allocation proceedings to frustrate and delay adoption of Edwin Armstrong's superior FM radio technology is oft told and well known.[34] It delayed widespread adoption of the technology for decades, well after it drove Armstrong to suicide in 1954. It was only in the 1970s that the number of FM receivers came to equal that of AM receivers, and it was only then that a significant new generation of DJs began experimenting with using the technology, particularly its ability to transmit stereo, to play longer format, non-top-40 music.[35] By the early 1980s FM radio far overtook AM, and music in particular was shifting to the higher fidelity, stereo-capable systems. AM needed something new, that did not suffer so much from the technical deficit. That something would turn out to be talk radio. And, as cable did for Turner's superstation model, satellite distribution to ground stations allowed national syndication on a scale and quality that transmission over copper wire had not, significantly increasing the potential reach of this new format.[36]

But for political talk radio to emerge, one regulatory piece had to fall in place. Driven by a deep ideological commitment to free markets, FCC Chair Mark Fowler, perhaps known best for his quip that a television is just a "toaster with pictures,"[37] led a campaign to repeal the fairness doctrine throughout most of his tenure in office. The doctrine had had a varied life since 1949. Throughout the '50s and '60s, first-generation right-wing media outlets saw the fairness doctrine as a direct threat to their ability to use radio. However, Nixon's use of the FCC and the increasingly sophisticated strategic use of fairness doctrine complaints by both conservatives and liberals alike evened out the partisan effects by the 1970s.[38] Fowler built a record of these complaints and worked over years until the FCC repealed the fairness doctrine as inconsistent with the First Amendment. The repeal was completed in 1987.

In 1988 Rush Limbaugh's daily three-hour shock-jock right-wing talk radio show became nationally syndicated. His visceral, emotional style; his unabashedly partisan exhortations and commentary; and his sheer capacity to sustain three hours a day of programming launched the second-generation right-wing media ecosystem (as well as saving AM radio). By 1990 he was reported to be syndicated on over 300 stations and reaching 5 million listeners a week.[39] In 1992 he was reported to have 14 million listeners every week, and launched his syndicated television program Rush Limbaugh Show, which was produced by Roger Ailes.[40] That year, Ronald Reagan sent Limbaugh a letter lauding him as "the number one voice for conservatism in our country."[41] In 1993 *National Review*'s cover anointed Limbaugh "The Leader of the Opposition."[42] When Republicans took the House in 1994, Limbaugh was feted as the "majority maker," an honorary member of the freshman class of the 104th Congress. Newt Gingrich's former press secretary described Limbaugh as the most important person other than Gingrich in achieving the new Republican majority,[43] and Tom DeLay credited him with giving the Republicans their ideological marching orders in the 1993–1994 run-up to their victory.[44] By 1996 the Pew report on voter media consumption already treated Limbaugh as one of the major sources of news for voters, noting that Limbaugh "has many more Republicans and twice as many conservatives in his audience than business magazines." In that survey, 37 percent of respondents said they got news about presidential candidates and the campaign from talk radio, and about 20 percent answered that question with Focus on the Family or the Christian Broadcasting Network.[45] The style Limbaugh developed, and has retained since, includes strong emotional appeals to audiences, continuous criticism of mainstream media aimed to undermine trust in media, systematic efforts to undermine trust in government whenever led by Democrats, and policing of Republican candidates and politicians to make sure they toed the conservative line.[46] In 1996 Limbaugh abandoned his syndicated television program and focused on radio, where he has been reported (occasionally with skepticism) to attract on the order of 14 to 20 million listeners weekly since the early 2000s.[47] Roger Ailes, in the meantime, found a new partner in Rupert Murdoch and launched Fox News.

Talk radio was supercharged beyond Limbaugh by the industry consolidation that followed the loosening of ownership limits in the Telecommunications Act of 1996. That act was the most extensive reform of communications law since 1934. Most of it dealt with enhancing competition in telecommunications. But the act also significantly reduced the ownership limits on radio stations and made mergers easier. Throughout the preceding decades, FCC radio regulation reflected a clear commitment to localism—to the idea that local radio stations should serve the local community—by preferring to license locally owned stations—and to competition, by setting clear caps on how many stations any single company could own, both nationally and locally. As Clinton Democrats came to embrace deregulation alongside Reagan Republicans, both constraints were loosened significantly. The result was a rapid consolidation in the radio station markets. Clear Channel Communications in particular went on a buying spree. By one account the firm owned 43 stations nationwide before the 1996 Act, and eight years later owned over 1,200 stations, reaching over 100 million listeners.[48] One of those purchases included Jacor Communications, which, like Clear Channel, had started to grow through acquisitions after 1996. But Jacor brought to Clear Channel more than its 230 stations. It also brought Premier Radio, the producer of the radio shows of Rush Limbaugh, Sean Hannity, and Glenn Beck. Hours of right-wing radio propaganda were now seamlessly syndicated throughout the United States; and radio, to this day, is the communications platform that reaches the most U.S. adults daily.[49] One politically liberal survey of talk radio in 2007 found that talk radio featured conservative programming over liberal programming by a 10:1 ratio.[50] Conservatives gladly acknowledge that talk radio is overwhelmingly their turf.[51] Air America, the liberal counterpart to conservative talk radio, largely failed as a commercial enterprise. Democracy Now! succeeded in establishing itself as a listener-supported daily radio broadcast in about 350 cities across the United States, initially on a handful of Pacifica radio stations and now occupying an hour a day, sometimes repeated for another hour. Lacking the benefits of Clear Channel's distribution network or commercial funding, the program is concentrated in relatively liberal states and regions. In part, the weakness of left-leaning radio may reflect the diversity of the liberal coalition. Conservative talk shows aim at and capture a large and relatively homogenous block—white, Christian, and older. Liberals include Black and Hispanic populations, each seen as its own market segment,[52] and liberal radio also had to contend with NPR, an enormously successful radio system that maintains a palpable liberal editorial tone while adhering to mainstream journalistic norms in reporting—in that regard more like a liberal version of the *Wall Street Journal*, than like Fox News or MSNBC. And in the 2000s liberals tuned into late night comedy, particularly John Stewart and then Stephen Colbert, for their mass media partisan diet. In the news segment of the market, nothing emerged to match Fox News as an alternative partisan news system, dedicated to providing sustained news coverage from a consistently partisan perspective until MSNBC shifted strategy in 2006, a decade after Fox News and nearly 20 years after Limbaugh.

Murdoch and Ailes's innovation was to capture market share in the 24-hour news channel not by competing on the same model as CNN, but by offering a similar 24-hour news format oriented to leverage the market that Limbaugh had proven—giving right-wing audiences an outlet they did not have within media constrained by professional journalistic norms.[53] Fox News combined the format of CNN's 24-hour news network model with the audience-segmentation strategy that had been developed by the Christian broadcasters and Limbaugh in the 1980s and early 1990s. Rather than serving the median viewer in hopes of capturing a share of it, which was the prevailing theory of how to compete in the three-network world of over-the-air broadcast, channel abundance made room for stark audience segmentation as a robust and successful strategy. Within five years of its launch, and particularly after September 11, 2001, Fox News caught up to and then passed its major rival, CNN. By the 2016 election cycle American right-leaning audiences had been exposed for two decades on television (and nearly three on radio) to a propagandist mass media outlet built on feeding its viewers with news that fit and reinforced their world view while constantly pointing fingers at all other media sources as biased. The strategy paid off for Fox in producing an immensely loyal viewership, and for the Republican Party with a core of support highly resilient to the vicissitudes of real-world failure or transient political winds.

Studies by Pew of the news habits of Republicans and Democrats demonstrate the significant difference between the two audiences. A 2014 study found that 47 percent of "consistently conservative" respondents identified Fox News as their "main source of news about government and politics."[54] Another 11 percent mentioned "local radio" as their main source, and in a breakdown of sources of news that meant that Hannity on radio, Limbaugh, Glenn Beck on radio, and Beck's "The Blaze" all ran ahead of ABC, CBS, or NBC, much less CNN.[55] By contrast, "consistently liberal" respondents were spread out much more evenly across various media, including primarily CNN (15 percent), NPR (13 percent), MSNBC (12 percent), and the New York Times (10 percent). Conservatives not only watch and listen to Fox News and talk radio, they also express high trust in these sources. A full 88 percent of consistently conservative viewers trusted Fox News, 62 percent trusted Hannity, and 58 percent trusted Limbaugh. Among "consistently liberal" respondents, NPR, PBS, and the BBC were the most trusted sources, hovering around 70 percent. MSNBC, which since 2006 has mounted the most explicit effort to mirror the Fox News strategy for the left, received only a 52 percent trust score from consistently liberal respondents and was trusted by fewer than half of the "mostly liberal" respondents, all of whom trust CNN and the major television networks to a degree largely consistent with the trust patterns of respondents who were "mixed" liberal and conservative (Figure 11.1).

This pre-election snapshot reflects one moment in a long trajectory of declining and divergent levels of trust in journalism between conservatives and liberals, Republicans and Democrats. Gallup has been measuring distrust in media since the mid-1990s.[56] In 1998 and 2000 party identifiers of both parties, and independents, were closest to each other in the level of trust in

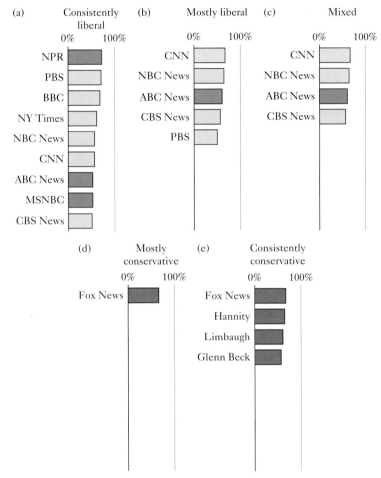

FIGURE 11.1 Trust in media by ideological identity.
Source: Pew Research Center.

media: 52-53-59 (R-I-D) in 1998, and 47-53-53 (R-I-D) in 2000. Election coverage separated democrats from Republicans in 2001, but 9/11 brought the two groups together in 2002: 39-52-65 in 2001, 49-52-59 in 2002. Republican trust in media dropped over the remainder of George W. Bush's first term in office, from 49 percent in 2002 to 31 percent in 2004, where it stayed fairly stable until 2015 and the beginning of the 2016 election cycle. In 2016, just before the election, it dropped precipitously to 14 percent and remained at that level in 2017. These patterns of extremely low trust in media are highly consistent with the pattern of attention that we observe in our data—with conservative audiences tweeting and sharing on Facebook stories from within an insular right-wing media ecosystem and largely ignoring most other sites. By contrast, Democrats' trust in media rose over the course of George W. Bush's first term, from 53 percent in 2000 up to between 60 percent and 65 percent until the first year of the Barack Obama presidency, after which it saw a gradual steady decline, down to 51 percent in 2016, followed by a sharp upswing in 2017 back to 72 percent, its highest value in the Gallup set and closely matched only by the 2005 Gallup poll (which likely coincided with coverage of Hurricane Katrina). Again, this trust is consistent with our behavioral observations about which sites users who are not on the right tend to share and amplify. The category of "independents" that show up in these polls should not in fact be treated as a completely distinct third group. Surveys suggest that this group is made up mostly of Republican and Democratic leaners (slightly more Republicans than Democrats), with only 15 percent of all independents truly not leaning toward one or the other party. Both sets of "lean-party" respondents are very similar to party identifiers of the party toward which they lean.[57] Unsurprisingly, independent trends "split the difference" between the responses of party identifiers. The pattern suggests (a) systematically less trust among Republicans throughout the period, and (b) a correlation between trust in media and the party of the president in power. If mainstream media are consistently somewhat critical of whoever happens to be in power, then partisans of that president will see media as less trustworthy whenever that party is in control and more trustworthy when the opposite party is in control.

The longest relevant time series on the question of trust in media is the General Social Survey's question on confidence in the press. Most revealing is the partisan breakdown of the question that is the inverse of Gallup's question. Where Gallup reports all those who have "a great deal" or a "fair amount" of trust in media, the GSS also collects data on everyone else—in particular, those who have "hardly any" trust in media (Figure 11.2).

Several patterns emerge. First, extreme distrust of the press media was very low in the 1970s and the immediate post-Watergate era, although it briefly bounced upward during that era among Republican Party identifiers. The Reagan-Bush years in the 1980s to 1992 saw Democrats jump in their high distrust from 14 percent to about 20 percent, while Republicans saw their distrust rate hover around 30 percent during the 1980s. Republicans saw a clear inflection point from 1990, when their "hardly any" category made up 29 percent of Republican respondents, to 47 percent in 1993, as Bill Clinton became president and on the eve of the Gingrich revolution. Republicans response remained stable until 1998, when it again inflected upward from 44 percent in 1998 to the upper-mid 50s (56–57 percent, up to 60–61 percent)

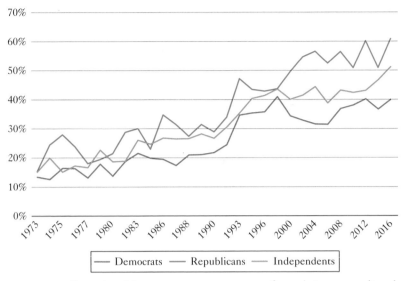

FIGURE II.2 General social survey responses: percent of population responding that they have "hardly any" confidence in the press (1973–2016).[58]

from 2002 until the 2016 election. Among Democrats, by contrast, there was an inflection point from 1990 to 1993 (22 to 35 percent), and distrust stayed at that level except for a brief peak (41%) during the Lewinsky affair in 1998 percent (which was also the Republican's lowest "hardly ever" answer, at 44 percent), from where it gradually declined until 2006. It again shifted upward from a low of 31 percent in 2006 to a high just under 40 percent over the course of the Obama years.

Given the great number of factors involved in broad, population-level trends of trust and distrust, it is impossible to identify a clear causal line from media coverage to levels of trust in media. It is hard, for example, to lay the 1990 dramatic increase of distrust in media at the feet of Rush Limbaugh, given that "hardly ever" responses among Democrats increased by 50 percent (from 22 percent to 35 percent) between 1990 and 1993, a very similar degree of change as that among Republicans during the same time period (29 percent to 47 percent). By contrast, the Republican inflection point in 1998 certainly could reflect a Fox News effect similar to the effect we describe at the end of this chapter. It is difficult to imagine that the sustained attacks on the credibility of the media by political leaders and the partisan press for over two decades have been entirely inert and have not contributed meaningfully to undermining their audience's confidence in the independent press. And it is difficult to imagine that attacks such as these by Fox News, the news source conservatives trust above all other news sources in the country, have no effect on the fact that precisely those conservatives who most trust Fox News also have the lowest trust in all other media. And the result is quite an outlier by international standards. The Reuters Institute found that U.S. media were more starkly polarized than in other countries, primarily in the sense that right-wing viewers did not look at most mainstream publications and that self-described right-leaning survey respondents showed much lower trust in news media than self-described left-leaning respondents.[59] The most powerful finding in the Reuters Institute report was that "[i]n the United States the headline rate (38%) is up, although there is a 15-point gap between this and trust in the sources you use (53%). Only Hungary, another deeply polarized country, has a bigger gap between general trust (31%) and the sources you use (54%)."[60]

Existing in a media ecosystem dominated by media whose role is to confirm your preconceptions and lead you to distrust any sources that might challenge your beliefs is a recipe for misinformation and susceptibility to disinformation. At the end of the day, if one side most trusts Fox News, Hannity, Limbaugh, and Beck, and the other side most trusts NPR, the BBC, PBS, and the *New York Times*, one cannot expect both sides to be equally informed or equally capable of telling truth from identity-confirming fiction.

As we discussed in more detail in Chapter 3, the propaganda feedback loop that creates the patterns of distrust and media attention and the dynamic way in which media production and consumption patterns feed into each other and into the behavior of political elites, seem sufficient to explain the sustained differences between Democrats and Republicans in their susceptibility to conspiracy theory and rumor.[61] The audiences of talk radio, Fox News, and other conservative media outlets are subject to a sustained flow of identity-confirming news and attacks on potential sources of error correction, and are informed by their political elites that certain facts and attitudes are identity consistent and that challenges to these facts reflect bias of the other side, rather than being the products of professional, objective norms. Right-wing audiences are systematically disconnected from potential sources of disconfirmation. As the dissonance between what they receive from their own media and what they receive from outside increases, a deeply asymmetric trust structure develops which associates identity-confirming news as trustworthy and identity-disconfirming news as suspect. This does not require any special psychological profile; it is merely a direct consequence of the architecture of the media system. And it means that a population with high trust in bias-confirming news and high distrust in bias-disconfirming, professional-norms-driven media will be more vulnerable to disinformation campaigns than a population that has generally higher trust in professional journalism on average, but lower trust in any given media outlet. The latter population will, on average, check and cross-reference rumors, conspiracy theories, and other modes of disinformation more than the former. And it is onto that baseline asymmetric structure—of media outlets, political elite practices, and media consumption and trust patterns—that the internet and social media were grafted. And, unsurprisingly, the different architectures of the two parts of the media ecosystem resulted in quite different susceptibility to the new techniques of network propaganda. As our case studies in Chapters 3 to 9 showed, Russian propaganda, commercial clickbait entrepreneurs, sockpuppets and botnets, and straight-up partisan disinformation campaigns all operated differently in the right-wing media ecosystem than in the center and left. And whatever solutions we will embrace, if all we do is treat the discrete, social-media-focused manifestations of the underlying structural difference, our answers will be partial and unstable.

What About the Internet?

In March 1995 the Drudge Report already had 1,000 email subscribers.[62] For perspective, the yahoo.com domain had only been registered in January of that year, and Microsoft would release its first version of Internet Explorer in August. At the time the internet enjoyed wide acclaim as a democratizing technology. In 1997 the Supreme Court hailed it as a platform on which "[t]hrough the use of chat rooms, any person with a phone line can become a town crier with a voice that resonates farther than it could from any soapbox. Through the use of web pages, mail exploders, and newsgroups, the same individual can become a pamphleteer."[63] That image captured what many of us writing about the internet at the time thought. Reduced costs of producing and sharing information, news, and perspectives would, for the first time since the emergence of mass circulation print and broadcast, enable citizens to participate in setting the public agenda and mobilize for action around our intense political concerns, rather than following the agenda set by media owners, the advertisers who paid, and political elites to whom they paid attention.[64] In a 1999 article, for example, one of us described a copyright lawsuit by the *Washington Post* and *Los Angeles Times* against the conservative Free Republic website, and argued that the amateur, citizen-produced commentary and speech produced on Free Republic offered an important new degree of diversity and free speech in the public sphere that would be lost if courts continued to prefer commercial organizations as the core speakers in the networked public sphere. Within a couple of years, however, a counternarrative emerged that blamed the internet for causing fragmentation and polarization,[65] phenomena that we, in Chapters 10 and 11, describe as a consequence of longer-term political processes and changes in the radio and television media ecosystems.

The first dozen or so years of the twenty-first century continued and deepened the pattern. Building on new empirical observations that online attention tended to follow power law,[66] rather than normal distributions— that is, a very small number of sites garnered a very large portion of the attention—several authors argued that in practice the internet replicates the broadcast model of attention, with a very small number of sites accounting for most of what people read or heard.[67] Some empirical studies, most prominently pioneering work by Nancy Glance and Lada Adamic, tended to support Cass Sunstein's arguments about polarization and fragmentation of political discourse, rather than a reconcentration on a small number of supernodes.[68] Importantly, those early efforts to map the blogosphere tended to observe a symmetric pattern of polarization. A different line of argument against the democratizing effects of the internet was that they simply were not that important. Markus Prior emphasized that most people were simply distracted—and enjoyed broad access to entertainment and other formats that left them simply uninformed—leaving only the more partisan and polarized to participate.[69] Matthew Hindman used extensive data analysis of blogs and their use to argue that the relative size of the political blogosphere was negligible in the overall scheme of internet usage, and that those who wrote the top blogs were as much a part of the elite as the op-ed writers.[70] Nonetheless, as we discuss in more detail in Chapter 12, throughout those years more of the academic work combined qualitative assessment, survey data, and quantitative analysis to argue that the internet had a more democratizing effect, whether emphasizing mobilization, diversity of view-points, or organizational transformation as the elements that made for a networked public sphere in which power to set the agenda and influence political discourse was more widely distributed.

Although Drudge and the Free Republic were early adopters, the "Web 2.0" period in the first decade of the twenty-first century saw more or less equal growth on the two sides of the partisan divide online. In one of the first studies that looked systematically at the differences between the left and the right in this period, one of us collaborating with Aaron Shaw showed that the primary differences during this period revolved around organization and action orientation.[71] Bloggers on the right tended to write many more sole-authored sites that primarily shared links to stories found online with brief comments. The Free Republic was, in this regard, unusual on the right. On the left there were more group blogs and blogs that enabled users to write their own diaries. The left also had much more of a focus on action orientation—raising funds in particular—than the right blogosphere did.[72] Daily Kos was the standard-bearer of this format. Howard Dean's insurgent presidential campaign in 2004 is generally celebrated as the first political campaign supported by the "netroots," young, mobilized, liberal, internet-based activists, which continued to play a significant role in the 2006 and 2008 campaigns,[73] but the decentralized, self-organizing approach was as central to Ron Paul's supporters on the libertarian right as it was for those of the netroots on the left. Of the highly visible sites during that early Web 2.0 period, several on both sides of the political divide continued to be influential in the 2016 cycle, such as the Daily Kos and Talking Points Memo on the left, or Michelle Malkin, Townhall, and RedState on the right. However, the most influential were either founded in that Web 2.0 period as media ventures, such as Huffington Post (2005), BuzzFeed (2006), or Breitbart (2007), or founded more recently, after 2010. Because the techniques and research questions that have been brought to bear in the last few years were not available at the time, we do not have a systematic study to which we can compare our current results to those that described the blogosphere in its first few years. Studies did not include mainstream media; they described much shorter snapshots of time, and often included blogrolls, as opposed to specifically story links, which means that they reflected to some extent affinity networks rather than authority or attention networks, as ours do. Because of the differences in what was possible and done at the time, we do not know whether the actual linking patterns were similarly asymmetric during the first few years of Web 2.0, or whether the networked public sphere was more symmetric then, unlike on TV and radio. The earliest analysis we have, from our data, goes back to the month before the 2012 election (Figure 11.3). And while the details are slightly different, and the overall architecture is less clearly segregated asymmetrically, it is structurally similar to what we found in our data from 2015 to 2018. We see a well-separated right-wing sphere, though it is more integrated and offers a more prominent place to media outlets we characterized as center-right in 2016, particularly the older conservative publications like the *National Review* or *Weekly Standard*. The rest of the media ecosystem was anchored around mainstream media in 2012 as it was in our present study. Because we only captured data for one month

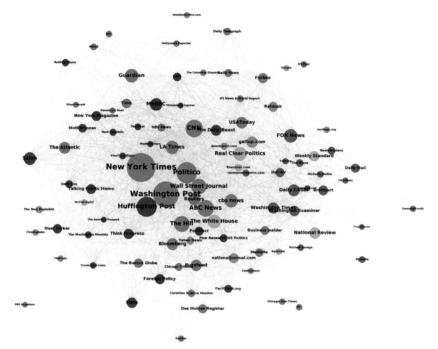

FIGURE 11.3 Network map of political media in the United States during the 2012 election. Nodes sized by media inlinks.

prior to 2012, this architecture is likely noisy and only indicative of the trend toward the patterns we now observe.

As social media, in particular Facebook, replaced Web 2.0 technologies central to the blogosphere, the debate took on the familiar structure of the prior decade and a half, triggered most powerfully by the Arab Spring (and before that the Iranian Green Wave moment) and the brief exhilaration associated with seeing a region long-plagued by repressive and corrupt regimes rising up to demand democracy.[74] Terms like "liberation technology"[75] or "emancipatory politics" [76] set the frame for Hillary Clinton's State Department to adopt its Internet Freedom Agenda as one of its core programs for expanding democracy throughout the world. The Arab Spring, and after it Occupy Wall Street and the Indignados in Spain, were the high-water mark for the argument that the internet democratizes and liberates. The apparent short-term media and attention victories were followed in most places by political losses, while the digital trails, particularly on Twitter, enabled a new generation of data-collection techniques to evaluate the structure of organization in online mobilization. Sandra González-Bailón and her collaborators' research on the Indignados movement showed that the structure of online mobilization was more hierarchical and centered on major influencers as central nodes.[77] Mayo Fuster Morell emphasized the ways in which the anti-austerity 15-M Movement in Spain was built on earlier mobilization efforts in the Free-Culture movement.[78] Zeynep Tufekci's analysis of these protest movements, from Tahrir to Gezi Park and Zucotti Park, led to a new ambivalence about the double-edged nature of social media for mobilization and the possibilities it opened for repression.[79] Nagla Rizk's analysis of the post-revolution networked public sphere in Egypt similarly underscored the rising role of both the Egyptian Army and the Muslim Brotherhood on Facebook, and their displacement of the earlier, more liberal Egyptian blogosphere, as central dynamics in the unfolding of the story of the Egyptian revolution,[80] with only Tunisia offering a major counterexample.[81] In all, as the dust settled from the Occupy movement and the Arab Spring, the liberating potential of decentralized social mobilization began to give way to the consideration of the benefits of more organizationally structured politics.

As networked discourse shifted from the open web to social media, large parts of the media ecosystem became much more opaque. While Twitter opened its data and gave rise to a generation of studies that have taught us most of what we know about discourse and mobilization on social media, Facebook created an enormously powerful platform that was in large parts unobservable by anyone who wanted to understand how the internet was affecting democracy. Anyone, that is, except Facebook scientists. The most significant study of polarization on Facebook was done by a team inside Facebook and published in *Science* in 2015.[82] Using data from the last six months of 2014, the team found that Facebook users who shared news did so in a polarized way, but that they did so primarily because they shared what their friends shared, and they were segregated into politically homogeneous communities. It was users' sharing patterns, not the design of Facebook's algorithms that led to the polarization. Setting aside the troubling self-serving nature of a team in Facebook publishing a study that exonerates Facebook from responsibility for polarization in American politics, using data the company would not share with outsiders except under a nondisclosure agreement, the pattern of polarization they describe dovetails quite well with what we observed. We showed that based on Facebook sharing, the two sides of the media ecosystem look more symmetrically polarized than when measured by tweets or inlinks, but nonetheless there was significant asymmetry, with the right being much more skewed. The 2015 Facebook paper similarly showed a broad symmetry, but with the more extreme right-wing content accounting for a larger share of right-oriented sharing than the most extreme left-wing sites accounting for sharing on the left, and sharing of sites on the left extending much further toward the middle of the ideological spectrum. The comparison is imperfect, because the Facebook team were not looking specifically to compare, but the published materials offer support for the proposition that the asymmetry we observe clearly since 2015, and was also visible in our 2012 data, was also there in this very large study conducted between our two observation periods.

As we look at the internet and its history, it seems that we have some anecdotal evidence of the early success of right-wing-oriented sites, but little evidence from the first dozen or so years of political speech on the internet of the asymmetries we observe today. We certainly have nothing like the sustained evidence of asymmetry in cable television or talk radio. By the second decade of the twenty-first century, however, we do in fact see such a differentiation, and our data from 2012 and early 2015 suggests that it is already well established by then, rather than that it first emerged during the 2016 presidential campaign. If we understand that online media and offline media interact in an integrated single large media ecosystem, we can also understand that online media on the right and the left faced different incentive structures and different constraints. As mainstream media came online, online left media had to contend with audiences that had a moderate trust in mainstream media and an architecture of use that exposed them extensively to mainstream professional media offline. Selling wild bias-confirming conspiracies risked harming a publication's reputation, or consigning it to amusement rather than news, because of negative feedback effects from that sphere's most trusted sources. Online left publications faced the reality-check dynamic. On the right, presented with an audience already highly attuned to talk radio and Fox News and deeply distrusting of all media outside their ecosystem, right-wing sites that came online—Breitbart, Daily Caller, and beyond—faced very different competitive pressures, and positive feedback reinforcement for bias-confirming news, irrespective of its veracity. Heightened partisanship was a positive differentiator, and manifest falsehood (as long as it was only pointed out by mainstream outlets that could be painted as corrupt and lying) was not a particularly costly practice. Indeed, when Hannity amplifies an Infowars story, the falsehood becomes a virtue. Right-wing online media had to adapt to a media ecosystem that was already a decade or two into the propaganda feedback loop. When Breitbart was launched in 2007, it had to compete for an audience that had already listened to Rush Limbaugh for 20 years, and to Fox News for 11. When the Huffington Post launched in 2005, Air America was barely a year old, and MSNBC had not yet shifted from trying to copy CNN to trying to differentiate as the mirror image of Fox.

It is not hard to explain why a population exposed to news outlets whose core professional commitment is to provide partisan bias-confirming news will be more susceptible to partisan identity-consistent rumor, conspiracy theory, and disinformation than a population whose media consumption habits are anchored in media committed to fact checking and objective reporting. Those who exist in a media ecosystem committed to objectivity (and the commitment need not be perfectly followed; it merely needs to restrict the practices in the main) will usually encounter no confirmation, or refutation, of the false information in the media they trust the most. By contrast, those who pay attention to the partisan media will not generally receive disconfirmation and will instead often receive confirmation and amplification of the false facts. When the Petra News Agency in Jordan was hacked and had a story planted supposedly exposing an interview with the Saudi now–crown prince boasting that the Saudis had funded 20 percent of Hillary Clinton's campaign, the story was reported on the Zero Hedge and then republished on the Fox News website and Infowars.[83] In addition to reinforcing the conspiracy theory fringe claims, the partisan media persistently reiterate for their readers, viewers, and listeners that the mainstream, professional media are the ones who are biased, partisan, and "fake," and that only they, the partisan media, are in fact those who offer "fair and balanced" reporting. This makes the corrective role of professional institutions asymmetrically available to the two populations.

We recognize that our findings and the media history we review could be explained by the work in political psychology that follows from the rigidity model developed by John Jost and collaborators.[84] Synthesizing decades of work stretching back to the 1950s, Jost and his coauthors proposed a theory that suggested that people adopted conservative political positions as a way of satisfying a particular combination of cognitive style, personality traits, and epistemic and existential needs. Many of these could certainly provide a simple answer to why Limbaugh or Fox News succeed on the right to a degree that Al Franken or MSNBC never did on the left. If dogmatism, intolerance of ambiguity, and a need for closure, order, and structure are strong predictors of politically conservative attitudes, these certainly would also predict a rapid conversion on a single authoritative source of news that offers only confirmation of belief-consistent news and reassures its viewers and listeners that other sources that raise doubt are liars. The observed patterns of media consumption on the right and the left are also consistent with this model. In particular, the significantly narrower menu of media sources used by consistently conservative audiences, and the high trust these respondents report in their own media sources combined with their high distrust of other sources, even when those other sources are highly trusted by everyone else, including nonpartisans of mixed views, are all consistent with the rigidity model.

Our own research does not, however, incorporate any measures that could deny or refute this effect. The rigidity model has long been contested by psychologists who view it as too partisan in its research orientation, and recent work in particular raises concerns about several core methodological concerns, in particular whether it captures the range of positions that count as conservative, particularly the overlap between economic and identity issues. More directly relevant to our findings, the critique questions whether the rigidity model can account for exposure of study subjects to discourse that would shape the alignment of their political answers more than their personality or cognitive style.[85]

Neither the propaganda feedback loop model we describe in Chapter 3 nor the political economy story we offer here for how that feedback loop emerged on the right in the United States between the 1980s and 2000s, depend on a psychological theory. They merely require that one side of the political ecosystem begin to adopt such a strategy before the other. The positive feedbacks between the benefits to elites, who gain a reliable audience, the benefits to the broadcasters, who gain a loyal market segment, and the beliefs and attitudes of the population begin to reinforce each other within the feedback loop. As we explained in Chapter 3, the mainstream media then become a source of confirmation for the opposite side of the political spectrum because they, on average, will find more lying in the bias-confirming media (because there will be more of it there, by design) and provide its opponents with truth-based reasons to reject their opponents claims. The side that adopts the hyperpartisan media strategy enjoys, in this regard, a first-mover advantage in a positive feedback dynamic that then both reinforces and disciplines those who are in it. Certainly, endowing the population of the side that chooses the bias-confirming media with a baseline personality that increases the prevalence of preferences for such media would make the tipping easier and faster. But the model does not require a differential psychological makeup for the propaganda feedback loop to emerge alongside, and in opposition to, media that continue to operate under the reality-check dynamic. Once the population being studied is pervasively served by a highly asymmetric media system, studies that depend on responses from that population will have to control for the asymmetric effects of media exposure and discourse on shaping the political beliefs of respondents.

Fox News vs. Internet: Political Impact Assessments

Moving from identifying patterns of media practice and consumption to outcomes is hard. We are most persuaded by three studies by economists that look at the effect of Fox News, and at the effects of the internet relative to Fox News, over the past 20 years. These studies all support the proposition that Fox was the more important component of the right-wing media ecosystem, even in the 2016 election.

Over the past decade, two major studies have sought to quantify the "Fox News Effect" on America political polarization. The work was pioneered by Stefano DellaVigna and Ethan Kaplan in an article published in the *Quarterly Journal of Economics*.[86] Because the cable industry and cable channel offerings were growing and changing fast in the late 1990s, Fox News was introduced at different times in different cities. In particular, Fox News's successful completion of carriage deals with major multiple-system operators like TCI (later bought by AT&T) sped up its adoption, while its failure to negotiate carriage on other cable carriers like Adelphia (taken over by Time Warner after its bankruptcy) delayed its adoption. This variation between towns in the timing of Fox News entering the market provided a natural experiment for the effect of Fox News on voter turnout and partisan voting. DellaVigna and Kaplan were able to show that introducing Fox News to a town increased the Republican vote share by 0.4 percent to 0.7 percent, and estimated that because it likely was responsible for about 200,000 more Republican votes nationwide in the 2000 election. In particular, they estimated that Fox News was likely responsible for slightly over 10,000 votes in Florida in an election won by George W. Bush by 537 votes. Because the effect was present even for Senate seat elections that were too local to be covered by a national cable channel like Fox News, DellaVigna and Kaplan argued that the Fox News effect acted at the general ideological activation level, rather than specific candidate support, and was particularly significant in increasing Republican turnout in otherwise Democratic districts.

DellaVigna and Kaplan's work covered the first election after Fox News began to play a significant role. By 2017, two other economists, Gregory Martin and Ali Yurukoglu, were able to replicate these results for 2000, improve their precision, and extend the analysis to cover the 2004 and 2008 results as well.[87] Martin and Yurukoglu combine several of the most sophisticated techniques available to analyze the partisan bias and effects of media on voting patterns. They used a novel instrumental variable (the placement of each of the 24-hour news channels on the dial) combined with text analysis to measure the degree of partisan slant of the program transcripts from CNN, Fox News, and MSNBC over the course of the 2000, 2004, and 2008 elections, applying a technique developed by Matthew Gentzkow and Jesse Shapiro to measure media bias in newspapers.[88] To these they add voter data, surveys, and Nielsen data to provide the most detailed and robust evidence of the central role Fox News has played in the partisan polarization of American media and voting patterns. In this study, Martin and Yurukoglu replicated and strengthened DellaVigna and Kaplan's original finding that Fox News made a critical difference in 2000. They further showed that because it increased both its viewership and its partisan slant, the effect of Fox News became more pronounced over time. While their data picked up the strategic shift MSNBC made in 2006 to try to mirror the Fox News strategy on the left, they did not find that MSNBC had a meaningful effect on voting behavior. Most importantly, Martin and Yurukoglu found that the primary effect of exposure to Fox News was on voters who started the election cycle as centrists or Democrats, and over the course of the election cycle were converted to Republicans. While this effect declined from 2000 to 2004 and to 2008, it was substantially higher than the impact MSNBC had on converting viewers who were originally Republicans.

Looking at the 2016 election, anyone assessing the impact of cable versus that of the internet has to contend with the fact that Trump supporters were, overall, primarily to be found in demographic groups that were the least attentive to online news sites and social media. Trump voters overwhelmingly reported tuning in to television: Fox News (40 percent), the networks (12 percent), and local TV (5 percent). Facebook was the primary source for only 7 percent.[89] Moreover, the relationship between social media and internet use for election news and support for Trump and Clinton, respectively, across age groups and gender raises doubt about the role of online media in Trump's rise. If anything, it seems use of social media is inversely related to support for Trump. Of white voters in the 18–29 age range, whose social media and internet use for election news was 53 percent,[90] fewer than 40 percent voted for Trump.[91] Trump's share of the vote increased with age. Trump's share of the white vote was over 54 percent in the 45–64 age range, and over 58 percent in the over 65 group, while social media use in these demographics was between 5 percent and 1 percent, respectively. Similarly, women reported using Facebook for news much more often than men do, by a ratio of 62 percent to 38 percent,[92] and supported Clinton over Trump by a healthy 12-point difference.[93] In another recent paper, Levi Boxell, Matthew Gentzkow, and Jesse Shapiro exploited these significant age-based differences in partisanship and internet use in a formal analysis of the contribution of the internet to polarization. Looking at eight different measures used across political science to measure partisan polarization, and at data ranging back to 1972, they found that most of the polarization that has happened since 1996, the first year for which there is regularly collected data on internet use, occurred in the populations least likely to be internet connected (those aged 65 and over), while polarization of those most likely to be online and use social media has been fairly stable over this period.[94] It is simply unreasonable to pin the blame for patterns of trust and distrust in media, or the rise of Trump, on a medium that is consistently used less by demographic groups that express that distrust or support the president and is used more by populations that hold the opposite position on both questions.

Can the Internet Survive Democracy?

AS WE WRITE this book in early 2018, the prevailing *zeitgeist* seems to be that all the promise of the internet has been swept away in a cloud of manipulation and abuse. Facebook finds itself under questioning on both sides of the Atlantic for its uses of the personal data of its users. If there are battles over who did what, they seem to be about who used the internet as one big manipulation platform, whether it was the Russians, Cambridge Analytica, or the Trump campaign, helped by Facebook and Google targeted advertising experts. If there was a sigh of relief after the German elections that the Russians did not interfere, it was explained as a function of the central role and high trust that traditional public broadcasters enjoy in the German media ecosystem.

It cannot be, however, that "the internet democratizes" when it enables people who think as we do to challenge institutionalized power that protects institutions we would rather challenge, but "the internet threatens democracy" when it allows people with whom we disagree to challenge institutionalized power that protects institutions we would rather protect. It strains credulity that the Trump candidacy or the Leave campaign were entirely the product of manipulation, Russian or otherwise, rather than the surprising political success of a campaign that tapped into attitudes and beliefs held by millions of people in the United States and the United Kingdom, respectively. One of the reasons it is so difficult, for example, to identify Russian campaigns in the American media ecosystem is that they were so often congruent with the organic online mobilization of people who in fact wanted to go out and protest against immigration or share memes that denigrate mainstream media. These views may be illiberal, but a media ecosystem that effectively suppresses widely held beliefs that are contrary to elite opinions is not more

Network Propaganda. Yochai Benkler, Robert Faris, and Hal Roberts.
© Yochai Benkler, Robert Faris, and Hal Roberts 2018. Published 2018 by Oxford University Press.

"democratic" if elite opinions happen to be pluralistic and egalitarian than it is when elite opinions merely protect oligarchy.

The fact that Donald Trump was able to spin up a campaign with little support from the Republican Party, is democratizing—in the sense that it enabled an insurgent campaign that was far from mainstream consensus to emerge and give voice to the anxieties and ambitions of millions in Americans who had not been heard so clearly before in the halls of power. Much of his success, as we documented earlier in the book, was due to the interaction between partisan media on the right and extensive mainstream media coverage; but his own campaign organization and spending suggest that the campaign itself was focused on using Facebook, Twitter, and online mobilization to attract millions. The fact that Bernie Sanders, a party outsider, was able to run a credible campaign and raise $230 million for his campaign, 60 percent of which was from small individual contributions, is democratizing in the sense of allowing outsiders to challenge the consensus establishment candidate.

The core argument that the internet was a democratizing technology had to do with the fact that in the mass mediated environment, agenda setting and framing of what mattered and what was a credible move in political contestation was centralized and depended on access to organizational and institutional power. The cost of production and distribution of news and opinions; the cost of mobilizing on a national scale; the credibility to assert in public what was, and was not, news or fact; all these were associated with a relatively concentrated power structure. Government, parties, professional commercial media, organized corporations, organized labor, to some extent national-scale membership organizations—all these were necessary to move an idea or a demand from the peripheries of late twentieth-century democracy to the core of its political debate. The internet promised to open new pathways for agenda setting, framing, and mobilization. People, with diverse viewpoints, were able to find each other.[1] Citizens and residents could mobilize into new, flatter organizational forms.[2] More of us could publish, and more of us could read a broader set of sources and viewpoints, and we could be more engaged when we did so.[3] These effects could then spill over into broader media because journalists would also read these decentralized media and their coverage could be shaped not only by political and corporate insiders but by a broader range of public authors.[4] These voices, amateur and professional, commercial and noncommercial, mobilized and otherwise, could together form a networked public sphere where power to set the agenda and frame political discourse was more widely distributed than it had been in the latter twentieth century.[5] Critically, the organizational literature focused on the distributed, nonhierarchical nature of these mobilization efforts, ushering in a new era where collective action did not depend on large political machines.[6]

All of these features are still true, and the affordances continue to be available for people to organize themselves around establishment organizations, rather than having to run through them. It is impossible to ignore the fact that the national debate on police shootings of black men was fundamentally altered not because one of the major parties took it up; not because the number of shootings increased; but because bystanders shot videos of police shootings, shared them online, and the Black Lives Matter movement developed, at first primarily online, around these shocking images. After the election of Donald Trump, activists organized through a Google Doc to organize the Indivisible movement, which coordinated citizens to appearance at town hall meetings to put pressure on congressional representatives. The Women's March on Washington could not have developed except through online engagement. The high school students who organized around school shootings and gun control follow the same pattern.

The second decade of the twenty-first century has taught us that while decentralization can support democratization, it is susceptible to five major failure modes. The first of these became clear after the Arab Spring and Occupy: leaderless, decentralized movements can form relatively easily online and focus on distinct great moments, like Tahrir, Gezi Park, or Zuccotti Park. But converting protest into action requires more structure, discipline, and longevity than many of these movements were able to develop, as Zeynep Tufekci captured so well in *Twitter and Teargas*.[7] The first failure mode is simply the failure to convert from a moment's surge of decentralized passion into a longer-term, sustained effort with competence to engage political institutions systematically over time.

The second failure mode is the failure to sustain the decentralized openness in the transition to more structured political organization. It turns out that marrying the energy of decentralized online action to the discipline of a party or government is far from easy. Howard Dean's 2004 primary campaign was the first significant political effort that leveraged the possibilities of the radically distributed network of activists to raise a campaign in a truly decentralized, peer-driven way.[8] That particular, fully decentralized, user-generated campaign was later foundational to the Ron Paul presidential primary campaign in 2008. While both campaigns benefited from enormous distributed energy, neither was able to harness and organize it. By 2008 "MyBarackObama.com" took over from the decentralized peers of the Dean and Paul campaigns and integrated it into this amazing new technology—the social network platform. MyBO provided a centralized platform, but still emphasized the decentralized capabilities—people creating their own meetups; raising their own campaign bundling efforts; communicating their own news. As Micah Sifry documented, however, the Obama transition team made a conscious choice to dismantle the grassroots army that had helped propel the new president into the White House in 2008.[9] By the end of the campaign, MyBO had two million active members, 70,000 of whom had started their own fundraising campaigns. Sifry describes how several key actors, most importantly Christopher Edley and Mitch Kapor, pushed hard for the new presidency to introduce a new, perpetual grassroots-engaged democracy, where the presidency and the people use the internet for continuous engagement and participation on a mass scale. Instead, Democratic Party insiders, threatened with loss of control, persuaded the incoming president to fold his online campaign into the DNC, turning MyBO into a new Organizing for America site. As Sifry describes it,

> Shunted into the DNC, MyBO's tools for self-organizing were dismantled within a year. Instead of calling on supporters to launch a voter registration drive or build a network of small donors or back state and local candidates, OFA deployed the campaign's vast email list to hawk coffee mugs and generate thank-you notes to Democratic members of Congress who backed Obama's initiatives. As a result, when the political going got rough, much of Obama's once-mighty army was AWOL. When the fight over Obama's health care plan was at its peak, OFA was able to drum up only 300,000 phone calls to Congress. After the midterm debacle in 2010, when Democrats suffered their biggest losses since the Great Depression, Obama essentially had to build a new campaign machine from scratch in time for his reelection effort in 2012.

Hierarchical, centralized organizations have very different interests and concerns than decentralized networks of activists and citizens. And Obama's 2012 campaign was the first test run of the third failure mode of the internet and democracy—the power of well-organized, data-informed central powers to move millions of people from the center out, instead of the other way around. It was there that the tide first turned from the internet as decentralized enablement platform to internet as data-driven control platform.

Hailed by many at the time as a success, the Obama 2012 campaign represented the first systematic use of big data and individualization for a campaign to target individual voters, particularly in the get-out-the-vote efforts. Instead of a campaign site like MyBO that had leveraged supporters own social networks to organize events, volunteers, and fundraising, it was the data geeks who were the new heroes. And the internet they used was more about surveillance through social media systems developed for marketing than about participatory mobilization. The title and subtitle of Alexis Madrigal's celebratory *Atlantic* story right after the election captures it all: "When the Nerds Go Marching In: How a Dream Team of engineers from Facebook, Twitter, and Google built the software that drove Barack Obama's reelection."[10] The triumphalism only gradually gave way to a more sober assessment of the implications of this shift toward the capacity of a campaign to control mass mobilization and how much it inverted the dynamics we had originally celebrated as the democratizing effect of the internet.

Soon thereafter, scientific papers from Facebook researchers—documenting how Facebook could manipulate the moods of Facebook users by altering the prevailing sentiment in their newsfeed or increase voter turnout with notifications that a friend had voted—launched a new set of concerns with algorithmic manipulation of politics.[11] Zeynep Tufekci's "Engineering the public: Big data, surveillance, and computational politics" became the first academic essay that highlighted the core affordances that made the American internet such a powerful vehicle for political manipulation.[12] Tufekci identified the ability of social media and internet platforms to leverage big-data techniques to provide individually tailored, experimentally validated, targeted communication that could leverage the most cutting-edge behavioral science to manipulate the beliefs and attitudes of users, using algorithmic processes that are entirely opaque to external review and accountability. In this story Facebook and Google, much more than Russia or any state, were the primary culprits, building platforms for refined, scientifically informed manipulation of human individuals at population scales and doing so in pursuit of profit under the newly emerging surveillance capitalism[13]—but with clear risks for the very possibility of democratic politics. The major threat to the internet as a democratizing force is not the abuse of the system but its intended use. Because the internet had been reengineered, primarily by Google and Facebook, into a preference manipulation platform, the two companies emerged as behemoths whose entire business model was built on producing fine-grained data at the individual level, running mass-scale experiments on millions of users, and developing the capacity to update the online interaction in real time to achieve behavioral manipulation made to order and sold to advertisers. As we described in Chapter 9, the evidence that these techniques were critical and effective in the 2016 election is sparse. But the fact that something has not yet been shown to have had the critical marginal impact is no reason to ignore it as a major threat or constraint on how we use the internet in a democratic society. And of all the major threats to democracy that we have encountered in this decade, it is the one most amenable to regulatory or policy intervention.

The fourth failure mode is that precisely what makes decentralized networks so effective at circumventing established forms of control can also make them the vehicles of repressive mobs. Here, the failure is not inefficacy, subversion by organizations, or reconcentration in the hands of centralized organizations that turn the network into a control system. It is rather that the methods or goals of the distributed network of actors are themselves repressive, rather than participatory. This critique of decentralized networks as democratizing followed the Gamergate controversy, as networked mobilization was turned into a harassment and intimidation campaign against women, game developers, and media critics, in the name of preserving geek masculinity and fighting for free speech against "social justice warriors" out to destroy it.[14] Adrienne Massanari analyzed the design and algorithms of Reddit, showing how these affordances enabled the Gamergate campaign to take off,[15] while Shira Chess and Adrienne Shaw focused on how the Gamergaters' attack on academic feminist studies of gaming culture exhibited the classic characteristics of the conspiracy theory-driven, paranoid style, in American politics.[16] What was different was not that earlier studies of the networked public sphere focused on left or liberal mobilization. These had always included examples for both left and right sites circumventing mainstream media to shape the agenda.[17] As Alice Marwick and Rebecca Lewis show, what Gamergate exposed was a new set of distributed attack techniques that went well beyond what could be considered still within democratic practice: doxxing (disclosing private documents) private individuals who expressed opposing positions; intimidation through personal death and rape threats; revenge porn and social shaming; all aggressively gendered and aimed at women. Moreover, Gamergate was the proving ground for a set of techniques that later developed as the core techniques of disinformation in the 2016 election: organized brigades of online harassment organized around hashtags or specific memes; use of sockpuppets to push topics and stories to prominence, and in particular to put them in front of mainstream influencers to propagate the message to society at large; and a networked coalition of loosely affiliated groups around core objects of hatred of the kind we saw more in the Unite the Right campaign in Charlottesville, Virginia. It was also where some of the core activists of the alt-right got their start.[18] Again, though, it is important to distinguish elements of the strategy that are expressive—like propagating memes or putting them in front of mainstream influencers, and elements that are about intimidating opponents. We focus here only on the latter, unless the expressive actions fall within what we defined and described throughout this book as disinformation. This mode is a "failure" even if it does not actually affect the outcomes of election or policy battles. Because intimidation campaigns can be personal and relatively nihilistic—not caring about discrete policy outcomes—even if they do not affect an outcome at the aggregate level, they can and do harm their targets.

The final failure mode is the susceptibility to disinformation and propaganda and is the motivating force behind this book. The critical thing to understand is that the internet democratizes, if it does, only through its interaction with preexisting institutions and organizations—working with them and around them, and creating new alternatives that interact with them. As one of us put it in an article in 2009, "Like other information goods, the production model of news is shifting from an industrial model— be it the monopoly city paper, IBM in its monopoly heyday, Microsoft, or Britannica—to a networked model that integrates a wider range of practices into the production system: market and nonmarket, large scale and small, for profit and nonprofit, organized and individual. We already see the early elements of how news reporting and opinion will be provided in the networked public sphere."[19] It would be the interaction between "surviving elements of the old system," changed, small-scale new, digital native commercial media, volunteer media like Daily Kos and Townhall, more effective nonprofits (more effective because they could do much more with less online than in the mass media era), and mobilized individuals that would form the networked fourth estate. The media ecosystem needed all these elements, including the healthy surviving element of traditional professional media and nonprofit professional journalism, to be able to benefit from the edgier, more partisan distributed, mobilized action. What we saw repeatedly in our case studies throughout the book was that this integrated system worked like a networked public sphere or fourth estate outside the right-wing media ecosystem thanks to the reality-check dynamic that characterized the interactions among professional media and newer online media, professional and amateur, for profit and nonprofit, fact-checking organizations and activists. But when the professional, commercial, and nonprofit think tanks, like Fox News, Breitbart, the Government Accountability Initiative, the Center for Immigration Studies, or Judicial Watch, all functioned to reinforce the disinformation campaigns, it was then that the networked public sphere turned into a networked propaganda system.

WE HAVE ONLY presented data here from the United States. It is entirely possible that observing the patterns in other countries will offer better evidence that it was, in fact, the internet or social media or just Facebook that has created the epistemic crisis we observe in the United States, Europe, and other democratic societies. But if our experience in America is representative, then any analysis of a perceived epistemic crisis anywhere must consider how the internet interacts with that country's entire media ecosystem, and how that system in turn interacts with that country's political-institutional system more generally.

We have presented in this Part Four an approach based on a broader sense of political economy than simply a media- or technology-centric view. We have suggested that many factors have contributed to and fed off of the asymmetric polarization in the positions of the two parties in America, with a conservative wing particularly focused on ideological purity and symbolic action. These factors include the long-term patterns of identity threat born of race relations and relatively open immigration policy; the economic insecurity born of policies aimed to reduce taxes and services, reduce labor power, and reduce regulatory oversight over businesses; and an increasing mismatch between a large, deeply religious population and an increasingly pluralistic and gender-egalitarian mainstream. These patterns laid the ground work for the 30-year ascendance of a commercially successful strategy of news and opinion media outlets committed to serving identity-confirming news and views for that conservative wing, while denigrating the veracity and honesty of all other outlets. Changes in technology (satellite and FM radio, cable transmission, and only later the internet), institutions (the deregulation of cable, repeal of the fairness doctrine, reduction in ownership limits, and reduced antitrust enforcement) and political culture have shaped the emergence of a network of media outlets, including radio, cable television, and internet sites, that operate in a distinctly partisan propagandist mode. While there were efforts of liberals to create a parallel but functionally similar system, these failed because the coalition that formed the rest of the polity simply did not have the same cohesion to support ideologically pure, reality-agnostic media. There were certainly elements of this coalition who were (and are) more than happy to consume and produce bias-confirming news and opinion. We have seen, from MSNBC and online, such examples in several of our chapters. But the coalition as a whole was too focused on functional results to support a dominant propagandist model. Its members were not willing to concentrate on bias confirmation to the exclusion of what professional journalism and expertise, whether commercial, governmental, or nonprofit, could offer, and once the conservative propagandist outlets took off, fact-based journalism offered a valuable source of credible, independent, but belief-consistent rebuttal for liberals. And so the media and information consumption habits of the two parts of the media ecosystem developed separately and distinctly. As we in the United States, and anyone else in any other democracy, turn to look at solutions, we must consider these background political institutional dynamics to understand where they are and where they are likely to go, what their susceptibilities to disinformation are, and what nationally specific sources of resilience they may be able to harness. It would be particularly unfortunate if countries that do not have the same decades-long processes that made the United States susceptible to propaganda and disinformation, foreign and domestic, will adopt measures that will undermine the democratizing aspects of the internet and social media even though they do not, in fact, face the same risks, or even though they have sources of resilience that are more robust than those we appear to have in America.

13

What Can Men Do Against Such Reckless Hate?

WE OPENED THIS book with a threat matrix: a description of the major sources of polluted information that have been blamed for threatening our ability to tell truth from fiction as a society. We noted that most public discussion of the threats focused on novel and technological causes, rather than long-term institutional and structural causes. As we come to the conclusion of our book, we can say with confidence that writing this chapter of possible solutions would have been easier had our analysis revealed a clear, technologically driven cause for our present epistemic crisis. It would be easier if we knew that the present crisis was caused by entrepreneurial teenagers running fake news sites on Facebook, Russian sockpuppet and bot accounts, targeted psychographics-informed advertising from Cambridge Analytica, or even technologically induced symmetrically partisan echo chambers.

But our studies have led us to the conclusion that these putative risks are, for the near future, not the major causes of disruption. We have argued throughout this book that none of these actors—Russians, fake news entrepreneurs, Cambridge Analytica, Facebook itself, or symmetric partisan echo chambers—were the major cause of the epistemic crisis experienced within the U.S. media ecosystem during the 2016 election or since. Instead of these technologically driven dynamics, which are novel but ultimately less important, we see longer-term dynamics of political economy: ideology and institutions interacting with technological adoption as the primary drivers of the present epistemic crisis. These dynamics, which play out across television, radio, and mainstream professional journalism at least as much as through the internet and social media, have been developing for 30 years and have resulted in a highly asymmetric media ecosystem that is the primary driver

Network Propaganda. Yochai Benkler, Robert Faris, and Hal Roberts.
© Yochai Benkler, Robert Faris, and Hal Roberts 2018. Published 2018 by Oxford University Press.

of disinformation and propaganda in the American public sphere. The right-wing media ecosystem in particular circulates an overwhelming amount of domestic disinformation and propaganda, and its practices create the greatest vulnerabilities to both foreign propaganda and nihilistic commercial exploitation by clickbait factories. Outside the right-wing media ecosystem, we observe efforts by partisans, Russians, and clickbait factories, but fact-checking norms and journalistic institutional commitments dampen the diffusion and amplification of disinformation. These dynamics are inverted in the insular right-wing network, and partisan identity-confirming assertions, however false, are accelerated and amplified.

In this chapter we take on a range of possible interventions that might strengthen media ecosystems and raise the level of public discourse and political reporting. While the options are many, there are no silver bullets. There are changes that might be led by media producers themselves on both sides of the political spectrum. There are a range of intended fixes underway by the large social media platforms and supporting mechanisms being proposed and developed by public interest organizations, and there are options for more aggressive government regulatory action. Because of the size of the problem, we are not optimistic that any of these changes will succeed on its own. But the lesson we take away from our work is that we as a society must lean more heavily toward fixing our currently broken media system. Unfortunately, most of the interventions we describe below have real costs in terms of uncomfortable acceptance of the partisan nature of the problem and of increased private and public control of content.

We divide this chapter into three parts. The first part is dedicated to the two major kinds of changes that may actually go to the root of the problem: political-institutional change on the right and a reorientation of how journalists pursue their professional commitments in a highly asymmetric media ecosystem. The former is the ultimate solution, we think, but is unlikely to occur unless the Republican Party suffers a series of political setbacks that will force such a fundamental reorientation. The latter is more feasible, and we think it can actually make a difference for much of the population. But it may have little or no effect on the roughly one-third of the population that actively and willingly inhabits the right-wing media ecosystem. The second part outlines the most widely discussed practical solutions to the more novel, technology-dependent explanations of crisis that have captured most of the public attention since 2016. These are primarily: increased control by intermediaries, particularly social media platforms and Google, of variously defined illegal or otherwise unacceptable content, and regulation of political advertising. The last part will offer a brief overview of various other approaches aimed to help reduce the supply of, and demand for, misinformation and bias-confirming propaganda.

Reconstructing Center-Right Media

There is nothing conservative about calling career law enforcement officials and the intelligence community the "deep state." The fact that the targets of the attack, like Robert Mueller, Rod Rosenstein, or Andrew McCabe, were life-long Republicans merely underscores that fact. There is nothing conservative about calling for a trade war. There is nothing conservative about breaking from long-held institutional norms for short-term political advantage. And there is nothing conservative about telling Americans to reject the consensus estimate of the CIA, the FBI, and the NSA that we were attacked by Russia and suggesting instead that these agencies are covering up for a DNC conspiracy. What has happened first and foremost to make all these things possible is that the Republican Party has been taken over by ever-more right-wing politicians. As an analysis published following Richard Lugar's primary defeat noted, when Lugar first became a senator in 1977, he was to the right of more than half of Senate Republicans. Despite moderating only a bit over his 36 years in the Senate, by his retirement he had moved from being the twenty-third-most moderate Republican to being the fifth-most moderate, and even if he had not moderated his views, would have been the twelfth-most moderate.[1] When Marco Rubio was elected as a senator in 2010, he was the firebrand Tea Party candidate, elected alongside Tea Party darling Pat Toomey, who had ousted moderate Republican Arlen Specter. By 2016 Rubio was identified as the "moderate" candidate, even though he had a DW-NOMINATE score to the right of the median Republican senator in the 113th Congress, while the final two candidates in the primary were the third-most right-wing senator, Ted Cruz, and Donald Trump. As we write these lines, we have no idea whether the 2018 mid-term elections, much less the 2020 election, will deliver losses or gains to the Republican Party. Perhaps the hard-right strategy will continue to pay off for Republicans in terms of short-term political gains. Perhaps a reversal will force a reorientation. The question is whether Republicans who would identify themselves with a Lugar, an Arlen Specter, or a John Kasich have a significant chance of recapturing their party without a significant reassertion of the role of center-right media.

One of our clearest and starkest findings is the near disappearance of center-right media. There is the *Wall Street Journal*, with its conservative editorial page but continued commitment to journalistic standards in its reporting; and to some extent *The Hill* plays a center-right role. Both sites appear in the center of the partisan landscape according to our data because readers on the right did not pay attention to these sites any more than readers on the left did. Fox News, as we showed in Chapter 2, has asserted its leadership role in the right-wing media ecosystem at the expense of becoming even more oriented inwardly, toward the insular right wing of the American public sphere. Several conservative commentators have emphasized the extent to which Fox News has skewed the Republican-oriented media system. David French and Matthew Sheffield wrote in the *National Review* during the run-up to the 2016 election that Fox News was "hurting the right" or "making the right intellectually deaf."[2] Libertarian Cato Institute Senior Fellow Julian Sanchez wrote early and presciently when he described the right as suffering what he called "epistemic closure":

> One of the more striking features of the contemporary conservative movement is the extent to which it has been moving toward epistemic closure. Reality is defined by a multimedia array of interconnected and cross promoting conservative blogs, radio programs, magazines, and of course, Fox News. Whatever conflicts with that reality can be dismissed out of hand because it comes from the liberal media, and is therefore ipso facto not to be trusted. (How do you know they're liberal? Well, they disagree with the conservative media!) This epistemic closure can be a source of solidarity and energy, but it also renders the conservative media ecosystem fragile.[3]

Our data could not be summed up more perfectly. The right wing of the American media ecosystem has been a breeding ground for conspiracy theory and disinformation, and a significant point of vulnerability in our capacity, as a country and a democracy, to resist disinformation and propaganda. We have documented this finding extensively throughout this book by describing both the architecture and flows of information and disinformation in the American media ecosystem in the past three years and by presenting distinct case studies of disinformation campaigns surrounding what we know to be Russian hacks of the DNC and Podesta emails and the investigation into Russian interference in the election—be it Seth Rich, the Forensicator, Uranium One, or the DNC and Podesta email-based stories like spirit cooking.

The question is, in part, whether there is enough will, and money, among centrist Republicans to address the fragility of the conservative media ecosystem by supporting publications that are centrally committed to reasserting a sense of reality. We are under no illusion that such a reorientation will be easy, and we are not even sure it is possible. Our observations regarding how Breitbart and Trump brought Fox News to heel toward the end of the primary season, and the propaganda feedback loop we outline in Chapter 3 suggest that this strategy will be exceedingly difficult to carry out, as does the extent to which long-standing conservative sites that opposed Trump were shunted aside during the primary. There just may not be appetite for reporting oriented more toward objectivity and less toward partisanship. But just as Robert and Rebekah Mercer invested heavily in creating Breitbart, the Government Accountability Initiative, and other elements of the far-right disinformation ecosystem, one might imagine that there are enough billionaires and millionaires who do not see themselves in the populist, anti-immigrant, anti-trade, and increasingly anti-rule-of-law Trump-Bannon image of the Republican Party. We have no basis in our own work to advise how such a Herculean feat may be achieved. Perhaps it could take the form of leadership or ownership change in Fox News, leveraging existing audience loyalty to gradually reintroduce a more reality-anchored but nonetheless conservative news outlet. Perhaps it would require launching a new media outlet. But without a significant outlet that is both committed to professional journalistic values in its news reporting and fact checking and trusted by conservatives when it reports what it reports, it is difficult to see how center-right, reality-based conservatives can reassert themselves within the Republican Party. And without such a reassertion, it is hard to see how the fragility of the right-wing media ecosystem does not continue to be a hotbed of bias-confirming disinformation and propaganda, foreign and domestic.

Professional Journalism in a Propaganda-Rich Ecosystem

We have dedicated most of this volume to mapping the media ecosystem, documenting its asymmetric structure, and understanding the role this asymmetry plays in the dissemination of disinformation. We nonetheless emphasized the critical role of mainstream media in this system. In Chapter 6, we showed how our work relates to the work of other scholars who looked at coverage during the election to underscore the extent to which mainstream media focused on horse race coverage, negative coverage, and scandals over issues, particularly when it came to Hillary Clinton. We showed how the

New York Times allowed itself to be used in a disinformation campaign, laundering politically motivated opposition research by Peter Schweizer by bestowing upon it the imprimatur and legitimacy of its name with coverage that raised questions in blaring headlines and buried caveats deep in the small print of the story. We similarly showed how coverage by other major outlets like the *Washington Post* and the Associated Press in August of 2016 led with the scandal-implying headline and buried the admission that evidence of corruption was thin at best. But we also showed in Chapters 3, 5, 6, and 8 how the reality-check dynamic in play across "the rest" of the media ecosystem was able to check disinformation and error on both sides, as mainstream and newer online media continuously checked each other's worst impulses and corrected error and overreaching.

Most Americans do not occupy the right-wing media ecosystem. Likely more than half of conservative and more independent viewers, readers, and listeners are exposed to CNN as well as to network and local television and mainstream news sites. The crossover audience, much more than the audience already fully committed to the perspective of Sean Hannity or Rush Limbaugh, is the most important audience that can be influenced by mainstream media. When mainstream professional media sources insist on coverage that performs their own neutrality by giving equal weight to opposing views, even when one is false and the other is not, they fail. In a famous 2004 study, Maxwell Boykoff and Jules Boykoff showed that the climate change coverage of major prestige papers—the *New York Times*, the *Washington Post*, the *Wall Street Journal*, and the *Los Angeles Times*—gave "balanced" coverage, providing a platform not only for arguments that climate change was anthropogenic but also to those that climate change was not caused by human activity, even though the scientific consensus was by then well established.[4] As more recent work by Derek Koehler showed, readers form erroneous assessments of the weight of the evidence even when they are explicitly told that one view they are reading reflects a near-consensus of experts while the other is held by a small minority.[5] The balanced-reporting norm in that context significantly muddied the waters on the politics of climate change, which was exactly the purpose of the propagandists. But they could only achieve their goal at the population level with the implicit support of mainstream journalists who reported on the two sides as more-or-less equal voices in the controversy. Our observations regarding the prevalence and diffusion of disinformation in the right-wing media ecosystem suggest that mainstream professional journalism needs to treat many statements associated with current American politics as it later came to deal with coverage of climate science and climate denial.

Practically, this means that professional journalism needs to recalibrate its commitment to objective reporting further toward transparent, accountable verifiability and away from demonstrative neutrality. As Thomas Patterson wrote in explaining the negative reporting in election coverage, consistently negative reporting allowed media outlets to demonstrate their independence and neutrality to their audiences. Given the highly asymmetric patterns of lying and disinformation coming from the two campaigns, media outlets avoided the appearance of bias by emphasizing negativity and criticism in their reporting of both sides. In practical terms, that created a broad public impression of equivalent unsuitability for office and a paucity of substantive coverage of positions.

Instead of engaging in this kind of public performance of neutrality, what we might call demonstrative neutrality, objectivity needs to be performed by emphasizing the transparency and accountability of journalists' sources and practices, what we might call accountable verifiability. We already see it to a degree in the ways in which mainstream media organizations dealt with some visible errors in Chapter 6. Some of this is simply emphasis and extension of existing practices—providing public access to underlying documentary materials, for example. Some would require developing institutional mechanisms for independent verification of sources, on the model of scientific access to materials and underlying code for reproducibility. Whether this should be done in a network of media outlets, as it is in peer review in science, by designating a set of independent nonprofit fact-checking organizations that will operate as quality assurance for journalistic enterprises and be provided with more access to underlying materials than under current practice, or at least initially by creating a more prominent role for internal "inspector generals" inside the most visible media remains to be seen. More controversially and harder to implement, these practices have to be applied equally to headlines and framing, where so much of the communicative value of the article is conveyed, as they are to discrete factual claims. None of this will persuade people who are already inside the propaganda feedback loop, nor need it be designed to satisfy them. It is intended to allow journalistic enterprises to avoid errors and gain enough confidence internally, and communicate enough objective truth seeking externally, so that they can abandon demonstrative neutrality and its attendant false impressions.

This broader reorientation should not postpone several narrower and more immediate adjustments in journalistic practice. Recognizing the asymmetry we document here requires editors to treat tips or "exclusives," as well as emails or other leaked or hacked documents with greater care than they have in the past few years. The "Fool me once, shame on you . . ." adage suggests that after, for example, the *New York Times*'s experience with Peter Schweizer and the Uranium One story, mainstream professional journalists need to understand that they are subject to a persistent propaganda campaign trying to lure them into amplifying and accrediting propaganda. This happens of course as normal politics from both sides of the partisan system, but our work here shows that one side is armed with a vastly more powerful engine for generating and propagating propaganda.

It is certainly possible to resist these attacks without particularly supporting one side over the other. In November 2017, for example, the right-wing disinformation outfit Project Veritas tried to trip up the *Washington Post*, offering the *Post* a fake informant who told the *Post* that Roy Moore had impregnated her when she was a teenager. The sting operation was intended to undermine the credibility of the *Post*'s reporting on Roy Moore's alleged pursuit and harassment of teens when he was a 30-something-year-old.[6] Rather than jumping at the opportunity to develop the Moore story, the *Washington Post*'s reporters followed the professional model—checked out the source, assessed her credibility, and ultimately detected and outed the attempt at manipulation. Mainstream media editors and journalists must understand that they are under a sustained attack, sometimes as premeditated and elaborate as this sting, usually more humdrum.

Russian and right-wing political actors have been particularly effective at using document dumps, particularly hacked emails, to lure journalists into over-reporting. The dynamic is clear. By offering real documents, activists and propagandists give journalists the illusion that they have both a trove of newsworthy documents—what could be more tempting than a tranche of secrets?—and complete control over the sources materials and ability to craft a narrative around them. After all, the journalist makes up her own mind about what matters and what does not. After a reporter spends hours or days pouring over materials, as other competitors are releasing juicy tidbits based on the documents, the pressure to produce something spectacular becomes powerful. It is not front-page news to report: "folks, we looked at these emails for days and they're pretty humdrum; not much to report." And yet, now we know that these document dumps are intended precisely to elicit attention-grabbing headlines followed by professional caveats buried in paragraph 12, on the model of "while there is no direct evidence of wrongdoing in these emails, they nonetheless raise legitimate questions. . . ." The DNC and Podesta email hacks, as well as the Judicial Watch FOIA-based email dumps, were all designed precisely to elicit this kind of predictable response. And the editors, reporters, and propagandists all know that very few readers will get to paragraph 12. It is irresponsible for professional journalists and editors to continue this practice given this pattern. We must develop new standards for evidence of wrongdoing before prominent publication of implied allegations of corruption. Likewise, we must develop new modes of investigative reporting that focus more on propagandists who create document dumps.

Similarly, researchers at the Data & Society Institute who have focused specifically on the nether-regions of the internet, like Joan Donovan, have questioned whether journalists and editors should curtail coverage of fake news and extremist memes.[7] Producers of this content thrive on such attention, and publication in major outlets only increases the diffusion of the falsehoods, whether debunked or not. What is perhaps gained with exposure and debunking may, according to these arguments, be more than outweighed by the encouragement the speakers receive from the attention and the exposure that the falsehoods received.[8] Our findings about the insularity of the right-wing media ecosystem suggest that for a given rumor or conspiracy theory to circulate outside right-wing media, it has to be picked up by outlets outside that insular system. Moreover, even inside that ecosystem, a story must be picked up by influencers or major outlets to escape obscurity. Decisions not to report such stories unless and until they hit a sufficiently influential node could in fact dampen distribution to people who would only be exposed to them from mainstream media. Whether this dampening effect would be outweighed by having the rumors circulate unchallenged should be addressed as an open research question.

Despite our various cautions, our findings are good news for professional journalistic organizations. The past decade has seen repeated claims that the sky is falling; that there is no more of a market for general interest professional journals; that audience attention is diffused around the internet; that audiences only want entertaining, bias-confirming news; and so forth. We find instead that professional mainstream media continue to play an enormously important role for most Americans. Indeed, the information abundance of this era makes professional mainstream media particularly valuable to those living at least partly outside the right-wing bubble. Going forward, professional journalists must offer precisely what makes them special: credible reporting, in organizations committed to journalistic norms, but with a heavier emphasis on verifiable and accountable truth and credibility rather than balance and neutrality. As long as the media ecosystem is highly asymmetric structurally and in its flow of propaganda, balance and neutrality amplify disinformation rather than combating it.

The Question of Platform Regulation

The primary focus of solutions-oriented conversations since 2016—in the United States, in Europe, and throughout the world—has been on changing how information is accessible, framed, shared, or remunerated on platforms, primarily on Facebook and Google. The big unanswered question is whether the time has come for new government regulation or whether the best of the imperfect options is to be patient and avoid invasive legal remedies while platforms muddle toward the right balance of content moderation tools and self-regulatory policies to satisfy their many constituencies, including investors, advertisers, and users.

There are a range of measures under consideration, some based on regulation, some on self-regulation or voluntary measures. They sometimes depend on algorithmic identification of false stories and sometimes on human detection and assessment; they usually focus on removal or treatment for falsehood or illegality, but sometimes for extreme views; sometimes such designations result in additional tagging and marking of the content, sometimes in removal or demotion; and sometimes they involve blocking advertising and payment to undermine the business model of the purveyors of bullshit.

The debate over misinformation and disinformation on online platforms has intersected with a growing concern over the degree of concentration that internet platforms enjoy in their respective markets. The core examples are Google and Facebook. Google dominates search and (through YouTube) video, while Facebook dominates social media, through the Facebook platform itself and through its ownership of Instagram and WhatsApp. But there is real tension between the goal of reducing concentration and increasing competition, on the one hand, and the goal of regulating a reasonably coherent public sphere, on the other hand. A Google search for "Gab" displays (at least in early 2018) a "people also searched for" box that includes "The Daily Stormer." Gab is a social media platform that developed as an alternative for far-right and alt-right users who were banned or constrained by Twitter, Facebook, and even Reddit. A crackdown by the platforms in the presence of competition diverted their communications to a semi-segregated platform but did not remove them from the internet. Whether robust competition is helpful for combating misinformation depends on whether the critical goal is to eliminate the disinformation or merely to segregate it and reduce its diffusion pathways. But segregation only works in a relatively concentrated market, where banishment from a handful of major platforms contains content within smaller communities. Current regulatory and activist effort is focused on the major platforms precisely because they have so much power and changing their diffusion patterns has a large impact on overall diffusion patterns online.

From the perspective of disinformation and misinformation, the trouble with concentrated platforms is that if and when they fail, or become bad actors or beholden to bad actors, the negative effect is enormous. The Cambridge Analytica story, with all the caveats about how much of it was true and how much was hype, offers a perfect example. Even in the most Facebook-supportive version of the story, the company's overwhelming influence and presence made it a single point of failure that enabled Cambridge Analytica, by abusing Facebook's terms of service, to inappropriately collect and use the private data of 87 million Facebook users. The story is no better if, instead of fingering Cambridge Analytica as the bad actor, it is Facebook itself, using permission it obtained by forcing people to click "I agree" on inscrutable terms of service, that sells to a political campaign the means to mount a targeted advertising campaign intended to microtarget black voters in Florida to suppress their votes. The acts of both Facebook and the campaign in Florida were legal. But the danger presented by a single company having such massive influence over large portions of the population is reason enough to focus either on ensuring greater competition that will diffuse that power or on tightly regulating how that company can use its market power. In this Facebook represents a parallel problem to the challenge created by media consolidation after the 1996 Telecommunications Act in the United States, where companies like Clear Channel and Sinclair Broadcasting were able to expand their audience reach dramatically while combining it with aggressive distribution of right-wing propaganda on radio and television. In all these cases, solutions that tend to reinforce centralized control over the network of content outlets, rather than reduce concentration and with it the degree to which any of them provides a single point of failure, seem to exacerbate rather than solve the problem.

Our experience in the few areas where there has been normative consensus in favor of harnessing the power of platforms to regulate content means that we are not in uncharted territory. Child pornography and copyright, with all their fundamental differences, have been areas where platforms have been regulated, and have even adopted voluntary mechanisms beyond what law requires, to contain the spread of information about which we have made moral or legal decisions. The problem is that political speech is very different from pedophilia and that the copyright wars have taught us well that platform control over speech can shade into censorship, both intentionally and unintentionally.

The Contentious Role of Government

The United States has generally taken a light touch approach to internet regulation, particularly in respect to political speech. Many other countries, especially more authoritarian countries such as China, Iran, and Saudi Arabia, have forcefully policed online speech. The most aggressive effort in a liberal democracy to respond to disinformation and hate speech on social media by regulating social media platforms is the German NetzDG law that became effective on January 1, 2018. The act applies to platforms with more than two million registered users in Germany, thereby preserving the possibility for smaller, more insulated platforms to exist without following these rules, as well as for new entrants to roll out and grow before they must incur the costs of compliance. The law requires these larger platforms to provide an easily usable procedure by which users can complain that certain content is "unlawful" under a defined set of provisions in the German criminal code. These provisions include not only hate speech against groups and Holocaust denial but also criminal prohibitions on insulting and defamatory publications.

On its face, this would seem to cover much of the immigration coverage we described in Chapter 4 and practically all of the personal attacks we described in Chapter 3 and Part Two. And while the German criminal code offers reduced penalties when the targets of defamation are political figures, it does not excuse the defamation. The NetzDG requires companies it covers to either delete the content if it is "manifestly unlawful" within 24 hours, or, if its unlawfulness is not "manifest," to take one of two actions. The company may decide on the content's lawfulness within seven days, or it may refer the content to an industry-funded tribunal that will be overseen by a public authority, which then has seven days to decide on the unlawfulness of the content. Violations can be sanctioned at various levels, all the way up to 50 million euros. Sharp criticism that the draft of the act was overly restrictive came from within Germany and outside. In response to the critiques, several of the definitions were tightened, an alternative dispute resolution mechanism was added, and provisions were added to allow users to challenge blocks of allegedly factually false content. These changes did not satisfy opponents, and blistering criticism continued from a broad range of observers, including Human Rights Watch.

Critics argued that, faced with a very short time to make decisions, companies would err on the side of over-censoring rather than take the risk of being found in violation of a law that carries very high fines. Examples cropped up as soon as the law began to be enforced. Comedian Sophie Passman poked fun at the far-right's claims that immigrants destroyed German culture with a tweet that said that, as long as the practice of airing "Dinner for One" on television on New Year's Eve remained a part of German cultural tradition, immigrants were totally welcome to come and destroy it. Her tweet was removed because some users misinterpreted it as espousing the rhetoric she was mocking. Less silly, but more threatening to democratic contestation, at least from an American perspective, were the rapid removals of tweets by leaders of the far-right Alternative for Germany (AfD) party. After the Cologne police tweeted out a New Year's message in Arabic, among several other foreign languages, Beatrix von Storch, deputy-leader of AfD, tweeted that the police were appeasing "barbaric, gang-raping Muslim hordes of men." Twitter removed von Storch's tweet. The company then also removed a tweet from AfD co-leader, Alice Weidel, arguing that "[o]ur authorities submit to imported, marauding, groping, beating, knife-stabbing migrant mobs."[9] In Germany, incitement to hatred is one of the criminal offenses to which the NetzDG applies, and it is difficult to argue that the words on their face fail that test—and yet the result is state-induced private censorship of the political viewpoints of the leaders of a party that represents the views of about 13% of the votes. The problem is that there is often a wide gap, filled by case law in common law countries and commentary and experience in civil law countries, between what a law says on its face and what will be prosecuted, and what may lead to a conviction. Think of how unimaginably broad the prohibition on insulting someone might be without working knowledge of German law and its application by the judicial system. Due to lack of public process or appeal, companies are expected to err on the side of caution (censoring arguably criminal speech to avoid the fine for inaction). Another major concern is that the NetzDG law legitimizes efforts in Singapore, the Philippines, Russia, Venezuela, and Kenya to adopt copycat models that incorporate more speech-repressive criminal provisions.

In grappling with the trade-off between free speech and extreme, counterdemocratic speech, Germany's experience with the rise of Nazism has led it to adopt a more aggressive model than the U.S. First Amendment permits. Britain's and France's forays into platform regulation focused more on countering terrorist recruitment and propaganda, but hate speech is generally regulated more tightly in Western Europe than it is in the United

States. And a 2017 European Commission report underscored that the model by which platforms regulate various forms of illegal speech is hardly new. From materials depicting the sexual abuse of children to materials that violate someone's intellectual property rights, democracies generally find some materials that they are willing to prohibit and then impose on platforms some obligation to take those materials down.

The basic concern of critics of the German NetzDG law—that fear of liability would lead firms to exercise private censorship well beyond what the legislature could constitutionally impose directly—was at the foundation of American legal protection for online platforms. In the United States, the Communications Decency Act of 1996 (CDA) section 230 and the Digital Millennium Copyright Act of 1998 (DMCA) are the foundational laws governing liability of platforms for content posted by their users. CDA section 230 gave platform providers broad immunity from liability for pretty much anything their users published and has been widely considered the foundation of the freewheeling speech culture on the net. Courts were happy to let platforms avoid liability for quite substantial interpersonal abuse on their platforms,[10] much less hate speech, which is mostly protected under the First Amendment. In the absence of legal constraint in the United States, pressure from users has occasionally moved some of the major platforms to regulate offensive speech, resulting in "community guidelines" approaches. These became the de facto content control rules of the platforms in most areas, enforced through end-user agreements as interpreted by the platform companies, and punctuated by moments of public outrage that nudge these practices one way or another.

Unlike other forms of disfavored speech, the U.S. Supreme Court has long held that when copyright is used as the reason to prohibit publication of words or images, there is usually no violation of the First Amendment. We will not here rehearse the decades of academic commentary that has explained why that interpretation of the relationship between copyright and the First Amendment is incoherent. It is the law of the land, and for our purposes it explains how, faced with relative constitutional license, Congress developed in the DMCA a much more restrictive "notice-and-takedown" regime for speech challenged as violating copyright. In doing so, it identified a structure that, while not as restrictive as the NetzDG, nonetheless has similar structural attributes. Here, platform providers can only escape copyright liability over the acts of their users if they maintain a system to allow copyright challenges. Those challenges allow copyright owners to challenge the use of specific pieces of content on grounds of copyright infringement and to take down that content unless the person posting the content submitted a counternotification. This approach would encounter strong constitutional headwinds in any context but copyright. In the United States it is easier to remove YouTube videos showing students performing a show tune at a school play than YouTube videos showing neo-Nazis singing the "Horst Wessel."

The approach taken by the CDA section 230 has been remarkably successful in supporting the development of online publishing platforms. This same architecture is ill-suited for fine-grained moderation of human interaction. Whether by government mandate or voluntary company action, applying online content moderation at massive scale is a particularly gnarly challenge. There are a range of options for dealing with problematic speech. It can be removed at the source, blocked from circulation by intermediaries, removed or demoted by a search engine, or flagged for audiences as problematic. The hard part is that someone must first determine standards and guidelines for what constitutes problematic speech, and second, design a process to weed through billions of online posts, determine which posts are problematic, and then find a way to review these decisions to be able to correct errors. In the United States the default answer to the first challenge is to leave it to companies to decide how to deal with transgressing actors and content. Germany has chosen a different path that will almost certainly result in the removal of considerably more content. Companies are meanwhile expanding the infrastructure for monitoring and sorting content at a massive scale, combining algorithms and human review. It is difficult to be optimistic about how this can be applied at such scale. The promise of machine learning and artificial intelligence to accurately separate the good from the bad has not been realized, and the interim solution is hiring tens of thousands of workers to review content with company instructions in hand. These processes are aided by flagging mechanisms that allow users to flag problematic content. Predictably, these mechanisms have their limits as they are easily gamed to attack rivals and political opponents. Our experiences, in the United States and elsewhere, with both over- and underinclusiveness in the determinations of existing systems for managing copyright or nudity, leave us very skeptical that these processes will work well, much less seamlessly.

Self-Regulation and Its Discontents

For the lack of better alternatives, the hardest questions of content moderation in the United States are being left in the hands of companies: whether to allow the Daily Stormer to be treated like any other web publisher, whether conspiracy theorists should have equal standing on YouTube and in the Facebook newsfeed, and whether anti-vaxxers should be allowed to freely distribute information that will result in sickness and death.

Over the course of 2017 and early 2018, both Google and Facebook announced various measures intended to combat "fake news," misleading information, and illegal political advertising. These measures combined various elements of the systems that are already in place and will almost certainly suffer from similar difficulties and imperfections, while delivering some higher enforcement. It is important not to get caught up in the supposed newness of the problem and to recognize that we are dealing with known problems with bad information—spam, phishing, sexual exploitation of children, hate speech, and so on.

The commercial bullshit or clickbait sites are the most familiar challenge. They are simply a new breed of spammers or search engine optimizers. It is feasible to identify them through some combination of machine learning based on traffic patterns, fact checking, and human judgment, likely outsourced to independent fact-checking organizations. Excluding clickbait factories is normatively the least problematic, since they are not genuine participants in the polity. That is why most of the announcements and efforts have been directed at this class of actors. Similarly, dealing with Russian or other foreign propaganda is normatively unproblematic, though technically more challenging because of the sophistication of the attacks.

The much more vexing problem is intentional political disinformation, including hyperpartisan hate speech that is harmful but not false. Perhaps in Germany it is imaginable to remove posts by the leader of a political party (AfD) supported by over 10 percent of the electorate. In the United States private platforms are allowed under current interpretations of the First Amendment to censor political speech for whatever reason they choose. But widespread political censorship by the major private platforms would certainly generate howls of protest from large swaths of the political spectrum. Moreover, the most effective propaganda generally builds on a core set of true facts and then constructs a narrative that is materially misleading. Efforts we ourselves, and many of our colleagues who are studying the landscape of disinformation, propaganda, and bullshit, have made to create well-defined research instruments that reliably permit trained coders to identify this kind of manipulative propaganda leave us skeptical that a reliable machine-learning algorithm will emerge to solve these questions in the near future.

There have been some successful efforts to pressure advertisers to remove ads from certain programs. Alex Jones of Infowars offers the clearest example of a publisher who has repeatedly published defamatory falsehoods, like Pizzagate, that have been debunked by many fact checkers. One company, AdRoll, suspended its advertising relationship with Infowars, but Google has not turned off advertising for Infowars videos. Some brands, however, have instructed Google not to run ads for their products alongside Infowars videos. In Jones's case, this may not be too great of a loss for him, since his business model is largely based on directly selling products he markets on his shows (over 20 percent of Infowars outgoing traffic is to the site's store, where Jones sells his own branded supplements for "male vitality," brain enhancement, and such). These campaigns may reduce the economic incentives for some disinformation sites, and they are cathartic for the activists pushing the companies to sever ties. But they do not appear to present a systematic, scalable, and long-term response to the broader phenomenon of disinformation in the media ecosystem. Many of the most widely visited, shared, or linked sites in the right wing of the American media ecosystem engage in disinformation regularly or episodically. Asking the platforms to solve the problem by blocking a broad swath of the right-wing media ecosystem would be palpably antidemocratic.

In 2013 Pew reported that about one-quarter of American adults watch only Fox News among the cable news channels.[11] A later Pew study found that the number of Americans who preferred getting news on radio, rather than television, was about one-quarter the number who preferred television news.[12] Yet a third Pew study found that, after Fox News, the most trusted news sources for consistently conservative respondents were the radio shows of Sean Hannity, Rush Limbaugh, and Glenn Beck.[13] These all suggest that somewhere between 25 and 30 percent of Americans willingly and intentionally pay attention to media outlets that consistently tell that audience what it wants to hear, and what that audience wants to hear is often untrue. For the rest of the population to ask a small oligopoly of platforms to prevent those 30 percent from getting the content they want is, to say the least, problematic. Platforms can certainly help with the commercial pollution, and to some extent they can help with foreign propaganda. But we suggest that asking platforms to solve the fundamental political and institutional breakdown represented by the asymmetric polarization of the American polity is neither feasible nor normatively attractive.

Political Advertising: Disclosure and Accountability

A much more tractable problem, for both law and self-regulation, is online political advertising. The problem presents three distinct aspects. First, online ads have been to this date exempt from the disclosure requirements that normally apply to television, radio, and print advertising. This is a holdover from an earlier, "hands off the internet" laissez-faire attitude that can no longer be justified given the size of the companies involved and the magnitude of the role they play in political advertising. Second, online advertising may be substantially more effective and narrowly targeted in ways that subvert judgment and are more amenable to experimentally validated behavioral manipulation. Cambridge Analytica's claims were likely overstated, and it is likely that the 2016 cycle did not see these developing techniques of psychographically informed behavioral marketing techniques deployed with any measureable success. But there is little doubt that the confluence of techniques for analysis of very large datasets, A/B testing in product marketing, and the rapidly developing fields of behavioral sciences will continue to improve techniques of emotional and psychological manipulation. The literature we reviewed in Chapter 9 makes clear that the claims of the effectiveness of narrowly targeted advertising are not yet scientifically proven. But the continued efforts of industry suggest that platforms will continue to increase their ability to individualize and will seek to increase their effectiveness at manipulating the preferences of their targets. The third problem is that, just as we saw with Russian sockpuppets and bots, behavioral marketing techniques often do not take the form of explicit advertising. Rather, they are paid influencers who deceptively manipulate genuine users. Any regime that focuses its definitions purely on explicit paid advertising, and does not address to some extent the problem of masked influence, will push propaganda and political marketing from the regulated and explicit to the unregulated underground.

The Honest Ads Act

The Honest Ads Act introduced by Senators Amy Klobuchar, Mark Warner, and John McCain was the first significant legislative effort to address the new challenges of network propaganda. The bill sought to do three things. First, it separated paid internet communications from unpaid communications, incorporating paid communications into the normal model adopted for communication generally, and leaving volunteer or unpaid communications alone. Second, it required disclaimers on online advertising, so that people exposed to political advertising can see that it is political advertising, not part of the organic flow of communications, and who is paying for it. And third, and perhaps most important, it required the creation of a fine-grained public database of online political *issue advertising*, reaching well beyond electioneering.

Paid Internet as Political Communication. First, the bill included "paid Internet, or paid digital communications" as part of the normal framework of contributions and expenditures, addressing what was an anachronistic exclusion given the dramatic increase in the significance of internet and social media as core modes of political communication. And the bill also expanded electioneering—express advocacy for or against a candidate by anyone just before an election—to include placement or promotion on an online platform *for a fee*. The use of "paid" and "for a fee" are clearly intended to exclude genuine grassroots campaigns. By doing so, the bill recognized the importance of preserving the democratizing aspect of the internet—its capacity to empower decentralized citizens to self-organize rather than depending on the established parties and wealthy donors. This latter provision is also the only one that might be interpreted to apply not only to communications made in payment to the platforms themselves, as with advertising, but also to behavioral social-media marketing firms that specialize in simulating social attention to a topic or concern by deploying paid human confederates or automated and semi-automated accounts—botnets and sockpuppets.

Disclaimers on Facebook and Google Ads. Second, the bill required online advertising to include the kinds of disclaimers television viewers have come to expect: "paid for by" or "I am so and so and I approve this message." These provisions of the bill emphasize the anomaly that inconclusive Federal Election Commission (FEC) advisory opinions have enabled Google and Facebook to market to political advertisers not only reach and focus but also the ability to remain masked. In 2010 Google persuaded a divided FEC that its ads were too short to include a full disclaimer, and the commissioners were split between those who wanted to simply exclude Google's ads from the requirements of disclaimer altogether, and those who wanted to condition the exclusion on the ad carrying a link to the advertiser's site, where the disclaimer would appear prominently.[14] In 2011 Facebook tried to piggyback on Google's effort by arguing that its own advertising was not only too brief to allow the disclaimer to show on its face, but that because much of the advertising directed not to a campaign site but to news stories supportive of a campaign, the FEC should adopt the more complete exclusion supported by some of its members in the 2010 opinion.[15] In other words, because Facebook's ads were designed to be short to fit with users' usage patterns, and because ads often sent users to media sites rather than to a campaign site where a disclaimer could be displayed, imposing any disclaimer requirement on Facebook advertising, even one satisfied merely by disclosure on the target site, was "impractical," a recognized exception to the disclaimer requirement in the act.

The Honest Ads Act would explicitly reject the possibility that advertising on social media and search would be covered by this "impractical" exception. The idea that the biggest and most sophisticated technology companies in the world can build driverless cars and optimize messaging and interfaces by running thousands of experiments a day, but cannot figure out how to include an economical indication that a communication is a political ad and construct a pop-up or other mechanism for letting users who want to figure out who is behind the act, is laughable. The bill simply states a clear minimal requirement: users have to know the name of the sponsor and have to be given the means to get all the legally required information about the sponsor without being exposed to any other information.

The necessity of this kind of provision is clear. We assess the credibility of any statement in the context of what we think the agenda of the speaker is. That's why we require political advertising to disclose its sponsor to begin with. If the Clinton campaign were to target evangelical voters with communications that emphasized her opponent's comments on the Hollywood Access video, these voters would treat the communications with more of a grain of salt even if its contents are true. The same would be true if the Trump campaign had targeted African American voters with narrowly tailored targeted ads quoting Hillary Clinton's use of the term "superpredator" in the context of a 1996 criminal law reform debate.[16] There is nothing wrong with trying to persuade your opponents' base that their candidate is unworthy of their support. But doing so behind a mask undermines those voters' ability to judge your statements fairly, including by discounting properly the reliability or honest intentions of the speaker.

In 2018 the Federal Election Commission invited comments on its own version of the disclosure requirements. These are tailored to the FEC's mandate to deal with electioneering, and largely deal with the nature of the disclaimer requirement. One option would simply treat online video like television, online audio like radio, and online text like print. The other tries to offer more flexibility for online platforms to tailor their disclosure to the technology. Presumably, the more flexibility the platforms have to design the disclosures, the easier it will be for them to design and test forms of disclosure that comply with the letter of the law but offer their clients the ability to minimize the number of recipients who are exposed to the disclosure. Our own sense is that, if in 2010 the internet companies deserved protection from overly onerous requirements, by 2018 the risk is inverted. Starting with a very demanding and strict requirement and then loosening the constraints through case-by-case advisory opinions, seems the more prudent course today.

A Public Machine-Readable Open Database of Political Issue Advertising

The major innovation of the bill is to leverage the technological capabilities of online advertising to create a timely, publicly open record of online advertising that would be available "as soon as possible" and would be open to public inspection in machine-readable form. This is perhaps the most important of the bill's provisions, because, executed faithfully, it should allow public watchdog organizations to offer accountability for lies and manipulation in almost real time. Moreover, this is the only provision of the bill that applies to issue campaigns as well as electoral campaigns, and so it is the only one where the American public will get some visibility into the campaign dynamics on any "national legislative issue of public importance."

The bill requires the very biggest online platforms (with over 50 million unique monthly U.S. visitors) to report all ads placed by anyone who spends more than $500 a year on political advertising to be placed in an open, publicly accessible database. The data would include a copy of the ad, the audience targeted, the views, and the time of first and last display, as well as the name and contact information of the purchaser. The online platforms already collect all this data as a function of their basic service to advertisers and their ability to price their ads and bill their clients. The additional requirement of formatting this data in an open, publicly known format and placing it in a public database is incrementally trivial by comparison to the investments these companies have made in developing their advertising base and their capacities to deliver viewers to advertisers. Having such a database, by contrast, would allow campaigns to be each other's watchdogs—keeping each other somewhat more honest and constrained—and perhaps more importantly, would allow users anywhere on the net, from professional journalists and nonprofits to concerned citizens with a knack for data, to see what the campaigns and others are doing, and to be able to report promptly on these practices to offer us, as a society, at least a measure of transparency about how our elections are conducted. This public database could allow the many and diverse organizations that have significant knowledge in machine learning and pattern recognition to deploy their considerable capabilities to identify manipulative campaigns by foreign governments and to help

Americans understand who, more generally, is trying to manipulate public opinion and how.

The database is particularly critical because Facebook and Google will continuously improve their ability to deliver advertisements finely tuned to very narrowly targeted populations. In the television or newspaper era, if a campaign wanted to appeal to neo-Nazis, it could only do so in the public eye, suffering whatever consequences that association entails with other populations. That constraint on how narrow, incendiary, or outright false a campaign candidates and their supporters can run is disappearing in an era when Facebook can already identify and target advertising to populations in the few thousands range—down to the level of American followers of a German far-right ultranationalist party.[17] Hypertargeted marketing of this sort frees a campaign from being associated with particularly controversial messages, while still being able to use them on very narrow populations where they appeal. A database that is publicly accessible and allows many parties to review and identify particularly false, abusive, or underhanded microtargeted campaigns will impose at least some pressure on campaigns not to issue messages that they cannot defend to the bulk of their likely voters.

In 2017 Google released a plan to voluntarily implement some of these affordances. It announced that it would publish a transparency report about who is buying election-related ads on Google platforms and how much money is being spent, a publicly accessible database of election ads purchased on AdWords and YouTube, with information about who bought each ad, and will implement in-ad disclosures—Google will identify the names of advertisers running election-related campaigns on Google Search, YouTube, and the Google Display Network via Google's "Why This Ad" icon. These are all desirable features, and they may offer some insight into how these elements may operate when adopted voluntarily, but the electoral system and its integrity is fundamentally a matter of public concern and should be regulated uniformly, across all companies and platform, and subject to appropriate administrative and judicial procedures. Falling back on private action may be the only first step available, given a dysfunctional legislative process, but it cannot be the primary permanent solution for a foundational piece of the democratic process.

What About Botnets, Sockpuppets, and Paid Social Promoters?

Addressing paid ads will not obviously address "astroturf" social influence—bots, sockpuppets, and paid influencers. Particularly in Chapter 8, in our discussion of Russian efforts, we saw that coordinated campaigns aim to simulate public engagement and attention, and to draw other, real citizens to follow the astroturfing networks in terms of agenda setting, framing of issues, and levels of credibility assigned to various narratives. This practice is used by marketing firms as well as foreign governments.

If regulation stopped at "paid advertising" as traditionally defined, the solution would be significant but partial even with regard to paid advertising. Historically, when a broadcast station or editor was a bottleneck that needed to be paid to publish anything on the platform, defining "paid" as "paid to the publisher" would have made sense. Here, however, a major pathway to communicating on a platform whose human users are provided the service for free is by hiring outside marketing firms that specialize in using that free access to provide a paid service to the person seeking political influence. Search engine optimizers who try to manipulate Google search results to come out on top, or behavioral marketing firms that use coordinated accounts, whether automated or not, to simulate social engagement, are firms that offer paid services to engage in political communication. The difficulty posed by such campaigns is that they will not appear *on the platforms* as paid advertising, because those who engage in these platforms are simulating accounts on the networks. The marketers—whether they are a Russian information operations center or a behavioral marketing firm—engage with the network through multiple accounts, as though they are authentic users, and control and operate the accounts from outside the platform.

The Honest Ads Act definition of "qualified Internet or digital communication" is "any communication which is placed or promoted for a fee on an online platform." This definition is certainly broad enough to encompass the products sold by third-party paid providers whose product is to use the free affordances of the online network to produce the effect of a political communication, and to do so for a fee. As a practical matter, such a definition would reduce the effectiveness of viral political marketing that uses botnets or sockpuppets to simulate authentic grassroots engagement, because each bot, sockpuppet, or paid influencer would have to carry a disclaimer as to the fact that they are paid and the source of payment. Although the whole purpose of such coordinated campaigns is to create the false impression that the views expressed are expressed authentically in the target Facebook or Twitter community, the burden on expression is no greater than the burden on any political advertiser who would have preferred to communicate without being clearly labeled as political advertising. The party seeking to communicate is still permitted to communicate, to exactly the same people (unless the false accounts violate the platform's terms of service, but it is not a legitimate complaint for the marketers to argue that the campaign disclosure rule makes it harder for them to violate the terms of service of the platforms they use). The disclaimer requirement would merely remove the misleading representation that the communication is by a person not paid to express such views.

While the general language of the definition of a qualified internet communication is broad enough to include paid bot and sockpuppet campaigns, and the disclaimer provisions seem to apply, the present text of the bill seems to exclude such campaigns from the provision that requires online platforms to maintain a public database of advertisements. The definition of "qualified political advertisement" to which the database requirement applies, includes "any advertisement (including search engine marketing, display advertisements, video advertisements, native advertisements, and sponsorships)." It would be preferable to include "coordinated social network campaigns" explicitly among the list of examples of "advertisement." It is possible and certainly appropriate for courts to read "native advertisements" to include a sockpuppet or bot pushing a headline or meme that supports a candidate or campaign. But there is a risk that courts would not. Furthermore, the provision requires platforms only to keep a record of "any request to purchase on such online platform a qualified political advertisement," and advertisers are only required to make information necessary for the online platform to comply with its obligations. It would be preferable to clarify that the advertisers owe an independent duty to disclose to the platform all the information they need to include paid coordinated campaigns in the database, even if the request for the advertisement and the payment are not made to the platform.

As with the more general requirements of disclaimer applied to explicit advertising, clarifying that the disclosure and disclaimer requirements apply to coordinated campaigns will not address every instance of media manipulation. A covert foreign information operation will not comply with new laws intended to exclude it any more that it complies with present laws designed for the same purpose. But just as the disclosure requirements and database for advertisements would limit the effectiveness of efforts by would-be propagandists (campaigns, activists, or foreign governments) to leverage the best data and marketing techniques that Google and Facebook have to offer, so too would an interpretation of the bill that extends to commercial marketing firms that provide synthetic social-behavioral marketing through paid sockpuppets, botnets, or human influencers. This will not address all propaganda, but it will certainly bring some of the most effective manipulation tactics into the sunlight.

A Public Health Approach to the Media Ecosystem

The public database called for in Honest Ads presents a model for a broader public health approach to our media ecosystem. At the moment, Twitter offers expensive but broadly open access to its data, which explains why so much of the best research on fake news, bots, and so forth is conducted on Twitter. Facebook, by contrast, offers very limited access to its data to outside researchers. Google occupies a position somewhere in the middle, with reasonable access to YouTube usage patterns, for example, but less visibility to other aspects of search and advertising. Each of these companies has legitimate considerations concerning protecting user privacy. Each of these companies has legitimate considerations in terms of their own proprietary interests. And as each of these companies considers its own commercial interests, these will often align imperfectly, if at all, with the public interest. In order to understand how our information environment is changing, we need a mechanism through which to offer bona fide independent investigators access to data that would allow us, as a society, to understand how various changes in how we communicate—whether driven by technological change, regulatory intervention, or business decisions—affect the levels of truth and falsehood in our media ecosystem or the degrees of segmentation and polarization.

Our communications privacy as individuals and citizens is an important concern, but not more so than our privacy interest in health data. And yet we develop systems to allow bona fide health researchers access, under appropriate legal constraints, contractual limitations, and technical protections to access the health data of millions of residents to conduct detailed analyses of patterns of disease, treatment, and outcomes. We can no more trust Facebook to be the sole source of information about the effects of its platform on our media ecosystem than we could trust a pharmaceutical company to be the sole source of research on the health outcomes of its drugs, or an oil company to be the sole source of measurements of particles emissions or levels of CO_2 in the atmosphere. We need a publicly regulated system that will regulate not only the companies but the researchers who access the data as well, so they do not play the role of brokers to companies like Cambridge Analytica.

What About Defamation Law?
Intentional or Reckless Falsehoods

As we brought this book to a close, the family of Seth Rich was suing Fox News for its false and disturbing story. Alex Jones was forced to retract his Pizzagate story, likely under threat of a lawsuit. Nothing under present or proposed election law would touch this kind of intentional lying. As Peter Thiel showed when he funded "Hulk Hogan's" lawsuit that bankrupted Gawker, a motivated actor with enough money and patience can find a case with which to shut down a publication, even under the very permissive American defamation law framework. Should we have a system that would allow Jeb Bush to sue Alex Jones for portraying him as having "close Nazi ties"? Under normal circumstances such a path should raise concerns for anyone who is properly concerned with robust political speech. Certainly, defamation has been used in many countries as a way of silencing the government's critics, and the strict limits under the *New York Times v. Sullivan* line of cases make this path appropriately difficult. The level of bile and sheer disinformation that characterized the 2016 election is such that perhaps raising the cost of reckless or intentional defamatory falsehood as a business model, at least, is a reasonable path to moderation of the most extreme instances of falsehood. But the persistence of the tabloid model in the United Kingdom, despite that country's very permissive defamation law, suggests that even this approach would be of only moderate use. Whether such an approach is worth the candle depends on one's empirical answer to the question of how much of the defamation comes from fly-by-night fake news outlets, which would be effectively judgment proof, and how much comes from a core number of commercial sites that have made it their business model to sell false information and peddle in conspiracy theory.

Institutionalizing Fact Checking

An approach that has received a good bit of public attention and some platform integration focuses on efforts to institutionalize fact checking and generate ground-truth labels and marking. First among these are existing fact-checking sites and the efforts by platforms to use their collective judgment to remove, demote, or label stories. These organizations, PolitiFact, Snopes, Factcheck. org, the *Washington Post*'s Fact Checker, are all efforts to institutionalize and professionalize the process of checking how true or false the facts in a given story are. Of these organizations only one, PolitiFact, systematically reports both true and false judgments by a media source or personality, so as to give some broad overall sense of the veracity of an outlet or speaker. All these organizations limit themselves to "fact" checking, so they are not useful in determining sites that are extremist or hyperpartisan, as opposed to simply false. And they all suffer from the one failure that most newer projects will also have to contend with. They are treated by the media outlets and users of the right-wing media ecosystem as systematically biased, and as our work and the work of other researchers finds, are generally not visited, shared, linked to, or believed by users on the right.

Despite being ignored by users and outlets on the right, fact-checking sites serve an important role for the majority of people outside the right. For centrists and people of mixed views, who are not entirely in the thrall of the right-wing network, they offer an anchor through which to assess what they read and see. For people on the left, they offer an anchor in reality—a way of persuading themselves that they are not in the simple mirror image of the right-wing propaganda network. Nonetheless, the empirical evidence on the effects of fact checking even for this population are mixed. There are some studies that suggest that correction and fact checking merely reinforces recall by repeating the story and that over time all that is left is a sense that "I've heard this before." Others suggest that correction fails, if it does, only for highly salient questions that conflict with a person's prior beliefs.[18] Furthermore, fact checking takes time and, at least for short-term belief formation, is likely too slow to influence immediate perceptions. Nonetheless, our case studies show that some conspiracy theories, like Uranium One or Seth Rich, remain prevalent for days or weeks. In these cases, it seems plausible that an independent source, trusted at least by people outside the echo chamber from which the false stories emerge, could play a useful role.

Regardless of their impact on media consumers, fact-checking organizations play a valuable role for academics seeking to study diffusion of falsehoods. Determining "ground truth" is an extremely expensive and difficult process, fraught with judgments. Most scientific research groups are not set up to produce such ground-truth judgments about politically salient news, and so referring to some minimal number of decisions by these independent sites becomes a "ground truth" on which analyses can then proceed. A problem with all of the fact-checking sites is that they can check only a fraction of the overall universe of statements, true and false, that can be made, and they systematically only spend their time on claims that are at least arguably false. Looking at their statistics systematically overstates the amount of falsehood, because the numerator of total stories includes only stories that are both (a) suspect and (b) sufficiently visible to draw the attention of one or usually more fact checkers. So while these organizations play an important role, they overestimate the prevalence of falsehoods in the media ecosystem. Several new projects, such as CrossCheck or the Credibility Coalition, are trying to redress some of these problems—particularly by developing a richer ontology of offensive and misleading forms. Another important reform for these organizations would be to invest in creating a baseline ratio of truth to fiction for media outlets and politically prominent institutions by dedicating some of their resources to assessing a properly randomized sample of stories and statements from these outlets and speakers.

It is demonstrably true that institutional fact checking has not prevented the continued worsening of the epistemic crisis we describe in this book. But more and better fact checking can at least help us better understand the nature and the scope of the problem.

Media Literacy Education

One class of interventions proposed has been media literacy education. This is a vitally important and active area of research, experimentation, and applied work. Survey after survey have demonstrated that many people are shockingly poor at effectively evaluating the accuracy of news reporting. A natural response is to improve education and explicitly train consumers to be more discerning about what they read and believe. Some programs are being rolled out to specifically address the "fake news" problem by teaching specific strategies to ferret out disinformation and propagation from online news sources. These are laudable projects and may help to chip away at the problem. This is not a panacea and will not by itself disarm the incredibly resilient psychological and social-identity-based factors that so often lead us astray. As foundations and government entities invest in developing these efforts, we suggest that they at least acknowledge how little evidence there is that media literacy training will relieve the kinds of pressures we identified in this volume. There appears to be little evidence that improvement on the ability to answer test or classroom media literacy questions actually translates into adoption of critical viewing and listening when students consume media in the real world.[19] A more recent, trenchant critique of media literacy comes from danah boyd, whose years of research with youth in media have led her to hypothesize that media literacy efforts have trained media consumers to be distrustful of all media and in a perverse way less discerning about what is credible and what is not.[20] Given the considerable faith and resources being invested in media literacy training, the apparent dearth of evidence, and the possibility of negative implications, we suggest that such programs be well instrumented to assess their positive and negative effects.

Thinking About Solutions

We began this chapter with the acknowledgement that our diagnosis of the present information disorder makes identifying solutions difficult. Solutions that are based on misdiagnosis, particularly on imagining that Facebook, or bots, or the Russians are the core threat, will likely miss their mark. Some level of effort from platforms, backed by legal liability as necessary, could help clean platforms of some of the garbage they now carry; but regulation informed by misdiagnosis, aimed at the wrong targets, will almost certainly lead to over-censorship. There are important discrete interventions that can help alleviate the present sense of disorder. In particular, we emphasize efforts to make sure that political advertising becomes more transparent and susceptible to public scrutiny because we see large scale preference manipulation as the core of the platform business, and we see that core business presenting a profound future threat to democracy.

But our central argument has been that the present source of information disorder in American political communications is the profound asymmetry between the propaganda feedback loop that typifies the right-wing media ecosystem and the reality-check dynamic that typifies the rest of the media system. The most important attainable change in the face of that asymmetry would be to the practice of professional journalism. Our findings make clear that mainstream professional journalists continue to influence the majority of the population, including crossover audiences exposed both to right-wing propaganda and to journalism in mainstream media. We argued in Chapter 6 that the present journalistic practice of objectivity as neutrality has perverse effects in the media ecosystem we document here. By maintaining the "one side says x, the other side says y" model of objectivity in the presence of highly asymmetric propaganda efforts, mainstream media become sources of legitimation and amplification for the propagandists. Here, we suggest that a shift in emphasis in how journalists practice objectivity, from demonstrative neutrality to accountable verifiability, could help counteract some of the reinforcement and legitimation that the present practice creates on the background of highly asymmetric propaganda practices. This will not change the perceptions of the 25 to 30 percent of the population that attends purely to the right-wing media ecosystem, but could make a significant difference to crossover audiences, and would prevent erosion of the present patterns of reliance on objective media in partisan audiences on the left.

A more foundational change is, at present, aspirational. It is that Republican leaders recognize the dangers that the propaganda feedback loop poses to American democracy, and find a way to lead their party and voters out of it. Only those who have credibility and power within the partisan media sphere stand a chance of breaking the destructive cycle. While the revolution in talk radio and Fox News has provided Republicans with a highly mobilized core of supporters, it has done so at the expense of pulling the party far to the right, disconnecting its base from reality, and disabling party leaders from delivering and acting on bad news where bad news turns out to be the case. It is extremely unlikely that this change will happen, however, as long as the propaganda feedback loop delivers electoral gains. And such an effort, even if undertaken, faces the daunting challenge of communicating with a population exposed to decades of propaganda that instilled in them a profound distrust of messages that do not conform to their partisan beliefs.

14

Conclusion

THE SECOND DECADE of the twenty-first century has seen dramatic new strains on the democratic project. The 1970s, '80s, and '90s saw the demise of the last authoritarian regimes in Western Europe followed by Latin America, Central and Eastern Europe, and to a degree East and Southeast Asia and Africa. By 2018 trends appear to have reversed, and illiberal majoritarian parties or authoritarian regimes are asserting themselves across the globe. As governments, civil society organizations, academics, and media tried to understand what was driving this global change, many focused on technology and technological change. Processes of technological progress that were out of human control were overwhelming our capacity to make sense of the world and govern ourselves as reasonable democracies. The most optimistic feature of our work is that the culprit was not technology.

Technology allowed us to analyze millions of stories published over a three-year period. Technology allowed us to analyze millions of tweets and links, and hundreds of millions of Facebook shares and words to make sense of these stories. And yet, all this technology-enabled research has led us away from technology as the primary explanatory variable of our present epistemic crisis.

Technology is not destiny. Technology interacts with institutions and ideology to shape how we make meaning, how we organize our affairs across economic, political, and personal domains, and how we make our culture and identity.

In the United States, a set of technological innovations rolled out since the 1970s, from FM radio, satellites, and cable, through the personal computer, the internet, and social media, have been adopted and adapted by two fundamentally different epistemic communities in two radically different ways. The civil rights revolution, the women's movement, and the

Network Propaganda. Yochai Benkler, Robert Faris, and Hal Roberts.
© Yochai Benkler, Robert Faris, and Hal Roberts 2018. Published 2018 by Oxford University Press.

emergence of self-actualization and individual liberty at the heart of both the New Left and the neoliberal moment created a new political reality and a new bifurcation of American polity in terms of how meaning and identity were defined and how these translated into practical political ambitions. On the left, a loose coalition of civil rights advocates, feminists, consumer advocates, environmentalists, and vestiges of organized labor reorganized to challenge an establishment seen as too white, male, and corporate. Some of this reorientation focused on identity; much of it was focused on gaining specific programmatic victories effected through law and policies aimed at achieving better practical outcomes for members of the coalition. On the right, starting in the South, white-identity backlash against the civil rights movement made common cause with the religious right, which itself emerged as a backlash against both the women's movement's challenge to the patriarchal family and the secularizing force of putting individual choice at the normative core of markets and morality.[1] These two pillars of the emerging conservative coalition were fundamentally about meaning and identity, rather than about programmatic achievement. The pro-business pillar of the emerging conservative coalition was very much about programmatic achievement, particularly deregulation and reduction of taxes, but found ways to translate its programmatic goals into articles of faith—most visibly in Grover Norquist's tax pledge. That pledge, initiated in 1986, commits politicians who take it to oppose "any and all" tax increases or reduction or elimination of credits, without qualification. Functionally, it has become a precondition to running for office as a Republican. And it transformed the most basic tool for economic and social policy at the heart of the power of the legislative branch into an article of faith divorced from practical considerations and immune to evidence of changed conditions.

The deregulation of cable and elimination of the fairness doctrine in broadcast in the 1970s and 1980s created the institutional conditions for divergent organizational strategies to explore the markets for listeners and viewers. The increased channel capacity provided first by AM radio, then cable, and finally the internet meant that strategies focused on intense engagement of large but still minority audiences became a viable market strategy. Audiences who made up the emerging conservative movement proved a lucrative market for merchants of angry, ideologically pure messages that expressed a shared sense of outrage and loss in the fast-moving, fast-changing world. Rush Limbaugh was the first major commercial success at selling this kind of sentiment since Father Coughlin was forced off the air at the beginning of World War II. Fox News followed, and deregulation allowed

Clear Channel to consolidate both radio stations and right-wing outrage content into a seamless distribution network for these messages, around the clock, in every corner of the country, to tens of millions of listeners. These outlets offered an ideological coordination point, a cathartic experience of shared anger, and a platform for disciplining political elites who did not hew to the pure message produced by these new right-wing media. Democrats, by contrast, never developed a sufficiently large and homogenous group to form the basis of a similarly successful strategy focused on ideological purity. The coalition the party represented was too diverse to support a single entity like Fox, or Rush Limbaugh in the late 1980s to mid-1990s. Its constituents spread their attention across too many outlets to sustain efforts, like Air America or MSNBC, to replicate the strategy that had succeeded so well on the right.

Thirty years of divergent organizational practices and market dynamics turn out to produce quite different markets, offerings, and consumption habits. When the market in question is the market in informing political beliefs and news, it turns out that this divergence produces very different views of what is going on in the world and who to believe about what is going on.

Our study offers a large-scale observation, sustained over a substantial period of time, of how the American political media ecosystem discusses presidential politics specifically and, by extension, national politics. We found that there is no single effect that the internet has on democracy, or on news media, or on people's ability to tell truth from fiction. In America, "the internet" is really two very different media ecosystems. One conforms to the very worst fears of those critical of the effects of the internet on democracy. It exhibits all the characteristics of an echo chamber that radicalizes its inhabitants, destabilizes their ability to tell truth from fiction, and undermines their confidence in institutions. The other is closer to the model of the networked public sphere. It combines distinct attention to professional media still pursuing norm-constrained journalism with diverse outlets for mobilizing activists, challenging agenda setting, and questioning mainstream media narratives. This larger part of the American media ecosystem certainly has its own share of propagators of disinformation and commercial clickbait, but these operate in an environment that contains their dissemination and limits their impact.

The differences between the two media ecosystems are palpable. Despite extensive efforts, we were unable to find an example of disinformation or commercial clickbait started on the left, or aimed from abroad at the left, that took hold and became widely reported and believed in the broader network that stretches from the center to the left for any meaningful stretch of time.

By contrast, as this book demonstrates amply, we found such instances repeatedly succeeding in the right-wing media ecosystem, with pervasive exposure and lasting effects on the beliefs reported by listeners, readers, and viewers within that network. Few if any moments more clearly capture the sheer dehumanization that such a dynamic can birth than the sight of the host of the fourth-most watched television news show in America, Laura Ingraham, tweeting to her two million followers, publicly mocking a 17-year-old high school senior, David Hogg, for not getting into the colleges of his choice. Hogg's crime, by which he merited public bullying by a Fox News host for the entertainment of her followers, was that he had shown remarkable leadership in the high school students protest movement in favor of gun control in the wake of the Marjory Stoneman Douglas High School shooting.

For those not focused purely on the American public sphere, our study suggests that we should focus on the structural, not the novel; on the long-term dynamic between institutions, culture, and technology, not only the disruptive technological moment; and on the interaction between the different media and technologies that make up a society's media ecosystem, not on a single medium, like the internet, much less a single platform like Facebook or Twitter. The stark differences we observe between the insular right-wing media ecosystem and the majority of the American media environment, and the ways in which open web publications, social media, television, and radio all interacted to produce these differences, suggest that the narrower focus will lead to systematically erroneous predictions and diagnoses. It is critical not to confound what is easy to measure (Twitter) with what is significantly effective in shaping beliefs and politically actionable knowledge in society. We are only at the very beginning of the ability to create the capacity to engage in such broad, cross-platform research. Television archival data is becoming available; talk radio is still observable only through sporadic transcripts. Facebook data in nonpublic- pages is largely inaccessible. Political ads are not available, but that is changing either through voluntary efforts of companies or through changes in campaign law. We need broad, publicly accessible databases for all these different media so that we can begin to apply the emerging array of data science techniques to a sufficiently broad and diverse set of media to actually represent how people get their news and how people come to learn about the world and understand it.

It is equally critical not to confound whether a phenomenon is observable and whether it actually has an impact. Throughout this book we have argued that many of the concerns over information disorder or the post-truth moment discussed in the past two years focus on what is observable and novel, without accounting for how impactful it has in fact been. Russian information operations penetrated American social media in ways that would have been considered the stuff of spy movies in 2012. The evidence supporting the existence of these efforts is real and persuasive, and the recent origin of the organizations perpetrating them suggest that these efforts are in fact novel. The fact that we observe these efforts strongly suggests we need to build capabilities to identify them in real time, and interdict and counter them as they occur. But simply because these efforts are observable and require a response does not mean that they actually had an impact. As we explained in Chapter 8, our own findings, when compared to the publicly disclosed accusations of interference, suggest that these efforts sought to build on and widen already existing fissures in American society but that they appear to have mostly amounted to little more than jumping on a bandwagon already well underway. Similarly, we do not challenge the veracity of some of the excellent journalistic reporting, particularly by Craig Silverman at BuzzFeed news, on the hyperpartisan commercial clickbait. These too are very real and do in fact pollute the environment. We have no systematic reason to think that they could not grow to become an even bigger problem, but our observations at present, and the work of others, suggest that these played a role not fundamentally dissimilar to that of the supermarket checkout-counter tabloid—a side entertainment, not a driver of discourse, opinion, or changes in beliefs at a population level.

Unique in our view among the putative novel suspected contributors to disinformation dissemination is targeted advertising. Here, as is true of the other major suspects, the effect sizes reported in the published science suggest that at least psychographically microtargeted advertising of the Cambridge Analytica variety is highly unlikely to have made a difference in the 2016 campaign. We have no similar evidence with which to confirm or refute the claims that Facebook put Donald Trump in office by selling his campaign the best of their microtargeted advertising capabilities. Nonetheless, the overall trajectory of the entire market in personal data collection and algorithmically delivered, personalized advertising across the online economy suggests that even the small documented effects may well amount to significant effects in the near future. Because effects will be extremely hard to measure, however, both candidate and issue campaigns are likely to invest heavily in these microtargeting techniques, and we will almost certainly not be able to measure their impact until it is too late. For this reason we dedicated a good bit of our solutions chapter to the regulation and transparency of political advertising broadly, not only during electoral campaigns, and believe that this is an area where many ounces of prevention are necessary and justified, even in the absence of proof of impact.

Our study is, ironically, both optimistic and pessimistic about the possibilities for democracy in an age of ubiquitously networked communications. It is optimistic because it suggests that the introduction of the internet and social media does not itself put pressure on democracy as such. Different countries, with different histories, institutional structures, and cultural practices of collective sense-making need not fear the internet's effects. There is no echo chamber or filter-bubble effect that will inexorably take a society with a well-functioning public sphere and turn it into a shambles simply because the internet comes to town. The American online public sphere is a shambles because it was grafted onto a television and radio public sphere that was already deeply broken. Even here, those parts of the American public sphere that were not already in the grip of a propaganda feedback loop and under the influence of hyperpartisan media dedicated to a propagandist project did not develop such a structure as a result of the internet's development. In fact, after the election of Donald Trump, online communications outside of the right-wing media ecosystem became more mainstream-focused, not less; and this was true even on Facebook, the most polluted of online platforms. These observations suggest that professional journalism continues to play a critical role in anchoring public debate in facts and evidence-based norms and that it functions within a vibrant network of nontraditional sites that constitute a more decentralized, participatory networked public sphere that can work around and through its interactions with the mainstream to diversify expression, counter some of the failure modes of the mainstream, and make mobilization more democratic.

But that happy image goes only as far as a country's politics and institutional history permit it. The pessimistic lesson of our work is that there is no easy fix for epistemic crises in countries where a politically significant portion of the population does occupy a hyperpartisan, propaganda rich environment. Regulation of, or self-regulation by, platforms can help deal with some of the commercial pollution effects. National security identification of foreign propaganda campaigns may be able to help cleanse public debate from them, although at the cost of substantial surveillance of the major platforms of public discourse. If, however, the origins of crisis are primarily domestic and comprised of intentional manipulation of large parts of the population by its own political leaders and preferred media, there is little that technocratic solutions can do consistent with a commitment to free expression. Here, the hard work of containing disinformation and hate-provoking messages falls heavily on those media most trusted by people who are still tuned in to the majority of the network but are at risk of falling into the disinformation vortex. Emphasizing truth seeking rather than neutrality in journalism may help. Regulators might seek to limit the market reach of any given platform, to avoid making any platform a single point of failure that can be used by a disinformation campaign. Public funding for reliable professional media and an educated public may help as well. We embrace these diverse measures because some of them may, in fact, begin to roll back some of the uncertainty and distrust. But if the fundamental problem has deep political roots and takes a political shape, it is hard to imagine that it will be solved by technocratic rather than political and cultural means.

Breathing new life into the truth-seeking institutions that operate on reason and evidence would require a revival of the idea that science, scholarship, journalism, law, and professionalism more generally offer real constraints on what one can say and do, and that they are not all simply modes of legitimating power. This is unimaginable without an underlying shift in political culture, a shift that would require either a successful internal effort from leaders on the right to extricate their party and its base from the propaganda feedback loop or a series of electoral defeats that would force such a transformation. The former is unlikely without the latter. These political and cultural developments will have to overcome not only right-wing propaganda, but also decades of left-wing criticism of objectivity and truth-seeking institutions. Developing such a framework without falling into high modernist nostalgia is the real answer to the threat of a post-truth era.

Notes

CHAPTER 1

1. Faiz Siddiqui and Susan Svrluga, "N.C. man told police he went to D.C. pizzeria with gun to investigate conspiracy theory," *Washington Post*, December 5, 2016, https://www.washingtonpost.com/news/local/wp/2016/12/04/d-c-police-respond-to-report-of-a-man-with-a-gun-at-comet-ping-pong-restaurant/?utm_term=.936da2eb2f42.

2. Belief in conspiracies largely depends on political identity, https://today.yougov.com/news/2016/12/27/belief-conspiracies-largely-depends-political-iden/.

3. Craig Silverman, "This Analysis Shows How Viral Fake Election News Stories Outperformed Real News on Facebook," *BuzzFeed News*, November 16, 2016, https://www.buzzfeed.com/craigsilverman/viral-fake-election-news-outperformed-real-news-on-facebook?utm_term=.vkaAjDkD2#.qfAX8rLrk.

4. "Assessing Russian Activities and Intentions in Recent US Elections," Intelligence Community Assessment, January 6, 2017, https://www.dni.gov/files/documents/ICA_2017_01.pdf.

5. Alex Jones, "Jeb Bush Close Nazi Ties Exposed," https://www.infowars.com/jeb-bush-close-nazi-ties-exposed/.

6. Tyler Durden, "Saudi Arabia has funded 20% of Hillary's Presidential Campaign, Saudi Crown Prince Claims," Fox Nation, June 14, 2016, http://nation.foxnews.com/2016/06/14/saudi-arabia-has-funded-20-hillarys-presidential-campaign-saudi-crown-prince-claims.

7. Robert Faris et al., "Partisanship, Propaganda, and Disinformation: Online Media and the 2016 U.S. Presidential Election," at 98, Berkman Klein Center for Internet and Society, August 2017 https://dash.harvard.edu/handle/1/33759251.

8. Gallup Knight Foundation Survey, "American Views: Trust, Media and Democracy," January 16, 2018, https://kf-site-production.s3.amazonaws.com/

publications/pdfs/000/000/242/original/KnightFoundation_AmericansViews_
Client_Report_010917_Final_Updated.pdf.

9. Nick Newman et al., "Reuters Institute Digital News Report 2017," n.d.; Amy Mitchell et al., "Publics Globally Want Unbiased News Coverage but Are Divided on Whether Their News Media Deliver" (Pew Research Center, January 11, 2018).

10. Robert H. Weibe, *The Search for Order 1877–1920* (New York: Hill and Wang, 1967), 111–132.

11. David Mindich, *Just the Facts: How "Objectivity" Came to Define American Journalism* (New York: New York University Press, 2000).

12. James C. Scott, *Seeing like a State: How Certain Schemes to Improve the Human Condition Have Failed*, Nachdr., Yale Agrarian Studies (New Haven, CT: Yale Univ. Press, 2008).

13. Claire Wardle and Hossein Derakhshan, "Information Disorder: Toward and Interdisciplinary Framework for Research and Policy Making," Council of Europe Report, September 27, 2017; Caroline Jack, "Lexicon of Lies: Terms for Problematic Information" (Data & Society, August 9, 2017).

14. Joshua Tucker et al., "Social Media Political Polarization and Political Disinformation: A Review of the Scientific Literature" (Hewlett Foundation, March2018),https://www.hewlett.org/wp-content/uploads/2018/03/Social-Media-Political-Polarization-and-Political-Disinformation-Literature-Review.pdf; Nathaniel Persily, "Can Democracy Survive the Internet?," *Journal of Democracy* 28, no. 2 (2017): 63–76, https://doi.org/10.1353/jod.2017.0019; Gabriel Emile Hine et al., "Kek, Cucks, and God Emperor Trump: A Measurement Study of 4chan's Politically Incorrect Forum and Its Effects on the Web," *ArXiv Preprint ArXiv:1610.03452*, 2016.

15. Samuel C. Woolley and Douglas R. Guilbeault, "Computational Propaganda in the United States of America: Manufacturing Consensus Online," n.d., http://comprop.oii.ox.ac.uk/wp-content/uploads/sites/89/2017/06/Comprop-USA.pdf; Denis Stukal et al., "Detecting Bots on Russian Political Twitter," *Big Data* 5, no. 4 (December 1, 2017): 310–324, https://doi.org/10.1089/big.2017.0038; Alice Marwick and Rebecca Lewis, "Media Manipulation and Disinformation Online" (New York: Data & Society Research Institute, 2017); Jacob Davey and Julia Ebner, "The Fringe Insurgency" (Institute for Strategic Dialogue, October 2017); David M.J. Lazer et al., "The Science of Fake News," *Science* 359, no. 6380 (March 9, 2018): 1094–1096, https://doi.org/10.1126/science.aao2998.

16. Emilio Ferrara, "Disinformation and Social Bot Operations in the Run up to the 2017 French Presidential Election," *First Monday* 22, no. 8 (July 31, 2017), https://doi.org/10.5210/fm.v22i8.8005; Alessandro Bessi and Emilio Ferrara, "Social Bots Distort the 2016 U.S. Presidential Election Online Discussion," *First Monday* 21, no. 11 (November 3, 2016), http://firstmonday.org/ojs/index.php/fm/article/view/7090; Woolley and Guilbeault, "Computational Propaganda in the United States of America"; Stefano Cresci et al., "The Paradigm-Shift of Social

Spambots: Evidence, Theories, and Tools for the Arms Race," in *Proceedings of the 26th International Conference on World Wide Web Companion* (International World Wide Web Conferences Steering Committee, 2017), 963–972, http://dl.acm.org/citation.cfm?id=3055135; Chengcheng Shao et al., "The Spread of Fake News by Social Bots," *ArXiv:1707.07592* [Physics], July 24, 2017, http://arxiv.org/abs/1707.07592.

17. Craig Silverman, *This Analysis Shows How Viral Fake Election News Stories Outperformed Real News on Facebook*, BuzzFeed News, November 16, 2016, https://www.buzzfeed.com/craigsilverman/viral-fake-election-news-outperformed-real-news-on-facebook?utm_term=.vkaAjDkD2#.qfAX8rLrk.

18. Craig Silverman and Lawrence Alexander, "How Teens In The Balkans Are Duping Trump Supporters With Fake News," *BuzzFeed*, November 3, 2016, https://www.buzzfeed.com/craigsilverman/how-macedonia-became-a-global-hub-for-pro-trump-misinfo?utm_term=.ak8V5PlP4#.fiEA7mqmO.

19. Scott Shane, "From Headline to Photograph, a Fake News Masterpiece," *New York Times*, January 18, 2017, sec. U.S., https://www.nytimes.com/2017/01/18/us/fake-news-hillary-clinton-cameron-harris.html; "The Bizarre Truth Behind the Biggest Pro-Trump Facebook Hoaxes | Inc.Com," accessed January 27, 2018, https://www.inc.com/tess-townsend/ending-fed-trump-facebook.html.

20. Ellen Nakashima, "Russian Government Hackers Penetrated DNC, Stole Opposition Research on Trump," *Washington Post*, June 14, 2016, sec. National Security, https://www.washingtonpost.com/world/national-security/russian-government-hackers-penetrated-dnc-stole-opposition-research-on-trump/2016/06/14/cf006cb4-316e-11e6-8ff7-7b6c1998b7a0_story.html.

21. ODNI Report January 2017.

22. Frank Pasquale, *The Black Box Society: The Secret Algorithms That Control Money and Information* (Cambridge, MA: Harvard University Press, 2015).

23. Zeynep Tufekci, "Engineering the Public: Big Data, Surveillance and Computational Politics," *First Monday* 19, no. 7 (July 2, 2014), http://firstmonday.org/ojs/index.php/fm/article/view/4901.

24. Daniel Kreiss and Shannon C. Mcgregor, "Technology Firms Shape Political Communication: The Work of Microsoft, Facebook, Twitter, and Google With Campaigns During the 2016 U.S. Presidential Cycle," *Political Communication*, October 26, 2017, 1–23, https://doi.org/10.1080/10584609.2017.1364814.

25. Alexis C. Madrigal, "When the Nerds Go Marching In," *The Atlantic*, November 16, 2012, https://www.theatlantic.com/technology/archive/2012/11/when-the-nerds-go-marching-in/265325/.

26. Marwick and Lewis, "Media Manipulation and Disinformation Online."

27. Marwick and Lewis; Davey and Ebner, "The Fringe Insurgency"; Hine et al., "Kek, Cucks, and God Emperor Trump."

28. Whitney Phillips, Jessica Beyer, and Gabriella Coleman, "Trolling Scholars Debunk the Idea That the Alt-Right's Shitposters Have Magic Powers," *Motherboard*,

March 22, 2017, https://motherboard.vice.com/en_us/article/z4k549/trolling-scholars-debunk-the-idea-that-the-alt-rights-trolls-have-magic-powers.

29. Amy Mitchell et al., "Political Polarization & Media Habits," *Pew Research Center's Journalism Project* (blog), October 21, 2014, http://www.journalism.org/2014/10/21/political-polarization-media-habits/.

30. Jeffrey Gottfried, Michael Barthel, and Amy Mitchell, "Trump, Clinton Voters Divided in Their Main Source for Election News," *Pew Research Center's Journalism Project* (blog), January 18, 2017, http://www.journalism.org/2017/01/18/trump-clinton-voters-divided-in-their-main-source-for-election-news/.

31. Thomas E. Patterson, "News Coverage of the 2016 General Election: How the Press Failed the Voters," 2016. Shorenstein Center on Media, Politics, and Public Policy, Harvard Kennedy School, December 7, 2016. https://shorensteincenter.org/news-coverage-2016-general-election/.

32. Duncan J. Watts and David M. Rothschild, "Don't Blame the Election on Fake News. Blame It on the Media.," *Columbia Journalism Review*, December 5, 2017, https://www.cjr.org/analysis/fake-news-media-election-trump.php.

33. Gallup Inc., "'Email' Dominates What Americans Have Heard About Clinton," *Gallup.com*, accessed January 30, 2018, http://news.gallup.com/poll/195596/email-dominates-americans-heard-clinton.aspx.

34. Matthew Gertz, "I've Studied the Trump-Fox Feedback Loop for Months. It's Crazier Than You Think.," *Politico Magazine*, accessed April 5, 2018, http://politi.co/2Av9vof; "Trump Tweets and the TV News Stories behind Them," *CNNMoney*, accessed April 5, 2018, http://money.cnn.com/interactive/media/trump-tv-tweets/index.html; Brian Feldman, "Here Are the Cable-News Segments That President Trump Is Cribbing Tweets From," *Select All*, accessed April 5, 2018, http://nymag.com/selectall/2017/02/trump-tweets-inspired-by-fox-an-exhaustive-list.html.

35. Jacob Pramuk, "House Speaker Paul Ryan talks up the spending bill on 'Fox & Friends' for an audience of one—President Donald Trump," *CNBC*, https://www.cnbc.com/2018/03/22/paul-ryan-talks-up-the-spending-bill-for-an-audience-of-one-on-fox-friends.html.

36. Alvin Chang, "We analyzed 17 months of Fox & Friends transcripts. It's far weirder than state-run media," *Vox*, https://www.vox.com/2017/8/7/16083122/breakfast-club-fox-and-friends.

37. Wardle and Derakhshan, "Information Disorder: Toward and Interdisciplinary Framework for Research and Policy Making"; Jack, "Lexicon of Lies: Terms for Problematic Information."

38. Harold Laswell, *Propaganda Technique in the World War* (New York: Alfred A. Knopf 1927); Harold D Lasswell et al., *Propaganda and Promotional Activities, an Annotated Bibliography* (Minneapolis: University of Minnesota Press, 1935), http://catalog.hathitrust.org/api/volumes/oclc/1013666.html.

39. Walter Lippmann, *Public Opinion*, 1st Free Press pbks. ed. (New York: Free Press Paperbacks, 1997), 158.

40. Edward Bernays, *The Engineering of Consent*, Annals of the American Academy of Political and Social Sciences, 1947.

41. Laswell, *Propaganda Technique in the World War,* 1927.

42. *United States Army Field Manual* No. 3-05.30, Psychological Operations, April 15, 2005, https://fas.org/irp/doddir/army/fm3-05-30.pdf.

43. Amanda Amos and Margaretha Haglund, "From social taboo to "torch of freedom": the marketing of cigarettes to women," Tobacco Control 9(1), http://tobaccocontrol.bmj.com/content/9/1/3.

44. Jacques Ellul, *Propaganda: The Formation of Men's Attitudes* (New York: Vintage Books, 1973), xviii.

45. Jay Black, "Semantics of Propaganda," *Journal of Mass Media Ethics*, 16(2&3), 121–137 (2001).

46. Edward S. Herman and Noam Chomsky, *Manufacturing Consent: The Political Economy of the Mass Media* (New York: Pantheon Books, 2002).

47. Yochai Benkler, *The Wealth of Networks: How Social Production Transforms Markets and Freedom* (New Haven, CT: Yale University Press, 2006), Chapters 6–7.

48. Gareth S. Jowett and Victoria O'Donnell, *Propaganda and Persuasion* (Sage, 1992).

49. Cass R. Sunstein ed., "Fifty Shades of Manipulation," in *The Ethics of Influence: Government in the Age of Behavioral Science*, Cambridge Studies in Economics, Choice, and Society (Cambridge: Cambridge University Press, 2016), 78–115, https://doi.org/10.1017/CBO9781316493021.005.

50. Anne Barnhill, "What Is Manipulation," in *Manipulation: Theory and Practice*, eds. Christian Coons and Michael Weber (Oxford University Press, 2014), https://doi.org/10.1093/acprof:oso/9780199338207.001.0001.

51. Yochai Benkler , "Networks of Power, Degrees of Freedom," *International Journal of Communication*, [S.l.], v. 5, p. 39, April 2011. ISSN 1932-8036. Available at http://ijoc.org/index.php/ijoc/article/view/1093/551.

52. Harry G. Frankfurt, *On Bullshit* (Princeton, NJ: Princeton University Press, 2005), 56.

53. Benkler, *Wealth of Networks*.

54. D.J. Flynn, Brendan Nyhan, and Jason Reifler, "The Nature and Origins of Misperceptions: Understanding False and Unsupported Beliefs About Politics: Nature and Origins of Misperceptions," *Political Psychology* 38 (February 2017): 127–150, https://doi.org/10.1111/pops.12394.

55. Jennifer L. Hochschild and Katherine Levine Einstein, *Do Facts Matter? Information and Misinformation in American Politics* (Norman: University of Oklahoma Press, 2015), 14.

56. Gary King, Jennifer Pan, and Margaret E. Roberts, "How the Chinese Government Fabricates Social Media Posts for Strategic Distraction, Not Engaged Argument," *American Political Science Review* 111, no. 03 (August 2017): 484–501, https://doi.org/10.1017/S0003055417000144.

57. https://www.theatlantic.com/international/archive/2014/09/russia-putin-revolutionizing-information-warfare/379880/.

58. Adam J. Berinsky, "Telling the Truth about Believing the Lies? Evidence for the Limited Prevalence of Expressive Survey Responding," *Journal of Politics* 80, no. 1 (January 2018): 211–224, https://doi.org/10.1086/694258.

59. Brittany Seymour et al., "When Advocacy Obscures Accuracy Online: Digital Pandemics of Public Health Misinformation Through an Antifluoride Case Study," *American Journal of Public Health* 105, no. 3 (March 2015): 517–523, https://doi.org/10.2105/AJPH.2014.302437; Rebekah Getman et al., "Vaccine Hesitancy and Online Information: The Influence of Digital Networks," *Health Education & Behavior*, December 21, 2017, 1090198117773967, https://doi.org/10.1177/1090198117739673.

CHAPTER 2

1. Amy Mitchell et al., "1. Pathways to News," *Pew Research Center's Journalism Project* (blog), July 7, 2016, http://www.journalism.org/2016/07/07/pathways-to-news/; Jeffrey Gottfried and Elisa Shearer, "Americans' Online News Use Is Closing in on TV News Use," *Pew Research Center* (blog), September 7, 2017, http://www.pewresearch.org/fact-tank/2017/09/07/americans-online-news-use-vs-tv-news-use/.

2. http://mediacloud.org.

3. We used a version of the bot-detection approach developed by the Menczer group in Indiana, as modified by Emilio Ferrara, formerly of that group, to study the French election. Emilio Ferrara, "Disinformation and Social Bot Operations in the Run up to the 2017 French Presidential Election," *First Monday* 22, no. 8 (July 31, 2017), http://firstmonday.org/ojs/index.php/fm/article/view/8005.

4. "Why the Trump Machine Is Built to Last Beyond the Election," *Bloomberg.com*, October 27, 2016, https://www.bloomberg.com/news/articles/2016-10-27/inside-the-trump-bunker-with-12-days-to-go.

5. Philip E. Converse, "The nature of belief systems in mass publics (1964)," *Critical Review* 18, no. 1-3 (2006): 1–74; John Zaller, *The Nature and Origins of Mass Opinion* (Cambridge University Press, 1992); Alan I. Abramowitz and Kyle L. Saunders. "Is polarization a myth?," *The Journal of Politics* 70, no. 2 (2008): 542–555.

6. John Nolte, "Trump-Effect: Fox News Channel's Brand Takes 50% Hit Among Republicans," *Breitbart*, February 27, 2016, http://www.breitbart.com/big-journalism/2016/02/27/trump-effect-fox-news-channels-brand-takes-50-hit-among-republicans/.

7. Ted Marzilli, "Fox News Hits Three Year Perception Low With Republicans," *BrandIndex*, February 24, 2016, http://www.brandindex.com/article/fox-news-hits-more-two-year-perception-low-republicans%E2%80%8B.

8. The table with descriptive statistics of linking practices is available in the online appendix.

9. Craig Silverman, "Publishers Are Switching Domain Names To Try To Stay Ahead Of Facebook's Algorithm Changes," *BuzzFeed*, accessed March 28, 2018, https://www.buzzfeed.com/craigsilverman/publishers-are-switching-domain-names-to-try-and-stay-ahead.

10. Amy Mitchell et al., "1. Pathways to News," *Pew Research Center's Journalism Project* (blog), July 7, 2016, http://www.journalism.org/2016/07/07/pathways-to-news/.

11. Jeffrey Gottfried et al., "The 2016 Presidential Campaign—a News Event That's Hard to Miss," *Pew Research Center's Journalism Project* (blog), February 4, 2016, http://www.journalism.org/2016/02/04/the-2016-presidential-campaign-a-news-event-thats-hard-to-miss/.

12. Hunt Alcott and Matthew Gentzkow, "Social Media and Fake News in the 2016 Election," *Journal of Economic Perspectives* 31, no. 2 (2017): 211–236, 212.

13. Jeffrey Gottfried, Michael Barthel, and Amy Mitchell, "Trump, Clinton Voters Divided in Their Main Source for Election News," *Pew Research Center's Journalism Project* (blog), January 18, 2017, http://www.journalism.org/2017/01/18/trump-clinton-voters-divided-in-their-main-source-for-election-news/.

14. Elisa Shearer and Jeffrey Gottfried, "News Use Across Social Media Platforms 2017" (Pew Research Center, September 7, 2017), http://www.journalism.org/2017/09/07/news-use-across-social-media-platforms-2017/.

15. Amy Mitchell et al., "The Modern News Consumer—1. Pathways to News" (Pew Research Center, July 7, 2016), http://www.journalism.org/2016/07/07/pathways-to-news/.

16. Gottfried and Shearer, "Americans' Online News Use Is Closing in on TV News Use."

17. Amy Mitchell et al., "1. Pathways to News," *Pew Research Center's Journalism Project* (blog), July 7, 2016, http://www.journalism.org/2016/07/07/pathways-to-news/.

18. Amy Mitchell et al., "Political Polarization & Media Habits," *Pew Research Center's Journalism Project* (blog), October 21, 2014, http://www.journalism.org/2014/10/21/political-polarization-media-habits/.

CHAPTER 3

1. R. Kelly Garrett, Brian E. Weeks, and Rachel L. Neo, "Driving a wedge between evidence and beliefs: How online ideological news exposure promotes political misperceptions," *Journal of Computer-Mediated Communication* 21, no. 5 (2016): 331–348.

2. Mark Hemingway, "Once Again, PolitiFact Struggles to Explain Data Showing They Treat GOP Unfairly," *Weekly Standard*, May 31, 2013, http://www.weeklystandard.com/once-again-politifact-struggles-to-explain-data-showing-they-treat-gop-unfairly/article/732009.

3. Lucas Graves, "What We Can Learn from the Factcheckers' Ratings," *Columbia Journal Review*, June 4, 2013, http://www.cjr.org/united_states_project/what_ we_can_learn_from_the_factcheckers_ratings.php; Paul Krugman, "Facts Have a Well-Known Liberal Bias," *New York Times*, December 8, 2017, https://www. nytimes.com/2017/12/08/opinion/facts-have-a-well-known-liberal-bias.html.

4. Glenn Kessler, "One Year of Fact Checking—an Accounting," *Washington Post*, December 30, 2011, https://www.washingtonpost.com/blogs/fact-checker/post/ one-year-of-fact-checking--an-accounting/2011/12/27/gIQARıtaOP_blog.html; Chris Mooney, "Reality Bites Republicans," *The Nation*, May 16, 2012, https:// www.thenation.com/article/reality-bites-republicans/.

5. We do not compare CBS or NBC because there are too few stories checked on those networks to provide a reasonable basis of comparison. NBC is qualitatively similar to ABC.

6. Lou Colagiovanni, "Trump Allegedly Tied-Up 13 Year-Old Girl He Raped, Struck Her In Face," *Occupy Democrats*, October 24, 2016, http://occupydemocrats.com/ 2016/10/24/trump-allegedly-tied-13-year-old-girl-raped-struck-face/.

7. Lisa Bloom, "Why the New Child Rape Case Filed Against Donald Trump Should Not be Ignored," *Huffington Post*, June 26, 2016, https://www.huffingtonpost.in/ entry/why-the-new-child-rape-ca_b_10619944.

8. Here, we use top 10 sites, excluding candidate sites and sites like WikiLeaks and Wikipedia, which were used as sources by others, and candidate sites as measured by most linked-to, most Twitter shared, and most Facebook shared over the course of the entire 18-month period under observation. Because the last two sites of the most linked-to sites on the right were World Net Daily and Gateway Pundit, two particularly pernicious conspiracy sites, we also ran the analysis without these two, and these reduced the number of sentences from 199 to 170, suggesting that these sites overcontributed slightly, but not to a degree that qualitatively effects the difference between the right and every other quintile observed.

9. https://www.theguardian.com/us-news/2016/jul/07/donald-trump-sexual-assault-lawsuits-norm-lubow.

10. https://jezebel.com/heres-how-that-wild-lawsuit-accusing-trump-of-raping-a-1782447083.

11. https://www.thedailybeast.com/trump-rape-accusers-turn-on-each-other.

12. Malia Zimmerman, "Flight Logs Show Bill Clinton Flew on Sex Offender's Jet Much More than Previously Known," *Fox News*, May 13, 2016, http://www. foxnews.com/us/2016/05/13/flight-logs-show-bill-clinton-flew-on-sex-offenders-jet-much-more-than-previously-known.html.

13. The RSS feed was captured on Media Cloud. The Facebook title appeared as of early 2018 on http://app.viralnewschart.com/News/News.aspx?linkId=174625641; but the URL was no longer accessible at the closing of this writing.

14. Breitbart News, "Report: Bill Clinton Flew on Jeffrey Epstein's Jet Without Secret Service Detail," *Breitbart*, May 13, 2016, http://www.breitbart.com/

big-government/2016/05/13/report-bill-clinton-flew-jeffrey-epsteins-jet-without-secret-service-detail/.

15. Geoff Earle and David Martosko, "Bill Clinton Jumped Aboard Disgraced Sex Offender Jeffrey Epstein's 'Lolita Express' Plane for Junkets 26 TIMES in Just Three Years," *Daily Mail Online*, May 13, 2016, http://www.dailymail.co.uk/news/article-3589628/Report-Bill-Clinton-jumped-aboard-disgraced-sex-offender-Jeffrey-Epstein-s-Lolita-Express-plane-junkets-26-TIMES-just-three-years.html.

16. Derek Hunter, "Bill Clinton Took Twice As Many Flights On 'Pedophile Island' Billionaire's 'Lolita Express' Than Previously Reported," *Daily Caller*, May 14, 2016, http://dailycaller.com/2016/05/14/bill-clinton-took-more-than-twice-as-many-flights-on-pedophile-island-billionaires-lolita-express-than-previously-reported/.

17. Douglas Ernst, "Bill Clinton Ditched Secret Service on Multiple 'Lolita Express' Flights: Report," *Washington Times*, May 14, 2016, https://www.washingtontimes.com/news/2016/may/14/bill-clinton-ditched-secret-service-on-multiple-lo/.

18. Megan Twohey and Michael Barbaro, "Crossing the Line: How Donald Trump Behaved With Women in Private," *New York Times*, May 14, 2016, https://www.nytimes.com/2016/05/15/us/politics/donald-trump-women.html.

19. "Woman in NYT Trump Piece Disputes Report," *NBC News*, May 16, 2016, https://www.msnbc.com/morning-joe/watch/woman-in-nyt-s-trump-piece-disputes-report-686463555992.

20. "MSNBC Live: MSNBCW: May 16, 2016 12:00pm–1:01pm PDT" (MSNBC, May 16, 2016), https://archive.org/details/MSNBCW_20160516_190000_MSNBC_Live/start/600/end/660; "MSNBC Live" (MSNBC, May 16, 2016), https://archive.org/details/MSNBCW_20160516_190000_MSNBC_Live/start/660/end/720.

21. Sean Hannity, "Carson: Press Has Shirked Its Duty to Be Honest; Exclusive: Former Bergdahl Platoon Mates Endorse Trump," *Fox News*, May 16, 2016, http://www.foxnews.com/transcript/2016/05/16/carson-press-has-shirked-its-duty-to-be-honest-exclusive-former-bergdahl.html.

22. Steve Guest, "Bill Clinton To Campaign Near Pedophile's 'Orgy Island' [VIDEO]," *Daily Caller*, May 16, 2016, http://dailycaller.com/2016/05/16/bill-clinton-to-campaign-near-pedophiles-orgy-island-video/.

23. Trent Baker, "'Morning Joe' Panel: Clinton Connection With Billionaire Pedophile Jeffrey Epstein Will 'Blow Up' Campaign," *Breitbart*, May 16, 2016, http://www.breitbart.com/video/2016/05/16/morning-joe-panel-clinton-connection-with-billionaire-pedophile-jeffrey-epstein-will-blow-up-campaign/.

24. "Special Report With Bret Baier: FOXNEWSW: May 17, 2016 3:00pm–4:01pm PDT" (Fox News, May 17, 2016), https://archive.org/details/FOXNEWSW_20160517_220000_Special_Report_With_Bret_Baier/start/2100/end/2160.

25. "Special Report With Bret Baier," https://archive.org/details/FOXNEWSW_20160517_220000_Special_Report_With_Bret_Baier/start/2160/end/2220.

26. Steve Guest, "Gingrich: Clinton Is 'A Target-Rich Environment' Regarding Relationships With Women [VIDEO]," *Daily Caller*, May 18, 2016, http://dailycaller.com/2016/05/18/gingrich-clinton-is-a-target-rich-environment-regarding-relationships-with-women-video/.

27. Trump Refers to Alleged Bill Clinton Assault as "Rape," http://www.foxnews.com/politics/2016/05/19/trump-refers-to-alleged-bill-clinton-sexual-indiscretions-as-rape.html?utm_source=feedburner&utm_medium=feed&utm_campaign=Feed%3A+foxnews%2Fpolitics+%28Internal+-+Politics+-+Text%29.

28. Breitbart TV, "Limbaugh Rips CNN's Gergen, 'Clinton Cash' Critics for Calling Book 'Discredited,'" *Breitbart*, June 23, 2016, http://www.breitbart.com/video/2016/06/23/limbaugh-rips-cnns-gergen-clinton-cash-critics-for-calling-book-discredited/.

29. Hannah Parry, "Billionaire Sex Offender Jeffrey Epstein Once Claimed He Helped Found Clinton Foundation as He Touted Close Relationship with Former President during Plea Bargain Negotiations," *Daily Mail Online*, July 7, 2016, http://www.dailymail.co.uk/news/article-3679023/Billionaire-sex-offender-Jeffrey-Epstein-claimed-helped-Clinton-Foundation-touted-close-relationship-former-president-plea-bargain-negotiations.html.

30. "BREAKING BOMBSHELL: NYPD Blows Whistle on New Hillary Emails: Money Laundering, Sex Crimes with Children, Child Exploitation, Pay to Play, Perjury," *True Pundit*, November 2, 2016, https://truepundit.com/breaking-bombshell-nypd-blows-whistle-on-new-hillary-emails-money-laundering-sex-crimes-with-children-child-exploitation-pay-to-play-perjury/. Craig Silverman at BuzzFeed locates the origin of the story three days earlier, in a tweet and blog post, which were transposed into a YourNewsWire story, all of which preceded the True Pundit story. Craig Silverman, "How The Bizarre Conspiracy Theory Behind 'Pizzagate' Was Spread," *BuzzFeed*, November 4, 2016, https://www.buzzfeed.com/craigsilverman/fever-swamp-election?bftwnews&utm_term=.esW37XrXv#.oyY5RoPoW. Because the True Pundit story introduced new elements that were those ultimately picked up by Erik Prince, and because its story was tweeted out by Michael Flynn, we treat the True Pundit story as the core source. But we acknowledge that the earlier tweets could have been the source, and if so, given how early and central the True Pundit story was, the basic overarching implication does not change much.

31. Sean Adl-Tabatabai, "NYPD: Hillary Clinton 'Child Sex Scandal' About To Break," *Your News Wire*, November 2, 2016, http://yournewswire.com/nypd-hillary-clinton-child-sex-scandal/.

32. Matthew Rosenberg, "Trump Adviser Has Pushed Clinton Conspiracy Theories," *New York Times*, December 5, 2016, https://www.nytimes.com/2016/12/05/us/politics/-michael-flynn-trump-fake-news-clinton.html.

33. John Hayward, "Erik Prince: NYPD Ready to Make Arrests in Anthony Weiner Case," *Breitbart*, November 4, 2016, http://www.breitbart.com/radio/2016/11/04/erik-prince-nypd-ready-make-arrests-weiner-case/.

34. "Source: FBI Has Evidence Hillary Visited 'Orgy Island,'" *WND*, November 4, 2016, http://www.wnd.com/2016/11/source-fbi-has-evidence-hillary-visited-orgy-island/.

PART TWO

1. M.E. McCombs and D.L. Shaw, "The agenda-setting function of mass media," *Public Opinion Quarterly* 36 no. 2 (1972): 176–187.
2. S. Iyengar, and D.R. Kinder, *News That Matters: Television and American Opinion* (Chicago: University of Chicago Press, 1987).
3. A particularly useful review is Dietram A. Scheufele and David Tewksbury, "Framing, Agenda Setting, and Priming: The Evolution of Three Media Effects Models," *Journal of Communication* 57 (2007): 9–20.

CHAPTER 4

1. Jonathan Capehart, "Opinion | Donald Trump's 'Mexican Rapists' Rhetoric Will Keep the Republican Party out of the White House," *Washington Post*, June 17, 2015, https://www.washingtonpost.com/blogs/post-partisan/wp/2015/06/17/trumps-mexican-rapists-will-keep-the-republican-party-out-of-the-white-house/.
2. Peter Holley, "'Radical Islamic Terrorism': Three Words That Separate Trump from Most of Washington," *Washington Post*, March 1, 2017, sec. The Fix, https://www.washingtonpost.com/news/the-fix/wp/2017/02/28/radical-islamic-terrorism-three-words-that-separate-trump-from-most-of-washington/.
3. TIME, *George H. W. Bush And Ronald Reagan Debate On Immigration In 1980 | TIME*, accessed April 11, 2018, https://www.youtube.com/watch?v=YsmgPp_nlok&feature=youtu.be.
4. Bradley Jones, "Americans' Views of Immigrants Marked by Widening Partisan, Generational Divides," *Pew Research Center* (blog), April 15, 2016, http://www.pewresearch.org/fact-tank/2016/04/15/americans-views-of-immigrants-marked-by-widening-partisan-generational-divides/.
5. Mark Hugo Lopez and Paul Taylor, "Latino Voters in the 2012 Election," *Pew Research Center's Hispanic Trends Project* (blog), November 7, 2012, http://www.pewhispanic.org/2012/11/07/latino-voters-in-the-2012-election/.
6. Republican National Committee, "Growth and Opportunity Project," December 2012, http://s3.documentcloud.org/documents/623664/republican-national-committees-growth-and.pdf.
7. Leslie Kaufman, "Breitbart News Network Plans Global Expansion," *New York Times*, February 16, 2014, sec. Media, https://www.nytimes.com/2014/02/17/business/media/breitbart-news-network-plans-global-expansion.html.

8. Jane Mayer, "The Reclusive Hedge-Fund Tycoon Behind the Trump Presidency," *New Yorker*, March 17, 2017, https://www.newyorker.com/magazine/2017/03/27/the-reclusive-hedge-fund-tycoon-behind-the-trump-presidency.

9. We include a list of the sites in each part of the training set in the online appendix.

10. Joseph Bernstein, "Here's How Breitbart And Milo Smuggled Nazi and White Nationalist Ideas Into The Mainstream," *BuzzFeed*, accessed April 23, 2018, https://www.buzzfeed.com/josephbernstein/heres-how-breitbart-and-milo-smuggled-white-nationalism.

11. Chuck Ross, "New Ties Emerge Between Clinton And Mysterious Islamic Cleric," *Daily Caller*, July 13, 2016, http://dailycaller.com/2016/07/13/new-ties-emerge-between-clinton-and-mysterious-islamic-cleric/.

12. Richard Pollock, "Wikileaks: Here's A Peek At Clinton's Free Private Jet Scam | The Daily Caller," *Daily Caller*, October 31, 2016, https://web.archive.org/web/20161101090958/http://dailycaller.com/2016/10/31/wikileaks-heres-how-the-clintons-free-private-jet-scam-works/.

13. Email from Ira Magaziner to John Podesta, 2011-11-22. https://wikileaks.org/podesta-emails/emailid/38048.

14. Richard Hofstadter, "The Paranoid Style in American Politics," *Harper's Magazine* 229, no. 1374 (1964): 77–86.

15. Richard Pollock, "Hillary's Two Official Favors To Morocco Followed By $28 Million For Clinton Foundation," *Daily Caller*, October 31, 2016, http://dailycaller.com/2016/10/31/hillarys-two-official-favors-to-morocco-resulted-in-28-million-for-clinton-foundation/.

16. Clinton Foundation Form 990 for 2013, at 7. https://www.clintonfoundation.org/sites/default/files/clinton_foundation_report_public_11-19-14.pdf.

17. Department of Justice, Environment and Natural Resources Division, Accomplishments Report FY 2010, April 28, 2011. https://www.justice.gov/sites/default/files/enrd/legacy/2015/04/13/ACCOMPLISHMENT_REPORT_2010_FINAL_5_18_11_Internet-508.pdf.

18. Department of Justice Press Release, https://www.justice.gov/opa/pr/major-fertilizer-producer-mosaic-fertilizer-llc-ensure-proper-handling-storage-and-disposal; EPA announcement, https://www.epa.gov/enforcement/mosaic-fertilizer-llc-settlement.

19. Richard Pollock, "Hillary's Two Official Favors To Morocco Resulted In $28 Million For Clinton Foundation," *Text.Article, Fox News*, October 31, 2016, http://www.foxnews.com/politics/2016/10/31/hillary-8217-s-two-official-favors-to-morocco-resulted-in-28-million-for-clinton-foundation.html.

20. "LEAK—Muslims Paid Hillary $28 MILLION To Do THIS, It's SICK," *Conservative Fighters* (blog), March 14, 2017, http://conservativefighters.com/news/leak-muslims-paid-hillary-28-million-sick/; "LEAK—Muslims Paid Hillary $28 MILLION To Do THIS, It's SICK," *The Angry Patriot*, March 14, 2017, http://www.angrypatriotmovement.com/muslims-paid-hillary-28-million/.

21. Saagar Enjeti, "Here's A (Dirty) Laundry List Of The Clinton Foundation's Most Questionable Foreign Donations," *Daily Caller*, October 31, 2016, http://dailycaller. com/2016/10/23/heres-a-dirty-laundry-list-of-the-clinton-foundations-most-questionable-foreign-donations/.

22. Alex Pfeiffer, "Hillary In Leaked Email: Saudi Arabia And Qatar Are Funding ISIS," *Daily Caller*, October 10, 2016, http://dailycaller.com/2016/10/10/hillary-in-leaked-email-saudi-arabia-and-qatar-are-funding-isis/.

23. http://endingthefed.com/its-over-hillarys-isis-email-just-leaked-its-worse-than-anyone-could-have-imagined.html.

24. Tyler Durden, "Saudi Arabia Has Funded 20% Of Hillary's Presidential Campaign, Saudi Crown Prince Claims," *Zero Hedge*, June 14, 2016, https://www.zerohedge. com/news/2016-06-13/saudi-arabia-has-funded-20-hillarys-presidential-campaign-saudi-crown-prince-claims.

25. Tyler Durden, "Saudi Arabia Has Funded 20% Of Hillary's Presidential Campaign, Saudi Crown Prince Claims," http://nation.foxnews.com/2016/06/14/saudi-arabia-has-funded-20-hillarys-presidential-campaign-saudi-crown-prince-claims. The story was still live when we accessed it for our August 2017 report, but has since been removed from Fox's site and blocked from the Internet Archive, so there is no live link to that republication.

26. Zero Hedge, "Saudi Arabia Has Funded 20% Of Hillary's Presidential Campaign, Saudi Crown Prince Claims," *Infowars*, June 14, 2016, https://www.infowars. com/saudi-arabia-has-funded-20-of-hillarys-presidential-campaign-saudi-crown-prince-claims/.

27. "Statement by Jordan News Agency" (Petra, June 14, 2016), http://www.petra.gov. jo/Public_News/Nws_NewsDetails.aspx?lang=2&site_id=1&NewsID=257423&CatID=13.

28. Rori Donaghy, "Jordan Says Hack Led to Posting of 'False News' That Saudi Funds Clinton," *Middle East Eye*, June 14, 2016, http://www.middleeasteye.net/news/deleted-official-report-says-saudi-key-funder-hillary-clinton-presidential-campaign-223282807.

29. The editor of the site, David Hearst, was previously an editor at the *The Guardian*, and the site has consistently refused to disclose its donors. Other members of its staff and its sole registered director have been the basis of criticism from a wide array of sites—from Saudi (http://www.ikhwan.whoswho/en/archives/854) and UAE media, to Breitbart (http://www.breitbart.com/london/2014/06/19/the-national-muslim-brotherhood-its-uk-connections-and-media-attacks-on-the-uae/) to the U.K.-based *Jewish News*, (http://jewishnews.timesofisrael.com/font-of-hatred-how-hamas-relies-on-two-uk-websites/), all claiming one basis or another for tying MEE to Qatar or the Muslim Brotherhood.

30. "Hackers Did It? Jordanian Media in Hot Water over 'Saudi Prince Funding Clinton Campaign' Report," *RT International*, June 14, 2016, https://on.rt.com/7fhe.

31. Patrick Wintour, "Russian Hackers to Blame for Sparking Qatar Crisis, FBI Inquiry Finds," *The Guardian*, June 7, 2017, http://www.theguardian.com/world/ 2017/jun/07/russian-hackers-qatar-crisis-fbi-inquiry-saudi-arabia-uae.

32. Karen DeYoung and Ellen Nakashima, "UAE Orchestrated Hacking of Qatari Government Sites, Sparking Regional Upheaval, According to U.S. Intelligence Officials," *Washington Post*, July 16, 2017, https://www.washingtonpost.com/ world/national-security/uae-hacked-qatari-government-sites-sparking-regional- upheaval-according-to-us-intelligence-officials/2017/07/16/00c46e54-698f-11e7- 8eb5-cbccc2e7bfbf_story.html.

33. Hannity, Fox News, October 11, 2016: https://archive.org/details/FOXNEWSW_ 20161012_050000_Hannity/start/2880/end/2940; https://archive.org/details/ FOXNEWSW_20161012_050000_Hannity/start/2940/end/3000; https://archive. org/details/FOXNEWSW_20161012_050000_Hannity/start/3000/end/3060; https://archive.org/details/FOXNEWSW_20161012_050000_Hannity/start/ 3060/end/3120; https://archive.org/details/FOXNEWSW_20161012_050000_ Hannity/start/3120/end/3180.

34. https://archive.org/details/FOXNEWSW_20161020_100000_FOX__Friends/ start/6189/end/6224.

CHAPTER 5

1. "Reince Priebus on Flynn, Russia and President Trump's Agenda; Rush Limbaugh Talks Trump's Relationship with the News Media | Fox News," accessed April 22, 2018, http://www.foxnews.com/transcript/2017/02/19/reince-priebus-on-flynn- russia-and-president-trump-agenda-rush-limbaugh-talks.html.

2. Glenn Greenwald, "The Deep State Goes to War With President-Elect, Using Unverified Claims, as Democrats Cheer," *The Intercept* (blog), January 11, 2017, https://theintercept.com/2017/01/11/the-deep-state-goes-to-war-with-president- elect-using-unverified-claims-as-dems-cheer/.

3. Tucker Carlson & Glenn Greenwald Gov't: Gov't Agencies vs. Donald Trump Cannel, Channel 11 News Today YouTube channel, https://www.youtube.com/ watch?v=_ff9YnnpAF8.

4. "Essay: Anatomy of the Deep State," *BillMoyers.com* (blog), February 21, 2014, https://billmoyers.com/2014/02/21/anatomy-of-the-deep-state/.

5. "Ron Paul: Trump Will Continue to Be Himself," *MovingImage, Fox Business*, November 10, 2016, http://video.foxbusiness.com/v/5205472770001/.

6. "Trump Should Resist Neocon & Shadow Gov't Influence to Justify People's Hopes—Ron Paul to RT—RT US News," accessed April 22, 2018, https:// www.rt.com/usa/366404-trump-ron-paul-crosstalk/?utm_source=rss&utm_ medium=rss&utm_campaign=RSS.

7. "Is A Real Civil War Possible? | Zero Hedge," accessed April 22, 2018, https://www. zerohedge.com/news/2016-11-12/real-civil-war-possible.

8. Adam Entous, Ellen Nakashima, and Greg Miller, "Secret CIA Assessment Says Russia Was Trying to Help Trump Win White House," *Washington Post*, December 9, 2016, sec. National Security, https://www.washingtonpost.com/world/national-security/obama-orders-review-of-russian-hacking-during-presidential-campaign/2016/12/09/31d6b300-be2a-11e6-94ac-3d324840106c_story.html.

9. "Silent Coup in Progress: American Intelligence Agencies Are Trying to Stop Trump From Taking Office," December 10, 2016, https://russia-insider.com/en/node/18123.

10. "Silent Coup in Progress"; Justin Raimondo, "Stop the CIA Coup," *Antiwar.com Original* (blog), December 11, 2016, https://original.antiwar.com/justin/2016/12/11/stop-cia-coup/; VNN, "Stop CIA Coup: Deep State versus Donald Trump," *Veterans News Now* (blog), accessed April 22, 2018, https://www.veteransnewsnow.com/2016/12/12/1011997-stop-the-cia-coup-the-deep-state-versus-donald-trump/; "Stop the CIA Coup : Information Clearing House—ICH," accessed April 22, 2018, http://www.informationclearinghouse.info/46019.htm.

11. Ben Schreckinger, "How Russia Targets the U.S. Military," *Politico*, https://www.politico.com/magazine/story/2017/06/12/how-russia-targets-the-us-military-215247.

12. Ben Schreckinger, "How Russia Targets the U.S. Military—POLITICO Magazine," accessed April 22, 2018, https://www.politico.com/magazine/story/2017/06/12/how-russia-targets-the-us-military-215247.

13. Virgil12 Dec 20164 and 174, "Virgil: The Deep State vs. Donald Trump," *Breitbart*, December 12, 2016, http://www.breitbart.com/big-government/2016/12/12/virgil-the-deep-state-vs-donald-trump/.

14. "Exclusive: Trump Operative Roger Stone Survives Assassination Attempt," *Infowars* (blog), January 17, 2017, https://www.infowars.com/exclusive-trump-operative-roger-stone-survives-assassination-attempt/; "Breaking: Deep State Targeting Journalists for Death," *Infowars* (blog), January 18, 2017, https://www.infowars.com/breaking-deep-state-targeting-journalists-for-death/.

15. Eli Lake, "The Political Assassination of Michael Flynn," *Bloomberg.com*, February 14, 2017, https://www.bloomberg.com/view/articles/2017-02-14/the-political-assassination-of-michael-flynn.

16. Saker as Tyler Durden, "'It's Over Folks' The Neocons & The 'Deep State' Have Neutered The Trump Presidency | Zero Hedge," accessed April 22, 2018, https://www.zerohedge.com/news/2017-02-14/its-over-folks-neocons-deep-state-have-neutered-trump-presidency.

17. "Intel Community Trying to Undermine Trump's Presidency?," *Fox Business*, accessed April 22, 2018, https://www.youtube.com/watch?v=7j_ZfKmcnSk&feature=youtu.be.

18. Chris Stirewalt, "Trump Knocks down 'Deep State' Claims," *Text.Article, Fox News*, February 16, 2017, http://www.foxnews.com/politics/2017/02/16/trump-knocks-down-deep-state-claims.html.

19. https://www.youtube.com/watch?v=cRZO4SiXWZQ.

20. "Lou Dobbs Tonight : FBC : March 8, 2017 7:00pm-8:01pm EST," March 9, 2017, http://archive.org/details/FBC_20170309_000000_Lou_Dobbs_Tonight.

21. Sean Hannity, "Sean Hannity: Trump Must Purge Deep-State Bureaucrats Now," *Text.Article, Fox News*, March 10, 2017, http://www.foxnews.com/opinion/2017/03/10/sean-hannity-trump-must-purge-deep-state-bureaucrats-now.html.

22. "Greenwald: Empowering the 'Deep State' to Undermine Trump Is Prescription for Destroying Democracy," *Democracy Now!*, accessed April 22, 2018, https://www.youtube.com/watch?v=jY1MiNfwcRg.

23. Sean Adl-Tabatabai, "DNC Election Fraud Whistleblower Found Murdered," *YourNewsWire*, July 12, 2016, http://yournewswire.com/dnc-election-fraud-whistleblower-found-murdered/.

24. Keegan Hankes and Alex Amend, "Alt-Right Celebrity @Ricky_Vaughn99 Suspended From Twitter," Southern Poverty Law Center, October 6, 2016, https://www.splcenter.org/hatewatch/2016/10/06/alt-right-celebrity-rickyvaughn99-suspended-twitter.

25. "WAS MURDERED 27 YEAR OLD DEMOCRAT Operative About To Blow The Whistle On VOTER FRAUD When He Was Shot In The Back? [VIDEO] * 100PercentFedUp.com," *100PercentFedUp.com*, July 16, 2016, https://100percentfedup.com/was-murdered-27-year-old-democrat-operative-about-to-blow-the-whistle-on-voter-fraud-when-he-was-shot-in-the-back-video/; Team DML, "People Claiming Murder of DNC's Seth Rich Connects to Clinton," Dennis Michael Lynch, July 16, 2016, http://dennismichaellynch.com/dc-conspiracy-death2/.

26. [deleted], "This Is Seth Conrad Rich, the DNC's 27 Year Old Data Director, Who Was Murdered. The Fact That They Do Not Want to Talk about Him Is Exactly Why We Should.," *Reddit*, July 28, 2016, https://www.reddit.com/r/The_Donald/comments/4v34fk/this_is_seth_conrad_rich_the_dncs_27_year_old/; MyKettleIsNotBlack, "DNC Data Director Seth Rich Was Likely Assassinated by the Clintons," *Reddit*, July 27, 2016, https://www.reddit.com/r/The_Donald/comments/4uua1j/dnc_data_director_seth_rich_was_likely/.

27. Alex Johnson, "Julian Assange: 'No Proof' Hacked DNC Emails Came From Russia," *NBC News*, July 25, 2016, https://www.nbcnews.com/news/us-news/wikileaks-julian-assange-no-proof-hacked-dnc-emails-came-russia-n616541.

28. TruthFeedNews, "VIDEO: DNC Staffer Set to Testify Against Hillary Clinton SHOT TWICE AND NOW DEAD," *Truthfeed*, July 30, 2016, http://truthfeed.com/video-dnc-staffer-set-to-testify-against-hillary-clinton-shot-twice-and-now-dead/14115/.

29. Archivist2001, "Deaths of Seth Conrad Rich & John Ashe—OAN 7-28-2016" (YouTube, 2016), https://www.youtube.com/watch?v=MikSx1-Maro.

30. Jim Hoft, "ANOTHER MYSTERIOUS DEATH => Activist and Sanders Supporter Who Served Papers to DNC on Fraud Case Found Dead," *Gateway Pundit*, August 4, 2016, http://www.thegatewaypundit.com/2016/08/breaking-lead-attorney-dnc-fraud-case-found-dead-1-week-serving-dnc-papers/.

31. Nieuwsuur, "Julian Assange on Seth Rich" (YouTube, 2016), https://www.youtube.com/watch?v=Kp7FkLBRpKg.

32. Michael S. Schmidt, "Comey Memo Says Trump Asked Him to End Flynn Investigation," *New York Times*, May 16, 2017, sec. Politics, https://www.nytimes.com/2017/05/16/us/politics/james-comey-trump-flynn-russia-investigation.html.

33. "Fox 5 Morning News" (Fox News, May 16, 2017), https://archive.org/details/WTTG_20170516_083000_Fox_5_Morning_News__430/start/0/end/60; "Fox 5 Morning News," https://archive.org/details/WTTG_20170516_083000_Fox_5_Morning_News__430/start/60/end/120; "Fox 5 Morning News," https://archive.org/details/WTTG_20170516_083000_Fox_5_Morning_News__430/start/120/end/180.

34. "Fox and Friends First" (Fox News, May 16, 2017), http://archive.org/details/FOXNEWSW_20170516_090000_Fox_and_Friends_First.

35. "Fox & Friends" (Fox News, May 16, 2017), http://archive.org/details/FOXNEWSW_20170516_100000_FOX__Friends.

36. "Fox & Friends," https://archive.org/details/FOXNEWSW_20170516_100000_FOX__Friends/start/4680/end/4740.

37. Malia Zimmerman, "Seth Rich, Slain DNC Staffer, Had Contact with WikiLeaks, Say Multiple Sources," May 16, 2017, https://web.archive.org/web/20170516114431/http://www.foxnews.com/politics/2017/05/16/slain-dnc-staffer-had-contact-with-wikileaks-investigator-says.html.

38. "Hannity" (Fox News, May 17, 2017), http://archive.org/details/FOXNEWSW_20170517_050000_Hannity.

39. "Hannity," https://archive.org/details/FOXNEWSW_20170517_050000_Hannity/start/540/end/600.

40. "Rod Wheeler Backtracks Statements about Seth Rich Investigation," *WTTG*, May 17, 2017, http://www.fox5dc.com/news/rod-wheeler-backtracks-statements-about-seth-rich-investigation.

41. Steven Levitsky and Daniel Ziblatt, *How Democracies Die*, First edition (New York: Crown, 2018), 146–75.

42. Lauren Carroll, "Baseless Claims That Slain DNC Staffer Was WikiLeaks Source," *PolitiFact*, May 23, 2017, http://www.politifact.com/punditfact/statements/2017/may/23/newt-gingrich/claim-slain-dnc-staffer-seth-rich-gave-emails-wiki/.

43. Eugene Kiely, "Gingrich Spreads Conspiracy Theory," *FactCheck.org*, May 22, 2017, https://www.factcheck.org/2017/05/gingrich-spreads-conspiracy-theory/.

44. "Statement on Coverage of Seth Rich Murder Investigation," *Fox News*, May 23, 2017, http://www.foxnews.com/politics/2017/05/23/statement-on-coverage-seth-rich-murder-investigation.html.

45. Scott Taylor, "EXCLUSIVE: A Look Inside 'Profiling Project: Seth Rich,'" *WJLA*, May 25, 2017, http://wjla.com/features/7-on-your-side/exclusive-a-look-inside-profiling-project-seth-rich-at-gwu.

46. Noah Lanard, "A Republican Lobbyist Went Hunting for Seth Rich's Murderer. Things Got Bizarre.," *Mother Jones* (blog), July 17, 2017, https://www.motherjones. com/politics/2017/07/a-lobbyist-detectives-strange-quest-to-find-seth-richs-murderer/.

47. Scott Taylor, "READ: Independent Group Releases New Report on Seth Rich's Murder Investigation," WFXL, June 20, 2017, http://wfxl.com/news/nation-world/read-new-report-released-on-seth-richs-murder-investigation.

48. RT, "CrossTalk: 'Seth Rich'" (YouTube, 2017), https://www.youtube.com/ watch?v=OT9wFXUAjMk.

49. Amended Complaint, Wheeler v. Twenty First Century Fox et al., Civil Action No.: 17-cv-05807 (GBD) (2017), https://www.courtlistener.com/recap/gov.uscourts. nysd.478367.56.0.pdf.

50. Data obtained through SimilarWeb Pro, March 11, 2018, https://pro. similarweb.com/#/website/worldwide-overview/yournewswire.com,reason. com,weeklystandard.com,nationalreview.com,thegatewaypundit.com/*/999/ 18m?webSource=Total.

51. Reports on Congress working toward protecting Mueller from being fired: Erin Kelly, "Special Counsel Mueller Is Investigating Facebook Ads Linked to Russia," *USA Today*, September 21, 2017, https://www.usatoday.com/story/news/politics/ 2017/09/21/congress-should-protect-evidence-gathered-mueller-russia-probe-experts-warn/685139001/. On September 21, Mueller asks for phone records from Air Force One surrounding the claim that Trump had dictated the response of Donald Trump Jr. over the June 9 meeting: Josh Dawsey, "Mueller Requested Phone Records about Air Force One Statement," *Politico*, September 21, 2017, http://politi.co/2DvhwE3. Salon has a breakdown of the week ending 9/22: "There are a number of threads to the story to pull together. The first is that special counsel Robert Mueller has sent requests to the White House asking for various documents pertaining to Trump'sTrump's actions as president. These include the firing of James Comey and Michael Flynn, as well as requests for telephone records from Air Force One on the day the president helped draft the false statement about Donald Trump Jr's June 2016 meeting with a purported representative of the Russian government, in hopes of getting dirt on Hillary Clinton". "(Heather Digby Parton, "Paul Manafort May Hold the Key: Who Was He Really Working For?," *Salon*, September 22, 2017, https://www.salon.com/2017/09/22/paul-manafort-may-hold-the-key-who-was-he-really-working-for/). "After a relatively quiet summer, September has seen a flurry of media reports that suggest special counsel Robert Mueller's Russian-interference investigation is heating up. Whether it's the FBI raid on former Trump campaign manager Paul Manafort's home, Mueller's demand for White House correspondence concerning Trump's firing of FBI director James Comey and other controversial actions, or Mueller's search warrant for Facebook accounts tied to Russian operatives, the investigation appears to be homing in on President Trump and his inner circle". (Arn Pearson, "Trump v.

Mueller?," *Huffington Post*, September 26, 2017, https://www.huffingtonpost.com/entry/trump-v-mueller_us_59ca4da8e4b0b7022a646dae).

52. Rep Jim McGovern and Tiffany Muller, "As Mueller Probes Russian Facebook Ads, Our Elections Are Vulnerable And Congress Does Nothing," Huffington Post, September 28, 2017, https://www.huffingtonpost.com/entry/as-mueller-probes-russian-facebook-ads-our-elections_us_59cd238fe4b04575111f390d; Dylan Byers, "Facebook: Russian Ads Reached 10 Million People," CNNMoney, October 3, 2017, http://money.cnn.com/2017/10/02/media/facebook-russian-ads-10-million/index.html?utm_source=feedburner&utm_medium=feed&utm_campaign=Feed%3A+rss.

53. Brad Heath, "Exclusive: Jared Kushner's Personal Email Re-Routed to Trump Organization Computers amid Public Scrutiny," *USA Today*, October 3, 2017, https://www.usatoday.com/story/news/politics/2017/10/03/exclusive-jared-kushners-personal-email-moved-trump-organization-computers-amid-public-scrutiny/728467001/; Josh Dawsey and Rea Peterson, "Hundreds of White House Emails Sent to Third Kushner Family Account," POLITICO, October 2, 2017, https://www.politico.com/story/2017/10/02/jared-kushner-email-account-white-house-243389).

54. Matt Apuzzo and Michael S. Schmidt, "Hoping to Have Trump Cleared, Legal Team Eases Resistance to Inquiry," *New York Times*, October 7, 2017, sec. Politics, https://www.nytimes.com/2017/10/07/us/politics/trump-russia-legal.html; Greg Price, "Will Trump Meet with Mueller to Discuss the Russia Probe?," *Newsweek*, October 12, 2017, http://www.newsweek.com/trump-mueller-meeting-russia-683376; Darren Samuelsohn, "President's Lawyers May Offer Mueller a Meeting with Trump," *Politico*, October 12, 2017, http://politi.co/2lZABHH.

55. "Hannity" (Fox News, October 24, 2017), http://archive.org/details/FOXNEWSW_20171024_070000_Hannity.

56. "Hannity," https://archive.org/details/FOXNEWSW_20171027_010000_Hannity/start/2591/end/2626.

57. Breitbart News, "Hillary Clinton's Brother Defends Haiti Gold Mine Deal: 'I Raise Money for a Lot of People,'" Breitbart, March 20, 2015, http://www.breitbart.com/big-government/2015/03/20/hillary-clintons-brother-defends-gold-mine-deal-i-raise-money-for-a-lot-of-people/.

58. Robert O'Harrow Jr., "Trump Adviser Received Salary from Charity While Steering Breitbart News," *Washington Post*, November 23, 2016, sec. Investigations, https://www.washingtonpost.com/investigations/trump-adviser-received-salary-from-charity-while-steering-breitbart-news/2016/11/22/75340778-af8a-11e6-8616-52b15787add0_story.html.

59. Carrie Levine, "Reclusive Mega-Donor Fueling Donald Trump's White House Hopes," Center for Public Integrity, October 7, 2016, https://www.publicintegrity.org/2016/10/07/20307/reclusive-mega-donor-fueling-donald-trumps-white-house-hopes.

60. Jo Becker and Mike McIntire, "Cash Flowed to Clinton Foundation Amid Russian Uranium Deal," *New York Times*, April 15, 2015, sec. U.S., https://www.nytimes.com/2015/04/24/us/cash-flowed-to-clinton-foundation-as-russians-pressed-for-control-of-uranium-company.html.

61. Michelle Ye Hee Lee, "The Facts behind Trump's Repeated Claim about Hillary Clinton's Role in the Russian Uranium Deal," *Washington Post*, October 26, 2016, sec. Fact Checker, https://www.washingtonpost.com/news/fact-checker/wp/2016/10/26/the-facts-behind-trumps-repeated-claim-about-hillary-clintons-role-in-the-russian-uranium-deal/.

62. Eugene Kiely, "No 'Veto Power' for Clinton on Uranium Deal," FactCheck.org, April 28, 2015, https://www.factcheck.org/2015/04/no-veto-power-for-clinton-on-uranium-deal/.

63. Linda Qiu, "Did Clinton Help Russia Obtain Uranium for Donations? Nope," *PolitiFact*, June 30, 2016, http://www.politifact.com/truth-o-meter/statements/2016/jun/30/donald-trump/donald-trump-inaccurately-suggests-clinton-got-pai/.

64. Jo Becker and Mike McIntire, "Cash Flowed to Clinton Foundation Amid Russian Uranium Deal," *New York Times*, April 15, 2015, sec. U.S., https://www.nytimes.com/2015/04/24/us/cash-flowed-to-clinton-foundation-as-russians-pressed-for-control-of-uranium-company.html.

65. Erik Wemple, "John Solomon Leaves Washington Times, Joins Circa Re-Launch," *Washington Post*, December 7, 2015, sec. Erik Wemple, https://www.washingtonpost.com/blogs/erik-wemple/wp/2015/12/07/john-solomon-leaves-washington-times-joins-circa-re-launch/.

66. "A Russian Nuclear Firm under FBI Investigation Was Allowed to Purchase US Uranium Supply," *Circa*, October 17, 2017, https://www.circa.com/story/2017/10/17/national-security/the-fbi-uncovered-russian-nuclear-kickback-scheme-months-before-the-obama-administration-passed-uranium-one-deal-with-moscow.

67. Styxhexenhammer666, "FBI Uncovered Russian Bribery Plot In 2009 Before Obama Sold Russia A Bunch of Uranium" (YouTube, 2017), https://www.youtube.com/watch?v=UwHzIC3Tu1U.

68. "The Left's Imploding Everywhere You Look," *Rush Limbaugh Show*, October 17, 2017, https://www.rushlimbaugh.com/daily/2017/10/17/the-lefts-imploding-everywhere-you-look/.

69. "After the Bell" (Fox Business, October 17, 2017), http://archive.org/details/FBC_20171017_200000_After_the_Bell; and a full segment is at https://archive.org/details/FBC_20171017_200000_After_the_Bell/start/2680/end/2715.

70. "Making Money With Charles Payne" (Fox Business, October 17, 2017), http://archive.org/details/FBC_20171017_220000_Making_Money_With_Charles_Payne.

71. "Lou Dobbs Tonight" (Fox Business, October 17, 2017), https://archive.org/details/FBC_20171017_230000_Lou_Dobbs_Tonight/start/660/end/720.

72. "Hannity: October 19, 2017 9:00pm–10:00pm PDT" (Fox News, October 20, 2017), http://archive.org/details/FOXNEWSW_20171020_040000_Hannity.

73. "Hannity," https://archive.org/details/FOXNEWSW_20171020_040000_Hannity/start/1860/end/1920.

74. "Hannity," https://archive.org/details/FOXNEWSW_20171020_040000_Hannity/start/2100/end/2160.

75. Mike Levine, "McCabe Claims Firing Part of 'Ongoing Assault' on Russia Probe," *ABC News*, March 16, 2018, http://abcnews.go.com/Politics/words-mccabe-claims-firing-part-ongoing-assault-russia/story?id=53807980.

76. "Hannity," https://archive.org/details/FOXNEWSW_20171020_040000_Hannity/start/2100/end/2160.

77. Nicole Hemmer, *Messengers of the Right: Conservative Media and the Transformation of American Politics, Politics and Culture in Modern America* (Philadelphia: University of Pennsylvania Press, 2016).

78. Kathleen Hall Jamieson and Joseph N. Cappella, *Echo Chamber: Rush Limbaugh and the Conservative Media Establishment* (Oxford; New York: Oxford University Press, 2008), 146–147.

79. "The Four Corners of Deceit: Prominent Liberal Social Psychologist Made It All Up," *Rush Limbaugh Show*, April 29, 2013, https://www.rushlimbaugh.com/daily/2013/04/29/the_four_corners_of_deceit_prominent_liberal_social_psychologist_made_it_all_up/.

80. Donald J. Trump, "And the FAKE NEWS Winners Are . . . ," Twitter, January 17, 2018, https://twitter.com/realDonaldTrump/status/953794085751574534; Team GOP, "The Highly Anticipated 2017 Fake News Awards," *GOP* (blog), January 17, 2018, https://gop.com/the-highly-anticipated-2017-fake-news-awards.

81. "Fox & Friends: October 20, 2017, 3:00am–6:00am PDT" (Fox News, October 20, 2017), http://archive.org/details/FOXNEWSW_20171020_100000_FOX__Friends.

82. "Hannity: October 24, 2017, 12:00am–1:00am PDT" (Fox News, October 24, 2017), http://archive.org/details/FOXNEWSW_20171024_070000_Hannity.

83. Hannity: October 26, 2017, 6:00pm–7:00pm PDT" (Fox News, October 27, 2017), 26, http://archive.org/details/FOXNEWSW_20171027_010000_Hannity.

CHAPTER 6

1. Frank Newport et al., "'Email' Dominates What Americans Have Heard About Clinton," *Gallup*, September 16, 2016, http://news.gallup.com/poll/195596/email-dominates-americans-heard-clinton.aspx.

2. Thomas E. Patterson, "News Coverage of the 2016 General Election: How the Press Failed the Voters," 2016.

3. Duncan J. Watts and David M. Rothschild, "Don't Blame the Election on Fake News. Blame It on the Media," *Columbia Journalism Review*, December 5, 2017, https://www.cjr.org/analysis/fake-news-media-election-trump.php.

4. Michael S. Schmidt, "Hillary Clinton Used Personal Email Account at State Dept., Possibly Breaking Rules," *The New York Times*, March 2, 2015, sec. Politics, https://www.nytimes.com/2015/03/03/us/politics/hillary-clintons-use-of-private-email-at-state-department-raises-flags.html.

5. Jonathan Mahler, "Group's Tactic on Hillary Clinton: Sue Her Again and Again," *New York Times*, October 12, 2016, https://www.nytimes.com/2016/10/13/us/politics/judicial-watch-hillary-clinton.html.

6. Jo Becker and Mike McIntire, "Cash Flowed to Clinton Foundation Amid Russian Uranium Deal," *New York Times*, April 15, 2015, sec. U.S., https://www.nytimes.com/2015/04/24/us/cash-flowed-to-clinton-foundation-as-russians-pressed-for-control-of-uranium-company.html.

7. Breitbart News, "11 Explosive Clinton Cash Facts Mainstream Media Confirm Are Accurate," *Breitbart*, April 26, 2015, http://www.breitbart.com/big-government/2015/04/26/11-explosive-clinton-cash-facts-mainstream-media-confirm-are-accurate/.

8. Breitbart News, "Free Global Broadcast of 'Clinton Cash' Documentary Online at Breitbart.Com," *Breitbart*, July 22, 2016, http://www.breitbart.com/2016-presidential-race/2016/07/22/global-airing-clinton-cash-documentary-breitbart-email-sign/.

9. Daily Caller News Foundation, "IRS Response Clinton Foundation July 2016," July 22, 2016, https://www.scribd.com/document/319384834/IRS-Response-Clinton-Foundation-July-2016. The entire relevant text of the letter was, "We have forwarded the information you submitted to our Exempt Organizations Examinations Program in Dallas. This program considers all referrals and will send you a separate acknowledgement letter when it receives your information."

10. Richard Pollack, "EXCLUSIVE: IRS Launches Investigation Of Clinton Foundation," *Daily Caller*, July 26, 2016, http://dailycaller.com/2016/07/26/exclusive-irs-launches-investigation-of-clinton-foundation/.

11. Fred Lucas et al., "IRS Looking into Clinton Foundation 'Pay-to-Play' Claims," *Fox News*, July 27, 2016, http://www.foxnews.com/politics/2016/07/27/irs-reviewing-clinton-foundation-pay-to-play-claims.html.

12. Post Editorial Board, "Why Didn't the Democrats Even Mention the Clinton Foundation?," *New York Post*, July 30, 2016, sec. Opinion, https://nypost.com/2016/07/29/why-didnt-the-democrats-even-mention-the-clinton-foundation/.

13. "Why Didn't Democrats Even Mention The Clinton Foundation?," *Fox News*, July 30, 2016, http://nation.foxnews.com/2016/07/30/why-didn-t-democrats-even-mention-clinton-foundation.

14. Breitbart News, "NY Post: Why Didn't the Democrats Even Mention the Clinton Foundation?," *Breitbart*, July 30, 2016, http://www.breitbart.com/

2016-presidential-race/2016/07/30/ny-post-why-didnt-the-democrats-even-mention-the-clinton-foundation/.

15.   "'Clinton Cash' Author Doubts IRS Will Thoroughly Investigate Clinton Foundation," *Fox News Insider*, July 30, 2016, http://insider.foxnews.com/2016/07/30/irs-launches-investigation-clinton-foundation-clinton-cash-author-reacts.

16.   Linda Qiu, "Did Clinton Help Russia Obtain Uranium for Donations? Nope," *PolitiFact*, June 30, 2016, http://www.politifact.com/truth-o-meter/statements/2016/jun/30/donald-trump/donald-trump-inaccurately-suggests-clinton-got-pai/.

17.   Michelle Ye Hee Lee, "Pro-Trump Ad Suggests Clinton Foundation Donations Contributed to Clintons' Net Worth," *Washington Post*, August 10, 2016, sec. Fact Checker, https://www.washingtonpost.com/news/fact-checker/wp/2016/08/10/pro-trump-ad-suggests-clinton-foundation-donations-contributed-to-clintons-net-worth/.

18.   "Judicial Watch Uncovers New Batch of Hillary Clinton Emails," *Judicial Watch*, August 9, 2016, https://www.judicialwatch.org/press-room/press-releases/judicial-watch-uncovers-new-batch-hillary-clinton-emails/.

19.   GDELT Summary, "Television Explorer," *GDELT*, n.d., https://api.gdeltproject.org/api/v2/summary/summary?DATASET=IATV&TYPE=SUMMARY&STARTDATETIME=&ENDDATETIME=.

20.   Mark Hensch, "Clinton Foundation Won't Accept Foreign Money If Hillary Wins," *The Hill*, August 18, 2016, http://thehill.com/blogs/ballot-box/presidential-races/291911-clinton-foundation-to-alter-donation-rules-if-hillary.

21.   Clinton Foundation, "Empowering People to Build Better Futures for Themselves, Their Families, and Their Communities," *Medium* (blog), August 22, 2016, https://medium.com/@ClintonFdn/empowering-people-to-build-better-futures-for-themselves-their-families-and-their-communities-99d5843391fb.

22.   Rosalind S. Helderman, Spencer S. Hsu, and Tom Hamburger, "Emails Reveal How Foundation Donors Got Access to Clinton and Her Close Aides at State Dept.," *Washington Post*, August 22, 2016, sec. Politics, https://www.washingtonpost.com/politics/emails-reveal-how-foundation-donors-got-access-to-clinton-and-her-close-aides-at-state-dept/2016/08/22/345b5200-6882-11e6-8225-fbb8a6fc65bc_story.html.

23.   Matthew Yglesias, "The AP's Big Exposé on Hillary Meeting with Clinton Foundation Donors Is a Mess," *Vox*, August 24, 2016, https://www.vox.com/2016/8/24/12618446/ap-clinton-foundation-meeting.

24.   Donald J. Trump, "And the FAKE NEWS Winners Are . . . ," Twitter, January 17, 2018, https://twitter.com/realDonaldTrump/status/953794085751574534.

25.   ABC News, "ABC News Statement on Michael Flynn Report," *ABC News*, December 2, 2017, http://abcnews.go.com/US/abc-news-statement-michael-flynn-report/story?id=51536475; Brian Ross, Matthew Mosk, and Josh Margolin, "Flynn Prepared to Testify That Trump Directed Him to Contact Russians about ISIS, Confidant Says," *ABC News*, December 1, 2017, http://abcnews.

go.com/Politics/michael-flynn-charged-making-false-statements-fbi-documents/
story?id=50849354.

26. Oliver Darcy, "ABC News Corrects Bombshell Flynn Report," *CNNMoney*,
December 1, 2017, http://money.cnn.com/2017/12/01/media/abc-news-flynn-
correction/index.html.

27. Brad Reed, "Mike Flynn 'Prepared to Testify against Trump and His Family' in
Mueller's Russia Probe: Report," *Raw Story*, December 1, 2017, https://www.
rawstory.com/2017/12/mike-flynn-prepared-to-testify-against-trump-and-his-
family-in-muellers-russia-probe-report/; Linley Sanders, "Who Told Michael Flynn
to Talk to Russians? He Will Name Trump, Confidant Says," *Newsweek*, December 1,
2017, http://www.newsweek.com/who-told-michael-flynn-talk-russians-728754.

28. Casey Michel, "This Is Why Flynn's Guilty Plea Should Terrify Trump,"
ThinkProgress, December 1, 2017, https://thinkprogress.org/mike-flynn-guilty-
plea-e5fb7c38a229/.

29. Bill Palmer, "Congressmen Say Jared Kushner's Arrest Is Coming and Donald
Trump Will Be Ousted from Office," *Palmer Report* (blog), December 1, 2017,
http://www.palmerreport.com/politics/congress-kushner-ousted/6387/.

30. Based on a review of all stories in our set that mentioned the words "Flynn" and
"Russia" in the same sentence in the period following the guilty plea.

31. Brad Reed, "Don Jr and Other Trump Campaign Officials Were Offered Secret
Link to WikiLeaks Hacks: Report," *Raw Story*, December 8, 2017, https://www.
rawstory.com/2017/12/don-jr-and-other-trump-campaign-officials-were-offered-
secret-link-to-wikileaks-hacks-report/.

32. Allegra Kirkland, "CNN Issues Major Correction To Story On Email
Pointing Trumps To Hacked Docs," *Talking Points Memo*, December 8, 2017,
https://talkingpointsmemo.com/muckraker/trump-campaign-sent-email-
with-access-hacked-wikileaks-documents.

33. Alex Kasprak, "'Raftergate' Explained: Was Trump's Pensacola Rally 'Packed to the
Rafters?,'" *Snopes*, December 9, 2017, https://www.snopes.com/news/2017/12/
09/was-trumps-pensacola-rally-packed-rafters/.

34. Gloria Borger et al., "Comey Unlikely to Judge on Obstruction," *CNN*, June 7,
2017, https://www.cnn.com/2017/06/06/politics/comey-testimony-refute-trump-
russian-investigation/index.html.

35. Paul Krugman, "What Happened on Election Day," *New York Times*, October 9,
2016, sec. Opinion, paul-krugman-the-economic-fallout.

36. The original link was http://www.cnn.com/2017/06/22/politics/russian-
investment-fund-under-investigation/index.htm. As we were preparing the book, it
was still available on the Internet Archive. It has since been removed.

37. Matthew Boyle, "Very Fake News: CNN Pushes Refurbished Russia Conspiracy,
Inaccurately Claims Investments Under Investigation," *Breitbart*, June 23, 2017,
http://www.breitbart.com/big-government/2017/06/23/very-fake-news-cnn-
pushes-refurbished-russia-conspiracy-inaccurately-claims-investment-fund-under-

investigation/; "Russian Investment Fund Denies CNN Report of US Sanctions Regime Violations," *Sputnik News*, June 23, 2017, https://sptnkne.ws/eHtq.

38. Jim Dalrymple II and Jon Passantino, "CNN Deleted A Story Linking Trump And Russia, Then Issued A Retraction After Questions Were Raised," *BuzzFeed*, June 24, 2017, https://www.buzzfeed.com/jimdalrympleii/cnn-deleted-a-story-linking-trump-and-russia-then-issued-a.

39. "Editor's Note," *CNN*, June 23, 2017, https://www.cnn.com/2017/06/23/politics/editors-note/index.html; Erik Wemple, "Three CNN Employees Resign over Retracted Story on Russia Ties," *Washington Post*, June 26, 2017, sec. Opinion, https://www.washingtonpost.com/blogs/erik-wemple/wp/2017/06/26/three-cnn-employees-resign-over-retracted-story-on-russia-ties/.

40. Ilya Arkhipov and Patrick Donahue, "Trump Aide Talks Investment With Sanctioned Kremlin Fund," *Bloomberg*, January 17, 2017, sec. Politics, https://www.bloomberg.com/news/articles/2017-01-17/in-davos-trump-aide-talks-deals-with-sanctioned-kremlin-fund.

41. Steven T. Mnuchin, "Mnuchin Response to Elizabeth Warren," January 30, 2017, https://www.warren.senate.gov/files/documents/Mnuchin_Response-20170130.pdf.

42. Lisa Friedman, "Scientists Fear Trump Will Dismiss Blunt Climate Report," *New York Times*, August 7, 2017, sec. Climate, https://www.nytimes.com/2017/08/07/climate/climate-change-drastic-warming-trump.html.

43. Oil Change International, "Leaked Government Report Sounds Alarm on Climate Change Before Trump Could Suppress It," *EcoWatch*, August 8, 2017, https://www.ecowatch.com/leaked-climate-change-report-2470544185.html.

44. Friedman, "Scientists Fear Trump Will Dismiss Blunt Climate Report."

45. Bob Kopp, "The Times' Leaked Draft Has Been on the Internet Archive since January, during the Public Comment Period," Twitter, August 7, 2017, https://twitter.com/bobkopp/status/894762578739515393?ref_src=twsrc%5Etfw&ref_url=https%3A%2F%2Fwww.washingtonpost.com%2Fblogs%2Ferik-wemple%2Fwp%2F2017%2F08%2F09%2Fnew-york-times-guilty-of-large-screw-up-on-climate-change-story%2F.

46. Katharine Hayhoe, "Important to Point Out That This Report Was Already Accessible to Anyone Who Cared to Read It during Public Review & Comment Time. Few Did.," Twitter, August 7, 2017, https://twitter.com/KHayhoe/status/894757321838010368?ref_src=twsrc%5Etfw&ref_url=http%3A%2F%2Fwww.foxnews.com%2Fpolitics%2F2017%2F08%2F08%2Fscientists-call-out-new-york-times-for-incorrect-claim-about-climate-report.html; Katharine Hayhoe, "The 3rd Order Draft of Climate Science Special Report Is Still Available via the National Academy of Sciences Public Access File, on Request," Twitter, August 8, 2017, https://twitter.com/KHayhoe/status/894932418347634688?ref_src=twsrc%5Etfw&ref_url=http%3A%2F%2Fwww.foxnews.com%2Fpolitics%2F2017%2F08%2F08%2Fscientists-call-out-new-york-times-for-incorrect-claim-about-climate-report.html.

47. Erik Wemple, "New York Times Guilty of Large Screw-up on Climate-Change Story," *Washington Post*, August 9, 2017, sec. Opinion, https://www.washingtonpost.com/blogs/erik-wemple/wp/2017/08/09/new-york-times-guilty-of-large-screw-up-on-climate-change-story/; Alex Pappas, "Scientists Call out New York Times for Incorrect Claim about Climate Report," *Fox News*, August 8, 2017, http://www.foxnews.com/politics/2017/08/08/scientists-call-out-new-york-times-for-incorrect-claim-about-climate-report.html.

CHAPTER 7

1. Andrew Marantz, "Trolls of Trump," *New Yorker*, October 31, 2016, https://www.newyorker.com/magazine/2016/10/31/trolls-for-trump.
2. Hannity.com Staff, "LEAKED EMAIL Appears To Link Clinton Campaign Chairman To Bizarre Occult Ritual," *Sean Hannity Show*, November 4, 2016, https://web.archive.org/web/20161107062645/http://www.hannity.com:80/articles/election-493995/leaked-email-appears-to-link-clinton-15270858/; Sean Hannity, "LEAKED EMAIL Appears to Link Clinton Campaign Chairman to Bizarre Occult Ritual Http://Bit.ly/2f2kyXP," Twitter post, November 4, 2016, https://twitter.com/seanhannity/status/794612729852166144; Edmund Kozak, "WikiLeaks: Clinton Campaign Chair Participated in Occult Magic," *LifeZette*, November 4, 2016, https://web.archive.org/web/20161109010216/http://www.lifezette.com:80/polizette/wikileaks-podesta-practices-occult-magic/?utm_content=buffer05465&utm_medium=social&utm_source=twitter.com&utm_campaign=buffer; Paul Joseph Watson, "'Spirit Cooking': Clinton Campaign Chairman Practices Bizarre Occult Ritual," *Infowars* (blog), November 4, 2016, http://www.drudgereportarchives.com/dsp/search.htm?searchFor=%22WIKI%20WICCAN%3A%20PODESTA%20PRACTICES%20OCCULT%20MAGIC%22; Douglas Ernst, "WikiLeaks: Podesta Invited to 'Spirit' Dinner; Host's Known 'recipes' Demand Breast Milk, Sperm," *Washington Times*, November 4, 2016, https://www.washingtontimes.com/news/2016/nov/4/wikileaks-john-podesta-invited-to-spirit-dinner-ho/.
3. Mike Cernovich, "Podesta Emails Reveal Clinton's Inner Circle as Sex Cult with Connections to Human Trafficking," *Danger & Play*, November 3, 2016, https://web.archive.org/web/20161104093838/http://www.dangerandplay.com/2016/11/03/podesta-emails-reveal-clintons-inner-circle-as-sex-cult-with-connections-to-human-trafficking/.
4. Liam Stack, "Who Is Mike Cernovich? A Guide," *New York Times*, April 5, 2017, https://www.nytimes.com/2017/04/05/us/politics/mike-cernovich-bio-who.html.
5. BBC Trending, "The Social Media Star Who Flipped to Trump," *BBC*, October 5, 2016, http://www.bbc.com/news/blogs-trending-37507542.
6. WikiLeaks, "The Podestas' 'Spirit Cooking' dinner? It's Not What You Think. It's Blood, Sperm and Breastmilk. But Mostly Blood.," Twitter post, November 4, 2016, https://twitter.com/wikileaks/status/794450623404113920.

7. Cassandra Fairbanks, "Internet Is On Fire With Speculation That Podesta Emails Contain Code for Child Sex," *We Are Change*, November 3, 2016, https://wearechange. org/internet-fire-speculation-podesta-emails-contain-code-child-sex/.

8. PleadingtheYiff, "BREAKING: I Believe I Have Connected a Convicted Child Abductor Who Was Caught Stealing Children in Haiti with the Clintons," *Reddit*, November 3, 2016, https://www.reddit.com/r/The_Donald/comments/5aupnh/ breaking_i_believe_i_have_connected_a_convicted/.

9. Charley Keyes, "State Department Rebuffs Call for Clinton Intervention in Haiti Case," February 9, 2010, http://www.cnn.com/2010/POLITICS/02/09/haiti. clinton.arrests/index.html; Jill Dougherty and Lonzo Cook, "U.S. Missionaries Sent to Separate Haitian Prisons; No Ruling on Bail," *CNN*, February 5, 2010, http://www.cnn.com/2010/CRIME/02/05/haiti.arrests/index.html.

10. Evens Sanon, "Haiti Prosecutors Seek 6 Months in Prison for US Woman Who Tried to Remove Kids after Quake," *Associated Press*, May 13, 2010, http://www.foxnews.com/world/2010/05/13/haiti-prosecutors-seek-months-prison-woman-tried-remove-kids-quake-1947670658.html.

11. Andrew Anglin, "Top Right-Wing Tweeter Jared Wyand Goes Full-1488, Condemns Jews," *Daily Stormer*, November 21, 2016, https://dstormer6em3i4km. onion.link/top-right-wing-tweeter-jared-wyand-goes-full-1488-condemns-jews/.

12. Private communications with a firm that conducted forensic research into Twitter campaigns involving Russian campaigns.

13. BedriddenSam, "SOMEONE TELL ME IM WRONG."

14. LiquidRitz, "Official Thread for Leaks and Evidence Regarding the Government Sex Ring: Keep All Posts in This Thread," *Reddit*, November 4, 2016, https://www. reddit.com/r/WikiLeaks/comments/5b4xt9/official_thread_for_leaks_and_ evidence_regarding/.

15. Fairbanks, "Internet Is On Fire."

16. dcpizzagate, "DC PizzaGate: A Primer UPDATED 07/07/17," *Suspected Pedophile Ring Exposed*, November 7, 2016, https://dcpizzagate.wordpress.com/2016/11/07/ first-blog-post/. "'Jimmy Comet': The Weak Link in Podesta Pedo Ring," *Reddit*, November 7, 2016, https://www.reddit.com/r/conspiracy/comments/5bp6ph/ jimmy_comet_the_weak_link_in_podesta_pedo_ring/.

17. Jim Hoft, "Wikileaks: Podesta Involved in 'Spirit Cooking' Dinners and Cult Activity," *Gateway Pundit*, November 4, 2016, http://www.thegatewaypundit. com/2016/11/wikileaks-podesta-involved-spirit-cooking-dinners-cult-activity/.

18. Alice Marwick and Rebecca Lewis, "Media Manipulation and Disinformation Online," *New York: Data & Society Research Institute*, 2017; Gabriel Emile Hine et al., "Kek, Cucks, and God Emperor Trump: A Measurement Study of 4chan's Politically Incorrect Forum and Its Effects on the Web," *ArXiv Preprint ArXiv:1610.03452*, 2016.

19. burninglegs, "Wikileaks Is Dropping a Huge Bombshell on 11/3/2016. This Is the Big One." *Reddit*, November 3, 2016, https://www.reddit.com/r/The_Donald/

comments/5axjjh/wikileaks_is_dropping_a_huge_bombshell_on_1132016/. The first Reddit post suggesting that WikiLeaks was about to release email and videos that would probe a pedophilia scandal seems to be have been published on November 3, 4:00 p.m. UTC, that is, late morning on the East Coast in the United States. It began with a screenshot from 4chan, purportedly by WikiLeaks.

20. followingthecolors, "[WARNING: GRAPHIC] I Don't Think You Guys Appreciate the Trauma /Pol/ Is Going through Tracking down the Absolutely off-the-Deep-End Shit Podesta Is Into. Here's a Small Taste.," *Reddit*, November 3, 2016, https://www.reddit.com/r/The_Donald/comments/5b08cy/warning_graphic_i_dont_think_you_guys_appreciate/; TigerClaws, "Wikileaks: Podesta Participates in 'Spirit Cooking,'" *Free Republic*, November 3, 2016, http://www.freerepublic.com/focus/f-news/3488913/posts.

21. BedriddenSam, "SOMEONE TELL ME IM WRONG!!! This Invite to A 'pizza Party' includes the Name Maya Harris, Whose Sister Is Kamal Harris Deputy District Attorney Who SPECIALIZEs IN CHILD SEXUAL ASSAULT CASES!!!," *Reddit*, November 3, 2016, https://www.reddit.com/r/The_Donald/comments/5azc9k/someone_tell_me_im_wrong_this_invite_to_a_pizza/.

CHAPTER 8

1. Peter Pomerantsev, *Nothing Is True and Everything Is Possible: The Surreal Heart of the New Russia* (United States of America: PublicAffairs, 2014).

2. Ben Nimmo, "Anatomy of an Info-War: How Russia's Propaganda Machine Works, and How to Counter It," May 19, 2015, http://www.stopfake.org/en/anatomy-of-an-info-war-how-russia-s-propagandamachine-works-and-how-to-counter-it/, quoted in Keir Giles, *Handbook of Russian Information Warfare*, NDC Fellowship Monograph Series 9 (NATO Defense College, Research Division, 2016), https://krypt3ia.files.wordpress.com/2016/12/fm_9.pdf.

3. Bruce Etling et al., "Public Discourse in the Russian Blogosphere: Mapping RuNet Politics and Mobilization," Berkman Center Research Publication (Berkman Klein Center for Internet & Society at Harvard University, October 19, 2010), https://papers.ssrn.com/sol3/papers.cfm?abstract_id=1698344.

4. Darrell M. West, "President Dmitry Medvedev: Russia's Blogger-in-Chief," *Brookings* (blog), November 30, 2001, https://www.brookings.edu/opinions/president-dmitry-medvedev-russias-blogger-in-chief/.

5. Vladimir Barash and John Kelly, "Salience vs. Commitment: Dynamics of Political Hashtags in Russian Twitter," Berkman Center Research Publication (Berkman Klein Center for Internet & Society at Harvard University, April 10, 2012); John Kelly et al., "Mapping Russian Twitter," Berkman Center Research Publication (Berkman Klein Center for Internet & Society at Harvard University, March 23, 2012), https://papers.ssrn.com/sol3/papers.cfm?abstract_id=2028158; Sergey Sanovich, "Computational Propaganda in Russia: The Origins of Digital

Misinformation," Computational Propaganda Research Project (Oxford Internet Institute, June 19, 2017), http://comprop.oii.ox.ac.uk/wp-content/uploads/sites/89/2017/06/Comprop-Russia.pdf.

6. @DFRLab, "The Russians Who Exposed Russia's Trolls," *DFRLab* (blog), March 8, 2018, https://medium.com/dfrlab/the-russians-who-exposed-russias-trolls-72db132e3cd1.

7. Ronald Deibert and Rafal Rohozinski, "Beyond Denial: Introducing Next-Generation Information Access Controls," in *Access Controlled: The Shaping of Power, Rights, and Rule in Cyberspace*, ed. John Palfrey et al. (Cambridge: The MIT Press, 2010). Anna Polyanskaya, Andrei Krivov, and Ivan Lomko, "Commissars of the Internet: The FSB at the Computer" (Vestnik Online, April 30, 2003), http://www.vestnik.com/issues/2003/0430/win/polyanskaya_krivov_lomko.htm.

8. *Id.*, at 28.

9. Evgeny Morozov, *The Net Delusion: The Dark Side of Internet Freedom* (New York: PublicAffairs, 2011).

10. Keir Giles, "HANDBOOK OF RUSSIAN INFORMATION WARFARE," n.d., 6–7; Timothy Thomas, "The Evolving Nature of Russia's Way of War," *Military Review*, no. July–August 2017 (2017): 34–42.

11. Michael D. Shear and Matthew Rosenberg, "Released Emails Suggest the D.N.C. Derided the Sanders Campaign," *New York Times*, July 22, 2016, sec. Politics, https://www.nytimes.com/2016/07/23/us/politics/dnc-emails-sanders-clinton.html; Jonathan Martin and Alan Rappeport, "Debbie Wasserman Schultz to Resign D.N.C. Post," *New York Times*, July 24, 2016, sec. Politics, https://www.nytimes.com/2016/07/25/us/politics/debbie-wasserman-schultz-dnc-wikileaks-emails.html.

12. "Russia: Hacker Hell, Scourge of the RuNet—Global Voices," *Global Voices* (blog), July 23, 2012, https://globalvoices.org/2012/07/23/russia-hacker-hell-scourge-of-the-runet/; Aleksandr Gorbachev On 7/9/15 at 6:43 AM, "Meet the Hacker Who Terrorized the Russian Blogosphere," *Newsweek*, July 9, 2015, http://www.newsweek.com/2015/07/17/gospel-according-hell-351544.html; Sergey Sanovich, "Computational Propaganda in Russia: The Origins of Digital Misinformation," n.d., 26.

13. Nakashima, "Russian Government Hackers Penetrated DNC, Stole Opposition Research on Trump," *Washington Post*, June 14, 2016, sec. National Security, https://www.washingtonpost.com/world/national-security/russian-government-hackers-penetrated-dnc-stole-opposition-research-on-trump/2016/06/14/cf006cb4-316e-11e6-8ff7-7b6c1998b7a0_story.html.

14. "Can a BEAR Fit Down a Rabbit Hole? State Board of Election Analysis," ThreatConnect | Enterprise Threat Intelligence Platform, September 2, 2016, https://www.threatconnect.com/blog/state-board-election-rabbit-hole/; "ThreatConnect Identifies FANCY BEAR World Anti-Doping Agency Breach," ThreatConnect | Enterprise Threat Intelligence Platform, August 19, 2016, https://

www.threatconnect.com/blog/fancy-bear-anti-doping-agency-phishing/; "Shiny Object? Guccifer 2.0 and the DNC Breach," ThreatConnect | Enterprise Threat Intelligence Platform, June 29, 2016, https://www.threatconnect.com/blog/guccifer-2-0-dnc-breach/; "ThreatConnect Identifies Additional Infrastructure in DNC Breach," ThreatConnect | Enterprise Threat Intelligence Platform, June 17, 2016, https://www.threatconnect.com/blog/tapping-into-democratic-national-committee/; "APT28: A Window into Russia's Cyber Espionage Operations?," *FireEye*, 28, accessed March 13, 2018, https://www.fireeye.com/blog/threat-research/2014/10/apt28-a-window-into-russias-cyber-espionage-operations.html.

15. "Joint Statement from the Department Of Homeland Security and Office of the Director of National Intelligence on Election Security" (Department of Homeland Security, October 7, 2016), https://www.dhs.gov/news/2016/10/07/joint-statement-department-homeland-security-and-office-director-national; "Joint Analysis Report: GRIZZLY STEPPE—Russian Malicious Cyber Activity" (Department of Homeland Security and Federal Bureau of Investigation, December 29, 2016), https://www.us-cert.gov/sites/default/files/publications/JAR_16-20296A_GRIZZLY%20STEPPE-2016-1229.pdf.

16. "Assessing Russian Activities and Intentions in Recent US Elections," Intelligence Community Assessment, January 6, 2017, https://www.dni.gov/files/documents/ICA_2017_01.pdf.

17. Indictment, United States of America vs. Internet Research Agency LLC et al. 2/16/18. https://www.justice.gov/file/1035477/download.

18. Jen Weedon, William Nuland, and Alex Stamos, "Information Operations and Facebook" (Facebook, April 27, 2017), https://fbnewsroomus.files.wordpress.com/2017/04/facebook-and-information-operations-v1.pdf; Alex Stamos, "An Update On Information Operations On Facebook" (Facebook, September 6, 2017), https://newsroom.fb.com/news/2017/09/information-operations-update/.

19. "Update: Russian Interference in 2016 US Election, Bots, & Misinformation" (Twitter, September 28, 2017), https://blog.twitter.com/official/en_us/topics/company/2017/Update-Russian-Interference-in-2016--Election-Bots-and-Misinformation.html.

20. Young Mie Kim, Jordan Hsu, David Neiman, Colin Kou, Levi Bankston, Soo Yun Kim, Richard Heinrich, Robyn Baragwanath, and Garvesh Raskutt, "The Stealth Media? Groups and Targets Behind Divisive Issue Campaigns on Facebook." Forthcoming *Political Communication*. Available at https://journalism.wisc.edu/wp-content/blogs.dir/41/files/2018/04/Kim.FB_.StealthMedia.re_.3.two-colmns.041718-1.pdf.

21. Mike Isaac and Daisuke Wakabayashi, "Russian Influence Reached 126 Million Through Facebook Alone," *New York Times*, October 30, 2017, sec. Technology, https://www.nytimes.com/2017/10/30/technology/facebook-google-russia.html; Colin Lecher, "Here Are the Russia-Linked Facebook Ads Released by Congress," *The Verge*, November 1, 2017, https://www.theverge.com/2017/11/1/16593346/

house-russia-facebook-ads; Nicholas Fandos, Cecilia Kang, and Mike Isaac, "House Intelligence Committee Releases Incendiary Russian Social Media Ads," *New York Times*, November 1, 2017, sec. Politics, https://www.nytimes.com/2017/11/01/us/politics/russia-technology-facebook.html.

22. Ben Collins, Kevin Poulsen, and Spencer Ackerman, "Exclusive: Russia Used Facebook Events to Organize Anti-Immigrant Rallies on U.S. Soil," *Daily Beast*, September 12, 2017, sec. Tech, https://www.thedailybeast.com/exclusive-russia-used-facebook-events-to-organize-anti-immigrant-rallies-on-us-soil.

23. Georgia Wells, "Russia-Linked Facebook Pages Pushed Divisions After Election, Including on Charlottesville," *Wall Street Journal*, October 3, 2017, sec. Tech, https://www.wsj.com/articles/russia-linked-facebook-pages-pushed-divisive-views-through-august-1507051387.

24. Scott Shane, "The Fake Americans Russia Created to Influence the Election," *New York Times*, September 7, 2017, sec. Politics, https://www.nytimes.com/2017/09/07/us/politics/russia-facebook-twitter-election.html.

25. @DFRLab, "The Russians Who Exposed Russia's Trolls."

26. "Russia Media Group That Angered Kremlin Is Sold," *Reuters*, June 16, 2017, https://www.reuters.com/article/us-russia-media-rbc-sale/russia-media-group-that-angered-kremlin-is-sold-idUSKBN1972KO.

27. "Расследование РБК: Как «фабрика Троллей» Поработала На Выборах в США," *Журнал РБК*, accessed March 13, 2018, https://www.rbc.ru/magazine/2017/11/59e0c17d9a79470e05a9e6c1.

28. Whitney Phillips, Jessica Beyer, and Gabriella Coleman, "Trolling Scholars Debunk the Idea That the Alt-Right's Shitposters Have Magic Powers," Motherboard, March 22, 2017, https://motherboard.vice.com/en_us/article/z4k549/trolling-scholars-debunk-the-idea-that-the-alt-rights-trolls-have-magic-powers.

29. @DFRLab, "The Russians Who Exposed Russia's Trolls."

30. Denis Stukal et al., "Detecting Bots on Russian Political Twitter," *Big Data* 5, no. 4 (December 1, 2017): 310–324, https://doi.org/10.1089/big.2017.0038; @DFRLab, "Human, Bot or Cyborg?," *DFRLab* (blog), December 23, 2016, https://medium.com/@DFRLab/human-bot-or-cyborg-41273cdb1e17.

31. @DFRLab, "The Russians Who Exposed Russia's Trolls."

32. Jane Lytvynenko, "InfoWars Has Republished More Than 1,000 Articles From RT Without Permission," *BuzzFeed*, accessed March 13, 2018, https://www.buzzfeed.com/janelytvynenko/infowars-is-running-rt-content.

33. "Sean Adl-Tabatabai on Being in the Eye of the 'Fake News' Storm | London Evening Standard," accessed March 13, 2018, https://www.standard.co.uk/lifestyle/london-life/sean-adltabatabai-on-being-in-the-eye-of-the-fake-news-storm-a3468361.html.

34. Kate Starbird, "Created a Domain Network Graph for 'White Helmets' Tweets May–Aug 2017. These Are Websites Connected by Users (Who Tweet to Both)," *Twitter* (blog), September 21, 2017, https://twitter.com/katestarbird/

status/910988793125023745?lang=en; "Killing the Truth" (The Syria Campaign, December 20, 2017), http://thesyriacampaign.org/wp-content/uploads/2017/12/KillingtheTruth.pdf.

35. https://www.zerohedge.com/news/2017-02-21/conflictual-relationship-between-donald-trump-and-us-deep-state-part-1.

36. https://www.politico.com/magazine/story/2017/06/12/how-russia-targets-the-us-military-215247.

37. Adam Carter, "Guccifer 2.0: Game Over," *Guccifer 2.0*, February 22, 2018, http://g-2.space.

38. нет, "Russia and WikiLeaks: The Case of the Gilded Guccifer," *Medium* (blog), February 21, 2017, https://web.archive.org/web/20170221231421/ https:// medium.com/@nyetnyetnyet/russia-and-wikileaks-the-case-of-the-gilded-guccifer-f2288521cdee.

39. нет, "This Fancy Bear's House Is Made of Cards: Russian Fools or Russian Frame-Up?," *Medium* (blog), March 8, 2017, https://web.archive.org/web/20170308190211/https://medium.com/@nyetnyetnyet/this-fancy-bears-house-is-made-of-cards-russian-fools-or-russian-frame-up-59a714243b91.

40. "Intelligence Committee Ranking Member Schiff Opening Statement During Hearing on Russian Active Measures," U.S. House of Representatives Permanent Selection on Intelligence Democratic Office, March 20, 2017, https://democrats-intelligence.house.gov/news/documentsingle.aspx?DocumentID=220.

41. Cassandra Fairbanks, "Pretty Sure Guccifer 2 Is Not A 'creature of Russia' @RepAdamSchiff," Twitter, March 20, 2017, 2, https://twitter.com/cassandrarules/status/843853011562708992?lang=en.

42. "Twitter DMs—Guccifer 2.0," *Guccifer 2.0*, n.d., http://g-2.space/sr/dms.html.

43. WikiLeaks, "Direct Messages from U.S. Alleged Russian Spy @GUCCIFER_2 to Actress-Model @robbin_young (according to the Latter)," Twitter, April 8, 2017, https://twitter.com/wikileaks/status/850692885062139904.

44. Tyler Durden, "'Guccifer 2.0' Chat With Nude Model Sparks New Conspiracy Theories About Seth Rich Murder," *Zero Hedge*, April 9, 2017, https://www.zerohedge.com/news/2017-04-09/guccifer-20-chat-nude-model-sparks-new-conspiracy-theories-about-seth-rich-murder.

45. Jim Hoft, "Report: Wikileaks Bombshell: Guccifer 2.0 Says 'Seth' Rich Was DNC Leaker," *Gateway Pundit*, April 8, 2017, http://www.thegatewaypundit.com/2017/04/wikileaks-bombshell-guccifer-2-0-admits-seth-rich-dnc-leaker/.

46. Crooked Hillary, "Fox News Report on Messages between Guccifer 2.0 and Robin Young Regarding Seth Rich" (YouTube, 2017), https://www.youtube.com/watch?v=s5h28kIcEAk.

47. Cassandra Fairbanks, "My Strange Interactions With Guccifer 2.0," *Big League Politics*, April 23, 2017, https://bigleaguepolitics.com/strange-interactions-guccifer-2-0/.

48. Cassandra Fairbanks, "Hacker: Guccifer 2.0 Planted Fake Russian Fingerprints On His Account," *Big League Politics*, April 25, 2017, https://bigleaguepolitics.com/hacker-guccifer-2-0-planted-fake-russian-fingerprints-account/.

49. Jo Becker, Matt Apuzzo, and Adam Goldman, "Trump Team Met With Lawyer Linked to Kremlin During Campaign," *New York Times*, July 8, 2017, sec. Politics, https://www.nytimes.com/2017/07/08/us/politics/trump-russia-kushner-manafort.html.

50. "Guccifer 2.0 NGP/VAN Metadata Analysis," *The Forensicator* (blog), July 9, 2017, https://theforensicator.wordpress.com/guccifer-2-ngp-van-metadata-analysis/.

51. Elizabeth Vos, "New Research Shows Guccifer 2.0 Files Were Copied Locally, Not Hacked," *Disobedient Media*, July 9, 2017, https://disobedientmedia.com/2017/07/new-research-shows-guccifer-2-0-files-were-copied-locally-not-hacked/.

52. "William Craddick | Zero Hedge," *Zero Hedge*, accessed April 5, 2018, https://www.zerohedge.com/users/william-craddick.

53. Zeiger, "New Analysis Disproves Russian Hacking Hoax Narrative," *Daily Stormer*, July 22, 2017, https://web.archive.org/web/20170722182420/https://www.dailystormer.com/new-analysis-disproves-russian-hacking-hoax-narrative/.

54. "New Analysis Suggests Guccifer 2.0 Files Copied Locally, Not Hacked by Russia," *RT International*, July 12, 2017, https://www.rt.com/usa/396056-guccifer-forensicator-hack-dnc/.

55. veganmark, "Implications of Recent Analyses by Adam Carter and Forensicator," Reddit, July 10, 2017, https://www.reddit.com/r/WayOfTheBern/comments/6mgjuy/implications_of_recent_analyses_by_adam_carter/."

56. "Intel Vets Challenge 'Russia Hack' Evidence," *Consortiumnews* (blog), July 24, 2017, https://consortiumnews.com/2017/07/24/intel-vets-challenge-russia-hack-evidence/.

57. Nicholas D. Kristof, "Save Our Spooks," *New York Times*, May 30, 2003, sec. Opinion, https://www.nytimes.com/2003/05/30/opinion/save-our-spooks.html.

58. Patrick Lawrence, "A New Report Raises Big Questions About Last Year's DNC Hack," *The Nation*, August 9, 2017, https://www.thenation.com/article/a-new-report-raises-big-questions-about-last-years-dnc-hack/.

59. Leonid Bershidsky, "Why Some U.S. Ex-Spies Don't Buy the Russia Story," *Bloomberg.com*, August 10, 2017, https://www.bloomberg.com/view/articles/2017-08-10/why-some-u-s-ex-spies-don-t-buy-the-russia-story.

60. Brian Feldman, "The Nation Article About the DNC Hack Is Too Incoherent to Even Debunk," *Select All*, August 10, 2017, http://nymag.com/selectall/2017/08/the-nation-article-about-the-dnc-hack-is-incoherent.html; Nancy LeTourneau, "Conspiracy Theories on the Left," *Washington Monthly*, August 11, 2017, https://washingtonmonthly.com/2017/08/11/conspiracy-theories-on-the-left/.

61. Danielle Ryan, "What If the DNC Russian 'hack' Was Really a Leak after All? A New Report Raises Questions Media and Democrats Would Rather Ignore," August 15, 2017, https://www.salon.com/2017/08/15/what-if-the-dnc-russian-hack-was-really-a-leak-after-all-a-new-report-raises-questions-media-and-democrats-would-rather-ignore.

62. Ian Mason, "Left-Wing Magazine The Nation Report Puts 'Russian Hack' DNC Narrative in Freefall," *Breitbart*, August 10, 2017, http://www.breitbart.com/

big-government/2017/08/10/left-wing-magazine-the-nation-report-puts-russian-hack-dnc-narrative-in-freefall/.

63. "Former NSA Official: Dems' Russia Hacking Story Likely Bogus," Fox News Insider, August 14, 2017, http://insider.foxnews.com/2017/08/14/russian-hacking-2016-election-nsa-member-says-trump-story-false.

64. Erik Wemple, "The Nation Is Reviewing a Story Casting Doubt on Russian Hack of DNC," *Washington Post*, August 15, 2017, sec. Opinion, https://www.washingtonpost.com/blogs/erik-wemple/wp/2017/08/15/the-nation-is-reviewing-a-story-casting-doubt-on-russian-hack-of-dnc/.

65. Various Contributors, "A Leak or a Hack? A Forum on the VIPS Memo: Independent Review," *The Nation*, September 1, 2017, https://www.thenation.com/article/a-leak-or-a-hack-a-forum-on-the-vips-memo/#independent-review.

66. Nathaniel Freitas, "Independent Review of Reporting and Analysis on the 2016 Compromise of the DNC Computer Network," *The Nation*, September 1, 2017, https://www.thenation.com/article/a-leak-or-a-hack-a-forum-on-the-vips-memo/#independent-review.

67. Thomas Drake, Scott Ritter, Lisa Ling, Cian Westmoreland, Philip M. Giraldi, and Jesselyn Radack, *The Nation*, September 1, 2017, When Facts are not Facts, https://www.thenation.com/article/a-leak-or-a-hack-a-forum-on-the-vips-memo/.

68. William Binney, Skip Folden, Ed Loomis, Ray Mcgovern, and Kirk Wiebe, "Why This Is Important," *The Nation*, September 1, 2017, When Facts are not Facts, https://www.thenation.com/article/a-leak-or-a-hack-a-forum-on-the-vips-memo/.

69. Oren Dorell, "Breitbart, Other 'alt-right' Websites are the Darlings of Russian Propaganda Effort," *USA Today*, August 24, 2017, https://www.usatoday.com/story/news/world/2017/08/24/breitbart-other-alt-right-websites-darlings-russian-propaganda-effort/598258001/.

70. Bethania Palma, "Was the Manchester Terror Attack a 'False Flag'?," *Snopes.com*, May 24, 2017, https://www.snopes.com/fact-check/manchester-attack-false-flag/.

71. "All Statements Involving YourNewsWire.Com | PolitiFact," *PolitiFact*, accessed April 6, 2018, http://www.politifact.com/personalities/yournewswirecom/statements/?list=speaker.

72. "L.A. Alt-Media Agitator (Not Breitbart) Clashes With Google, Snopes," *Hollywood Reporter*, accessed March 13, 2018, https://www.hollywoodreporter.com/features/hollywoods-hidden-alt-media-firebrands-1041157.

73. Richard Godwin, "Sean Adl-Tabatabai on Being in the Eye of the 'Fake News' Storm," *London Evening Standard*, February 16, 2017, https://www.standard.co.uk/lifestyle/london-life/sean-adltabatabai-on-being-in-the-eye-of-the-fake-news-storm-a3468361.html; Josh Boswell, "Mother Churns out Stories for Master of Fake News," *Sunday Times*, January 29, 2017, sec. News, https://www.thetimes.co.uk/article/mother-churns-out-stories-for-master-of-fake-news-fcmzco5sx.

74. Tracy Alloway and Luke Kawa, "Unmasking the Men Behind Zero Hedge, Wall Street's Renegade Blog," *Bloomberg*, April 29, 2016.

75. "Re: No Shit," email, *WikiLeaks*, May 5, 2016, https://wikileaks.org/dnc-emails/emailid/11508.

76. Brent Johnson, "The 12 Questions and Answers of Donald Trump's Reddit AMA," *NJ.com*, July 27, 2016, http://www.nj.com/politics/index.ssf/2016/07/the_9_questions_and_answers_of_donald_trumps_reddit_ama.html.

77. Associated Press, "Republican-Authored Voting Laws in Wisconsin and Kansas Overturned," *The Guardian*, July 29, 2016, http://www.theguardian.com/us-news/2016/jul/29/wisconsin-kansas-republican-voting-laws-unconstitutional.

78. Charlie Nash, "Roger Stone on The Milo Show: How Trump Can Fight Voter Fraud," *Breitbart*, July 29, 2016, http://www.breitbart.com/milo/2016/07/29/roger-stone-milo-show-trump-can-fight-voter-fraud/.

79. Katherine Krueger, "Trump: 'I'm Afraid' The General Election's 'Gonna Be Rigged,'" *TPM*, August 1, 2016, https://web.archive.org/web/20160803151821/http:/talkingpointsmemo.com:80/livewire/trump-general-election-rigged-potential-challenge, Internet Archive record.

80. Allan Smith, "DONALD TRUMP: 'I'm Afraid the Election Is Going to Be Rigged,'" *Business Insider*, August 1, 2016, http://www.businessinsider.com/donald-trump-rigged-election-2016-8.

81. "Donald Trump: The Election in November Will Be Rigged," video, *Fox News*, August 1, 2016, http://video.foxnews.com/v/5067615849001/.

82. Ian Schwartz, "Trump: People Without Identification 'Are Going To Vote 10 Times,'" video, *RealClearPolitics*, August 2, 2016, https://www.realclearpolitics.com/video/2016/08/02/trump_people_are_going_to_vote_10_times.html.

83. A.J. Katz, "August 2016 Ratings: Fox News Is Most-Watched Cable Network for a Second Straight Month," *TVNewser*, August 30, 2016, http://adweek.it/2bGKntn.

84. "Why Is Trump Saying the Election Is Rigged?," *Rush Limbaugh Show* (blog), August 2, 2016, https://www.rushlimbaugh.com/daily/2016/08/02/why_is_trump_saying_the_election_is_rigged_/.

85. "Donald Trump Transcript: The Republican Nominee in His Own Words—The Washington Post," *Washington Post*, August 2, 2016, https://www.washingtonpost.com/politics/donald-trump-transcript-the-republican-nominee-in-his-own-words/2016/08/02/77e9fa68-58eb-11e6-831d-0324760ca856_story.html?postshare=2641470192244004&utm_term=.e72406c83220.

86. "Pelosi, Reid Call for All Leaders to Join in Affirming Fairness of Our Democratic Process," Democratic Leader Nancy Pelosi, October 17, 2016, https://www.democraticleader.gov/newsroom/pelosi-reid-call-for-all-leaders-to-join-in-affirming-fairness-of-our-democratic-process/.

87. Zachary Roth, "Analysis: Trump Not the First to Claim Voter Fraud Will Rig Elections—NBC News," *NBC News*, August 3, 2016, https://www.nbcnews.com/politics/2016-election/trump-not-first-claim-voter-fraud-will-rig-elections-n622421.

88. Katherine Q. Seelye, "McCain's Warning About Voter Fraud Stokes a Fiery Campaign Even Further—The New York Times," *New York Times*, October 26, 2008, https://www.nytimes.com/2008/10/27/us/politics/27vote.html?_r=0.

89. Tom Jensen, "ACORN," *Public Policy Polling* (blog), November 19, 2009, https://publicpolicypolling.blogspot.com/2009/11/acorn.html.

90. "2016 Election Results: Michigan Exit Polls," *CNN*, November 9, 2016, http://www.cnn.com/election/2016/results/exit-polls/michigan/president.

91. Joshua Green and Sasha Issenberg, "Inside the Trump Bunker, With 12 Days to Go," *Bloomberg*, October 27, 2016, https://www.bloomberg.com/news/articles/2016-10-27/inside-the-trump-bunker-with-12-days-to-go.

92. Daniel Kreiss and Shannon C. Mcgregor, "Technology Firms Shape Political Communication: The Work of Microsoft, Facebook, Twitter, and Google With Campaigns During the 2016 U.S. Presidential Cycle," *Political Communication*, October 26, 2017, 1–23, https://doi.org/10.1080/10584609.2017.1364814.

93. Collins, Poulsen, and Ackerman, "Exclusive."

94. "Alex 'Never Giving Up' Jones Gives Up," accessed March 13, 2018, https://www.thedailybeast.com/alex-never-giving-up-jones-gives-up.

95. Alex Riggins, Nathan Brown, and Julie Wootton, "UPDATED: Story of Syrian Refugees Raping Idaho Girl Is Wrong, Prosecutor Says | Idaho Statesman," *Idaho Statesman*, June 20, 2016, http://www.idahostatesman.com/news/state/idaho/article84829787.html; Rocky Barker, "Breitbart's Chobani Coverage Is a Reminder of Idaho's Experience with the Alt-Right," *Idaho Statesman*, November 16, 2016, http://www.idahostatesman.com/news/local/news-columns-blogs/letters-from-the-west/article115283313.html.

96. Scott Shane, "Purged Facebook Page Tied to the Kremlin Spread Anti-Immigrant Bile," *New York Times*, September 12, 2017, sec. Politics, https://www.nytimes.com/2017/09/12/us/politics/russia-facebook-election.html.

97. Bence Kollanyi, Philip N. Howard, and Samuel C. Woolley, "Bots and Automation over Twitter during the U.S. Election," Computational Propaganda Research Project (Oxford Internet Institute, November 17, 2016), 1–4, http://comprop.oii.ox.ac.uk/wp-content/uploads/sites/89/2016/11/Data-Memo-US-Election.pdf.

98. Onur Varol et al., "Online Human-Bot Interactions: Detection, Estimation, and Characterization," *ArXiv Preprint ArXiv:1703.03107*, 2017, https://arxiv.org/abs/1703.03107; Clayton Allen Davis et al., "BotOrNot: A System to Evaluate Social Bots," in *Proceedings of the 25th International Conference Companion on World Wide Web, WWW '16 Companion* (Republic and Canton of Geneva, Switzerland: International World Wide Web Conferences Steering Committee, 2016), 273–274, https://doi.org/10.1145/2872518.2889302; Alessandro Bessi and Emilio Ferrara, "Social Bots Distort the 2016 U.S. Presidential Election Online Discussion," *First Monday* 21, no. 11 (November 3, 2016), http://firstmonday.org/ojs/index.php/fm/article/view/7090.

99. Stukal et al., "Detecting Bots on Russian Political Twitter."

100. Stefano Cresci et al., "The Paradigm-Shift of Social Spambots: Evidence, Theories, and Tools for the Arms Race," in *Proceedings of the 26th International Conference on World Wide Web Companion* (International World Wide Web Conferences Steering Committee, 2017), 963–972, http://dl.acm.org/citation.cfm?id=3055135.

101. In full disclosure, the email reports that experts were consulted, including at the Berkman Center at Harvard, where all three of us were then, in the preparation of this memo. None of us remember whether we were consulted, but Yochai later wrote a detailed article explaining why WikiLeaks had to be treated no differently from the *New York Times* or the *Guardian*, which had also published the war logs and cables, and then participated in the defense of Chelsea Manning's prosecution for aiding the enemy.

102. "Under Intense Pressure to Silence Wikileaks, Secretary of State Hillary Clinton Proposed Drone Strike on Julian Assange," *True Pundit* (blog), October 2, 2016, https://truepundit.com/under-intense-pressure-to-silence-wikileaks-secretary-of-state-hillary-clinton-proposed-drone-strike-on-julian-assange/.

103. "Kremlin-Linked Network Amplifies 'alt-Right' Media."

CHAPTER 9

1. Joshua Green and Sasha Issenberg, "Inside the Trump Bunker, With Days to Go," *Bloomberg*, October 27, 2016, https://www.bloomberg.com/news/articles/2016-10-27/inside-the-trump-bunker-with-12-days-to-go.

2. Philip Bump, "Donald Trump's Campaign Manager Is Out. Here Are the Brutal Numbers That Tell Us Why.," *Washington Post*, June 20, 2016, sec. The Fix, https://www.washingtonpost.com/news/the-fix/wp/2016/06/19/the-brutal-numbers-behind-a-very-bad-month-for-donald-trump/.

3. Philip Bump, "How Facebook Plans to Become One of the Most Powerful Tools in Politics," *Washington Post*, November 26, 2014, sec. The Fix, https://www.washingtonpost.com/news/the-fix/wp/2014/11/26/how-facebook-plans-to-become-one-of-the-most-powerful-tools-in-politics/.

4. Jeanne Cummings, "Rove's Patented Strategies Will Endure," *Politico*, August 13, 2007, https://www.politico.com/news/stories/0807/5375.html.

5. Alexis C. Madrigal, "When the Nerds Go Marching In," *The Atlantic*, November 16, 2012, https://www.theatlantic.com/technology/archive/2012/11/when-the-nerds-go-marching-in/265325/.

6. Darren Samuelsohn, "Hillary's Nerd Squad," *Politico*, March 25, 2015, https://www.politico.com/story/2015/03/hillarys-nerd-squad-116402.html.

7. Mike Allen and Kennth P. Vogel, "Inside the Koch Data Mine," *Politico*, December 8, 2014, http://www.politico.com/story/2014/12/koch-brothers-rnc-113359.html.

8. Jane Mayer, "The Reclusive Hedge-Fund Tycoon Behind the Trump Presidency," *The New Yorker*, March 27, 2017, https://www.newyorker.com/magazine/2017/03/27/the-reclusive-hedge-fund-tycoon-behind-the-trump-presidency.

9. Daniel Kreiss and Shannon C. McGregor, "Technology Firms Shape Political Communication: The Work of Microsoft, Facebook, Twitter, and Google With Campaigns During the 2016 U.S. Presidential Cycle," *Political Communication* 35, no. 2 (October 26, 2017): 155–177, https://doi.org/10.1080/10584609.2017.1364814.

10. Green and Issenberg, "Trump Bunker."

11. Nicholas Confessore and Karen Yourish, "$2 Billion Worth of Free Media for Donald Trump," *New York Times*, March 15, 2016, sec. The Upshot, https://www.nytimes.com/2016/03/16/upshot/measuring-donald-trumps-mammoth-advantage-in-free-media.html.

12. Zeynep Tufekci, "Beware the Big Data Campaign," *New York Times*, November 16, 2012, sec. Opinion, https://www.nytimes.com/2012/11/17/opinion/beware-the-big-data-campaign.html.

13. Zeynep Tufekci, "Engineering the Public: Big Data, Surveillance and Computational Politics," *First Monday* 19, no. 7 (July 7, 2014), https://doi.org/10.5210/fm.v19i7.4901.

14. Dipayan Ghosh and Ben Scott, "#Digitaldeceipt: The Technologies Behind Precision Propaganda on The Internet" (New America Foundation and the Shorenstein Center at Harvard Kennedy School, January 2018), https://na-production.s3.amazonaws.com/documents/digital-deceit-final-v3.pdf.

15. Michal Kosinski, David Stillwell, and Thore Graepel, "Private Traits and Attributes Are Predictable from Digital Records of Human Behavior," *Proceedings of the National Academy of Sciences* 110, no. 15 (April 9, 2013): 5802–5805, https://doi.org/10.1073/pnas.1218772110.

16. Nicholas Confessore and Danny Hakim, "Data Firm Says 'Secret Sauce' Aided Trump; Many Scoff," *New York Times*, March 6, 2017, sec. Politics, https://www.nytimes.com/2017/03/06/us/politics/cambridge-analytica.html.

17. Will Oremus, "The Real Scandal Isn't Cambridge Analytica. It's Facebook's Whole Business Model.," *Slate Magazine*, March 20, 2018, https://slate.com/technology/2018/03/the-real-scandal-isnt-cambridge-analytica-its-facebooks-whole-business-model.html.

18. "Revealed: Trump's Election Consultants Filmed Saying They Use Bribes and Sex Workers to Entrap Politicians," *Channel 4 News*, March 19, 2018, https://www.channel4.com/news/cambridge-analytica-revealed-trumps-election-consultants-filmed-saying-they-use-bribes-and-sex-workers-to-entrap-politicians-investigation.

19. As the Cambridge Analytica story was exploding, a discussion on a listserv of academics working on fake news and disinformation raised several thoughtful considerations that suggest a good deal of skepticism about the likelihood that microtargeting based on Facebook data is in fact that much more efficient or

effective than the already-existing arsenal of tools at the disposal of political campaign operatives. The next few paragraphs are based on research we did to flesh out comments made on that list by Duncan Watts, Brendan Nyhan, David Lazer, and David Rand. Any errors here are our own.

20. Wu Youyou, Michal Kosinski, and David Stillwell, "Computer-Based Personality Judgments Are More Accurate than Those Made by Humans," *Proceedings of the National Academy of Sciences* 112, no. 4 (January 27, 2015): 1036–1040, https://doi.org/10.1073/pnas.1418680112.

21. S.C. Matz et al., "Psychological Targeting as an Effective Approach to Digital Mass Persuasion," *Proceedings of the National Academy of Sciences* 114, no. 48 (November 28, 2017): 12714–12719, https://doi.org/10.1073/pnas.1710966114.

22. Michael A. Bailey, Daniel J. Hopkins, and Todd Rogers, "Unresponsive and Unpersuaded: The Unintended Consequences of a Voter Persuasion Effort," *Political Behavior* 38, no. 3 (September 2016): 713–746, https://doi.org/https://doi.org/10.1007/s11109-016-9338-8.

23. Eitan D. Hersh and Brian F. Schaffner, "Targeted Campaign Appeals and the Value of Ambiguity," *Journal of Politics* 75, no. 2 (April 1, 2013): 520–534, https://doi.org/10.1017/S0022381613000182.

24. David Nickerson and Todd Rogers, "Political Campaigns and Big Data," HKS Working Paper No. RWP13-045 (February 25, 2014), https://doi.org/https://doi.org/10.2139/ssrn.2354474.

25. Randall A. Lewis and Justin M. Rao, "The Unfavorable Economics of Measuring the Returns to Advertising," *SSRN Electronic Journal*, September 18, 2014, https://doi.org/https://doi.org/10.2139/ssrn.2367103.

26. Samidh Chakrabarti, "Hard Questions: What Effect Does Social Media Have on Democracy?," *Facebook Newsroom* (blog), January 22, 2018, https://newsroom.fb.com/news/2018/01/effect-social-media-democracy/.

27. Elisa Shearer and Jeffrey Gottfried, "News Use Across Social Media Platforms 2017" (Pew Research Center, September 7, 2017), http://www.journalism.org/2017/09/07/news-use-across-social-media-platforms-2017/.

28. Craig Silverman et al., "Inside The Partisan Fight For Your Facebook News Feed," *BuzzFeed*, August 8, 2017, https://www.buzzfeed.com/craigsilverman/inside-the-partisan-fight-for-your-news-feed.

29. Daniel Kahneman, *Thinking, Fast and Slow* (New York: Farrar, Straus and Giroux, 2011).

30. "Campaign '92: Survey VIII" (Pew Research Center, July 8, 1992), http://www.people-press.org/1992/07/08/campaign-92-survey-viii/.

31. Craig Silverman et al., "Hyperpartisan Facebook Pages Are Publishing False And Misleading Information At An Alarming Rate," *BuzzFeed*, October 20, 2016, https://www.buzzfeed.com/craigsilverman/partisan-fb-pages-analysis.

32. Hunt Allcott and Matthew Gentzkow, "Social Media and Fake News in the 2016 Election," *Journal of Economic Perspectives* 31, no. 2 (January 19, 2017): 211–236.

33. Andrew Guess, Brendan Nyhan, and Jason Reifler, "Selective Exposure to Misinformation: Evidence from the Consumption of Fake News during the 2016 U.S. Presidential Campaign," Jan 9, 2018, 49, http://www.dartmouth.edu/~nyhan/fake-news-2016.pdf.

PART FOUR

1. Nathaniel Persily, "Can Democracy Survive the Internet?," *Journal of Democracy* 28, no. 2 (April 2017): 63–76.
2. Cass R. Sunstein, *Republic.com* (Princeton, NJ: Princeton University Press, 2001).
3. Donald J. Trump, Twitter, March 17, 2018, https://twitter.com/realDonaldTrump/status/975057131136274432.

CHAPTER 10

1. Congressman Charlie Dent, "Dent Statement on Decision Not to Seek 8th Term," Congressman Charlie Dent, September 8, 2017, https://dent.house.gov/2017/9/dent-statement-on-decision-not-to-seek-8th-term.
2. "List of U.S. Congress Incumbents Who Are Not Running for Re-Election in 2018—Ballotpedia," *Ballotpedia*, accessed April 4, 2018, https://ballotpedia.org/List_of_U.S._Congress_incumbents_who_are_not_running_for_re-election_in_2018.
3. Clio Andris et al., "The Rise of Partisanship and Super-Cooperators in the U.S. House of Representatives," *PLOS ONE* 10, no. 4 (April 21, 2015), https://doi.org/10.1371/journal.pone.0123507.
4. Ira Katznelson, *When Affirmative Action Was White: An Untold History of Racial Inequality in Twentieth-Century America* (New York; London: W.W. Norton, 2006).
5. Bill D. Moyers, *Moyers Oon America: A Journalist and His Times* (New York: Anchor Books, 2005).
6. Warren Weaver Jr., "The Emerging Republican Majority," *The New York Times*, September 21, 1969, http://www.nytimes.com/packages/html/books/phillips-emerging.pdf.; James Boyd, "Nixon's Southern Strategy," *The New York Times*, May 17, 1970, https://timesmachine.nytimes.com/timesmachine/1970/05/17/354962432.pdf.
7. Kevin Phillips, *The Emerging Republican Majority*, James Madison Library in American Politics Series (Princeton, NJ: Princeton University Press, 2014).
8. Warren Weaver Jr., "The Emerging Republican Majority."
9. Nolan McCarty, Keith T. Poole, and Howard Rosenthal, *Polarized America: The Dance of Ideology and Unequal Riches* (Cambridge: MIT Press, 2006), https://mitpress.mit.edu/books/polarized-america.

10. "Introduction," *Studies in American Political Development* 30, no. 2 (2016): 95–96, https://doi.org/10.1017/S0898588X16000109.

11. Nolan McCarty, "In Defense of DW-NOMINATE," *Studies in American Political Development* 30, no. 2 (October 2016): 172–184, https://doi.org/10.1017/S0898588X16000110.

12. Jacob S. Hacker and Paul Pierson, *Winner-Take-All Politics: How Washington Made the Rich Richer—and Turned Its Back on the Middle Class* (New York: Simon & Schuster, 2010).

13. Matthew Grossmann and David A. Hopkins, *Asymmetric Politics: Ideological Republicans and Group Interest Democrats* (New York: Oxford University Press, 2016).

14. Morris P. Fiorina, "Has the American Public Polarized?," *Hoover Institution Essays on Contemporary American Politics* 2 (September 2016): 1–24; Marc J. Hetherington, "Putting Polarization in Perspective," *British Journal of Political Science* 39, no. 2 (2009): 413–448; Matthew Levendusky, *The Partisan Sort: How Liberals Became Democrats and How Conservatives Became Republicans* (Chicago: University of Chicago Press, 2009).

15. Yphtach Lelkes, "Mass Polarization: Manifestations and Measurements," *Public Opinion Quarterly* 80, no. S1 (January 1, 2016): 392–410, https://doi.org/10.1093/poq/nfw005.

16. Matthew Levendusky, *The Partisan Sort.*

17. Lelkes, "Mass Polarization."

18. Alan I. Abramowitz and Kyle L. Saunders, "Is Polarization a Myth?," *The Journal of Politics* 70, no. 2 (April 1, 2008): 542–555, https://doi.org/10.1017/S0022381608080493.

19. Morris P. Fiorina, "Has the American Public Polarized?"

20. Fiorina, Morris P., Samuel J. Abrams, and Jeremy Pope. *Culture war?: The Myth of a Polarized America.* New York: Pearson Longman, 2005.

21. American National Election Studies, "Data Center," http://www.electionstudies.org/studypages/download/datacenter_all_NoData.php.

22. Abramowitz and Saunders, "Is Polarization a Myth?"

23. Fiorina, Morris P., and Samuel J. Abrams. *Disconnect: The Breakdown of Representation in American Politics.* Vol. 11 (Norman: University of Oklahoma Press, 2012).

24. Abramowitz, Alan I., and Kyle L. Saunders. "Is polarization a myth?." *The Journal of Politics* 70, no. 2 (2008): 542–555.

25. David E. Broockman, David E. "Approaches to studying policy representation," *Legislative Studies Quarterly* 41, no. 1 (2016): 181–215.

26. Philip E. Converse, "The Nature of Belief Systems in Mass Publics," *Critical Review* 18, no. 1–3 (1964): 1–74, https://doi.org/10.1080/08913810608443650.

27. Donald R. Kinder and Nathan P. Kalmoe, *Neither Liberal Nor Conservative: Ideological Innocence in the American Public* (Chicago: University of Chicago Press, 2017).

28. Christopher H. Achen and Larry M. Bartels, *Democracy for Realists: Why Elections Do Not Produce Responsive Government* (Princeton, NJ: Princeton University Press, 2016), https://doi.org/10.1002/polq.12663.

29. Angus Campbell et al., *The American Voter* (New York: John Wiley, 1960).

30. Converse, "The Nature of Belief Systems in Mass Publics."

31. Donald R. Kinder and Nathan P. Kalmoe, *Neither Liberal Nor Conservative: Ideological Innocence in the American Public* (Chicago: University of Chicago Press, 2017), 133.

32. Gabriel S. Lenz, *Follow the Leader?: How Voters Respond to Politicians' Policies and Performance* (Chicago: University of Chicago Press, 2012); John Zaller, *The Nature and Origins of Mass Opinion* (Cambridge: Cambridge University Press, 1992).

33. David E. Broockman and Daniel M. Butler, "The Causal Effects of Elite Position-Taking on Voter Attitudes: Field Experiments with Elite Communication," *American Journal of Political Science* 61, no. 1 (December 2015): 208–221, https://doi.org/https://doi.org/10.1111/ajps.12243.

34. Michael Barber, "Does Party Trump Ideology? Disentangling Party and Ideology in America," n.d., https://www.dropbox.com/s/ofh5bzwnt4ixwdj/Does_Party_Trump_Ideology%3F.pdf?dl=0.

35. David A. Graham, "Trump Is Radicalizing the Democratic Party," *The Atlantic*, October 27, 2017, https://www.theatlantic.com/politics/archive/2017/10/symmetric-polarization/544059/.

36. Donald P. Green, Bradley Palmquist, and Eric Schickler, *Partisan Hearts and Minds: Political Parties and the Social Identities of Voters* (New Haven, CT: Yale University Press, 2002), https://doi.org/10.1017/S1537592703510428.

37. Leonie Huddy, Lilliana Mason, and Lene Aarøe, "Expressive Partisanship: Campaign Involvement, Political Emotion, and Partisan Identity," *American Political Science Review* 109, no. 1 (February 2015): 1–17, https://doi.org/10.1017/S0003055414000604.

38. Lilliana Mason, "Why Are Americans so Angry This Election Season? Here's New Research That Helps Explain It.," *Washington Post*, March 10, 2016, sec. Monkey Cage, https://www.washingtonpost.com/news/monkey-cage/wp/2016/03/10/why-are-americans-so-angry-this-election-season-heres-new-research-that-helps-explain-it/.

39. Lilliana Mason, "'I Disrespectfully Agree': The Differential Effects of Partisan Sorting on Social and Issue Polarization," *American Journal of Political Science* 59, no. 1 (2015): 128–145.

40. Donald R. Kinder and Cindy D. Kam, *Us Against Them: Ethnocentric Foundations of American Opinion* (Chicago: University of Chicago Press, 2010), https://doi.org/10.1111/j.1467-9221.2011.00833.x.

41. Miller, Patrick R., and Pamela Johnston Conover. "Red and blue states of mind: Partisan hostility and voting in the United States." *Political Research Quarterly* 68, no. 2 (2015): 225–239.

42. Dimock, Michael, Carroll Doherty, Jocelyn Kiley, and Russ Oates. "Political polarization in the American public." *Pew Research Center* (2014).

43. Shanto Iyengar and Sean J. Westwood, "Fear and Loathing across Party Lines: New Evidence on Group Polarization," *American Journal of Political Science* 59, no. 3 (2015): 690–707.

44. Shanto Iyengar, Gaurav Sood, and Yphtach Lelkes, "Affect, Not Ideology: A Social Identity Perspective on Polarization," *Public Opinion Quarterly* 76, no. 3 (September 2012): 405–431, https://doi.org/10.1093/poq/nfs038.

45. Iyengar and Westwood, "Fear and Loathing across Party Lines."

46. Alan I. Abramowitz and Steven W. Webster, "Negative Partisanship: Why Americans Dislike Parties But Behave Like Rabid Partisans," *Political Psychology* 39 (February 1, 2018): 119–135, https://doi.org/10.1111/pops.12479.

CHAPTER 11

1. Quoted in: Nicole Hemmer, *Messengers of the Right: Conservative Media and the Transformation of American Politics*, Politics and Culture in Modern America (Philadelphia: University of Pennsylvania Press, 2016), 157.

2. Jeffrey M. Berry and Sarah Sobieraj, *The Outrage Industry: Political Opinion Media and the New Incivility*, Studies in Postwar American Political Development (Oxford; New York: Oxford University Press, 2014), 12–13; "November 2012 Ratings: Fox News Daytime Shows Have Best Months Ever," accessed February 14, 2018, http://www.adweek.com/tvnewser/november-2012-ratings-fox-news-daytime-shows-have-best-months-ever/157704.

3. A.J. Katz, "November 2016 Ratings: Fox News Has Most-Watched Month Since 2012," *Adweek*, November 30, 2016, http://adweek.it/2gWcPfF.

4. A.J. Katz, "November 2017 Ratings: Fox News Is Basic Cable's Most-Watched Network For 17 Months," November 29, 2016, http://adweek.it/2i1MToL.

5. Jeffrey Gottfried, Michael Barthel, and Amy Mitchell, "Trump, Clinton Voters Divided in Their Main Source for Election News," *Pew Research Center's Journalism Project* (blog), January 18, 2017, http://www.journalism.org/2017/01/18/trump-clinton-voters-divided-in-their-main-source-for-election-news/.

6. Berry and Sobieraj, *The Outrage Industry*.

7. *Id.* Berry and Sobieraj, at 39–41.

8. *Id.* Berry and Sobieraj, at 42–45.

9. Joanne M. Miller, Kyle L. Saunders, and Christina E. Farhart, "Conspiracy Endorsement as Motivated Reasoning: The Moderating Roles of Political Knowledge and Trust," *American Journal of Political Science* 60, no. 4 (2016): 824–844, https://doi.org/10.1111/ajps.12234. Adam J. Berinsky, "The Roots of False Beliefs: Political Rumors in America from 2010–2017" draft chapter.

10. Theda Skocpol and Vanessa Williamson, *The Tea Party and the Remaking of Republican Conservatism* (New York: Oxford University Press, 2016), 125–126.

11. Michael Schudson, *Discovering the News: A Social History of American Newspapers*, (New York, NY: Basic Books, 1995).

12. David Harvey, *The Condition of Postmodernity: An Enquiry into the Origins of Cultural Change* (Oxford, [England]; Cambridge, MA, USA: Blackwell, 1989); James C. Scott, *Seeing Like a State: How Certain Schemes to Improve the Human Condition Have Failed,* Nachdr., Yale Agrarian Studies (New Haven, CT: Yale University Press, 2008); Charles S. Maier, "Between Taylorism and Technocracy: European Ideologies and the Vision of Industrial Productivity in the 1920s," *Journal of Contemporary History* 5, no. 2 (1970): 27–61; Charles S. Maier, "The Politics of Productivity: Foundations of American International Economic Policy after World War II," *International Organization* 31, no. 04 (1977): 607–633.

13. *Masses Publishing Co. v. Patten*, 244 F. 535 (S.D.N.Y. 1917).

14. *Schenck v. United States*, 249 U.S. 47 (1919).

15. *Abrams v. United States*, 250 U.S. 616 (1919).

16. Sheldon Marcus, *Father Coughlin: The Tumultuous Life of the Priest of the Little Flower*, 1st ed. (Boston: Little, Brown, 1973).

17. Institute for Propaganda Analysis, Alfred McClung Lee, and Elizabeth (Briant) Lee, eds., *The Fine Art of Propaganda* (New York: Octagon Books, 1972).

18. Victor Pickard "'Whether the Giants Should Be Slain or Persuaded to Be Good'": Revisiting the Hutchins Commission and the Role of Media in a Democratic Society," *Critical Studies in Media Communication* Vol. 27, No. 4, (October 2010): pp. 391–411.

19. Ira Katznelson, *When Affirmative Action Was White: An Untold History of Racial Inequality in Twentieth-Century America* (New York; London: W.W. Norton, 2006).

20. Hemmer, *Messengers of the Right.*

21. *Id.* Hemmer, at 3–48.

22. *Id.* Hemmer, at 167–170.

23. Tom W. Smith, Peter Marsden, Michael Hout, and Jibum Kim, *General Social Surveys, 1972–2016* [machine-readable data file]. Data accessed from the GSS Data Explorer website at http://gssdataexplorer.norc.org.

24. Edward S. Herman and Noam Chomsky, *Manufacturing Consent: The Political Economy of the Mass Media* (New York: Pantheon Books, 2002).

25. Ben H. Bagdikian, *The Media Monopoly*, 5th ed. (Boston: Beacon Press, 1997).

26. Yochai Benkler, *The Wealth of Networks: How Social Production Transforms Markets and Freedom* (New Haven, CT: Yale University Press, 2006).

27. Stanley M. Besen and Robert W. Crandall, "The Deregulation of Cable Television," *Law and Contemporary Problems* 44, no. 1 (1981): 77–124, https://doi.org/10.2307/1191387.

28. "Campaign '92: Survey VIII" (Pew Research Center, July 8, 1992), http://www.people-press.org/1992/07/08/campaign-92-survey-viii/.

29. Peter G. Horsfield, *Religious Television: The American Experience* (New York: Longman Press, 1984), 8.

30. Jeffrey K. Hadden and Anson D. Shupe, *Televangelism: Power and Politics on God's Frontier* (New York: H. Holt, 1988), 8–10.

31. *Id.* Jeffrey K. Hadden and Anson D. Shupe, at 138.

32. Razelle Frankl, *Televangelism: The Marketing of Popular Religion* (Carbondale: Southern Illinois University Press, 1986), Table 2, 92. Razelle Frankl, 118.

33. Jeffrey K. Hadden and Anson D. Shupe, *Televangelism: Power and Politics on God's Frontier*, 155–159.

34. Paul Starr, *The Creation of the Media: Political Origins of Modern Communications* (New York: Basic Books, 2004), 382–383; Tim Wu, *The Master Switch: The Rise and Fall of Information Empires*, 1st Vintage Books ed. (New York: Vintage Books, 2011), chap. 9.

35. Brian Regal, *Radio: The Life Story of a Technology*, Greenwood Technographies (Westport, CT: Greenwood Press, 2005).

36. Kathleen Hall Jamieson and Joseph N. Cappella, *Echo Chamber: Rush Limbaugh and the Conservative Media Establishment* (Oxford; New York: Oxford University Press, 2008), 45–46.

37. Brent Staples, "Just a Toaster with Pictures," *The New York Times*, February 8, 1987, https://www.nytimes.com/1987/02/08/books/just-a-toaster-with-pictures.html.

38. Hemmer, *Messengers of the Right*.

39. Lewis Grossberger, "The Rush Hours," *The New York Times Magazine*, December 16, 1990, https://www.nytimes.com/1990/12/16/magazine/the-rush-hours.html.

40. Hemmer, *Messengers of the Right*, 256–57.

41. *Id.* Hemmer, at 270–271.

42. *Id.* Hemmer, at 271.

43. Jamieson and Cappella, *Echo Chamber*, xiv; Hemmer, *Messengers of the Right*, 171.

44. Jamieson and Cappella, *Echo Chamber*, 46.

45. "TV News Viewership Declines," TV News Viewship Declines (Pew Research Center, May 13, 1996), http://www.people-press.org/1996/05/13/other-important-findings-12/.

46. Jamieson and Cappella, *Echo Chamber*.

47. *Id.* Jamieson and Cappella, at 46; "Is Rush Limbaugh's Business Model in Trouble?," *Politico Magazine*, accessed February 9, 2018, https://www.politico.com/magazine/story/2016/05/is-rush-limbaugh-in-trouble-talk-radio-213914; "Rush Limbaugh's Audience May Be So Much Smaller Than You Think"— *Business Insider*, accessed February 9, 2018, http://www.businessinsider.com/rush-limbaughs-audience-may-be-so-much-smaller-than-you-think-2012-3.

48. Maria Figueroa, Damone Richardson, and Pam Whitefield, *The Clear Picture on Clear Channel Communications, Inc.: A Corporate Profile* (Ithaca: ILR School, Cornell University, 2004).

49. "State of the Media—Audio Today 2017" (Nielsen, June 22, 2017), 3, http://www.nielsen.com/us/en/insights/reports/2017/state-of-the-media-audio-today-2017.

50. John Halpin et al., "The Structural Imbalance of Political Talk Radio," June 22, 2007, https://cdn.americanprogress.org/wp-content/uploads/issues/2007/06/pdf/talk_radio.pdf.

51. Skocpol and Williamson, *The Tea Party and the Remaking of Republican Conservatism*, 125–126.

52. "Audio Today: Radio 2016—Appealing Far and Wide," (Nielsen, February 25, 2016), http://www.nielsen.com/us/en/insights/reports/2016/audio-today-radio-2016-appealing-far-and-wide.

53. Bruce Bartlett, "How Fox News Changed American Media and Political Dynamics," *SSRN Electronic Journal*, June 3, 2015, http://dx.doi.org/10.2139/ssrn.2604679.

54. Amy Mitchell et al., "Political Polarization & Media Habits," *Pew Research Center's Journalism Project* (blog), October 21, 2014, http://www.journalism.org/2014/10/21/political-polarization-media-habits/.

55. Mitchell et al., 5. http://www.journalism.org/2014/10/21/political-polarization-media-habits/pj_2014-10-21_media-polarization-11/.

56. Gallup Inc., "Democrats' Confidence in Mass Media Rises Sharply From 2016," *Gallup.com*, accessed March 1, 2018, http://news.gallup.com/poll/219824/democrats-confidence-mass-media-rises-sharply-2016.aspx.

57. Samantha Smith, "5 Facts about America's Political Independents," *Pew Research Center* (blog), July 5, 2016, http://www.pewresearch.org/fact-tank/2016/07/05/5-facts-about-americas-political-independents/.

58. Tom W. Smith, Peter Marsden, Michael Hout, and Jibum Kim. General Social Surveys, 1972–2014 [machine-readable data file]/Principal Investigator, Tom W. Smith; Co-Principal Investigator, Peter V. Marsden; Co-Principal Investigator, Michael Hout; Sponsored by National Science Foundation. NORC ed. (Chicago: NORC at the University of Chicago) [producer and distributor].

59. Nic Newman with Richard Fletcher, Antonis Kalogeropoulos, David A.L. Levy, and Rasmus Kleis Nielsen, *Reuters Institute Digital News Report* 2017, http://www.digitalnewsreport.org/.

60. *Id.* at 19.

61. Miller, Saunders, and Farhart, "Conspiracy Endorsement as Motivated Reasoning: The Moderating Roles of Political Knowledge and Trust."; Adam J. Berinsky, "The Roots of False Beliefs: Political Rumors in America from 2010–2017" draft chapter.

62. Blumenthal v. Drudge and America Online, Inc., April 22 1998. https://epic.org/free_speech/blumenthal_v_drudge.html.

63. *Reno v. American Civil Liberties Union*, 521 U.S. 844, 870 (1997).

64. Yochai Benkler, "Free as the Air to Common Use: First Amendment Constraints on Enclosure of the Public Domain," *New York University Law Review* 74, no. 2

(May 1999): 354–446; Yochai Benkler, "From Consumers to Users: Shifting the Deeper Structures of Regulation Toward Sustainable Commons and User Access" *Federal Communications Law Journal* 52 (2000): 561–579.

65. Cass R. Sunstein, *Republic.Com* (Princeton, NJ: Princeton University Press, 2001).

66. Albert-László Barabási and Réka Albert, "Emergence of Scaling in Random Networks," *Science* 286, no. 5439 (October 15, 1999): 509–512, https://doi.org/10.1126/science.286.5439.509.; Lada A. Adamic, Lada A., and Bernardo A. Huberman., "Power-Law Distribution of the World Wide Web.," *Science* 287, no. 5461 (2000): 2115–2115.

67. Erzsébet Ravasz and Albert-László Barabási, "Hierarchical Organization in Complex Networks," *Physical Review E* 67, no. 2 (February 14, 2003), https://doi.org/10.1103/PhysRevE.67.026112.; Matthew Scott Hindman, *The Myth of Digital Democracy* (Princeton, NJ; Oxford: Princeton University Press, 2009).

68. Lada A. Adamic and Natalie Glance, "The Political Blogosphere and the 2004 U.S. Election: Divided They Blog," in *Proceedings of the 3rd International Workshop on Link Discovery*, 2005, https://doi.org/10.1145/1134271.1134277.

69. Markus Prior, *Post-Broadcast Democracy: How Media Choice Increases Inequality in Political Involvement and Polarizes Elections*, Cambridge Studies in Public Opinion and Political Psychology (New York: Cambridge University Press, 2007).

70. Hindman, *The Myth of Digital Democracy*.

71. Others who had looked at this question on a smaller scale or more based on experience were Bowers, C., & Stoller, M. (2005)., *Emergence of the Progressive Blogosphere: A New Force in American Politics*, New Politics Institute (2005). Available at: http://www.newpolitics.net/node/87?full_report=1; David Karpf, (2008b). "Understanding blogspace," *Journal of Information Technology and Politics* 5, (no. 4) (2008b): 369–385. M.R. Kerbel, M. R. (2009). *Netroots: Online Progressives and the Transformation of American Politics.* (Boulder, Colo. CO: Paradigm Publishers, 2009).

72. Aaron Shaw and Yochai Benkler, "A Tale of Two Blogospheres: Discursive Practices on the Left and Right," *American Behavioral Scientist* 56, no. 4 (April 2012): 459–487, https://doi.org/10.1177/0002764211433793.

73. Micah L. Sifry, *The Big Disconnect Why the Internet Hasn't Transformed Politics (Yet)* (New York: OR Books, 2014).

74. Zeynep Tufekci and& Christopher Wilson, "Social media and the decision to participate in political protest: Observations from Tahrir Square," *Journal of Communication* 62, no. (2) (2012): 363–379 (2012).

75. Larry Diamond, "Liberation Technology," *Journal of Democracy* 21 (July 2010): 69–83.

76. Philip N. Howard, *The Digital Origins of Dictatorship and Democracy: Information Technology and Political Islam*, Oxford Studies in Digital Politics (Oxford; New York: Oxford Univesity Press, 2010).

77. Sandra González-Bailón, Javier Borge-Holthoefer, and Yamir Moreno, "Broadcasters and Hidden Influentials in Online Protest Diffusion," *American Behavioral Scientist* 57 (July 2013): 943–965.

78. Mayo Fuster Morell, "The Free Culture and 15M Movements in Spain: Composition, Social Networks and Synergies," *Social Movement Studies* 11, no. 3–4 (August 1, 2012): 386–392, https://doi.org/10.1080/14742837.2012.710323.

79. Zeynep Tufekci, *Twitter & Teargas* (2016).

80. Nagla Rizk, Lina Attalah, and Nadine Weheba, *The Networked Public Sphere and Civic Engagement in Post-2011 Egypt: A Local Perspective.*, http://www.arabnps.org/egypt/.

81. Escander Nagazi, Jazem Halioui, and Fares Mabrouk, *An Accelerated Story of the Emergence and Transformation of the Networked Public Sphere: The Case of Tunisia*, http://www.arabnps.org/tunisia/.

82. E. Bakshy, S. Messing, and L.A. Adamic, "Exposure to Ideologically Diverse News and Opinion on Facebook," *Science* 348, no. 6239 (June 5, 2015): 1130–1132, https://doi.org/10.1126/science.aaa1160.

83. Tyler Durden, "Zero Hedge, Saudi Arabia Has Funded 20% Of Hillary's Presidential Campaign, Saudi Crown Prince Claims," http://www.zerohedge.com/news/2016-06-13/saudi-arabia-has-funded-20-hillarys-presidential-campaign-saudi-crown-prince-claims; republished http://nation.foxnews.com/2016/06/14/saudi-arabia-has-funded-20-hillarys-presidential-campaign-saudi-crown-prince-claims; https://www.infowars.com/saudi-arabia-has-funded-20-of-hillarys-presidential-campaign-saudi-crown-prince-claims/.

84. John T. Jost et al., "Political Conservatism as Motivated Social Cognition.," *Psychological Bulletin* 129, no. 3 (2003): 339–375, https://doi.org/10.1037/0033-2909.129.3.339.

85. Ariel Malka, Yphtach Lelkes, and Christopher J. Soto, "Are Cultural and Economic Conservatism Positively Correlated? A Large-Scale Cross-National Test," *British Journal of Political Science*, May 30, 2017, 1–25, https://doi.org/10.1017/S0007123417000072.; Ariel Malka, Yphtach Lelkes, and Nissan Holzer, "Rethinking the Rigidity of the Right Model," *in* Jarret T. Crawford and Lee J. Jussim, eds., *The Politics of Social Psychology*, Frontiers of Social Psychology (NewYork: Routledge, Taylor & Francis Group, 2018).

86. Stefano DellaVigna and Ethan Kaplan, "The Fox News Effect: Media Bias and Voting," 122(3) *QJE* 122 no. 3 (August 2007): 1187–1234.

87. Gregory J. Martin and Ali Yurukoglu, *Bias in Cable News: Persuasion and Polarization.*, NBER Working Paper, April 5, 2017.

88. Matthew Gentzkow and Jesse M. Shapiro, "What drives media slant? Evidence from US daily newspapers," *Econometrica*, 2010, 78 no. (1), (2010): 35–71.

89. Gottfried, Barthel, and Mitchell, "Trump, Clinton Voters Divided in Their Main Source for Election News."

90. Pew Jan. 12–27 2016 survey., http://www.journalism.org/2016/02/04/the-2016-presidential-campaign-a-news-event-thats-hard-to-miss/.

91. "How the 2016 Vote Broke Down by Race, Gender, and Age—Decision Desk HQ," accessed April 6, 2018, https://decisiondeskhq.com/data-dives/how-the-2016-vote-broke-down-by-race-gender-and-age/. (based on CCES Common Content 2016).

92. Elisa Shearer and Jeffrey Gottfried, "News Use Across Social Media Platforms 2017," *Pew Research Center's Journalism Project* (blog), September 7, 2017, http://www.journalism.org/2017/09/07/news-use-across-social-media-platforms-2017/.

93. Alec Tyson and Shiva Maniam, "Behind Trump's Victory: Divisions by Race, Gender, Education," *Pew Research Center* (blog), November 9, 2016, http://www.pewresearch.org/fact-tank/2016/11/09/behind-trumps-victory-divisions-by-race-gender-education/.

94. Levi Boxell, Matthew Gentzkow, and Jesse M. Shapiro, *PNAS* 114, no.(40) (October 3, 2017): 10612–10617 (Oct. 3, 2017), http://www.pnas.org/cgi/doi/10.1073/pnas.1706588114.

CHAPTER 12

1. Henry Farrell, "The Consequences of the Internet for Politics," *Annual Review of Political Science* 15, no. 1 (June 15, 2012): 35–52, https://doi.org/10.1146/annurev-polisci-030810-110815.

2. Bruce A. Bimber, *Information and American Democracy: Technology in the Evolution of Political Power*, Communication, Society, and Politics (Cambridge, UK; New York: Cambridge University Press, 2003); David Karpf, *The MoveOn Effect: The Unexpected Transformation of American Political Advocacy*, Oxford Studies in Digital Politics (New York: Oxford University Press, 2012).

3. Eszter Hargittai, Jason Gallo, and Matthew Kane, "Cross-Ideological Discussions among Conservative and Liberal Bloggers," *Public Choice* 134, no. 1–2 (November 20, 2007): 67–86, https://doi.org/10.1007/s11127-007-9201-x; Eric Lawrence, John Sides, and Henry Farrell, "Self-Segregation or Deliberation? Blog Readership, Participation, and Polarization in American Politics," *Perspectives on Politics* 8, no. 01 (March 2010): 141, https://doi.org/10.1017/S1537592709992714; Matthew Gentzkow and Jesse M. Shapiro, "Ideological Segregation Online and Offline," The *Quarterly Journal of Economics* 126, no. 4 (2011): 1799–1839.

4. Henry Farrell and Daniel W. Drezner, "The Power and Politics of Blogs," *Public Choice* 134, no. 1–2 (November 20, 2007): 15–30, https://doi.org/10.1007/s11127-007-9198-1; Kevin Wallsten, "Agenda Setting and the Blogosphere: An Analysis of the Relationship between Mainstream Media and Political Blogs: Agenda Setting and the Blogosphere," *Review of Policy Research* 24, no. 6 (December 17, 2007): 567–587, https://doi.org/10.1111/j.1541-1338.2007.00300.x.

5. Yochai Benkler, *The Wealth of Networks: How Social Production Transforms Markets and Freedom* (New Haven, CT: Yale University Press, 2006).

6. *Id.* Benkler; Clay Shirky, *Here Comes Everybody: The Power of Organizing without Organizations: [With an Updated Epilogue]*, Nachdr. (New York, NY; Toronto; London: Penguin Books, 2009); Bruce Bimber, Andrew Flanagin, and Cynthia Stohl, "Collective Action in Organizations: Interaction and Engagement in an Era of Technological Change: Cambridge University Press, New York, 2012, 224 Pp., Appendices, References, Index, $29.99 (Paperback)," *Voluntas: International Journal of Voluntary and Nonprofit Organizations* 25, no. 3 (June 2014): 847–848, https://doi.org/10.1007/s11266-013-9413-2; W. Lance Bennett and Alexandra Segerberg, "THE LOGIC OF CONNECTIVE ACTION: Digital Media and the Personalization of Contentious Politics," *Information, Communication & Society* 15, no. 5 (June 2012): 739–768, https://doi.org/10.1080/1369118X.2012.670661.

7. Zeynep Tufekci, *Twitter and Tear Gas: The Power and Fragility of Networked Protest* (New Haven, CT; London: Yale University Press, 2017).

8. Micah L Sifry, *The Big Disconnect Why the Internet Hasn't Transformed Politics (Yet)* (New York: OR Books, 2014); "The Decembrist: Dean's Penguin, or Technology and the Nature of Political Interaction," accessed January 29, 2018, http://markschmitt.typepad.com/decembrist/2003/12/deans_pengun_or.html.

9. Micah L. Sifry, "Obama's Lost Army," *The New Republic*, February 9, 2017, https://newrepublic.com/article/140245/obamas-lost-army-inside-fall-grassroots-machine.

10. Alexis C. Madrigal, "When the Nerds Go Marching In," *The Atlantic*, November 16, 2012, https://www.theatlantic.com/technology/archive/2012/11/when-the-nerds-go-marching-in/265325/.

11. Adam D.I. Kramer, Jamie E. Guillory, and Jeffrey T. Hancock, "Experimental Evidence of Massive-Scale Emotional Contagion through Social Networks," *Proceedings of the National Academy of Sciences* 111, no. 24 (June 17, 2014): 8788–8790, https://doi.org/10.1073/pnas.1320040111.

12. Zeynep Tufekci, "Engineering the Public: Big Data, Surveillance and Computational Politics," *First Monday* 19, no. 7 (July 7, 2014), https://doi.org/10.5210/fm.v19i7.4901.

13. Shoshana Zuboff, "Big Other: Surveillance Capitalism and the Prospects of an Information Civilization," *Journal of Information Technology* 30, no. 1 (March 2015): 75–89, https://doi.org/10.1057/jit.2015.5.

14. For a brief overview, see Alice Marwick and Rebecca Lewis, "Media Manipulation and Disinformation Online" (Data & Society, May 15, 2017), 7–9, https://datasociety.net/pubs/oh/DataAndSociety_MediaManipulationAndDisinformationOnline.pdf. For the leading academic treatments, see Andrea Braithwaite, "It's About Ethics in Games Journalism? Gamergaters and Geek Masculinity," *Social*

Media + Society 2, no. 4 (November 2016): 205630511667248, https://doi.org/
10.1177/2056305116672484.

15. Adrienne Massanari, "#Gamergate and The Fappening: How Reddit's Algorithm, Governance, and Culture Support Toxic Technocultures," *New Media & Society* 19, no. 3 (March 1, 2017): 329–346, https://doi.org/10.1177/1461444815608807.

16. Shira Chess and Adrienne Shaw, "A Conspiracy of Fishes, or, How We Learned to Stop Worrying About #GamerGate and Embrace Hegemonic Masculinity," *Journal of Broadcasting & Electronic Media* 59, no. 1 (March 11, 2015): 208–220, https://doi.org/10.1080/08838151.2014.999917.

17. The Free Republic Forum was one of the first such examples on the right. See Yochai Benkler, "Free As the Air to Common Use: First Amendment Constraints on Enclosure of the Public Domain," *New York University Law Review* 74, no. 2 (May 1999): 354–446. The Dan Rather takedown was every bit as prominent as Trent Lott's demise in the early discussions of online mobilization. See Yochai Benkler, *The Wealth of Networks: How Social Production Transforms Markets and Freedom* (New Haven, CT: Yale University Press, 2006), chap. 7.

18. Marwick and Lewis, "Media Manipulation and Disinformation Online."

19. Yochai Benkler, "CORRESPONDENCE: A New Era of Corruption?," *The New Republic*, March 4, 2009, https://newrepublic.com/article/61997/correspondence-new-era-corruption.

CHAPTER 13

1. Nolan McCarty, "Polarization Is Real (and Asymmetric)," *The Monkey Cage* (blog), May 15, 2012, http://themonkeycage.org/2012/05/polarization-is-real-and-asymmetric/; David Karol, "Defining Dissidence Down," *The Monkey Cage* (blog), May 9, 2012, http://themonkeycage.org/2012/05/defining-dissidence-down/.

2. Matthew Sheffield, "The Conservative Media Echo Chamber Is Making the Right Intellectually Deaf," *National Review*, August 4, 2016, https://www.nationalreview.com/2016/08/fox-news-conservative-media-echo-chamber-hurts-conservatives/; David French, "The Drive to Become 'Fox News Famous' Hurts the Right," *National Review*, August 30, 2016, https://www.nationalreview.com/2016/08/fox-news-hurts-conservative-movement/.

3. Julian Sanchez, "Frum, Cocktail Parties, and the Threat of Doubt," *Julian Sanchez* (blog), March 26, 2010, http://www.juliansanchez.com/2010/03/26/frum-cocktail-parties-and-the-threat-of-doubt/.

4. Maxwell T. Boykoff and Jules M. Boykoff, "Balance as Bias: Global Warming and the US Prestige Press," *Global Environmental Change* 14, no. 2 (July 2004): 125–136, https://doi.org/10.1016/j.gloenvcha.2003.10.001.

5. Derek J. Koehler, "Can Journalistic 'False Balance' Distort Public Perception of Consensus in Expert Opinion?," *Journal of Experimental Psychology: Applied* 22, no. 1 (March 2016): 24–38, https://doi.org/10.1037/xap0000073.

6. Bill Chappell, "'Washington Post' Says It Foiled Apparent Sting By James O'Keefe's Activist Group," *NPR*, November 28, 2017, https://www.npr.org/sections/thetwo-way/2017/11/28/566911256/washington-post-says-it-foiled-apparent-sting-by-james-okeefes-activist-group.

7. Danah Boyd, "You Think You Want Media Literacy … Do You?," Data & Society: Points, March 9, 2018, https://points.datasociety.net/you-think-you-want-media-literacy-do-you-7cad6af18ec2.

8. Nic Dias and Claire Wardle, "10 Questions to Ask before Covering Misinformation," *First Draft*, September 29, 2017, https://firstdraftnews.org/10-questions-newsrooms/.

9. Philip Oltermann and Pádraig Collins, "Two Members of Germany's Far-Right Party Investigated by State Prosecutor," *The Guardian*, January 2, 2018, http://www.theguardian.com/world/2018/jan/02/german-far-right-mp-investigated-anti-muslim-social-media-posts.

10. *Zeran v. America Online, Inc.*, 129 F.3d 327 (4th Cir. 1997); *Jones v. Dirty World Entertainment Recordings LLC*, 755 F.3d 398 (6th Cir. 2014).

11. Kenneth Olmstead et al., "How Americans Get TV News at Home" (Pew Research Center, October 11, 2013), http://www.journalism.org/2013/10/11/how-americans-get-tv-news-at-home/.

12. Amy Mitchell et al., "The Modern News Consumer—3. Loyalty and Source Attention" (Pew Research Center, July 7, 2016), http://www.journalism.org/2016/07/07/loyalty-and-source-attention/.

13. *Id.*

14. Matthew S. Petersen, "FEC Advisory Opinion 2010-19: Concurring Statement of Chairman Matthew S. Petersen," *Perma.cc*, December 30, 2010, https://perma.cc/WK2L-CHZ5.

15. Marc Eric Elias, "Facebook Request for Advisory Opinion," *Perma.cc*, April 26, 2011, https://perma.cc/6543-DUD6.

16. Joshua Green and Sasha Issenberg, "Inside the Trump Bunker, With Days to Go," *Bloomberg*, October 27, 2016, https://www.bloomberg.com/news/articles/2016-10-27/inside-the-trump-bunker-with-12-days-to-go.

17. Julia Angwin, Madeleine Varner, and Ariana Tobin, "Facebook Enabled Advertisers to Reach 'Jew Haters,'" *ProPublica*, September 14, 2017, sec. Machine Bias, https://www.propublica.org/article/facebook-enabled-advertisers-to-reach-jew-haters.

18. David M.J. Lazer et al., "The Science of Fake News," *Science* 359, no. 6380 (March 9, 2018): 1094–1096, https://doi.org/10.1126/science.aao2998.

19. Hans Martens, "Evaluating Media Literacy Education: Concepts, Theories and Future Directions," *Journal of Media Literacy Education* 2 (January 2010): 1–22.
20. danah boyd, "You Think You Want Media Literacy...Do You?," March 9, 2018, https://points.datasociety.net/you-think-you-want-media-literacy-do-you-7cad6af18ec2.

CHAPTER 14

1. Yochai Benkler, "Network Pragmatism: Towards an Open Social Economy," in *Towards a Participatory Society: New Roads to Social and Cultural Integration*, ed. M. Archer, P. Donati, and M. Sánchez Sorondo, Proceedings of the Pontifical Academy of Social Sciences, Acta 21, Vatican City, 2017.

Index

Note: Page numbers followed by the italicized letters *f*, *n*, or *t* indicate material found in figures, notes or tables.

ABC News
  Clinton Foundation stories on, 199
  cross media inlinks to, 63
  Facebook shares of, 54*t*, 70*f*
  FBI coverage by, 181
  as media source, 50*t*
  in open web link economy, 49
  popularity of, 283*t*
  Ross's reporting on, 216
  Trump's Fake News award to, 183
  trust in, 325*f*
  Twitter shares of, 52*t*, 69*f*
  on voter fraud, 260
Abedin, Huma, 95, 96, 203, 211–212, 230
Abramovic, Marina, 227, 231
Abramowitz, Alan, 301–303, 308
Abrams, Samuel J., 302
Achen, Christopher, 304
Acorn, 261
activists
  agenda setting and, 213
  on the alt-right, 223, 347
  campaign role of, 12, 331
  in centralized/decentralized
    organizations, 343–344
  in deep state frame, 151
  disinformation and, 367
  document dumps and, 358
  focus/ideological positions of, 76, 78
  internet effect and, 383
  on-line media use by, 73

  as percent of electorate, 302
  polarization of, 303, 309
  Russian interference and, 102
  social media influence and, 240–241
actors, in information disorder. *See also*
    bots; Cambridge Analytica
  alt-right trolls, 11–13, 21*f*, 22*f*,
    225, 232
  Facebook News Feed algorithm, 10–11,
    280, 287
  "fake news" entrepreneurs, 9, 11, 41,
    71, 351
  mainstream media, 16–18, 148*f*, 149*f*,
    189–196, 214–220, 317, 318
  mapping of, 20–23
  online echo chambers and, 10–11
  political clickbait fabricators, 9, 15, 23,
    33, 41, 92, 269, 279–288
  right-wing media ecosystem, 13–16
  Russian hackers, 9–10, 21*f*, 22*f*, 102,
    159, 192
  sockpuppets, 9–10, 21–22*f*, 102,
    240–243, 254, 259, 329, 346,
    368–369, 372–374
  white supremacists, 11–13, 132
Adamic, Lada, 330
Addicting Info, 54, 54*t*, 70, 70*f*, 86, 87*f*,
    282*t*, 283, 285*t*, 287
Adl-Tabatabai, Sean, 244, 253
ads. *See* dark ads; Honest Ads Act;
    political advertising

Network Propaganda. Yochai Benkler, Robert Faris, and Hal Roberts.
© Yochai Benkler, Robert Faris, and Hal Roberts 2018. Published 2018 by Oxford University Press.

Adweek, 311
affective polarization, 306–307
African American voters, 242, 260,
    270–271, 370
agenda setting, 17, 98, 101–102, 106–114,
    258–259, 291, 342, 373, 383
Agnew, Spiro, 318
Ailes, Roger, 321–323
Alcott, Hunt, 71, 286
All Channel Receiver Act, 319–321
Allcott, Hunt, 286
Alternative for Germany (AfD) party,
    363, 366
alt-right trolls
    definition of, 11–13
    in on-line echo chambers, 22*f*
    in media echo system, 21*f*, 225, 232
Amazon, 50*t*
America First Committee, 182, 316
"America First" message, 107
The American Prospect, 316
The American Voter (study of voter
    behavior), 304
AM radio, 320–321, 382
Amusing Ourselves to Death
    (Postman), 28
Andris, Clio, 296
anti-semitism, 103, 125, 128, 130–131
Arab Spring, 147, 149, 332–333, 343
Armstrong, Edwin, 321
*Army Field Manual of Psychological
    Operations*, 26
Assange, Julian, 140, 147, 159, 161, 163,
    248, 266
Associated Press (AP), 176, 207, 213–214,
    356
*Asymmetric Politics: Ideological Republicans
    and Group Interest Democrats*
    (Grossman and Hopkins), 300
asymmetry/asymmetric polarization.
    See also network maps; talk radio;
    trust/distrust in media/journalism
    cable deregulation and, 319, 348, 382
    cross media inlinks, 63*f*
    Facebook-based, 53–54
    internet/technology and, 329–337
    open web view of, 48–51

origins of, 313–318
partisan distribution, 55*f*, 56*f*, 63*f*
patterns of authority/attention in,
    54–56
political impact assessment of, 337–339
in post-election period, 60–65
presentation of data, 46–48
social media patterns in, 65–73
top 50 sites of left/right, 64*t*
Twitter-based, 51–53
The Atlantic, 50*t*, 69, 70*f*, 282*t*, 341
attention backbone, 33

Baer, Steve, 92
Bagdikian, Ben, 28, 318
Baier, Bret, 94, 96, 97, 215, 311
Baker, C. Edwin, 28, 314, 318
Band, Doug, 203, 211–212
Bannon, Steve, 40, 54, 97, 131–132, 167,
    196–197, 214, 262, 275, 355
Barnhill, Anne, 30
Bartels, Larry, 304
BBC, 15, 50*t*, 69*f*, 70*f*, 73, 114*t*, 184, 227,
    244, 282*t*, 324, 325*f*, 328
Beck, Glenn, 15, 83, 98, 323–324, 325*f*,
    328, 367
Beeley, Vanessa, 244
behavioral marketing, 21–22*t*, 41, 223,
    269, 272–274, 276, 278–279, 361,
    385, 426n19
Berinsky, Adam, 312
Bernays, Edward, 26, 27
BernieSanders.com, 50*t*, 282*t*
Berry, Jeffrey, 311–312
Bershidsky, Leonid, 249
bias confirmation
    liberal media and, 348–349
    in on-line media, 334–336
    in media ecosystem, 74, 328, 355
    media strategy of, 84–85
    polarization and, 290
    professional journalistic organizations
        and, 359
    in propaganda feedback loop, 80–82
    in realty-check dynamic, 78–79
    in Trump rape stories, 92
Bias of Communications (Innis), 281

Big League Politics, 247

Binney, William, 248, 250–253, 250*f*

Bipartisan Report, 54, 54*t*, 70, 70*f*, 86, 87*f*, 282, 282*t*, 283, 285*t*, 287

"black box" algorithms, 10–11

Blackburn, Marsha, 138, 201–202

Black Lives Matter, 227, 343

black propaganda. *See* propaganda

Blacktivist, 242, 262

blogosphere, 237, 311, 312, 330–333

Bloom, Lisa, 91

Bloomberg, 152–153, 176, 208*f*, 218, 249, 254, 262, 270

Botometer, 264

bots
    definition of, 9–10
    difficulty spotting/finding, 43, 264–265
    in echo chamber creation, 4
    in epistemic crisis, 20, 21–22*t*
    influence of, 52–53, 240, 372, 375, 379
    Russian interference and, 236–237, 242–243, 254, 259, 267–268

Boxell, Levi, 339

Boxer, Barbara, 211–212

Boykoff, Jules, 356

Boykoff, Maxwell, 356

Brazile, Donna, 194–195, 195*f*

Breitbart
    on California motor voter law, 35
    Clinton Cash coverage, 167, 171, 197, 199, 201–202, 255
    on Clinton Foundation, 132–133, 214
    on Clinton pedophilia frame, 96–97
    "deep state" coverage, 151–153, 155, 158, 176, 245
    in disinformation ecosystem, 348, 355
    DNC hack coverage, 250
    Facebook shares of, 54*t*, 68*f*, 115–117*t*, 207
    founding of, 81, 331
    Fox News comparison, 61, 63, 66–67, 67*t*, 69, 71, 93
    "globalist" term usage on, 129–130
    on immigration, 4, 18, 59, 101, 103, 108–109, 108–109*f*, 111–112, 111*f*, 114, 124–129, 132, 263, 268

    influence/prominence of, 56, 57–60
    inlinks to, 64*t*
    as media source, 50*t*, 51–54, 52*t*
    monthly visits to, 158*f*
    most linked-to stories on, 121–123*t*
    in open web link economy, 49
    in positive feedback loops, 220, 224
    radicalization and, 14
    Trump election and, 7
    Twitter-shared stories, 47, 68*f*, 113*t*, 118–120*t*
    on voter fraud, 260

Brexit, 4, 28. *See also* European Union

Breyer, Jessica, 12

Broderick, Juanita, 95

Brown, Jerry, 35, 35*f*, 115*t*

Buchanan, Pat, 4, 107

"bullshit," definition of, 24, 32–33

Burkman, Jack, 163–164

Bush, George H. W., 7, 106

Bush, George W., 7, 14, 107, 181, 312, 325–326, 337

Bush, Jeb, 3, 14, 57, 268, 292, 376

Business Insider, 50*t*, 69*f*, 114*t*, 283*t*

Business Week, 49, 50*t*, 52*t*, 283*t*

Butkowsky, Ed, 163

BuzzFeed
    "Ending the Fed" site and, 232
    "fake news" term/stories in, 3, 9, 269
    influence of, 331
    journalistic reporting on, 385
    media inlinks for, 50*t*
    on Pizzagate story, 398*n*30
    popularity rank of, 282*t*
    Scaramucci story and, 218
    social media shares, 52*t*, 69*f*, 140
    Steele Dossier publication, 147, 153

cable deregulation, 319, 348, 382

cable news, 19, 45, 292, 311

Cambridge Analytica, 11, 41, 43, 71, 223, 269–272, 275–279, 290, 341, 351, 361, 368, 375, 385

Campbell, Duncan, 252

Cardin, Ben, 219

Carlson, Tucker, 145, 148, 154, 156, 179, 250, 250*f*, 311

Carter, Adam, 246–249, 251
Casey, Doug (Tyler Durden), 150–151
Cato Institute, 354
Cavuto, Neil, 179
CBS News, 50*t*, 69*f*, 282*t*, 325*f*
Center for Immigration Studies (CIS), 108*f*, 109, 109*t*, 111–112, 348
Cernovich, Mike, 225–227, 229–233
Chagoury, Gilbert, 203
Chess, Shira, 346
Chomsky, Noam, 27–28, 318
Christian broadcasting, 319–320, 322
Christian Broadcasting Network (CBN), 320, 322
Christians. *See* evangelical Christians
Circa News, 173, 176, 180
Civil Rights Act (1964), 297
Clark, Justin, 231
Clear Channel Communications, 322–323
clickbait fabricators
    as commercial bullshit, 33
    definition of, 9
    Facebook algorithms and, 279–288
    "fake news" focus of, 269
    partisanship and, 15, 23
    political purpose and, 92
    skepticism about, 41
Clinton, Bill
    Clinton Foundation and, 135–136, 167, 174, 177, 180, 199, 202–205, 207, 211, 213
    pedophilia/sex scandal frame and, 39, 85, 93–97, 229–230
Clinton, Hillary. *See also* hillaryclinton.com
    automated/fake account messages and, 10
    campaign funding and, 3
    corruption frame, 103–104
    email investigation, 95, 96, 102
    email-related stories, 189–196, 190*f*, 193–194*f*
    immigration frame, 119*t*, 122*t*
    media coverage of, 17, 40, 262
    media ecosystem and, 99
    Muslims/Islamic terrorism frame, 115*t*, 116*t*, 117*t*, 118*t*

open web mentions of, 17*f*
pedophilia libel and, 3, 39, 82, 85–91, 92–93, 96–97, 99
Republican Party radicalization and, 7
in right-wing media ecosystem, 36–37
Trump's conspiracy theories about, 201
2016 presidential election, 48
voters' news sources, 72
Clinton Cash, 115*t*, 143, 167–168, 170–171, 185, 197, 199–201, 203, 204–206*f*, 255
Clinton Foundation
    EPA/Mosaic Fertilizer story, 137–139
    Islamophobia and, 132–137
    news segment mentions on, 209–210*f*
    online linking practices for stories on, 202*f*, 211*f*
    open web mentions of, 204–207*f*
    Podesta email dump and, 139–144
    reports of investigations on, 201–202
    right-wing media coverage of, 197, 198*f*
    social media shares about, 211–212, 212*f*
    television coverage of, 203, 205, 207
Clinton Health Access Initiative (CHAI), 135–136
Cloudflare, 12
CNN
    attention/social attention to, 67
    Blacktivist coverage, 242
    cable deregulation and, 319
    Clinton Foundation coverage by, 205, 207, 208*f*
    "deep state" stories on, 154*f*
    on DNC emails, 256
    Donna Brazile and, 195
    error detection/correction and, 216–219
    Facebook shares of, 54*t*, 68*f*
    Fake News Awards and, 183
    false equivalency and, 16
    Fox News comparison, 83–85, 311, 323, 335
    ideological positions and, 325*f*
    immigration mentions on, 108*f*, 109*f*, 127*f*
    Limbaugh on, 183

as media source, 50*t*, 72, 108, 110*t*, 324
in open web link economy, 48–50, 52
partisan slant of, 338
PolitiFact scoring for, 84*f*, 85*f*
popularity of, 282*t*
Seth Rich conspiracy theory and, 163, 165
Twitter shares of, 52*t*, 68*f*
Uranium One conspiracy theory/story on, 186*f*
Cohn, Gary D., 131
Colbert, Stephen, 323
Cold War, 243, 316
Coleman, Gabriella, 12
Comet Pizza, 3, 231. *See also* "Pizzagate" conspiracy
Comey, James, 39, 95, 96, 154*f*, 161–162, 175–176, 179, 181, 191–192, 193*f*, 217, 255, 270, 406*n*51
Committee on Political Information, 27
Committee on Public Information, 25
Communications Decency Act (CDA), 364–365
conservative media
audience for, 328
Breitbart/Fox News influence, 57–60
confrontations in, 312
epistemic closure and, 354
magazines/publications in, 316
vs. mainstream media, 317
on PolitiFact, 82
reach of, 318
Uranium One conspiracy theory in, 170
conspiracy theories. *See also* deep state; "Pizzagate" conspiracy; Seth Rich conspiracy theory; Uranium One conspiracy theory/story
on left/right news site comparison, 15
Trump's embrace of, 18
Converse, Philip, 304
Coughlin, Charles (Father Coughlin), 314, 316, 382
Council of Europe, 23
Craddick, William, 248
Creel Committee, 25
"Crossfire" (CNN), 107

CrowdStrike, 239, 248
Cruz, Ted, 18, 108*f*, 353
cyborgs, 240, 243. *See also* bots

Dacey, Amy, 256
Daily Beast, 50*t*, 52*t*, 64*t*, 69*f*, 70*f*, 91–92, 151, 242, 263, 282
Daily Caller
on Clinton Foundation, 133–139, 135*f*, 197, 201–202, 214
on Clinton pedophilia frame, 93–95
on deep state frame, 176
Facebook shares of, 54*t*, 70, 70*f*
immigration stories in, 108, 108*f*, 114*t*, 127, 127*f*
inlinks to, 64*t*
on ISIS funding email, 141
as media source, 50*t*, 52
media source sharing and, 47
in open web link economy, 49
popularity of, 284*t*
radicalization and, 14
in right-wing media ecosystem, 82, 334
Twitter shares of, 52*t*, 69*f*
Daily Kos, 52, 52*t*, 54, 54*t*, 69–70*f*, 74, 282*t*, 331, 347
Daily Mail, 49, 50*t*, 64*t*, 69*f*, 70*f*, 91, 93, 95, 114*t*, 284*t*
Daily Stormer, 12, 124, 127*f*, 230, 248, 360, 365
dark ads, 223, 274, 290. *See also* political advertising
Data & Society Institute, 23, 359
DCLeaks, 239, 242, 246, 255
Dean, Howard, 331, 343–344
deep state
in center right media, 353
conspiracy theories about, 195
Dobbs on, 215
in Fox News' framing, 39, 103, 147–158, 226
Gateway Pundit on, 176
Hannity on, 163, 292
media inlinks to, 156*f*
news segment mentions on, 154*f*
Russian interference and, 244–246, 248, 253, 268

deep state (*Cont.*)
  term usage, 147
  in top media, 149*f*
  Trump's references to, 18, 145
  in 2016 election, 103
defamation laws, 376
Deibert, Ronald, 238
DeLay, Tom, 322
DellaVigna, Stefano, 337–339
democracy
  echo chambers and, 5
  folk theory of, 304
  survival of, 289–293
  threats to, 4
"Democracy Now!" 155, 323
Democratic National Committee. *See*
    DNC email hacking/leaking
Democratic National Convention,
    132, 163, 190, 196, 199, 201, 214,
    239, 255
Dent, Charlie, 295
Department of Justice (DOJ), 138, 154*f*,
    174–175, 181, 184–185, 193*f*
Derakhshan, Hossein, 23
Deutsch, Donny, 94
Digital Millennium Copyright Act
    (DMCA), 364
Dimitriev, Kirill, 218
Disconnect (Fiorina and Abrams), 302
disinformation. *See also* "Fake News"
    entrepreneurs
  activists and, 367
  definition of, 24, 32
  hate speech and, 366
  prevalence of, 71
  in right-wing media ecosystem, 13
  Russian campaigns of, 3
  susceptibility/vulnerability to, 8, 268,
    329, 347–348
  through social media, 6
  trust/distrust in media/journalism
    and, 387
Disobedient Media, 248, 251
disorientation
  definition of, 24
  propaganda and, 36–37
distraction, propaganda and, 35

distrust. *See* trust/distrust in media/
    journalism
DNC email hacking/leaking, 9–10, 146,
    159, 239–240, 242, 245–250, 255–257,
    256–257*t*
Dobbs, Lou, 130, 130*f*, 153–154, 168, 178,
    178*f*, 179, 185, 214
DonaldJTrump.com, 50*t*, 64*t*, 110*t*,
    284*t*
doxxing, 239, 245, 255, 346
Drake, Thomas, 252
Drudge Report, 81, 223, 225, 226, 231, 233,
    245, 329–330
Durden, Tyler (Doug Casey), 150–151
DW-NOMINATE, 297–299

echo chambers
  creation of, 4
  definition of, 10–11
  in pluralist democracies, 5
EcoWatch, 219
Einstein, Katherine Levine, 34
Eisenhower, Dwight D., 148
Ellul, Jacques, 27, 28
emails
  Clinton investigation and, 95, 96, 102
  Clinton related stories for, 189–196,
    190*f*, 193–194*f*
  Clinton Foundation and Podesta
    dump of, 139–144
  DNC hacking/leaking of, 9–10, 146,
    159, 239–240, 242, 245–250,
    255–257, 256–257*t*
  Sean Hannity on ISIS funding and,
    143–144
  Clinton coverage in mainstream
    media of, 189–196
  Podesta dump of, 136, 163, 192, 194–195,
    240, 245, 255, 265, 358
  Washington Post stories about, 144,
    195, 213–214, 216–217, 256
The Emerging Republican Majority
    (Phillips), 297
Ending the Fed, 70, 86, 87*f*, 140–144,
    231–232, 282, 284, 284*t*, 285*t*, 288
"Engineering of Consent," 25
"epistemic closure," 354

epistemic crisis
  causes of/explanations for, 11, 20, 351
  Clinton pedophilia libel and, 96–97
  in democratic societies, 348
  Facebook and, 269
  fact checking and, 378
  left/center-left in, 71
  open web and, 51
  partisan shape of, 16, 20–21
  regulation/self-regulation and, 386
  social-identity theory and, 166
  technology and, 22–23, 42, 138, 381
  threat models of, 21*f*, 22*f*
Epstein, Jeffrey, 91, 92–96, 229–230
Erdoğan, Recep Tayyip, 134
error detection/correction (in
    journalism), 214–220
Etling, Bruce, 124, 237
European Union, 4, 235, 238–239,
    253, 289
evangelical Christians, 7, 297, 299, 309,
    319, 320, 370
Evening Standard, 244

Facebook. *See also* Cambridge Analytica
  automated/fake accounts and, 10
  Clinton pedophilia frame and,
      91, 93, 99
  discrimination claims against, 288
  engagement from Trump supporters, 9
  engagement with news stories on, 3
  in first year of Trump
      presidency, 65–72
  immigration discussions/stories on,
      113–114*t*, 115–117*t*
  media sharing on, 54*t*, 68*f*
  media sources on, 285*t*
  microtargeted behavioral marketing
      on, 21–22*t*, 41, 223, 269, 272–274,
      276, 278–279, 361, 385, 426*n*19
  partisan distribution on, 67*f*
  Russian advertising on, 10
  second-tier media source shares
      on, 70*f*
  Seth Rich story shares on, 165*f*
  Trump digital campaign and, 270–274
  in 2016 election period, 53–54

Facebook News Feed algorithm,
    10–11, 280, 287. *See also* clickbait
    fabricators
fact checking, institutionalization of,
    376–378
fact checking sites, 82–85
FactCheck.org, 163, 376
Fairbanks, Cassandra, 226–227, 229–233,
    245–248
Fair Deal/New Deal, 297, 298, 314–316
fairness doctrine (FCC), 314, 317–318,
    321, 348, 382
"fake news" as term, 3
"Fake News Awards," 4, 15, 183*f*, 215,
    217–218, 220
"fake news" entrepreneurs
  definition of, 9
  disinformation and, 71
  epistemic crisis and, 11, 351
  Facebook-based culprits and, 41
false statements
  by political alignment, 85*f*
  prevalence of, 82–85
Falwell, Jerry, 297. *See also* evangelical
    Christians
Faulkner, Harris, 179
fear/fear mongering
  appeals to, 31
  Cambridge Analytica and, 276
  by campaigns, 274
  of immigrants, 132
  of internet effects, 383, 386
  of liability, 364
  mobilization of, 132
  of Muslims/Islamist terrorism, 18, 101,
      114, 117, 123
  paranoid reasoning and, 138–139
  of retaliation, 242
  social divides and, 273
  stories to elicit, 4
  white supremacists and, 12
Federal Communications Commission
    (FCC), 314, 317–322
"50 Cent Army," 35, 242
The Filter Bubble (Pariser), 290
filter bubbles, 10–11, 41, 289. *See also* echo
    chambers

Fiorina, Morris, 302
First Amendment
  FCC and, 321
  interpretations of, 366
  protections/violations, 363–364
  Supreme Court and, 313
  white supremacists and, 12
FiveThirtyEight, 50t
Flynn, D. J., 35
Flynn, Michael, 39, 96, 97, 151–153, 154f,
  155, 161, 166, 216, 246, 406n51
FM radio, 321, 348, 381
Focus on the Family, 322
"folk theory" of democracy, 304
Forbes, 50t, 74, 114t, 283t
Forensicator, 155, 245, 247–249, 251–252,
  251f, 354
Fowler, Mark, 321
Fox and Friends, 19, 162–163, 184, 184f,
  215, 247
Fox News. *See also* Uranium One
    conspiracy theory/story
  amplification of radical sites by, 14
  attacks on party of Reagan by, 7
  bias/truth and, 15
  Breitbart comparison, 67t
  on Clinton pedophilia frame, 92–97
  deep state frame and, 147–158
  false equivalency and, 16
  immigration coverage, 127
  vs. Internet, 337–339
  monthly visits to, 158f
  as president's propaganda network,
    145–146
  on Seth Rich conspiracy theory,
    159–166
"Fox News Effect," 337
frames/framing
  of immigration issue/debate, 114, 124
  of issues, 101–102
  use of social media to introduce,
    258–262
Frank, LoBiondo, 295
Frankfurt, Harry, 32
Freedom of Information Act (FOIA),
  137, 192, 203, 207, 213, 225, 255, 358

Free Republic, 329, 330–331
Freitas, Nathan, 252
French, David, 354

Gamergate controversy, 12, 346
Gateway Pundit
  in conservative feedback cycle, 268
  DNC leaks and, 257
  emotionally evocative language in, 31
  Facebook and, 54t, 70, 165, 284
  false equivalency and, 16
  immigration headlines of, 122–123
  manipulation and, 31
  monthly visits to, 158f
  radicalization and, 14
  Russiagate and, 248
  Seth Rich conspiracy theory and,
    160–161, 247
  spirit cooking story and, 231
  Twitter and, 52, 69f, 70–71, 288
  Uranium One story and, 176
  YouTube and, 155
Gawker, 91–92, 93, 255, 376
General Social Survey, 318, 326, 327f
Gentzkow, Matthew, 71, 286, 338–339
Germany
  content removal in, 365–366
  NetzDG law, 12–13, 21, 362–363
  public media in, 21–22, 267
Ghosh, Dipayan, 273, 274
Gingrich, Newt, 94, 95, 97, 163, 167, 168,
  179, 185, 291, 322, 326
Glance, Nancy, 330
"globalist" term usage, 128–131, 129–130f
GoDaddy, 12
González-Bailón, Sandra, 332–333
Goodman, Amy, 155
Google/Google searches, 12, 154f
Gorka, Sebastian, 143, 167, 179, 185
government, role of, 362–365
Government Accountability Initiative
    (GAI), 167, 197, 348, 355
Graepel, Thore, 275
Graham, Franklin, 7. *See also* evangelical
    Christians
gray propaganda. *See* propaganda

Green, Joshua, 270–271
Greenwald, Glenn, 147–148, 152, 154*f*, 155, 236, 245, 252
Grossman, Matthew, 300
groupthink, 238, 252
Guardian, 50*t*, 52*t*, 54*t*, 67, 68*f*, 69*f*, 70, 91–92, 109*f*, 113*t*, 127*f*, 199, 260, 282*t*, 401*n*29, 425*n*101
Guardian Project, 252
Guccifer 2.0, 155, 159–160, 227, 245–247, 249, 251, 251*f*, 253, 255
Guess, Andrew, 286–287
Gulen, Fethullah, 134

Hacker, Jacob, 300
hacking. *See* DNC email hacking/leaking
Hamilton 68 project, 253, 267
Hannity, Sean
    Breitbart and, 115*t*, 123*t*
    "deep state" frame and, 150, 153–154, 292
    Drudge Report and, 225–226
    false statement ratio of, 83, 311
    on ISIS funding email, 143–144
    on journalism, 145
    misdirection of, 180–182
    propaganda feedback loop and, 94–95
    talk radio and, 323
    trust patterns and, 73, 324, 325*f*
    Uranium One story and, 167, 177–179, 185
    on Wikileaks, 162–164
hate speech
    in Europe, 363
    First Amendment and, 364
    as intentional political disinformation, 366
    NetzDG Law and, 13, 21, 362
Hemmer, Nicole, 317
Herman, Edward, 27–28, 318
Hewitt, Hugh, 94
The Hill, 49, 50*t*, 52, 52*t*, 54*t*, 63, 66–67, 68*f*, 91, 109*f*, 110*t*, 114*t*, 127*f*, 166, 170, 171, 173–177, 180–181, 185, 197, 283*t*, 354
hillaryclinton.com, 50*t*, 64*t*, 70*f*, 282*t*
Hindman, Matthew, 330

Hoaxy, 264
Hochschild, Jennifer, 34
Hofstadter, Richard, 136
Hollywood Reporter, 253
Honest Ads Act, 368–371, 373, 375
Hopkins, David, 300
House Intelligence Committee, 154*f*, 231, 235, 241, 246, 274, 292
Huffington Post, 14, 49–50, 50*t*, 52, 52*t*, 54, 54*t*, 64*t*, 67, 71, 82, 86, 91, 92, 110*t*, 114*t*, 195, 282*t*, 331, 334
Human Events (magazine), 182, 316, 317
Hutchins Commission, 314–315

identity confirmation, 77–79, 79*f*, 80–81, 328, 335, 348, 352
IJR (right-wing site), 96
immigration
    agenda setting on, 106–114
    Breitbart's framing/stories on, 4, 59, 108, 121–123*t*
    Facebook-shared stories, 115–117*t*
    fear of Muslims/Islamic terrorism, 114, 117, 123–125, 127
    link-based map of stories on, 111, 111–112*f*
    media outlet mentions of, 108*f*, 109*f*
    "Muslim ban" and, 105–106
    Republican Party and, 106–107
    sites discussing, 109–110*t*, 110*f*, 113–114*t*, 113*f*
    Twitter-shared stories on, 118–120*t*
    white nationalist stories, 126–127*f*
information, sources of political, 45
Infowars, 14, 16, 32, 69*f*, 70–71, 114*t*, 141–142, 143*f*, 158*f*, 245, 253, 263, 268, 284, 284*t*, 288, 334–335, 366–367
Ingraham, Laura, 226, 311, 384
Innis, Harold, 281
Institute for Propaganda Analysis, 26
The Intercept, 147, 152, 155, 251, 252, 256, 283*t*
Internet
    as data-driven control platform, 344–345

Internet (*Cont.*)
democracy's survival and, 289–293
as democratizing technology, 8, 318,
329–337, 341, 342, 345–346, 349, 369
vs. Fox News, 337–339
leaderless/decentralized movements
and, 343
repressive mobs and, 346–347
structured political organizations and,
343–345
susceptibility to disinformation/
propaganda, 347–348
Internet Archive, 73, 141, 205, 219,
401n25, 412n36
Internet Freedom Agenda, 332
Internet Research Agency (IRA), 237,
240–243, 262
interventions/solutions
defamation law and, 376
disclosure/accountability and,
367–368
Honest Ads Act, 367–371, 373, 375
institutionalization of fact checking,
376–378
media literacy education, 378
paid social promotion and, 372–375
platform regulation, 360–362
professional journalism and, 355–359
public health approach, 375
public machine-readable open
database, 371–372
reconstructing center-right media,
353–355
role of government, 362–365
self-regulation, 365–367
Islamophobia, Clinton Foundation and,
132–137
Issenberg, Sasha, 270–271

Jack, Caroline, 23
Jackson, Lisa, 137–138
Jacor Communications, 322–323
Jezebel, 91–92
Johnson, Lyndon, 297, 316
Jones, Alex, 32, 128, 152, 176, 232–233, 253,
263, 366, 376
Jost, John, 335

journalism. *See also* trust/distrust in
media/journalism
disinformation and, 387
error detection/correction in, 214–220
as institutionalized profession, 5–6
objective attributes of, 6
professional journalistic
organizations, 359
in propaganda-rich ecosystem, 355–359
Jowett, Gareth, 28
Judge Jeannine, 168, 178
Judicial Watch, 70f, 114t, 152, 178f, 192,
199, 203, 205, 207, 213–214, 255,
348, 358

Kalmoe, Nathan, 304
Kaplan, Ethan, 337–338
Kasich, John, 353
Khan, Khizr, 115–116t, 143, 197
Kim, Young Mie, 241, 265, 273
Kinder, Donald, 304, 307
King, Gary, 35
King, Martin Luther, Jr., 31, 217
Klobuchar, Amy, 368
Koch brothers, 272
Kogan, Alexander, 275
Kosinski, Michal, 275–276
Kreiss, Daniel, 272
Krugman, Paul, 217
Kucinich, Dennis, 153
Kushner, Jared, 131, 216

Lake, Eli, 152–153
Lane, Rowan Brewer, 93–94
Laswell, Harold, 24, 26
LawNewz, 92
Lawrence, Patrick, 249, 251
Leave campaign (Brexit), 4, 289, 341. *See
also* European Union
Levine, Mark, 312
Lewandowski, Corey, 271
Lewis, Rebecca, 12, 346
lies on TV, prevalence of, 82–85
LifeZette, 226
Limbaugh, Rush
bias/truth and, 15
Congress and, 322

"deep state" frame and, 147, 153
false statement ratio of, 83
"four corners of deceit" and, 37, 183
in political psychology, 335
propaganda feedback loop and, 95, 97
right-wing media development and,
    81, 182
talk radio and, 321
on Trump's voter fraud claim, 261
trust patterns and, 73, 324, 325*f*, 327
on Uranium One story, 176
Lippmann, Walter, 25, 26–27
LiveJournal, 237
Lofgren, Mike, 150
"Lolita Express," 85, 92–97, 137, 214–215,
    220, 230–231, 255
Loomis, Ed, 248
Los Angeles Times, 50*t*, 114*t*, 329, 356
Lubow, Norm, 92
Lucas, Shawn, 247
Luce, Henry, 314
Lugar, Richard, 353

MacArthur, Douglas, 151
Maddow, Rachel, 83, 311
Madrigal, Alexis, 345
mainstream media. *See also* Clinton
    Foundation
  balance/scoop culture of, 189
  circumvention of, 346
  Clinton email coverage in, 189–196
  Clinton Foundation coverage by, 133,
    207, 214
  vs. conservative media, 317
  "deep state" frame and, 148*f*, 149*f*
  definition of, 16–18
  error detection/correction, 214–220
  "fake news" and, 217
  feedback loops and, 336
  Hannity on, 180, 182
  in information disorder, 16–18
  internet democratization and,
    341–342
  in media ecosystem, 331
  national security establishment
    and, 318
  online presence of, 334

PolitiFact scoring for, 85, 85*f*
right-wing criticism of, 317–318, 322
role/influence of, 355–356, 359
sustained attacks on, 358
Trump campaign coverage by, 273
truth-seeking goals of, 81
Malkin, Michelle, 231, 331
Manafort, Paul, 39, 155, 166, 271,
    406*n*51
Manion, Clarence, 316–318
"Manion Forum," 316, 318
manipulation, definition/elements of,
    30–32
Manning, Chelsea, 147, 265, 425*n*101
manufacture of consent, 25
*Manufacturing Consent: The Political
    Economy of the Mass Media*
    (Herman and Chomsky), 27, 318
Marantz, Andrew, 225
Marshall, Brad, 256
Martin, Gregory, 337–338
Marwick, Alice, 12, 346
Mason, Lilliana, 306
Massanari, Adrienne, 346
McAuliffe, Terry, 175
McCabe, Andrew, 175, 181, 353
McCain, John, 261, 368
McCarthyism, 153, 316
McCarty, Nolan, 298
McChesney, Robert, 28, 318
McConnell, Mitch, 83
McGregor, Shannon, 272
"The McLaughlin Group," 107
McMullin, Evan, 130, 130*f*
Media, Markets, and Democracy (Baker),
    28
media literacy education, 378–379
Media Monopoly (Bagdikian), 28, 318
media outlets/sources. *See also* trust/
    distrust in media/journalism;
    specific media outlets
  asymmetric structure of, 291, 318, 348
  "deep state" frame and, 226
  errors/failures in, 104, 220
  Facebook shares in, 54*t*, 165
  fact checking and, 377–378
  fairness doctrine and, 321

media outlets/sources (*Cont.*)
  immigration mentions/debate in,
    108*f*, 132
  most popular, 282–284*t*
  negative coverage emphasis, 40
  network propaganda and, 201
  neutrality/objectivity and, 357
  overlap/interaction between, 48
  partisan-confirming news in, 78
  post-election coverage, 67
  prevalence/success of
    disinformation in, 71
  professional norms and, 236
  propaganda feedback loop and, 33–34,
    233, 328–329
  in realty-check dynamic, 77*f*
  Russia/Russian interference and, 36,
    243
  top 50 sources, 50*t*
  trust/distrust in, 182, 184
  Twitter shares of, 52*t*
Medvedev, Dmitry, 237
memes/meme campaigns, 12–13, 97,
    223, 225–226, 232, 259, 274, 341,
    346–347
Menczer, Filippo, 264
Mercer, Rebekah, 355
Mercer, Robert, 7, 108, 167, 197, 272, 275,
    355
Merlan, Anna, 91
Michigan model (voter theory), 304
microtargeted behavioral marketing,
    21–22*t*, 41, 223, 269, 272–274, 276,
    278–279, 361, 385, 426*n*19
Middle East Eye (MEE), 141–142
military-industrial complex, 148
Miller, Joanne, 312
Miller, Zeke, 217
Mills, Cheryl, 203
misinformation
  definition of, 6, 24
  propaganda and, 37–38
misperceptions, propaganda and, 34–35
Mnuchin, Steven, 219
Moore, Roy, 7, 16, 358
Moral Majority, 297. *See also* evangelical
  Christians

Morell, Mayo Fuster, 333
"Morning Joe," 94
Morozov, Evgeny, 238
Mosaic Fertilizer story, 137–139
Mother Jones, 16, 38, 49, 50*t*, 52*t*, 54, 54*t*,
    69, 69*f*, 70*f*, 74, 282*t*, 316
Moyers, Bill, 150, 297
Moynihan, Daniel Patrick, 6
MSNBC
  asymmetry/asymmetric polarization
    and, 311, 313
  Clinton Cash and, 199
  Clinton Foundation stories on,
    207, 208*f*
  on Clinton pedophilia frame, 94
  deep state mentions by, 154*f*
  Facebook shares of, 54*t*, 70*f*
  Fox News comparison, 83–85, 312, 335
  ideological positions and, 325*f*
  immigration stories on, 127*f*
  influence of, 65
  media inlinks to, 62, 64*t*
  as media source/outlet, 49, 50*t*, 72, 319,
    324
  media strategy of, 323, 383
  partisan slant of, 338
  PolitiFact scoring for, 84–85*f*
  popularity of, 282*t*
  Twitter shares of, 52*t*, 69, 69*f*
  Uranium One conspiracy theory/story
    on, 177–178*f*, 178, 186*f*
Mueller, Robert, 18, 37, 39, 146, 154, 154*f*,
    161, 166–167, 170, 175–176, 181, 184,
    237, 240, 258, 263, 353, 406*n*51
Murdoch, Rupert, 322, 323
Muslims/Islamic terrorism frame, 105–106
MyBarackObama.com (MyBO),
    344–345

Napolitano, Andrew, 153
The Nation, 38, 249–252, 316
National Academies of Sciences, 219
National Review, 20, 49, 50*t*, 166, 283*t*,
    311, 316, 331, 354
national security establishment
  deep state frame and, 248
  Fox News vs., 147–158

Guccifer 2.0 story and, 245, 247
mainstream media and, 318
Republican Party and, 7
Trump on, 145
Nazi content, 12
NBC News, 50*t*, 52*t*, 54*t*, 69*f*, 70*f*, 91, 282*t*, 325*f*
"negative partisanship," 308
negativity
balance and, 189–196
in media coverage, 17, 357
neo-Nazi sites, 12, 124
The Net Delusion (Morozov), 238
network maps
of Clinton Foundation topic, 133*f*
of "Clinton pedophilia" stories, 90*f*
of deep state stories, 156*f*
of election media sources, 48*f*
of Forensicator theory of Guccifer 2.0, 251*f*
of open web media, 49*f*
of political media, 332*f*
of Seth Rich mentions, 164
of Trump coverage, 61*f*, 62*f*
of "Trump rape" stories, 90*f*
of Twitter media sharing, 51*f*, 52*t*, 58*f*, 60*f*, 65*f*
of Uranium One stories, 171–173*f*
network propaganda. *See also* propaganda
definition of, 24, 33
effect of, 22
Fox News and, 92, 146
legislation and, 368
media outlets/sources and, 201, 226
repetition of claims and, 137, 201
reworking of stories for, 139
susceptibility/vulnerability to, 329
system of, 348
as threat to democracy, 38
NetzDG law, 12–13, 21, 362–364
NeverTrumpers, 92, 163
New Deal/Fair Deal, 297, 298, 314–316
The New Republic, 316
New York Daily News, 50*t*
New Yorker, 50*t*, 54*t*, 69, 70*f*, 225, 282*t*, 285

New York Magazine, 50*t*, 91, 249
New York Post, 49, 50*t*, 52, 108, 176, 201, 260, 284*t*
New York Times
bias/truth and, 15
centrality of, 49–50
climate change coverage and, 219–220, 356
on Clinton corruption frame, 104
on data-fueled political campaigns, 273
Facebook shares of, 68*f*, 197, 199
immigration stories in, 109*f*, 109*t*, 111, 113*t*, 242
journalistic norms and, 15
Limbaugh's description of, 183
manipulation of, 40
as media source, 50*t*, 52, 54*t*, 56, 67, 72, 91, 282*t*, 324
New York Times v. Sullivan, 376
reporting on Clinton, 167–168, 171, 191–192, 194, 197, 199, 201–203, 207, 214, 281, 356
reporting on Trump, 93–94, 131–132, 247
study of, 16
trust/distrust in, 328
Twitter shares of, 47, 52*t*, 68*f*
Uranium One stories in, 170, 358
Nix, Alexander, 276, 278
Nixon, Richard, 107, 297, 316, 318, 321
Norquist, Grover, 300
Nothing Is True and Everything is Possible (Pomerantsev), 36
NPR, 15, 50*t*, 62, 64*t*, 65, 69*f*, 70, 70*f*, 72, 73, 114*t*, 282*t*, 323–324, 325*f*, 328
Nyhan, Brendan, 34, 286–287

Obama, Barack, 108, 326, 345. *See also* MyBarackObama.com (MyBO)
Obama administration, 37, 146, 151, 174, 176, 179–180, 185, 249
objectivity, practice/norms of, 14, 16, 23, 42, 81, 104, 196, 215, 313, 318, 320, 335, 355, 357, 379, 387
Occupy Democrats, 54, 54*t*, 68*f*, 69, 71, 86, 87*f*, 92, 281, 282*t*, 283, 285*t*, 287
Occupy Wall Street, 332

October surprise, 181, 270
O'Donnell, Lawrence, 311
O'Donnell, Victoria, 28
Office of the Director of National
    Intelligence (ODNI), 3, 147, 240,
    244, 245
open web media
    aggregate view of, 48*f*
    Clinton Foundation stories on, 198*f*,
        204–207*f*
    "globalist" term usage in, 129*f*
    media network map, 49*f*
    shift to social media, 333–334
    topics related to Trump/Clinton, 191*f*
    2016 presidential election
        mentions, 17*f*
    Uranium One mentions on, 169–170*f*
O'Reilly, Bill, 83, 260, 311
"Orgy Island" story, 37, 85, 92–97, 182, 220
The Outrage Industry (Berry and
    Sobieraj), 311

Pacifica Radio, 316, 323
Palmer Report, 69, 70, 70*f*, 71, 216
Pan, Jennifer, 35
Pariser, Eli, 290
Parscale, Brad, 270–273, 275
Passman, Sophie, 363
Patterson, Thomas, 16–17, 191, 196, 357
Paul, Ron, 150, 245, 331, 343
PBS, 15, 73, 184, 260, 281, 324, 325*f*, 328
Pelosi, Nancy, 83, 261
Pence, Mike, 152
Persily, Nathaniel, 289
Petra News Agency, 141, 335
Pew Research Center, 109*t*, 111, 307
Phillips, Kevin, 297
Phillips, Whitney, 12
Pierson, Paul, 300, 300
Pirro, Jeannine. *See* Judge Jeannine
pizza, as code word, 230–231, 231*f*
"Pizzagate" conspiracy, 3, 160, 227, 229,
    233, 244, 245, 255, 263, 367, 376
Podesta, John
    email hack/dump, 136, 163, 192,
        194–195, 240, 245, 255, 265, 358
    ISIS funding email, 139, 144

mentions per day during election
    period, 193*f*
Pizzagate and, 229–230
Podesta Group and, 142
in right-wing media ecosystem, 37
Russian propaganda and, 10
Spirit Cooking event and,
    226–227, 354
Podesta, Tony, 142, 227
Podesta Group, 142
polarization. *See also* asymmetry/
    asymmetric polarization
    media dynamics and, 308–310
    of political elites, 295–300
    political identity and, 303–306
    of the public, 300–303
    social identity and, 306–308
    symmetry and, 14
    in U.S. Congress, 299*f*
political advertising, 41–42, 240, 270–271,
    273, 276–277, 366–368, 370–371, 373,
    379, 380, 385
political clickbait fabricators. *See*
    clickbait fabricators
political communications
    architecture of, 46
    asymmetry in, 379
    Cambridge Analytica and, 275
    choices of social media/internet
        firms, 291
    Facebook and, 270
    mechanisms of, 101
    misinformation and, 38
    online platforms in, 45
    paid advertising as, 373
    paid internet as, 369
    Russian interference and, 41
    Tufekci on, 273
political elites
    "deep state" frame and, 226
    internet/technology and, 329
    Islamophobia and, 132
    partisanship and, 139, 302, 308
    platforms for, 383
    polarization of, 291, 295–300, 303–306
    in political landscape, 76, 98
    in propaganda feedback loop, 33, 328

political information, sources of, 45
politicians
  media outlets and, 76
  in realty-check dynamic, 77*f*, 80
Politico, 49, 50*t*, 52, 52*t*, 68*f*, 70*f*, 109*f*,
  110*t*, 127*f*, 195, 197, 207, 216, 245,
  256, 272, 282*t*
PolitiFact, 50*t*, 64*t*, 69*f*, 82–85, 84*f*,
  85*f*, 163, 168, 170, 202, 253, 282*t*,
  311, 376
Pomerantsev, Peter, 36
Pompeo, Mike, 252
Poole, Keith, 298, 299
Postman, Neil, 28
Premier Radio, 323
Priebus, Reince, 107
Prigozhin, Yevgeny, 240
priming, 101–102
Prince, Erik, 96, 97, 233, 398*n*30
Prior, Markus, 330
The Progressive, 316
Project Alamo, 271
Project Veritas, 358
propaganda. *See also* network
  propaganda
  definition/elements of, 6, 24,
    29–30, 80
  effects of, 34–38
  intellectual history of, 24–29
  in markets, 27
  white-/gray-/black-, 32, 95, 159–160,
    239–240, 243–245, 253, 267
Propaganda and Persuasion (*Jowett and*
  O'Donnell), 28
propaganda feedback loop
  definition of, 33
  influence of, 41
  model of, 79*f*
  psychological theory and, 336–337
  vs. reality check dynamic, 85–91
  Republican Party radicalization and, 7
  right-wing media and, 42
"Propaganda Model," of mass media, 27
propaganda pipeline
  definition of, 33–34, 223, 225
  importance of, 12, 40
  spirit cooking story in, 232

transmission of narratives through, 233,
  245
Propaganda: The Formation of Men's
  Attitudes (Ellul), 27
protest orchestration, 263–264
psychographic data, 11, 276
public
  consumption of news by, 76
  in realty-check dynamic, 77*f*
Public Opinion (Lippman), 3, 25, 26
Public Policy Polling, 261
pundits, media outlets and, 76
Putin, Vladimir, 36, 174–175, 180, 235,
  237, 242, 249, 254

Radack, Jesselyn, 252
radicalization, of right-wing media
  ecosystem, 14–16
Raines, Howell, 183
rallies/protests, 263–264
rape accusation, against Donald
  Trump, 91–92
rational voter theory, 304
Raw Story, 52, 52*t*, 54*t*, 69–70, 69–70*f*,
  216–217, 282*t*, 284
Reagan, Ronald, 7, 106–107, 144, 321, 322,
  326
Real Clear Politics, 50*t*, 110*t*, 283*t*
"reality-check dynamic"
  media ecosystem and, 77–78, 80
  model of, 77*f*
Reason, 127*f*, 166, 253, 283*t*
Reddit/subreddit threads, 12, 13, 40, 93,
  161, 223, 226–227, 229, 245, 248, 259,
  346, 360, 416*n*19
RedState, 69–70*f*, 127*f*, 283*t*, 285*t*, 331
regulation, of platforms, 360–362,
  365–367
Reid, Harry, 261
Reifler, Jason, 34, 286–287
religious broadcasting, 314, 319. *See also*
  evangelical Christians
Republican National Committee
  (RNC), 107, 271–272
Republican Party
  "fake news" and, 4
  governance difficulties and, 16

Republican Party (*Cont.*)
  populist right-wing politics and, 4
  Trump Party takeover of, 7
Reuters, 50*t*, 52*t*, 63, 69*f*, 70, 109*t*, 113*t*,
  283*t*
Rich, Seth, 39, 103, 146, 155, 159–166, 160*f*,
  162*f*, 164*f*, 165*f*, 182, 214–215, 220,
  240
Rich Media, Poor Democracy
  (McChesney), 28
right-wing media ecosystem
  behavior of, 13–16
  early success of, 334
  first generation of, 42, 317–319, 321
  second-generation of, 182, 319, 321
Risen, James, 252
Roberts, Margaret, 35
Rohozinski, Rafal, 238
Romney, Mitt, 107, 130, 130*f*
Rooney, Francis, 7
Rosenstein, Rod, 37, 161, 167, 175–176,
  181, 353
Rosenthal, Howard, 298, 299
Ross, Brian, 216
Ross, Dennis, 138
Roth, Zachary, 261
Rothschild, David, 16, 191, 196
Rove, Karl, 272
RT (formerly Russia Today), 36, 142, 150,
  164, 239–240, 243–245, 248–249,
  266*f*, 267
Rubio, Marco, 57, 353
Rusher, William, 311
Russian Direct Investment Fund, 218
Russian interference hypothesis
  conclusions about, 267–268
  cyberattacks on American targets, 235
  existence vs. impact, 239, 241, 245–246,
    250, 252, 254–255
  hacking/doxxing and, 9–10, 239–240,
    255–262
  origins of, 237–239
  propaganda and useful idiots, 243–254
  protest orchestration, 263–264
  skepticism about, 235–236, 245, 247,
    252, 289
  social media influence, 240–243,
    262–263

  Twitter bots and, 264–267
  Ukrainian crisis, 238–239
Russian propaganda
  activists and, 12
  in American media ecosystem, 40–41,
    225, 236
  clickbait factories and, 264
  conspiracy theories and, 160
  disorientation and, 36
  email hacking and, 192, 239
  European Union and, 253
  Facebook and, 10
  generalized trust and, 268
  in German elections, 22
  in right-wing media ecosystem, 329
  RT content and, 244
  sites as pathways for, 254
  susceptibility to, 23
  targets of, 99
  True Pundit and, 267
  in US elections, 235
  WikiLeaks and, 245
Rusyayeva, Polina, 242
Ryan, Paul, 7, 19, 83, 115*t*, 116*t*, 118*t*, 120*t*,
  123*t*

The Saker (pseudonym), 152, 245
Salon, 16, 46, 50*t*, 52, 52*t*, 54, 54*t*, 64*t*,
  69*f*, 70*f*, 195, 250, 282*t*, 406*n*51
Sanchez, Julian, 354
Sanders, Bernie, 193*f*, 199, 200, 227, 239,
  247–248, 255–256, 270, 272, 342.
  See also BernieSanders.com
Sarnoff, David, 320–321
Saunders, Kyle, 301
Scaife, Richard Mellon, 192, 194
Scaife Foundation, 192
Scaramucci, Anthony, 218
Schiff, Adam, 246
Schudson, Michael, 313
Schulz, Debbie Wasserman, 163
Schumer, Chuck, 83
Schweizer, Peter, 166–168, 171, 174, 185,
  197, 199, 202, 214, 356, 358
Scott, Ben, 273, 274
Secured Borders, 241–242, 263
Senate Select Committee on Intelligence,
  246–247

Sessions, Jeff, 119*t*, 181, 185

Seth Rich conspiracy theory, 39, 103, 146, 155, 159–166, 160*f*, 162*f*, 164*f*, 165*f*, 182, 214–215, 220, 240

Seymour, Brittney, 38

Shapiro, Jesse, 338–339

Shaw, Aaron, 330

Shaw, Adrienne, 346

Sheffield, Matthew, 354

Sifry, Micah, 344

Silsby, Laura, 229, 248

Silverman, Craig, 3, 9, 269, 385

Simonyan, Margarita, 244

Sinclair Broadcasting, 163, 173, 361

Skocpol, Theda, 312

Slate, 49, 50*t*, 54, 54*t*, 64*t*, 69, 69*f*, 70*f*, 282*t*

Snowden, Edward, 147, 249

Sobieraj, Sarah, 311–312

social identity/social identity theory, 166, 300, 306–308, 378

social media
  infiltration of, 258–262
  influence of, 240–243
  support for Trump and, 338
  to suppress/split vote, 262–263

social media entrepreneurs, 9, 236

sockpuppets, 9–10, 21–22*f*, 102, 240–243, 254, 259, 329, 346, 368–369, 372–374

Solomon, John F., 173–174, 176

solutions/interventions
  defamation law and, 376
  disclosure/accountability and, 367–368
  Honest Ads Act, 367–371, 373, 375
  institutionalization of fact checking, 376–378
  media literacy education, 378
  paid social promotion and, 372–375
  platform regulation, 360–362
  professional journalism and, 355–359
  public health approach, 375
  public machine-readable open database, 371–372
  reconstructing center-right media, 353–355
  role of government, 362–365
  self-regulation, 365–367

sorting process, of voters, 301

Southern Poverty Law Center, 124, 160

Southern Strategy, 297, 299

Specter, Arlen, 353

Spirit Cooking event, 226–227, 228*f*, 231

Sputnik News, 36, 218, 226, 227, 232, 239, 243–247, 249

Steele Dossier, 147, 153

Stein, Jill, 227, 240, 262

Stelter, Brian, 225

Stewart, Jon, 323

Stillwell, David, 275–276

Stone, Roger, 152, 260

Strange, Lucas, 16

Strategic Culture Foundation, 245

Sunstein, Cass, 30, 290, 330

Talking Points Memo, 50*t*, 62, 64*t*, 69*f*, 217, 331

talk radio, 20, 42, 45, 72, 81, 147, 176, 273, 310–312, 314, 319–329, 334, 380, 384

Tampa Bay Times, 83. *See also* PolitiFact

Tea Party, 4, 312, 353

TEN_GOP, 242, 259, 261

Thiel, Peter, 376

Think Progress, 52*t*, 114*t*, 216, 282*t*

Tillerson, Rex, 19

Toomey, Pat, 353

Townhall, 331, 347

Trans-Pacific Partnership, 270

Treasury Department, 218

trolls, 233, 237, 243. *See also* alt-right trolls

True Pundit, 95–96, 155, 253, 266–267, 266*f*, 288, 398*n*30

Trump, Donald. *See also* DonaldJTrump.com
  as candidate/president, 18–20, 105
  digital campaign of, 270–274
  election of, 3, 7
  embrace of conspiracy theories by, 18
  "Fake News Awards" of, 4, 15, 183*f*, 217–218, 220
  "fake news" term usage, 9
  immigration agenda of, 105–106
  media coverage of, 17*f*, 61*f*, 62*f*, 190*f*
  use of Twitter by, 18–19

Trump, Donald, Jr., 166, 216, 227, 247, 406*n*51

Trump rape frame
    coverage of, 85–91, 87–90*f*
    Jane Doe accusation, 91–92
Trump Tower meeting, 154, 166, 247, 251
trust/distrust in media/journalism
    asymmetry and, 311, 318
    disinformation and, 387
    in Germany, 22, 341
    Hannity on, 182
    by ideological identity, 325*f*
    media literacy education and, 377–378
    online/offline media and, 334–336
    partisan-confirming news and,
        78–80, 380
    patterns of, 4–5, 20, 73, 98, 184, 339
    propaganda feedback loop and, 79*f*
    in realty-check dynamic, 77*f*
    by Republicans, 188
    right-wing media ecosystem and, 13, 15,
        354–355
    Russian interference and, 267–268
    standards/responsibility and, 218
    studies/surveys on, 324–329, 327*f*, 367
    systematic undermining of, 322
Truthfeed, 14, 54, 54*t*, 66, 69*f*, 70–71, 86,
    87*f*, 155, 161, 176, 231, 280, 282, 284,
    284*t*, 285*t*, 287
Tucker, Joshua, 264
Tufekci, Zeynep, 273–274, 333, 343, 345
Turnbull, Mark, 276
Turner Broadcasting Station (TBS),
    319–320
21stcenturywire.com, 244–245, 253
Twitter
    automated/fake accounts and, 10
    deep state frame on, 155, 157*f*
    in first year of Trump
        presidency, 65–71
    immigration discussions on, 113–114*t*
    media sharing on, 51*f*, 52*t*, 58*f*, 60*f*,
        65*f*, 68*f*
    open web stories on, 154*f*
    partisan distribution on, 66*f*
    Russian bots on, 264–268
    Russian interference and, 10
    second-tier media source shares
        on, 69*f*

Trump's use of, 18–19, 145*f*
    in 2016 election period, 51–53
Twitter and Teargas (Tufekci), 343
2016 presidential elections
    asymmetric architecture of news
        media, 23
    asymmetric polarization in, 46–48
    Breitbart/Fox News influence
        during, 57–60
    epochal change reflected by, 7
    Facebook in, 53–54
    misleading information in, 3
    open web media mentions during, 17*f*,
        48–51
    patterns of authority/attention
        during, 54–56
    post-election asymmetry, 60–65
    Twitter in, 51–53

Uranium One conspiracy theory/story
    case study on, 166–188
    Clinton Cash film and, 167–168
    fact checking and, 377
    Fox News framing of, 39, 139, 146,
        177–185, 214–215
    investigative reporting on, 173–177
    on-line coverage of, 169–173
    news segment mentions on, 186*f*
    New York Times coverage of, 203, 358
    open web mentions of, 186*f*
    in political media ecosystem, 220, 354
    Trump's embrace of, 18
    videos about, 177–178*f*
USA Today, 49, 50*t*, 52*t*, 69*f*, 70*f*, 110*t*, 127*f*,
    283*t*
useful idiots, 243, 253

Vanity Fair, 219–220
Van Susteren, Greta, 95, 97
VDARE, 124, 127*f*, 128, 132
Veselnitskaya, Natalia, 247
Veteran Intelligence Professionals for
    Sanity (VIPS), 248–250, 252
Veterans News Now, 151
Virgil (pseudonym), 151, 245
voter fraud, 258–261, 259*f*, 260*f*
voter suppression, 260, 262, 270, 279

voting patterns
 advertising and, 278
 ideological positions and, 298
 media effect on, 338
 partisanship in, 296*f*
Vox, 49, 50*t*, 52*t*, 54, 54*t*, 64*t*, 65, 69, 69*f*,
  70*f*, 110*t*, 127*f*, 166, 282*t*

Wallace, George, 4
Wallace, Mike, 153
Wall Street Journal, 38, 49, 50*t*, 52*t*, 63,
  69*f*, 70*f*, 74, 75, 108, 108*f*, 112, 113*t*,
  207, 242, 283*t*, 323, 353, 356
Wardle, Clair, 23
Warner, Mark, 368
Warren, Elizabeth, 219
Washington Examiner, 49, 50*t*, 52*t*, 64*t*,
  65, 69*f*, 70*f*, 110*t*, 114*t*, 197, 284*t*
Washington Monthly, 250
Washington Post
 center-left popularity of, 282*t*
 climate change coverage and, 220, 356
 critique of Fox, 165
 "deep state" framing and, 151
 email-related stories, 195, 213–214,
  216–217, 256
 in Facebook-based network, 54*t*, 68*f*,
  211
 fact checking and, 83, 168, 170, 203,
  376
 Free Republic lawsuit, 329
 Hannity on, 182
 immigration mentions on, 109*f*, 109*t*,
  111, 114*t*
 journalistic norms and, 15
 media attention and, 207
 in open web link economy, 48–51
 pre-/post-election attention, 67
 Project Veritas and, 358
 sensationalist headlines in, 281, 356
 structure of attention and, 56
 Trump's "Fake News Awards" and, 183,
  217
 in Twitter-based network, 47, 52, 68*f*
 used to legitimize claims, 199, 202
 on voter fraud, 260–261
 WikiLeaks' emails dump, 144

Washington Times, 49, 50*t*, 52, 64*t*,
  69*f*, 93, 114*t*, 173, 176, 226, 228*f*,
  231, 284*t*
Wasserman, Casey, 211–212
Watson, Paul Joseph, 151
Watts, Duncan, 16, 191, 196
WeAreChange, 177*f*, 178, 178*f*, 227, 230,
  231*f*, 245, 246
Weaver, Warren, Jr., 297
Webster, Steven, 308
Weekly Standard, 166, 253, 283*t*, 331
Weidel, Alice, 363
Weigel, Dave, 217
Weiner, Anthony, 95
well-informed rational voter theory, 304
Western Journalism, 54, 54*t*, 70, 70*f*,
  86, 87*f*, 96, 231, 282, 284, 284*t*,
  285*t*, 287
Westwood, Sean, 308
Wheeler, Rod, 162–164, 166
white-identity, 102, 132, 179, 240, 297,
  299, 382
white-nationalist publications/sites,
  124–127
white propaganda. *See* propaganda
white supremacists, 11–13, 132
Wiebe, Kirk, 248
WikiLeaks
 on Clinton Foundation, 134–136, 144
 DNC email leak, 239, 242,
  245–249, 255
 effect of, 265
 false reports and, 216
 inlinks to, 64*t*, 266*f*
 on ISIS funding email, 140–141, 140*f*
 Pizzagate and, 231–232
 popularity of, 284*t*
 Russian interference and, 159
 Seth Rich conspiracy theory and,
  162–163
 Spirt Cooking event and, 226–227
Wikipedia, 124, 396*n*8
Williamson, Vanessa, 312
Winner-Take-All-Politics (Hacker and
  Pierson), 300
WND (right-wing site), 96, 231
World Anti-Doping Agency, 230, 232

Wyand, Jared (@JaredWyand), 161, 230, 232
Wylie, Chris, 276

Yahoo! News, 50t, 52t, 69f, 70f, 114t, 176,
    197, 283t
Yglesias, Matthew, 213
Young, Robbin, 247
YourNewsWire, 95–96, 160, 165, 244,
    253, 288, 398n30
YouTube
    ad purchases on, 372
    analysis of, 73
    campaign-related stories on, 200f
    centrality of, 165
    Clinton Cash on, 199–200
    "deep state" frame and, 151–153, 155–156,
        157f

distribution of information on,
    365–366
as media source, 50t
public interest and, 375
right-wing media ecosystem and,
    176–177
Russian interference and, 242
Uranium One conspiracy theory/story
    on, 178f, 179
Yunnus, Muhammad, 213
Yurukoglu, Ali, 337–338

Zakharov, Andrei, 242
Zero Hedge, 14, 141–142, 143f,
    150–153, 158f, 245, 247–248,
    253–254, 335
Zimmerman, Malia, 95, 162, 163, 214